# Instant
# JavaScript

## Martin Webb

**McGraw-Hill**
New York   Chicago   San Francisco   Lisbon
London   Madrid   Mexico City   Milan   New Delhi
San Juan   Seoul   Singapore   Sydney   Toronto

# McGraw-Hill

A Division of The **McGraw·Hill** Companies

1 2 3 4 5 6 7 8 9 0   DOC/DOC   0 5 4 3 2 1

P/N 212993-X

Part of ISBN 0-07-212994-8

*The sponsoring editor for this book was Rebekah Young, the editing supervisor was Penny Linskey, and the production manager was Claire Stanley. It was set in Century Schoolbook by Victoria Khavkina of McGraw-Hill's Professional Book Group composition unit, in cooperation with Spring Point Publishing Services.*

*Printed and bound by R. R. Donnelley & Sons Co.*

This book is printed on recycled, acid-free paper containing a minimum of 50% recycled, de-inked fiber.

# CONTENTS

**iii**

# Contents

# Contents

# Contents

# INTRODUCTION

This book is loosely divided into two parts. The first part is primarily concerned with the different components in JavaScript, from basic mathematical expressions to the use of cookies to store persistent state between pages. Each chapter in this section explores in detail the possibilities surrounding the components, showing by way of practical, everyday, reusable example applications how to make use of the components. Chapters in this section include:

## Chapter 2—Maths and Numbers

This chapter describes two calculators written in JavaScript, a standard calculator, and a scientific calculator. Shows how to use a random number generator to display random quotes. Includes several number utility functions that are reused many times throughout the remainder of the book.

## Chapter 3—Strings and Regular Expressions

This chapter shows how to find and replace strings within other strings, along with a practical demonstration with a copyright boilerplate. It also shows how to create scrolling text links, how to manipulate a contacts list, and how to manipulate strings to apply Gourad shading. This chapter describes how to parse text strings, and finally how to use Regular Expressions to validate form data input.

## Chapter 4—Arrays and Objects

This chapter shows how to hold data as objects and how to hold objects within arrays, to show how to visit one of many web sites in an automated tour. It also explores how to search data held in a database, along with a multiple-choice test, and finally how to sort an array of objects.

## Chapter 5—Location and Links

This chapter describes how to interact with the current location to provide automatic redirection to a new location, shows how to automate previous and next buttons between different pages, and automate links between portions of the same page, describes how JavaScript can be used to manage a ring of related web-sites. It shows how to extract the browsers preferred language and loads an appropriately written web page. There's also information on how to password protect resources and verify the entered password, and finally how to write a JavaScript link crawler to crawl through all the links in a connected set of pages.

## Chapter 6—Windows and Frames

This chapter shows how to target the entries in a select form list to various windows in a frame set. It describes how to read the entries in a directory listing and describes a tool to generate your own popup windows. The use of popup windows in a dictionary lookup is also illustrated, along with the use of frames to hold data between page views to provide a family tree application. The chapter addresses how popup windows can be used to debug your own applications, followed by a popup date selector application, and finally code to stop other sites framing your own pages, while at the same time provide a means to ensure your pages are correctly framed within their own frame set.

## Chapter 7—Date and Time

This chapter explores how to work with and manipulate the current date and time. It shows how to extract the day of the week for any date, how to validate an input date, and display a different page based on the time of day. It describes how to show a yearly calendar, how to count forwards and backwards to different dates, how to calculate an age in years, months and days, and shows how to work with the zodiac and Chinese calendars. The chapter includes applications to show events, religious celebrations and birthdays associated with a date, and finally shows how to work out the current time anywhere around the world.

## Chapter 8—Form

This chapter first shows how HTML forms and JavaScript can interact and includes applications to show how to send email forms, how to interact with drop down menus, and how to pass data from one form to another. It covers how to provide a generic and dynamic thank you page following a form submission and includes applications to pass data from one form to another by way of cookies and emails. It describes how to disable form fields in HTML 4, and includes a technique to control form data entry. It also covers how to filter data input, and how to generate a new form component to spin date values up and down through a list, and finally shows how to provide a generic sales order form to calculate the sub-totals and total along with any necessary taxes.

## Chapter 9—Images

This chapter covers the ubiquitous highlighting of images, and a fast implementation of image rollovers, with a variation that fades the images in and out. It demonstrates how to use image maps with applications that show an image slide show, and bar chart generation. It also shows how to count the number of images downloaded, popup windows to hold images, including an image counter, random banner adverts, and an image toolbar.

## Chapter 10—Cookies

This chapter addresses general-purpose cookies functions for saving, retrieving and deleting cookies, and shows how to combine cookies with HTML to mark items as new. Intelligent cookies that avoid continual writing of cookies when disabled within the browser are also covered. The chapter's cookie tracker application demonstrates how cookies can be used to track a visitor's movement around a web site, and the personal calendar application shows how cookies can be used to store personalization information.

The second part of the book builds on the first part to generate far more complex applications, and at the same time build a cross-browser code library to support Dynamic HTML techniques in both Netscape

Navigator (versions 4 and 6) and Internet Explorer (versions 4 and 5). Chapters in this section include:

## Chapter 11—Dynamic HTML

This chapter describes the Document Object Model, including those available in Internet Explorer 5 and Netscape Navigator 6. Builds a cross-browser compatible library for manipulating the DOM. It demonstrates the use of a cross-browser library to collapse content, dynamically change the cascading style sheet used to display the page, display tool tips that float above the document, handle multi-dialog forms, and toolbar menus with drop-down content. The library is also used to automatically generate a table of contents from the heading tags within a document, to slide tabbed content from the sides of the document, along with a hierarchical menu structure that can be opened and closed to show different leafs within a tree structure. The final application demonstrates a dynamic advert that interacts with the user.

## Chapter 12—Applications

This chapter shows fully fledged applications, including two versions of a shopping cart application, one using simple hypertext links and form buttons to interact with the user, and the second using drag n' drop techniques. The myPage.com application shows how the user can personalize their view of your page. The computer builder/selector demonstrates how different complex views of several products can be generated from a simple database of products and components. The book catalog applications show how JavaScript can interact with an XML document the DOM and style sheets all within one application.

## Chapter 13—Utilities

Various uses of JavaScript are covered in this chapter. The color picker allows you, the author, to experiment with mixing background and foreground colors. The onscreen keyboard shows how users can interact with the page even when a keyboard isn't present. The automated scrolling application demonstrates how the page can be scrolled automatically without user intervention. The homepage script can be used to select the current page as the users default homepage. The final application shows how to detect for support of plugins and ActiveX components, both of which extend the basic browser beyond what it is capable of.

## Chapter 14—Fun Stuff

The final chapter covers the more fun aspects of JavaScript, including three JavaScript games—from the simple icon match game to the more interesting JavaScript versions of Tetris and Columns. The amusing mouse trail application shows how interesting DHTML techniques can be used to follow the mouse pointer around the screen, while the final application of the book, the personality test, can be used to rate the user's personality, or lack thereof.

All of the examples in this book are exactly that: examples. Examples that can be adapted to your needs, or perhaps provide inspiration of what JavaScript is capable of. Rather than a dry, and perhaps dull reference book on JavaScript, this book instead illustrates JavaScript applications, nearly 100 in total, that can be used as they stand or built on to provide even more complex and interesting programs.

## Accompanying CD-ROM

All the example code, including the applications, is included on the accompanying CD-ROM, as denoted by the CD-ROM icon. There should be no need to type in the code by hand. If, however, you decide to do this you should first check the code on the CD-ROM before reporting any problems with your code.

If you do have problems with the code on the CD-ROM then you can report these along with any errors or omissions in the book, or any suggestions for improvements in future editions of the book, to Martin Webb at *martin@irt.org*. Any updates or errata found after the book has gone to print will be detailed online at the supporting web page at *http://www.irt.org/instant/*.

As the book progresses less and less of the code is presented in the book. This is to first highlight the most important aspects of the code, and secondly to reduce the size of the overall book. However, the accompanying CD-ROM includes all the code for all the applications in full. The first few chapters of the book do however include all the necessary JavaScript code and HTML markup.

# JavaScript
# Overview

# JavaScript, JScript, DHTML, and the DOM

Brendan Eich created JavaScript for use within Netscape Navigator 2 back in 1995. It was included to allow the client browser to generate HTML on the fly and execute JavaScript code resulting in a page that the user sees or interacts with. JavaScript statements embedded in an HTML page can respond to user events such as mouse clicks, form input, and page navigation. The specific term *JavaScript* implicitly refers to Netscape's implementation within Netscape Navigator browsers, whereas *JScript* is Microsoft's implementation of JavaScript within Internet Explorer. This book covers both Netscape's JavaScript and Microsoft's JScript, as used with Netscape Navigator and Internet Explorer. The general term *JavaScript* will be used through the remainder of this book to refer to both.

Dynamic HTML (DHTML), although not a term that is well defined, is generally accepted as being the combination of HTML, JavaScript, the Document Object Model (DOM), and Cascading Style Sheets (CSS). DHTML is covered in detail in Chapter 11 "Dynamic HTML" and supported by further DHTML applications in Chapter 12 "Applications." The World Wide Web Consortium (W3C) states that "The Document Object Model is a platform- and language-neutral interface that will allow programs and scripts to dynamically access and update the content, structure, and style of documents."

JavaScript is not Java, and similarly Java is not JavaScript. JavaScript was developed independently of Java. It was originally developed as a product called LiveScript, but was renamed when Netscape announced support for Java in Netscape Navigator 2.0. JavaScript is a scripting language that is, usually, interpreted at runtime by a JavaScript interpreter within the browser. The code can be embedded within an HTML page or as an external JavaScript file. Java, on the other hand, is compiled into byte code and then run within a Java Virtual Machine (JVM), either stand-alone, or again within a browser. JavaScript is not a pure 100 percent object-oriented language, although it can easily be described as an object-based language. Java is a pure object-oriented language.

The syntax between the two is very similar, although not identical. In Netscape Navigator it is possible to invoke Java code from within JavaScript—this feature is termed LiveConnect. Both Java and LiveConnect are outside the scope of this book.

## JavaScript Standards

The European standards body, ECMA, publishes the ECMAScript language specification. The first release was based on Netscape's JavaScript 1.1 implementation. The most current version, release 3, is based on Netscape's JavaScript 1.5 implementation and was published in December 1999. It is available as a Microsoft Word document (*http://www.mozilla. org/js/language/E262-3.doc*) or as an Acrobat PDF file (*http://www.mozilla. org/js/language/E262-3.pdf*). ECMA-262 has also been adopted by the ISO/IEC JTC 1 as ISO/IEC 16262. The ECMAScript is a language specification, and so in itself it does not define the object model (beyond a small set of "native objects.")

A Web browser's object model, or DOM, which is used by scripting languages has been standardized by the W3C (*http://www.w3.org*). There are three DOM levels: Level 0 DOM was the object model provided in Netscape Navigator 3.x and Internet Explorer 3.x; Level 1 DOM is a current W3C recommendation (*http://www.w3.org/TR/REC-DOM-Level-1*); Level 2 DOM is also a current W3C recommendation (*http://www.irt.org/TR/*). The third DOM level is currently a W3C working draft.

Apart from the ECMAScript and W3C documentation, probably the most relevant documentation is the browser vendor's own JavaScript documentation. JScript is documented on the Microsoft website at *http://msdn. microsoft.com/scripting/default.htm?/scripting/jscript/default.htm,* and JavaScript is documented on the Netscape website at *http://developer. netscape.com/tech/javascript/index.html.*

## Where to Place the JavaScript Code

Where exactly does JavaScript go within a page? This question is usually the first asked by someone when he or she encounters JavaScript. The simple answer is that JavaScript is located between an opening and closing script tag. A sample JavaScript code, our first, would perhaps look like the following:

 **chapter1/examples/sample.htm**

```
<html>

<head>
```

```
<title>Sample Code</title>
</head>

<body>

<script language="JavaScript"><!--
document.write('Hello World');
//--></script>

</body>

</html>
```

The characters `<!--` and `//-->` are a combination of HTML start (`<!`) and end (`-->`) comment tags along with JavaScript comment characters (`//`) to effectively hide the contents of the script tags from browsers that do not support JavaScript. If omitted, then on browsers that do not support JavaScript, the contents of the script tags would be rendered as normal text on the page.

The placement of JavaScript code depends on what you want the JavaScript code to do. If you simply want the JavaScript code to perform some processing as the page loads and possibly affect the page as it is rendered to the screen, as above, then the answer is to include inline JavaScript code in between script elements in the body of the page. If, however, you want to define blocks of reusable JavaScript code that might possibly be used several times through the life of a page, then placing the JavaScript code in a function block, perhaps declared between script tags in the head of a document, is a more suitable place. If you want JavaScript to react to events triggered by the user, then placing JavaScript code inside HTML attributes of appropriate HTML tags is another possibility, perhaps also supported by JavaScript code in function blocks. Another possibility, used extensively through this book, is placing reusable JavaScript code in external libraries of JavaScript source code. All these possibilities are explained and described further.

It is recommended that any JavaScript code that does not write out to the document should be placed within the head of the document. In the following example, we define a block of code, actually just one line, as `functionName()`. This code can be invoked just by referencing its name followed by an empty set of parentheses. A JavaScript variable identified as `text` is also defined and initialized to the text string value `Hello World`. As neither of these impacts the rendering of the page, they are suitably situated within the head document.

A second use of JavaScript code in this example is the generation of HTML markup output in between the body element tags. This use of JavaScript is perhaps the more well used aspect of JavaScript (i.e., generating HTML markup based on runtime settings—for example, the browser being used, the time of day, and information passed in the URL).

**NOTE.** *Since the JavaScript code writes out content to the page while the page is being rendered, the code has to execute before the page has finished loading; otherwise, if JavaScript is used to write to the document after the page has loaded, then the current page, HTML markup, and the JavaScript code currently being executed will be replaced by the newly generated output. This may well be what is required, but this is usually the problem first encountered by those who are not familiar with JavaScript.*

The actual content of the markup written out to the document also illustrates a third use of JavaScript. The `onClick` attribute of the button form field detects the user clicking the form button and intercepts the action by invoking the `nameFunction()` function defined in the head of the document:

**chapter1/examples/functionName.htm**

```
<html>

<head>

<script language="JavaScript"><!--
function functionName() {
   alert(text);
}

var text = 'Hello World';
//--></script>

</head>

<body>

<script language="JavaScript"><!--
document.write(
  '<form>' +
  '<input type="button" value="Click Here" ' +
  'onClick="functionName()"></form>'
);
//--></script>

</body>

</html>
```

Defining the JavaScript functions within the head of the document ensures that the JavaScript function definitions have been loaded by the browser before they are required. It also makes it slightly easier to maintain the JavaScript code if it can always be found in the head of the document.

JavaScript source files can be used from Netscape Navigator 3 and from Microsoft Internet Explorer 3.01 onward to hold JavaScript code in an external JavaScript file that can be embedded in one or many HTML files. The benefit is that, once downloaded into the browser's cache, it is instantly available for other HTML pages to reuse.

The JavaScript source file then effectively acts as a library of reusable JavaScript code. However, before using code within a source file from within the HTML file, you should perform a test to ensure that the source file has actually loaded and that its contents are available for use. Here again we use an event handler to invoke the `hello()` function when the page has completely loaded, but only if the *library.js* JavaScript source file has been loaded and thus has a property named `hello`. In other words, the function named `hello()` has been declared and defined as a property of the current window:

**chapter1/examples/library.htm**

```
<html>

<head>
<title>JavaScript Source File</title>
<script src="library.js"></script>
</head>

<body onLoad="if (window.hello) hello()">
</body>

</html>
```

And then the function is defined within the *library.js* JavaScript source file simply by the following JavaScript code, omitting the usual opening and closing `script` tags:

**chapter1/examples/library.js**

```
function hello() {
  alert('Hello World');
}
```

**NOTE.** *Care must be taken when using JavaScript source files in Microsoft Internet Explorer 3.01, as using* `document.write()` *from within an external source file does not write to the document and, in some instances, may cause the browser to crash.*

**NOTE.** *If you must develop code, or wish to use the applications in this book that make use of JavaScript source files, for browsers that do not support JavaScript source files, simply cut and paste the contents of the external JavaScript source files in between opening and closing* `script` *tags in the head of the document.*

## Problems Unique to Client-Side JavaScript

In most programming languages, source code is compiled on one machine and then executed on the same machine or possibly on another target machine. In either case, the resultant program will run on a known and stable environment.

JavaScript source code is interpreted (or compiled) at the time it is used by the client computer it is being used on. When writing JavaScript source code, it is difficult to predict exactly what hardware, operating system, or browser will be used. This means that you cannot write JavaScript code expecting to use the most up-to-date version of JavaScript with all the latest features and then expect it to run on all browsers currently in use, as a minority of people may still be using older versions. Therefore, it is necessary to either restrict ourselves to only those aspects of JavaScript available in JavaScript 1.0 or write code that degrades safely in browsers with a lower version of JavaScript code than that which is required. It is also important to note that JavaScript code written today may still be used 5 or 10 years from now on a browser that could not possibly be envisaged. It is thus extremely important to write code that is as browser-independent as possible. In Chapter 9 "Images," we describe in the Highlighting Images application the problem encountered when code written to support a particular browser failed when the next version of the browser was released, along with how, as other browsers were released with support for image-swapping techniques, code changes were required to "turn on" support for additional browsers.

These problems do exist with other programming languages, but not to the extent to which JavaScript code is used on many web pages and websites all around the world, which can be viewed and processed on any client machine by anyone, anywhere using many different combinations of hardware platforms, operating systems, and web browsers. Web pages are supposed to be truly universal. JavaScript code usage should aim to be as well.

## JavaScript Versions

Probably at least two dozen versions of JavaScript are in use today. Table 1-1 details the main JavaScript versions used by the two major browser vendors.

The JavaScript engine within Microsoft's Internet Explorer can be updated independently of the browser version. There are also differences in the versions depending on the platform the browser is used on. The Mac, for example, suffers many incomplete or buggy versions of JScript on Microsoft Internet Explorer. You may be wondering why Netscape Navigator 5 does not appear in Table 1-1; this is because version 5 was the version number given to the source code released by Netscape to the Mozilla organization (*http://www.mozilla.org*), who then effectively rewrote the browser from the ground up. This rewritten browser was then subsequently released by Netscape as Netscape Navigator 6.

The `language` attribute within the `script` element—for example, `<script language="JavaScript">`—is deprecated in HTML 4.01. Although in this book we attempt at all times to follow the appropriate standards, there are sound reasons for ignoring this particular deprecation. We use this attribute to explicitly state that the required scripting

**Table 1-1**

*JavaScript Versions*

| Vendor | Browser | Browser Version | JavaScript Version |
|--------|---------|-----------------|--------------------|
| Netscape | Navigator | 2.x | JavaScript 1.0 |
| Netscape | Navigator | 3.x | JavaScript 1.1 |
| Netscape | Navigator | 4.0x | JavaScript 1.2 |
| Netscape | Navigator | 4.5x | JavaScript 1.3 |
| Netscape | Navigator | 4.7x | JavaScript 1.4 |
| Netscape | Navigator | 6.x | JavaScript 1.5 |
| Microsoft | Internet Explorer | 3.x | JScript 1.x, 3.x or 5.x |
| Microsoft | Internet Explorer | 4.x | JScript 3.x or 5.x |
| Microsoft | Internet Explorer | 5.x | JScript 5.x |
| Microsoft | Internet Explorer | 5.5 | JScript 5.5 |

language is JavaScript and not an alternative scripting language, like VBScript, which is supported in Internet Explorer. We also use this attribute to specify the version of the JavaScript language that is required by the code contained inside the script tags:

 **chapter1/examples/version.htm**

```html
<html>

<head>
<title>JavaScript Version</title>
</head>

<body>

<script language="JavaScript"><!--
document.write('<p>Supports JavaScript</p>');
//--></script>

<script language="JavaScript1.1"><!--
document.write('<p>Supports JavaScript 1.1</p>');
//--></script>

<script language="JavaScript1.2"><!--
document.write('<p>Supports JavaScript 1.2</p>');
//--></script>

<script language="JavaScript1.3"><!--
document.write('<p>Supports JavaScript 1.3</p>');
//--></script>

<script language="JavaScript1.4"><!--
document.write('<p>Supports JavaScript 1.4</p>');
//--></script>

<script language="JavaScript1.5"><!--
document.write('<p>Supports JavaScript 1.5</p>');
//--></script>

</body>

</html>
```

Although it is possible to explicitly state the scripting language with the recommended alternative attribute `type="text/javascript"`, it is not possible to use this to specify the language version consistently across all browsers. It is, however, straightforward to convert from `language="JavaScript"` to `type="text/javascript"` at a later date when browser vendors provide a consistent mechanism for detecting the language version.

# JavaScript Fundamentals

The following is a brief introduction to the fundamentals of JavaScript. For a full description of all the statements, objects, methods, and properties available and supported by each browser, you should view the browser vendor's own documentation as detailed earlier in "JavaScript Standards."

## Expressions and Variables

JavaScript expressions are evaluated at runtime, and normally the result of an expression is assigned to a variable, or as input to some other expression, or a function or method. We have already seen expressions in use in the few examples shown so far in this chapter. For example, the last code used an expression to *add* a text string to the value returned by `navigator.appName`. More common examples are shown in the following, where the results of the expressions are assigned to a variable and then the variables themselves are used in further expressions:

 **chapter1/examples/expressions.htm**

```
<html>

<head>
<title>Expressions</title>
</title>

</head>

<body>

<script language="JavaScript"><!--
var x = 2 + 2;
var y = x * 2;
var z = x * y / 10;
//--></script>

</body>

</html>
```

The expression 2 + 2 will equate to 4 at runtime. This value is then assigned to the variable x. The expression x * 2 will equate to 8, and is then assigned to the variable y. The expressions x * y / 10 will equate to 3.2, and is then assigned to the variable z. The preceding JavaScript code is not optimized by the browser, so if it is present many times, or the code is invoked many times by the browser, then the expressions are evaluated each time they occur or are processed in the running of a JavaScript program. A variable is a reference to the data value. In JavaScript it is easy to amend and use the value of a variable in expressions.

## Statements

As can be seen in the preceding section, a JavaScript expression does not actually do anything other than become evaluated at runtime. To actually do something, a JavaScript statement is required. A JavaScript statement is either a single line of code or a block of code lines surrounded by braces. For example, the following statement displays the text *Hello World* on the document:

 **chapter1/examples/statement.htm**

```
<html>

<head>
<title>Statement</title>
</head>

<body>

<script language="JavaScript"><!--
document.write('Hello World');
//--></script>

</body>

</html>
```

A block of code lines is also regarded as a statement. For example, the following statement block displays information about the browser on the document, using three single-line statements:

 **chapter1/examples/block.htm**

```html
<html>

<head>
<title>Statement block</title>
</head>

<body>

<script language="JavaScript"><!--
{
  document.write('Browser vendor: ' + navigator.appName);
  document.write('<br>');
  document.write('Browser version: ' + navigator.appVersion);
}
//--></script>

</body>

</html>
```

Why we would use a statement block instead of two single-line code statements will become clearer in a moment when we discuss conditions and functions.

*NOTE.   When we nest code—for example, in a statement block—for clarity and readability, we indent the code by two spaces. The actual layout of the code does not affect the processing. It is done purely to aid understanding of the code.*

# Conditions

JavaScript conditions allow tests to be performed at runtime, so that the flow of the program can be altered. For example, the following code will display the name of the browser on the document, but only if it is Internet Explorer. Otherwise, the code will display an alternative message:

 **chapter1/examples/if.htm**

```html
<html>

<head>
<title>If condition</title>
</head>

<body>
```

```
<script language="JavaScript"><!--
if (navigator.appName == 'Microsoft Internet Explorer')
  document.write(navigator.appName);
else
  document.write('You are not using a Microsoft browser');
//--></script>

</body>

</html>
```

**NOTE:** *An assignment operator* (=) *assigns the result of the right-hand side of the operator to the left-hand side of the operator. In other words, in the statement* var x = 3 + 4, *the expression* 3 + 4 *is evaluated to 7, and then the value 7 is assigned to the variable* x. *The equivalent operator* (==), *on the other hand, performs a Boolean test comparing the right-hand side of the operator with the left-hand side, returning a Boolean* true *if they are equal or* false *if not.*

A JavaScript condition will perform one statement or another depending on the result of the condition. As explained previously, a statement can be a block of statements. Therefore, we can perform more interesting process flows by wrapping several lines of JavaScript code in statement blocks. Before we do this, let's see the result of changing the previous example to use braces to signify statement blocks:

```
<script language="JavaScript"><!--
if (navigator.appName == 'Microsoft Internet Explorer') {
  document.write(navigator.appName);
}
else {
  document.write('You are not using a Microsoft browser');
}
//--></script>
```

As you can see, the only change is the addition of opening and closing braces around each statement. A more complex multiline statement block example is as follows:

**chapter1/examples/if-block.htm**

```
<html>

<head>
<title>If condition block</title>
</head>
```

```
<body>

<script language="JavaScript"><!--
if (navigator.appName == 'Microsoft Internet Explorer') {
  document.write(navigator.appName);
  document.write(' version: ' + navigator.appVersion);
}
else {
  document.write('You are not using a Microsoft browser');
  document.write(' instead you are using ');
  document.write(navigator.appName);
}
//--></script>

</body>

</html>
```

Since a JavaScript condition is also a statement, it is possible to include nested conditions within conditional statement blocks.

## Loops

JavaScript would not be complete without the ability to loop around statements. JavaScript supports the normal looping statements `for`, `while`, and so on. For example, looping through the length of a text string printing out the letters one at a time can simply be achieved as follows:

**chapter1/examples/for.htm**

```
<html>

<head>
<title>for loop</title>
</head>

<body>

<script language="JavaScript"><!--
var message = 'Hello World';
for (var i = 0; i < message.length; i++) {
  document.write(message.substring(i, i+1) + '<br>');
}
//--></script>

</body>

</html>
```

The `for` loop first defines and initializes a variable `i` to zero, and then loops through the statement that follows (in this case, a single-line statement block) while the value of `i` is less than the value of the `message` variable's length. At the end of each loop, the value of the `i` variable is incremented by 1. At the start of each loop, including the first, the test is performed again. Therefore, if the `message` variable is an empty string, the code will not loop through at all, but instead will skip to the line after the statement block. The example code uses a string method to extract one character at a time from the message variable. Chapter 3 "Strings and Regular Expressions" covers the use of string methods in more detail.

## Functions

As previously mentioned, functions allow blocks of code to be identified by name and then invoked by using the name of the function. Functions can also additionally accept a fixed or variable number of parameters or arguments and optionally return a value to the statement that invoked the function. For example, the following code illustrates a function named `product` that accepts two parameters `a` and `b`, and then returns the product of the two parameters:

 **chapter1/examples/function.htm**

```
<html>

<head>
<title>Function</title>
</head>

<body>

<script language="JavaScript"><!--
function product(a, b) {
  var p = a * b;
  return p;
}

document.write(product(2, 2));
document.write(product(product(4, 5), 6));
if (product(10, 10) == 100) document.write('100!');
//--></script>

</body>

</html>
```

The first use of the product() function is to simply display the return result (4) on the document. In the next use, the return value (20) is used as input to yet another product() function call, and then its return result (120) is displayed on the document. In the last use, the product() function returns the result (100) in an if expression.

## Objects

Most components within an HTML document are also represented as objects within an internal browser object model. An object is attached to an object hierarchy, with the topmost object being the window object for the current window. For example, all the frames within a window are also included in a frames object array, which can be accessed as window.frames. The object that represents the document within the browser window is the document object, which is accessed as window.document in the model. JavaScript can control this hierarchy of objects that the browser makes available via the object model. Figure 1-1 shows the objects accessible to JavaScript 1.0, 1.1, and 1.2.

**Figure 1-1**
Browser object model accessible from JavaScript 1.0, 1.1, and 1.2.

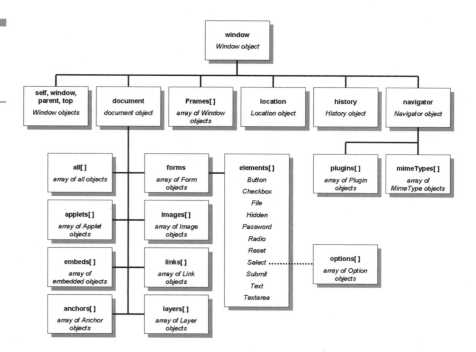

Using this object model as a reference allows code to be quickly written to traverse the objects in a window or document. For example, to check how many links the current browser window contains, we simply need to check the `length` property of the `links` object via the `window` object's `document` object. This is achieved by placing a period character (.) in between each object or property—for example, `window.document.links.length`.

 **chapter1/examples/links.htm**

```html
<html>

<head>
<title>Number of links</title>
</head>

<body>
<a href="http://www.microsoft.com">Microsoft</a><br>
<a href="http://www.netscape.com">Netscape</a><br>

<script language="JavaScript"><!--
document.write('Links = ' + window.document.links.length);
//--></script>

</body>

</html>
```

However, you should be aware of several points when accessing the objects shown in Figure 1-1:

- The `Anchor` object provides little functionality in JavaScript 1.0. The `Link` object should be used in preference.

- The `Image` object is not fully supported in Microsoft Internet Explorer prior to version 4.

- The `Layer`, `Plugin`, and `MimeType` objects are not supported in Microsoft Internet Explorer.

- The `All` object is not supported in Netscape Navigator.

- The `Arguments`, `Applet`, and `Embed` objects are only available in JavaScript 1.1 and higher.

Where an object has been introduced into the object model since JavaScript 1.0, before you attempt to make use of the object, its support within the browser should first be established. For example, before using the vendor-specific `All` or `Layer` objects, you should test their support by checking that the `document` object has an `all` or `layers` array property:

**chapter1/examples/object.htm**

```html
<html>

<head>
<title>Object detection</title>
</head>

<body>

<script language="JavaScript"><!--
if (window.document.all) {
  document.write('Supports the All object');
}
else if (window.document.layers) {
  document.write('Supports the Layer object');
}
//--></script>

</body>

</html>
```

This then allows a small amount of future proofing for when later browser versions provide additional object support.

## Object Properties

An object property is an otherwise JavaScript variable that is assigned as a property of an instance of an object. For example, the window object has a title property: window.title. Every window that is opened by the browser has an associated window object, each with its own unique title property.

Not all object properties are available in all versions of JavaScript. As JavaScript has been adapted and extended, so have the objects and their properties. If you cannot restrict yourself just to the object properties available since JavaScript 1.0, then ensure that your code is not executed by a browser without support for the object property you are using. The check is similar to the previous object detection example. For example, to test if the current browser supports the language or browserLanguage properties of the navigator object:

**chapter1/examples/property.htm**

```
<html>

<head>
<title>Properties test</title>
</head>

<body>

<script language="JavaScript"><!--
if (navigator.language) {
  document.write('Preferred language ');
  document.write(navigator.language);
}
else if (navigator.browserLanguage) {
  document.write('Preferred language ');
  document.write(navigator.browserLanguage);
}
//--></script>

</body>

</html>
```

## Object Methods

An object method is an otherwise JavaScript function that is assigned as a function to a type of object. In other words, the method is defined once against a particular object type—for example, a document object—and is then available to all instances of that object type. We have already seen and used the document object's write() method. As with properties, new methods are introduced with each version of JavaScript. Therefore, you need to test support for a non-JavaScript 1.0 object method before attempting to use it. The following code illustrates this by testing that the window object's print() method is supported, before attempting to use the method to print out the current document:

 **chapter1/examples/method.htm**

```
<html>

<head>
<title>Method test</title>
</head>

<body>

<script language="JavaScript"><!--
if (window.print) {
```

```
    alert('Printing document...');
    window.print();
}
//--></script>

</body>

</html>
```

As before, it is possible to omit the window reference when using window methods—for example, `alert('Hello world')`. However, there are certain occasions when you should avoid omitting the window reference—for example, when using the `open()` method, as both the `document` and `window` objects have an `open()` method. It is important to specify in detail the correct object hierarchy in these circumstances—for example, `window.open()` or `document.open()`.

## Events and Event Handlers

An event in JavaScript is triggered either as the result of the browser completing something—for example, the document completely loading—or as a result of the user interacting with the browser—for example, clicking a form button. Events have associated event handlers. For instance, the completion of the document loading into the browser fires a *load* event, which can be intercepted by JavaScript with the inclusion of an `onLoad` event handler within the HTML body element:

 **chapter1/examples/event.htm**

```
<html>

<head>
<title>Event handler</title>
</head>

<body onLoad="alert('Page completely loaded')">

</body>

</html>
```

An increasing number of events and event handlers are being introduced in each browser release. Fortunately, because of the way that HTML attributes are ignored if not recognized, you can include event handlers that are not supported by all browsers. For example, the following, although syntactically correct, will not cause a JavaScript error message and will never actually cause the enclosed JavaScript code to be executed (unless, of course, kettles start to have embedded JavaScript code):

```
<a href="page.htm"
  onKettleBoiled="alert('Hello World')">Click Here</a>
```

It is, however, important to realize that JavaScript code is case-sensitive. Therefore, the case of event handlers must be correct or there is a danger that browsers will not recognize them. For example, onMouseover is incorrect, whereas onMouseOver is correct. It is also important to note that JavaScript event handlers form part of the HTML tag attributes, and as such, they should be valid event handlers as defined within the HTML 4.0 specification (*http://www.w3.org/TR/html401/*). Invalid event handlers might cause problems with a future browser release.

## Double and Single Quotes

Use double quotes (") for HTML attributes and single quotes (') for JavaScript text strings. When you are writing HTML, the general practice is to use double quotes for tag attributes. For example:

```
<img src="picture.gif">
```

When you are writing JavaScript, the general practice is to use single quotes for text strings:

```
<script language="JavaScript"><!--
document.write('Hello World');
//--></script>
```

In general, these quoting styles then complement one another when you are outputting HTML using JavaScript:

```
<script language="JavaScript"><!--
document.write('<img src="picture.gif">');
//--></script>
```

Where nested quotes are required, use the Escape character (\) to escape the quotes:

```
<script language="JavaScript"><!--
document.write('Don\'t forget to escape apostrophes');
//--></script>
```

## The `noscript` tag

Use the `noscript` tag to provide alternative text for JavaScript-disabled browsers. The HTML markup within the `noscript` tag is only rendered if the browser does not support JavaScript and thus does not recognize the `noscript` tag. Browsers that support JavaScript should ignore the contents of the `noscript` tags.

 **chapter1/examples/noscript.htm**

```
<html>

<head>
<title>noscript</title>
</head>

<body>

<script language="JavaScript"><!--
document.write('Last modified: ');
document.write(document.lastModified);
//--></script>

<noscript>
Last modified: January 2001
</noscript>

</body>

</html>
```

## Summary

This book is not a JavaScript reference book that sits on a shelf. Instead, it is a book that focuses on providing instant JavaScripts that you can use or take apart to build other applications. The code on the CD-ROM allows you to concentrate on the explanations throughout this book that describe how the code works—why it does what it does—without having to worry about typing out the code by hand and then having to debug any errors introduced in this process. This chapter has explained what JavaScript is, where the code sits in the document, and the basic fundamentals that the rest of the book builds upon. Without further delay, let's move on to the applications.

CHAPTER **2**

# Maths and
# Numbers

Mathematics and numbers constitute a large amount of the work that takes place within most JavaScript applications—adding, subtracting, looping through lists of items and so on. In this chapter we introduce the JavaScript `Math` object and its mathematical methods. We describe a basic and advanced calculator, which can be used as a replacement for the desktop calculator. We look at converting strings into numbers and numbers into strings, and how to use numbers in both decimal and hexadecimal number bases.

We then discuss how to make use of random numbers to show random quotes. Finally, we end the chapter with the inclusion of several number utility functions for formatting numbers in various ways.

**Standard Calculator ../chapter2/calculator/standard.htm**
**Scientific Calculator .. /chapter2/calculator/scientific.htm**
**Random Quote of the Day ../chapter2/quotes/quote.htm**
**Number Utilities ../chapter2/number/utilities**

# Standard Calculator

The Standard Calculator is a simple but effective introduction to JavaScript. It makes use of image links for the calculator buttons, a form field for the calculator display, and `Math` and `String` objects to perform the behind-the-scene calculations.

Although using strings within a calculator may seem strange, they provide easy locations to store the user's input, which entered digit-by-digit, needs to be added together one digit at a time. This is where string concatenation—that is, adding one text string to another—excels. Adding two numbers together would result in the sum of the two numbers. For example, `3 + 4` would result in the numeric value `7`. Concatenating two text strings, on the other hand, would result in a larger text string. For example, `'3' + '4'` would result in the string value `'34'`.

Converting string values back to numeric values can be achieved in two ways: the textbook way using the `parseInt()` and `parseFloat()` global methods—for example, `parseInt('3')`, which would result in an integer value `3`—or the code hacker's way by subtracting zero. Subtracting zero from a string converts the string to a number—as long as the string represents a valid number, then there shouldn't ever be a problem. For example, `'3' - 0` would result in a numeric value 3. The `parseFloat()` global method is used to extract a floating-point number from a string. For example, `parseFloat('3.05xxxxx')` would result in a numeric value 3.05, whereas `parseInt('3.05xxxxx')` would result in an integer value 3.

Converting a number to a string can again be achieved in two ways: the textbook way using the `Number` object's `toString()` method—for example, `(3+4).toString()`, which would result in the string value 7—or the code hacker's way by adding an empty string—for example `'' + (3 + 4)`, which again would result in the string value 7. A word of caution: If we changed the last example to `'' + 3 + 4`, then the result would be the string value 34. In other words, the 3 has been converted to a string before the 4 is added. This is because of operator precedence. The use of parentheses ensures that the numbers are correctly summed before the result is converted to a string.

Another extremely useful method is the global `eval()` method, which evaluates the passed string argument. For example, if the two variables `lhs` and `rhs` were assigned the values 2 and 3, and the `op` variable was assigned the value `*`, then the expression `eval(lhs + op + rhs)` would produce the numeric value 6. In other words, the string value `2*3` would be passed to the `eval()` function, which would then evaluate this as a JavaScript expression. This allows the capability of evaluating runtime expressions, where the user controls the complete mathematical expression, which is then interpreted using `eval()`.

Figure 2-1 shows the results of the square root of 2—that is, the result of the user first pressing the 2 button and then pressing the `sqrt` button.

As this is a fairly complex application to write, debugging the code can be difficult. To assist with the debugging on JavaScript applications, several techniques can be employed. The simplest is the use of carefully placed `alert()` statements to highlight the state of variables when the code is running.

Another option, employed within the Standard Calculator, is the use of a form to hold visible copies of internal settings. The calculator makes use of several internal settings to describe the current state of the calculator: `lhs` represents the numeric value to the left in a mathematical expression, `op` represents the operand in the middle of the expression, `rhs` the numeric value to the right of the operand, `res` represents the result of the expression, `mem` represents the calculator's memory value, and `old` represents the previous value of `res`. There is also a `done` setting that is used to indicate that the user has finished entering the `lhs` or `rhs` value. These seven values are extremely useful when debugging

**Figure 2-1**
Standard Calculator—
Displaying the
Square Root of 2.

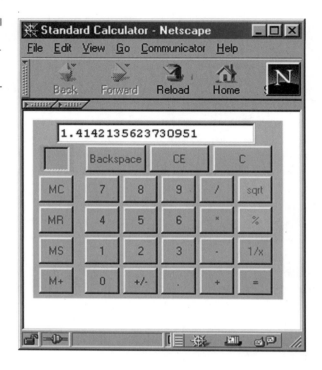

the application. Therefore, being able to see the current values may help you understand what is happening when problems start to occur within the code. The code includes a debug form with a form field for each of the seven values. Whenever the main process within the code updates the internal settings, it also updates the debug form fields. Enabling the debug form is as simple as setting a debug variable to true or false. This then allows us to debug the calculator at a later date without having to reintroduce the debugging code.

Figure 2-2 shows the debug code in operation, displaying the current values of the calculator's internal settings.

## Standard Calculator Source Code

On the CD

../chapter2/calculator/standard.htm

```html
<html>

<head>
<title>Standard Calculator</title>
```

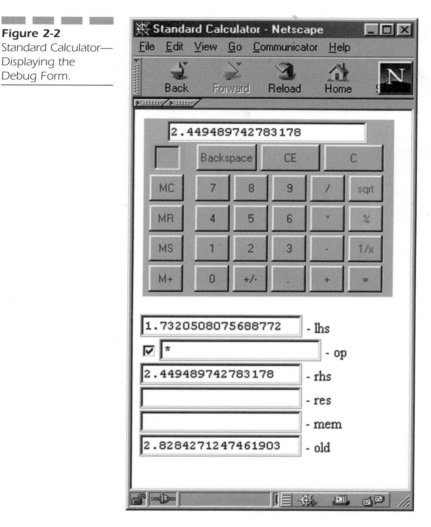

Here we use a style sheet to define the background color of all `table` elements:

```
<style><!--
table { background:#cccccc; }
//--></style>
```

Here we use the `script` element to embed JavaScript code within the HTML:

```
<script language="JavaScript"><!--
```

We first define several global variables—global in the sense that they are available to all of the JavaScript code in the current page. The debug Boolean variable, set to false, controls whether diagnostic data is shown on the screen, which is useful when initially creating the application:

```
var debug = false;
```

The nan Boolean variable is used to trap invalid mathematical values (for example, division by zero, which produces the special Infinity value, or cases of indeterminacy such as zero multiplied by "infinity," which can produce the special NaN value—Not a Number) and to stop the user from continuing until he or she cancels the current display:

```
var nan = false;
```

We can define and initialize several variables in one go to save space. Here we define and initialize lhs, op, rhs, res, mem, and old variables all to hold empty string values:

```
var lhs = op = rhs = res = mem = old = '';
```

The done Boolean variable controls whether the user can enter a leading zero. This avoids the generation of octal numbers (octal numbers—base 8— are indicated as such by the presence of a leading zero):

```
var done = false;
```

The update() function is the key process within the whole Standard Calculator code. It updates the calculator display and optionally updates the debug form fields:

```
function update() {
```

Only if debug is set to true will we update the debug form fields. Each of the six internal calculator variables (lhs, op, rhs, res, mem, old, and mem) plus the done variable have a corresponding debug form field, which is updated using the form hierarchy document.formName.formFieldName.value:

```
if (debug) {
  document.debug.lhs.value = lhs;
  document.debug.op.value = op;
  document.debug.rhs.value = rhs;
```

```
    document.debug.res.value = res;
    document.debug.mem.value = mem;
    document.debug.old.value = old;
    document.debug.done.checked = done;
}
```

Chapter 8 "Forms" presents more details on the use of forms with JavaScript. To show the appropriate value in the calculator's display, we use the local variable `dis`. The `dis` variable is local to the scope of the `update()` function—that is, the `dis` variable and its value is not available to any of the JavaScript code outside the scope of the `update()` function. Its initial value is set to zero to indicate an empty display:

```
var dis = '0';
```

Then depending on the value of the `res`, `rhs`, or `lhs` variables, the `dis` variable is updated to show the first variable that doesn't contain an empty string:

```
if (res != '') dis = res;
else if (rhs != '') dis = rhs;
else if (lhs != '' && op == '') dis = lhs;
```

In the last line we also check that the value of the `op` variable is not an empty string. This allows the initial zero value of `dis` to be maintained—and stops `dis` from being set to an empty string.

As most calculators display a value followed by a decimal point, we will do likewise. However, first we need to check that the `dis` variable does not already hold a floating-point number. We first ensure that `dis` contains a string by prefixing it with an empty string, then we use the `String` object's `indexOf()` method to find the first instance of any decimal point within `dis`. If none is found, then `-1` is returned by the `indexOf()` method. If one is not found—that is, the value returned by the `indexOf()` method is less than ($<$) zero—then we add a decimal point using the `+=` operator:

```
if (('' + dis).indexOf('.') < 0) dis += '.';
```

The expression `dis += '.'` is a shorthand version of `dis = dis + '.'`, It is used frequently throughout JavaScript. Strings are covered in detail in Chapter 3 "Strings and Regular Expressions."

We then update the calculator display by updating the `value` property of the `calc` form's `result` form field with the value of `dis`:

```
document.calc.result.value = dis;
```

Before continuing we check to see if the current display value shows a nonnumeric value—in other words, the result of bad expression or the result of a division by zero. If an expression uses a nonnumeric input, then the result will produce the value NaN. If a division by zero occurs, then the result will produce Infinity or -Infinity. We set the nan Boolean variable to true if either the value of dis equals NaN. (note the trailing decimal point), or dis contains the substring Infinity:

```
if (dis == 'NaN.' || dis.indexOf('Infinity') > -1)
  nan = true;
```

Finally we return false to whatever invoked the update() function:

```
  return false;
}
```

The e() function is used to evaluate the current calculator settings. It is invoked when the calculator's equal sign (=) is pressed:

```
function e() {
```

As in nearly all the remaining functions, we first check the nan Boolean variable. If its true, then we simply return false—effectively canceling the user's action:

```
  if (nan) return false;
```

We now evaluate the res using the eval() global method, using the expression lhs + op + rhs if rhs is not empty:

```
  if (rhs != '')     res = '' + eval(lhs + op + rhs);
```

Or using the expression lhs + op + lhs if op is not empty:

```
  else if (op != '') res = '' + eval(lhs + op + lhs);
```

Or simply the expression lhs if lhs is not empty:

```
  else if (lhs != '') res = '' + eval(lhs);
```

The eval() global method evaluates a string containing JavaScript code. For instance, if lhs contained the string 9, and op contained + and rhs contained 10, then the string passed to eval() would be 9+10, which eval() would evaluate to the numeric value 19.

We set the lhs, op, and rhs variables to empty strings ready for the next calculation:

```
lhs = op = rhs = '';
```

Once the expression has been evaluated we then finish of by setting the done Boolean to true, invoking the update() function to update the display, setting old to be the current value of res, setting res to an empty string, and finally returning false:

```
done = true;
update();
old = res;
res = '';
return false;
}
```

The o() function is used to hold one-of-a-kind options—in this case, a percent calculation. A string containing the character % is passed as the option argument when the % key is pressed by the user:

```
function o(option) {
  if (nan) return false;
```

If the passed option is the % character, we calculate a percentage value depending on which of the rhs, op, and lhs variables are not empty:

```
if (option == '%') {
  if (rhs != '')       rhs = '' + (lhs*rhs/100), res = rhs;
  else if (op != '')   rhs = '' + (lhs*lhs/100), res = lhs;
  else if (lhs != '')  lhs = '';
}
```

Note that we ensure the result of the expression is converted back into a string by appending an empty string.

```
done = true;
return update();
}
```

We'll be extending the o() function in the "Scientific Calculator" section later in this chapter.

The f() function is used to calculate various mathematical functions, depending on the value of the passed func argument. At the moment, just sqrt and 1/x are passed when the sqrt or 1/x keys are pressed by the user:

```
function f(func) {
  if (nan) return false;
```

Rather than work out which of the variables rhs, lhs, res, or old to use when performing the calculation, within each separate mathematical function, we work it out up front and then store the variables' value in the local tmp variable:

```
var tmp;
if (rhs != '') tmp = rhs;
else if (lhs != '') tmp = lhs;
else if (res != '') tmp = res;
else if (old != '') tmp = old;
else tmp = 0;
```

Now rather than performing the calculation in several different ways, we perform it just the once using the tmp value.

For the sqrt request, we use the Math objects sqrt() method passing tmp as an argument, assigning the result back to the tmp variable:

```
if (func == 'sqrt')     tmp = Math.sqrt(tmp);
```

For the 1/x request, we simply divide 1 by tmp:

```
else if (func == '1/x') tmp = 1 / tmp;
```

We then perform the reverse of the checks performed at the start of the f() function, setting the appropriate rhs or lhs variable to the value of tmp converted to a string:

```
if (rhs != '')      rhs = '' + tmp;
else if (lhs != '') lhs = '' + tmp;
else if (res != '') lhs = '' + tmp;
else lhs = tmp;

done = true;
return update();
}
```

The m() function is used to control the calculators memory store. The passed memory argument can have the value of MC, MR, MS, or M+:

```
function m(memory) {
  if (nan) return false;
```

If MC (Memory Cancel), we simply set the global mem variable to an empty string:

```
if (memory == 'MC') mem = '';
```

If MR (Memory Recall), we set either the value of lhs or rhs to mem:

```
else if (memory == 'MR') {
  if (op == '') lhs = mem; else rhs = mem;
}
```

If MS (Memory Store), we set the value of mem to either rhs, lhs, or res:

```
else if (memory == 'MS') {
  if (rhs != '')        mem = rhs;
  else if (lhs != '')   mem = lhs;
  else if (res != '')   mem = res;
}
```

If M+ (Memory Add), we add rhs, lhs, or res to the existing value of mem, making sure to convert the values to numeric by subtracting zero from each one:

```
else if (memory == 'M+') {
  if (rhs != '')        mem = (mem - 0) + (rhs - 0);
  else if (lhs != '')   mem = (mem - 0) + (lhs - 0);
  else if (res != '')   mem = (mem - 0) + (res - 0);
  mem += '';
}
```

To indicate to the user that the calculator memory holds a value, we change the src attribute of the memory image to either *empty.gif* or *full.gif*—but only for browsers that support the Image object (images will be covered in detail in Chapter 9 "Images"):

```
if (document.images && mem == '')
  document.images.memory.src = 'empty.gif';
if (document.images && mem != '')
  document.images.memory.src = 'full.gif';

done = true;
return update();
}
```

The n() function is used to process the user's selection of numeric keys, along with the negate key (+/-) and the decimal point key:

```
function n(num) {
  if (nan) return false;
```

The negate key (+/-) is used to prefix a minus character (-) to either the lhs, rhs, or res variables or to remove a leading minus character, using the indexOf() method to check if one exists already within the string, and with the String objects substring() method with an argument value of 1 to return a string value minus the first character of the string:

```
if (num == '+/-') {
  if (op == '' && lhs != '') {
    if (lhs.indexOf('-') < 0) lhs = '-' + lhs;
    else lhs = lhs.substring(1);
  }
  else if (rhs != '') {
    if (rhs.indexOf('-') < 0) rhs = '-' + rhs;
    else rhs = rhs.substring(1);
  }
  else lhs = (res * (-1)) + '', res = '';
}
```

Similarly a decimal point is only appended to the end of the lhs, rhs, or res variable if one is not already present within the string:

```
else if (num == '.') {
  if (op == '') {
    if (lhs.indexOf('.') < 0) {
      if (lhs == '') lhs = '0'; lhs += '.';
    }
  }
  else if (rhs.indexOf('.') < 0) {
    if (rhs == '') rhs = '0'; rhs += '.';
  }
}
```

Finally, we deal with the numeric keys 0 through 9. If the done Boolean variable is set to true, we set the value of the lhs or rhs variables to the passed num value, but only if the num value is not zero:

```
else if (done) {
  if (op == '') { if (num != '0') lhs = '' + num; }
  else { if (num != '0') rhs = '' + num; }
}
```

Otherwise, we append the passed num value to either the lhs or rhs variables, but not if the existing variable value is empty and the passed num value is zero:

```
else {
  if (op == '') {
    if (!(lhs == '' && num == '0')) lhs += num;
  }
  else {
    if (!(rhs == '' && num == '0')) rhs += num;
  }
}
```

As can be seen in the previous code, the done Boolean variable prevents the user from entering leading zeros. Now that the value of lhs or rhs contains a value, we set the done Boolean variable to false:

```
  done = false;
  return update();
}
```

The s() function processes all the operand key presses: +, -, /, and *:

```
function s(sign) {
  if (nan) return false;
```

If the lhs variable is empty but the old variable isn't, we first bring forward the old variable into the lhs variable, then reset old to empty, before assigning the passed sign argument to the op variable:

```
  if (lhs == '' && old != '') lhs = old, old = '', op = sign;
```

However, if both the lhs and rhs variables already contain values, we invoke the e() function directly to evaluate the mathematical expression, before setting the values of lhs, old, and op as in the previous line:

```
  else if (lhs != '' && rhs != '') {
    e(); lhs = old, res = '', op = sign;
  }
```

Finally, as long as the lhs variable is not empty, we simply assign the value of sign to the op variable:

```
  else if (lhs != '') op = sign;

  done = true;
  return update();
}
```

The c() function processes the user's request to cancel or clear the calculator's internal settings. The user can either delete the last entered digit using the Backspace button, clear the displayed number using the CE button, or clear the current calculation using the C button:

```
function c(cancel) {
```

When the user presses the Backspace key, the passed cancel argument contains back:

```
  if (cancel == 'back') {
```

Until now, if the nan Boolean variable was set to true, we have always abandoned the function by returning false. Here we only do so if the user is attempting to delete the last entered digit:

```
if (nan) return false;
```

If the rhs variable is not empty, we trim the last character using the String object's substring() method. Starting at the first character, we extract all the characters from the start of the rhs string, for the length of the string minus 1:

```
if (rhs != '')
    rhs = rhs.substring(0,rhs.length-1);
  else if (lhs != '' && op == '')
```

We do likewise for the lhs variable, but only if an op variable has not been populated with an operand by a call to the s() function:

```
    lhs = lhs.substring(0,lhs.length-1);
}
```

When the passed cancel argument contains CE, we need to clear the current lhs or rhs variable:

```
else if (cancel == 'CE') {
```

However, if the nan Boolean is set to true, we treat the CE key as a C key—and clear everything:

```
if (nan) lhs = op = rhs = res = old = '';
else if (rhs != '') rhs = '';
else lhs = op = '';
}
```

Finally, if the user presses the C key, we clear everything:

```
else if (cancel == 'C') {
  lhs = op = rhs = res = old = '';
}

done = false;
nan = false;
return update();
}
//--></script>
</head>
```

Now that we have discussed all the JavaScript code, let's turn our attention to the HTML. We use a load event handler (onLoad) within the body element to invoke the `update()` function when the page has completely loaded. This ensures that the calculator settings are initialized correctly:

```
<body onLoad="update()">
```

A form is used to display the calculator display as a text input field. To be able to correctly identify the text form field, we name the form `calc` using the `name` attribute:

```
<form name="calc">

<table border="0" width="265">
<tr><td>
<center>
```

The text input form field is named `result`, again using the `name` attribute. It also captures the focus event, triggered when the user clicks the mouse into the text field, using the `onFocus` event handler. The event handler uses a reference to the current text field (`this`) to invoke the `blur()` method on it, which defocuses the text field to prevent the user from typing into the text area:

```
<input type="text" size="25" name="result"
  onFocus="this.blur()">
<br>
```

An *empty.gif* image is used to indicate that the calculator's memory is empty. To alter the image, we name the image, using the `name` attribute, as `memory`:

```
<img src="empty.gif" name="memory">
 
```

We then use image links for each of the calculator's buttons, capturing the click events using the a element's `onClick` event handler to invoke the appropriate JavaScript function, returning the result of the function (in each case a `false` return value) back to the originating click event. This then cancels the default action of the event, which is to jump to an anchor within the current page:

```
<a href="#" onClick="return c('back')"><img src="back.gif"></a>
<a href="#" onClick="return c('CE')"><img src="CE.gif"></a>
<a href="#" onClick="return c('C')"><img src="Cancel.gif"></a>
<br>
<a href="#" onClick="return m('MC')"><img src="MC.gif"></a>
 
<a href="#" onClick="return n(7)"><img src="7.gif"></a>
```

```
<a href="#" onClick="return n(8)"><img src="8.gif"></a>
<a href="#" onClick="return n(9)"><img src="9.gif"></a>
<a href="#" onClick="return s('/')"><img src="div.gif"></a>
<a href="#" onClick="return f('sqrt')"><img src="sqrt.gif"></a>
<br>
<a href="#" onClick="return m('MR')"><img src="MR.gif"></a>
 
<a href="#" onClick="return n(4)"><img src="4.gif"></a>
<a href="#" onClick="return n(5)"><img src="5.gif"></a>
<a href="#" onClick="return n(6)"><img src="6.gif"></a>
<a href="#" onClick="return s('*')"><img src="mul.gif"></a>
<a href="#" onClick="return o('%')"><img src="percent.gif"></a>
<br>
<a href="#" onClick="return m('MS')"><img src="MS.gif"></a>
 
<a href="#" onClick="return n(1)"><img src="1.gif"></a>
<a href="#" onClick="return n(2)"><img src="2.gif"></a>
<a href="#" onClick="return n(3)"><img src="3.gif"></a>
<a href="#" onClick="return s('-')"><img src="minus.gif"></a>
<a href="#" onClick="return f('1/x')"><img src="1divx.gif"></a>
<br>
<a href="#" onClick="return m('M+')"><img src="Mplus.gif"></a>
 
<a href="#" onClick="return n(0)"><img src="0.gif"></a>
<a href="#" onClick="return n('+/-')"><img src="neg.gif"></a>
<a href="#" onClick="return n('.')"><img src="dot.gif"></a>
<a href="#" onClick="return s('+')"><img src="plus.gif"></a>
<a href="#" onClick="return e()"><img src="equal.gif"></a>
</center>
</td></tr>
</table>
</form>
```

Note that in order to avoid a blue outline around each of the image links, a `border` attribute with a value of zero can be additionally included within each of the `img` tags.

Finally, we optionally write a separate form out to the page using JavaScript. This can quickly aid the testing and debugging of an application while it is being developed:

```
<script language="JavaScript"><!--
```

We only write the form if the `debug` Boolean variable is set to `true`:

```
if (debug) {
```

We use the `document` object's `write()` method to write a string of text (in this case a form named `debug`) out to document:

```
document.write(
  '<form name="debug">' +
```

```
      '<input type="text" name="lhs"> - lhs<br>' +
      '<input type="checkbox" name="done">' +
      '<input type="text" name="op"> - op<br>' +
      '<input type="text" name="rhs"> - rhs<br>' +
      '<input type="text" name="res"> - res<br>' +
      '<input type="text" name="mem"> - mem<br>' +
      '<input type="text" name="old"> - old' +
      '</form>'
    );
}
```

The update() function updates the values of each of the debug forms lhs, rhs, res, mem, and old text form fields, and done checkbox—depending on the value of the debug Boolean variable.

```
//--></script>

</body>
</html>
```

# Scientific Calculator

The Standard Calculator—as the name suggests—is fairly standard. You could probably find several instances of similar-looking calculators on the Internet. A Scientific Calculator, however, would be more difficult to find—if it even exists. Figure 2-3 shows the Scientific Calculator.

As seen in the Standard Calculator, JavaScript provides a Math object instance—that is, an object that already exists—with several static functions and constants. A complete list of the static functions is shown in Table 2-1.

All bar one of the functions have been available since the first release of JavaScript—the Math.random() method was introduced in JavaScript 1.1. Prior to JavaScript 1.1, we would have had to write our own pseudo-random-number function. Fortunately, the days of supporting JavaScript 1.0-enabled browsers have long gone.

Table 2-2 shows the complete list of the Math object constants.

We make use of many of the static methods and a couple of the constants within the Scientific Calculator. We even create a factorial function to calculate the factorial of the passed argument. With knowledge of mathematical expressions and equations, it is possible to add further features to the calculator.

**Figure 2-3**
Scientific Calculator
in Decimal Mode.

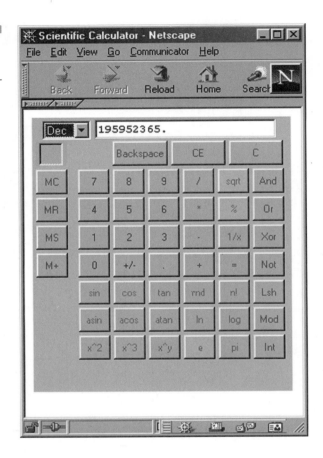

The Scientific Calculator also works in two base number systems: decimal and hexadecimal. The decimal base system is easy enough—it just uses the digits 0 through to 9. Hexadecimal numbers are also supported in JavaScript. A hexadecimal number is represented with the addition of a leading 0x sequence. For example, decimal 255 is represented in hexadecimal by 0xFF or 0xff. As shown in the Standard Calculator, we store the internal calculator settings within strings. Within the Scientific Calculator, this foundation allows the easy inclusion of the alpha characters A through F; we simply concatenate the characters to the existing internal settings.

The difficult part comes when we need to convert the string value FF to a value suitable for use within an expression. This can be achieved by concatenating 0x with FF, and then using the eval() method to evaluate the string. For example, eval('0x'+'FF') would return the value 255. Figure 2-4 shows the calculator in the hexadecimal mode. As you

**TABLE 2-1**

*Math object static functions.*

| Functions | Description |
|---|---|
| Math.abs() | Returns the absolute value of a number. |
| Math.acos() | Returns the arccosine of a number. |
| Math.asin() | Returns the arcsine of a number. |
| Math.atan() | Returns the arctangent of a number. |
| Math.atan2() | Returns the arctangent of the quotient of its arguments. |
| Math.ceil() | Returns the smallest integer greater than or equal to the number. |
| Math.cos() | Returns the cosine of a number. |
| Math.exp() | Return the exponent of $e$, i.e., $e^x$. |
| Math.floor() | Returns the largest integer less than or equal to a number. |
| Math.log() | Returns the natural logarithm of a number. |
| Math.max() | Returns the greater of two numbers. |
| Math.min() | Returns the lesser of two numbers. |
| Math.pow() | Returns $x$ to the power of $y$, i.e., $x^y$. |
| Math.random() | Returns a random number between 0 and 1. |
| Math.round() | Returns the value of a number rounded to the nearest integer. |
| Math.sin() | Returns the sine of a number. |
| Math.sqrt() | Returns the square root of a number. |
| Math.tan() | Returns the tangent of a number. |

**TABLE 2-2**

*Math object constants.*

| Constants | Description |
|---|---|
| Math.E | Constant $e$ and the base of natural logarithms |
| Math.LN10 | Natural logarithm of 10 |
| Math.LN2 | Natural logarithm of 2 |
| Math.LOG10E | Base 10 logarithm of $e$ |
| Math.LOG2E | Base 2 logarithm of $e$ |
| Math.PI | Constant $\Pi$—ratio of the circumference of a circle to its diameter |
| Math.SQRT1_2 | Square root of 1/2; equivalently, 1 over the square root of 2 |
| Math.SQRT2 | Square root of 2 |

**Figure 2-4**
Scientific Calculator in Hexadecimal Mode.

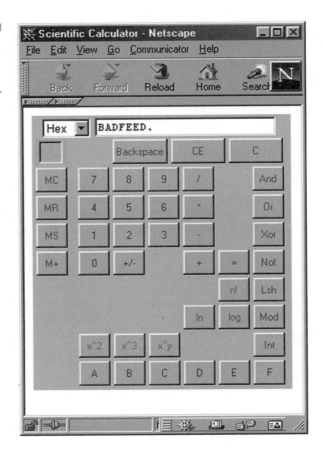

can see, several of the buttons visible in the decimal mode become hidden, whereas the buttons for the characters A through F now become visible. This uses image-swapping techniques, which are covered in detail in Chapter 9 "Images."

## Scientific Calculator Source Code

On the CD

../chapter2/calculator/scientific.htm

As the source code for the Scientific Calculator builds on the code used in the Standard Calculator, we will only concentrate on the differences between the two:

```
<html>

<head>
<title>Scientific Calculator</title>

<style><!--
table { background:#cccccc; }
//--></style>

<script language="JavaScript"><!--
var debug = false;
var nan = false;
var lhs = op = rhs = res = mem = old = '';
var done = false;
```

Two global integer variables are defined: base to indicate the current number base being used (decimal -10, or hexadecimal - 16) and oldbase to indicate the previous value of base, and to indicate a recent change in the number base being used:

```
var base = 10;
var oldbase = 16;
```

Two new global string variables are also defined: noHex, which is a string containing a list of keys not acceptable when base 16 is not being used, and noDec, which is a string containing a list of keys not acceptable when base 10 is not being used:

```
var noHex = 'ABCDEF';
var noDec = 'sqrt % 1/x dot rnd asin acos atan e pi';

function update() {
  if (debug) {
    document.debug.lhs.value = lhs;
    document.debug.op.value = op;
    document.debug.rhs.value = rhs;
    document.debug.res.value = res;
    document.debug.mem.value = mem;
    document.debug.old.value = old;
    document.debug.done.checked = done;
  }

  var dis = '0';
  if (res != '') dis = res;
  else if (rhs != '') dis = rhs;
  else if (lhs != '' && op == '') dis = lhs;
```

A new form field is included within the calculator display. This time a select options list is included to allow the user to select either a decimal or hexadecimal calculator display. We obtain a reference to the select options list, named base, using the hierarchy document.formName. fieldName, and assign the reference to the what variable:

```
var what = document.calc.base;
```

Using the reference `what`, we retrieve the string value of the `base` select field's selected option, subtract zero from it to convert it into a numerical value, and then assign the value to the global `base` variable:

```
base = what.options[what.selectedIndex].value - 0;

if (('' + dis).indexOf('.') < 0) dis += '.';
dis = ('' + dis).toUpperCase();

document.calc.result.value = dis;
if (dis == 'NAN.' || dis.indexOf('INFINITY') > -1)
  nan = true;
```

If the current value of `base` isn't equal to the current value of `old-base`, then a change has just been made to the base number system by the user—the `set()` function is invoked, passing the `what` reference as an input argument:

```
if (base != oldbase) set(what);

return false;
}
```

To avoid multiple instances of JavaScript code to convert numbers from decimal format to hexadecimal format and vice versa, two utility functions are defined. The `dec()` function converts a string into a decimal number:

```
function dec(h) {
```

The passed `h` string argument is first prefixed with `0x` to represent a hexadecimal string, which is then evaluated using the `eval()` method. This converts the hexadecimal string into a decimal number, which is then converted into a string by prefixing it with an empty string:

```
var d = '' + eval('0x'+h);
```

If the result was a zero, then this is replaced with an empty string:

```
if (d == '0') d = '';
return  d;
}
```

The `hex()` function converts a string into a decimal number:

```
function hex(d) {
```

The passed d string argument is converted to a number by subtracting zero from it. It is then converted to a string using the Number object's toString() method with an input argument of 16—indicating which number base to use:

```
var h = (d-0).toString(16);
if (h == '0') h = '';
```

The returned result is first converted to uppercase using the String object's toUpperCase() method. This ensures that the letters a to f are converted to A to F:

```
  return h.toUpperCase();
}
```

The ox() function is used to prefix an 0x string to the start of a number—but only if the current number base is 16 and the passed h string argument is not empty:

```
function ox(h) {
  if (base == 16 && h != '') return '0x' + h; return h;
}
```

The set() function is invoked whenever a base number change is detected. It is used to suppress or unsuppress several of the calculator buttons unsuitable for decimal of hexadecimal mode, and also to convert the internal calculator settings from decimal to hexadecimal or vice versa:

```
function set(what) {
```

The current base value is retrieved from the base select option, using the passed what form field reference argument:

```
  base = what.options[what.selectedIndex].value - 0;

  if (base == 16) {
```

If the base value is 16, then the internal calculator settings are converted from decimal to hexadecimal using the hex() function:

```
    lhs = hex(lhs);
    rhs = hex(rhs);
    res = hex(res);
```

If the browser supports the image object, then the src property of the named images A, B, C, D, E, and F is altered so that the hexadecimal calculator buttons are shown:

```
if (document.images) {
   document.images['A'].src = 'A.gif';
   document.images['B'].src = 'B.gif';
   document.images['C'].src = 'C.gif';
   document.images['D'].src = 'D.gif';
   document.images['E'].src = 'E.gif';
   document.images['F'].src = 'F.gif';
```

The src property of the several of the scientific images are altered so that they are hidden from view, replacing each one with a *space.gif* image:

```
      document.images['sqrt'].src = 'space.gif';
      document.images['percent'].src = 'space.gif';
      document.images['1divx'].src = 'space.gif';
      document.images['dot'].src = 'space.gif';
      document.images['sin'].src = 'space.gif';
      document.images['cos'].src = 'space.gif';
      document.images['tan'].src = 'space.gif';
      document.images['rnd'].src = 'space.gif';
      document.images['asin'].src = 'space.gif';
      document.images['acos'].src = 'space.gif';
      document.images['atan'].src = 'space.gif';
      document.images['ee'].src = 'space.gif';
      document.images['pi'].src = 'space.gif';
   }
}
else {
```

If base value is 10, then the internal calculator settings are converted from hexadecimal to decimal using the dec() function:

```
   lhs = dec(lhs);
   rhs = dec(rhs);
   res = dec(res);

   if (document.images) {
```

If the browser supports the image object, then the src property of the named images A, B, C, D, E, and F is altered so that the hexadecimal calculator buttons are hidden, replacing each one with a *space.gif* image

```
      document.images['A'].src = 'space.gif';
      document.images['B'].src = 'space.gif';
      document.images['C'].src = 'space.gif';
      document.images['D'].src = 'space.gif';
      document.images['E'].src = 'space.gif';
      document.images['F'].src = 'space.gif';
```

The src property of the several of the scientific images are altered so that they are shown:

```
document.images['sqrt'].src = 'sqrt.gif';
document.images['percent'].src = 'percent.gif';
document.images['1divx'].src = '1divx.gif';
document.images['dot'].src = 'dot.gif';
document.images['sin'].src = 'sin.gif';
document.images['cos'].src = 'cos.gif';
document.images['tan'].src = 'tan.gif';
document.images['rnd'].src = 'rnd.gif';
document.images['asin'].src = 'asin.gif';
document.images['acos'].src = 'acos.gif';
document.images['atan'].src = 'atan.gif';
document.images['ee'].src = 'ee.gif';
document.images['pi'].src = 'pi.gif';
  }
}
```

Finally, the value of base is copied into oldbase:

```
oldbase = base;
}

function e() {
  if (nan) return false;
```

Before evaluating the calculation in the e() function, we first convert the lhs and rhs values from strings to numeric values using the ox() function—which, if necessary, converts the hexadecimal strings that lhs or rhs contain into decimal values:

```
lhs = ox(lhs), rhs = ox(rhs);
```

A new evaluate expression x^y is included within the calculator. This is used to raise either lhs to the power of rhs or lhs to the power of lhs using the Math object's pow() method:

```
if (op == 'x^y') {
  if (rhs != '')        res = '' + Math.pow(lhs, rhs);
  else if (lhs != '') res = '' + Math.pow(lhs, lhs);
  lhs = op = rhs = '';
}
else {
  if (rhs != '')        res = '' + eval(lhs + op + rhs);
  else if (op != '')  res = '' + eval(lhs + op + lhs);
  else if (lhs != '') res = '' + eval(lhs);
  lhs = op = rhs = '';
}
```

If the base is 16, then the hex() function is used to convert the res variable to a hexadecimal string value:

```
    if (base == 16) res = hex(res);

    done = true;
    update();
   .old = res;
    res = '';
    return false;
}

function o(option) {
  if (nan) return false;
```

Before we allow the user to use one of the one-off options in the `o()` function, we first check if it is a valid `option` for the hexadecimal mode. If the passed option argument appears within the `noDec` string, we return `false`:

```
    if (base == 16 && noDec.indexOf(option) > -1) return false;
```

Before using the `lhs` and `rhs` variables in the one-off expressions, we again use the `ox()` function:

```
    lhs = ox(lhs), rhs = ox(rhs);

    if (option == '%') {
      if (rhs != '')        rhs = '' + (lhs*rhs/100), res = rhs;
      else if (op != '')    rhs = '' + (lhs*lhs/100), res = lhs;
      else if (lhs != '') lhs = '';
    }
```

Several new one-off options are included. The `rnd` option generates a random number between 0 and 1 using the `Math` object's `random()` method:

```
    else if (option == 'rnd') {
      if (lhs == '' || op == '') lhs = '' + Math.random();
      else rhs = '' + Math.random();
    }
```

The pi option returns the value of constant $\prod$ using the Math object's PI constant:

```
    else if (option == 'pi') {
      if (lhs == '' || op == '') lhs = '' + Math.PI;
      else rhs = '' + Math.PI;
    }
```

The `e` option returns the value of constant `e` using the `Math` object's `E` constant:

```
    else if (option == 'e') {
      if (lhs == '' || op == '') lhs = '' + Math.E;
      else rhs = '' + Math.E;
    }
```

Again, if the base is 16, then the hex() function is used to convert the res variable to a hexadecimal string value:

```
    if (base == 16) res = hex(res);

    done = true;
    return update();
  }

  function f(func,y) {
    if (nan) return false;
```

Again, we limit the functions that can be used in hexadecimal mode:

```
    if (base == 16 && noDec.indexOf(func) > -1) return false;

    var tmp;
    if (rhs != '') tmp = rhs;
    else if (lhs != '') tmp = lhs;
    else if (res != '') tmp = res;
    else if (old != '') tmp = old;
    else tmp = 0;
```

This time we prefix the tmp variable with 0x if in hexadecimal mode:

```
    tmp = ox(tmp);

    if (func == 'sqrt')      tmp = Math.sqrt(tmp);
    else if (func == '1/x') tmp = 1 / tmp;
```

Many new scientific functions are included, the sine, cosine, tangent, arcsine, arccosine, and arctangent values using the appropriate Math object methods:

```
    else if (func == 'sin') tmp = Math.sin(tmp);
    else if (func == 'cos') tmp = Math.cos(tmp);
    else if (func == 'tan') tmp = Math.tan(tmp);
    else if (func == 'asin') tmp = Math.asin(tmp);
    else if (func == 'acos') tmp = Math.acos(tmp);
    else if (func == 'atan') tmp = Math.atan(tmp);
```

The bitwise not operator using the ~ unary operator to reverse all the bits in the tmp variable:

```
else if (func == 'Not') tmp = (~tmp);
```

Rounding a number down using the `Math` object's `floor()` method:

```
else if (func == 'Int') tmp = Math.floor(tmp);
```

Calculating the natural logarithm using the `Math` object's `log()` method:

```
else if (func == 'ln')  tmp = Math.log(tmp);
```

Calculating the squared or cubed value of `tmp` using the additionally passed `y` argument:

```
else if (func == 'pow') tmp = Math.pow(tmp,y);
```

Calculating the base 10 natural logarithm using the `Math` object's `LOG10E` constant and `log()` method:

```
else if (func == 'log') tmp = (Math.LOG10E * Math.log(tmp));
```

Calculating the factorial value of `tmp` using the `factorial()` function, but first trapping negative numbers and setting their resultant value to NaN:

```
    else if (func == 'fac') {
      if (tmp < 0) tmp = NaN;
      else tmp = factorial(tmp-0);
    }

    if (base == 16) tmp = hex(tmp);

    if (rhs != '')        rhs = '' + tmp;
    else if (lhs != '') lhs = '' + tmp;
    else if (res != '') lhs = '' + tmp;
    else lhs = tmp;

    done = true;
    return update();
  }

  function m(memory) {
    if (nan) return false;

    if (memory == 'MC') mem = '';
    else if (memory == 'MR') {
      if (op == '') lhs = mem; else rhs = mem;
    }
    else if (memory == 'MS') {
      if (rhs != '')        mem = rhs;
```

```
      else if (lhs != '') mem = lhs;
      else if (res != '') mem = res;
    }
    else if (memory == 'M+') {
```

When adding a value to the existing `mem` memory store, we use the `ox()` function to append an `0x` to the values if in hexadecimal mode:

```
    if (rhs != '')        mem = (ox(mem) - 0) + (ox(rhs) - 0);
    else if (lhs != '') mem = (ox(mem) - 0) + (ox(lhs) - 0);
    else if (res != '') mem = (ox(mem) - 0) + (ox(res) - 0);
    if (base == 16) mem = hex(mem);
    mem += '';
    }

    if (document.images && mem == '')
      document.images.memory.src = 'empty.gif';
    if (document.images && mem != '')
      document.images.memory.src = 'full.gif';

    done = true;
    return update();
  }

  function n(num) {
    if (nan) return false;
```

When in decimal mode, we restrict the use of the hexadecimal keys A through F:

```
    if (base == 10 && noHex.indexOf(num) > -1) return false;

    if (num == '+/-') {
      if (op == '' && lhs != '') {
        if (lhs.indexOf('-') < 0) lhs = '-' + lhs;
        else lhs = lhs.substring(1);
      }
      else if (rhs != '') {
        if (rhs.indexOf('-') < 0) rhs = '-' + rhs;
        else rhs = rhs.substring(1);
      }
      else lhs = (res * (-1)) + '', res = '';
    }
    else if (num == '.') {
      if (op == '') {
        if (lhs.indexOf('.') < 0) {
          if (lhs == '') lhs = '0'; lhs += '.';
        }
      }
      else if (rhs.indexOf('.') < 0) {
        if (rhs == '') rhs = '0'; rhs += '.';
      }
    }
    else if (done) {
      if (op == '') { if (num != '0') lhs = '' + num; }
      else { if (num != '0') rhs = '' + num; }
```

```
      }
      else {
        if (op == '') {
          if (!(lhs == '' && num == '0')) lhs += num;
        }
        else {
          if (!(rhs == '' && num == '0')) rhs += num;
        }
      }

      done = false;
      return update();
    }

    function s(sign) {
      if (nan) return false;

      if (lhs == '' && old != '') lhs = old, old = '', op = sign;
      else if (lhs != '' && rhs != '') {
        e(); lhs = old, res = '', op = sign;
      }
      else if (lhs != '') op = sign;

      done = true;
      return update();
    }

    function c(cancel) {
      if (cancel == 'back') {
        if (nan) return false;

        if (rhs != '')
          rhs = rhs.substring(0,rhs.length-1);
        else if (lhs != '' && op == '')
          lhs = lhs.substring(0,lhs.length-1);
      }
      else if (cancel == 'CE') {
        if (nan) lhs = op = rhs = res = '';
        else if (rhs != '') rhs = '';
        else lhs = op = '';
      }
      else if (cancel == 'C') {
        lhs = op = rhs = res = '';
      }

      done = false;
      nan = false;
      return update();
    }
```

The factorial() function calculates the factorial value of the passed n argument simply by looping through all the values from 1 to n and multiplying each one together before returning the value:

```
function factorial(n) {
  var r=1; for (var i = 1; i<=n; i++) r *= i; return r;
}
```

The code `i++` uses the postfix increment operator to increment the value of `i` by 1. This is shorthand for `i = i + 1`:

```
//--></script>
</head>
```

There is one small change to the `onLoad` event handler within the `body` element, to invoke the `set()` function passing a reference to the `calc` form's `base` select field, before invoking the `update()` function as in the Standard Calculator:

```
<body onLoad="set(document.calc.base);update()">

<form name="calc">

<table border="0" width="300">
<tr><td>
<center>
```

The additional `select` element allows the user to switch between decimal and hexadecimal modes—the `value` attribute of each `option` element is used to indicate the number base. The `select` element's `onChange` event handler captures the change event, fired when the user changes the selected option, which invokes the `set()` function, passing a reference to itself (`this`), and then invokes the `update()` function:

```
<select name="base" onChange="set(this);update()">
<option value="10" selected>Dec</option>
<option value="16">Hex</option>
</select>
<input type="text" size="25" name="result"
  onFocus="this.blur()">
<br>
<img src="empty.gif" name="memory">
 
<img src="space.gif">
```

Additional `img` tags are used to represent more calculator buttons:

```
<a href="#" onClick="return c('back')"><img src="back.gif"></a>
<a href="#" onClick="return c('CE')"><img src="CE.gif"></a>
<a href="#" onClick="return c('C')"><img src="Cancel.gif"></a>
<br>
<a href="#" onClick="return m('MC')"><img src="MC.gif"></a>
 
<a href="#" onClick="return n(7)"><img src="7.gif"></a>
<a href="#" onClick="return n(8)"><img src="8.gif"></a>
<a href="#" onClick="return n(9)"><img src="9.gif"></a>
<a href="#" onClick="return s('/')"><img src="div.gif"></a>
```

Images that require suppressing—depending on which mode is being used—have an additional `name` attribute to uniquely identity the image. Images and image manipulation is covered in detail in Chapter 9 "Images."

```
<a href="#" onClick="return f('sqrt')"><img src="sqrt.gif"
   name="sqrt"></a>
<a href="#" onClick="return s('&')"><img src="And.gif"></a>
<br>
<a href="#" onClick="return m('MR')"><img src="MR.gif"></a>
 
<a href="#" onClick="return n(4)"><img src="4.gif"></a>
<a href="#" onClick="return n(5)"><img src="5.gif"></a>
<a href="#" onClick="return n(6)"><img src="6.gif"></a>
<a href="#" onClick="return s('*')"><img src="mul.gif"></a>
<a href="#" onClick="return o('%')"><img src="percent.gif"
   name="percent"></a>
<a href="#" onClick="return s('|')"><img src="Or.gif"></a>
<br>
<a href="#" onClick="return m('MS')"><img src="MS.gif"></a>
 
<a href="#" onClick="return n(1)"><img src="1.gif"></a>
<a href="#" onClick="return n(2)"><img src="2.gif"></a>
<a href="#" onClick="return n(3)"><img src="3.gif"></a>
<a href="#" onClick="return s('-')"><img src="minus.gif"></a>
<a href="#" onClick="return f('1/x')"><img src="1divx.gif"
   name="1divx"></a>
<a href="#" onClick="return s('^')"><img src="Xor.gif"></a>
<br>
<a href="#" onClick="return m('M+')"><img src="Mplus.gif"></a>
 
<a href="#" onClick="return n(0)"><img src="0.gif"></a>
<a href="#" onClick="return n('+/-')"><img src="neg.gif"></a>
<a href="#" onClick="return n('.')"><img src="dot.gif"
   name="dot"></a>
<a href="#" onClick="return s('+')"><img src="plus.gif"></a>
<a href="#" onClick="return e()"><img src="equal.gif"></a>
<a href="#" onClick="return f('Not')"><img src="Not.gif"></a>
<br>
<img src="space.gif">
 
<a href="#" onClick="return f('sin')"><img src="sin.gif"
   name="sin"></a>
<a href="#" onClick="return f('cos')"><img src="cos.gif"
   name="cos"></a>
<a href="#" onClick="return f('tan')"><img src="tan.gif"
   name="tan"></a>
<a href="#" onClick="return o('rnd')"><img src="rnd.gif"
   name="rnd"></a>
<a href="#" onClick="return f('fac')"><img src="fac.gif"></a>
<a href="#" onClick="return s('<<')"><img src="Lsh.gif"></a>
<br>
<img src="space.gif">
 
<a href="#" onClick="return f('asin')"><img src="asin.gif"
   name="asin"></a>
<a href="#" onClick="return f('acos')"><img src="acos.gif"
   name="acos"></a>
<a href="#" onClick="return f('atan')"><img src="atan.gif"
```

```
      name="atan"></a>
<a href="#" onClick="return f('ln')"><img src="ln.gif"></a>
<a href="#" onClick="return f('log')"><img src="log.gif"></a>
<a href="#" onClick="return s('%')"><img src="Mod.gif"></a>
<br>
<img src="space.gif">
 
<a href="#" onClick="return f('pow',2)"><img src="xp2.gif"></a>
<a href="#" onClick="return f('pow',3)"><img src="xp3.gif"></a>
<a href="#" onClick="return s('x^y')"><img src="xpy.gif"></a>
<a href="#" onClick="return o('e')"><img src="ee.gif"
      name="ee"></a>
<a href="#" onClick="return o('pi')"><img src="pi.gif"
      name="pi"></a>
<a href="#" onClick="return f('Int')"><img src="Int.gif"></a>
<br>
<img src="space.gif">
 
<a href="#" onClick="return n('A')"><img src="space.gif"
      name="A"></a>
<a href="#" onClick="return n('B')"><img src="space.gif"
      name="B"></a>
<a href="#" onClick="return n('C')"><img src="space.gif"
      name="C"></a>
<a href="#" onClick="return n('D')"><img src="space.gif"
      name="D"></a>
<a href="#" onClick="return n('E')"><img src="space.gif"
      name="E"></a>
<a href="#" onClick="return n('F')"><img src="space.gif"
      name="F"></a>
</center>
</td></tr>
</table>

</form>

<script language="JavaScript"><!--
if (debug) {
   document.write(
      '<form name="debug">' +
      '<input type="text" name="lhs"> - lhs<br>' +
      '<input type="checkbox" name="done">' +
      '<input type="text" name="op"> - op<br>' +
      '<input type="text" name="rhs"> - rhs<br>' +
      '<input type="text" name="res"> - res<br>' +
      '<input type="text" name="mem"> - mem<br>' +
      '<input type="text" name="old"> - old' +
      '</form>'
   );
}
//--></script>

</body>
</html>
```

With a bit of thought, the Scientific Calculator could be extended to use other number bases. The Number object's toString() method supports number bases from 2 through 36. As well as decimal and hexadecimal numbers, JavaScript also provides support for octal—indicated with a leading zero. Using binary, for example, would require simple JavaScript functions to convert a decimal number into a string of 1s and 0s and back again.

# Random Quote of the Day

Presenting a different page content every time the user visits gives the impression that the page is constantly changing—and therefore encourages people to revisit. Adding a random feature using JavaScript can add a simple but effective change of content to an otherwise static web page. Displaying random humorous quotes may encourage a visitor to simply carry on browsing through a site to catch the next random quote. Figures 2-5 and 2-6 show typical random quotes displayed on an otherwise mundane page.

Using a simple array of text strings, we can use the Math object's random() method to select one string at random to display. The trick is converting the random floating-point number between 0 and 1 to an integer that represents an item in our string array.

The number of random quotes available with the Random Quote of the Day code is slightly over 500. Holding all these quotes within the

**Figure 2-5**
Random Quote of the Day—A Typical Quote.

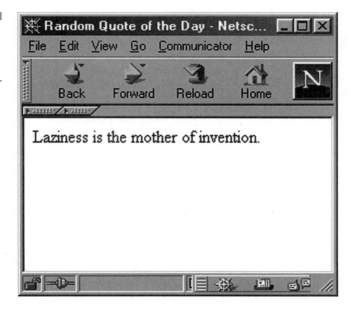

**Figure 2-6**
Random Quote of
the Day—Another
Typical Quote.

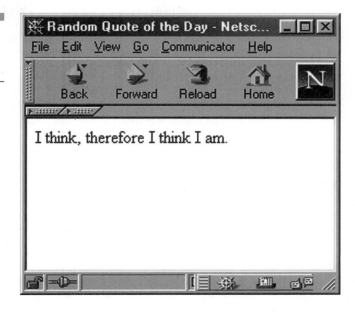

JavaScript code embedded in a page not only adds a large overhead (approximately 22 Kb of data), it also means that if added to another page, it would again add another large overhead. This is where the use of external JavaScript source files comes in handy.

So far, we have embedded JavaScript code directly within the page in between SCRIPT tags. As well as doing this, we can refer to external JavaScript source files using the HTML syntax: `<script language="JavaScript" src="quote.js"></script>`. Note that we still need to use the closing `script` tag. The code within the *quote.js* file is retrieved at the same time as the HTML, and then it is included within the page at the point the `script` tag appears. The code within the *quote.js* file is pure JavaScript code—there is no need to use `script` tags within the file itself.

The benefit of using external JavaScript source files is that we can reuse the *quote.js* file within other pages. Once the file has been loaded into the browser's cache, it is immediately available again to other pages without the user waiting for it to be downloaded from the server.

As we want our users to revisit often, we really need to ration the number of quotes that they can see in any one day. This can easily be achieved by using separate external JavaScript files, each with a different filename, one for each day of the month—for instance, *quote1.js* through *quote31.js*. We then just need to load the appropriate file within our HTML page. Rather than updating the HTML to change the filename each and every day, we can use JavaScript to perform this for us.

JavaScript code can be used to output HTML to a page while it is being rendered to the browser. It can also be used to write `script` tags to the page. This technique is used to dynamically write the appropriate `script` tag requesting an external JavaScript source file for the current date.

## Random Quote Source Code

 ../chapter2/quotes/quote.htm

The Random Quote of the Day is controlled by only a few lines of JavaScript code. This code can be placed within any number of pages. There are two fundamental parts. The first, which is placed inside the head of the HTML, loads the appropriate external JavaScript source file. The second writes one of the quotes out to the document. This second part can be used many times within the page, perhaps to place random quotes at the top and bottom of the page or at different locations throughout a long document.

```
<html>

<head>
<title>Random Quote of the Day</title>

<script language="JavaScript"><!--
```

The `rndInteger()` function is used to return any random integer from zero up to the value of the passed n argument:

```
function rndInteger(n) {
```

The `Math` object's `random()` method is used to generate a random floating-point number between 0 and 1. This is then multiplied with the value of n—which gives a floating-point number between 0 and n. This is then passed as input to the `Math` object's `floor()` function, which rounds the number down. The result is then returned:

```
  return Math.floor(Math.random() * n);
}
```

To retrieve the current day of the month, we first create a new `Date` object representing the current date using the `Date()` object constructor without any arguments:

```
var today = new Date();
```

Using the `Date` object's `getDate()` method, we can retrieve the days of the month (1 through to 31):

```
var day = today.getDate();
```

The `file` variable then contains the name of the external JavaScript source code for the current day:

```
var file = 'quote' + day + '.js';
```

We use this when writing a script tag out to the document:

```
document.write(
    '<script language="JavaScript" src="' + file + '"><\/script>'
);
//--></script>
</head>

<body>
```

Note that we escaped the forward slash character (/) within the `write()` method with a backslash character (\). Otherwise, the browser is likely to treat this as the end of the current JavaScript code.

The contents of the external JavaScript source file is then included within the current page at this point. As seen later, each of the external JavaScript source quote files defines a `qs` string array. If the file is loaded correctly, then a `qs` variable will be defined within the current page. If, for whatever reason, the quote file is not loaded then the `qs` variable will not be defined.

Before attempting to use the `qs` variable, we first check to see if it exists as a property of the current `window` object:

```
<script language="JavaScript"><!--
if (window.qs) {
```

If the `qs` variable exists, then we generate a random integer using the `rndInteger()` function passing the `length` property of the `qs` array as input. This will then generate a random integer from zero up to the value of the `length` property, which is assigned to the `rnd` variable:

```
var rnd = rndInteger(qs.length);
```

Using the `rnd` variable, we retrieve the value of the string at that location within the `qs` array and write it out to the document:

```
document.write(qs[rnd]);

}//--></script>

</body>
</html>
```

## JavaScript quote1.js Source Code

../chapter2/quotes/quote1.js

The source code for just one of the 31 different quote files, *quote1.js*, is shown in full below. Note that the file contains just JavaScript source code without any HTML tags. The file contains just one line of JavaScript code, to create an array of strings. Arrays will be covered in detail in Chapter 4 "Arrays and Objects."

In this particular file, the `qs` array contains 16 different quotations. The number of items within the `qs` array is obtained using the `length` property—in other words, `qs.length`. This will return the value `16`. The first item within the `qs` array is located at index position zero—arrays usually start from position zero. The last item is in position 15. Retrieving the value of one of the strings is achieved using `qs[position]`, where `position` ranges from zero to 15. Therefore, `qs[5]` contains the string `The early worm gets the bird.`:

```
var qs = new Array(
"There is much Obi-Wan did not tell you.",
"The bozos are coming.",
"The heart is wiser than the intellect.",
"The greatest remedy for anger is delay.",
"The future lies ahead.",
"The early worm gets the bird.",
"The die is cast.",
"The coast was clear.",
"The bigger the theory, the better.",
"The better part of valour is discretion.",
"The best prophet of the future is the past.",
"The adverb always follows the verb.",
"That that is is not that that is not.",
"TANSTAAFL.",
```

```
"Talkers are no good doers.",
"SYSTEM RESTARTING, WAIT."
);
```

## Number Utilities

JavaScript is particularly weak when it comes to providing number formatting functions. Before we end this chapter, we will include few utility functions to enable the easy formatting of numbers. These functions can then be dropped into any script and be reused at will.

### Rounding Numbers to Several Decimal Places

Whenever dealing with numbers, especially where the JavaScript language performs calculations on floating-point numbers, it is possible that the result can have two many digits trailing the decimal point. The following round() function rounds a number down to a certain number of decimal places. For instance, round(9.909, 2) will produce the result 9.9, and round(1.234567, 3) will produce 1.234.

 **../chapter2/number/utilites.htm**

```
function round(number,x) {
  return Math.round(number * Math.pow(10,x)) / Math.pow(10,x);
}
```

### Displaying Monetary Amounts

Displaying prices to users, perhaps after calculating taxes and delivery charges, can result in values that are not properly formatted with the necessary number of decimal places. For example, one dollar and 20 cents could end up as 1.2—an odd monetary amount. The following cents() function accepts either a numeric or string value, and then reuses the previous round() function to round the amount to two decimal places. Finally, it pads the amount with the required number of trailing zeros, returning a string value:

**../chapter2/number/utilites.htm**

```
function cents(amount) {
  amount -= 0;

  amount = round(amount, 2);

  if (amount == 0)
    amount += '.00';
  else if (amount == Math.floor(amount))
    amount += '.00';
  else if (amount*10 == Math.floor(amount*10))
    amount += '0';

  return '' + amount;
}
```

## Formatting Large Numbers with Commas

Large numbers are traditionally grouped into three sets of digits and separated by commas. For instance, 7562309476, which is too large a number to visually recognize, is easier to understand if formatted as 7,562,309,476. The following commas() function does just that; it accepts an integer and then returns a string value.

**../chapter2/number/utilites.htm**

```
function commas(integer) {
  integer = '' + Math.round(integer);

  if (integer.length > 3) {
    var mod = integer.length%3;

    var output = (mod > 0 ? (integer.substring(0,mod)) : '');

    for (i=0 ; i < Math.floor(integer.length/3) ; i++) {
      if ((mod ==0) && (i ==0))
        output+= integer.substring(mod+3*i,mod+3*i+3);
      else
        output+= ',' + integer.substring(mod+3*i,mod+3*i+3);
    }
    return output;
  }
  return integer;
}
```

## Formatting Monetary Amounts with Commas

Although the previous Commas() function formats large integers with commas, it doesn't cope with floating-point values. It actually rounds the amount down to an integer before adding the commas. The following monetary() function reuses the cents() and commas() functions to combine the two to produce formatted monetary amounts:

 ../chapter2/number/utilites.htm

```
function monetary(amount) {
var integer = Math.floor(amount);
  var floating = amount - integer;
  return commas(integer) + cents(floating);
}
```

## Formatting 99 as Ninety-Nine

The following tu() function converts a tens and units number (i.e., any number from zero to 99) into its corresponding text equivalent. The code defines a numbers array to hold the text strings, representing one through to nineteen, and then twenty through to ninety:

 ../chapter2/number/utilites.htm

```
var numbers = new Array(
  '','one','two','three','four','five','six','seven',
  'eight','nine','ten','eleven','twelve','thirteen','fourteen',
  'fifthteen','sixteen','seventeen','eighteen','nineteen',
  '','','twenty','thirty','fourty','fifty','sixty', 'seventy',
  'eighty','ninety'
);

function tu(u) {
  var t = 0;
  if (u>=20) t = (u - u % 10) / 10, u = u - (u - u % 10);
  return numbers[t+20] + ((t>0 && u>0) ? '-' : '') + numbers[u];
}
```

## Formatting 999 as Nine Hundred and Ninety-Nine

The following `htu()` function—that is, hundreds, tens, and units—reuses the previous `tu()` function to convert any number from zero to 999 into its corresponding text equivalent:

 **../chapter2/number/utilites.htm**

```
function htu(number) {
  var hs = (number - number % 100) / 100;
  var tus = number - hs * 100;

  return tu(hs) + (hs>0 ? ' hundred' : '') +
         (tus>0 && hs>0 ? ' ':'') + tu(tus);
}
```

The `htu()` function uses the ternary operator, so called because it takes three operands—a condition and two alternative values. The syntax for the ternary operator is `condition ? truevalue : falsevalue`. The expression `hs>0 ? ' hundred' : ''` will return the text string `'hundred'` if `hs` is greater than zero; otherwise, it returns an empty string. The ternary operator is extremely effective where you need to include one of two values within an expression.

## Formatting Large Monetary Amounts as Text Strings

The following `monetaryText()` function returns the text string value of large monetary amounts (up to hundreds of billions). For example `1566324599.99` is formatted as `One billion, five hundred sixty-six million, three hundred twenty-four thousand, five hundred ninety-nine dollars and ninety-nine cents`. The `monetaryText()` function uses the `HTU()` function, which reuses the previous `htu()` function.

 **../chapter2/number/utilites.htm**

```
function monetaryText(input) {
  var dollars = Math.floor(input - 0);
  var cents = Math.floor(input*100 - dollars*100);

  var billions = (dollars - dollars % 1000000000) / 1000000000;
  dollars  -= billions * 1000000000;
  var millions = (dollars - dollars % 1000000) / 1000000;
  dollars  -= millions * 1000000;
  var thousands = (dollars - dollars % 1000) / 1000;
  dollars -= thousands * 1000;

  var o = '';

  o += HTU(billions, ' billion', ', ');
  o += HTU(millions, ' million', ', ');
  o += HTU(thousands, ' thousand', ', ');
  o += HTU(dollars, ' dollars', ', ');
  o += HTU(cents, ' cents', ' and ');

  and = false;

  return o.substring(0,1).toUpperCase() + o.substring(1);
}

var and = false;

function HTU(number, text, add) {
  if (number <= 0) return '';
  var output = '';
  if (and) output += add;
  output += htu(number) + text;
  and = true;
  return output;
}
```

All that is now required is an example use for all these number utilities. The following simple HTML form uses all the number utilities to accept a user-entered number and then displays it in both the two different formats available.

 On the CD

**../chapter2/number/utilites.htm**

```
<form>
<input type="text" name="i">
<br>
<input type="text" name="o1">
<br>
<input type="button" value="Convert"
  onClick="this.form.o1.value=monetary(this.form.i.value);
    this.form.o2.value=monetaryString(this.form.i.value)">
<br>
<textarea name="o2" rows="5" cols="70" wrap="virtual">
</textarea>
</form>
```

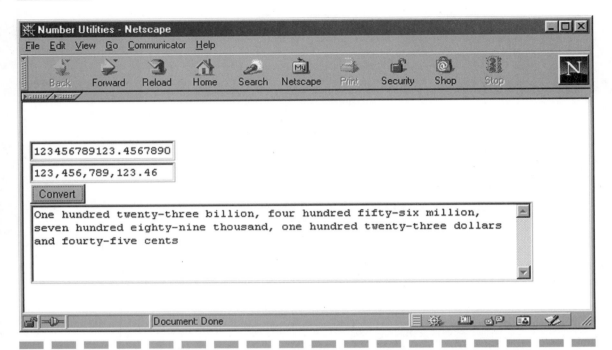

**Figure 2-7** Number Utilities—Formatting Numbers into Comma-Separated Data and as Text Strings.

Figure 2-7 shows the results of entering a large amount and then pressing the Convert form button to convert the value into the two different formats.

*NOTE: Note that as this simple form example stands, there is no validation of the user input. It is therefore too easy to enter data that breaks the number utilities. In Chapter 3, "Strings and Regular Expressions," we look at using regular expressions to validate text strings.*

Hopefully, these last few utility functions have shown that with care a library of reusable routines can be quickly built up in JavaScript. Once a function has been developed and fully tested, it can be reused again and again in other JavaScript applications, drastically reducing the development time.

## Summary

This chapter has shown how mathematics forms the basis for most of the work performed within JavaScript applications. Although we have shown mathematical calculators in this chapter, the real use of mathematics is shown in the last few utility functions, where we have manipulated the numbers and the content of strings. As you progress through the remainder of the book, you will see examples like these time and time again.

# Strings and Regular Expressions

When working within the confines of a browser, the vast majority of the time we are dealing with what the user can see—more often than not, this is text-based. Being able to manage strings of text, whether they are held in arrays, in form fields, or simply in string objects, allows JavaScript developers to control what the user can see or do.

This chapter covers finding and replacing strings within strings, the generation of specific text output using generic boilerplate text, scrolling text links, a contacts list that can be viewed in many different ways, using Gourad shading to color both text strings and table cells, the parsing of text strings to extract different elements, and the use of regular expressions to validate string patterns.

Not surprisingly, the manipulation of strings does not stop with this chapter. Many of the examples throughout this book will build on the some of the techniques used and explained in this chapter.

Find and Replace ../chapter3/replace/replace.htm
Copyright Boilerplate ../chapter3/replace/copyright.htm
Scrolling Text ../chapter3/scroll/text.htm
Scrolling Text Links ../chapter3/scroll/links.htm
Contacts List ../chapter3/contact/database.htm
String Gourad Shading ../chapter3/gourad/string.htm
Table Gourad Shading ../chapter3/gourad/table.htm
Parsing Strings ../chapter3/parse/literal.htm
Validating Strings ../chapter3/validate/form.htm

# Find and Replace

There are many occasions within JavaScript where it is necessary to replace a string or character with another. Often this replacement has to be performed within the middle of a larger string—for instance, replacing instances of the word *Draft* with *Issue*, or a double quote character (") with a single quote character ('). This example will introduce String object methods that can be used to perform the Find and Replace function with ease. Once written, the function can then be reused in other applications, saving time on development and testing.

## Source Code for Find and Replace

We use the `String` objects `indexOf()` or `lastIndexOf()` methods to find strings or characters (the search) within another string (the target). These two methods return the position of the search string within the target string, or `-1` if the search string is not found. Combined with the length of the search string, we have the ability to find the start and end locations within the target string.

Once found, we cannot simply update the characters insitu, as there are no `String` object methods to do so. We must split the target string into three substrings using the `String` objects `substring()` method: the substring preceding the found search string, the found search string itself, and the substring following the search string. Using the first and last, we can create a new string by concatenating the first along with a replacement string followed by the last substring.

 **../chapter3/replace/replace.htm**

```
<script language="JavaScript"><!--
```

We first define a JavaScript function called `replace()`, which accepts three parameters, the target `string` to be manipulated, the search `text` to be replaced, and the text to replace it with (`by`):

```
function replace(string,text,by) {
```

The first thing that is done is to use the `String` object's `length` property to find the length of both the target `string` and search `text`:

```
var strLength = string.length;
var txtLength = text.length;
```

If either is empty then the function returns the search string unchanged:

```
if ((strLength == 0) || (txtLength == 0))
  return string;
```

The `String` object's `indexOf()` method is used to find the first occurrence of the search `text` within the target `string`. The value returned is then held in the `i` variable:

```
var i = string.indexOf(text);
```

If the search `text` is not found within the target `string`, then the `indexOf()` method returns `-1`, in which case we return the value of the `string` unchanged:

```
if (i == -1)
    return string;
```

At this point we have found a match. We now need to add the replacement `by` string to the `target` substring up to the found location. Using the `String` object's `substring()` method we concatenate the substring from character location `0` (the start of the string) up to the found location (`i`) with the replacement `by` string creating a new string (`newstr`):

```
var newstr = string.substring(0,i) + by;
```

At this point we have replaced the first occurrence with the `target` string. However, there may well be many more occurrences in the remainder of the `target` string. What we need to do at this point is replace any occurrence of the search `text` within the `target` string with the replacement `by` string. Sounds familiar? We have just written and explained a function that performs this role, so why not reuse it? This is exactly what we do. We call the `replace()` function from within the `replace()` function, this time passing the remainder of the `target` string retrieved using the `substring()` method to extract the substring following the found search `text` up to the length of the `target` string (`strLength`), the results of which are concatenated to the end of the `newstr` variable:

```
newstr +=
    replace(string.substring(i+txtLength,strLength),text,by);
```

This process is called *iteration* and is used quite often in JavaScript to iterate through a string performing the same action many times until the entire string has been processed.

Finally, we return the results:

```
    return newstr;
}
//--></script>
```

The following code shows how to simply make use of the `replace()` function, replacing the single occurrence of `Draft` with `Issued` in the first `message1` string before writing out the results to the document, and then replacing all the double quotes with single quotes in `message2` before again writing out the results to the document:

```
<script language="JavaScript"><!--
var message1 = 'The status of this document is Draft.';

document.write(replace(message1,'Draft','Issued') + '<br>');

var message2 = '"quoted" text can be "useful"';

document.write(replace(message2,'"','\'') + '<br>');
//--></script>
```

Replacement of text can become very flexible, using the results of one replacement as the input to another. The following example replaces all the lowercase vowels with uppercase vowels a vowel at a time, starting with letter `a` and ending with letter `u`:

```
<script language="JavaScript"><!--
var message3 = 'This message uses vowels';

document.write(
  replace(
    replace(
      replace(
        replace(
          replace(message3,'a','A'),
          'e','E'),
        'i','I'),
      'o','O'),
    'u','U')
+ '<br>'
);
//--></script>
```

One potential use of the `replace()` function is to highlight a particular phrase. For example, the following example, which uses a helper `highlight()` function to invoke the `replace()` function indirectly, does not simply replace one string with another but with a variation of itself using the `String` object's `bold()` method, which wraps the string in `<b>` and `</b>` tags:

```
<script language="JavaScript"><!--
function highlight(string,phrase) {
  return replace(string,phrase,phrase.bold());
}

var message4 = 'JavaScript is extremely versatile';

document.write(highlight(message4,'JavaScript') + '<br>');
//--></script>
```

Another is to remove items from a string. The next example removes all the lowercase o characters:

```
<script language="JavaScript"><!--
document.write(replace('oOoOoOoOoOoOoOo','o','') + '<br>');
//--></script>
```

All the results of the previous scripts are show below:

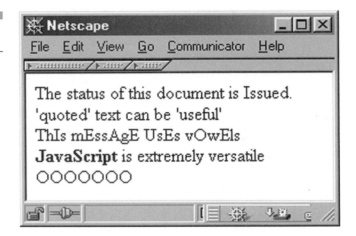

# Copyright Boilerplate

To show how the Find and Replace function can be used, we show a simple copyright boilerplate that can be automated to show different copyright messages for similar products.

This example demonstrates how to not only replace generic terms through the template, but also to highlight text using String object methods, and how to replace special characters, e.g. the newline (\n) character with HTML tags.

## Source Code for Copyright Boilerplate

../chapter3/replace/copyright.htm

```
<script language="JavaScript"><!--
function replace(string,text,by) {
  var strLength = string.length;
  var txtLength = text.length;

  if ((strLength == 0) || (txtLength == 0))
    return string;

  var i = string.indexOf(text);

  if (i == -1)
    return string;

  var newstr = string.substring(0,i) + by;

  newstr +=
    replace(string.substring(i+txtLength,strLength),text,by);

  return newstr;
}
```

After the inclusion of the `replace()` function, we first define our copyright boilerplate string. The text `$YEAR`, `$NAME`, and `$PRODUCT` are all generic terms that can be replaced with specific terms depending on the current product being described. The newline character (\n) is normally used in form textareas to break text over several lines:

```
var copyright =
  '\n\nCopyright (c) $YEAR by $NAME\n\n' +
  'Please freely copy and distribute $PRODUCT.\n\n' +
  '$PRODUCT is distributed on an "AS IS" basis, WITHOUT ' +
  'WARRANTY OF ANY KIND, either express or implied.\n\n' +
  'The Original is $PRODUCT.';
```

Next, we define the variables to hold the specific terms for the current product being described:

```
var year = 2000;
var name = 'ABC Company';
var product = 'This Copyright Statement';
```

Now we just need to use the `replace()` function to find and replace the generic terms with the specific values:

```
copyright = replace(copyright,'$YEAR',year);
copyright = replace(copyright,'$NAME',name);
copyright = replace(copyright,'$PRODUCT',product.bold());
copyright = replace(copyright,'\n','<br>');
```

Finally, we display the copyright message

```
document.write(copyright);
//--></script>
```

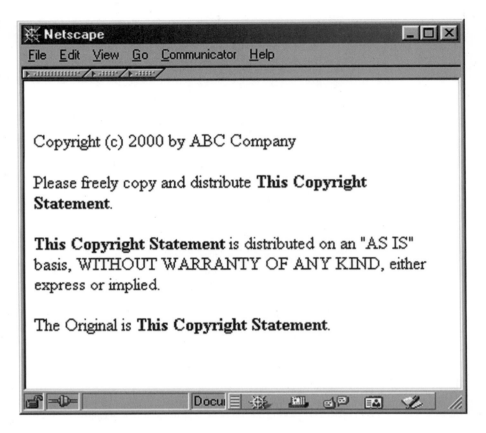

When we need to display the copyright message for a separate product, all that needs to be changed are the three lines that define the specific values for year, name, and product. This has direct implications toward large-scale document management; global changes can readily be made when the above JavaScript code is used in a file referred to externally from several HTML and XHTML 1.0 documents.

## String Methods

Table 3-1 describes some of the String object's methods. The String object only has one property: length.

**TABLE 3-1**

String object
methods.

| Method | Description |
|--------|-------------|
| indexOf | Searches the string for a character or substring. For example:<br><br>`var s = 'abcabc'; var p = s.indexOf('b');`<br>p will equal 1. |
| lastIndexOf | Searches the string backward for a character or substring. For example:<br><br>`var s = 'abcabc'; var p = s.lastIndexOf('b');`<br>p will equal 4. |
| substring | Extracts a substring of the string. For example:<br><br>`var s = 'abcdef'; var p = s.substring(1,3);`<br>p will equal bc. |
| toLowerCase | Returns a copy of the string in lowercase. For example:<br><br>`var s = 'ABCdef'; var p = s.toLowerCase();`<br>s will equal ABCdef, and p will equal abcdef. |
| ToUpperCase | Returns a copy of the string in uppercase. For example:<br><br>`var s = 'ABCdef'; var p = s.toUpperCase();`<br>s will equal ABCdef, and p will equal ABCDEF. |
| replace | Performs a search and replace operation. For example:<br><br>`var s = 'abcabc'; var p = s.replace('b', 'B');`<br>s will equal abcdef, and p will equal aBcabc. Also performs search and replace using regular expressions. For example:<br><br>`var s = 'abcabc'; var p = s.replace(new RegExp('b', 'g'), 'B');`<br>s will equal abcdef, and p will equal aBcaBc. |
| split | Splits a string into an array of strings. For example:<br><br>`var s = 'abc 123 xyz'; var p = s.split(' ');`<br>s will equal abc 123 xyz, p[0] will equal abc, p[1] will equal 123, and p2[] will equal xyz. Can also split using regular expressions. |

# Scrolling Text Links

**../chapter3/scroll/text.htm**

Stock ticker tapes, news bulletins, weather forecasts, sports results—too large to display all of it on a page—ideal for scrolling. Scrolling text is a relatively simple trick. You take a string, display it, then remove a character or two from the front of the string and append it to the end, and then redisplay the string. Then you repeat this process *ad nauseam*. Being able to display scrolling text that is context-sensitive and when clicked takes you to a new page is slightly harder; you need to account for the text link being split into two parts at either end of the larger string.

This example uses dynamic HTML techniques to write to an absolute positioned document layer. As such, it works on Internet Explorer 4 and 5 and Netscape Navigator 4 only. Extending the example to work on Netscape Navigator 6 will require extensive knowledge of the Document Object Model covered in Chapter 11 "Dynamic HTML." For now we will keep the code light and easy to understand.

Figure 3-1 shows a snapshot of the Scrolling Text Links code in action.

**Figure 3-1**
Scrolling Text Links—
In action.

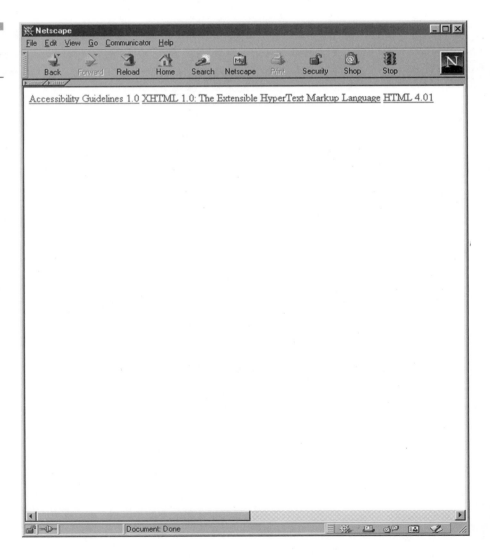

## Scrolling Text Link Source Code

 ../chapter3/scroll/links.htm

```
<script language="JavaScript"><!--
```

The first thing that we do is define two arrays: `textArray` to hold all the text values for the links and `urlArray` to hold all the URLs for the links:

```
var textArray = new Array();
var urlArray = new Array();
```

Next, we initialize a `links` counter:

```
var links = 0;
```

We initialize `currentLink` to -1, which is used in the `prepareLinks()` function where its first action is to increment the value of `currentLink`—that is, to zero, which maps to the first elements in the two arrays:

```
var currentLink = -1;
```

We define and initialize the three global variables—`string1`, `string2`, and `string3`:

```
var string1 = string2 = string3 = '';
```

The Boolean `scrolling` variable is initially set to `false`; it is used later to control the suspension of the scrolling text links:

```
var scrolling = false;
```

We declare but do not initialize the `timer` variable, which is later used to set and cancel a running timer:

```
var timer;
```

We declare a `link()` function that accepts two arguments for the text and link, which populates the `textArray` and `urlArray` and then increments the `links` count:

```
function link(text, link) {
  textArray[links] = text;
  urlArray[links] = link;
  links++;
}
```

Next, we use the `link()` function to add all the links, passing the text to appear in the link, along with the relative or absolute URL:

```
link(
  "Authoring Tool Accessibility Guidelines 1.0",
  "http://www.w3.org/TR/ATAG10"
);
link(
  "XHTML 1.0: The Extensible HyperText Markup Language",
  "http://www.w3.org/TR/xhtml1"
);
link(
  "HTML 4.01 Specification",
  "http://www.w3.org/TR/html401"
);
link(
  "XSL Transformations (XSLT) Version 1.0",
  "http://www.w3.org/TR/xslt"
);
link(
  "XML Path Language (XPath) Version 1.0",
  "http://www.w3.org/TR/xpath"
);
link(
  "Associating Style Sheets with XML documents",
  "http://www.w3.org/TR/xml-stylesheet"
);
link(
  "Web Content Accessibility Guidelines 1.0",
  "http://www.w3.org/TR/WAI-WEBCONTENT"
);
link(
  "Resource Description Framework (RDF) Model",
  "http://www.w3.org/TR/REC-rdf-syntax"
);
link(
  "WebCGM Profile",
  "http://www.w3.org/TR/REC-WebCGM"
);
link(
  "Namespaces in XML",
  "http://www.w3.org/TR/REC-xml-names"
);
link(
  "Document Object Model (DOM) Level 1",
  "http://www.w3.org/TR/REC-DOM-Level-1"
);
link(
  "Synchronized Multimedia Integration Language (SMIL) 1.0",
  "http://www.w3.org/TR/REC-smil/"
);
link(
```

```
    "PICS Signed Labels (DSig) 1.0 Specification",
    "http://www.w3.org/TR/REC-DSig-label/"
);
link(
    "Cascading Style Sheets, level 2 (CSS2) Specification",
    "http://www.w3.org/TR/REC-CSS2"
);
link(
    "Extensible Markup Language (XML) 1.0 Specification",
    "http://www.w3.org/TR/REC-xml"
);
link(
    "PICSRules 1.1 Specification",
    "http://www.w3.org/TR/REC-PICSRules"
);
link(
    "HTML 3.2 Reference Specification",
    "http://www.w3.org/TR/REC-html32"
);
link(
    "Cascading Style Sheets (CSS1) Level 1 Specification",
    "http://www.w3.org/TR/REC-CSS1"
);
link(
    "PICS 1.1 Rating Services and Rating Systems",
    "http://www.w3.org/TR/REC-PICS-services"
);
link(
    "PICS 1.1 Label Distribution",
    "http://www.w3.org/TR/REC-PICS-labels"
);
link(
    "PNG (Portable Network Graphics) Specification",
    "http://www.w3.org/TR/REC-png"
);
```

The `formatLink()` function returns a string representing a text link made from the passed `text` and `link` arguments. We include two event handlers—onMouseover, which invokes the `stopScroll()` function, and onMouseout, which invokes `startScroll()` function:

```
function formatLink(text,link) {
    return '<a href="' + link + '"' +
        ' onMouseover="stopScroll()"' +
        ' onMouseout="startScroll()">' +
        text + '<\/a> ';
}
```

The `prepareLinks()` function is called whenever a new link appears at the start of the scrolling text. It updates the three global string variables: string1, string2, and string3. The string1 contains the complete text for the link at the start of the scrolling text, string2 contains all the other links (each one created using the `formatLink()` function), and string3 remains empty.

```
function prepareLinks() {
```

First, we increment the `currentLink` value using the pre-increment operative, and then use the modulus operator (`%`) to calculate the remainder of `currentLink` divided by the number of `links`. This ensures that `currentLink` wraps back to zero when it reaches the value of the number of `links`:

```
currentLink = ++currentLink % links;
```

Next, we set the value of `string1` to the value held in the `textArray[]` array's `currentLink` element:

```
string1 = textArray[currentLink];
```

The values of `string2` and `string3` are set to empty strings:

```
string2 = '';
string3 = '';
```

We now add text links using the `formatLink()` function for all the remaining elements left in the `textArray[]` array (and the corresponding `urlArray[]` array), starting from the element one after the `currentLink`:

```
var i=currentLink + 1;
while (i < links) {
  string2 += formatLink(textArray[i], urlArray[i]);
  i++;
}
```

We now add text links using the `formatLink()` function for all the preceding elements in the `textArray[]` array (and the corresponding `urlArray[]` array), starting from the first element (i.e., position zero) up to the element one before the `currentLink`:

```
var i = 0;
while (i<currentLink) {
  string2 += formatLink(textArray[i], urlArray[i]);
  i++;
}
}
```

The `prepareLinks()` function is invoked to set the initial values for `string1` and `string2` and to initialize (yet again) `string3`:

```
prepareLinks();
```

With the introduction of Netscape Navigator 4 and Internet Explorer 4, Cascading Style Sheets (CSS) support was introduced. This meant that rather than using presentation style HTML tags (e.g., `font`, `i`, `b`) to mark up the presentation of the page content, the style could be indicated within an HTML tags `style` attribute. For example, to indicate that a paragraph of text should be rendered in a red bold Arial font, the following could be used: `<p style="font-weight: bold; font-family: Arial; color: red;">This is red bold Arial</p>`. Not only does CSS provide much more control over the presentation of the content, but it also removes the need to use HTML tags to do it, leaving the HTML tags to simply structure the content—the original intention behind HTML.

In Netscape Navigator 4, creating an absolute positioned element has the effect of creating another document layer, one that can be written into using the `document` object's `write()` method. We have seen instances of the `document.write()` statement being used to write to the current document. If, however, we were to use this after the document has completely loaded, then the effect would be to replace the current document with whatever we write to the document. Thus, we cannot use a simple `document.write()` on its own to dynamically alter content. We either have to write to another window or frame, or in the case of Netscape Navigator 4, into another document layer.

In Netscape Navigator 4, access to document layers is achieved via the `document` object's `layers` object array, using the syntax `document.layers[]`. In our case, as we will use a `div` element with an `id` attribute, we can access the document layer using `document.layers['myDiv']`. To write into the document layer, we can use `document.layers['myDiv'].document.write()`.

Unlike Netscape Navigator 4, Internet Explorer does not use the `document` object's `write()` method to write into a document layer. Instead, Internet Explorer allows us to change the content of an HTML element using the `innerHTML` and `innerText` properties. In fact, Internet Explorer does not require an absolute positioned element or document layer, as it can update any HTML tag using these properties. In Internet Explorer 4 and 5, Microsoft has provided an alternative way to access HTML tags, using the `document` object's `all` object array. This method uses the syntax `document.all[]`, which again in our case can be used as `document.all['myDiv']`.

Note that the two methods are totally incompatible with one other. What works on one browser will not work on the other.

The `update()` function provides a generic way to update the content of an HTML tag in Internet Explorer 4 and 5, and an absolute positioned document layer in Netscape Navigator 4. Two arguments passed to the update() function are what being the id attribute value of the HTML tag or layer to be updated (in our case myDiv) and output being the new content:

```
function update(what,output) {
```

As the two methods are incompatible with one another, we first need to detect which browser the user is using. Testing for browser support of a particular object is one of the easiest (and generally one of the most reliable) ways of detecting browser support for one feature or another. We first test to see whether the browser supports the document object's all object:

```
if (document.all) {
```

If the browser being used is Internet Explorer 4 or 5, then the expression will evaluate to true. In this case, we update the content of the element using the innerHTML property. In other words, we replace the current contents of the myDiv element with the new contents:

```
document.all[what].innerHTML = output;
}
```

If the browser being used is Netscape Navigator 4, then the second test, testing whether the browser supports the document object's layers object, will evaluate to true:

```
else if (document.layers) {
```

In this case, we first open the layers document using the open() method:

```
document.layers[what].document.open();
```

Then we write the new content into the document using the write() method:

```
document.layers[what].document.write(output);
```

Finally, we close the document using the close() method:

```
document.layers[what].document.close();
    }
}
```

Note that we need to refer to what appears to be two documents: the current documents layer, and then the document within that layer. Confusing at first, but once understood, it allows us to create truly dynamic content. The scrollLinks() function controls the scrolling link text:

```
function scrollLinks() {
```

The value of a local scrollingText variable is built from three constituent parts:

```
var scrollingText =
```

The results of passing the string1 variable and the urlArray[] array's currentLink value to the formatLink() function, which creates a text link using whatever text is held in the string1 variable:

```
formatLink(string1, urlArray[currentLink]) +
```

plus the already prepared text links held in string2:

```
string2 +
```

Plus the results of passing the string3 variable and the urlArray[] arrays currentLink value to the formatLink() function, which creates a text link using whatever text is held in the string3 variable:

```
formatLink(string3, urlArray[currentLink]);
```

Then we pass the value of the scrollingText variable to the update() function to update the contents of the myDiv div element:

```
update('myDiv', scrollingText);
```

We now move one character from the start of string1 and add it to the end of string3 using the substring() method, but only if string1 is not empty (i.e., we have something left to move):

```
if (string1 != '') {
  string3 += string1.substring(0,1);
  string1 = string1.substring(1);
}
```

If there is nothing left to move then we invoke the prepareLinks() method to prepare the global variables string1, string2, and string3 for the next text link to be sliced and diced:

```
else {
  prepareLinks();
}
```

To allow the scrolling text link to scroll across the screen at a reasonable rate, and to also give the browser the opportunity to update the screen, we need to stop the currently running JavaScript code and then restart it again after a short interval. Starting a script after an interval is trivial. We simply set a timer using the `setTimeout()` method, passing it a string to be evaluated and a delay interval in milliseconds. The following line effectively says "execute the `scrollLinks()` function again in 50 milliseconds time." A handle to the running timer is returned by the call to the `setTimeout()` method, which is held in the global `timer` variable:

```
  timer = setTimeout('scrollLinks()',50);
}
```

The links created using the `formatLink()` function included `onMouseout` and `onMouseover` event handlers to call the `startScroll()` and `stopScroll()` functions, respectively. The `startScroll()` function checks that we are not already scrolling and then sets the Boolean `scrolling` variable to `true` and invokes the `scrollLinks()` function:

```
function startScroll() {
  if (!scrolling) {
    scrolling = true;
    scrollLinks();
  }
}
```

The `stopScroll()` function checks that we are already scrolling and then sets the Boolean `scrolling` variable to `false` and invokes the `clearTimeout()` method to cancel the running timer.

```
function stopScroll() {
  if (scrolling)
    clearTimeout(timer);

  scrolling = false;
}
//--></script>
</head>
```

The `body` tag includes an `onLoad` event handler that starts the scrolling text links by invoking the `startScroll()` function:

```
<body onLoad="startScroll()">
```

The contents of the page is extremely simple, just the one `div` element:

```
<div id="myDiv"
  STYLE="position:absolute; clip:rect(0px 1280px 20px 0px);">
</div>

</body>

</html>
```

The one `div` element offers enormous potential. The starting `div` tag has an `id` property with a value of `myDIV` and a `style` attribute with what might appear to some people as a strange value `position:absolute;` `clip:rect(0px 1280px 20px 0px);`. The `style` attribute value `position:absolute;` declares that the content of the `div` element is to be absolutely positioned on the page. The `style` attribute value `clip:rect(0px 1280px 20px 0px);` clips the visible area of the `div` element to a short, wide area 20 pixels high by 1280 pixels wide. This has the effect of only showing the first line of text within the `div` element—hiding the remainder.

# Contacts List

Using data held with a forms textarea, we can make use of several of the `String` object methods to split the data into strings, place them into string arrays, and then further manipulate them to reorder the contents. This example will demonstrate a very simple Contacts List that can be used to hold the name, e-mail address, and phone number details of people within your organization or team. Figure 3-2 shows the initial state of the Contacts List. The Contacts List allows a user to sort the data on various columns and also allows the user to filter the data by entering a search string. Figure 3-3 shows the results sorted on the contact e-mail address. All the results are redisplayed within the text area, so this example will work on all browsers that support the JavaScript 1.1 `String` object. Figure 3-4 shows the results of first sorting by the phone number, and then filtering on the string `John`.

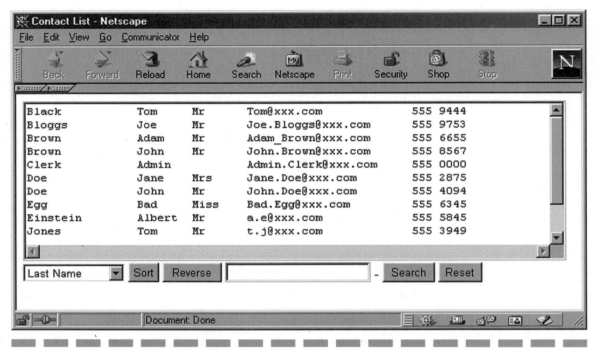

**Figure 3-2** Contacts List—Initial view.

## Contacts List Source Code

../chapter3/contact/database.htm

```html
<html>

<head>
<title>Contact List</title>
</head>

<body>
```

The onSubmit event handler for the contactForm form invokes the doSearch() function and then cancels the form submission by returning false to the submit event:

```html
<form name="contactForm" onSubmit="doSearch();return false">
```

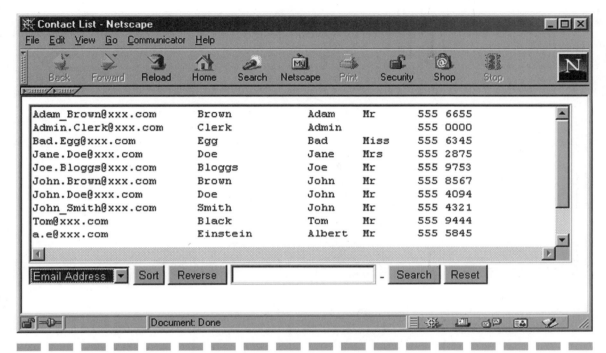

**Figure 3-3**    Contacts List—Sorted by e-mail address.

The form includes a `textarea` element named `data`, which contains the contact details as comma-delimited strings padded out with spaces so that the data is aligned correctly:

```
<textarea name="data" cols="78" rows="10">
Black     ,Tom   ,Mr  ,Tom@xxx.com         ,555 9444
Bloggs    ,Joe   ,Mr  ,Joe.Bloggs@xxx.com  ,555 9753
Brown     ,Adam  ,Mr  ,Adam_Brown@xxx.com  ,555 6655
Brown     ,John  ,Mr  ,John.Brown@xxx.com  ,555 8567
Clerk     ,Admin ,    ,Admin.Clerk@xxx.com ,555 0000
Doe       ,Jane  ,Mrs ,Jane.Doe@xxx.com    ,555 2875
Doe       ,John  ,Mr  ,John.Doe@xxx.com     ,555 4094
Egg       ,Bad   ,Miss,Bad.Egg@xxx.com     ,555 6345
Einstein  ,Albert,Mr  ,a.e@xxx.com         ,555 5845
Jones     ,Tom   ,Mr  ,t.j@xxx.com         ,555 3949
Smith     ,John  ,Mr  ,John_Smith@xxx.com  ,555 4321
T         ,Cue   ,Miss,cutie@xxx.com       ,555 4984
</textarea>
```

The `onChange` event handler within the `select` option list named `item` invokes the `doFormat()` function, passing a reference to itself

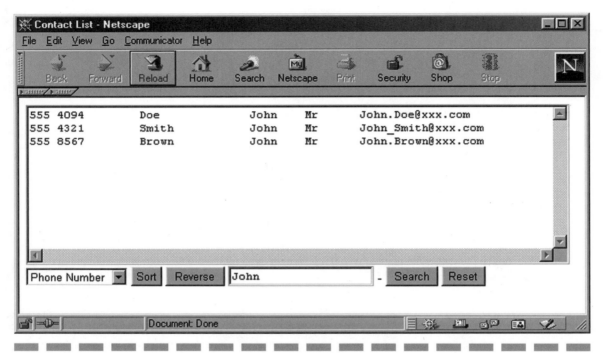

**Figure 3-4**    Contacts List—Sorted by phone number and filtered on John.

(this), and it places the result into the global contacts variable, before invoking the doSort() function:

```
<select name="item" onChange="contacts =
doFormat(this);doSort()">
<option selected>Last Name</option>
<option>First Name</option>
<option>Salutation</option>
<option>Email Address</option>
<option>Phone Number</option>
</select>
```

The Sort button invokes the doSort() function when clicked:

```
<input type="button" onClick="doSort()" value="Sort">
```

The Reverse button invokes the doReverse() function when clicked:

```
<input type="button" onClick="doReverse()" value="Reverse">
```

The `Search` button invokes the `doSearch()` function when clicked, which will use the contents of the text field named `search`:

```
<input type="text" name="search"> -
<input type="button" onClick="doSearch()" value="Search">
```

The `Reset` button invokes the `doReset()` function when clicked:

```
<input type="button" onClick="doReset()" value="Reset">
</form>

<script language="JavaScript"><!--
```

We include the generic `replace()` function discussed in the previous Find and Replace example:

```
function replace(string,text,by) {
  var strLength = string.length;
  var txtLength = text.length;

  if ((strLength == 0) || (txtLength == 0))
    return string;

  var i = string.indexOf(text);

  if (i == -1)
    return string;

  var newstr = string.substring(0,i) + by;

  newstr +=
    replace(string.substring(i+txtLength,strLength),text,by);

  return newstr;
}
```

We define and initialize the value of several global variables. The `search` variable holds the value of the current search request. When empty, it matches each of the contact entries:

```
var search = '';
```

The `item` variable holds the index value of the selected option (`selectedIndex`), which is used to control which column is shown first within the `textarea` element and therefore which column is used to sort the data:

```
var item;
```

The `rawdata` variable is used to hold the original contents of the contactForm form's data textarea value, but not before using the replace() function to replace every occurrence of the comma character (,) with a tab character (\t):

```
var rawdata = replace(document.contactForm.data.value,',','\t');
```

This modified value is then used to update the value of the contactForm form's data textarea value:

```
document.contactForm.data.value = rawdata;
```

The String object's split() method is used to split the value of the rawdata variable into an array (contacts[]) of strings split at every carriage return (\r) and newline characters (\n):

```
var contacts = rawdata.split('\r\n');
```

Next, we declare all the remaining functions: The doFormat() function is invoked when the user selects one of the options in the item select list:

```
function doFormat(what) {
```

The what argument, which accepts the this reference passed from the onChange event handler, allows the doFormat() function to retrieve the selectedIndex value of the item select list:

```
item = what.selectedIndex;
```

We declare and initialize a local output variable:

```
var output = '';
```

We resplit the rawdata string into an array of strings—the contacts[] array:

```
var contacts = rawdata.split('\r\n');
```

We then loop through each string within the contacts[] array using the length property to know when we have reached the end of the loop:

```
for (var i=0; i<contacts.length; i++) {
```

It is possible that the last line of data in the form's data textarea generates a blank string in the `contacts[]` array. To avoid using this blank string, we check that the `length` of the current string in the `contacts[]` array is not zero before proceeding:

```
if (contacts[i].length != 0) {
```

The current string being processed in the `contacts[]` array is then split at every tab character (`\t`) using the `split()` method into a `splitString[]` array:

```
var splitString = contacts[i].split('\t');
```

The string element in the `splitString[]` array that corresponds to the selected `item` option is then entered as the first item in the `output` variable:

```
output += splitString[item];
```

Then we loop through each of the strings in the `splitString[]` array, adding a tab character (`\t`) and the string element to the end of the `output` variable—all, that is, except the element already entered at the start of the `output` variable:

```
for (var j=0; j<splitString.length; j++) {
  if (j != item)
    output += '\t' + splitString[j];
}
```

A carriage return (`\r`) and a newline (`\n`) character are then added to the end of the `output` variable:

```
    output += '\r\n';
  }
}
```

Finally, we split the `output` variable using the `String` object's `split()` method at the carriage return (`\r`) and a newline (`\n`) character, sort the resulting array using the `Array` object's `sort()` method, and return the results back to the `onChange` event handler—which uses the returned results to update the value of the global `contacts[]` array:

```
  return output.split('\r\n').sort();
}
```

The `redisplay()` function is used in several places to update the data textarea value:

```
function redisplay() {
```

We declare and initialize an output variable:

```
var output = '';
```

We then loop through each entry in the contacts[] array:

```
for (var i=0; i<contacts.length; i++) {
```

We check that the entry is not blank:

```
if (contacts[i].length != 0)
```

Then we check using the String object's indexOf() method to see if the search string appears within the lowercase value (created using the String object's toLowerCase() method) of the current contacts[] array element:

```
if (contacts[i].toLowerCase().indexOf(search) > -1)
```

If it does, we append the value of the current contacts[] element plus the obligatory carriage return (\r) and new line (\n) characters to the output variable:

```
output += contacts[i] + '\r\n';
}
```

The output variable is then used to update the contactForm form's data textarea value:

```
document.contactForm.data.value = output;
}
```

The doSort() function sorts the contacts[] array using the Array object's sort() method and then invokes the redisplay() function:

```
function doSort() {
  contacts.sort();
  redisplay();
}
```

The doReverse() function sorts the contacts[] array into reverse order using the Array object's reverse() method and then invokes the redisplay() function:

```
function doReverse() {
  contacts.reverse();
  redisplay();
}
```

The doSearch() function retrieves the contactForm forms search text field value into the global search variable and then invokes the redisplay() function:

```
function doSearch() {
  search = document.contactForm.search.value.toLowerCase();
  redisplay();
}
```

The doReset() function resets everything back to its initial state before invoking the redisplay() function:

```
function doReset() {
  document.contactForm.search.value = '';
  document.contactForm.item.selectedIndex = 0;
  search = '';
  contacts = rawdata.split('\r\n');
  redisplay();
}
//--></script>

</body>
</html>
```

# Gourad Shading

*Gourad shading* is where two colors are joined together through a color gradient from one to the other such that the two end colors seem to slowly merge. Using JavaScript to write HTML content to the document, we are able to set both the font and bgcolor attributes of text and table cells. By applying different colors to each character of a string or each table cell, we are able to create stunning visual effects.

We include two examples. The first uses a string to perform *Gourad shading* throughout the length of the string, as shown in Figure 3-5. The second slightly adapted version uses tables to create various sized and colored Gourad shaded table cells, as shown in Figure 3-6.

Before we dive into the code, a few words about colors. In HTML, we can set the color in two ways: using a named color—for instance, <font color="red">—or by using a hexadecimal color format—for instance, <font color="#FFCC99">. The hexadecimal number FFCC99 dictates

**Figure 3-5**
String Gourad
shading.

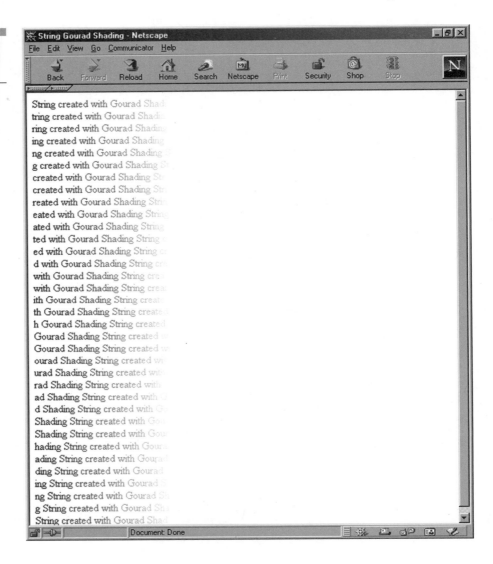

the various strengths of the three primary colors red, green, and blue. The first two characters (FF) represent the color red, the second two (CC) represent green, and the last two (99) represent blue. The larger the number, the stronger the primary color. Therefore, the color represented by FFCC99 will have more red than green and will have more green than blue. Each primary color can range in strength from 0x00 to 0xFF (or in decimal, 0 to 255). As the color black is the absence of any color, its value

**Figure 3-6**

Table Gourad
shading.

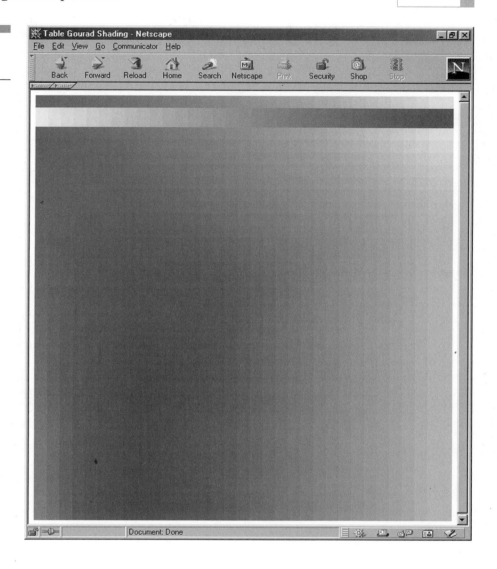

is 000000, whereas white, which is the combination of all the three primary colors in full strength, has a value of FFFFFF. Within an HTML tag
attribute, we specify a hexadecimal color with the # prefix. In JavaScript
code, we specify a hexadecimal number with the 0x prefix. Therefore, in
JavaScript, the integer that represents white is 0xFFFFFF. With these
words in mind, the following two examples should be that much easier to
understand.

## String Gourad Shading Source Code

The first version presented here, the String Gourad Shading example, accepts a string, a start color, and a finish color, and then proceeds to alter each letter of the string so that it is colored using one of the many colors between the start and finish colors, resulting in a color gradient. The amended string is then written to the document.

../chapter3/gourad/string.htm

```html
<html>

<head>
<title>String Gourad Shading</title>

<script language="JavaScript"><!--
```

The `gradient()` function accepts the three named arguments: `string`, `startcolor`, and `endcolor` (both colors are passed as hexadecimal numbers):

```javascript
function gradient(string, startcolor, endcolor) {
```

The first thing we do is retrieve the `length` of the `string` and assign its value to the local `len` variable (note that strings longer than 256 characters will not result in a Gourad shade being applied due to a maximum of 256 shades of each color component, red, green, and blue):

```javascript
var len = string.length;
```

The local `output` variable is declared and initialized:

```javascript
var output = '';
```

Next, we break the passed `startcolor` hexadecimal number down into the color components that represent `red`, `green`, and `blue`:

```javascript
var red    = startcolor >> 16;
var green  = (startcolor & 0x00FF00) >> 8;
var blue   = startcolor & 0x0000FF;
```

This code requires further explanation. The right shift operator (>>)

shifts the binary value of `startcolor` 16 bits to the right. For example, the hexadecimal number `0xFF0000` (which represents the color `#FF0000`) has a binary value of `111111110000000000000000`, which when shifted 16 bits to the right produces the new value `00000000000000000011111111`. This value has a hexadecimal value of `0xFF`, which represents the value of the red component.

The value for the green component is treated slightly differently. We first need to rid ourselves of the red constituent using the bitwise AND operator (`&`), note that this is different to the logical AND operator (`&&`), and then using the right shift operator (`>>`) to shift the binary value eight bits to the right.

Using the bitwise `&` operator performs a boolean AND operation on each bit of the two binary integers to produce a new integer. For example, the expression `0xAAAAAA & 0x00FF00` produces the result `0x00AA00`. Table 3-2 explains the mathematics behind this.

The second integer acts rather like a mask, only allowing the bits set to 1 in the second byte through to the result. Finally, the green component is retrieved just by applying a `&` bitwise operator to mask just the last 8 bits.

Exactly the same operations are performed on the `endcolor` variable to set the value of the `ered`, `egreen`, and `eblue` variables:

```
var ered   = endcolor >> 16;
var egreen = (endcolor & 0x00FF00) >> 8;
var eblue  = endcolor & 0x0000FF;
```

We next calculate the step values between the start colors and the end colors necessary to step the color from one to another over the length of the string. We subtract the start color from the end color, divide the result by the one less than the `len` variable, before using the `Math` object's `round()` method to roundoff the result to the nearest integer:

```
var ired   = Math.round((ered - red) / (len - 1));
var igreen = Math.round((egreen - green) / (len - 1));
var iblue  = Math.round((eblue - blue) / (len - 1));
```

**TABLE 3-2**

The result of using the & bitwise operator.

| Symbol | Hexadecimal Operation | Binary Representation |
|--------|----------------------|----------------------|
|        | 0xAAAAAA             | 101010101010101010101010 |
| &      | 0x00FF00             | 000000001111111100000000 |
| =      | 0x00AA00             | 000000001010101000000000 |

Now all we have to do is loop through the length of the string, wrapping a font tag around each character with the appropriate color attribute.

```
for (var x=0; x<len; x++) {
```

The color variable is built up using the current values of the red, green, and blue color variables, using the left shift operator (<<) to shift the binary value of the red component 16 bits to the left, and the green component 8 bits to the left. Then we use the bitwise OR operator ( | ) to perform a Boolean OR operation on all three values. Finally, we use the Number object's toString() method with a radix of 16 to convert the integer to a hexadecimal string:

```
var color = (red << 16 | green << 8 | blue).toString(16);
```

Using the bitwise | operator performs a Boolean OR operation on each bit of the binary integers to produce a new integer. For example, the expression 0xFF0000 | 0x00FF00 | 0x0000FF produces the result 0xFFFFFF. Table 3-3 explains the mathematics behind this.

The result of using the Number object's toString() method with a radix of 16 is to convert a decimal integer into a string representing its hexadecimal value so that (1044480).toString(16) produces the string FF000. Unfortunately, we cannot use this hexadecimal value to represent a color, as it is too short. We must have a six-character hexadecimal number, with leading zeros where appropriate. The following line of code does just that; it adds additional leading zeros up to a maximum of six to the start of the color string variable:

```
color = ('000000').substring(0, 6 - color.length) + color;
```

Finally, we can now use the color string variable within our output variable to set the font color of the current character within our string

**TABLE 3-3**

The result of using the | bitwise operator

| Symbol | Hexadecimal Operation | Binary Representation |
|--------|----------------------|----------------------|
|        | 0xFF0000             | 111111110000000000000000 |
| \|     | 0x00FF00             | 000000001111111100000000 |
| \|     | 0x0000FF             | 000000000000000011111111 |
| =      | 0xFFFFFF             | 111111111111111111111111 |

variable, using the `String` object's `charAt()` method to retrieve the current character at position x:

```
output += '<font color="#' + color + '">' +
          string.charAt(x)  +
          '<\/font>';
```

We now increment the values of the red, green, and blue color variables with the ired, igreen, and iblue color increment variables, by passing the sum of the two as input to the fix() function, and then assigning the result to the appropriate red, green, and blue color variable:

```
red   = fix(red + ired);
green = fix(green + igreen);
blue  = fix(blue + iblue);
}
```

Once we have looped through all the characters in the string, we return the value of the local output variable back to the caller of the gradient() function:

```
return output;
}
```

The fix() function called from within the gradient() function ensures that the passed color value remains within the bounds 0 to 255:

```
function fix(color) {
  if (color < 0) return 0;
  if (color > 255) return 255;
  return color;
}
//--></script>

</head>

<body>

<script language="JavaScript"><!--
```

All we have to do now is actually make use of the gradient() function. We first declare a text string:

```
var text = 'String created with Gourad Shading ';
```

Then to make things more interesting, we loop through the entire length of the text string:

```
for (var i=0; i<text.length; i++) {
```

We invoke the `gradient()` function, passing the `text` string, along with a start and finish color value, both in hexadecimal format. The results are written out to the document:

```
document.write(gradient(text, 0x000000, 0xFFFFFF) + '<BR>');
```

We then move the first character of the text string to the end of the text string (reminiscent of the Scrolling Text Links example earlier in this chapter:

```
text = text.substring(1) + text.substring(0,1);
}
//--></script>

</body>
</html>
```

## Table Gourad Shading Source Code

We are not just restricted to shading text strings. We can also apply the same techniques to the background color of table cells by just making a few adjustments to the original source code.

../chapter3/gourad/table.htm

```
<html>

<head>
<title>Table Gourad Shading</title>

<script language="JavaScript"><!--
```

The amended `gradient()` function now accepts four named arguments: the start and end colors, the number of columns, and the height of the table row:

```
function gradient(startcolor, endcolor, numCol, rowHeight) {
```

Whereas in the original code we used the length of a string argument to set the local `len` variable, here we use the value of the `numCol` argument:

```
var len = numCol;
var output = '';

var red    = startcolor >> 16;
var green  = (startcolor & 0x00FF00) >> 8;
var blue   = startcolor & 0x0000FF;

var ered   = endcolor >> 16;
var egreen = (endcolor & 0x00FF00) >> 8;
var eblue  = endcolor & 0x0000FF;

var ired   = Math.round((ered - red) / (len - 1));
var igreen = Math.round((egreen - green) / (len - 1));
var iblue  = Math.round((eblue - blue) / (len - 1));
```

Before starting to mix the colors, we first add the necessary HTML tags to the output variable to define the settings of the table, including the `height` attribute, which is set to the `rowHeight` argument:

```
output += '<table border="0" cellpadding="0" ' +
          'cellspacing="0" width="100%" height="' +
          rowHeight + '"><tr>';
for (var x=0; x<len; x++) {
  var color = (red << 16 | green << 8 | blue).toString(16);
  color = ('000000').substring(0, 6 - color.length) + color;
```

Instead of setting the font color of the current character, we add a table cell using the `td` tags to the `output` variable, setting the `bgcolor` attribute to the value of the `color` variable:

```
output += '<td bgcolor="#' + color + '"> <\/td>';

red   = add(red + ired);
green = add(green + igreen);
blue  = add(blue + iblue);
}
```

We need to ensure that we close the table using the appropriate HTML table tags:

```
output += '<\/tr><\/table>';

return output;
}

function add(color) {
  if (color < 0) return 0;
  if (color > 255) return 255;
  return color;
}
//--></script>

</head>
```

```
<body>

<script language="JavaScript"><!--
```

It's not until we come to use the table version of the gradient() function that we see much change in the code. The following two lines create two tables using different start and finish colors, but both specify 32 columns, although the row height is different in each case:

```
document.write(gradient(0xFF0000, 0xFFFF00, 32, 10));
document.write(gradient(0xFFFF00, 0xFF0000, 32, 30));
```

The following code calls the gradient() function 32 times, specifying slightly different start and finish colors each time:

```
var output = '';
for (var i=0; i<32; i++) {
  output +=
    gradient(0xFF0000 + i*16/2, 0xFFFF00 - (i*32 << 16), 32, 10);
}
document.write(output);
//--></script>

</body>
</html>
```

# Parsing Strings

Browsers supporting JavaScript 1.1 benefit from the added advantage of regular expressions support. Regular expressions, popular in Perl and other similar languages, provide the ability to match, search, and replace patterns within strings. At their simplest they offer the ability to search for strings or characters, and at their most complex, nothing is impossible except that which is limited by your imagination and, more importantly, your understanding of regular expressions.

This example introduces a simple regular expression that allows a string of text to be parsed into its separate components. The literal string a list of (key words) or "a phrase" can be said to have six components. If we were to use the String object method's split(), substring(), and indexOf(), it may well be possible to break the literal string down, but it would require a large amount of JavaScript code to do so. This is where regular expressions excel.

# Parsing Strings Source Code

 **../chapter3/parse/literal.htm**

```
<script language="JavaScript"><!--
```

First, we declare and initialize our `string` literal:

```
var string = 'a list of (key words) or "a phrase"';
```

We next create a Regular Expression variable named `re`:

```
var re = /"[^"]*"|\(([^(]*\)|\w+/g;
```

Note that the regular expression does not need quotes. Instead, it uses the forward slash character (/) as delimiters. The above `re` Regular Expression will match three different substrings as it uses the alternation character (|) to alternate on the three matches, the first match being `"[^"]*"`, which means this: Match a double quote character, the `"`, followed by any character except a double quote character, the `[^"]`, many times, the `*`. The second possible match is `\(([^(]*\)`, which means this: Match a left bracket character, the `\(`, followed by any character except a left bracket, the `[^(]`, many times, the `*`. The third possible match is `\w+`, which means this: Match any word character, the `\w`, one or more times, the `+`. The `re` Regular Expression also uses a regular expression attribute, in this case `g`, which means perform a global match. In other words, find all matches throughout the target string, and don't stop after the first—which would have happened if we had omitted the attribute.

Next, we declare a `splitArray` variable and assign the result of the `match()` method on the `string` passing the `re` Regular Expression as input to the `match()` method. This returns an array of all the found matches:

```
var splitArray = string.match(re);
```

We then loop through all the string elements in the `splitArray[]` array, writing each one out to the document:

```
for (var i=0; i<splitArray.length; i++) {
  document.write(splitArray[i] + '<br>');
}
//--></script>
```

The following shows the results of parsing the string literal: `a list of (key words) or "a phrase"`:

## Validating Strings Using Regular Expressions

Ensuring that user-entered data is valid and follows certain criteria can help eliminate corrupt data being passed and processed on the server. Informing the user that his or her data is invalid at the point the user enters it allows the user to immediately remedy the faults. Without the use of regular expressions, validating string data requires JavaScript code to test every single character within the string one at a time. Writing code to do this is laborious and prone to error. With the use of regular expressions, we can specify patterns that can be used to validate data. If the data follows the pattern, then the data is marked as valid, and if not, then the data can be highlighted as invalid.

Performing the data validation on the client reduces the load on the server, since it reduces the amount of invalid data that reaches the server in the first place, and results in fewer failures being returned to the browser for remedy. However, it does not eliminate the need for revalidation of the data on the server. It is good practice to validate the data again on the server, as it is possible that the browser may have skipped the validation if either JavaScript is disabled or the browser does not support JavaScript.

The example shown here validates typical user data: first name, last name, age, phone number, IP address, e-mail address, and credit card number, as shown in Figure 3-7. If the data is invalid in any way, then all the data items that fail validation are highlighted, as shown in Figure 3-8.

**Figure 3-7**
Validating Strings—
Valid form data.

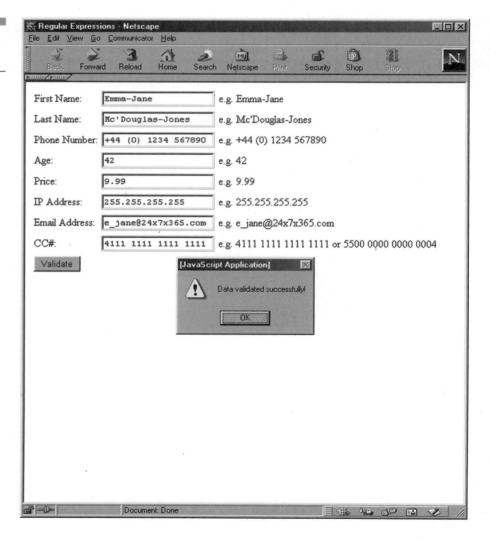

**Figure 3-8**
Validating Strings—
Invalid form data.

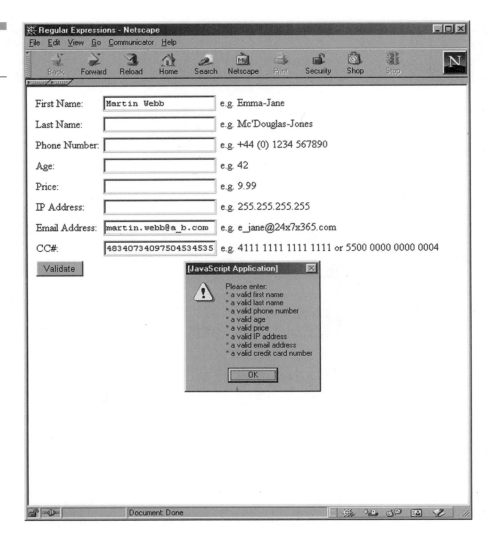

Armed with these simple to complex regular expressions, you can adapt them further to match any weird and wonderful patterns of data that you need to validate.

## Validating Strings Source Code

../chapter3/validate/form.htm

```
<html>

<head>
<title>Regular Expressions</title>
```

Regular expressions are only supported in JavaScript 1.2. Therefore, we set the script tag's `language` attribute to `JavaScript1.2`. Setting it to `JavaScript1.2` means only allowing browsers that support JavaScript 1.2 to process the enclosed JavaScript code:

```
<script language="JavaScript1.2"><!--
```

**First Name** We define several regular expressions using the forward slash characters to delimit the regular expressions. The first regular expression `isFirstName` can be used to match any alphabetical characters or the hyphen character (`-`). The metacharacter `^` indicates the start of the string, and the metacharacter `$` indicates the end of the string. The square brackets (`[` and `]`) indicate a valid range of literal characters: `A-Z` indicating all uppercase alphabetical characters from A through to Z, `a-z` indicating all lowercase alphabetical characters from a to z. To allow a hyphen character (`-`) within a range, we must escape it using a backslash character (`\`).

```
isFirstName = /^[A-Za-z\-]+$/;
```

The backslash character can be used to escape what would otherwise be treated as metacharacters to produce the literal character within regular expressions. For example, `\/`, `\\`, `\.`, `\*`, `\+`, `\?`, `\|`, `| (, \)`, `\[, \], \{`, and `\}`.

**Last Name** The `isLastName` regular expression is similar to `isFirstName`, except that it also allows single quote characters (`'`) within the string:

```
isLastName  = /^[A-Za-z'\-]+$/;
```

**Phone Number** The `isPhone` regular expression can be used to match international phone numbers:

```
isPhone     = /^(\+\d+ )?(\(\d+\) )?[\d ]+$/;
```

The digits 0, 1, 2, 3, 4, 5, 6, 7, 8, and 9 are represented using the character class `\d`. Repetition characters state how many times the preceding character or group of characters can appear at this point within a match. The characters ? - match zero or one occurrence only, + - matches one or more occurrences, and * - matches zero or more occurrences.

Parentheses—that is, ( and )—allow characters to be grouped together within an expression. This then allows metacharacters to act on the whole group and not just the preceding character. Therefore, in the isPhone regular expression, the portion ^(\+\d+ )? states that the start of the string could have zero or one occurrence of: one plus character followed by one or more digits followed by a space caracter.

The next portion (\(\d+\) )? states that the next part of the string (which could even be the start of the string) can contain zero or one occurrence of: one or more digits within a set of brackets followed by a space character.

The last portion [\d ]+$ states that the end of the string must contain one or more: digits or spaces.

**Age**   The isAge regular expression matches any string contain the numeric value 0 through to 129—any reasonable age. It uses the | character to allow matches on one or other of the two alternatives: 1[0-2]\d a 1 followed by 0, 1 or 2, followed by any digit, or \d{1,2} any digit followed by one or two other digits. The braces—that is, { and }—allow precise specification of repetition characters, in this case, a minimum of one and a maximum of two of the previous character or charactes:

```
isAge      = /^(1[0-2]\d|\d{1,2})$/;
```

**Money**   The isMoney regular expression matches on a floating-point number with at least one digit before the decimal point and exactly two after the decimal point:

```
isMoney    = /^\d+\.\d{2}$/;
```

**E-mail Address**   The validation of an e-mail address uses a slightly different approach. We specify two separate regular expressions, isEmail1 and isEmail2, with an isEmail() function, which shows how a string (s) can use the RegExp object's test() method to test that its regular expression matches on the passed string. Using the local AND operator (&&), we can test both at once and return true if both match or false if either the first doesn't, or if the first does but the second doesn't:

```
function isEmail(s) {
  return (isEmail1.test(s) && isEmail2.test(s));
}
```

The `isEmail1` regular expression is used to quickly match an e-mail address for groups of alphabetical characters, indicated by the character class `\w`—that is, a word character equivalent to `[a-zA-Z0-9_]` separated by hyphen or periods:

```
isEmail1    = /^\w+([\.\-]\w+)*\@\w+([\.\-]\w+)*\.\w+$/;
```

Breaking this expression down into stages:

- `^\w+` indicates that the e-mail address must start with one or more word characters.
- `([\.\-]\w+)*\@` indicates that zero or more occurrences of a hyphen or period character followed by one or more word characters must appear before the @ character.
- `\w+` indicates that one or more word characters must follow the @ character.
- `([\.\-]\w+)*` indicates that zero or more occurrences of a hyphen or period character followed by one or more word characters must appear.
- `\.\w+$` - indicates the e-mail address must finish with a period followed by one word character.

Unfortunately, the word character class `\w` includes a underscore character (_), which is not valid in a domain name. As `isEmail1` stands, it will incorrectly allow an e-mail address through of the format `first.second@domain_name.com`, where `domain_name.com` is invalid. The `isEmail2` regular expression overcomes this by not allowing the underscore character to appear after the @ character:

```
isEmail2    = /^.*@[^_]*$/;
```

We first match any and all characters up to the @ character using `^.*@`. The period metacharacter matches any character, the * repetition character matches zero of more occurrences of the previous character (i.e., the period metacharacter). Then we used negated character range using the caret character (^) to negate all the characters in the range—in this case, just the underscore character (_)—so that we match any character except the underscore character from the @ character to the end of the string.

If you think this will catch all valid and invalid e-mail addresses, think again. It will only vet the simplest forms of e-mail addresses, but this should be enough for our purposes.

**IP Address**  The `isIPAddress` regular expression uses yet another approach to create a regular expression. An IP address has the basic form `255.255.255.255`, where the four numbers can be anything from 0 through to 255. There appears to be a lot of repetition, so rather than create a long regular expression by hand, we can use the `RegExp` object constructor to build up a large regular expression using small string components.

First, we define an `ip` string that holds a regular expression to represent a number 0 through to 255. Note that as it is a string, we must escape any backslash characters with a preceding backslash character:

```
ip = '(25[0-5]|2[0-4]\\d|1\\d\\d|\\d\\d|\\d)';
```

Next, we define an `ipdot` string to represent the regular expression for the IP number followed by a period character. Again, the backslash character must be escaped:

```
ipdot = ip + '\\.';
```

We next create the Regular Expression using the `RegExp` object constructor combining three `ipdot` strings and one `ip` string:

```
isIPaddress = new RegExp('^'+ipdot+ipdot+ipdot+ip+'$');
```

**Credit Card Numbers**  We can even create regular expressions to validate the patterns of credit card numbers.

A Visa card number starts with 4 followed by 14 or 15 other digits:

```
isCCvisa        = /^4\d{14,15}$/;
```

A MasterCard number starts with 51, 52, 53, 54, or 55 followed by 14 other digits:

```
isCCmastercard = /^5[1-5]\d{14}$/;
```

An American Express number starts with 34 or 37 followed by 13 other digits:

```
isCCamex        = /^3[47]\d{13}$/;
```

A Diners Club card number starts with 300, 301, 302, 304, 305, 360, or 380 followed by 11 other digits:

```
isCCdinerscard = /^(30[0-5]|360|380)\d{11}$/;
```

A Discover card number starts with 6011 followed by 12 other digits:

```
isCCdiscover    = /^6011\d{12}$/;
```

An enRoute card number starts with 2014 or 2149 followed by 11 other digits:

```
isCCenroute     = /^(2014|2149)\d{11}$/;
```

A JCB card number starts with 2132 or 1800 followed by 11 other digits or starts with 3 and is followed by 15 other digits:

```
isCCjcb         = /^$((2131|1800)\d{11})|(3\d{15})/;
```

Rather than accept one credit card type and then vet it using the appropriate regular expression, the isCC() function accepts a string argument s for the credit card number and then uses each and every regular expression to attempt to find a matching credit card company.

```
function isCC(s) {
```

Before using any of the regular expressions to find a match, the RegExp object's replace() method is used to replace any whitespace characters, using the \s character class, with an empty string:

```
s = s.replace(/\s/g,'');
```

Each credit card regular expression is tested using the RegExp object's test() method. If a match is found, the test() method returns true. In this case we return the results of the call to the isLUHN() method, passing the s string as input for all credit card companies except for enRoute:

```
if (isCCvisa.test(s))       return isLUHN(s);
if (isCCmastercard.test(s)) return isLUHN(s);
if (isCCamex.test(s))       return isLUHN(s);
if (isCCdinerscard.test(s)) return isLUHN(s);
if (isCCdiscover.test(s))   return isLUHN(s);
if (isCCenroute.test(s))    return true;
if (isCCjcb.test(s))        return isLUHN(s);
```

Finally, if no credit card company has been matched, we simply return the results of the call to the isLUHN() function, again passing the s string:

```
    return isLUHN(s);
}
```

**LUHN Formula (Mod 10)**    To test if a credit card number is valid, we
need to use the LUHN Formula (Mod 10). Double the value of the alternate digits of the credit card number beginning with the second digit
from the right. Add the individual digits of the doubled number together.
Then add the unused digits from the credit card number. If the sum is
divisible by 10, then the credit card number passes the LUHN Formula.

This is exactly what the isLUHN() function does:

```
function isLUHN(s) {
```

Declare and initialize a local string variable x:

```
var x = '';
```

Declare and initialize a local integer variable l to hold the length of
the passed s argument:

```
var l = s.length;
```

Declare and initialize a local integer variable t to hold the sum:

```
var t = 0;
```

Loop through the entire length of the s string:

```
for (var i=0; i<l; i++)
```

We either append the current digit within the s string to the x string
using the String object's charAt() method or append the doubled current digit value, depending on whether we are on an alternate number or
not. This is dictated by the modulo 2 value of length of the string (l)
minus the current position within the string (i):

```
if ((l-i)%2) x+=s.charAt(i); else x+=''+s.charAt(i)*2;
```

At this point we have all the alternate doubled digits and all the
unused digits in a long concatenated string (x). We simply need to loop
the x string, adding all the digits to the t integer:

```
for (var i=0; i<x.length; i++)
  t += x.charAt(i) - 0;
```

We simply return the negated (!) modulo 10 value of the t integer. If the modulo 10 result is 0 (i.e., no remainder), then the negated value of 0 (false) is 1 (true):

```
    return !(t%10);
}
```

**Validating the Form Data**    The validate() function is called when the form's Validate button is clicked and passed a reference to the form as the what argument. It uses the previously defined regular expressions to validate the data entered into the form fields:

```
function validate(what) {
```

We declare and initialize an error message string to be initially empty:

```
    var message = '';
```

The value of the form's firstname field is passed as an argument to the isFirstName regular expression object's test() method. If a match is made, the data is valid. If not (!), then we append an error string to the message variable:

```
    if (!isFirstName.test(what.firstname.value))
        message += '* a valid first name\n';
```

Exactly the same thing is done with the lastname, phone, age, price, and ipaddress form fields:

```
    if (!isLastName.test(what.lastname.value))
        message += '* a valid last name\n';

    if (!isPhone.test(what.phone.value))
        message += '* a valid phone number\n';

    if (!isAge.test(what.age.value))
        message += '* a valid age\n';

    if (!isMoney.test(what.price.value))
        message += '* a valid price\n';

    if (!isIPaddress.test(what.ipaddress.value))
        message += '* a valid IP address\n';
```

When it comes to the email form field, instead of testing the regular expression directly, we call the isEmail() function to perform the test, passing the value of the email form field:

```
if (!isEmail(what.email.value))
  message += '* a valid email address\n';
```

And again with the `creditcard` form field, this time using the `isCC()` function:

```
if (!isCC(what.creditcard.value))
  message += '* a valid credit card number\n';
```

If any of the tests have failed, then the local `message` variable will contain an error message to display. Otherwise, the `message` variable will be empty, in which case we display a success message:

```
if (message == '')
  alert("Data validated successfully!")
else
  alert('Please enter:\n' + message);
}
//--></script>

</head>

<body>
```

The remainder of the code displays a form with input form fields on the page:

```
<form>

<table>
<tr>
<td>First Name:</td>
<td><input type="text" name="firstname"></td>
<td>e.g. Emma-Jane</td>
</tr><tr>
<td>Last Name:</td>
<td><input type="text" name="lastname"></td>
<td>e.g. Mc'Douglas-Jones</td>
</tr><tr>
<td>Phone Number:</td>
<td><input type="text" name="phone"></td>
<td>e.g. +44 (0) 1234 567890</td>
</tr><tr>
<td>Age:</td>
<td><input type="text" name="age"></td>
<td>e.g. 42</td>
</tr><tr>
<td>Price:</td>
<td><input type="text" name="price"></td>
<td>e.g. 9.99</td>
</tr><tr>
<td>IP Address:</td>
<td><input type="text" name="ipaddress"></td>
```

```
<td>e.g. 255.255.255.255</td>
</tr><tr>
<td>Email Address:</td>
<td><input type="text" name="email"></td>
<td>e.g. e_jane@24x7x365.com</td>
</tr><tr>
<td>cc#:</td>
<td><input type="text" name="creditcard"></td>
<td>e.g. 4111 1111 1111 1111 or 5500 0000 0000 0004</td>
</tr><tr>
```

When the `Validate` form button is clicked, we first check to see if `validate` is true—before calling the `validate()` function, passing a reference to the current (`this`) input field's `form`. The test on `validate` will only return `true` if the browser supports JavaScript 1.2, in which case the `validate()` function will be defined. If the browser does not support JavaScript 1.2, the JavaScript code will be skipped, the `validate()` function not defined, and therefore the test on `validate` will result in false:

```
<td><input type="button" value="Validate"
  onClick="if (validate) validate(this.form)"</td>
</tr>
</table>

</form>

</body>
</html>
```

## Regular Expressions

Anchor characters, shown in Table 3-4, dictate where in a string a match may be made.
Character classes, shown in Table 3-5, allow a range of characters to be combined.
Repetition characters, shown in Table 3-6, control how few or many times a character or group of characters occurs.

**TABLE 3-4**

*Regular expression anchor characters.*

| Anchor Character | Description |
|---|---|
| ^ | Matches the start of the string |
| $ | Matches the end of the string |

**TABLE 3-5**

*Regular expression character classes.*

| Character Class | Description |
|---|---|
| . | Matches any character |
| \w | Matches a word character, i.e., A-Z, a-z, 0-9, and the underscore character |
| \W | Matches a non-word character |
| \w+ | Matches a whole word, i.e., all word characters up to a whitespace character |
| \s | Matches a whitespace character, e.g., newline (\n), tab (\t), carriage return (\r), form feed (\f), or vertical tab (\v) character |
| \S | Matches a non-whitespace character |
| x\|y | Matches x or y |
| \d | Matches one digit character ranging from 0 to 9 |
| \D | Matches one nondigit character |
| [abc] | Matches a or b or c |
| [0-9] | Matches one digit character, ranging from 0 to 9 |
| [A-Za-z] | Matches one alphabetical character, uppercase or lowercase |
| [^A-Za-z] | Matches one nonalphabetical character |

**TABLE 3-6**

*Repetition characters.*

| Repetition Character | Description |
|---|---|
| ? | Matches one or none of the preceding character |
| + | Matches one or more of the preceding character |
| * | Matches none or all of the preceding character |
| {x,y} | Matches a minimum of x and a maximum of y instances of the preceding character |

**TABLE 3-7**

*Grouping.*

| Parertheses | Description |
|---|---|
| (abc)+ | Matches one or more occurrences of abc |

Parentheses allows characters to be grouped together, as shown in Table 3-7.

**TABLE 3-8**

Escaped
characters.

| Escaped Character | Description |
| --- | --- |
| \/ | Matches / |
| \\ | Matches \ |
| \. | Matches . |
| \* | Matches * |
| \+ | Matches + |
| \? | Matches ? |
| \| | Matches \| |
| \( | Matches ( |
| \) | Matches ) |
| \[ | Matches [ |
| \] | Matches ] |
| \{ | Matches { |
| \} | Matches } |

**TABLE 3-9**

Regular expression
modifiers.

| Modifier | Description |
| --- | --- |
| /abc/ | Global—matches all instances of abc. |
| /abc/i | Ignore case—Matches first instance of abc or ABC. |
| /abc/gi | Global and ignore case—Matches all instances of abc or ABC. |

If you wish to search for one of the special characters, you must first delimit it with a backslash character (\), as shown in Table 3-8.

Modifiers, shown in Table 3-9, can be added after the regular expression to control how it searches through the string.

# Summary

Although mathematics is the workhorse under the hood of JavaScript applications, strings are generally the data being manipulated, whether it is the string value of form fields or the string value of the current window location. These strings all need to be manipulated, processed, and searched. Even when we move on to more sophisticated arrays and objects in the next chapter, we still need to use basic mathematics and string processing techniques shown in this and the previous chapter.

# Arrays and Objects

Being able to store and manipulate data is one of the most fundamental aspects of JavaScript. Although technically not an object-oriented programming language, almost everything can be considered an object in JavaScript, from the most primitive data types, such as Number, String, and Boolean, to specialized data types, such as Date, RegExp, Math, Function, Array, and Event, and to specialized browser objects, such as window, document, history, location, image, and link.

It doesn't stop there, though. JavaScript allows the creation of user-defined objects. All that is needed to create user-defined objects is a constructor method and a new statement to create a new instance of the object. As with most objects, an object instance on its own doesn't provide us any major achievement. It is not until we have many objects of the same type, with each one representing a different instance of the object class (e.g., a car, a birth date or a description of a technical article), that we can begin to appreciate the usefulness of creating our own user-defined objects. When we have created many object instances, we need to be able to manage and hold them all. The in-built JavaScript array object is the most appropriate mechanism to do this.

This chapter introduces user-defined objects and object arrays. It shows how to use constructors to create object instances, how to store objects in an array, how to retrieve the values of object properties, and finally how to sort an array of objects.

Touring Web Sites ../chapter4/tour/tour.htm
**Searching a Database (frames version) ../chapter4/search1/search.htm**
**Searching a Database (non frames version) ../chapter4/search2/search.htm**
**Multiple-Choice ../chapter4/multiple/choice.htm**
**Object Array Sorting ../chapter4/sort/sort.htm**

# Touring Web Sites

Showing people your favorite locations on the Web can be difficult to do without providing a list of URLs. Once you've done this, it is then impossible to provide any commentary on each of the URLs without sitting down with your audience and explaining what you find interesting about each page. Unfortunately, we don't all have the time and energy to provide this level of customer service. This example shows how you can prepare a list of URLs, link them together—even though there may not be any physical connection between them—and also provide a running commentary in either a separate frame or window. For our example, we will use books available on Amazon.com as the remote pages to tour, which will be combined with our own book review comments.

## Touring Web Sites Components

The example demonstration is made up of several basic HTML files:

- *tour.htm*, which is the container frameset (to hold the navigational toolbar and work area)
- *tour-nav.htm*, which contains the navigation buttons
- *tour-comment.htm*, which contains another frameset (to hold comments and book pages)
- Our supplementary book review comment files
- The Amazon.com books to visit in the tour

Note that the files do not need to be called these names. They are just what we have used in this example. Also, the files that make up the tour can be anywhere—on your own site or on totally separate and unrelated websites. There is also no restriction on the number of files that make up the tour.

## Touring Web Sites Frameset Structure

The tour use frames to hold everything: a frame to hold the navigational form buttons that enables the user to move forward and backward through the tour, a frame to hold the running commentary, and a frame to hold the current page in the tour.

We nest one frameset within another, as this allows us to display an optional commentary page with the actual tour page. The frameset structure is shown in Figure 4-1.

However, since most other sites on the Web would probably prefer not to have their contents framed within someone else's site, we provide an option to display the current page in the tour in a separate pop-up window. The frameset structure for this option is shown in Figure 4-2.

The results can therefore look different depending on the option chosen in the JavaScript code. Figure 4-3 shows how a tour might look using just the straightforward frameset structure, whereas Figure 4-4 shows the option with the tour page in a separate pop-up window.

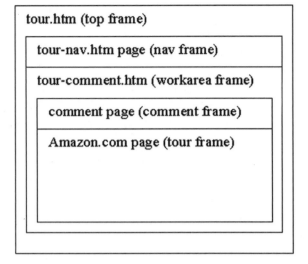

**Figure 4-1**
Touring Web Sites
frameset structure.

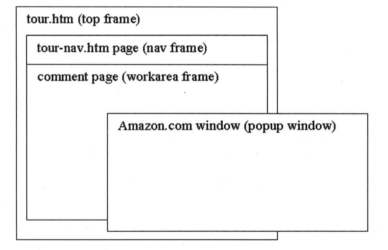

**Figure 4-2**
Touring Web Sites
alternative frameset
structure with pop-up
window.

## Touring Web Sites Source Code

### Source Code for tour.htm

**../chapter4/replace/tour.htm**

The *tour.htm* file contains HTML to define the size, position, and initial contents of two frames, the data that defines the pages to be toured, as well as almost all the JavaScript code necessary to control the navigation through the tour.

**Figure 4-3**
Sample Touring Web
Sites frameset.

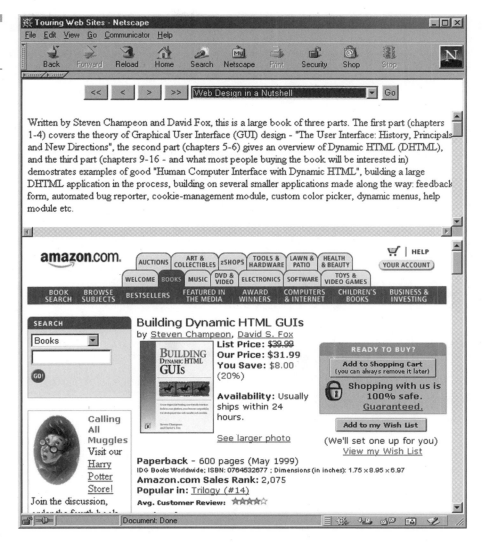

The `usePopup` Boolean variable is set to `false`. This means the code will use frames (amending this to `true` will result in the code using a pop-up window):

```
var usePopup = false;
```

The `Link()` function is used as an object constructor. To create a new `Link()` object, we simply use the new operator and assign the result to a variable. For example, the `var myObject = new Link();` Our

**Figure 4-4**
Sample Touring Web
Sites frameset with
pop-up window.

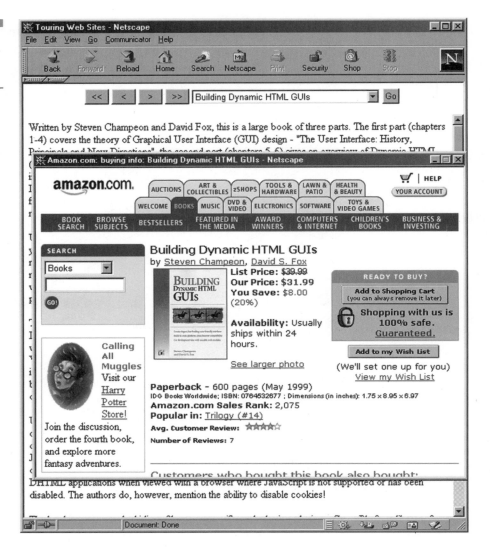

`Link()` constructor accepts three arguments: `href`, `text`, and `commentary`. As with all object constructors, a reference to the newly created `Link` object is passed to the `Link` object constructor and held in the `this` keyword. The `Link` object constructor uses the three input arguments along with the `this` reference to declare, define, and assign three `Link` object properties to the current `Link` object being constructed—`href`, `text`, and `commentary`:

```
function Link(href,text,commentary) {
  this.commentary = commentary;
  this.href = href;
  this.text = text;
}
```

The setLink() function creates Link objects, adding each one to the end of the MyLink[] array:

```
function setLink(href,text,commentary) {
  myLink[item++] = new Link(href,text,commentary);
}
```

The code item++ uses the postfix increment operator to increment the value of item by 1 after it has been used in the current statement. For example, if the current value of item is 10, then the object referenced returned by new Link() is placed into the tenth position in the MyLink[] object array. The value of item is then increased by 1 to 11.

We define and declare the initial value of item to be 0 (as in most computer languages, arrays start from index position 0):

```
var item = 0;
```

Here we define an empty Array object using the in-built JavaScript Array constructor and assign it to the myLink variable:

```
var myLink = new Array();
```

We create five Link objects to hold the data for each tour page. The setLink() function is invoked, passing an absolute URL of the tour page into the href argument, a string comment into the text argument, and a local relative URL into the commentary argument:

```
setLink(
  'http://www.amazon.com/exec/obidos/ISBN=0764532677/',
  'Building Dynamic HTML GUIs',
  'comment1.htm'
);
setLink(
  'http://www.amazon.com/exec/obidos/ISBN=1565923928/',
  'JavaScript : The Definitive Guide 3rd Edition',
  'comment2.htm'
);
setLink(
  'http://www.amazon.com/exec/obidos/ISBN=0201442078/',
  'Creating Dynamic Web Sites',
  'comment3.htm'
);
setLink(
```

```
    'http://www.amazon.com/exec/obidos/ISBN=1565925157/',
    'Web Design in a Nutshell',
    'comment4.htm'
);
setLink(
    'http://www.amazon.com/exec/obidos/ISBN=1565921496/',
    'Programming Perl, 2nd Edition',
    'comment5.htm'
);
```

We can now retrieve the value of any of our `Link` object's properties by using the syntax `myLink[index].property`, where `index` is the index position within the `myLink[]` object array (e.g., 0 to 4) and `property` is one of `href`, `text`, or `commentary`. For example, `myLink[1].text` has the string value `JavaScript : The Definitive Guide 3rd Edition`.

The `n` variable is used to hold the current position within the tour. It is defined and declared with a value of 0—that is, the first position within the tour:

```
var n = 0;
```

The `go()` function controls the loading of the tour and associated commentary pages:

```
function go() {
```

We test the value of the `usePopup` Boolean variable:

```
    if (usePopup) {
```

If `true`, we create a new window using the `window` object's `open` method, passing three arguments—the `href` property of the nth `Link` object in the `myLink[]` object array as the page to be loaded into the pop-up window, the name of the pop-up window (`myPopup`), and the width and height of the pop-up window:

```
        window.open(myLink[n].href,'myPopup','width=640,height=480');
```

We then load the associated commentary page into the `workarea` frame using the `commentary` property of the nth `Link` object in the `myLink[]` object array:

```
        self.workarea.location.href = myLink[n].commentary;
    }
    else {
```

However, because we have defined the `usePopup` Boolean variable to be `false`, we instead set the `href` property of the `workarea` frame's `location` to be equal to `tour-comment.htm?` plus the current value of the n variable (i.e., the position within the tour). This has the effect of loading the *tour-comment.htm* page into the bottom half of the current window:

```
      self.workarea.location.href = 'tour-comment.htm?' + n;
   }
}
```

At the start of the tour, this would result in a location of *tour-comment.htm?0*, and as we progress though the tour, this changes to *comment.htm?1*, *comment.htm?2*, *comment.htm?3*, and finally *comment.htm?4*. As shown later, the JavaScript code within the *tour-comment.htm* page uses the data after the question mark (?) character to load the appropriate tour and commentary pages into its own frameset.

The four functions `goFirst()`, `goBack()`, `goForward()`, and `goLast()` are used later in the *tour-nav.htm* page to navigate backward and forward through the tour pages:

```
function goFirst() {
   if (n != 0) { n = 0; go(); }
}

function goBack() {
   if (n != 0) { n--; go(); }
}

function goForward() {
   if (n != (item - 1)) { n++; go(); }
}

function goLast() {
   if (n != item -1) { n = item - 1; go(); }
}
```

A check is made in each one to ensure the ends of the tour are not being passed. Then the value of the n variable is altered appropriately. Finally, a call to the `go()` method is made to load the appropriate pages.

In addition to form buttons within the *tour-nav.htm* page to navigate backward and forward through the tour, there is also a form select options list of all the tour pages that can be used by the user to jump to any one of the pages. The select options list within the *tour-nav.htm* page uses the `goTo()` function here in the *tour.htm* page. A reference (`object`) to the select options is passed to the `goTo()` function:

```
function goTo(object) {
```

If the value of the select option's `selectedIndex` (i.e., the index value of the selected option) is not the same as the current tour page, then the value of the n variable is changed to the value of `selectedIndex` and the `go()` function is invoked to load the appropriate pages:

```
if (n != object.selectedIndex) { n = object.selectedIndex; go(); }
```

We finally return a `false` Boolean value to the caller of the `goTo()` function:

```
   return false;
}
```

All that is left is the definition of the frameset:

```
<frameset frameborder="0" framespacing="0" rows="50,*"
onLoad="go()">

<frame scrolling="no" frameborder="0" name="nav" noresize
src="tour-nav.htm">

<frame frameborder="0" name="workarea" noresize
src="about:blank">

</frameset>
```

Here a thin 50-pixel-high nav frame is defined along with workarea frame that then fills up the remaining available window height, indicated by the asterisk (*). The *tour-nav.htm* page is loaded into the nav frame, and the *about:blank* page is loaded into the workarea frame. The *about:blank* page is simply a blank page generated by the browser; it avoids having to retrieve a blank page from the server.

Finally, we use the onLoad event handler within the frameset tag to capture the event that notifies us that both the *tour-nav.htm* and *about:blank* pages have completely loaded, and invoke the go() function to load the first page in the tour.

**Source Code for tour-nav.htm**

**../chapter4/replace/tour-nav.htm**

The *tour-nav.htm* file contains a form that allows the user to navigate through the tour:

```
<form name="form1"
```

If the `form1` form is submitted, the `onSubmit` event handler catches the submit event and invokes the `goTo()` function on the `parent` frame:

```
onSubmit="return parent.goTo(document.form1.select1)">
```

The *tour-nav.htm* page is loaded into the `nav` frame. Therefore, the parent frame contains the *tour.htm* page. The call to the `goTo()` function includes a reference to the `form1` form's `select1` element, where `select1` is the name given to the select options list later in the form. The `goTo()` function, as detailed in the *tour.htm* page, takes the `selectedIndex` value of the select options list and uses that to jump to the appropriate tour page. The value returned from the `goTo()` function (`false`) is handed back to the `submit` event to cancel the form submission.

The four buttons labeled <<, <, >, and >> are used to navigate backward and forward through the tour. Each button's `onClick` event handler captures the mouse click and calls the appropriate function in the parent frame to navigate through the tour. They then set the `selectedIndex` value of the `form1` form's `select1` select options list to the new value of the `parent` frame's n variable—thus updating the select list to show the option that reflects the current tour page:

```
<input type="button" value=" << "
  onClick="parent.goFirst();
           document.form1.select1.selectedIndex = parent.n">

<input type="button" value="  <  "
  onClick="parent.goBack();
           document.form1.select1.selectedIndex = parent.n">

<input type="button" value="  >  "
  onClick="parent.goForward();
           document.form1.select1.selectedIndex = parent.n">

<input type="button" value=" >> "
  onClick="parent.goLast();
           document.form1.select1.selectedIndex = parent.n">
```

The actual options within the `select1` select options list are built dynamically from the `parent` frame's `myLink[]` object array:

```
<select name="select1">

<script language="JavaScript"><!--
```

We loop through each object within the `myLink[]` using the `parent` frame's `item` variable to control the end of the loop:

```
for (var i=0; i < parent.item; i++)
```

We use the `document` object's `write()` method to write an `option` tag to the document for each `Link` object, setting the text associated with the option to equal the `Link` object's `text` property:

```
document.write('<option>' +
               parent.myLink[i].text +
               '<\/option>');
//--></script>

</select>
```

The form's Submit button allows the user to select an option within the list and then hit the Go button to trigger a `submit` event:

```
<input type="submit" value="Go">
```

When the page is initially loaded, we ensure that the `form1` form's `select1` select option's `selectedIndex` is set to highlight the current page in the tour:

```
<body onLoad="document.form1.select1.selectedIndex = parent.n">
```

### Source Code for tour-comment.htm

../chapter4/replace/tour-comment.htm

Finally the *tour-comment.htm* page, which is loaded into the `workarea` frame if the `usePopup` Boolean variable is set to `false`, is used to define yet another frameset with initially empty commentary and tour frames, along with the necessary JavaScript code to interpret the current page's URL and load the appropriate commentary and tour pages.

The `load()` function is called from the `frameset` tag's `onLoad` event handler:

```
function load() {
```

First we extract the data passed after the question mark (?) character in the URL using the `location` object's `search` property. We remove the actual question mark character using the `String` object's `substring` method:

```
var n = location.search.substring(1);
```

Effectively, `substring(1)` says "give me a portion of the string starting at index position 1." For example, `var s = "01234"; var t = s.substring(1);` will result in `t` holding the value `1234`. Using `var n = location.search.substring(1)` retrieves the value of n appended to the URL, so that a URL of `comment.htm?0` will retrieve `0`, `comment.htm?1` will retrieve `1`, and so on.

Based on this passed `search` value, we load the appropriate commentary page into the `comment` frame:

```
self.comment.location.href = top.myLink[n].commentary;
```

And the appropriate tour page into the `tour` frame:

```
    self.tour.location.href = top.myLink[n].href;
}
```

Note that we use the `top` frame's `myLink[]` object array to retrieve the `commentary` and `href` properties of the nth `Link` object. Up to now we have being using a `parent` reference to obtain variables, arrays, and objects in the parent frame. However, now that we have one frame nested in another, we either use a `parent.parent` reference or cut straight to the top frame using `top`.

The `onLoad` event handler invokes the `load()` function when both the `comment` and `tour` frames have completely loaded the *about:blank* pages:

```
<frameset frameborder="0" framespacing="0" rows="200,*"
onLoad="load()">
```

# Searching a Database.

In the previous Touring Web Sites code, we showed how to create our own JavaScript objects (the `Link` object) with its own properties (`href`, `text`, and `commentary`) and how to store those objects in an object array. This enabled us to load different pages into the browser using the properties of any one of the `Link` objects.

In this section we will show how we can search through the properties of an array of objects and use the results to write the output of our findings to the browser, providing the ability for the user to search a client side database of technical articles. We will demonstrate two versions of the code, one that works using frames (in a similar manner to the Touring Web Sites example), and another version that works without using frames.

As with many client-side applications, the data has to be first downloaded to the client. Of course, this can cause problems if the data to be downloaded is very large, which is why these two examples should be used with caution. If the data is too large, the user may well move on before seeing the full benefit of the client-side search application. The advantage of a client-side search application over a server-side search application is that once the data has been downloaded, the user no longer has to be connected to the Internet. In fact, while the user is querying the database, there are no requests going back to the server, which means that the response time of the query is instantaneous.

## Frames-Based Searching

The hierarchy of the frames-based components consists of a parent frame (*search.htm*) and two child frames, named `tools` and `results`. The `tools` frame (*tools.htm*) holds the navigational form elements, and the `results` frame (*results.htm*) initially shows the complete client-side database, as shown in Figure 4-5. However, it is then reused to show the results of the user's database queries.

The code allows the user to select the level of detail shown in the search results—from all the details (title, URL, description, techniques, and date, as shown in Figure 4-6) to a partial selection (title and date, as shown in Figure 4-7.)

## Frames Source Code

**Source code for search.htm**

../chapter4/search1/search.htm

The *search.htm* page forms the parent frameset *tools.htm* and *results.htm* pages. It contains the database information using an object

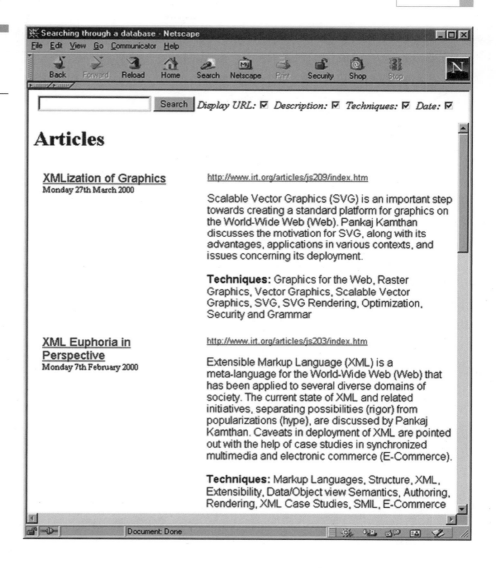

**Figure 4-5**
Searching through a database—Initial display.

array similar to that used in the Touring Web Sites example. Also contained within *search.htm* are several variables that are used to control the output of the search.

The four Boolean variables (`vhref`, `vdesc`, `vtech`, and `vdate`) are all initially defined and declared to be `true`—meaning the search results will display the URL, description, techniques, and date properties, along with the title link, which is always displayed:

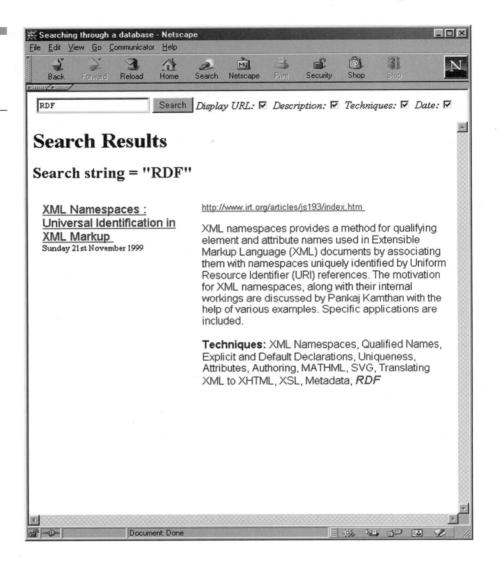

**Figure 4-6**
Searching through
a database—Full
search query results
on "RDF."

```
var vhref = true;
var vdesc = true;
var vtech = true;
var vdate = true;
```

The `searchtext` string variable is initialized as an empty string. This has the effect of matching on all items in the database, so that when initially loaded, all items in the database are displayed:

```
var searchtext = '';
```

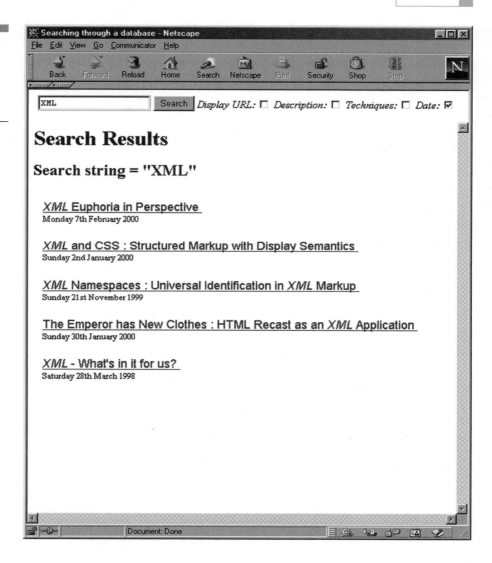

**Figure 4-7**
Searching through a database—Title and date search query results on "XML."

We create two arrays to hold the days of the week and the months of the year.

```
var days = new Array(
  'Sunday','Monday','Tuesday','Wednesday','Thursday',
  'Friday','Saturday'
);

var months = new Array(
  'January','February','March','April','May','June','July',
  'August','September','October','November','December'
);
```

The `articleObject()` constructor not only creates typical properties based on the passed arguments, it also creates other properties:

```
function articleObject(href,text,desc,tech,date) {
  this.href = href;
  this.text = text;
  this.desc = desc;
  this.tech = tech;
```

The `date` property is not initialized straight from the passed `date` argument, but it uses the `date` argument in a call to the `convert_date()` function:

```
this.date = convert_date(date);
```

The additional HREF, TEXT, DESC, TECH, and DATE properties are just uppercase versions of the lowercase versions, created using the `String` object's `toUpperCase()` method:

```
  this.HREF = href.toUpperCase();
  this.TEXT = text.toUpperCase();
  this.DESC = desc.toUpperCase();
  this.TECH = tech.toUpperCase();
  this.DATE = this.date.toUpperCase();
}
```

The `convert_date()` function converts the `date` string from its YYYYMMDD format to a full human-readable date string (e.g., it converts the string `20000207` to `Monday 7th February 2000`):

```
function convert_date(string) {
```

Using the `String` object's `substring()` method, the `convert_date()` function extracts the YYYY, MM, and DD portions of the passed string to create a new `Date` object:

```
var date = new Date(string.substring(0,4),
                    (string.substring(4,6)-1),
                    string.substring(6,8));
```

The results of the call to the `fulldate()` function using the newly constructed `date` object is finally returned:

```
  return fullDate(date);
}
```

The `Date` constructor excepts (among other combinations) three arguments: the year, the month (starting from zero), and the date of the month. For instance, `new Date(2000,1,7);` would create a `date` object for the `February 7th 2000`. The `fulldate()` function formats the passed `date` object:

```
function fullDate(date) {
```

The `days` array is used to retrieve the full name of the day of the week:

```
return days[date.getDay()] + ' ' +
```

The `date` object's `getDate()` method returns the date of the month:

```
date.getDate() +
```

The `nths()` function is used to work out the date ordinal (e.g. `1st`, `2nd`, `3rd`, or `4th`):

```
nths(date.getDate()) + ' ' +
```

The `months` array is used to retrieve the full name of the month of the year:

```
months[date.getMonth()] + ' ' +
```

The `y2k()` function is used to ensure a fully compliant Y2K year is displayed:

```
(y2k(date.getYear()));
}
```

Details on how to manipulates dates further will be covered in Chapter 9 "Images".

**Source code for tools.htm**

 **../chapter4/search1/tools.htm**

The *tools.htm* file contains a form that allows the user to enter the search query string and dictate the amount of detail shown in the search results. The `goSearch()` function's `form` argument holds the passed form reference:

```
function goSearch(form) {
```

The form's checkboxes and text fields are all individually named (`vhref`, `vdec`, `vtech`, `vdate`, and `searchtext`), which enables the `goSearch()` function to use the passed `form` argument to update the like named Boolean and string variables in the `parent` frame:

```
parent.vhref = form.vhref.checked;
parent.vdesc = form.vdesc.checked;
parent.vtech = form.vtech.checked;
parent.vdate = form.vdate.checked;
parent.searchtext = form.searchtext.value;
```

The *results.htm* page is then reloaded into the `results` frame:

```
parent.results.location.href = "results.htm";
}
```

The `onSubmit` event handler in the `form` tag invokes the `goSearch()` function (passing a `this` form reference) and returns `false` to cancel the forms submit event:

```
<form onSubmit="goSearch(this);return false">
```

### Source code for results.htm

**../chapter4/search1/results.htm**

The *results.htm* page is reloaded every time the user enters a query. It checks through each of the `articleObjects` held in the `parent` frame's `articleArray[]` array matching on the `parent` frame's `searchtext`.

First, we define and initialize several global variables—global in that they are available through the entire JavaScript code in the current page, even within functions:

```
var position = 0;
var old = 0;
var last = 0;
var out = '';
var OUT = '';
```

Next, the `searchtext` is retrieved from the `parent` frame and placed in a global `searchtext` variable:

```
var searchtext = parent.searchtext;
```

We check to see if a search query has been entered:

```
if (parent.searchtext != '') {
```

If a search query has been entered, then two lines of HTML markup are written to the document, one using the h1 element and the other using the h2 element:

```
    document.write('<h1>Search Results<\/h1>');
    document.write('<h2>Search string = "'+searchtext+'"<\/h2>');
}
else {
```

If a search query has not been entered, we simply write the content using a single h1 element to the document:

```
    document.write('<h1>Articles<\/h1>');
}
```

Now that we have finished displaying the value of the searchtext, we convert its value to uppercase so that any later string comparisons ignore any potential differences in case:

```
searchtext = searchtext.toUpperCase();
```

The output is displayed within a table, so a table tag is written out to the document:

```
document.write('<table>');
```

The code then loops through all the articleObject objects within the parent frame's articleArray[]:

```
for (var i=0; i < parent.articleIndex; i++) {
```

We test to see if the value of the searchtext variable is present within the uppercase versions of the articleObject properties HREF, TEXT, DESC, TECH, or (||) DATE:

```
    if (
      (parent.articleArray[i].HREF.indexOf(searchtext) != -1) ||
      (parent.articleArray[i].TEXT.indexOf(searchtext) != -1) ||
      (parent.articleArray[i].DESC.indexOf(searchtext) != -1) ||
      (parent.articleArray[i].TECH.indexOf(searchtext) != -1) ||
      (parent.articleArray[i].DATE.indexOf(searchtext) != -1)
```

If it is found, then the output() function is invoked:

```
    ) output();
}
```

The `String` object's `indexOf()` method returns the position of the first occurrence of the `searchtext` value within the string. If it is not found, then the `indexOf()` method returns `-1`.

Note that because the `searchtext` value is initially an empty string (`''`), the preceding test will match on all of the `articleObject` objects, so the `output()` function will be invoked for each and every one. Therefore, the articles are all displayed when the code is initially loaded.

Finally the table tag is closed:

```
document.write('<\/table>');
```

The `output()` function, which is invoked when a match is found, controls how the `articleObject` is displayed on the document. First, the lowercase versions of the `articleObject` properties `href`, `desc`, `text`, `tech`, and `date` property values are retrieved and held in local variables—local in that they are only available within the scope of the current function:

```
function output() {
  var href = parent.articleArray[i].href;
  var desc = parent.articleArray[i].desc;
  var text = parent.articleArray[i].text;
  var tech = parent.articleArray[i].tech;
  var date = parent.articleArray[i].date;
```

We initialize the `output` string variable to be an empty string:

```
var output = '';
```

We then start to build up the `output` string to contain all the HTML code to be written to the document:

```
output += '<tr>';
output += '<td valign="top>"';
output += '<font face="Arial, Helvetica" size="4">';
```

Here, we append a text link to the `output` string using the local `href` and `text` variables:

```
output += '<a href="' + href + '" target="_parent">';
output += show(text)+'<\/a>';
output += '<\/font>';
```

However, note that we've actually written the text for the link using the results of the show() function using text as an input argument.

Here we test the value of the parent frame's vdate Boolean variable:

```
if (parent.vdate)
```

If true, we append the results of the call to the show() function, this time passing date:

```
output += '<font size="2"><br>'+show(date)+'<\/font>';
output += '<\/td>';
output += '<td valign="top">';
output += '<font face="Arial" size="3">';
```

If the user had unchecked the date checkbox, then the output would not include the date.

Again, if the parent frame's vhref Boolean variable is true, we display the local href property wrapped in a link, and again we use the show() function, this time passing href:

```
if (parent.vhref)
    output += '<font size="2">' +
             '<a href="' + href + '" target="_parent">' +
             show(href) +
             '<\/a>' +
             '<\/font>';
```

Likewise with the desc variable:

```
if (parent.vdesc)
    output += '<p>' +show(desc) + '<\/p>';
```

And again with the tech variable:

```
if (parent.vtech)
    output += '<p><b>Techniques:<\/b> ' + show(tech) + '<\/p>';

output += '<\/font>';
output += '<\/td>';
output += '<\/tr>';
```

Before finally writing the value of the output string to the document:

```
document.write(output);
}
```

We could have written out to the document all the HTML formatting required to display the article step-by-step, but rather than doing that, we place everything into the output string variable, concatenating more and more information to it, until we finally write the contents out to the document at the end of the output() function. Writing a whole load of information to the document in one go is far quicker that writing lots of little bits individually.

The string concatenation operator (+=) adds the string expression on the right-hand side of the operator to the value of the string variable on the left-hand side of the operator, placing the results into the string variable. For example, var x = 'abc'; var y = 'def'; x+=y; will result in x containing the value abcdef. This is a shorthand way of saying x = x + y, and this is used quite often in JavaScript code.

The show() function, which we have used several times in the output() function, highlights any occurrence of the searchtext within the passed property:

```
function show(property) {
```

If searchtext is an empty string, we immediately return the property unchanged:

```
    if (searchtext == '') return property;
```

We update the value of the global variable out to hold the passed property argument:

```
    out = property;
```

We update the value of the global variable OUT to hold an uppercase version of the passed property argument:

```
    OUT = property.toUpperCase();
```

We update the value of the global position variable to hold the first occurrence of searchtext within the OUT and last to hold the last occurrence:

```
    position = OUT.indexOf(searchtext);
    last = OUT.lastIndexOf(searchtext);
    old = -(property.length);
```

We also update the value of the global old variable to the negative value of the searchtext string's length.

If we have a match, then we return the results of the find() function. Otherwise, we again return the property unchanged:

```
  if (position != -1) return find(); else return property;
}
```

The `find()` function highlights the first occurrence of the found string and then continually calls itself (iterates) until all occurrences have been found and highlighted:

```
function find() {
```

Here we use the `substring()` method to extract the found `search-text`, wrap it up in HTML tags to highlight it using a large blue font, and assign the result to the local `string` variable.

```
var string = out.substring(old+searchtext.length,position) +
    '<i><font color="#0000FF" size="+1">' +
    out.substring(position,position+searchtext.length) +
    '<\/font><\/i>';
```

The `old` position is set to the value of the current `position`:

```
old = position;
```

We attempt to locate the position of the next occurrence:

```
position = OUT.indexOf(searchtext,position+searchtext.length);
```

If we have found another occurrence then the `find()` function calls itself to do it all over again:

```
if ((position != -1) && (old != last))
  string += find();
```

Note that the result of the `find()` method is appended to the `string` variable:

```
else
```

Otherwise, we just append the remainder of the `out` string to the `string` variable:

```
string += out.substring(old+searchtext.length,out.length);
```

before finally returning the result—either back to the `show()` function or any previous `find()` function that called this instance of the `find()` function:

```
  return string;
}
```

# Non-Frames-Based Searching

The frames-based search application has several advantages. It works on almost all versions of JavaScript. Also, it doesn't require any interaction with the server once the pages have been downloaded, and as a result, it is very quick.

There are, however, disadvantages to using frames—namely, search engines allow visitors to enter a site at any level, with the result that the correct frameset structure, required for your application to function correctly, is not loaded. As it stands, the frames-based search application only allows the user to search for one keyword. Try entering more than one keyword, and unless the keywords are present one after another in the exact same order entered in the search form, you'll not find them.

The next version that we present overcomes this limitation as it makes use of regular expressions introduced in JavaScript 1.2. We can now perform searches using several keywords, as shown in Figure 4-8.

JavaScript 1.2 support was introduced in both Internet Explorer 4 and Netscape Navigator 4. As such, the script will not work in earlier versions of these two browsers. We take the opportunity that presents itself when writing code for later versions of JavaScript to make use of new features not available in previous versions—for example, external JavaScript source files and the JavaScript 1.2 `String` object methods `replace()` and `split()`.

Using external JavaScript source files allows us to remove all or parts of our JavaScript code and place it into a library file with a *js* extension. For this non-frames-based search application, we will remove the article database from the HTML and place it in a *database.js* file. All we then need to do is include it within our page using a variation on the `script` tag:

```
<script language="JavaScript" src="database.js"></script>
```

One disadvantage with the non-frames-based search application is that the HTML is continually loaded from the server. This is because the URL changes each time the user submits a form request. The browser, not knowing that we don't need to actually go back to the server, still does anyway. Storing the database in a separate external JavaScript source file goes some way to reducing the size of the file downloaded, as

**Figure 4-8**
Non-frames-based
searching with
multiple search
keywords.

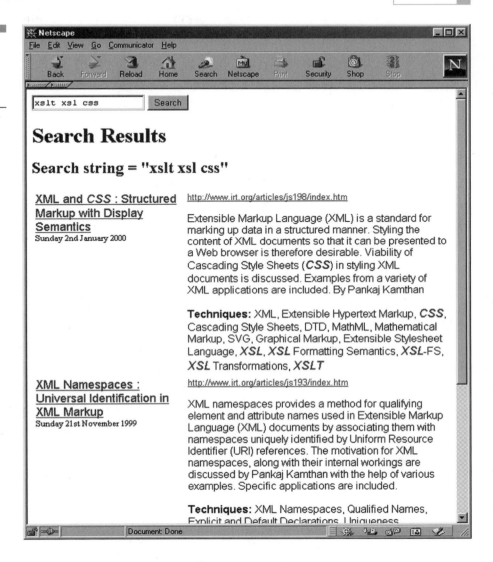

**Figure 4-8**
Non-frames-based searching with multiple search keywords.

only the generic HTML and JavaScript code is continually downloaded not the database itself.

Another disadvantage is that the code does not work from a local hard drive in Internet Explorer. However, once placed online, it will work correctly.

# Non-Frames Source Code

### Source code for database.js

 ../chapter4/search2/database.js

The *database.js* file just contains the database-specific data. It relies on the `setArticle()` function being previously defined earlier in the code. Note that *database.js* includes no HTML tags—not even the `script` tags:

```
setArticle(
  'http://www.irt.org/articles/js209/index.htm',
  'XMLization of Graphics',
  'Scalable Vector Graphics (SVG) is an important step ...',
  'Graphics for the Web, Raster Graphics, Vector Graphics ...',
  '20000327'
);

setArticle(
  'http://www.irt.org/articles/js203/index.htm',
  'XML Euphoria in Perspective',
  'Extensible Markup Language (XML) is a meta-language ...',
  'Markup Languages, Structure, XML, Extensibility ...',
  '20000207'
};

setArticle(
  'http://www.irt.org/articles/js198/index.htm',
  'XML and CSS : Structured Markup with Display Semantics',
  'Extensible Markup Language (XML) is a standard for ...',
  'XML, Extensible Hypertext Markup, CSS, Cascading...',
  '20000102'
);

setArticle(
  'http://www.irt.org/articles/js193/index.htm',
  'XML Namespaces : Universal Identification in XML Markup',
  'XML namespaces provides a method for qualifying...',
  'XML Namespaces, Qualified Names, Explicit and Default...',
  '19991121'
);

setArticle(
  'http://www.irt.org/articles/js192/index.htm',
  'The Emperor has New Clothes : HTML as an XML Application',
  'HTML (Hypertext Markup Language), the definitive...',
  'XHTML, SGML, HTML, XML, XHTML Syntax and Semantics...',
  '20000130'
);

setArticle(
```

```
'http://www.irt.org/articles/js072/index.htm',
'XML - What\'s in it for us?',
'Written by Janus Boye. If you\'re designing ...',
'XML, HTML, XSL, CSS, SGML, CDF, OSD, ICE',
'19980328'
);
```

### Source code for search.htm

 On the CD    **../chapter4/search2/search.htm**

First, a complete list of the entire search.htm source code:

```
<html>

<head>
<script language="JavaScript1.2"><!--

var days = new Array(
   'Sunday','Monday','Tuesday','Wednesday','Thursday',
   'Friday','Saturday'
);

var months = new Array(
   'January','February','March','April','May','June','July',
   'August','September','October','November','December'
);

function nths(day) {
   if (day == 1 || day == 21 || day == 31)
      return 'st';
   else
      if (day == 2 || day == 22)
         return 'nd';
      if (day == 3 || day == 23)
         return 'rd';
      else return 'th';
}

function y2k(number) {
   return (number < 1000) ? number + 1900 : number;
}

function fullDate(date) {
   return days[date.getDay()] + ' ' +
          date.getDate() +
          nths(date.getDate()) + ' ' +
          months[date.getMonth()] + ' ' +
          (y2k(date.getYear()));
}

function convert_date(string) {
   var date = new Date(string.substring(0,4),
                       (string.substring(4,6)-1),
```

```
                          string.substring(6,8));
    return fullDate(date);
}

function articleObject(href,text,desc,tech,date) {
  this.href = href;
  this.text = text;
  this.desc = desc;
  this.tech = tech;
  this.date = convert_date(date);

  this.HREF = href.toUpperCase();
  this.TEXT = text.toUpperCase();
  this.DESC = desc.toUpperCase();
  this.TECH = tech.toUpperCase();
  this.DATE = this.date.toUpperCase();
}

var articleIndex = 0;

var articleArray = new Array();

function setArticle(href,text,desc,tech,date) {
  articleArray[articleIndex++] =
    new articleObject(href,text,desc,tech,date);
}
//--></script>

<script language="JavaScript1.2" src="database.js"></script>

<script language="JavaScript1.2"><!--
function show(property) {
  for (var j=0; j < splitUp.length; j++) {
    property = property.replace(
                new RegExp(splitUp[j], 'g'),
                '{' + splitUp[j] + '}'
              );
  }

  property = property.replace(
              new RegExp('{','g'),
              '<i><font color="#0000FF" size="+1">'
            );
  property = property.replace(
              new RegExp('}','g'),
              '<\/font><\/i>'
            );

  return property;
}
function output() {
  var href = articleArray[i].href;
  var desc = articleArray[i].desc;
  var text = articleArray[i].text;
  var tech = articleArray[i].tech;
  var date = articleArray[i].date;

  var output = '';
  output += '<tr>';
  output += '<td valign="top">';
```

```
      output += '<font face="Arial, Helvetica" size="4">';

      output += '<a href="' + href + '" target="_parent">';
      output += show(text)+'<\/a>';

      output += '<\/font>';

      output += '<font size="2"><br>'+show(date)+'<\/font>';

      output += '<\/td>';
      output += '<td valign="TOP">';
      output += '<font face="Arial" size="3">';

      output += '<font size="2">' +
                '<a href="' + href + '" target="_parent">' +
                show(href) +
                '<\/a>' +
                '<\/font>';

      output += '<p>' +show(desc) + '<\/p>';

      output += '<p><b>Techniques:<\/b> ' + show(tech) + '<\/p>';

      output += '<\/font>';
      output += '<\/td>';
      output += '<\/tr>';

      document.write(output);
}
var searchtext = window.location.search;
searchtext = unescape(searchtext);
searchtext = searchtext.substring(12);
while (searchtext.indexOf('+')>-1)
 searchtext = searchtext.replace('+','');

var splitUp = searchtext.toUpperCase().split(' ');
//--></script>

</head>
<body>

<form name="form1" method="get">
<input type="text" name="searchtext" value="">
<input type="submit" value="Search">
</form>

<script language="JavaScript1.2"><!--
document.form1.searchtext.value = searchtext;

if (searchtext != '') {
  document.write('<h1>Search Results<\/h1>');
  document.write('<h2>Search string = "'+searchtext+'"<\/h2>');
}
else {
  document.write('<h1>Articles<\/h1>');
}

document.write('<table>');

for (var i=0; i < articleIndex; i++) {
  var Found = true;
```

```
    if (searchtext != '') {
      Found = false;
      for (var j=0; j < splitUp.length; j++) {
        if (
          (articleArray[i].HREF.indexOf(splitUp[j]) != -1) ||
          (articleArray[i].DESC.indexOf(splitUp[j]) != -1) ||
          (articleArray[i].TEXT.indexOf(splitUp[j]) != -1) ||
          (articleArray[i].TECH.indexOf(splitUp[j]) != -1) ||
          (articleArray[i].DATE.indexOf(splitUp[j]) != -1)
        ) {
          Found = true;
          continue;
        }
      }
    }
    if (Found) output()
  }

document.write('</table>');
//--></script>

</body>
</html>
```

The *search.htm* page contains the unchanged date functions, the
objectArticle() constructor, articleIndex property, articleArray[]
array, and setArticle() function.

The contents of the *database.js* file are loaded into the current position
of the page:

```
<script language="JavaScript1.2" src="database.js"></script>
```

At this point, the code uses the setArticle() function to create all the
objectArticle objects.

We retrieve any passed search string:

```
var searchtext = window.location.search;
```

The JavaScript unescape() global function is used to unescape the
searchtext string:

```
searchtext = unescape(searchtext);
```

When form data is submitted using the get method, the browser automatically escapes any non-ASCII alphabetic characters into the form
%xx (where xx is the Latin-1 encoding of the character), so that the data
can be passed over the Internet. For example, the string "Hello
World" will be passed as %22Hello+World%22, the double quote characters (") are converted to %22, and the space character is converted to a

plus character (+). Note that this is not unlike the JavaScript `escape()` global function that performs a similar effect. For example, `escape('"Hello World"')` results in `%22Hello%20World%22`, the difference being that the plus character (+) is converted to `%20`.

As described before, the `substring()` method can be used to extract the remainder of a string. Here we use it to extract any part of the `searchtext` string after the 12th character, so that `?searchtext=abc` will result in `abc`:

```
searchtext = searchtext.substring(12);
```

We use the JavaScript 1.2 string `replace()` method to replace all occurrences of the plus character (+) with a space character:

```
searchtext = searchtext.replace(new RegExp('\+','g'),' ');
```

The `replace()` method accepts two arguments: The first is the string or regular expression to be replaced, and the second is the string to replace it with. We are using a regular expression, created using the `RegExp()` object constructor, as the item to be replaced. The `RegExp()` constructor accepts one or two parameters. The first is the regular expression—in this case, a plus character, which must be escaped with a leading backward slash character (\). Otherwise, the plus character is treated as a regular expression repetitive character; on its own, the plus character is used to signify that the regular expression should match one or more of the previous items). The second optional argument is a regular expression attribute—in this case, g—which performs a global match.

We use the JavaScript 1.2 string `split()` method to split the upper-case `searchtext`, using the space character as the character to split on, into an array of strings:

```
var splitUp = searchtext.toUpperCase().split(' ');
```

We display a simple form named `form1`, which when submitted will reload the current page into the browser at the same time as passing any entered form input data as part of the `location` object's `search` property:

```
<form name="form1" method="get">
<input type="text" name="searchtext" value="">
<input type="submit" value="Search">
</form>
```

When a form is submitted, it passes any named form fields and their content to whatever the `action` attribute says is the next page to get. If we do not specify any `action` attribute, then the default action is to load the current page. So, for example, if the user enters the text `XML XSL` into the `searchtext` form field and then submits the form, the action will be to load the page:

```
http://www.somewhere.com/pathname/search.htm?searchtext=XML+XSL
```

As shown earlier, we can retrieve this search string data in the newly loaded page as input to our JavaScript code.

One of the first things we do with the manipulated `searchtext` is to repopulate the `searchtext` form field. This allows the user to easily amend and resubmit their search query without having to retype the original search query:

```
document.form1.searchtext.value = searchtext;
```

As with the frames-based version, we loop though all of the `articleObject` objects in the `articleArray[]` array:

```
for (var i=0; i < articleIndex; i++) {
```

This time, however, instead of testing for a single `searchtext`, we have to test to see of any of the substrings within the `searchtext` string appear in any of the object properties—that is, an implied Boolean `OR` is used throughout, such as `XML OR XSL`. First, we define and declare a Found Boolean variable to `true`:

```
var Found = true;
```

If the `searchtext` is not empty, we first set Found to `false`. In other words, we'll not display the article unless we explicitly find a match:

```
if (searchtext != '') {
  Found = false;
```

We then continue by looping through each of the strings in the `splitUp[]` array:

```
for (var j=0; j < splitUp.length; j++) {
```

We test each of the current `articleObject` object's properties against the current `splitUp[]` array element:

```
if (
  (articleArray[i].HREF.indexOf(splitUp[j]) != -1) ||
```

```
                 (articleArray[i].DESC.indexOf(splitUp[j]) != -1) ||
                 (articleArray[i].TEXT.indexOf(splitUp[j]) != -1) ||
                 (articleArray[i].TECH.indexOf(splitUp[j]) != -1) ||
                 (articleArray[i].DATE.indexOf(splitUp[j]) != -1)
            ) {
```

If a match is made, we set `Found` to `true` and immediately exit the loop using the `continue` statement:

```
         Found = true;
         continue;
      }
   }
}
```

If `Found` is set to `true`, either as a result of making a match or the `searchtext` being empty, we call the `output()` function to display the article:

```
   if (Found) output()
}
```

The `output()` function remains almost unchanged. However, the `show()` function that highlights any occurrence of the search query has changed to make use of regular expressions:

```
function show(property) {
```

First, we again loop through all of the strings in the `splitUp[]` array:

```
   for (var j=0; j < splitUp.length; j++) {
```

We then use the `replace()` method to replace all occurrences of the search current `splitUp[]` string with that same string, but this time it is wrapped in braces:

```
      property = property.replace(
              new RegExp(splitUp[j], 'g'),
              '{' + splitUp[j] + '}'
           );
   }
```

If the user searched for the keyword `XML`, then a property value of `this article describes XML in detail` would at this point produce `this article describes {XML} in detail`. This allows us to replace all occurrences of all the `searchtext` substrings without introducing any more text into the property, which would otherwise have the potential to cause a false match.

Once all the matches have been highlighted with braces, we then replace all occurrences of the braces with HTML code to highlight the matches—again using regular expressions:

```
property = property.replace(
        new RegExp('{','g'),
        '<i><font color="#0000FF" size="+1">'
    );
property = property.replace(
        new RegExp('}','g'),
        '<\/font><\/i>'
    );
```

Finally, the highlighted `property` string is returned:

```
    return property;
}
```

## Extending the Search Database Code

The code can very easily be extended to include support for different article databases simply by altering how the external JavaScript source file is loaded. At the moment, we load the database using the following static line of HTML code:

```
<script language="JavaScript1.2" src="database.js"></script>
```

We can use JavaScript code itself to write out this line of HTML code:

```
<script language="JavaScript1.2"><!--
document.write(
  '<script language="JavaScript1.2" src="database.js"><\/script>'
);
//--></script>
```

In this case, we can then choose to load a different external JavaScript source file, perhaps based on the first substring within the `searchtext` string:

```
<script language="JavaScript1.2"><!--
document.write(
  '<script language="JavaScript1.2" src="' +
    splitUp[0] + '.js"><\/script>'
);
//--></script>
```

Note if your database contains braces within the data, you'll need to use other characters to wrap the matches. Two foolproof characters that you can use are the unprintable ASCII character codes 01 and 02. These can easily be generated in JavaScript with `var x1 = unescape('%01');` `var x2 = unescape('%02');` and then the variables `x1` and `x2` can be used in the previous regular expressions in place of the braces.

# Multiple-Choice Test

You should by now have a good understanding of how to create your own objects and how to store them in an object array. This example demonstrates how to present a multiple-choice test to your user. We again use an external JavaScript source file to hold the database—this time a database of questions and answers. Not only does this allow us to create a generic HTML page that can be used with any set of questions and answers, it also makes it slightly harder for the user to see the answers to the questions. The user cannot simply view the page source to see the answers; instead, they would have to retrieve the JavaScript source file from the browsers cache—not an easy task.

With this example we will introduce a small amount of Dynamic HTML—the ability to update the current document without reloading it. So far, we have shown how to load information into the current document into another frame, and how to reload the current document to redisplay the page differently. Being able to update the displayed content without reloading the page is a very useful technique.

To keep the code fairly light and readable, we will only provide a solution that works in Internet Explorer 4 and 5 and Netscape Navigator 4. Writing code that works in Netscape Navigator 6 would distract from the code. We will cover solutions for Netscape Navigator 6 in later chapters.

## Multiple-Choice Test Source Code

### Source code for questions.js

../chapter4/multiple/questions.js

Here we have used a slightly different approach to create our objects. Whereas before we have used a helper function to both create the objects and increment the item object count, we create the choice objects directly, incrementing the `item` object count using the post-increment operator

(++). Although it does mean we lose the ability to reuse the code within the helper function, this approach does give us more flexibility. In the previous examples, the number of arguments to the object constructor were fixed. Here we have used a varying number of arguments, which allows us to pass the question, the number of the answer, and an unknown number of multiple-choice answers:

```
myChoice[item++] = new Choice(
  'What is JavaScript?',
  3,
  'A cut down version of Java',
  'Just a server side scripting language',
  'A client and server side scripting language'
);

myChoice[item++] = new Choice(
  'Which browsers support the Image object?',
  4,
  'All browers',
  'Internet Explorer only',
  'Netscape Navigator 2 and Internet Explorer 3 up',
  'Netscape Navigator 3 and Internet Explorer 4 up'
)

myChoice[item++] = new Choice(
  'How do you open a new popup window in JavaScript?',
  2,
  "window.open('page.htm','myWindow','width=480, height=640'",
  "window.open('page.htm')",
  "open.window('page.htm','myWindow')",
  "open.window('page.htm','myWindow','width=480,height=640')"
)

myChoice[item++] = new Choice(
  'Can JavaScript count how many people visit a page?',
  1,
  'No',
  'Yes',
  'Only in Netscape Navigator'
)
```

The preceding first and last questions both have three possible answers, whereas the second and third questions have four. The person setting the questions and answers for a real-world implementation of this code therefore has the flexibility to include as many possible incorrect answers along with the one correct answer, without having to alter the object constructor in any way.

**Source code for choice.htm**

**../chapter4/multiple/choice.htm**

The *choice.htm* page controls the complete multiple-choice test, displaying the questions and multiple answers, vetting the user's input, keeping the score of the correct answers, and then finally displaying the total score, along with the user's correct and wrong answers.

The `Choice()` object constructor is unusual in that it accepts only two named arguments, `question` and `correct`:

```
function Choice(question, correct) {
  this.question = question;
```

To keep this example simple, we allow the question setter to pass the value of the correct answer as a numeric integer, where 1 signifies that the first multiple-choice answer is correct, and 4 signifies the fourth is correct. As arrays usually start at zero, we actually set the value of the `correct` property to 1 less than the passed argument:

```
this.correct = correct - 1;
```

We include an `answers[]` array as one of the `Choice` objects properties. Instead of it being a simple string or integer property, it's actually an array property that holds strings:

```
this.answers = new Array();
```

To access any other non-named arguments, we use the `Choice` constructor's `arguments[]` array. Every function, method, and constructor has an `arguments[]` array, which can be used to access the arguments passed to it. The arguments are held in the array in the order that they are passed. So, for example, `Choice.arguments[0]` would hold the same value as the named `question` argument. Therefore, both the first two entries within the `Choice()` constructor's `argument` array are already catered for. All we have to do is check the `arguments[]` array's `length` to retrieve the remainder:

```
for (var i=2; i<Choice.arguments.length; i++) {
```

For each extra argument passed, we place the value within an `answers[]` array:

```
  this.answers[i-2] = Choice.arguments[i];
}
```

Finally, we declare and define an extra `answer` property with a value of `-1`. The `answer` property will hold the value of the users chosen multiple-choice answer. It is initially set to -1 so that we can easily test if the user has chosen an answer:

```
    this.answer = -1;
}
```

The code defines and declares a current question counter q to indicate which question we are on:

```
var q = 0;
```

As we progress through the test, the value of q will be incremented and then used to tell when we have asked the last question.

The contents of the page is extremely simple, just the one div tag:

```
<div id="myDiv" style="position:absolute; left:100; top:30;"></div>
```

The onLoad event handler within the body tag kicks off the multiple-choice test by calling the show() function:

```
<body onLoad="show()">
```

The show() function serves several purposes. It displays a multiple-choice question, validates the answer, and finally displays the results of the test:

```
function show() {
```

We first check if the test has finished—that is, when the question counter (q) is equal to the number of questions (myChoice.length):

```
    if (q < myChoice.length) {
```

While the test hasn't finished, we build up the next question using the output variable:

```
        var output = '';
        output += '<form>';
```

We include the current Choice object's question property (i.e, the question text itself):

```
        output += '<b>' + myChoice[q].question + '<\/b><br>';
```

We then loop through each multiple-choice answer (i.e., each string within the answers[] array):

```
for (var i=0; i<myChoice[q].answers.length; i++) {
```

For each multiple-choice answer, we include both a form radio button and the answer string:

```
output +=
    '<input type="radio" name="answer"' +
```

The radio button has an `onClick` event handler dynamically generated so that when the radio button is clicked, it sets the `answer` property of the current question (q) to the value of the current multiple-choice answer (i):

```
    'onClick="myChoice[' + q + '].answer=' + i + '">' +
    myChoice[q].answers[i] + '<BR>';
}
```

We include a form button to allow the user to signify completion of the answer:

```
output +=
    '<input type="button" value="Next" ' +
```

The form button has a dynamically generated `onClick` event handler that tests that the `answer` property of the current question (q) is no longer -1 before proceeding to the next question or the end of the test by invoking the `show()` function:

```
    'onClick="if (myChoice[' + q + '].answer!=-1) show()">';
    output += '<\/form>';
```

The `output` is then written into the `myDiv` div tag using the generic `update()` function:

```
update('myDiv',output);
```

The current question counter is incremented:

```
    q++;
}
else {
```

If the end of the test has been reached, we don't display another question. Instead, we display the test results. We first initialize the `score` and `output` variables:

```
var score = 0;
```

```
var output = '';
```

Then for each question we tally up the score and build up the output response:

```
for (var i=0; i<myChoice.length; i++) {
```

We first display the question property:

```
output += '<p>Q: ' + myChoice[i].question
```

If the user's answer equals the correct answer, then we increment the score:

```
if (myChoice[i].answer == myChoice[i].correct) {
  score++;
```

We also display the user's selected answer from the answers[] array:

```
    output += '<br>You correctly answered: ' +
            myChoice[i].answers[myChoice[i].answer];
  }
  else {
```

If the user incorrectly answered, then we display both his or her incorrect answer and the correct answer from the answers[] array:

```
    output += '<br>You incorrectly answered: ' +
            myChoice[i].answers[myChoice[i].answer] +
            '<br>The correct answer was: ' +
            myChoice[i].answers[myChoice[i].correct];
  }
}
var output = '<h1>You scored ' +
            score +
            ' out of ' +
            myChoice.length +
            '<\/h1>' +
            output;
```

Finally, we use the generic update() function to show the test results into the myDiv div tag:

```
    update('myDiv',output);
  }
}
```

The way the multiple-choice test has been designed allows the user to change his or her mind and select another answer. It insists that the user

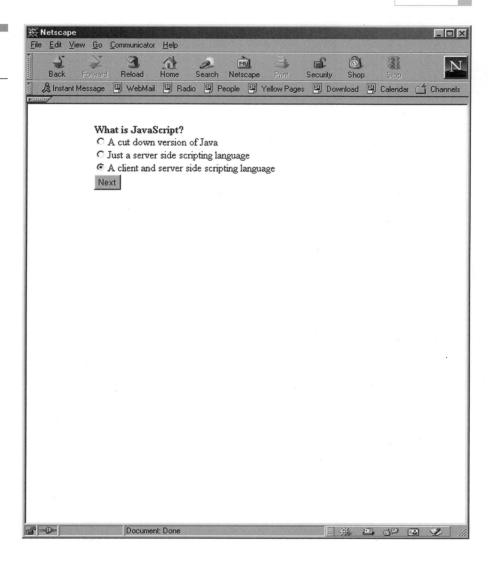

**Figure 4-9**
A sample multiple-choice test.

choose an answer before moving on to the next question. A sample test and results page are shown in Figures 4-9 and 4-10.

## Object Array Sorting

So far within this chapter we have always displayed the output of our object arrays in the order that we create the objects. This may not always be the best way to display the data. This next example shows how to sort

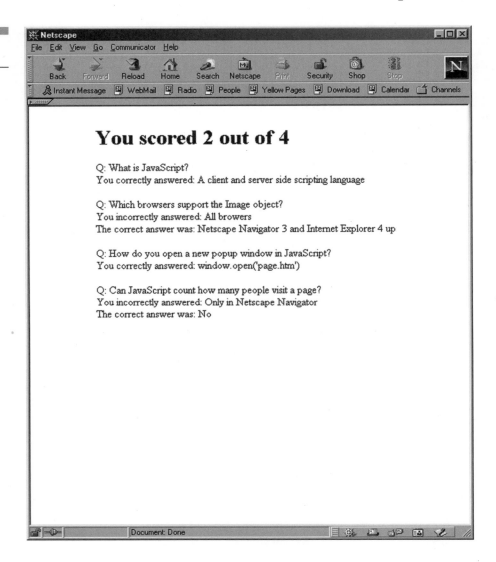

an object array, something that would seem to be easy to do with the JavaScript 1.1 `Array` object's `sort()` method. However, it soon becomes apparent that object arrays cannot use this method. Before we dive into the code, a short explanation on the `sort()` method is required.

JavaScript 1.1 introduced support for the `Array` object's `sort()` method. Before JavaScript 1.1 we would have had to write our own code to sort arrays—possibly a simple bubble sort function. With JavaScript 1.1, sorting arrays becomes relatively easy, although at the same time extremely flexible. Consider the following code snippet:

```
<script language="JavaScript"><!--
function show() {
  var string = myArray.join(' ');
  document.write(string + '<br>');
}

var myArray = new Array(
  'Red', 'Orange', 'Yellow', 'Green', 'Blue', 'Indigo', 'Violet'
);

show();

myArray.sort();
show();

function reverse(a, b) { return a<b; }
myArray.sort(reverse)
show();

function length(a, b) { return a.length-b.length }
myArray.sort(length)
show();
//--></script>
```

We first create a simple string array (it just happens to be the colors of the rainbow) and then use the show() method to output each array element to the document in their current order. The first use of the sort() array method simply sorts the array lexicographically (in dictionary order)—thus, Blue comes before Green, and so on.

The second use of the sort() array method uses a reverse function literal (i.e., the name of the previously declared reverse() function). The sort() method then uses the reverse() function when comparing each array element. The reverse() function returns a negative number if the first argument (a) should appear before the second (b), a positive number if the first argument (a) should appear after the second argument (b), and zero if the order does not matter. In the reverse() function, the expression a<b equates to true (1) if a is less than b, in which case their order is swapped, or false (0) if a is greater than or equal to b—in which case their order is unchanged. Thus, Green comes before Blue.

The third use of the sort() array method uses a length function literal. The length() function allows us to sort the array elements using the length of the array element. Thus, Blue comes before Green, as its value is shorter. The results of our code snippet are as follows:

Array object sort()
results

However, when it comes to sorting object arrays, the value of an array element is [object Object]—that is, its value indicates that it is an object of type Object, or a user-defined object. We can solve this by providing the object with a toString() method. The sort() method uses any available toString() method when converting the value of the object to a string.

The remainder of this example will show how to add dynamic toString() methods to an object and how to sort a database of celebrity birth dates on different object properties. Figure 4-11 shows the initial output of the Object Array Sorting code. By default, the object array is sorted by name.

### Source Code for birthdays.js

**../chapter4/sort/birthday.js**

The JavaScript source file *birthdays.js* contains all the data for the birth dates. Rather than show the whole file, we'll just show the first four lines—each of which call the setBirthday() function, passing in an integer representing the date of birth (in the format YYYYMMDD) and the person's name.

```
setBirthday(18820118,"A.A. Milne");
setBirthday(18090212,"Abraham Lincoln");
setBirthday(18890420,"Adolf Hitler");
setBirthday(18900915,"Agatha Christie");
```

**Figure 4-11**
Object Array
Sorting—Sorted by
name.

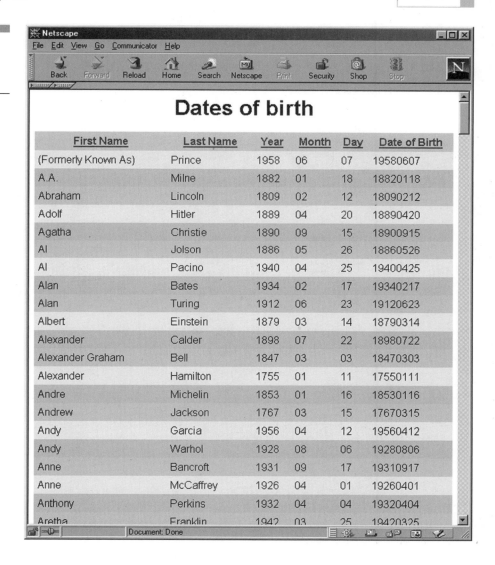

**Source code for sort.htm**

../chapter4/sort/sort.js

The *sort.htm* page defines the `Birthday` object constructor, includes the external JavaScript source file *birthdays.js*, creates an array of `Birthday` objects, and then displays a table of sorted births:

```
<html>

<head>
<script language="JavaScript"><!--
function Birthday(dob,who) {
  this.dob = dob;
  this.who = who;

  this.firstname =
    who.substring(0,who.lastIndexOf(' '));
  this.lastname =
    who.substring(who.lastIndexOf(' '),who.length);

  this.year = dob.toString().substring(0,4);
  this.month = dob.toString().substring(4,6);
  this.day = dob.toString().substring(6,8);
}

function setBirthday(dob,who) {
  myBirthday[birthdayIndex++] = new Birthday(dob,who);
}
var birthdayIndex = 0;

var myBirthday = new Array();
//--></script>

<script language="JavaScript" SRC="birthdays.js"></script>

<style type="TEXT/CSS"><!--
h1, td, th { font-family: Arial; }
tr.color0 { background: #ccffcc; }
tr.color1 { background: #ccccff; }
tr.color2 { background: #ffcccc; }
//--></style>
</head>

<body>

<h1>Dates of birth</h1>

<table border="0" cellspacing="0" cellpadding="5" width="100%">

<tr class="color2">
<th><a href="sort.htm?firstname">First Name</a></th>
<th><a href="sort.htm?lastname">Last Name</a></th>
<th><a href="sort.htm?year">Year</a></th>
<th><a href="sort.htm?month">Month</a></th>
<th><a href="sort.htm?day">Day</a></th>
<th><a href="sort.htm?dob">Date of Birth</a></th>
</tr>

<script language="JavaScript"><!--
var output = '';

var searchtext = location.search.substring(1);

if (searchtext == '')
  Birthday.prototype.toString = new Function('return this.who');
else
```

```
      Birthday.prototype.toString =
        new Function('return this.' + searchtext + ';');

  function mySort(a,b) { return a>b; }

  myBirthday.sort(mySort);

  for (var i=0; i < birthdayIndex; i++) {
    output += '<tr class="color' + i%3 + '">';
    output += '<td>' + myBirthday[i].firstname + '<\/td>';
    output += '<td>' + myBirthday[i].lastname + '<\/td>';
    output += '<td>' + myBirthday[i].year + '<\/td>';
    output += '<td>' + myBirthday[i].month + '<\/td>';
    output += '<td>' + myBirthday[i].day + '<\/td>';
    output += '<td>' + myBirthday[i].dob  + '<\/td>';
    output += '<\/tr>';
  }

  document.write(output);
  //--></script>

  </table>

  </body>

  </html>
```

The `Birthday` object constructor accepts the date of birth (`dob`) and the name of the person (`who`):

```
function Birthday(dob,who) {
   this.dob = dob;
   this.who = who;
```

Using the `who` argument, the `firstname` and `lastname` properties are generated using the last space character in the `who` argument to split it into two parts:

```
   this.firstname =
     who.substring(0,who.lastIndexOf(' '));
   this.lastname =
     who.substring(who.lastIndexOf(' '),who.length);
```

The last three properties are constructed by first converting the `dob` integer value into a string by using the built-in `Integer` object's `toString()` method, and then using the `String` object's `substring()` method to extract the relevant portion of the date:

```
   this.year = dob.toString().substring(0,4);
   this.month = dob.toString().substring(4,6);
   this.day = dob.toString().substring(6,8);
}
```

The contents of the *birthdays.js* file are then loaded into the document—which causes all the `Birthday` objects to be constructed:

```
<script language="JavaScript" src="birthdays.js"></script>
```

We mentioned using CSS style attributes in the previous example. Here we declared an inline style sheet using the `style` tag:

```
<style type="TEXT/CSS"><!--
```

The first line indicates that the font family of the content of any `h1` or `td` or `th` tag should be `Arial`:

```
h1, td, th { font-family: Arial; }
```

The next three lines declare three `tr` tag class styles with different values for the background color. These three `tr` class styles can be reference by using a matching `class` attribute within any `tr` tag:

```
tr.color0 { background: #ccffcc; }
tr.color1 { background: #ccccff; }
tr.color2 { background: #ffcccc; }
//--></style>
```

All the birth dates are displayed on the page using a table. The table column headers not only indicate the description of the data contained in each column, but they also contain a text link that when clicked reloads the *sort.htm* page with search data already hard-coded into the link:

```
<tr class="color2">
<th><a href="sort.htm?firstname">First Name</a></th>
<th><a href="sort.htm?lastname">Last Name</a></th>
<th><a href="sort.htm?year">Year</a></th>
<th><a href="sort.htm?month">Month</a></th>
<th><a href="sort.htm?day">Day</a></th>
<th><a href="sort.htm?dob">Date of Birth</a></th>
</tr>
```

The six hard-coded search data values match six of the `Birthday` object properties, allowing the user to choose which property to sort on. This particular table row uses a `class` attribute with a value `color2`. This matches the earlier `color2` class definition, causing the background color of the whole table row to be set to `#ffcccc`—a red pastel color.

We retrieve the value of any passed search data and place it into the `searchtext` variable:

```
var searchtext = location.search.substring(1);
```

We then check if the `searchtext` string is an empty string:

```
if (searchtext == '')
```

If the `searchtext` is an empty string, a `toString()` prototype object method is added to the `Birthday` object. We use the `Function` constructor (i.e., `new Function()`) to create a `toString()` method that returns the value of the current (`this`) `Birthday` object's `who` property:

```
Birthday.prototype.toString = new Function('return this.who');
```

Each constructor class (i.e., the constructor definition) for both built-in objects and user-defined objects has a `prototype` object. Using this object, we can add properties or methods to either built-in objects (e.g., `Date`, `String`) or user-defined objects. The property or method, rather than being held in each instance of an object, is inherited by each instance of the objects. This means that in our example, although there is only one copy of the `Birthday` object's `toString()` method, it is shared by all instances of the `Birthday` object.

If the `searchtext` is not an empty string, we again add a `toString()` prototype object method to the `Birthday` object. But this time, the `toString()` method returns the current (`this`) `Birthday` object's property that corresponds to the `searchtext` variable:

```
else
  Birthday.prototype.toString =
    new Function('return this.' + searchtext + ';');
```

If, for example, the current URL is `sort.htm?dob`, then the method will contain `return this.dob;`.

We define a `mySort()` function that sorts the a and b values into dictionary order:

```
function mySort(a,b) { return a>b; }
```

Then we sort the `myBirthday[]` object array using the `mySort` function literal:

```
myBirthday.sort(mySort);
```

The actual a and b values passed into the `mySort()` function are based on the `Birthday` object's `toString()` method. Depending on the contents of the `toString()` method, different string values are passed into the `mySort()` function.

The remainder of the *sort.htm* code simply loops through all the `Birthday` objects in the sorted `myBirthday[]` object array, creating a table row displaying six out of the seven `Birthday` object properties:

```
for (var i=0; i < birthdayIndex; i++) {
```

The one noteworthy item of interest is the use of JavaScript to set the `tr` tag's `class`. We concatenate the string `color` with the value returned by `i%3`, where `%` is the `modulo` operator—which returns the remainder of `i` divided by 3. This in turn will only ever return 0, 1, or 2, resulting in one of the three `tr` class styles being used—`color0`, `color1`, or `color2`:

```
    output += '<tr class="color' + i%3 + '">';
    output += '<td>' + myBirthday[i].firstname + '<\/td>';
    output += '<td>' + myBirthday[i].lastname + '<\/td>';
    output += '<td>' + myBirthday[i].year + '<\/td>';
    output += '<td>' + myBirthday[i].month + '<\/td>';
    output += '<td>' + myBirthday[i].day + '<\/td>';
    output += '<td>' + myBirthday[i].dob  + '<\/td>';
    output += '<\/tr>';
}

document.write(output);
```

Figure 4-12 shows the result of the user electing to sort the data by date of birth.

## Array Methods

We have already used the `join()` and `sort()` array methods, but several other JavaScript 1.1 `Array` object methods, shown in Table 4-1, are available. Like the `String` object, the `Array` object only has one property: `length`.

## Summary

Once we move away from simple strings or numbers, being able to hold multiple property values within an object allows single object references to be passed around within our code, rather than multiple variables. Object constructors can be used to initialize objects so that they all con-

**Figure 4-12**
Sorting Object
Arrays—Sorted by
date of birth.

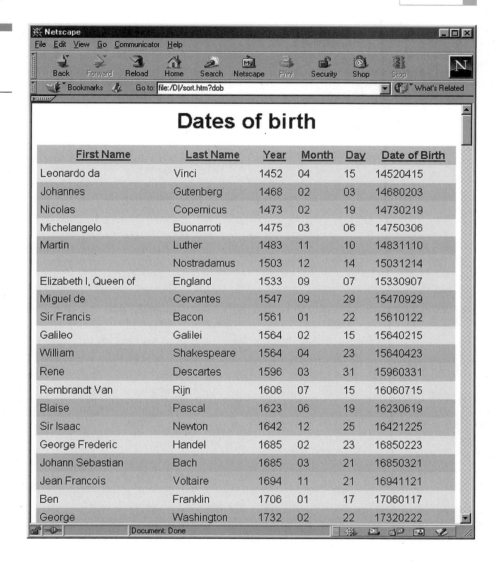

# Dates of birth

| First Name | Last Name | Year | Month | Day | Date of Birth |
|---|---|---|---|---|---|
| Leonardo da | Vinci | 1452 | 04 | 15 | 14520415 |
| Johannes | Gutenberg | 1468 | 02 | 03 | 14680203 |
| Nicolas | Copernicus | 1473 | 02 | 19 | 14730219 |
| Michelangelo | Buonarroti | 1475 | 03 | 06 | 14750306 |
| Martin | Luther | 1483 | 11 | 10 | 14831110 |
| | Nostradamus | 1503 | 12 | 14 | 15031214 |
| Elizabeth I, Queen of | England | 1533 | 09 | 07 | 15330907 |
| Miguel de | Cervantes | 1547 | 09 | 29 | 15470929 |
| Sir Francis | Bacon | 1561 | 01 | 22 | 15610122 |
| Galileo | Galilei | 1564 | 02 | 15 | 15640215 |
| William | Shakespeare | 1564 | 04 | 23 | 15640423 |
| Rene | Descartes | 1596 | 03 | 31 | 15960331 |
| Rembrandt Van | Rijn | 1606 | 07 | 15 | 16060715 |
| Blaise | Pascal | 1623 | 06 | 19 | 16230619 |
| Sir Isaac | Newton | 1642 | 12 | 25 | 16421225 |
| George Frederic | Handel | 1685 | 02 | 23 | 16850223 |
| Johann Sebastian | Bach | 1685 | 03 | 21 | 16850321 |
| Jean Francois | Voltaire | 1694 | 11 | 21 | 16941121 |
| Ben | Franklin | 1706 | 01 | 17 | 17060117 |
| George | Washington | 1732 | 02 | 22 | 17320222 |

tain the same properties, perhaps with different values, easily and consistently. Using arrays to hold our objects completes the equation because it allows us to manipulate one of many different objects at any one time by simply referencing an object at a particular position within an array.

**TABLE 4-1**

JavaScript 1.1
Array object
methods.

| Method | Description |
|---|---|
| `join` | Concatenates array elements with optional separator to return a string. For example, in the following:<br><br>`var a = new Array('A', 'B', 'C');`<br><br>`var b = a.join('-');`<br><br>a will still contain the array elements A, B, and C, but b will contain the string value A-B-C. |
| `reverse` | Reverses the elements in an array. For example, in the following:<br><br>`var a = new Array('A', 'B', 'C');`<br><br>`a.reverse();`<br><br>a will now contain the array elements C, B, and A. |
| `sort` | Sorts the elements in an array. For example, in the following:<br><br>`var a = new Array(321, 2345, 62345, 54);`<br><br>`a.sort();`<br><br>a will now contain the array elements 2345, 321, 62345, and 54—that is, sorted alphabetically. Also accepts an optional function literal to specify the sort criteria. For example, in the following:<br><br>`function numericsort(a, b) { return a-b; }`<br><br>`var a = new Array(321, 2345, 62345, 54);`<br><br>`a.sort(numericsort);`<br><br>a will now contain the array elements 54, 321, 2345, and 62345—that is, sorted numerically |
| `toString` | Returns the array elements as a string of comma separated string values. For example, in the following:<br><br>`var a = new Array('a', 'b', 'c');`<br><br>`var b = a.toString();`<br><br>a will still contain the array elements a, b, and c, but b will contain the string a, b, c. |

# Location and Links

Location is important on the World Wide Web (WWW)—the location of an HTML page in particular. Referencing one page from another can be achieved with links, linking the source page to the target page using either a full absolute reference, specifying the protocol, the server, the directory and finally the filename itself, or by using a relative reference—that is, relative to the current source page, such as up one directory, down another, and then the filename.

No matter how a page is linked, once it is loaded into the browser, the browser populates a `location` object, setting the different properties to hold for example the `protocol`, the `hostname`, the complete absolute `href`, and the `search` arguments or `hash` anchor name passed as part of the link. While the page is being loaded into the browser, the browser also populates a `links` array, holding each of the `href` attributes of all the links found in the page.

This chapter discusses both the `location` object and the `links` array in detail, showing how to:

■ Redirect the browser from the current page on one domain to its new location on another

■ Automatically add Previous and Next buttons to like-named pages or directories on either side of the current one as part of a list of like-named articles

■ Add automated anchors and links within a page to facilitate easier navigation between large sections of content on a long page

■ Create a web ring using just client-side JavaScript

■ Trap the browser's preferred language and present a different page holding a pretranslated version

■ Allow access to a hidden page using a password entry form, that validates the password and presents an attractive error page if invalid

■ Crawl through all the links of related web pages.

**Automatic Redirection ../chapter5/redirection/index.htm**
**Automated Links (text version) ../chapter5/links/text.htm**
**Automated Links (image version) ../chapter5/links/image.htm**
**A JavaScript Web Ring ../chapter5/webring/test.htm**
**What Is Your Language? ../chapter5/language/index-en.htm**
**Password Protection and Verification ../chapter5/password/ index.htm**
**Site Link Crawler ../chapter5/crawler/index.htm**

# Automatic Redirection

Over time, websites move from one location to another, perhaps as a result of acquiring a vanity domain name or as a result of increasing popularity. A problem then arises where old bookmarks that people have hanging around in their browser or search engines that seem reluctant to update the new location still refer people to the old location. It is possible to use a non-JavaScript technique to refer browsers automatically to the new location using a `meta` tag:

```
<meta http-equiv="Refresh"
    content="URL=http://www.newdomain.com/">
```

This will redirect the browser to the new domain as soon as the browser reads the `meta` information.

There are several issues with this approach, however. If the user clicks the browser's Back button, the browser will reread the `meta` tag and redirect back to the new location—effectively trapping the user in a browser loop. This can be remedied with the addition of a small delay:

```
<meta http-equiv="Refresh"
    content="15;URL=http://www.newdomain.com/">
```

This version of the `meta` tag will redirect after 15 seconds.

As the `meta` tag stands at the moment, it will redirect the browser to the URL http://www.newdomain.com/. If you need the old pages at the old location to redirect to different pages at the new location, then every single `meta` tag has to be hand-crafted to point to the new location. For example, from an old *page1.htm* to the new *page1.htm*:

```
<meta http-equiv="Refresh"
    content="15;URL=http://www.newdomain.com/page1.htm">
```

And from an old *page2.htm* to the new *page2.htm*:

```
<meta http-equiv="Refresh"
    content="15;URL=http://www.newdomain.com/page2.htm">
```

There is the possibility of using an *.htaccess* file on Apache web servers to detail the old-to-new mappings in one file. However, if you don't have access to this file, then the JavaScript code presented here allows intelligent redirection from old locations to new locations based on the current directory path and filename. Figure 5-1 shows the page as presented to the user prior to the automatic redirection.

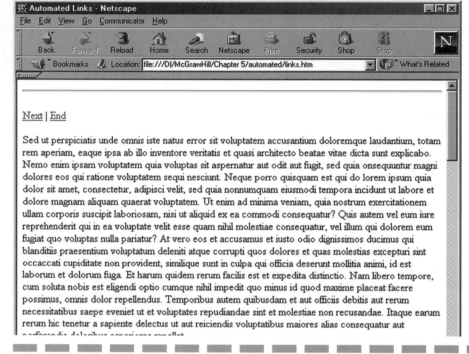

**Figure 5-1**   Automatic Redirection—Warning message that page location has changed.

## Automatic Redirection Source Code

**../chapter5/redirection/index.htm**

First, the HTML of the page needs to be redirected:

```
<html>
<head>
<title>Automatic Redirection</title>
```

We include a line to load in an external JavaScript source file *redirect.js:*

```
<script language="JavaScript" src="redirect.js"></script>

</head>

<body>
```

The message() function is invoked, but only if a message object exists (i.e., only if it has been loaded within the *redirect.js* file):

```
<script language="JavaScript"><!--
if (window.message) message();
//--></script>
</body>

</html>
```

The external JavaScript source file *redirect.js* controls the complete JavaScript redirection code. The file may be located relative to the page to be redirected (as in this case), or it may be referenced using an absolute URL to either a file on the old domain or for ease of control to a file on the new domain.

**../chapter5/redirection/redirect.js**

The *redirect.js* file first defines and initializes several global variables. The newDomain variable holds the URL of the new domain:

```
var newDomain    = 'http://www.newdomain.com';
```

The thisPage variable holds the pathname property of the current window's Location object:

```
var thisPage     = window.location.pathname;
```

The newLocation variable holds the concatenated values of the newDomain and thisPage variables:

```
var newLocation = newDomain + thisPage;
```

The go_now() function, when invoked, changes the href property of the current window's location object to the value of the newLocation variable. This in effect loads the new location into the browser:

```
function go_now () {
  window.location.href = newLocation;
}
```

The message() function is used to display a message informing the user that the page has moved location and giving the user the opportunity to click through to the new location straight away without having to wait for the delayed automatic redirection to kick in:

```
function message() {
  var out = '<h1>Location Changed<\/h1>';

  out += '<p>';
  out += 'Please note the new location of this page is:';
  out += '<br>';
  out += '<a href="' + newLocation + '">' + newLocation + '<\/a>';
  out += '<\/p>';

  out += '<p>';
  out += 'This page will automatically redirect in 10 seconds.';
  out += '<\/p>';

  document.write(out);
}
```

Finally, to kick the automatic redirection off, the `setTimeout()` method is used to set a timer running, which after 10 seconds, will invoke the `go_now()` function to load the new page:

```
setTimeout("go_now()",10000);
```

The `location` object used in this simple script provides access to the various components that make up the current window location, which uses the following format:

```
protocol://hostname:port/pathname?search#hash
```

For a hypothetical URL:

```
http://www.xxx.com:80/dir/subdir/file.htm?name=value#anchorname
```

The various elements can be extracted using the appropriate `location` object properties, shown in Table 5-1.

# Automated Previous and Next Buttons

JavaScript can be used not only to add richer functionality to a site but also to aid the maintenance of a site. Take, for example, some documentation that is published regularly. You may be in a position where you

**TABLE 5-1**

Location object properties.

| Property | Example |
|----------|---------|
| protocol | http: |
| host | www.xxx.com:80 |
| hostname | www.xxx.com |
| port | 80 |
| pathname | /dir/subdir/file.htm |
| search | ?name=value |
| hash | #anchorname |
| href | http://www.xxx.com:80/dir/subsir/file.htm?name=value#anchorname |

publish daily, weekly, or monthly material. Your visitors are presented with the newest material, but you need to provide links back to previous items or forward to the next item in the list.

For example, if you publish a series of pages—for example, *page1.htm*—then *page2.htm* and *page3.htm*, the only difference between them is the increasing sequence of numbers. If, on the other hand, you publish material into individual directories—for instance, *folder001/index.htm*, *folder002/index.htm* and *folder003/index.htm*, then the three digits within the folder name again make an increasing sequence of numbers.

In both these examples, we can easily provide links to the page before and after the current page. We simply work out the number for the current page and then subtract 1 for the page before and add 1 for the page after. The difficulty comes when reaching the ends of the list—that is, stopping the code from pointing to nonexistent pages.

The code included here provides the ability to link between like-named files in the same directory or identical named files in like-named directories without crashing off the ends of the list. Figures 5-2, 5-3, and 5-4 show the first, next, and last items within a series of 10 pages.

## Automated Previous and Next Buttons Source Code

Adding the buttons to a page is very simple. There are two versions, one suitable for files in the same directory, and another for files in separate directories. First, let's consider the case of same directory. Including the

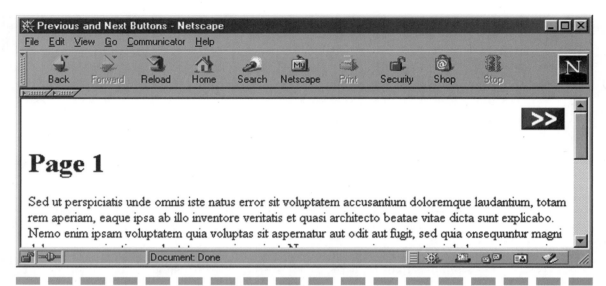

**Figure 5-2**    Automated Previous and Next Buttons—The first item.

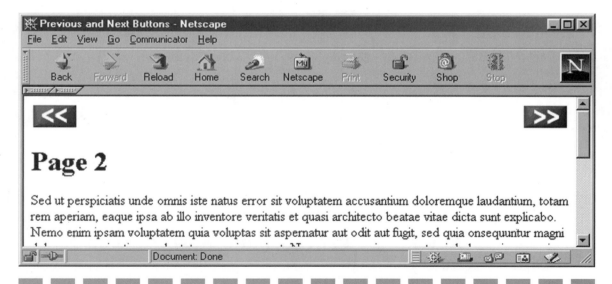

**Figure 5-3**    Automated Previous and Next Buttons—The next item.

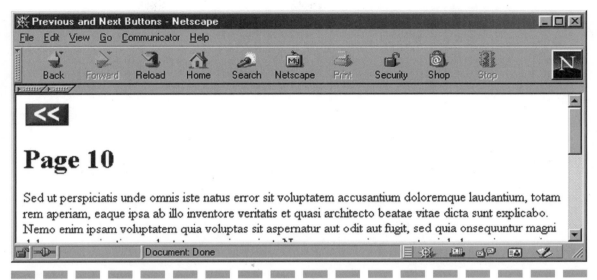

**Figure 5-4**   Automated Previous and Next Buttons—The last item.

following line in the head section of a page loads the external JavaScript source library *buttons.js*.

**../chapter5/nextprev/page1.htm**

```
<script language="JavaScript" src="buttons.js"></script>
```

To display the buttons, we invoke the showButtons() function but only if a showButtons object (i.e., the showbuttons() function declaration) exists within the current page:

```
<script language="JavaScript"><!--
if (window.showButtons) showButtons();
//--></script>
```

These three lines can be placed anywhere and any number of times within the page.

The different directories version uses a different external JavaScript source library—this time the *directories.js* file located in the parent directory (signified by the leading ../):

../chapter5/nextprev/folder098/index.htm

```
<script language="JavaScript" src="../directories.js"></script>
```

To display the buttons, we this time invoke the `showDirectory Buttons()` function:

```
<script language="JavaScript"><!--
if (window.showDirectoryButtons) showDirectoryButtons();
//--></script>
```

## Automated Previous and Next Buttons
## buttons.js Source Code

The external JavaScript source library *button.js* outputs a table with appropriate image links to the previous and next pages within the current directory. Two variables, `first` and `last`, are defined and initialized to indicate the first and last pages in the series. Whenever a new page is added to the series, the only change that needs to be made so that the new page is automatically included is to update the value of the `last` variable:

../chapter5/nextprev/button.js

```
var first = 1;
var last  = 10;
```

The two variables `prefix` and `suffix` are used to hold the parts of the relative filename either side of the sequential page number—for example, `page9.htm`:

```
var prefix = 'page';
var suffix = '.htm';
```

The `prev` and `next` variables hold the text for `src` and `alt` string for use in `img` tags:

```
var prev = 'src="prev.gif" alt="previous page"';
var next = 'src="next.gif" alt="next page"';
```

To retrieve the filename from the current (i.e., `self`) window location's `href` property, we use the `String` object's `indexOf()` method to locate the `prefix` and `suffix` strings and then extract the current sequential number as `num`:

```
var url  = self.location.href;
var pos1 = url.indexOf(prefix);
var pos2 = url.indexOf(suffix);

var num = url.substring(pos1 + prefix.length, pos2) - 0;
```

The `showButtons()` function is invoked to display the button image links:

```
function showButtons() {
  var o = '';

  o += '<table width="100%" border="0"><tr>';
```

If the value of `num` is greater than the value of the `first` item in the series, then we display the `prev` image wrapped within a link to the previous item (`num-1`):

```
if (num > first) {
  o += '<td>';
  o += '<a href="' + prefix + (num-1) + suffix + '">';
  o += '<img border="0" ' + prev + '><\/a>';
  o += '<\/td>';
}

o += '<td width="100%"> <\/td>';
```

If the value of `num` is less than the value of the `last` item in the series, then we display the `next` image wrapped within a link to the next item (`num+1`):

```
if (num < last) {
  o += '<td>';
  o += '<a href="' + prefix + (num+1) + suffix + '">';
  o += '<img border="0" ' + next + '><\/a>';
  o += '<\/td>';
}
o += '<\/tr><\/table>';
```

We then write out the HTML code to the document:

```
  document.write(o);
}
```

# Automated Previous and Next Buttons directories.js Source Code

The external JavaScript source file *directories.js* is almost identical to the previous *buttons.js* file. It is used where index pages within separately directories are to be linked together.

The two variables `first` and `last` are defined and declared, but whereas in the previous code the `first` variable started at 1, here we show that the `first` variable does not need to start at 1, As long as `first` is less than or equal to `last`, then the navigation between all the files will work correctly.

 **../chapter5/nextprev/directories.js**

```
var first = 98;
var last  = 111;
```

Again, the two variables `prefix` and `suffix` are used to hold the parts of the relative directory and filename either side of the sequential page number—for example, `folder999/index.htm`:

```
var prefix = 'folder';
var suffix = '/index.htm';
```

The `prev` and `next` variables hold the text for `src` and `alt` string for use in `img` tags. Note that the images are in the parent directory (signified by the `../` prefix). This allows us to provide just the one copy of the images rather than a copy per directory:

```
var prev = 'src="../prevdir.gif" alt="previous directory"';
var next = 'src="../nextdir.gif" alt="next directory"';
```

We once again extract the sequence number from the `location` object's `href` property:

```
var url  = self.location.href;
var pos1 = url.indexOf(prefix);
var pos2 = url.indexOf(suffix);

var num = url.substring(pos1 + prefix.length, pos2) - 0;
```

The `pad()` function is used to ensure that we have a three-digit sequential number with one or two leading zeros if required:

```
function pad(num, size) {
  num = '' + num;
  while (num.length < size) num = '0' + num;
  return num;
}
```

The `showDirectories()` function is invoked to display the button image links:

```
function showDirectoryButtons() {
  var o = '';

  o += '<table width="100%" border="0"><tr>';

  if (num > first) {
    o += '<td>';
```

The first change is the use of a reference to the parent directory (`../`) to be used when navigating to the relevant sibling directory and the use of the `pad()` function to pad out the passed `num` argument:

```
    o += '<a href="../' + prefix + pad(num-1,3) + suffix + '">';
    o += '<img border="0" ' + prev + '><\/a>';
    o += '<\/td>';
  }

  o += '<td width="100%"> <\/td>';

  if (num < last) {
    o += '<td>';
```

The second change is again to reference the parent directory and to use the `pad()` function:

```
    o += '<a href="../' + prefix + pad(num+1,3) + suffix + '">';
    o += '<img border="0" ' + next + '><\/a>';
    o += '<\/td>';
  }

  o += '<\/tr><\/table>';

  document.write(o);
}
```

If the directory names simply use a sequential directory number without any leading zeros, then you can omit the use of the `pad()` function in the above code or simply replace the second argument to the `pad()` function with the value 1.

# Automated Links

Large documents can be difficult to navigate. Providing links to the top and bottom of the document can easily be done with the inclusion of two named anchors—for example, `<a name="top"></a>` and `<a name="end"> </a>`. If links are then located at the end of each main paragraph, the user can quickly jump to the top or bottom of the document—for instance, `<a href="#top">top</a>` and `<a href="#end">end</a>`.

This doesn't help the user navigate backward or forward a paragraph at a time. A solution would be to hand-code individual anchors throughout the document, uniquely labeling each anchor, and then include links to jump backward or forward a paragraph. The problem with this approach is that not only is it laborious, it is also prone to human error, such as forgetting to increment the anchor name and committing typing errors. It is also likely to break if at some later date extra paragraphs are included in the document.

The script presented here dynamically adds the appropriate anchors and text links after each paragraph. All that is needed is the cutting and pasting of one simple line of code. We also present an enhanced version of the code that uses image links instead of text links.

Figure 5-5 shows the initial state of the loaded document; the location bar ends with `text.htm`. Figure 5-6 shows the document after clicking the first `next` text link in the document; the location bar changes to end with `text.htm#1`—the anchor named 1 in the document—and the document is repositioned to just after the anchor. Figure 5-7 shows the effect of clicking any one of the end text links; the location bar ends in `text.htm#end`, and the document is repositioned at the end of the document. Figure 5-8 shows the enhanced version using image links instead of text links.

## Automated Links Source Code—Text Version

**../chapter5/links/text.htm**

```
<html>

<head>
<title>Automated Links</title>

<script language="JavaScript"><!--
```

**Figure 5-5**
Automated Links—
The top of the
document.

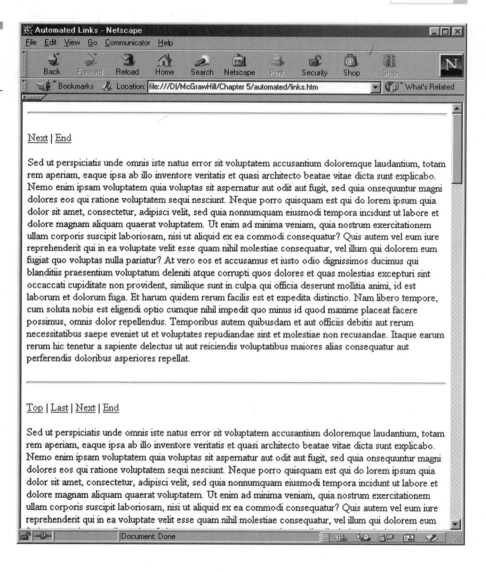

The global variable `textlink` is used to uniquely number each anchor throughout the document:

```
var textlink = 0;
```

The `textlinks()` function is used to output a set of anchors and text links. It accepts one optional argument—`last`—a Boolean value that indicates that an end anchor is to be output. This is the only complicated

**Figure 5-6**
Automated Links—
Jumped to #1.

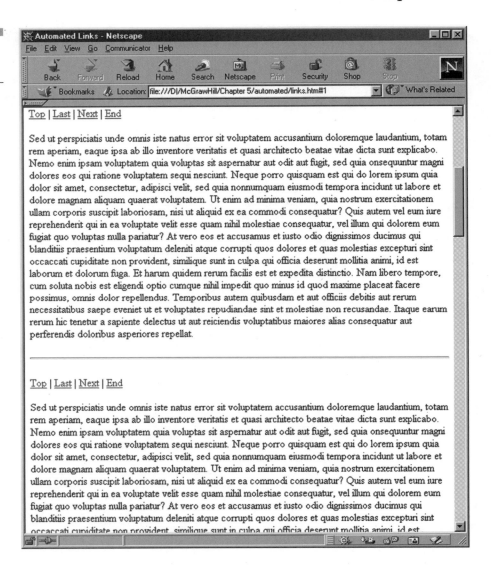

part of the whole process; you must remember to ensure that the last use of the `textlinks()` function in your document passes a `true` Boolean value.

```
function textlinks(last) {
```

A local output variable is initialized:

```
var output = '';
```

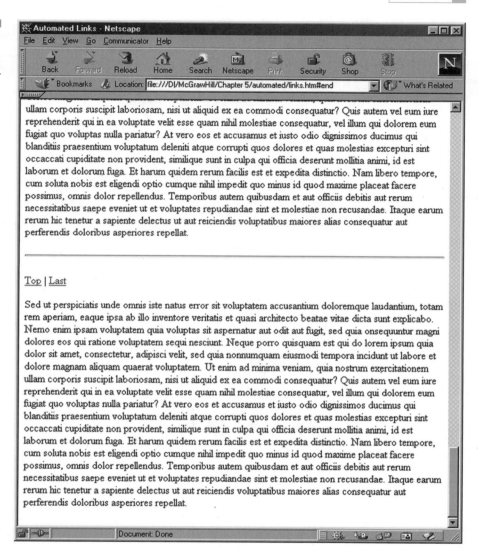

**Figure 5-7**
Automated Links—
Jumped to the #end.

If the `last` Boolean variable is `true`, we append an appropriate end anchor tag to the `output` variable:

```
if (last) output += '<a name="end"><\/a>';
```

A horizontal rule is also appended to the `output` variable. This may be omitted if not required:

```
output += '<hr><p>';
```

**Figure 5-8**
Automated Links—
Enhanced version
with image links.

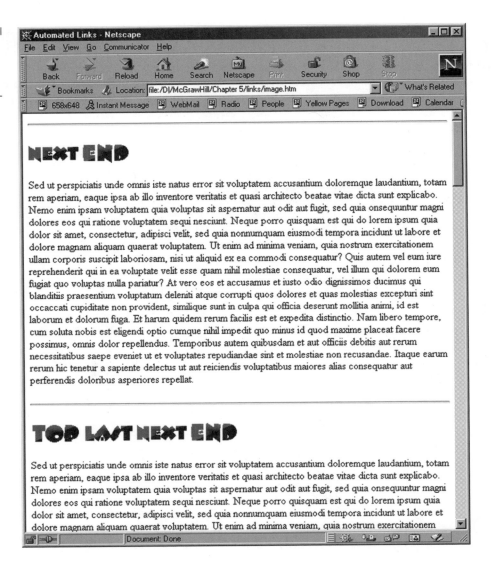

If the `textlink` variable is not zero—that is, this is not the first call to the `textlinks()` function—then we append a link to the top anchor, followed by a text link to the previous anchor (`textlink-1`). Note that a vertical bar (|) is used as a visual separator between the two links:

```
if (textlink != 0) {
  output += '<a href="#top">Top<\/a> | ';
  output += '<a href="#' + (textlink-1) + '">Last<\/a>';
}
```

If the `textlink` variable is not zero and the `last` Boolean variable is not `true`, then another vertical bar is appended to the `output` variable:

```
if ((textlink != 0) && (!last)) output += ' | ';
```

An anchor is appended to the `output` variable, its `name` attribute value set to the current value of the `textlink` variable, which is then post-incremented (i.e., its value is incremented after it has been used in the current expression):

```
output += '<a name="' + (textlink++) + '"><\/a>';
```

If the `last` Boolean variable is not `true`, then a link to the next (as yet unwritten) anchor is appended, followed by a link to the (as yet unwritten) end anchor:

```
if (!last) {
  output += '<a href="#' + textlink + '">Next<\/a> | ';
  output += '<a href="#end">End<\/a>';
}

output += '<\/p>';
```

Finally, we write the `output` variable to the document:

```
  document.write(output);
}
//--></script>

</head>

<body>
```

Using the `textlinks()` function throughout the body of the document is extremely straightforward. The following line of code is simply added wherever an anchor and text links needs to appear:

```
<script language="JavaScript">textlinks();</script>
```

Note, however, that the last call to the `textlinks()` function must pass a `true` Boolean value. Otherwise, the end anchor will never be written to the document, which will result in broken links throughout your document:

```
<script language="JavaScript">textlinks(true);</script>
```

# Automated Links Source Code—Image Version

../chapter5/links/image.htm

The enhanced version of the code uses image links instead of text links:

```
<html>

<head>
<title>Automated Links</title>

<script language="JavaScript"><!--
```

We initialize a global `imagelink` variable:

```
var imagelink = 0;
```

Four additional global variables are defined to hold the HTML code for the four required images—`topImage`, `lastImage`, `nextImage`, and `endImage`:

```
var topImage  = '<img src="top.gif" border="0">';
var lastImage = '<img src="last.gif" border="0">';
var nextImage = '<img src="next.gif" border="0">';
var endImage  = '<img src="end.gif" border="0">';
```

Instead of using a `textlinks()` function, we use an `imagelinks()` function:

```
function imagelinks(last) {
  var output = '';

  if (last) output += '<a name="end"><\/a>';

  output += '<hr><p>';

  if (imagelink != 0) {
```

Instead of appending text links, image links are appended using the `topImage` and `lastImage` variables:

```
    output += '<a href="#top">' + topImage +'<\/a> ';
    output += '<a href="#' + (imagelink-1) + '">' + lastImage + '<\/a> ';
}
```

```
    output += '<a name="' + (imagelink++) + '"><\/a>';

    if (!last) {
```

Again, instead of appending text links, image links are appended using the nextImage and endImage variables:

```
    output += '<a href="#' + imagelink + '">' + nextImage +'<\/a> ';
    output += '<a href="#end">' + endImage + '<\/a>';
}

output += '<\/p>';

document.write(output);
}
//--></script>

</head>

<body>
```

Using the imagelinks() function is as simple as the textlinks() function. Whenever you want an anchor and image links to appear, add the following line to your document:

```
<script language="JavaScript">imagelinks();</script>
```

Remember to pass a Boolean true value in the last imagelinks() call:

```
<script language="JavaScript">imagelinks(true);</script>
```

Note that in Netscape Navigator 3 problems can occur if you are placing JavaScript code within a table cell—the page is not rendered correctly. If you need to support Netscape Navigator 3 and you need to place the JavaScript code within table cells, amend the imagelinks() or textlinks() functions to output an entire table row. In other words, prefix the output variable with <tr><td> and append a postfix of <\/td><\/tr> to the output variable.

# A JavaScript Web Ring

The expression "Build it and they will come" does not always hold true with websites. You can build a spectacular website that no one visits. In WWW, the operative word is *Web*. The Web is by its very definition a web of interweaving links from one website to another. Unless people are informed about your website, they will not know that it exists, and they will not come.

After the actual creation, actually getting visitors to your website is the hardest part. It can be solved in many ways: promotion, registration on search engines, word of mouth, mutual links between websites, and last but by no means least, a web ring.

The web ring has become popular with groups of related websites—for instance, music fan websites, specialized interest groups, and sports websites. The vast majority of web rings are operated via a server-side process. You place hard-coded HTML links on your page to a central web server, and then it deals with the visitors clicking on these links to take the visitors to the next or previous website within the ring. The server-side process normally requires access to a CGI script on the server. Unfortunately, not everyone has administrative level access to run CGI scripts, and therefore, if you want to create your own web ring, you may have to rely on a third party to host it for you.

The example in the section shows how a web ring can be completely controlled using client-side JavaScript code. All that is needed is a central website that holds a publicly available JavaScript source file and that each site within the web ring refers to that file from within its HTML page. Because this JavaScript source file is simply a static file that any server can serve, you can host this file yourself; you do not need a third party. Figure 5-9 shows the images used by this particular web ring. You can replace the images—in fact, we recommend it. Figure 5-10 shows how the image links might look on a site within a typical web ring.

## A JavaScript Web Ring Source Code— Cut and Paste HTML

The following three lines of HTML are all that is needed to be placed within the HTML of each site within the web ring. This simply loads the external JavaScript source reference in the src attribute. Wherever the web master of a website wishes the web ring HTML to appear within their page, that's where they paste the following HTML.

 **../chapter5/webring/test.htm**

```
<script language="JavaScript"
  src="http://www.irt.org/webring/webring.js">
</script>
```

**Figure 5-9**
JavaScript Web
Ring—Typical web
ring control buttons.

**Figure 5-10**
JavaScript Web
Ring—A typical
display of a site
within a web ring.

Note that the value of the src attribute needs to be altered to the actual location of your own web ring.

## A JavaScript Web Ring Source Code—The webring.js JavaScript

../chapter5/webring/webring.js

The actual contents of the *webring.js* file need to be adapted for your own instances of the web rings. The addition of URLs for each of the sites within your web ring need to be used instead of the four examples used in this version of the source.

First, we declare and initialize several global variables. The WhereInRing variable is used indicate where in the web ring the script has been invoked from. This enables the code to calculate the next and previous sites in the web ring in relation to the current location:

```
var WhereInRing = 0;
```

The NumInWebRing variable is used to hold the number of sites in the web ring:

```
var NumInWebRing = 0;
```

The WebRing array is used to hold the URLs of all the sites in the web ring:

```
var WebRing = new Array();
```

The base variable contains the hard-coded location/directory of the controlling *webring.js* file. This needs to be altered to match the location/directory of your own webring:

```
var base = 'http://www.irt.org/webring/';
```

The output variable, as in most scripts, is used to hold the HTML code ready for writing to the document:

```
var output = '';
```

The WebRingObject() function is a constructor used to create a WebRingObject. Each WebRingObject contains just the one property—href:

```
function WebRingObject(href) {
  this.href = href;
}
```

The `Add()` function creates instances of the `WebRingObject` using the `href` argument as the input parameter to the `WebRingObject()` constructor:

```
function Add(href) {
```

The object returned by the constructor is appended to the `WebRing[]` array, and then the value of `NumInWebRing` is incremented by 1:

```
WebRing[NumInWebRing++] = new WebRingObject(href);
```

A check is made to see if the value of the `href` parameter is found as a substring within the current `href` property of the `location` object (i.e., the URL of the current window). If it is, then `WhereInRing` is set to the value of `NumInWebRing`:

```
if (location.href.indexOf(href) > -1)
  WhereInRing = NumInWebRing;
}
```

Next, we add all the websites within the web ring using the `Add()` function. This list can be as long as required, but it must have at least three entries:

```
Add("http://www.btinternet.com/~aredfern/");
Add("http://www.btinternet.com/~michael.coppins/");
Add("http://www.btinternet.com/~red.dragon/");
Add("http://www.btinternet.com/~markrsmith/");
```

We next calculate the sites on either side of the current site in the web ring. The `PrevInRing` variable is set as 1 less than either the `NumInWebRing` or the `WhereInRing` variables, depending on whether we are at the start of the web ring:

```
if (WhereInRing == 0)
  PrevInRing = NumInWebRing - 1;
else
  PrevInRing = WhereInRing - 1;
```

The `NextInRing` variable is set as either zero of 1 more than `WhereInRing`, depending on whether we are at the end of the web ring:

```
if (WhereInRing == NumInWebRing - 1)
  NextInRing = 0;
```

```
else
  NextInRing = WhereInRing + 1;
```

Testing for the start and end of the web ring completes the ring of websites, so that it does not matter where in the web ring a particular site is located. The site will always link to, and be linked from, the site on either side of it in the ring.

Finally we simply need to create image links to the previous and next sites within the web ring:

```
var output =
```

The `href` property of the `WebRingObject` object at index entry `PrevInRing` within the `WebRing` array is used as the `href` attribute for a image link back to the previous site:

```
'<center>' +

'<a href="' + WebRing[PrevInRing].href + '" target="_top">' +
'<img src="' + base + 'left.gif" border="0"></a>' +
```

We additionally provide a means for new websites to join the web ring by providing a link to an *index.htm* page at the `base` website:

```
'<a href="' + base + 'index.htm" target="_top">' +
'<img src="' + base + 'middle.gif" border="0"></a>' +
```

The `href` property of the `WebRingObject` object at index entry `NextInRing` within the `WebRing` array is used as the `href` attribute for a image link forward to the next site:

```
'<a href="' + WebRing[NextInRing].href + '" target="_top">' +
'<img src="' + base + 'right.gif" border="0"></a>' +

'<center>';
```

Finally, the HTML is written out to the document:

```
document.write(output);
```

The `src` attributes of the `img` tags use the `base` variable as a prefix to the image filename. This allows only one copy of the images to ever be loaded, no matter how many sites within the web ring a particular browser visits.

# What Is Your Language?

A global audience demands a global website. Not everyone can or wants to read English. Providing alternative pages using other languages can broaden your number of potential visitors. This example does not show how to translate from English to another language; that's your responsibility. What it does is show how to detect the preferred language set within the visitor's browser and then switch to an appropriate page that matches that language preference, giving the visitor the opportunity to read your website in their preferred language.

With Netscape Navigator 4, Netscape provided support for a new property against the `navigator` object called `language`. At the same time, Internet Explorer 4 also provided support for a new property against the `navigator` object but called `browserLanguage`. Fortunately, we can test whether the current browser supports as a minimum JavaScript 1.2, which both these two browser versions support, and then fork the code depending on which browser (i.e., Netscape Navigator or Internet Explorer) is being used.

The `language` or `browserLanguage` property provides simple access to the preferred language the browser has been configured to provide to servers when requesting pages. This setting allows servers the ability to offer pages written in different languages. Table 5-2 shows all the values that the `language` or `browserLanguage` property can hold and an indication of the actual language they represent.

For the example we present here we will restrict ourselves to detecting for the following language prefixes: `fr`, `de`, `it`, `en`, `es`, and `pt`, which represent the generic languages French, German, Italian, English, Spanish, and Portuguese.

## What Is Your Language? Source Code

 ../chapter5/language/index-en.htm

The following file is the English language version of a welcome page named *index-en.htm*. There needs to be five other versions, one each for the other five languages: *index-fr.htm*, *index-de.htm*, *index-it.htm*, *index-es.htm* and *index-pt.htm*. These other five do not need to include the JavaScript code necessary to detect the preferred language, since hope-

**TABLE 5-2**

language and
browserLanguage
values and their
meaning.

| Value | Meaning |
|-------|---------|
| af | Afrikaans |
| ar-ae | Arabic (U.A.E.) |
| ar-bh | Arabic (Bahrain) |
| ar-dz | Arabic (Algeria) |
| ar-eg | Arabic (Egypt) |
| ar-iq | Arabic (Iraq) |
| ar-jo | Arabic (Jordan) |
| ar-kw | Arabic (Kuwait) |
| ar-lb | Arabic (Lebanon) |
| ar-ly | Arabic (Libya) |
| ar-ma | Arabic (Morocco) |
| ar-om | Arabic (Oman) |
| ar-qa | Arabic (Qatar) |
| ar-sa | Arabic (Saudi Arabia) |
| ar-sy | Arabic (Syria) |
| ar-tn | Arabic (Tunisia) |
| ar-ye | Arabic (Yemen) |
| be | Belarusian |
| bg | Bulgarian |
| ca | Catalan |
| cs | Czech |
| da | Danish |
| de-at | German (Austrian) |
| de-ch | German (Swiss) |
| de-li | German (Liechtenstein) |
| de-lu | German (Luxembourg) |
| de | German (Standard) |
| el | Greek |
| en-au | English (Australian) |
| en-bz | English (Belize) |
| en-ca | English (Canadian) |
| en-gb | English (British) |

**TABLE 5-2**

language and browserLanguage values and their meaning. (Continued)

| Value | Meaning |
| --- | --- |
| en-ie | English (Ireland) |
| en-jm | English (Jamaica) |
| en-nz | English (New Zealand) |
| en-tt | English (Trinidad) |
| en-us | English (United States) |
| en-za | English (South Africa) |
| en | English |
| en | English (Caribbean) |
| es-ar | Spanish (Argentina) |
| es-bo | Spanish (Bolivia) |
| es-cl | Spanish (Chile) |
| es-co | Spanish (Colombia) |
| es-cr | Spanish (Costa Rica) |
| es-do | Spanish (Dominican Republic) |
| es-ec | Spanish (Ecuador) |
| es-gt | Spanish (Guatemala) |
| es-hn | Spanish (Honduras) |
| es-mx | Spanish (Mexican) |
| es-ni | Spanish (Nicaragua) |
| es-pa | Spanish (Panama) |
| es-pe | Spanish (Peru) |
| es-pr | Spanish (Puerto Rico) |
| es-py | Spanish (Paraguay) |
| es-sv | Spanish (El Salvador) |
| es-uy | Spanish (Uruguay) |
| es-ve | Spanish (Venezuela) |
| es | Spanish (Spain—Modern Sort) |
| es | Spanish (Spain—Traditional Sort) |
| et | Estonian |
| eu | Basque |
| fa | Farsi |

**TABLE 5-2**

language and
browserLanguage
values and their
meaning.
(Continued)

| Value | Meaning |
|-------|---------|
| fi | Finnish |
| fo | Faeroese |
| fr-be | French (Belgian) |
| fr-ca | French (Canadian) |
| fr-ch | French (Swiss) |
| fr-lu | French (Luxembourg) |
| fr | French (Standard) |
| gd-ie | Gaelic (Irish) |
| gd | Gaelic (Scots) |
| he | Hebrew |
| hi | Hindi |
| hr | Croatian |
| hu | Hungarian |
| in | Indonesian |
| is | Icelandic |
| it-ch | Italian (Swiss) |
| it | Italian (Standard) |
| ja | Japanese |
| ji | Yiddish |
| ko | Korean |
| ko | Korean (Johab) |
| lt | Lithuanian |
| lv | Latvian |
| mk | Macedonian |
| ms | Malaysian |
| mt | Maltese |
| nl-be | Dutch (Belgian) |
| nl | Dutch (Standard) |
| no | Norwegian (Bokmal) |
| no | Norwegian (Nynorsk) |
| pl | Polish |

**TABLE 5-2**

language and browserLanguage values and their meaning. (Continued)

| Value | Meaning |
|-------|---------|
| pt-br | Portuguese (Brazilian) |
| pt | Portuguese (Standard) |
| rm | Rhaeto-Romanic |
| ro-mo | Romanian (Moldavia) |
| ro | Romanian |
| ru-mo | Russian (Moldavia) |
| ru | Russian |
| sr | Serbian (Cyrillic) |
| sb | Sorbian |
| sk | Slovak |
| sl | Slovenian |
| sq | Albanian |
| sr | Serbian (Latin) |
| sv-fi | Swedish (Finland) |
| sv | Swedish |
| sx | Sutu |
| sz | Sami (Lappish) |
| th | Thai |
| tn | Tswana |
| tr | Turkish |
| ts | Tsonga |
| uk | Ukrainian |
| ur | Urdu |
| ve | Venda |
| vi | Vietnamese |
| xh | Xhosa |
| zh-cn | Chinese (PRC) |
| zh-hk | Chinese (Hong Kong) |
| zh-sg | Chinese (Singapore) |
| zh-tw | Chinese (Taiwan) |
| zu | Zulu |

*Source:* ISO 639:1988 (E) "Code for the representation of names of languages," ISO, Geneva, 1988.

fully by the time we reach them, the user-preferred language has been detected already.

The first thing we need to do is restrict the execution of the JavaScript code to only browsers that support at least JavaScript 1.2. By providing a `language` attribute, although deprecated in HTML 4, with a value of `JavaScript1.2`, we can guarantee that only browsers that support JavaScript 1.2 or above will execute the code within the `script` tags:

```
<script language="JavaScript1.2"><!--
```

The `getFileName()` function is a simple reusable utility function that when passed a URL (e.g., `http://www.domainname.com/foldername/filename.ext`) returns just the name of the file (e.g., `filename.ext`). Because the code can potentially be run offline as well as online, it includes checks for both the forward slash character (/) and an escaped backslash character (\) within the `s` argument, which returns everything after the last one found in the string:

```
function getFileName(s) {
  if (s.indexOf('/') != -1)
    return s.substring(s.lastIndexOf('/') + 1, s.length);
  else
    return s.substring(s.lastIndexOf('\\') + 1, s.length);
}
```

The `showpage()` function is passed a two-character string representing the browser's preferred language setting, which it uses to load an alternative page into the browser:

```
function showpage(code) {
```

The current window's `location` object's `href` property is retrieved. This maps to the current URL, which is then passed to the `getFileName()` function. The function then returns the filename of the current document:

```
var file = getFileName(window.location.href);
```

The position of the first dash character (-) within the filename is held in the local `dash` variable:

```
var dash = file.indexOf('-');
```

Two local variables, `prefix` and `suffix`, are defined and initialized:

```
var prefix = '';
var suffix = '';
```

If a dash character was found within the filename, then the `prefix` variable is set to the substring of the filename from the first character up to and including the dash character:

```
if (dash > -1) {
  prefix = file.substring(0, dash + 1);
}
```

Otherwise, the `prefix` variable is set to the substring of the filename from the first character up to the first dot character (`.`) plus an appended dash character:

```
else {
  prefix = file.substring(0, file.indexOf('.')) + '-';
}
```

The `suffix` variable is set to the substring from the character after the first dot to the last character:

```
suffix = file.substring(file.indexOf('.'), file.length);
```

So, for example, if the filename contained `index-es.htm`, then `prefix` would contain `index-` and `suffix` would contain `.htm`. On the other hand, if the filename contained `index.htm`, then `prefix` would contain `index-` and `suffix` would contain `.htm`.

The `href` property of the current window's `location` object is then changed to load the page built up from the concatenation of the three variables `prefix`, `code`, and `suffix`:

```
  window.location.href = prefix + code + suffix;
}
```

So in our previous example, if the two-character string `xx` is passed to the `showpage()` function, then the page `index-xx.htm` would be loaded into the current window.

While the page is loading, we detect the browser's preferred language, storing the results in the `language` variable using either the `navigator` object's `language` property for Netscape Navigator, or alternatively the `navigator` object's `browserLanguage` property:

```
if (navigator.appName == 'Netscape')
  var language = navigator.language;
else
  var language = navigator.browserLanguage;
```

Once retrieved, the first two characters of the `language` variable are extracted and placed in the variable:

```
var = language.substring(0,2);
```

Only if the `l` variable is equal to `fr`, `de`, `it`, `es`, or `pt` is it then subsequently passed as an input parameter to the `showpage()` function:

```
if (l=='fr' || l=='de' || l=='it' || l=='es' || l=='pt')
  showpage(l);
//--></script>
```

The remainder of the page is then the default English version of the page, which is displayed if either the preferred language does not match one of the five alternatives, or if the preferred language happens to be English.

If you need to capture the preferred language on all your pages, then place the above JavaScript code less the actual `script` tags into an external JavaScript source file—say, `language.js`—and then include the following HTML in between the head tags of each page:

```
<script language="JavaScript1.2" src="library.js"></script>
```

This will then only load the *library.js* source file with browsers that support JavaScript 1.2 and cause the page to be redirected to an alternate translated version of the current page. Again, the translation of your page needs to be done yourself, although you could make use of the AltaVista translation service at *http://babelfish.altavista.digital.com*, which can be used to prepare pretranslated English to French, German, Italian, Spanish, and Portuguese. The AltaVista translation service is not very accurate, since it does not take textual context into account when translating, but it can nevertheless be a useful start.

# Password Protection and Verification

Restricting access to information on a website appears to be a common requirement. The most reliable solution is to password-protect access to a particular directory using a server-side mechanism—for example, on the Apache web server, placing an *.htaccess* file within the directory to be password-protected with the username of the people who are allowed access. When requested for a file within the document, the server will ask for verification before serving the page, causing the browser to prompt the user for a username and password. Once verified, the page is then subsequently served to the browser. Any further requests for files are served without any further interaction with the user as the browser caches the username and password details for the duration of the browsers' session.

Many hosted websites do not provide support for *.htaccess* files. As a result, it is impossible to password-protect directories. Therefore, people resort to using security by obscurity. In other words, if you don't know the name of the file, you can't request it. This is a poor mechanism for protecting files, because as soon as the name of the file becomes publicly available, the file is no longer protected. To ensure that there is some semblance of protection, the name of the file must be protected at all costs:

- The file must not be linked to from another page. Otherwise, it is possible to reach it indirectly, possibly even from a search engine that has crawled through various links to reach your protected page.

- The name of the file must not be hidden within the source of a page. If someone were to read the source of your page, they would find your "hidden" password.

Once you have hidden your page by not revealing its filename, you need to provide access to it for those that have the password. This is usually performed by creating a page containing a form with two form fields: one for the user identity and one for the password. Once submitted, the form retrieves the two values entered by the user and uses them as parts of a URL to the actual file being protected. For example, if the user identity is `martin` and the password is `abracadabra`, then these might be used to retrieve a document located at `http://www.domain.com/martin/abracadabra.htm`. As long as the directory name `martin` and the filename `abracadabra.htm` are unknown to anyone except the user or users holding the identity `martin` and the password `abracadabra`, then the page has some form of protection.

Problems arise when the user enters incorrect information or when someone tries to guess the access details; the document that maps to the incorrect details will, generally, not exist, and the server will return a `404` error return code, which the browser then displays as a browser-specific not-found message. Figure 5-11 shows the not-found message as displayed by Netscape Navigator. Figure 5-12 shows the not-found message as displayed by Internet Explorer.

**Figure 5-11**
Netscape Navigator
404—Not Found.

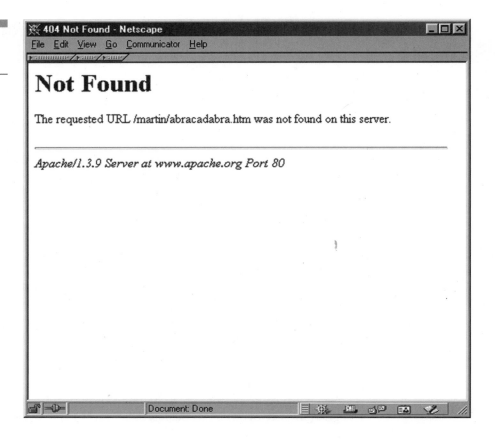

This example demonstrates not only how to create the necessary form and JavaScript code to load a page based on the user's identity and password, it also traps the condition where the resultant page does not actually exist and informs the user that his or her credentials are invalid. This provides an attractive user interface to what would otherwise result in a server-specific error message. As a result, you can have the look and feel of the trapped error page match the remainder of your well-designed website. See Figure 5-13.

Before we get into the code, an explanation of the various components and how they interact is in order. First, we have the *index.htm* page. This contains the form for the user to enter his or her credentials. It also loads a *blank.gif* image as a 1 pixel wide by 1 pixel high image with a transparent background color. When the user enters his or her credentials and submits the form, the JavaScript code intercepts the form submission,

**Figure 5-12**
Internet Explorer
404—The page
cannot be found.

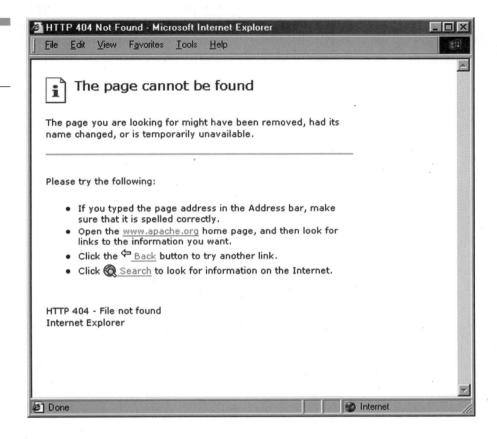

retrieves the identify and password values from the form, and attempts to load an image file using the relative URL format `identity/pass-word.gif`. If the image is successfully loaded, the image's `onLoad` event handler causes the password-protected page to be loaded using the relative URL format `identify/password.htm`. If the image fails to load, due perhaps to the user entering the wrong credential information and thus requesting an image that doesn't exist, then the image's `onError` event handler triggers the loading of the *error.htm* page to inform the user that he or she entered incorrect credentials and to try again.

The code additionally provides support for Internet Explorer 3, which does not support the manipulation of images from within JavaScript. The solution requires the use of an inline frame—that is, a frame embedded within the *index.htm* page itself. This initially holds a *blank.htm* page, which is replaced when the user submits the form with a temporary helper

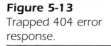

**Figure 5-13**
Trapped 404 error
response.

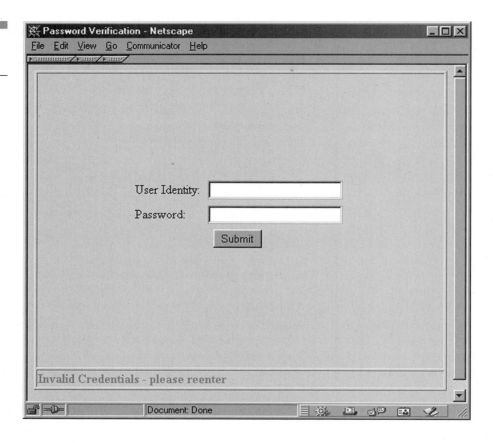

page using the relative URL format `identity/epassword.htm`. The contents of this page then load into the parent frame the password-protected page using the relative URL format `identity/password.htm`. Again, if the user enters the wrong credentials, then the temporary helper page will not be loaded into the inline frame. Although this failure cannot be detected using JavaScript, it at least avoids the default 404 error page being displayed by the browser. Hopefully, the number of people requiring password access using Internet Explorer 3 are constantly decreasing all the time.

Thus, the following files are required for the system to operate successfully:

*index.htm*—Identity and password entry page

*blank.gif*—Transparent 1x1 image

*blank.htm*—Empty page loaded into an inline frame by Internet Explorer 3 error.*htm*—Slightly amended version of index.htm

identity/password.*gif*—Transparent 1x1 password-protected image

identity/password.*htm*—Password-protected page

identity/*e*password.*htm*—Temporary helper page used by Internet
   Explorer 3

# Password Protection and Verification Source Code

The *index.htm* page contains a `logon` form to allow users to enter their
`identity` and `password`:

**../chapter5/password/index.htm**

```
<form name="logon" onSubmit="return testForIt()">
User Identity:
<input type="password" name="identity" value="">
Password:
<input type="password" name="password" value="">
<input type="submit" value="Submit">
</form>
```

When the `Submit` button is clicked, the `form` tag's `onSubmit` event
handler invokes the `testForIt()` function, returning the result back to
the event handler. If the result is `false`, then the form submission is
effectively cancelled.

Several global Boolean variables are defined and initialized to
`false`—`request` - indicates whether the user has submitted their credentials for verification, `useImage` - indicates that the browser supports images, and `useFrame` - indicates that the browser is Internet
Explorer 3, and instead of images, an inline frame should be used:

```
var request = false;
var useImage = false;
var useFrame = false;
```

Next, the code detects support for the `document` object's `images` property, and if present, it sets the global `useImage` Boolean variable to
`true`:

```
if (document.images)
  useImage = true;
```

Otherwise, if the browser is Internet Explorer 3, as identified by the substring `MSIE 3` within the `navigator` object's `appVersion` property, then the global `useFrame` Boolean variable is set to `true`:

```
else
  if (navigator.appVersion.indexOf('MSIE 3') > -1)
    useFrame = true;
```

If `useImage` is set to `true`, the code writes out the HTML necessary to display the transparent 1x1 *blank.gif* image (named `testImage`) with both `onLoad` a `onError` event handlers, which invoke the `loadIt()` and `failIt()` functions, respectively:

```
if (useImage)
  document.write(
    '<img src="blank.gif" name="testImage" alt="." width="1"' +
    ' height="1" onLoad="loadIt()" onError="failIt()">'
  );
```

Otherwise, if `useFrame` is set to `true`, the code writes out the HTML necessary to display a hidden 1x1 inline frame with `blank.htm` as its content:

```
else if (useFrame)
  document.write(
    '<iframe src="blank.htm" marginheight="0" marginwidth="0"' +
    ' frameborder="0" width="1" height="1"><\/iframe>'
  );
```

The `testForIt()` function is invoked when the user clicks the `logon` form's `Submit` button:

```
function testForIt() {
```

Only if both the `identity` and `password` form fields have nonempty `value` properties do we attempt to load the password-protected page:

```
if (document.logon.identity.value != '' &&
    document.logon.password.value != '') {
```

If the global `useImage` Boolean variable is `true` we attempt to load the image associated with the password-protected page:

```
if (useImage) {
```

First, the global `request` Boolean variable is set to `true` to indicate that the user has just requested authentication of their credentials:

```
request = true;
```

Next, an attempt is made to load the password-protected image by altering the `src` property of the `testImage` image:

```
    document.images["testImage"].src =
        document.logon.identity.value + '/' +
        document.logon.password.value + '.gif';
}
```

If, however, the global `useFrame` Boolean variable is set to `true`, then the temporary helper page is loaded into the hidden inline frame by altering the `href` property of the inline frame's `location` object:

```
    else if (useFrame) {
      document.frames[0].location.href =
        document.logon.identity.value + '/' +
        'e' + document.logon.password.value + '.htm';
    }
```

If neither of the two global Boolean variables, `useImage` or `useFrame`, are set to `true`, then an attempt is made to load the password-protected page. This ensures that any JavaScript-enabled browsers that don't support scripting of the image object at least attempt to load the password-protected page, just without the prerequisite check for its existence first:

```
    else {
      location.href =
        document.logon.identity.value + '/' +
        document.logon.password.value + '.htm';
    }
  }
```

The `testForIt()` function always returns `false` back to the `logon` form's `onSubmit` event handler so as to cancel the form submission:

```
  return false;
}
```

The `loadIt()` function is invoked whenever the `testImage` image's `onLoad` event handler is triggered. As the `onLoad` event handler for an `img` tag is triggered when an image has completely loaded, it will trigger at least twice for each successful credential verification: once when the initial *blank.gif* has loaded and once more when the password-protected image has loaded. The code must therefore discriminate between these two invocations. The first will occur as a result of the credential entry page being loaded by the browser; the second will occur when the user has submitted the form, and thus the `testForIt()` function will have set the global `request` Boolean variable to `true`. It is this Boolean that the `loadIt()` function tests to ensure that a call to the `loadIt()` function is as a result of the user submitting the form:

```
function loadIt() {
```

Only if the global `request` Boolean variable is `true` will the remainder of the function be executed:

```
   if (request) {
```

First, `request` is set to `false`:

```
      request = false;
```

Then the password-protected page is loaded:

```
      window.location.href =
         document.logon.identity.value + '/' +
         document.logon.password.value + '.htm';
   }
}
```

The `failIt()` function is invoked when the user supplies invalid credentials—that is, when the combination of `identify` and `password` do not result in the successful loading of a password protected image:

```
function failIt() {
```

Only when `request` is set to `true` do we highlight a credential verification failure:

```
   if (request) {
```

First, `request` is reset to `false`:

```
      request = false;
```

Second, the background color of the `document` object is changed to a pastel red color using the `bgColor` property:

```
document.bgColor = '#FFCCCC';
```

Next, the *error.htm* page is loaded. We change the color first, so as to give the user a visual clue that something is wrong while we are waiting for the error page to load:

```
window.location.href = 'error.htm';
}
```

Finally, the incorrect verification information held in the form fields is cleared:

```
document.logon.identity.value = '';
document.logon.password.value = '';
}
```

 **../chapter5/password/error.htm**

The *error.htm* page is almost an exact copy of the *index.htm* page. The only differences are a different background color (which matches the background color change made in the `failIt()` function):

```
<body bgcolor="#FFCCCC">
```

And instead of loading an error page in the `failIt()` function, it instead uses `alert` to warn the user that he or she has again failed to enter correct credential information:

```
alert('Incorrect credentials - please reenter');
```

All that remains is an explanation of the contents of the appropriate temporary helper page used in Internet Explorer 3. As we can't use images in Internet Explorer 3, we attempt to load a page almost identical to the password-protected page. For example, if the password-protected page is held in a file called *abracadabra.htm*, then an equivalent temporary helper page called *eabracadabra.htm* is required. Its contents are fairly short. It simply loads the password-protected page into the parent frame, using the `value` properties of the `logon` form's `identity` and `password` fields as the basis for the name of the file:

 **../chapter5/password/martin/eabracadabra.htm**

```
parent.location.href =
    parent.document.logon.identity.value + '/' +
    parent.document.logon.password.value + '.htm';
```

## Site Link Crawler

Crawling through all the links in a website, or part of a website, reporting back information on the number of pages, the number of links, the number of duplicate links, and the relationship between one page and another can provide extremely useful information about the structure of a website. This simple Site Link Crawler can be used to crawl through all the links of either files stored locally, or of a particular website, as long as the Site Link Crawler is located on the website itself, or in Netscape Navigator 4 of any remote website after requesting extra browser privileges. When run locally, Netscape Navigator politely indicates when a page cannot be linked to, as shown in Figure 5-14. This shows how the Site Link Crawler can be used to find broken links before uploading the pages online.

Usually, a script running in a page from one domain cannot access the data (script, objects, methods, variables, and so on) of a page from another domain. This is so that malicious scripts cannot hide in hidden frames or windows and monitor the user's browsing habits. The vendors employ security models in their products to stop this from happening. Generally, browser security bugs, often highlighted in the online news media, are a result of one or other of the vendors' security models being shown not to provide the level of security necessary to stop extremely talented JavaScripters from accessing information that they shouldn't be allowed to access.

**Figure 5-14**
Error message displayed when Netscape Navigator cannot find a file on the local file system.

Unfortunately, the downside to the security models is that it is harder, if not impossible, to provide extremely sophisticated interfaces in JavaScript that allow interaction between two pages from different domains. Fortunately, the security model employed in Netscape Navigator 4 supports a Java Capabilities API (the *netscape.security* package) that allows inline Java code within JavaScript to request extra browser privileges from the user, which the user can then grant or deny.

For example, JavaScript code could be written to read universal browser data in Netscape Navigator 4. Before the code is allowed access to the universal browser data, an otherwise protected data source, the code must first request that the `UniversalBrowserRead` privilege be enabled. This request prompts the user, as shown in Figure 5-15, to either grant or deny the requested privilege. Based on the user's experience of the site requesting the extra privilege, the type of privilege being requested, and his or her understanding of the loss of functionality resulting from denying the request, the user can hopefully make an informed decision as to whether to grant or deny the request. Before making a decision, the user can query the details of the request, shown in Figure 5-16, to see what effect the granting of the request would have.

Once the privilege has been granted, it persists for the duration of the

**Figure 5-15**
JavaScript code requesting Read access to universal browser data.

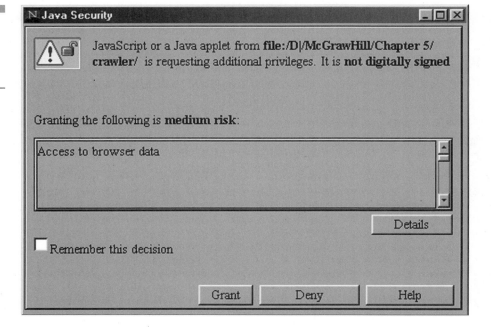

browser session—but only for the specific JavaScript code that has requested the privilege. If other JavaScript code requests similar privileges, then it too will require consent from the user.

Requesting extra privileges is extremely simple, the following Java code invokes the `PrivilegeManager` class's `enablePrivilege` method to request that the `UniversalBrowserRead` privilege should be enabled:

```
netscape.security.PrivilegeManager.enablePrivilege(
  "UniversalBrowserRead"
);
```

Once finished with, the privilege should be disabled, by invoking the `PrivilegeManager` class's `disablePrivilege` to disable the `UniversalBrowserRead` privilege:

```
netscape.security.PrivilegeManager.disablePrivilege(
  "UniversalBrowserRead"
);
```

Internet Explorer supports a security model that allows extra permissions to be requested within Java (using the *com.ms.security* package). However, there is no ability in Internet Explorer to include inline Java code within JavaScript—the solution would be to include all the processing in a Java applet, which is outside the scope of this book. Nevertheless, the code here will still work in Internet Explorer, but it will only allow local or relative files to be crawled.

Figure 5-17 shows the crawler in action, crawling through the links accessible from the local file named *file:///D|/McGrawHill/Chapter 5/crawler/* and detailing a snapshot of a total of 4 pages being searched, one of which has been completed, with 3 left to do, with 3 pages rejected and 12 duplicate links. Figure 5-18 shows the complete results, after scrolling down through the contents of the bottom frame to show all the referrers for each page searched.

## Site Link Crawler Source Code—index.htm

On the CD

../chapter5/crawler/index.htm

The *index.htm* page defines the three main frames that are used to hold an input form (`inputFrame`), the output display of the current page being crawled (`contentFrame`), and the output log of the complete crawl

**Figure 5-16**
Detailed description
of general effects of
granting Read access
to universal browser
data.

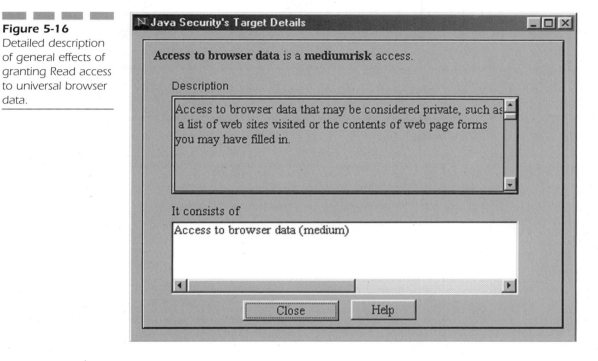

**Figure 5-17**
The Site Link Crawler
in action—Searching
the links accessible
from
file:///DI/McGrawHill
/Chapter 5/crawler/.

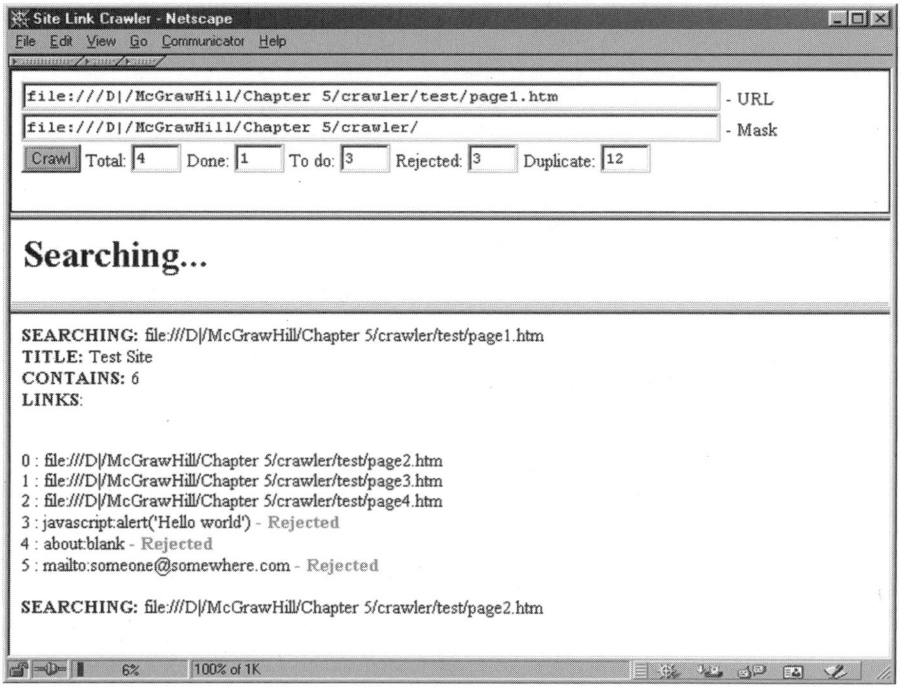

**Figure 5-18**
The Site Link
Crawler—Showing
the finished results.

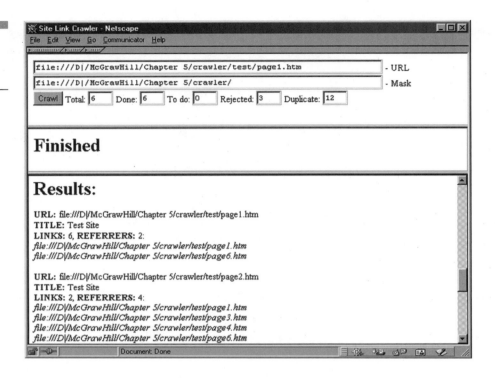

**Figure 5-18**
The Site Link
Crawler—Showing
the finished results.

(outputFrame). Note that to start with, both the contentFrame and outputFrame load a *blank.htm* page, which is essentially empty:

```html
<html>

<head>
<title>Site Link Crawler</title>
</head>

<frameset rows="125,200,*">
    <frame src="input.htm" name="inputFrame">
    <frame src="blank.htm" name="contentFrame">
    <frame src="blank.htm" name="outputFrame">
</frameset>

</html>
```

# Site Link Crawler Source Code—input.htm

 On the CD

**../chapter5/crawler/input.htm**

The *input.htm* page, loaded into the inputFrame frame, is the only page that initially displays any content. It is used to allow users to select which URL they wish to start the Site Link Crawler at, as well as what directory path mask should be applied, so as to avoid the Site Link Crawler straying from the intended directory path. For example, the user could select to start at the page *file:///D | /test/page1.htm* and restrict the crawl to pages within the directory path: *file:///D | /test/*.

The basic HTML for the inputForm form, has several input fields:

```
<form name="inputForm" onSubmit="return false">
```

The first (url) is a hidden input field (i.e., it is not shown on the page) used to track the current position within the *crawl*:

```
<input name="url" type="hidden">
```

The *visible* input field allows the user to enter the start position of the crawl:

```
<input name="visible" type="text" size="70"> - URL
```

The mask input field allows the user to enter the mask to be used when deciding which links to follow when crawling:

```
<input name="mask" type="text" size="70"> - Mask
```

When clicked, the Crawl form button invokes the startcrawl() function, passing the value property of the current form's (this.form) visible form field:

```
<input type="button" value="Crawl"
  onClick="startcrawl(this.form.visible.value)">
```

There are also five additional input fields (total, done, todo, rejected, and duplicate), each of which has an onFocus event handler that invokes the current input field's (this) onBlur() method—effectively preventing the user from amending the contents of these five input fields:

```
Total: <input type="text" name="total" size="4"
  onFocus="this.blur()">
Done: <input type="text" name="done" size="4"
  onFocus="this.blur()">
```

```
To do: <input type="text" name="todo" size="4"
  onFocus="this.blur()">
Rejected: <input type="text" name="rejected" size="4"
  onFocus="this.blur()">
Duplicate: <input type="text" name="duplicate" size="4"
  onFocus="this.blur()">
</form>
```

The global variable `startat` holds the relative URL of the default crawl—for instance, `test/page1.htm`. This can be changed to suit your own needs:

```
var startat = 'test/page1.htm';
```

To avoid repeated use of the long references to two other sibling frames (`outputFrame` and `contentFrame`), each of which have to be referenced via the `parent` frame, we define two global variables, `of` and `cf`:

```
var of = parent.outputFrame;
var cf = parent.contentFrame;
```

Once the HTML for the form has completely defined the form, it is then possible from that point onward to access the form through JavaScript. Again, to avoid repeated use of a long form reference, a global variable `form` is defined:

```
var form = document.inputForm;
```

The `getFullPath()` function is invoked, passing the `href` property of the current window's `location` object, assigning the result to the global `mask` variable.

```
var mask = getFullPath(window.location.href);
```

The `value` of the form's `mask` input field is updated with the value of the global `mask` variable:

```
form.mask.value = mask;
```

The value of the form's `visible` input field is updated with the concatenated value of the global `mask` variable and the `startat` variable:

```
form.visible.value = mask + startat;
```

As a result of these last two lines of code, the form is initialized so that the user can start a test crawl without having to do anything other than pressing the `Crawl` button.

The `myEntry` array is used to hold the URLs of all the pages that have been crawled or are to be crawled:

```
var myEntry = new Array();
var entryIndex = 0;
```

Two global variables (`rejected` and `duplicate`) are defined and initialized. They are used to hold the count of the number of pages rejected as unsuitable for following and duplicate pages (i.e., those that have already been added to the `myEntry` array):

```
var rejected = 0;
var duplicate = 0;
```

To restrict the path of crawl even further than that provided by the mask, it is necessary to declare certain types of URLs as off-limits—for example, any URL containing `javascript:`—which is a JavaScript link. The `rejectList` array holds examples of strings that, if present in a URL, would mark that URL as being unsuitable to be followed:

```
var rejectList = new Array(
  'res:',
  'javascript:',
  'about:',
  'mailto:'
);
```

Providing a list of unsuitable strings does not predicate against following an as yet undefined bad URL. The `acceptList` array holds examples of strings that, if present in a URL, would mark that URL as being suitable to be followed. At least one of the strings in the `acceptList` array must be present in the URL; otherwise, the URL will, once again, be marked as unsuitable:

```
var acceptList = new Array(
  '.htm'
);
```

The `getFullPath()` function, used previously to populate the value of the global `base` variable, returns the value of its `s` input parameter, generally a URL, minus the filename. In other words, it's the opposite of the `getFileName()` function described in the previous Password Protection and Verification code:

```
function getFullPath(s) {
  if (s.indexOf('/') != -1)
    return s.substring(0,s.lastIndexOf('/') + 1);
  else
    return s.substring(0,s.lastIndexOf('\\') + 1);
}
```

The `startcrawl()` function, invoked when the user clicks the `Crawl` button, starts the *crawler* off on its adventures using the passed `url` parameter as its starting point:

```
function startcrawl(url) {
```

The `of` frames document is opened ready for output to be written directly to it. Whatever content the `of` frame contained is instantly wiped out:

```
of.document.open();
```

The value of the hidden `url` form field is updated with the value of the `visible` form fields value:

```
form.url.value =
  form.visible.value;
```

If the `entryIndex` global variable is not equal to zero, then each entry in the `myEntry` array is set to `null`—in effect, deleting each element in the array:

```
if (entryIndex != 0)
  for (var i=0; i<entryIndex; i++)
    myEntry[i] = null;
```

The three global variables `entryIndex`, `rejected`, and `duplicate` are reinitialized:

```
entryIndex = 0;
rejected = 0;
duplicate = 0;
```

The `crawl()` function is invoked, passing the `url` parameter as an input argument:

```
crawl(url);
}
```

The `crawl()` function, although a one-line function, needs to be separated from the previous `startcrawl()` function as it is called from separate places within the code—once at the start and once for each and every page crawled through looking for links. It simply loads the *frame.htm* page into the `cf` frame:

```
function crawl(url) {
  cf.location.href = 'frame.htm';
}
```

Now might be a good time to skip forward to the description of the *frame.htm* page. Once understood, jump back here for the remaining description of the *input.htm* page.

If you had skipped forward to the *frame.htm* page, then you'll know that the page loads a frameset into the `cf` frame. One frame is the *search.htm* page, and the other is the page loaded using the current value of the `url` form field. Once loaded, the *search.htm* page reads all of the links in the `links` array, passing each `url` in turn as input to the `addEntry()` function, along with the `title`, number of `links`, and a Boolean `searched` value. The `addEntry()` function is called at least once—usually twice and maybe more—for every page crawled through by the *crawler*: once when a link to the page is found in another page and again when the page is finally loaded and scanned for links. In the first instance, the `searched` parameter is set to `false`. In the other instance, it is set to `true`. Other instances are usually as a result of duplicate links to the same page.

```
function addEntry(url, title, links, searched) {
```

The `url` parameter is passed as input to the `tidyupURL()` function, and the result is assigned back to `url`:

```
url = tidyupURL(url)
```

The tidied value of the `url` is passed as input to the `unAcceptable()` function, its result treated as a Boolean value in the `if` statement:

```
if (unAcceptable(url)) {
```

If the `unAcceptable()` function returns `true`, then the `rejectEntry()` function is invoked:

```
rejectEntry();
```

And the current `addEntry()` function ends as it returns back to its invokee:

```
    return;
}
```

If the unAcceptable() function returned false, then each entry in the myEntry array is checked to ensure that the url has not already been added to the array. The code loops through each entry in turn:

```
for (var entry=0; entry<entryIndex; entry++) {
```

The myEntry array contains, as will be seen later, Entry objects built using an Entry() object constructor. Each one of these objects has several properties. Some of these properties—for instance, url—are populated by the constructor. Others—for instance, title, links—are simply initialized to spaces or zero. This is necessary, because when a URL is added to the array, we know its URL, but not the title of the page or how many links it contains.

Each Entry object in the myEntry array has its url property compared against the current url parameter:

```
if (myEntry[entry].url == url) {
```

If the current url matches the url property of one of the Entry objects, and if the Entry object's links property is zero, both the title and links property are updated using the addEntry() function's title and links input parameters:

```
if (myEntry[entry].links == 0) {
  myEntry[entry].title = title;
  myEntry[entry].links = links;
}
```

If the Entry object's searched property is set to false, then the searched property is updated using the addEntry() function's searched input parameter:

```
if (!myEntry[entry].searched) {
  myEntry[entry].searched = searched;
}
```

If the searched parameter is set to false, then this function call is a result of the link being found in a page. In this case, since we have already found the url in the myEntry array, this is a duplicate link. Each Entry object contains a referURLs array. The current url is appended to this array, and the referrers property is incremented, before invoking the duplicateEntry() function:

```
   if (!searched) {
     myEntry[entry].referURLs[myEntry[entry].referrers++] =
       form.url.value;
     duplicateEntry();
   }
```

Finally, as we have found a match while looping through all the entries in the myEntry array, we jump out of the loop and out of the function, using the return statement:

```
     return;
   }
 }
```

If a match isn't found, then the setEntry() function is invoked:

```
   setEntry(url, title, links, searched)
 }
```

The tidyupURL() function simply strips any hash or search argument from the end of the url parameter. For example, if url contains http://www.domain.com/page.htm#anchor or http://www.domain.com/page.htm?search, then the returned result will just contain http://www.domain.com/page.htm. This avoids the crawler crawling through the same page many times but with different hash or search arguments.

```
function tidyupURL(url) {
  var hash = url.indexOf('#');
  var question = url.indexOf('?');

  if (hash > -1) url = url.substring(0, hash);

  if (question > -1) url = url.substring(0, question);

  return url;
}
```

The unAcceptable() function returns true if the url is not acceptable for crawling purposes, or false it is acceptable:

```
function unAcceptable(url) {
```

The first test is to ensure that the url parameter contains the value of the mask form field at position zero:

```
   if (url.indexOf(form.mask.value) != 0)
```

If not, it is not an acceptable url. Therefore, the function returns true:

```
return true;
```

Next, each entry within the `rejectList` array is tested:

```
for (var i=0; i<rejectList.length; i++)
   if (url.indexOf(rejectList[i]) > -1)
```

If an entry is found within the `url` parameter, then again it is not acceptable and the function returns `true`:

```
return true;
```

Next, each entry within the `acceptList` array is tested:

```
for (var i=0; i<acceptList.length; i++)
   if (url.indexOf(acceptList[i]) > -1)
```

If any one entry is found within the `url` parameter, then this time it is deemed as being acceptable and so the function returns `false`:

```
return false;
```

Finally, if no positive match is found in the `acceptList` array, the `url` is deemed by default to be unacceptable, so the function returns `true`:

```
return true;
}
```

The `rejectEntry()` function appends HTML output to the end of the of frame, then increments the value of the `rejected` variable and assigns the new value to the `value` of the `rejected` form field:

```
function rejectEntry() {
   of.document.write(
     '<font color="#FF0000"><b> - Rejected<\/b><\/font><br>'
   );
   form.rejected.value = ++rejected;
}
```

Likewise, the `duplicateEntry()` function appends HTML output to the end of the of frame, then increments the value of the `duplicate` variable and assigns the new value to the `value` of the `duplicated` form field:

```
function duplicateEntry() {
   of.document.write(
```

```
    '<font color="#FF9933"><b> - Duplicate<\/b><\/font><br>'
  );
  form.duplicate.value = ++duplicate;
}
```

The finishedSearch() function, invoked by the *search.htm* page, when it has finished passing all the links to the addEntry() function, checks to see if all the current entries in the myElement array have been searched. If not, it starts the crawler on the next page to be crawled; otherwise, it invokes the displayEntries() function to show the results of the crawlers adventures:

```
function finishedSearch() {
```

The first unsearched Entry object in the myEntry array is found by finding the first entry with a searched property of false:

```
var entry=0;
while (entry<entryIndex && myEntry[entry].searched)
  entry++;
```

Both the values of the done and todo form fields are updated, with the number of entries searched (entry), and the current number left to search (entryIndex - entry):

```
form.done.value = entry;
form.todo.value = entryIndex - entry;
```

If entry is less than entryIndex, then there is at least more one page to search through:

```
if (entry<entryIndex) {
```

In this case, the value of the hidden url form field is updated with the url property of the first unsearched Entry object:

```
form.url.value = myEntry[entry].url;
```

And the crawl() function is invoked to start yet another search:

```
crawl(myEntry[entry].url);
}
else {
```

Otherwise, all the Entry objects have been searched, in which case the displayEntries() function is invoked to display the results:

```
      displayEntries();
   }
}
```

The `displayEntries()` function simply loops through all the `Entry` objects in the `myEntry` array, appending HTML to the `output` variable:

```
function displayEntries() {
  var output = '<H1>Results:<\/H1>';

  for (var entry=0; entry<entryIndex; entry++) {
    output += '<p>';

    output +=
      '<b>URL:<\/b> ' + myEntry[entry].url + '<br>' +
      '<b>TITLE:<\/b> ' + myEntry[entry].title + '<br>' +
      '<b>LINKS:<\/b> ' + myEntry[entry].links + ', ' +
      '<b>REFERRERS:<\/b> ' + myEntry[entry].referrers + ':<br>';

    for (var i=0; i<myEntry[entry].referrers; i++)
      output += '<i>' + myEntry[entry].referURLs[i] + '</i><br>';

    output += '<\/p>';
  }
```

The `cf` frame is opened (causing the current content to be cleared) and a `Finished` heading is output:

```
cf.document.open();
cf.document.write('<h1>Finished<\/h1>');
cf.document.close();
```

The HTML contents of the `output` variable are finally written out to the `of` frame:

```
of.document.write(output);
of.document.close();
}
```

The `Entry()` function is actually the constructor for `Entry` objects. It creates and initializes `Entry` objects based on the passed arguments:

```
function Entry(url, title, links, searched) {
  this.url = url;
  this.title = title;
  this.links = links;
  this.searched = searched;
  this.referrers = 0;
```

One of the properties of the `Entry` object (`referURLs`) is actually an empty array, which is slowly populated with a list of all the pages that refer to the URL represented by an instance of the `Entry` object:

```
    this.referURLs = new Array();
```

The `Entry` constructor actually populates the first element of the `referURLs` array with the `value` of the form's `url` form field:

```
    this.referURLs[this.referrers++] = form.url.value;
}
```

The `setEntry()` function, invoked from the `addEntry()` function whenever a `url` is deemed to have passed the reject and duplicate checks, creates `Entry` objects by invoking the `Entry` constructor, and appends the resultant object reference to the `myEntry` array. At the same time the `value` of the form's `total` form field is updated with the value of the `entryIndex` variable:

```
function setEntry(url, title, links, searched) {
  myEntry[entryIndex++] =
    new Entry(url, title, links, searched);
  form.total.value = entryIndex;
}
```

## Site Link Crawler Source Code—frame.htm

 ../chapter5/crawler/frame.htm

As mentioned previously, whenever the crawler is required to load a `url` page to be searched for links, it loads the *frame.htm* page into the `cf` frame. Although this appears at first sight to be a strange way of loading the `url` page, it actually allows the code to be informed that the `url` page has successfully loaded without amending the `url` page in any way—useful when the `url` page is on a site that you have no control over.

Normally the `onLoad` event handler in a `body` tag is used to indicate when a page has completely loaded. The `frameset` tag also has an `onLoad` event handler that indicates when all the frames in the frameset have completely loaded.

Because the `url` page is not known at the time we create the code for the *frame.htm* page, the JavaScript code needs to dynamically build the HTML for the frameset based on the value of the hidden `url` form field in the `parent` frame's `inputFrame` frame. The *frame.htm* page defines two frames: `searchFrame` and `dataFrame`. The `searchFrame` initially contains the *loading.htm* page, which simply contains a "Loading..." message. Once the *url* page has been completely loaded into the `dataFrame`, the `frameset` tag's `onLoad` event handler loads the *search.htm* page into the `searchFrame`:

```
var output = '';

output += '<frameset rows="100%,*" ' +
  'onLoad="this.searchFrame.location = \'search.htm\'">' +
  '<frame src="loading.htm" name="searchFrame">' +
  '<frame src="' +
  parent.inputFrame.document.inputForm.url.value +
  '" name="dataFrame"><\/frameset>';

document.write(output);
```

## Site Link Crawler Source Code—search.htm

**../chapter5/crawler/search.htm**

The *search.htm* page loops through all the elements in the `links` array of the page contained in the sibling `dataFrame` frame. As mentioned at the start of the Site Link Crawler introduction, Netscape Navigator 4 supports a Java Capabilities API that allows extra privileges to be requested and enabled. To allow the crawler to access the properties of a page from another domain other than the one hosting the *search.htm* page, we can request from the user that they grant `UniversalBrowserRead` privilege to the JavaScript code in *search.htm*. Thus, the first page of the *search.htm* page does just that.

First, we test that the browser is Netscape Navigator by testing that the `appName` (application name) property of the `navigator` object contains the value "`netscape`":

```
if (navigator.appName == "Netscape" &&
```

Also, we check if Java is enabled using the `navigator` object's `javaEnabled()` method, which returns `true` if enabled or `false` if disabled:

```
navigator.javaEnabled()) {
```

Before finally invoking the *netscape.security* package's `Privilege-Manager` class's `enablePrivilege()` method, requesting that the user grant `UniversalBrowserRead` privileges:

```
netscape.security.PrivilegeManager.enablePrivilege(
  "UniversalBrowserRead"
);
}
```

If the user grants the required privilege, then any access to otherwise protected data is successful, if not, then access to otherwise protected data fails with an "access disallowed from scripts at search.htm to documents at another domain" error message, as can be seen in Figure 5-19.

As in the *input.htm* page, we provide shortcut references to other frames:

```
var df = parent.dataFrame;
var of = top.outputFrame;
```

The url variable holds the href property of the df frame's location object:

```
var url = df.location.href;
```

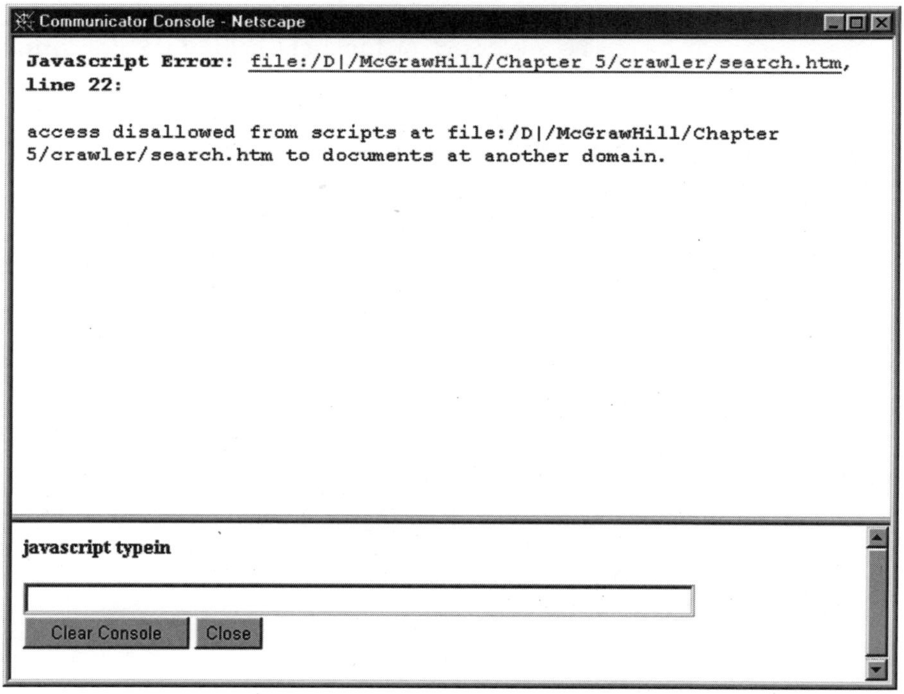

**Figure 5-19**
*JavaScript error generated in Netscape Navigator when user denies privilege request.*

The `title` variable holds the `title` property of the df frame's document object:

```
var title = df.document.title;
```

The `links` variable holds a reference to the `links` array in the df frame's document object:

```
var links = df.document.links;
```

The `length` variable holds the number of `links` in the links array reference:

```
var length = links.length;
```

HTML output is written directly to the of frame, displaying the details captured so far about the contents of the df frame:

```
of.document.write('<p>');
of.document.write('<b>SEARCHING:<\/b> ' + url + '<br>');
of.document.write('<b>TITLE:<\/b> ' + title + '<br>');
of.document.write('<b>CONTAINS:<\/b> ' + length + '<br>');
of.document.write('<b>LINKS<\/b>:');
of.document.write('<\/p>');
```

The `addEntry()` function, held in the top frame's inputFrame child frame, is invoked, passing the url (converted to a string), title, and length variables along with a true Boolean variable, indicating that this particular url has been searched:

```
top.inputFrame.addEntry(
  url.toString(), title, length, true
);
```

The code then loops through all the elements of the links array reference, invoking the `addEntry()` function, held in the top frame's inputFrame child frame, passing the href property, an empty string, and zero—for the `addEntry()` functions title and length parameters, respectively:

```
for (var i=0; i<length; i++) {
  of.document.write(i + ' : ' + links[i].href);
  top.inputFrame.addEntry(links[i].href, '', 0);
}
```

To be completely tidy, we disable the `UniversalBrowserRead` privilege:

```
if (netscape) {
  netscape.security.PrivilegeManager.disablePrivilege(
    "UniversalBrowserRead"
  );
}
```

Finally, the `finishedSearch()` function, held in the `top` frame's `inputFrame` child frame, is invoked:

```
top.inputFrame.finishedSearch();
```

Internet Explorer cannot be used to crawl through pages on another domain. When attempted a "`Permission denied`" error is generated, as indicated by a yellow exclamation warning sign in the bottom left-hand corner of the browser window. When double-clicked, the icon reveals the error message, as shown in Figure 5-20.

**Figure 5-20**
Permission denied error message revealed in Internet Explorer when attempting to access the properties of a page from another domain.

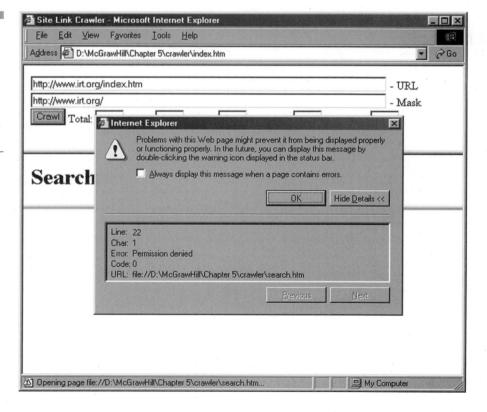

# Summary

As JavaScript accesses the properties of the current URL, it can make decisions based on where the current page is located in the site structure, make references to other pages around it, and also directly influence the pages loaded in the current window or another frame/window by amending the value of the `href` property.

Being able to access the links within a HTML page, not only allows JavaScript to progressively walk through all the links in page but also provides the ability to provide another view of the links with a page. This is shown to good effect in the Chapter 6, with the Reading a Directory application.

With the use of external JavaScript source files, we can begin to see how code can be shared and reused amongst several pages. We will see external JavaScript source files being use extensively throughout the remainder of the book.

CHAPTER **6**

# Windows and Frames

Not all websites reside in one single window or one single frame of a window. Some sites use frames to partition the site into menu and content frames, thereby reducing the overhead of having navigation menus in each and every page. Some sites open up remote or pop-up windows separate from the main browser window. Combinations of frames and extra windows allow web designers to emulate the more traditional client-side applications, providing richness in dialogs that assist, and possibly distract, the user in his or her interaction with a website.

This chapter includes useful applications of pop-up windows and multiple frames. The first, the Jump Box tool, shows how JavaScript can be used to target different frames and windows from a form select dropdown box. The Reading a Directory application, shows how a hidden frame directory listing can be read and then redisplayed in whatever form we choose, perhaps by filtering on file type.

The Pop-up Window Generator is a useful JavaScript tool that you can use to define the perfect pop-up window for your application. Once defined, you can cut and paste the JavaScript code for use within your main code. The Dictionary Pop-up shows how data can be passed between the main window and the pop-up window to affect the contents of the pop-up window, providing a dictionary lookup facility.

The Family Tree application shows how feature-rich applications that dynamically change the page view and display details of many people within a complex family tree can be used to good effect, with JavaScript code and variable data held in the invisible parent frame, safe from being overwritten.

As JavaScript programs become increasingly complicated, it becomes increasingly harder to debug them. The JavaScript Debugging Window shows techniques for writing debugging information to a separate pop-up window that, when disabled, doesn't affect the working or the performance of the debugged application. The Pop-up Date Selector shows how a generic calendar library (discussed further in Chapter 7 "Date and Time") can be used within a pop-up window application, without the library knowing anything about pop-up windows.

Finally, the strangely titled Un-Framing and Re-Framing example shows how some of the more irritating aspects of frames can be overcome—for instance, pages not held within their frameset, held within someone else's frameset, and not containing the correct surrounding frames.

# Jump Box Tool

This particular script solves the problem that first started my interest in JavaScript. The problem I had was loading one of many pages into another frame, but at the same time, allowing the user to select which frame the page appeared in—for example, a frame at the top of the browser's display or another at the bottom. (I never did solve the problem—not because it couldn't be solved, but because I spent the next four years being sidetracked by more complicated JavaScript code).

The code presented here uses a drop-down select form field to hold the description and location of several pages. Once selected, the user can press the Go button to load the relevant page into the required frame or additionally into a new window.

Figure 6-1 shows the effect of first loading Microsoft's MSDN site into the top frame and the Netscape's DevEdge site into the bottom frame.

## Jump Box Tool Source Code—index.htm

../chapter6/jumpbox/index.htm

The *index.htm* page defines a simple frameset to hold the *control.htm* page, and two initially blank target frames frame1 and frame2. Note how there are essentially two framesets, one nested within the other. This allows us to specify that the first frameset should be made up of columns, one 200 pixels wide and the other to take up the remaining

**Figure 6-1**    Jump Box tool—MSDN in the top frame; DevEdge in the bottom frame.

browser's window width (signified by the *). It also lets us specify that this second area should then be made up of two further frames held in rows, both taking up 50% of the available height:

```
<frameset cols="200,*">
  <frame src="control.htm">
  <frameset rows="50%,50%">
    <frame src="about:blank" name="frame1">
    <frame src="about:blank" name="frame2">
  </frameset>
</frameset>
```

Once the *index.htm* page has been loaded and the frameset has been defined, the browser will populate the current `window` object's `frames` array with three `window` objects, one for each frame element in the *index.htm* page. Using `window.frames[n]` where *n* is 0, 1, or 2, we are able to directly access the `window` objects that relate to the three pages loaded into the three frames.

## Jump Box Tool Source Code—control.htm

 ../chapter6/jumpbox/control.htm

The *control.htm* page contains the necessary JavaScript and form HTML to allow the user to dictate which frame the selected page should be loaded into. It also allows the user to indicate that a new window should be used instead. First, let's focus on the HTML markup for the form.

The `jump` form contains three radio buttons all named `where`, the `value` attribute of which is used later on to indicate where the page should load. When radio buttons are included with a form, the resultant form object holds a reference to each of the radio buttons using an array named after the name of the radio buttons. Therefore, the `jump` form object holds a `where` array of three entries, each of which correspond to the three radio buttons:

```
<form name="jump">

<input type="radio" name="where" value="frame1"> - Frame 1
<input type="radio" name="where" value="frame2"> - Frame 2
<input type="radio" name="where" value="popup"> - New window
```

The `places` select drop-down list uses `option` tags to hold both the `value` of the URL, and the `text` description of the page to be loaded. Note that some of the `option` tags do not have a `value` associated with them:

```
<select name="places">
<option>Select:
<option>===========
<option value="http://www.irt.org/">irt.org
<option value="http://msdn.microsoft.com/">MSDN
<option value="http://developer.netscape.com/">DevEdge
<option value="http://www.w3.org/">W3C
<option>===========
<option value="http://webreview.com/">webreview.com
<option value="http://developer.earthweb.com/">developer.com
</select>
```

The user selects an option from the list and then presses the following Go form button, which invokes the onClick event handler, which in turn calls the go() function, passing a reference to this current form:

```
<input type="button" value="Go" onClick="go(this.form)">
</form>
```

If you prefer to use an image instead of a form button, the following additional code reproduces similar functionality. When the user clicks on the image link, the onClick event handler invokes the go() function, passing a reference to the document object's jump form:

```
<a href="#" onClick="return go(document.jump)"
   onMouseOver="mouseOver(document.jump);return true"
   onMouseOut="mouseOut();return true"
><img src="go.gif" border="0"></a>
```

The image link additionally calls the mouseOver() and mouseOut() functions when the onMouseOver and onMouseOut event handlers are invoked. As these two functions alter the window's status bar, the two event handlers must return a true Boolean value to the event that triggered the handler; otherwise, the change will be ignored.

The go() function first ensures that a valid option has been selected by the user—that is, one with a nonempty value attribute—and then controls where the page is loaded. The form reference passed into the go() function is held in the what parameter:

```
function go(what) {
```

The value property of the selected option is retrieved by passing the reference to the what form's places select object to the getAnOptionValue() function:

```
    var URL = getAnOptionValue(what.places);
```

Only if the returned value of the URL variable is not empty do we attempt to load a page:

```
    if (URL != '') {
```

Depending on which radio button is checked, we load the page referenced by the URL variable in one of four possible ways. If either the first or second radio buttons are checked (i.e., what.where[0] or what.where[1] have a checked property with a Boolean value of true), then the `loadFrame()` function is called, passing the URL and the value property of the radio button that corresponds to its `value` attribute:

```
if (what.where[0].checked)
   loadFrame(URL, what.where[0].value);

else if (what.where[1].checked)
   loadFrame(URL, what.where[1].value);
```

If the third radio button is checked, then the `loadPopup()` function is invoked, again passing the URL and `value` property:

```
else if (what.where[2].checked)
   loadPopup(URL, what.where[2].value);
```

Finally, if none of the radio buttons are checked the `loadPage()` function is called, passing just the URL:

```
   else
      loadPage(URL);

}

return false;
}
```

The `loadPage()` function simply loads the page reference by the passed `url` parameter into the current page:

```
function loadPage(url) {
  location.href = url;
}
```

The `loadFrame()` function loads the page into one of the frames in the `parent` frame's `frames` array, using the passed `frame` parameter to signify the name of the frame to be used:

```
function loadFrame(url, frame) {
  parent.frames[frame].location.href = url;
}
```

The `loadPopup()` function creates a new window to load the page into, using the `window` object's `open()` method:

```
function loadPopup(url, name) {
  window.open(url, name, 'width=640,height=480,scrollbars=1');
}
```

The `getAnOptionValue()` function returns the `value` property of the selected option. The passed `what` parameter references the select object; therefore, `what.options` references the select object's `options` array, and the value of `what.options.selectedIndex` indicates which option is currently selected:

```
function getAnOptionValue(what) {
  return what.options[what.options.selectedIndex].value;
}
```

The `getAnOptionText()` function likewise returns the `text` property of the selected option:

```
function getAnOptionText(what) {
  return what.options[what.options.selectedIndex].text;
}
```

The `mouseOver()` function retrieves and then displays the `text` property of the currently selected option within the window's status bar by updating the `status` property of the *current* window object, but only if the `value` property of the selected option is not empty:

```
function mouseOver(what) {
  if (getAnOptionValue(what.places) != '') {
    var text = getAnOptionText(what.places);
    window.status = text;
  }
}
```

The `mouseOut()` function simply resets the window's status bar:

```
function mouseOut() {
  window.status = '';
}
```

# Reading a Directory

If allowed by a server, a directory listing of all the files in a directory can be displayed if the URL entered ends in the name of the directory that we wish to see the contents of. For example, if we enter `http://www.domain.com/directoryname`, then it may be possible to see all the files held in the directory `directoryname`. Figure 6-2 shows the results of displaying a directory on the local file system within Netscape Navigator.

As you can see, for each and every file in the directory there is an

**Figure 6-2**
Directory listing of
a local file system
within Netscape
Navigator.

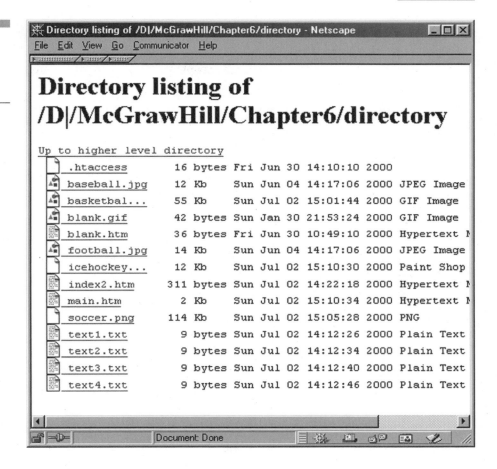

**Figure 6-2**
Directory listing of a local file system within Netscape Navigator.

entry with a link to that file, plus a link back up the directory tree to the directory above this one. The actual directory listing is a dynamically generated HTML page with links to the files in the directory.

However, when performed in Internet Explorer, the results are totally different. The Windows operating system displays not a web page containing links to the files, but instead a view of the directory using File Explorer, as shown in Figure 6-3.

The actual directory display is dependent on both the browser and operating system being used, or when displaying a directory of a remote server, it is dependent on the web server itself. The amount of details—for instance, file size, timestamp, and file description—may vary from one web server to another. However, the one constant is the filename and a link to the file itself.

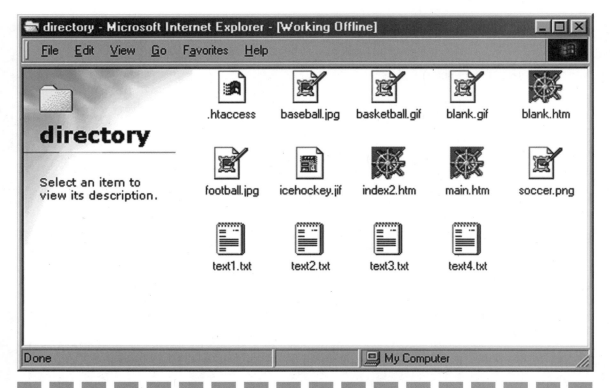

**Figure 6-3**    *Directory listing of a local file system within Internet Explorer.*

Whether a web server displays a directory listing depends on how the server has been configured and what the directory contains. Usually, if a directory contains a file named *index.htm* or *index.html*, then instead of the server showing a directory listing, it shows the file. Even if the directory does not contain one of these or other similarly configured filenames, the server may be configured to refuse to display a directory listing, as shown in Figure 6-4. In this case, if the server is an Apache web server, it may be possible to override this server-wide configuration by placing a *.htaccess* file within the directory containing the following server directive: Options +Indexes.

JavaScript may not be able to perform a directory query itself, but it can be used to read the links within a page, as demonstrated in the Web Site Crawler application in Chapter 5 "Location and Links." This application will demonstrate how we can read the links of a directory listing in one hidden frame and then use the results to selectively display links

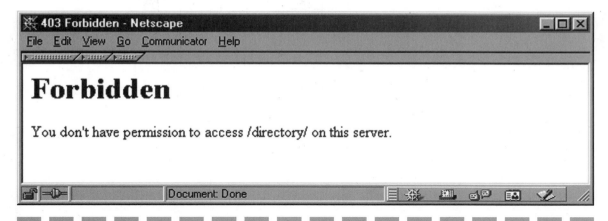

**Figure 6-4**    Forbidden—A server configured to refuse directory listings.

in interesting ways. Figure 6-5 shows the effects of the application described here on the previous directory listing.

## Reading a Directory Source Code— index2.htm

The *index2.htm* page (note it is not called index.htm—as this would defeat the directory listing being displayed) contains a frameset made of two frames, `main` and `directory`:

 **../chapter6/directory/index2.htm**

```
<frameset rows="100%,*" onLoad="reload_main()">
<frame src="about:blank" name="main">
<frame src="../directory/" name="directory">
</frameset>
```

The `main` frame, initially containing a blank page, takes up `100%` of the available browser window, whereas since there is no available space left, the `directory` frame, which contains a directory listing of the *current* directory (up one level to the parent directory, i.e., `../`, and then back into `directory/`), appears at the very bottom of the browser win-

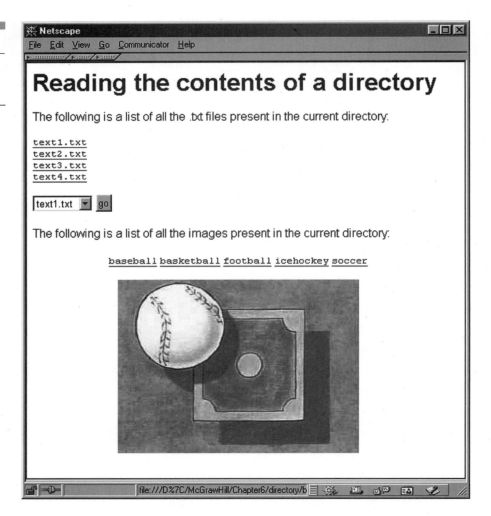

dow—effectively invisible. The `onLoad` event handler, which is invoked when all the pages in the frameset have successfully loaded, calls the `reload_main()` function to load the *main.htm* page into the main frame:

```
function reload_main() {
  window.main.location.href = "main.htm";
}
```

## Reading a Directory Source Code—main.htm

Once the `onLoad` event handler within the `index.htm` frameset has triggered and subsequently loaded the *main.htm* page into the `main` frame, we can be certain that the `directory` frame contains a document that lists the files in the relevant directory. Now all we need to do is access the `links` array within the document in the `directory` frame. Rather than simply looping through all the entries in the `links` array, the code presented here uses an array of strings, each of which is used as a filter for valid files that we want to use within our *main.htm* page.

../chapter6/directory/main.htm

For example, the following code creates a `filter` array of file extensions that is than passed to the `vetLinks()` function. The `vetLinks()` function uses the passed `filter` array to filter all the links in the document loaded into the `directory` frameset, returning a `files` array of only the links that match one or other of the passed file extensions. The `href` property of the `location` of the directory listed in the `directory` frame is passed along with the `files` to both the `showLinks()` and `showOptions()` functions, which use the data to output the filtered `files` array either as a list of text links or as options in a select dropdown list:

```
var filter = new Array('.txt');
var files = vetLinks(filter);
showLinks(parent.directory.location.href, files);
showOptions(parent.directory.location.href, files);
```

The following code works in a similar fashion. The `filter` array is a list of all the acceptable file types for images. Once vetted, the `files` array is then passed to the `showImages()` function, which formats the output as links with appropriate `onMouseOver` and `onMouseOut` event handlers that swap the `src` attribute of a dummy blank image:

```
var filter = new Array('.jpg', '.gif', '.png', '.jif');
var files = vetLinks(filter);
showImages(parent.directory.location.href, files);
```

The `vetLinks()` function accepts the passed `filter` array of file extensions and returns a `files` array of all the matching filenames:

```
function vetLinks(filter) {
  var files = new Array();
  var index = 0;
  var length = parent.directory.document.links.length;
```

The function loops through all of the entries in the `links` array of the parent frame's `directory` frame using the `length` of the `links` array to control the loop:

```
for (var i = 0; i < length ; i++) {
```

The filename of the current entry in the `links` array minus the directory path is then retrieved and held in the `file` variable using the `getFileName()` function described previously in the section "What Is Your Language?" in Chapter 5.

```
var link = parent.directory.document.links[i].href;
var file = getFileName(link);
```

Within the outer loop, there is an inner loop that loops through all the entries in the `filter` array, testing to see if the current entry in the `filter` appears within the current entry in the `links` array:

```
for (var j = 0; j<filter.length; j++) {
```

If it does, then the value of `file` is appended to the end of the `files` array before breaking out of the inner loop:

```
    if (file.indexOf(filter[j]) > -1) {
      files[index++] = file;
      break;
    }
  }
}
```

Once the outer loop has finished, the `files` array is returned back to the caller of the function:

```
  return files;
}
```

The `showLinks()` function, which is passed the directory location as `dir`, and the filtered `files` array simply looks through each entry writing out a text link for each one:

```
function showLinks(dir, files) {
  for (var i = 0; i < files.length; i++)
    document.write(
      '<a href="' + dir + files[i] + '">' + files[i] + '</a>' +
      '<br>'
    );
}
```

The showOptions() function, on the other hand, writes out a new form and select drop-down list with an option for each entry in the filtered files array:

```
function showOptions(dir, files) {
  document.write('<form><select name="list">');

  for (var i = 0; i < files.length; i++)
    document.write(
      '<option name="list" value="' + dir + files[i] + '">' +
      files[i] + '<\/option>'
    );
  document.write(
    '<\/select> <input type="button" value="go" ' +
    'onClick="go(this.form.list)"><\/form>'
  );
}
```

The HTML generated in the preceding showOptions() function uses the following go() function when the user clicks the Go form button to load the selected file into the current window:

```
function go(what) {
  location.href =
    what.options[what.options.selectedIndex].value;
}
```

The showImages() function formats the passed filtered files array, generating an img element for each one with appropriate onMouseOut and onMouseOver event handlers, which invoke the show() function to image-swap a blank image held in the page with the image associated with link that the mouse pointer moves across:

```
function showImages(dir, files) {
  for (var i = 0; i < files.length; i++)
    if (files[i] != 'blank.gif')
      document.write(
        '<a href="' + dir + files[i] + '" ' +
        'onMouseover="show(\'' + dir + files[i] + '\')" ' +
        'onMouseout="show(\'blank.gif\')">' +
        files[i].substring(0,files[i].indexOf('.')) + '</a> '
      );
}
```

Notice how the backslash character (\) is used to escape the single quote characters (') needed within nested quotation marks in both the img element's onMouseOver and onMouseOut attributes.

The HTML generated by the previous showImages() function uses the following show() function to swap the image held in the sports image with the passed img image:

```
function show(img) {
  if (document.images)
    document.images['sports'].src = img;
}
```

The following HTML defines a blank sports image, which is then swapped with an appropriate image by the previous show() function:

```
<img name="sports" src="blank.gif" width="320" height="240">
```

Image-swapping techniques are covered in detail in Chapter 9 "Images."

The important thing to note about the showLinks(), showOptions(), and showImages() functions is that once a filtered list of files has been passed to the function, the HTML formatting carried out by the function is totally flexible. You can change, adapt, or create new functions to meet your own formatting requirements.

# Pop-up Window Generator

The Pop-up Window Generator presented here can be used to interactively play with all the settings available in both Internet Explorer and Netscape Navigator when creating remote pop-up windows. Figure 6-6 shows the Pop-up Window Generator in action, and Figure 6-7 shows an example pop-up window created and opened by the generator.

The Pop-up Window Generator uses colored backgrounds to indicate what each browser supports. As such, it can be used to quickly generate the required JavaScript code (displayed in the textarea) to support both the major vendors' browsers. The JavaScript code can then be cut and pasted into your own scripts to create your ideal pop-up window.

The example pop-up window shown in Figure 6-7 has no tool, status, or scroll bars of any kind, and is 200 pixels wide by 200 pixels high. As has been seen in previous examples, the syntax of the window object's open() method is fairly straightforward:

Figure 6-6

The Pop-up Window Generator in action.

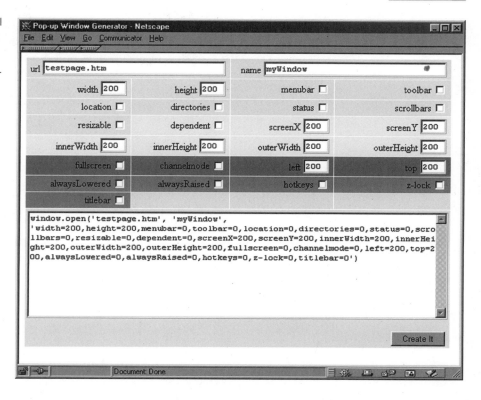

Figure 6-7

A generated pop-up window.

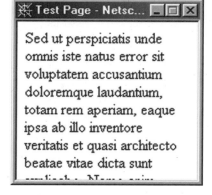

```
handle = window.open(URL, name, features)
```

The three parameters specify the URL to be loaded into the pop-up window, the name of the pop-up window, and the pop-up window's features. Once created, a reference or handle to the pop-up window is returned by the `open()` method. For example, the following JavaScript code will create a new window, named `myWindow` and loaded with `myPage.htm`, with a `width` of `640` pixels and a `height` of `480` pixels:

```
var handle = window.open(
  'myPage.htm',
  'myWindow',
  'width=640,height=480'
);
```

The window reference held in the `handle` variable can be used to close the window at a later time with:

```
handle.close();
```

The status of the window can also be detected to see if the window is closed with:

```
if (handle.closed) { ... }
```

or still open with:

```
if (!handle.closed) { ... }
```

The contents of the window can be changed with:

```
handle.href = 'another.htm';
```

The name of the window can be used as a target within a link with:

```
<a href="more.htm" target="myWindow">text link</a>
```

The `features` parameter needs further explanation. It is a string of comma-separated lists of name/value pairs. Each pair specifies the name and value of a particular window feature—for example, width and height, whether toolbars should be shown, and so on. Note that it is extremely important that there are no spaces within the `features` string parameter.

## Pop-up Window Generator Source Code

../chapter6/generator/index.htm

The *index.htm* page contains the two forms that allow the user to specify the window features and the generator to display the cut and paste code, along with the JavaScript code necessary to read the form values and then generate the pop-up window itself.

The global `windowHandler` variable is used later to hold the reference returned by the `open()` method. It needs to be a global variable and not a local variable within a function somewhere. Otherwise, the reference will be lost once the function ends:

```
var windowHandle;
```

The `createWindow()` function accepts two parameters that reference the `input` and `output` forms, and it builds up the data used to create a pop-up window:

```
function createWindow(input, output) {
```

First, the `value` property of the `url` form field is retrieved and held in local `url` variable:

```
var url = input.url.value;
```

Then the `value` property of the `name` form field is retrieved and held in the local `name` variable:

```
var name = input.name.value;
```

The local features variable is initialized:

```
var features = '';
```

The function then loops through all the elements in the `input` form, appending the `name` and either the value of the `checked` property of any form field with a `type` property equal to `checkbox`, or the `value` property of any form field with a `type` property of `text` not named `url` or `name`, to a local `features` variable, each prefixed with a comma character ( , ):

```
for (var i=0; i<input.elements.length; i++) {
   if (input.elements[i].type == 'checkbox')
      features += ',' + input.elements[i].name + '=' +
                     (input.elements[i].checked - 0);

   if (input.elements[i].type == 'text' &&
       input.elements[i].name != 'url' &&
       input.elements[i].name != 'name')
```

```
        features += ',' + input.elements[i].name + '=' +
                    (input.elements[i].value);
  }
```

The first comma character is stripped from the start of the `features` variable value:

```
  features = features.substring(1);
```

If a pop-up window has already been opened by the generator—that is, `windowHandle` is not `null` and the window referenced by the `windowHandle` global variable has not been closed—then the `windowHandle` window is closed using the `window` object's `close()` method:

```
  if (windowHandle && !windowHandle.closed)
    windowHandle.close();
```

The pop-up window is then opened using the values of the local variables `url`, `name`, and `features`, passing the returned window reference to the global `windowHandle` variable:

```
  windowHandle = window.open(url, name, features);
```

Finally, the `output` form's `debug` form field's `value` is updated to display the typical JavaScript code necessary to open a pop-up window of the required window features:

```
  output.debug.value =
    'window.open(\'' + url + '\', \'' +
    name + '\', \'' + features + '\')';
}
```

The `input` form, minus the table HTML markup, simply contains several `text` and `checkbox` form fields, each of which is named after either the `open()` method parameter or window feature they represent:

```
<form name="input">
<input type="text" size="35" name="url" value="testpage.htm">
<input type="text" size="35" name="name" value="myWindow">
<input type="text" size="4" name="width" value="200">
<input type="text" size="4" name="height" value="200">
<input type="checkbox" name="menubar">
<input type="checkbox" name="toolbar">
<input type="checkbox" name="location">
<input type="checkbox" name="directories">
<input type="checkbox" name="status">
<input type="checkbox" name="scrollbars">
<input type="checkbox" name="resizable">
```

```
<input type="checkbox" name="dependent">
<input type="text" size="4" name="screenX" value="200">
<input type="text" size="4" name="screenY" value="200">
<input type="text" size="4" name="innerWidth" value="200">
<input type="text" size="4" name="innerHeight" value="200">
<input type="text" size="4" name="outerWidth" value="200">
<input type="text" size="4" name="outerHeight" value="200">
<input type="checkbox" name="fullscreen">
<input type="checkbox" name="channelmode">
<input type="text" size="4" name="left" value="200">
<input type="text" size="4" name="top" value="200">
<input type="checkbox" name="alwaysLowered">
<input type="checkbox" name="alwaysRaised">
<input type="checkbox" name="hotkeys">
<input type="checkbox" name="z-lock">
<input type="checkbox" name="titlebar">
</form>
```

The `output` form contains a `textarea` named `debug` to hold the generated JavaScript code, as well as a `button` form field that when clicked invokes the `createWindow()` function, passing a reference to both the `input` and `output` forms:

```
<form name="output">
<textarea name="debug" rows="10" cols="80" wrap="virtual">
</textarea>
<input type="button" value=" Create It "
 onClick="createWindow(document.input, this.form)">
</form>
```

The Pop-up Window Generator can be used again and again to try out different window feature settings and then apply them immediately to see the result.

## Window Features

A complete list of all the available window features and which version of JavaScript or browser they are supported by is shown in Table 6-1.

# Dictionary Pop-up

The Dictionary Pop-up application shows how to make use of pop-up windows to display the dictionary definition of words or phrases in hypertext links. Rather than load a whole new page into the current window to display the dictionary definition, a pop-up window allows the user to see the definition without losing his or her place in the main window.

**TABLE 6-1**

Complete list of window features used in the window object's open() method.

| Feature | Supported by | Description |
| --- | --- | --- |
| width | JavaScript 1.0 | Specifies the width in pixels of the window. In Navigator requires UniversalBrowserWrite privilege to set the value to less than 100. |
| height | JavaScript 1.0 | Specifies the height in pixels of the window. In Navigator requires UniversalBrowserWrite privilege to set the value to less than 100. |
| menubar | JavaScript 1.0 | Controls the display of the menu bar. Value is either 1, 0, yes, or no. |
| toolbar | JavaScript 1.0 | Controls the display of the toolbar. Value is either 1, 0, yes, or no. |
| location | JavaScript 1.0 | Controls the display of the location bar. Value is either 1, 0, yes, or no. |
| directories | JavaScript 1.0 | Controls the display of the directory bar. Value is either 1, 0, yes, or no. |
| status | JavaScript 1.0 | Controls the display of the status bar. Value is either 1, 0, yes, or no. |
| scrollbars | JavaScript 1.0 | Controls the display of the scroll bars. Value is either 1, 0, yes, or no. |
| resizable | JavaScript 1.0 | Specifies whether the window can be resized. Value is either 1, 0, yes, or no. |
| dependent | Navigator 4 | Specifies whether the pop-up window is closed automatically when the opener window is closed. Value is either 1, 0, yes, or no. |
| screenX | Navigator 4 | Specifies the x-coordinate in pixels of the windows. Requires UniversalBrowserWrite privilege to place the window off-screen. |
| screenY | Navigator 4 | Specifies the y-coordinate in pixels of the window. Requires UniversalBrowserWrite privilege to place the window off-screen. |
| innerWidth | Navigator 4 | Specifies the width in pixels of the document. |
| innerHeight | Navigator 4 | Specifies the height in pixels of the document. |
| outerWidth | Navigator 4 | Specifies the total width in pixels of the window. |
| outerHeight | Navigator 4 | Specifies the total height in pixels of the window. |
| fullscreen | Explorer 4 | Specifies whether the window is opened in full-screen mode. Value is either 1, 0, yes, or no. |

**TABLE 6-1**

Complete list of window features used in the window object's open() method. (Continued)

| Feature | Supported by | Description |
|---------|--------------|-------------|
| channelmode | Explorer 4 | Specifies whether the window is opened in channel mode. Value is either 1, 0, yes, or no. |
| left | Explorer 4 | Specifies the x-coordinate in pixels of the windows. |
| top | Explorer 4 | Specifies the y-coordinate in pixels of the window. |
| alwaysLowered | Navigator 4 | Specifies whether the window should always remain beneath all other windows. Value is either 1, 0, yes, or no. Requires UniversalBrowserWrite privilege. |
| alwaysRaised | Navigator 4 | Specifies whether the window should always remain above all other windows. Value is either 1, 0, yes, or no. Requires UniversalBrowserWrite privilege. |
| hotkeys | Navigator 4 | Specifies whether keyboard hot keys should be enabled. Value is either 1, 0, yes, or no. Requires UniversalBrowserWrite privilege. |
| z-lock | Navigator 4 | Value is either 1, 0, yes, or no. Requires UniversalBrowserWrite privilege. |
| titlebar | Navigator 4 | Specifies whether the window should always remain in its current position above and beneath other windows. Value is either 1, 0, yes, or no. Requires UniversalBrowserWrite privilege. |

The application is sensitive to the text within the hypertext link. It first opens the pop-up window and then loads one of many different external JavaScript source files, each containing the definition of a range of words or phrases. This avoids having to load the entire dictionary when the user is interested in the definition of just one word.

**NOTE:** *As the Dictionary Popup application passes data from the main window to the pop-up window using the search property of a URL, it will not work offline in Internet Explorer.*

# Dictionary Popup Source Code—index.htm

**../chapter6/dictionary/index.htm**

The *index.htm* page is just a typical web page with several hypertext links, which instead of loading a normal page uses the `onClick` event handler to invoke the `d()` function, passing a reference to `this` current link:

```
<a href="#" onClick="return d(this)">connect</a> a
<a href="#" onClick="return d(this)">telephone line</a> to a
<a href="#" onClick="return d(this)">computer</a> using a
<a href="#" onClick="return d(this)">modem</a> to enable you to
<a href="#" onClick="return d(this)">send</a> electronic
<a href="#" onClick="return d(this)">messages</a>
<a href="#" onClick="return d(this)">around</a> the world
```

The `d()` function opens a pop-up window to contain the dictionary definition of the `text` property of the passed `what` link reference. The `text` property is first escaped using the global `escape()` method (to convert any non-alphanumeric characters into an equivalent Latin-1 encoded character) and then appended to the URL `define.htm?`, which is then used as the first parameter to the `window` object's `open()` method

```
function d(what) {
  myFloater = window.open(
    'define.htm' + '?' + escape(what.text),
    'myWindow',
    'width=300,height=300'
  )
```

The `d()` function returns `false` to the `onClick` event handler to cancel the link's default action—which would have been to jump to the top of the current page:

```
  return false;
}
```

If the user clicks on the hypertext link for `telephone line`, then the `d()` function would load the URL `define.htm?telephone%20line` into the pop-up window. The space character has been converted by the global `escape()` function into `%20`.

Figure 6-8 shows a page with hypertext links and the resultant pop-up window that shows the dictionary definition for `modem`.

**Figure 6-8**
Dictionary Pop-up
showing the
dictionary definition
of modem.

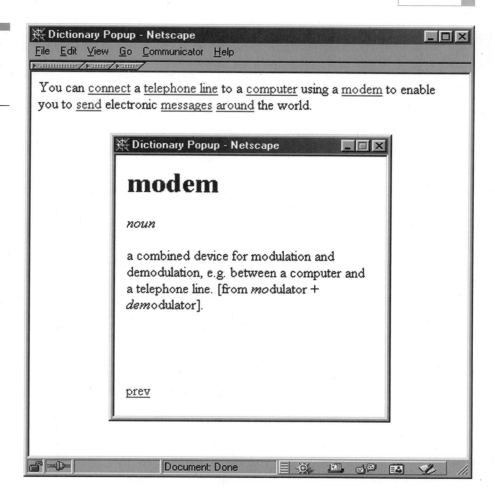

## Dictionary Pop-up Source Code—define.htm

../chapter6/dictionary/define.htm

The *define.htm* page, loaded into the pop-up window, extracts the passed `search` property, loads the relevant external JavaScript source file containing the dictionary definition, and then displays the definition.

The external JavaScript source files each create many instances of the `Def` object. The *define.htm* page includes both the `Def` object constructor and a `myDef` array to hold all the `Def` objects created by one of the external JavaScript source files. Chapter 4 "Arrays and Objects" explains how to define and use object constructors in detail. The `Def` object constructor accepts three parameters—`word`, `type`, and `def`, each of which are used to initialize the values of like-named properties:

```
function Def(word, type, def) {
  this.word = word;
  this.type = type;
  this.def  = def
}

function setDef(word, type, def) {
  myDef[item++] = new Def(word, type, def);
}

var item = 0;

var myDef = new Array();
```

The `search` property of the current `window` object's `location` is retrieved and then unescaped using the global `unescape()` method, the result of which is assigned to the global `word` variable:

```
var word = unescape(window.location.search.substring(1));
```

The first character of the `word` variable is obtained using the `String` object's `substring()` method and assigned to the global `letter` variable:

```
var letter = word.substring(0,1);
```

The `letter` variable along with the suffix `.js` is then used as the `src` attribute of the start script tag written out to the document:

```
document.write(
  '<script language="JavaScript" src="' + letter + '.js">' +
  '<\/script>'
);
//--></script>
```

At this point, the existing JavaScript code is ended with an end script tag. This forces the browser to immediately load and run the external JavaScript source file. Once the external JavaScript source file has loaded and has created all the necessary `Def` objects, we can continue with the rest of the JavaScript code in the *define.htm* page:

```
<script language="JavaScript"><!--
```

A global Boolean `found` variable is initialized to `false`:

```
var found = false;
```

The code then loops through every `Def` object held in the `myDef` array until either the end of the array is reached or the global Boolean `found` variable is no longer `false`:

```
for (var i=0; i<item || !found; i++) {
```

If the global `word` variable is found anywhere within the current `Def` object's `word` property, then the global Boolean `found` variable is set to `true`. Also, the local `output` variable is built up to contain the HTML markup necessary to display the dictionary definition of the current `Def` object and then written out to the document, before finally breaking out of the loop using the `break` statement:

```
if (word.indexOf(myDef[i].word) != -1) {
  found = true;

  var output = '';

  output +=
    '<table width="100%" height="100%">' +
    '<tr><td valign="top">' +
    '<h1>' + myDef[i].word + '</h1>' +
    '<p><em>' + myDef[i].type + '</em></p>' +
    '<p>' + myDef[i].def + '</p>' +
    '</td></tr></table>';

  document.write(output);
  break;
  }
}
```

Once the loop finishes, if the dictionary definition was not found, then a "Definition not found" message is displayed:

```
if (!found)
  document.write(
    '<h1>' + word + '</h1>' +
    '<p>Definition not found</p>'
  );
```

It is important to note that the first successful match ends the loop. Therefore, if you include definitions for words with similar roots—for example, `telephone`, `telephone line`, and `telephone call`—and if you want a hypertext link for `telephone` to give the definition of `tele-phone` as opposed to `telephone line`, then the definition of `tele-`

phone **must appear before** telephone line **in the appropriate external JavaScript source file.**

## Dictionary Popup Source Code—External JavaScript Source File

../chapter6/dictionary/*.js

A typical external JavaScript source file simply contains one or many calls to the setDef() function held in the *define.htm* page, which calls the Def constructor and then adds the newly created Def object to the myDef array:

```
setDef(
  'computer',
  'noun',
  'an electronic machine that arranges information and ' +
  'stores it on disks or tapes, using a set of instructions ' +
  'called a program.'
);
setDef(
  'connect',
  '</em><strong>connects connecting connected</strong><em> verb',
  'to link up two things.<p><em><strong>Connecting</strong> ' +
  'telephone to a computer</em>.'
);
```

The Dictionary Pop-up source code on the CD-ROM additionally allows the user to navigate backward and forward between all the dictionary definitions within the currently loaded external JavaScript source code.

# Family Tree

The Family Tree application uses two frames to display two views representing each person within a family tree. The top half of the browser contains a frame that shows the father, mother, spouse, and children of the current person being viewed in the tree. The bottom half of the browser contains a page that shows the details of the current person—for instance, date and place of birth/death, age in years, months and days, and names of spouse and children. When the mouse pointer moves across one hypertext link in the top half of the browser window, the details in the bottom half are updated with the details of the person represented by the hypertext link. When the hypertext link is clicked, the displayed tree structure in the top half is replaced with a clicked-on person's tree structure, and the bottom half of the browser is updated to show that clicked-on person's details.

Figure 6-9 shows the Family Tree application in action, displaying the details for Queen Elizabeth II, and all her direct relations, including mother, father, spouse, and children.

Figure 6-10 shows the effect of moving the mouse pointer over the hypertext link for the spouse of Queen Elizabeth (i.e., Prince Philip).

Figure 6-11 shows the effect of clicking on the hypertext link for the eldest child of Queen Elizabeth (i.e., Prince Charles).

**Figure 6-9**
The immediate family tree for Queen Elizabeth.

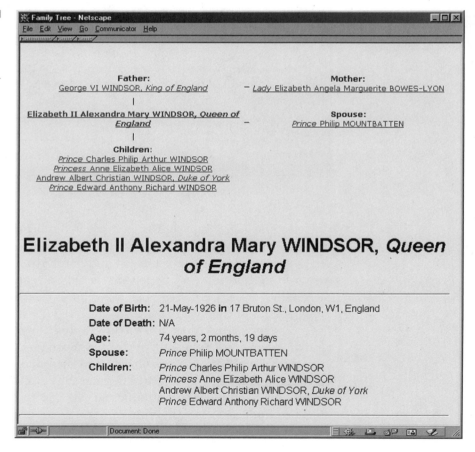

**Figure 6-10**
The details for Prince
Philip, spouse of
Queen Elizabeth.

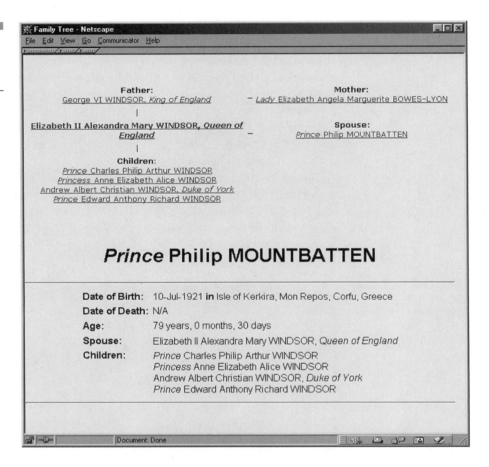

**Figure 6-10**
The details for Prince Philip, spouse of Queen Elizabeth.

It soon becomes apparent that there is duplication of data among all the people in a particular family tree—for instance, the father of one person is the son, brother, or spouse of another. Rather than hold this duplicate information in every page that would be required to hold the complete family tree, we instead use a `Person` object to represent each and every person in the family tree.

Once a `Person` object has been created for each person, we then resolve everyone's relations by first referencing their father, mother, spouse, and children `Person` objects and then updating the properties of each individual `Person` object to include the details of its relation's properties. For example, the value of the `father` property of one `Person` object is updated with the value of the `name` property of the `Person` object that represents its father.

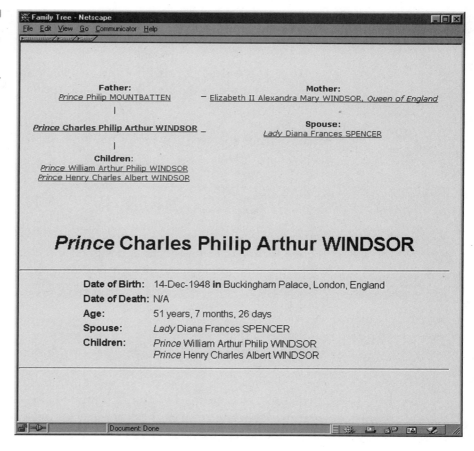

**Figure 6-11**
The immediate family tree for Prince Charles.

## Family Tree Source Code—index.htm

The *index.htm* includes the frameset definition along with nearly all the JavaScript code in the Family Tree application. An external JavaScript source file containing all the code necessary to generate a specific family tree—in this case the British Royal Family—is loaded into *index.htm*. Because both two frames are overwritten during the running of the application, it is necessary to hold the code and object references safe while pages are being overwritten; otherwise, the code and object references will be lost. Therefore, we hold the code and object references in the top frameset container document, since it will not be overwritten or replaced while the application is running.

*On the CD*

**../chapter6/tree/index.htm**

The `pad()` and `y2k()` utility functions seen and described in earlier examples are used in the Family Tree application but not shown here to save space.

As the Family Tree application calculates and displays the age of each person within the tree, an array named `months` holds all the month names of the year:

```
var months = new Array(
  'Jan','Feb','Mar','Apr','May','Jun',
  'Jul','Aug','Sep','Oct','Nov','Dec'
);
```

The current date and time is assigned to the global `today` variable using the `Date` constructor, which is then used to extract the current year (`thisYear`), the current month (`thisMonth`), and the current date of the month (`thisDay`):

```
var today     = new Date();
var thisYear  = y2k(today.getYear());
var thisMonth = today.getMonth()+1;
var thisDay   = today.getDate();
```

The `HowOld()` utility function accepts the day, month, and year of two separate dates and returns the difference between the two dates (i.e., the age) in years, months, and days:

```
function HowOld(day,month,year,Day,Month,Year) {
  var years = Year - year, months = days = 0;

  if (Month >= month) months = Month - month;
  else { years—; months = Month + 12 - month; }

  if (Day >= day) days = Day - day;
  else {
    if (months > 0) months—;
    else { years—; months+=11; }
    days = Day + 31 - day;
  }

  if (years < 0) return '';
  if ((years == 0) && (months == 0) && (days == 0)) return '';

  return years  + ' years, ' +
         months + ' months, ' +
         days   + ' days';
}
```

Chapter 7 "Date and Time" describes the HowOld() function, along with other date and time functions, in more detail.

The setPerson() function is invoked to create Person objects using the Person object constructor and to append the resultant object reference to the PersonArray array:

```
function setPerson(
    name, dobDay, dobMonth, dobYear, dobLocation,
        dodDay, dodMonth, dodYear, dodLocation) {
    return PersonArray[PersonArrayIndex++] =
    new Person(name, dobDay, dobMonth, dobYear, dobLocation,
                dodDay, dodMonth, dodYear, dodLocation);
}
```

The Person object constructor initializes the Person object based on the passed parameters:

```
function Person(
    name, dobDay, dobMonth, dobYear, dobLocation,
        dodDay, dodMonth, dodYear, dodLocation) {
```

The No property is set to the position of this Person object within the PersonArray array. This is used later to allow hypertext links to reference Person object by number rather than by an object reference:

```
    this.No = PersonArrayIndex - 1;
    this.name = name;
```

If the dobDay, dobMonth, and dobYear date of birth parameters are all nonzero (i.e., the date of birth is known), then the birth property is set to a formatted date string. Otherwise, it is set to 'unknown':

```
    if (dobDay != 0 && dobMonth !=0 && dobYear !=0)
      this.birth =
        pad(dobDay,2) + '-' + months[dobMonth] + '-' +
        y2k(dobYear) + ' <strong>in</strong> ' + dobLocation;
    else
      this.birth = 'unknown';
```

This is the same with the date of death, except that if the date of birth is known (signified by the birth property not being set to 'unknown'), then the age of the person is calculated, either using his or her date of death or the current date, and assigned to the age property using the HowOld() function:

```
    if (dodDay != 0 && dodMonth !=0 && dodYear !=0) {
      this.death =
```

```
          pad(dodDay,2) + '-' + months[dodMonth] + '-' +
          y2k(dodYear) + ' <strong>in</strong> ' + dodLocation;
       if (this.birth != 'unknown')
          this.age = HowOld(dobDay, dobMonth, dobYear,
                            dodDay, dodMonth, dodYear);
       else
          this.age = 'unknown';
    }
    else {
       this.death = 'N/A';
       if (this.birth != 'unknown')
          this.age = HowOld(dobDay, dobMonth, dobYear,
                            thisDay, thisMonth, thisYear);
       else
          this.age = 'unknown';
    }
```

At this point, when a `Person` object is being created, it is highly likely that the `Person` objects for the immediate relatives have not yet been constructed. Therefore, the properties that relate to the person's father, mother, spouse, and children are simply left initialized as either empty strings or as zero. Once all the `Person` objects have been created, each `Person` object's relatives will be resolved:

```
// The following details will all be resolved later:

this.father = ''; this.fatherNo = 0;
this.mother = ''; this.motherNo = 0;
this.spouse = ''; this.spouseNo = 0;
this.children = 0;
```

The `details` property is just initialized with the minimum of HTML markup. It is updated later with the HTML markup necessary to display all of a persons immediate relations:

```
this.details = '<body bgcolor="papayawhip"></body>';
```

Here we see our first-ever use of our own object method. The `setRelations` property is set to the name of another JavaScript function—in this case `resolveRelations()`. Therefore, whenever a `Person` object's `setRelations()` method is used, the `resolveRelations()` function is invoked. The difference is that whenever a method is used, it is passed a reference to the object it is being used on—that is, the `this` reference:

```
    this.setRelations = resolveRelations;
}
```

The `resolveRelations()` function is the function used whenever a `Person` object's `setRelations()` method is invoked. It is used to resolve the partly initialized `Person` object properties, and is therefore used on each `Person` object and passed a reference to each `Person` object that represents the father, mother, spouse, and children:

```
function resolveRelations(father, mother, spouse) {
```

It may initially look as though we simply accept `father`, `mother`, and `spouse` parameters, but this is not the case as will be seen a little later.

Every person that ever lived, with the exception of Adam and Eve, has a mother and father. An individual's mother or father may not be known—in which case an anonymous `Person` object is used. However, it seems sensible to always expect, as a minimum, a `father` and `mother` object reference with an optional `spouse` object reference as input to the `resolveRelations()` function.

The function updates the `this` object's `father`, `mother`, `fatherNo`, and `motherNo` properties, using the `name` and `No` properties of the `father` and `mother` objects:

```
this.father   = father.name;
this.fatherNo = father.No;
this.mother   = mother.name;
this.motherNo = mother.No;
```

If a `spouse` object reference was passed as input to the function (i.e., the `spouse` parameter is not null), then the function updates the `this` object's `spouse` and `spouseNo` properties, using the `name` and `No` properties of the `spouse` object:

```
if (spouse) {
  this.spouse = spouse.name;
  this.spouseNo = spouse.No;
}
```

Unlike a person's mother and father, where it is usual to only register one each in a family tree, it is usual for a person to have none, one, or many children. This varying number of children object references makes it awkward to specify a known number of named parameters as input to the function. Therefore, we resort to unnamed function parameters or arguments. Each function has an `arguments` array, and each element directly relates to a passed input parameter. To access the `arguments` array, we simply use the name of the function followed by the `arguments` array—for example, `resolveRelations.arguments`. Because the `father`, `mother`, and `spouse` parameters relate directly to the first three elements of the array (i.e., `resolveRelations.arguments[0]`,

resolveRelations.arguments[1], and resolveRelations.argu-
ments[2]), we loop from the next-possible element (i.e.,
resolveRelations.arguments[3]) to the end of the array using the
arguments array's length property:

```
var length = resolveRelations.arguments.length;
for (var i = 3; i < length; i++, this.children++) {
```

For each additional object reference passed as input to the function,
additional childXX and childXXNo properties are added to the this
object, where XX is an increasing integer, with the values of the current
arguments object references name and No properties:

```
this['child' + this.children] =
   resolveRelations.arguments[i].name;
this['child' + this.children + 'No'] =
   resolveRelations.arguments[i].No;
}
```

At this point all of the Person object's immediate relatives have been
resolved. All that is needed is to populate the details property with the
HTML markup necessary to display all of a person's details:

```
var details =
  '<center><h1><font face="Arial">' +
  this.name + '</font></h1><hr><table>' +

  '<tr><td valign="top"><font face="Arial">' +
  '<strong>Date of Birth:</strong>' +
  '</font></td><td valign="top"><font face="Arial">' +
  this.birth +
  '</font></td></tr>' +

  '<tr><td valign="top"><font face="Arial">' +
  '<strong>Date of Death:</strong>' +
  '</font></td><td valign="top"><font face="Arial">' +
  this.death +
  '</font></td></tr>' +

  '<tr><td valign="top"><font face="Arial">' +
  '<strong>Age:</strong>' +
  '</font></td><td valign="top"><font face="Arial">' +
  this.age +
  '</font></td></tr>' +

  '<tr><td valign="top"><font face="Arial">' +
  '<strong>Spouse:</strong>' +
  '</font></td><td valign="top"><font face="Arial">' +
  this.spouse +
  '</font></td></tr>' +
```

```
'<tr><td valign="top"><font face="Arial">' +
'<strong>Children:</strong>' +
'</font></td><td valign="top"><font face="Arial">';

for (var i=0; i<this.children; i++)
  details += this['child' + i] + '<br>';

details += '</font></td></tr></table></center><hr>';

this.details =
  '<body bgcolor="papayawhip">' + details + '</body>';
}
```

All that is needed now is the creation of all the `Person` objects to be held in a family tree. Before we do so, to enable dates to be entered as easily identifiable values, we define integer variables for each month of the year. This allows dates of birth and dates of death to be passed as input to the `setPerson()` function using the format `4, Jan, 1965`, (i.e., the 4th of January 1965):

```
var Jan=1, Feb=2, Mar=3, Apr=4, May=5, Jun=6,
    Jul=7, Aug=8, Sep=9, Cct=10, Nov=11, Dec=12;
```

The `PersonArrayIndex` variable and `PersonArray` array are initialized:

```
var PersonArrayIndex = 0;
var PersonArray = new Array();
```

An anonymous `Person` object is created (anon). This object, positioned at element zero of the `PersonArray` array, is used as a terminator. In other words, beyond this point, we know no further information. This can be used to signify an unknown father or mother:

```
// Define an unknown person:

var anon = setPerson('','',0,0,0,'',0,0,0,'','','');
```

The *royal.js* external JavaScript source file contains code to create `Person` objects for each and every person in the British Royal Family. Once created, each `Person` object's `father`, `mother`, `spouse`, and `children` properties are resolved using the aforementioned `resolveRelations()` function.

```
<script language="JavaScript" src="royal.js"></script>
```

Finally, we include a frameset to load the *topframe.htm* page into the topFrame frame, and *botframe.htm* into the botFrame frame:

```
<frameset rows="50%,*">
<frame src="topframe.htm" name="topFrame">
<frame src="botframe.htm" name="botFrame">
</frameset>
```

There are two remaining functions in *index.htm* that we have not discussed. The showTree() function is invoked from within the topFrame frame whenever it is loaded. The function is passed an index parameter of a Person object in the PersonArray array, which it uses to build up a tree view of that person and their immediate relations.

Each person in this tree is represented with a hypertext link, which when hovered over invokes the updateDetails() function (held within the *topframe.htm* page held in the topFrame frame), passing the value of their entry position within the PersonArray array, and when clicked invokes the show() function in the parent frame (i.e., the *index.htm* page).

```
function showTree(index) {
```

First, we initialize the local variables fatherNo, motherNo, and spouseNo to the values of the fatherNo, motherNo, and spouseNo properties of the index Person object within the PersonArray array:

```
var fatherNo = PersonArray[index].fatherNo;
var motherNo = PersonArray[index].motherNo;
var spouseNo = PersonArray[index].spouseNo;
```

Next, we initialize a local output variable:

```
var output = '';
```

The output variable is used to build up the HTML to be passed back to the topFrame frame:

```
output +=
  '<center>' +
  '<table height="100%"><tr><td>' +

  '<table>' +

  '<tr><td align="center"><strong>Father:</strong><br>' +
  '<a href="javascript:parent.show(' + fatherNo + ')" ' +
  'onMouseover="updateDetails(' + fatherNo + ')">' +
  PersonArray[index].father + '</a></td>' +
```

```
'<td>_</td>' +

'<td align="center"><strong>Mother:</strong><br>' +
'<a href="javascript:parent.show(' + motherNo + ')" ' +
'onMouseover="updateDetails(' + motherNo + ')">' +
PersonArray[index].mother + '</a></td></tr>' +

'<tr><td align="center">|<td></td></td><td></td></tr>' +
'<tr><td align="center">' +
'<a href="javascript:parent.show(0)" ' +
'onMouseover="updateDetails(' + index + ')" ><strong>' +
PersonArray[index].name + '</strong></a></td>' +

'<td>_</td>' +
'<td align="center"><strong>Spouse:</strong><br>' +
'<a href="javascript:parent.show(' + spouseNo + ')" ' +
'onMouseover="updateDetails(' + spouseNo + ')">' +
PersonArray[index].spouse + '</a></td></tr>' +

'<tr><td align="center">|</td><td></td><td></td></tr>' +

'<tr><td align="center"><strong>Children</strong>:<br>';
for (var i=0; i<PersonArray[index].children; i++) {
var childNo = PersonArray[index]['child' + i + 'No'];

output +=
   '<a href="javascript:parent.show(' + childNo + ')" ' +
   'onMouseover="updateDetails(' + childNo + ')">' +
   PersonArray[index]['child' + i] + '</a><br>';
}

output +=
   '</td><td></td><td></td></tr></table>' +
   '</td></tr></table>' +
   '</center>';
```

Finally, the value of the `output` variable is passed back to the `topFrame` frame, which then writes it out to the document:

```
   return output;
}
```

The `show()` function is invoked whenever a user clicks on one of the hypertext links within the `topFrame` frame:

```
function show(index) {
```

If the passed `index` parameter is not zero—that is, the user hasn't clicked the link representing the central person within the tree—then the global `PersonToShow` variable is updated with the value of the `index` parameter, and both the `topFrame` and `botFrame` frames have their contents reloaded, causing the family tree to be redisplayed with a new person at the center:

```
if (index != 0) {
  PersonToShow = index;
  window.topFrame.location.href = 'topframe.htm';
  window.botFrame.location.href = 'botframe.htm';
}
}
```

# Family Trees Source Code - royal.js

../chapter6/tree/royal.js

The *royal.js* external source file contains all the code necessary for a specific family tree—in this case, the British Royal Family. For your own application, you only need to replace this file with another and update the *index.htm* page to point to your own source file.

We first define all the Person objects in the complete family tree using the setPerson() function, passing the person's name; day, month, and year of birth; place of birth; day, month, and year of death; and finally place of death. We use friendly global variable names to hold the returned object reference, in this case, gVI, which stands for *George the Sixth*. It makes it easier to resolve relations later on:

```
var gVI = setPerson(
  'George VI WINDSOR, <em>King of England</em>',
  14,Dec,1895,
  'York Cottage, Sandringham, Norfolk, England',
  6,Feb,1952,
  'Sandringham, Norfolk, England'
);
```

Where a person is still living, the day, month, and year of death are all passed as zeros, and the place of death as an empty string:

```
var e_a_m = setPerson(
  '<em>Lady</em> Elizabeth Angela Marguerite BOWES-LYON',
  4,Aug,1900,
  'London, England',
  0,0,0,
  ''
);

var eII = setPerson(
  'Elizabeth II Alexandra Mary WINDSOR, <em>Queen of England</em>',
  21,Apr,1926,
  '17 Bruton St., London, W1, England',
```

```
     0,0,0,
     ' '
);

var pp = setPerson(
  '<em>Prince</em> Philip MOUNTBATTEN',
  10,Jun,1921,
  'Isle of Kerkira, Mon Repos, Corfu, Greece'
  ,0,0,0,
  ' '
);

var pc = setPerson(
  '<em>Prince</em> Charles Philip Arthur WINDSOR',
  14,Nov,1948,
  'Buckingham Palace, London, England',
  0,0,0,
  ' '
);

 var psa = setPerson(
  '<em>Princess</em> Anne Elizabeth Alice WINDSOR',
  15,Aug,1950,
  'Clarence House, St. James, England',
  0,0,0,
  ' '
);

 var pa = setPerson(
  'Andrew Albert Christian WINDSOR, <em>Duke of York</em>',
  19,Feb,1960,
  'Belgian Suite, Buckingham Palace, England',
  0,0,0,''
);

 var pe = setPerson(
  '<em>Prince</em> Edward Anthony Richard WINDSOR',
  10,Mar,1964,
  'Buckingham Palace, London, England',
  0,0,0,
  ' '
);
```

Once all the `Person` objects have been defined, we now need to resolve each person's relations. To indicate boundaries, we use the anonymous anon terminator `Person` object as the father and mother object references for both *George the Sixth* (`gVI`) and *the Queen Mother* (`e_a_m`), but we pass the *Queen Mother* (`e_a_m`) as the spouse of *George the Sixth*, then *George the Sixth* as the spouse of the *Queen Mother*, and then *Queen Elizabeth* (`eII`) and *Princess Margaret* (`psm`) as children of both *George the Sixth* and the *Queen Mother*:

```
gVI.setRelations(anon, anon, e_a_m, eII, psm);
e_a_m.setRelations(anon, anon, gVI, eII, psm);
```

With *Queen Elizabeth* we pass *George the Sixth* and the *Queen Mother* as father and mother, respectively, *Prince Philip* (pp) as spouse, and then the four children references *Prince Charles* (pc), *Princess Anne* (psa), *Prince Andrew* (pa), and *Prince Edward* (pe):

```
eII.setRelations(gVI, e_a_m, pp, pc, psa, pa, pe);
```

Once all the relatives of all the persons in the tree are resolved, we pick the default person who should be displayed initially and hold the value in both the global variables details and PersonToShow, in this case *Queen Elizabeth*:

```
var details = PersonToShow = eII.No;
```

# Family Trees Source Code— topframe.htm

../chapter6/tree/topframe.htm

The *topframe.htm* page loaded into the topFrame frame performs three purposes. It invokes the parent frame's showTree() function, passing the parent frame's PersonToShow global variable, and then writes the returned value to the document—thus showing the family tree around a central person.

When any of the hypertext links written out to the document are hovered over with the mouse pointer, the updateDetails() function is invoked, which opens, writes, and then closes the parent frame's botFrame frame, using as output the value of the parent frame's PersonArray array's index entries' Person object's details property, but only if the parent frame's details global variable is not already equal to index, before then setting it as such:

```
function updateDetails(index) {
  if (index != parent.details) {
    parent.botFrame.document.open();
    parent.botFrame.document.write(
      parent.PersonArray[index].details
    );
    parent.botFrame.document.close();
    parent.details = index;
  }
}

document.write(parent.showTree(parent.PersonToShow));
```

As an indirect result of the frame having its contents reloaded by the show() function in *index.htm*, the entire page is rewritten based on the new value of the parent frame's PersonToShow global variable.

# Family Tree Source Code— botframe.htm

../chapter6/tree/botframe.htm

The botframe.htm page loaded into the botFrame frame serves two purposes. When first loaded, it writes out to the document the value of the details property of the parent frame's PersonArray array's parent. PersonToShow entries' Person object:

```
document.write(
  parent.PersonArray[parent.PersonToShow].details
);
```

Again, as an indirect result of the frame having its contents reloaded by the show() function in *index.htm*, the entire page is rewritten based on the new value of the parent frame's PersonToShow global variable.

The Family Tree application on the CD-ROM includes an extended version of the British Royal Family Tree.

# A JavaScript Debugging Window

Writing an application as complicated as the previous family tree can be painful at times. Without knowing what is happening within the code, it can be extremely difficult to find and fix bugs in the code. One possible solution is to include document.write() statements through the code to highlight the status of variable, object properties, and function input parameters, but this can and does affect the page while it is being rendered, and the visible information can be lost when a page is reloaded. Another alternative is to use alert() statements to highlight the information. This can soon become annoying when used inside loops, as it becomes impossible to close the ever-increasing number of alert message windows.

This is where a debugging window comes to the rescue. Rather than create an individual alert message for each debug information required to be seen, we create one debug window. Rather than write out information to the current window, we write it to the debug window instead.

The Debugging Window code is written as an external JavaScript source file. This can then be included within any application code and then invoked using the publicly available debugging functions listed in Table 6-2.

If the debug.js is then removed from the application code at a later date, due to the way the function calls are always preceded with a test for the a window object's debug property, the debugging functions are not called and thus do not generate JavaScript errors.

**TABLE 6-2**

debug.js debugging functions.

| Function | Description |
|---|---|
| debug(msg) | Displays the optional msg message inside the debugging window. If invoked from within a function, also includes name of function. |
| | Usage: |
| | `if (window.debug) debug('Starting... ');` |
| forinDebug(ref, msg) | Displays all the accessible properties of the passed ref object reference with the optional msg message inside the debugging window. If invoked from within a function, also includes name of function. |
| | Usage: |
| | `if (window.debug) forinDebug(window.frames, 'frames!');` |
| startDebug() | If invoked from within a function, includes name of function and a list of the values of all the passed arguments. Also increases the indentation of the debugging window output. |
| | Usage: |
| | `if (window.debug) startDebug();` |
| endDebug() | If invoked from within a function, includes name of function. Also decreases the indentation of the debugging window output. |
| | Usage: |
| | `if (window.debug) endDebug();` |

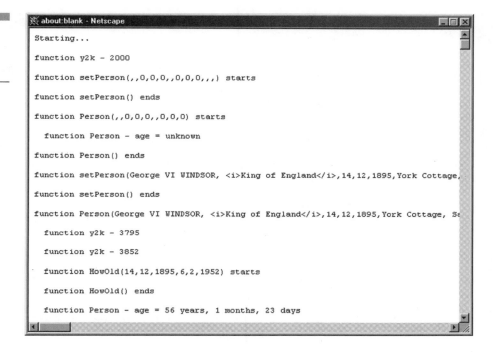

**Figure 6-12**
Debugging the
Family Tree
application 1.

Figure 6-12 shows the debugging window in operation, showing the initial debugging messages output from the Family Tree application.

Figure 6-13 shows the debugging window, this time showing the Family Tree application at the point where the resolveRelations() function/method is invoked, and showing the results of a forinDebug() on a Person object.

# A JavaScript Debugging Window Source Code

**../chapter6/debug/debug.js**

Although all the following global variables are contained within the *debug.js* external JavaScript source file, they may as easily be contained in the application being debugged. In this case, you can provide different values for different applications.

The doDebug global Boolean variable turns on debugging when true and off when false:

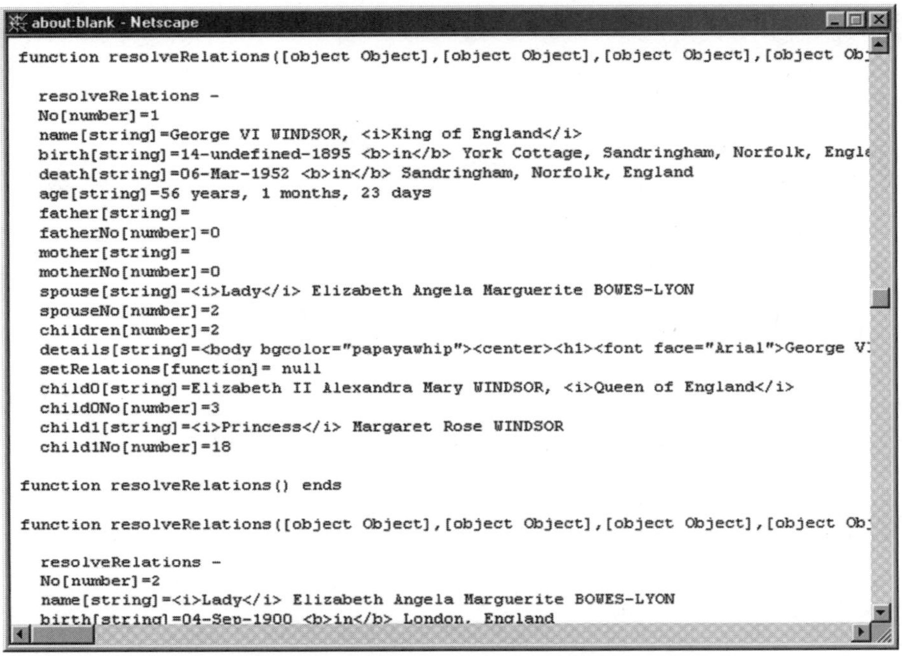

**Figure 6-13**
Debugging the
Family Tree
application 2.

```
about:blank - Netscape                                                    _ □ ×

function resolveRelations([object Object],[object Object],[object Object],[object Ob

  resolveRelations -
  No[number]=1
  name[string]=George VI WINDSOR, <i>King of England</i>
  birth[string]=14-undefined-1895 <b>in</b> York Cottage, Sandringham, Norfolk, Engl
  death[string]=06-Mar-1952 <b>in</b> Sandringham, Norfolk, England
  age[string]=56 years, 1 months, 23 days
  father[string]=
  fatherNo[number]=0
  mother[string]=
  motherNo[number]=0
  spouse[string]=<i>Lady</i> Elizabeth Angela Marguerite BOWES-LYON
  spouseNo[number]=2
  children[number]=2
  details[string]=<body bgcolor="papayawhip"><center><h1><font face="Arial">George V
  setRelations[function]= null
  child0[string]=Elizabeth II Alexandra Mary WINDSOR, <i>Queen of England</i>
  child0No[number]=3
  child1[string]=<i>Princess</i> Margaret Rose WINDSOR
  child1No[number]=18

function resolveRelations() ends

function resolveRelations([object Object],[object Object],[object Object],[object Ob

  resolveRelations -
  No[number]=2
  name[string]=<i>Lady</i> Elizabeth Angela Marguerite BOWES-LYON
  birth[string]=04-Sep-1900 <b>in</b> London, England
```

```
var doDebug = true;
```

The `htmlDebug` global Boolean variable converts left and right angle brackets to `&lt;` and `&gt;` HTML entities suitable for debugging generated HTML markup when `true`. Otherwise, it leaves them alone when `false`:

```
var htmlDebug = true;
```

The `maxDebug` global integer variable controls how many debug messages are written before debugging automatically stops:

```
var maxDebug = 2000;
```

The `cntDebug` global integer variable counts how many debug messages have been written:

```
var cntDebug = 0;
```

The `nstDebug` global string variable holds the current value to be prefixed before all debug messages. It is used for nesting debug messages within debug messages:

```
var nstDebug = '';
```

The `txtDebug` global string variable defines the string prefix to be appended to the `nstDebug` string:

```
var txtDebug = '  ';
```

The `winDebug` global variable holds the Debugging Window's window reference when later opened in the code:

```
var winDebug;
```

The `preDebug` global Boolean variable is used to indicate that a starting prefix tag (i.e., `<pre>`) has been output to the Debugging Window:

```
var preDebug = false;
```

The `nameDebug` global string variable holds the name to be assigned to the Debugging Window when later opened in the code:

```
var nameDebug = 'windowName';
```

If the `doDebug` global Boolean variable is `true`, then a new pop-up window is opened using the name held in `nameDebug`. It assigns the resultant window object reference to `winDebug`, before opening up the `winDebug` window's document ready for writing. It does this using the document object's `open()` method:

```
if (doDebug) {
  winDebug = window.open(
    'about:blank',
    nameDebug,
    'width=700,height=500,scrollbars=1,resize=1'
  );

  winDebug.document.open();
}
```

The `updateDebug()` function, which should not be invoked directly by any application code, writes out the passed `text` parameter to the `winDebug` window:

```
function updateDebug(text) {
```

If the `preDebug` global Boolean is `false`, then a `pre` tag is first output—this only happens once:

```
if (!preDebug) {
   preDebug = true;
   winDebug.document.write('<pre>');
}
```

If the `htmlDebug` global Boolean is `true`, then all instances of left angle (`<`) and right angle (`>`) brackets are replaced with the `&lt;` and `&gt;` HTML entities:

```
if (htmlDebug) {
  text = text.replace(/</g,'&lt;');
  text = text.replace(/>/g,'&gt;');
}
```

Finally, the value of the `text` variable is output to the `winDebug` window:

```
  winDebug.document.write(text + '\n\n');
}
```

The `debugging()` function, which tests if debugging is currently enabled, removes the need for duplicate tests throughout the publicly available debugging methods by placing the test in one place. This allows the test to be extended at a later date without affecting all the debugging functions. It currently returns `true` if `doDebug` is `true`, if `cntDebug` is less than `maxDebug`, and if the `winDebug` window is not closed:

```
function debugging() {
   return (doDebug && (cntDebug++ < maxDebug) && !winDebug.closed);
}
```

The `debug()` function, which is similar to the rest of the publicly available debugging functions, attempts to retrieve the name of the calling function and invokes the `updateDebug()` function to output the results:

```
function debug(msg) {
```

Exit the function if `debugging()` returns `false`:

```
  if (!debugging()) return;
```

If the `msg` parameter is not passed (i.e., it is `null`), then `msg` is set to an empty string:

```
  if (!msg) msg = '';
```

A local c variable is initialized:

```
var c = '';
```

Each function has a `caller` property, which provides access to the caller of the current function. The `caller` property is accessed via an object reference, which is the same as the name of the current function—for example, `debug.caller`.

If called by another function, then the `caller` property is not `null`. In this case the value of the caller property is converted to a string via its `toString()` method. In other words, it returns the definition of the function, which is then used in a regular expression `match()` method to retrieve the first word following the "function" text (i.e., the name of the calling function):

```
if (debug.caller)
    c = 'function ' +
        debug.caller.toString().match(/function (\w*)/)[1] +
        ' - ';
```

The name of the function, if available, is passed to the `updateDebug()` function along with the `msg` parameter value, prefixed with the current value of the `nstDebug` string:

```
    updateDebug(nstDebug + c + msg);
}
```

The `forinDebug()` function loops through all the accessible properties of the passed x object reference, building up a list of property names and values, which it then displays along with the optional `msg` parameter:

```
function forinDebug(x, msg) {
    if (!debugging()) return;
    if (!msg) msg = '';

    var o = nstDebug;

    if (forinDebug.caller)
     o += forinDebug.caller.toString().match(/function (\w*)/)[1] +
        ' - ';

    o += msg;
```

The `for (i in x)` statement is a special type of `for` loop. It loops through each of the properties in the x object, assigning the name of the property to the i variable. The value of the property can be retrieved using the name of the property (i.e., i) within an associate array (e.g., x[i]), instead of the more usual way of accessing a property value using the syntax x.propertyName.

```
for (var in x) {
  o += '\n' + nstDebug;
```

Append the name of the current property in the loop (i.e., i) to the o variable:

```
  o += i;
```

The typeof statement returns a string indicating its operand's data type. Here typeof(c[i]) is used to append the data type of the current properties value to o:

```
  o += '[' + typeof(x[i]) + ']';
```

If the property value is not null and the data type is not function, then the property value is appended to o:

```
  if (x[i] != null && typeof(x[i]) != 'function') {
    o += '=' + x[i];
  }
```

Otherwise, if it is null, then we append a string to say as much to o:

```
  else if (x[i] != null) {
    o += '= null';
  }
}
```

Finally the updateDebug() function is used to update the Debugging Window:

```
  updateDebug(o);
}
```

The startDebug() function, used as the first line inside a function, outputs the name of the function and all its parameter values to the Debugging Window, and then increments the value of nstDebug with the value of txtDebug to ensure that any debug messages output between now and the end of the function are indented:

```
function startDebug() {
  if (!debugging()) return;

  var a = c = '';
```

```
if (startDebug.caller) {
  c = 'function ' +
    startDebug.caller.toString().match(/function (\w*)/)[1];
```

We loop through all the entries within the `startDebug()` function's `caller` function's `arguments` array, appending the value of the array entry to the `a` variable:

```
for (var i=0; i<startDebug.caller.arguments.length; i++) {
  a += startDebug.caller.arguments[i] + ',';
  }
}
```

For tidiness, we trim the trailing character (a comma character) from the end of the `a` variable:

```
if (a.length > 0) a = a.substring(0,a.length-1);
```

The `updateFunction()` is used to update the Debugging Window:

```
updateDebug(nstDebug + c + '(' + a + ') starts');


  nstDebug += txtDebug;
}
```

The `endDebug()` function used immediately prior to any exit from a function (and there may be more than one—that is, more than one `return` statement) decreases the value of `nstDebug` by the value of `txtDebug`, so as to end the current level of indentation, and then it outputs the name the function just ending:

```
function endDebug() {
  if (!debugging()) return;

  var c = '';

  if (endDebug.caller)
    c = 'function ' +
      endDebug.caller.toString().match(/function (\w*)/)[1];

  if (nstDebug.indexOf(txtDebug) > -1)
    nstDebug = nstDebug.substring(txtDebug.length);

  updateDebug(nstDebug + c + '() ends');
}
```

The Debugging Window code on the CD-ROM uses an amended version of the Family Tree application to show debugging in action.

# Pop-up Date Selector

The Popup Date Selector uses a pop-up window to allow to user to select a date from a calendar—rather like the calendars available in Personal Information Manager applications (e.g., Microsoft Outlook). The actual calendar application is covered in detail in Chapter 7 "Date and Time." The Popup Date Selector application will concentrate on the public interface between the main window and the pop-up window.

The Popup Date Selector can be used to populate the value of form fields with a preformatted date in the format dd/mm/yyyy; however, this can be easily changed to meet your own requirements. The selector can be used to populate one of many form fields on the page. It is not restricted to just the one form field. Therefore, it can be used again and again throughout the page, perhaps for completing an order date, a delivery date, and a billing date. Once a date has been selected, the application remembers the chosen date, so that if the user needs to update it, the selector repositions the calendar to the same month and year.

Figure 6-14 shows the main page with several date form fields with individual form buttons. When a form button is clicked, the Popup Date selector is launched, as shown in Figure 6-15. When the user has made his or her selection, the form field in the main window is updated and the pop-up window closed.

## Pop-up Date Selector Source Code—index.htm

**../chapter6/selector/index.htm**

The *index.htm* page holds the form fields for displaying the dates and the form buttons for launching the Popup Date Selector. In this example, we have four form fields and four form buttons. Each of the form fields uses an `onFocus` event handler to stop the form field gaining the text caret—thus preventing the user from typing in a date directly. Each of the form buttons invokes the `cal()` function when the button is clicked, passing the reference to the `this` form's text field that is to be updated:

```
<form>
<input type="text" name="date1" size="10" onFocus="this.blur()">
<input type="button" value="Date" onClick="cal(this.form.date1)">
<br>
<input type="text" name="date2" size="10" onFocus="this.blur()">
```

**Figure 6-14**
Main page completed with three of four dates.

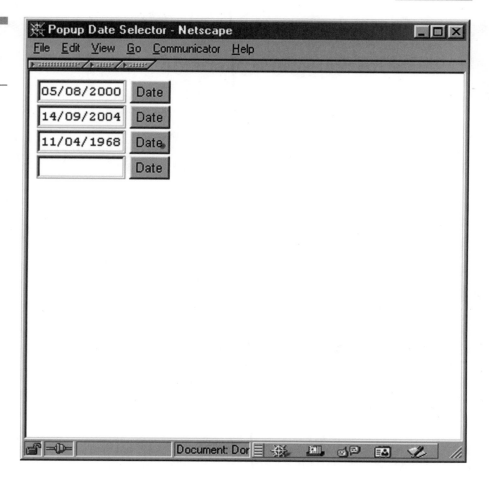

```
<input type="button" value="Date" onClick="cal(this.form.date2)">
<br>
<input type="text" name="date3" size="10" onFocus="this.blur()">
<input type="button" value="Date" onClick="cal(this.form.date3)">
<br>
<input type="text" name="date4" size="10" onFocus="this.blur()">
<input type="button" value="Date" onClick="cal(this.form.date4)">
</form>
```

There are several global variables defined while the page is loading: today holds the current date and time, day holds the day of the month, month holds the month of the year, and year holds the current year:

```
var today = new Date();
var day   = today.getDate();
```

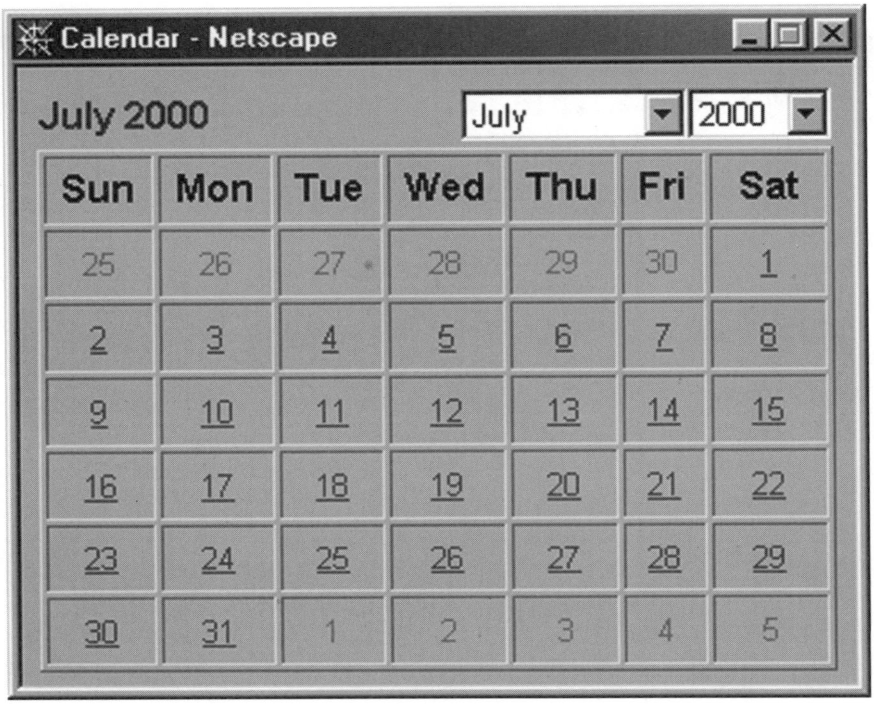

**Figure 6-15**
The Pop-up Date
Selector.

```
var month = today.getMonth() + 1;
var year  = y2k(today.getYear());
```

The `whichFormField` global variable, defined but not initialized, is used to hold a reference to the text form field, which needs to be updated once the Pop-up Date Selector has been used to choose a date:

```
var whichFormField;
```

The `popupCalendar` global variable is used to hold the window reference of the Pop-up Date Selector window:

```
var popupCalendar;
```

The `cal()` function, invoked when one of the four form buttons is clicked, first checks that a current Pop-up Date Selector window in not already open. If one is already open, then we exit the function using the `return` statement:

```
function cal(field) {
  if (popupCalendar && !popupCalendar.closed) return;
```

The function accepts the form text field reference as `field`, and then assigns the value to the global `whichFormField` variable:

```
whichFormField = field;
```

If the current value of the `field` form field is 10 characters long (for the 10 characters dd/mm/yyyy), we extract the day, month, and year constituent parts and assign the values to the global variables `day`, `month`, and `year`:

```
if (field.value.length == 10) {
  day   = field.value.substring(0,2) - 0;
  month = field.value.substring(3,5) - 0;
  year  = field.value.substring(6,10) - 0;
}
```

A new window is opened containing *cal.htm*. The returned window reference is assigned to the global `popupCalendar` variable:

```
popupCalendar = window.open(
  'cal.htm',
  'myname',
  'resizable=no,width=350,height=270'
);
}
```

Once the user has selected a date in the Pop-up Date Selector, the application invokes the `restart()` function in the opener window (i.e., from the *index.htm* page in the main window).

```
function restart() {
```

The `restart()` function updates the value of the form text field referenced by the global `whichFormField` variable with a formatted date containing the `day`, `month`, and `year` global variables. It uses the `pad()` utility function described in Chapter 5 "Location and Links."

```
whichFormField.value = '' + pad(day, 2) +
  '/' + pad(month, 2) + '/' + year;
```

Finally, the pop-up window is closed:

```
popupCalendar.close();
}
```

Note that although we have used form text fields to hold the selected dates, we didn't need to. We could have simply held the dates in hidden form fields, variables, arrays, or even cookies.

## Popup Date Selector Source Code—cal.htm

**../chapter6/selector/cal.htm**

The *cal.htm* page is loaded into the popup window whenever one of the four form buttons is clicked. The *cal.htm* page uses a *calendar.js* external JavaScript source file, which contains the generic code for displaying a calendar:

```
<script language="JavaScript" src="calendar.js"></script>
```

The contents of this *calendar.js* library are covered in Chapter 7 "Date and Time." The *calendar.js* library expects three functions to have been defined by whatever code makes use of it: changeMonth(), changeYear(), and changeDay(). These three functions are invoked whenever the user changes the month or year or selects a day from the calendar. Holding these three functions outside of the *calendar.js* library allows the library to remain generic, with the actual implementation of the three functions to be decided by developers making use of the *calendar.js* library. Here the three functions changeMonth(), changeYear(), and changeDay() accept the value of the *calendar.js* library's CalendarMonth, CalendarYear, and CalendarDay global variables and updates the opener window's month, year, and day global variables. Both the changeMonth() and changeYear() functions reload the *cal.htm* page within the pop-up window, causing the calendar to be rewritten based on the new values of the opener window's month and year variables. The changeDay() function, on the other hand, invokes the opener window's restart() function before closing the current (self) pop-up window:

```
function changeMonth() {
  opener.month = CalendarMonth + '';
  location.href = 'cal.htm';
}

function changeYear() {
  opener.year = CalendarYear + '';
  location.href = "cal.htm";
}
```

```
function changeDay(day,mpnth,year) {
  opener.day = CalendarDay + '';
  opener.restart();
  self.close();
}
```

The above functions avoid the *calendar.js* library from knowing anything about the fact that it is used within a pop-up window, and that the changes affect the pop-up window's `opener` window. This decouples the generic *calendar.js* library from its specific application. This makes it easier to reuse the *calendar.js* library within frames or Dynamic HTML applications, where they may only ever be the one main window.

Global variables are defined and initialized to the values of the corresponding `opener` window's variables:

```
var day = opener.day;
var month = opener.month;
var year = opener.year;
```

Finally, the actual `CalendarSelect()` method, held in the *calendar.js* library, is invoked, passing the values of the `opener` window's `month` and `year` global variables, along with an indicator of the first day of the week. In other words, `0` indicates that Sunday is the first day of the week, whereas `1` indicates that Monday is the first day of the week, all the way up to `6`, which indicates that Saturday is the first day of the week. The `CalendarSelect()` function builds up and returns the HTML markup necessary to describe the monthly calendar for the required month and year, with the required first day of the week, which is then written out to the pop-up window's document:

```
if (window.CalendarSelect)
  document.write(CalendarSelect(opener.month,opener.year,0));
```

# Pop-up Date Selector Source Code— calendar.js

 **../chapter6/selector/calendar.js**

The code contained in the *calendar.js* library is described in detail in Chapter 7 "Date and Time."

# Un-Framing and Re-Framing

This application attempts to solve several different problems:

- Detecting when a page has been framed within the correct frameset
- Detecting when a page has been framed within an incorrect/alien frameset and reloading it within the correct frameset
- Detecting when a page has not been framed and then loading it within the correct frameset
- Detecting when a page is being printed and leaving it alone
- Loading different title and menu frames to complement the current main frame
- Providing a solution that degrades gracefully in browsers that don't support JavaScript, or that have had JavaScript disabled
- Providing a solution that works without errors on as many versions of Netscape Navigator and Internet Explorer as possible
- Providing a solution that is extensible—in other words, that can be adapted to include any number of frames

To explain the problems that this application solves, imagine you have a frameset carefully laid out to the correct sizes to hold framed menu pages providing quick navigational access throughout your site and these frames are essential for the correct operation of your site. Your site is then indexed by a search engine, linked to from another site, or the URL is given out by someone, all without the correct page for the frameset, but for one nonframed page within your site. Perhaps the frames are sensitive to the main page being viewed, or perhaps your page is contained within some other site's frameset, destroying the carefully designed look and feel of your site.

This application detects of all these problems, and after the page has loaded, proceeds to break out of alien framesets and reload the user-requested page within your own frameset with the required surrounding frames.

Immense thanks are due to two people who helped with the development of this particular application: First, Jan Ehrhardt, who continues to this day to answer the oft-asked question on the Usenet newsgroup news:comp.lang.javascript, "How do I ensure that my page is correctly loaded within its frameset when referred to by…," and who helped test this application on a variety of platforms, and also to Ivan Peters who came up with a few enhancements to the ever-increasingly complicated script that unfolded.

## Un-Framing and Re-Framing Source Code—frameset.htm

../chapter6/unframing/frameset.htm

The *frameset.htm* page is an atypical frameset page. It contains the required JavaScript code to detect that the frameset is not itself being framed, and if it is, it unframes itself. It creates a frameset definition using JavaScript and provides names to each of the frames that contains a unique or key prefix—which is used later to detect that your own pages are framed by your own frameset. It also contains a `synchronize()` function that can be used by a page within the frameset to synchronize the contents of the other frames in the frameset.

```
<html>

<script language="JavaScript"><!--
```

The global `key` variable contains a unique random sequence of characters. As such, you should amend its value and every occurrence of the `ergi87143548_` character sequence with your own unique sequence of characters. Otherwise, if too many people use the `ergi87143548_` sequence, then the application will fail to live up to its promise.

```
var key = 'ergi87143548_';
```

The default pages to be loaded into the three frames (`menu`, `title`, and `main`) are defined:

```
var menu = 'menu.htm';
var title = 'title.htm';
var main = 'main.htm';
```

The `search` property of the `location` object is assigned to the `s` variable, and a `tmp` variable is declared:

```
var s = location.search;
var tmp;
```

The `location` object's `search` property is used to pass data back into the *frameset.htm* document, indicating which pages should be loaded into which frames. Therefore, a URL request for `frameset.htm?menu=menu.htm&title=title.htm&main=main.htm` indicates that *menu.htm* should be loaded in the `menu` frame, that *title.htm* should be loaded in the `title` frame, and that *main.htm* should be loaded in the `main` frame.

The `getParm()` function is invoked once for each frame in the frameset, passing the value of `s` and the name of the frame to be retrieved from the `s` variable. If the returned value, `tmp`, is not an empty string, then this value is used to update the value of the global variables `menu`, `title`, and `main`—that is, overwriting the default values with the values passed in the `search` property:

```
tmp = getParm(s, 'menu'); if (tmp != '') menu = tmp;
tmp = getParm(s, 'title'); if (tmp != '') title = tmp;
tmp = getParm(s, 'main'); if (tmp != '') main = tmp;
```

The `getParm()` function searches through the passed `string` parameter, looking for the passed `parm` parameter as part of a *name=value* pair, returning the value of the *name=value* pair if found. Otherwise, it returns an empty string:

```
function getParm(string,parm) {
```

The position of the `parm` variable value in front of an equal sign within the `string` string is retrieved and assigned to the `startPos` local variable:

```
var startPos = 0 + string.indexOf(parm + '=');
```

If it was found, then the function proceeds to extract the value of the *name=value* pair:

```
if (startPos > -1) {
```

The position of the first character following the equal sign within the `string` string is calculated and assigned to the `startPos` variable:

```
startPos = startPos + parm.length + 1;
```

The position of the first ampersand character (`&`) after the current `startPos` position in the `string` string is found and assigned to the `endPos` variable:

```
        var endPos = 0 + string.indexOf('&',startPos);
```

If an ampersand character is not found, the value of the endPos variable is set to the length of the string string:

```
    if (endPos == -1)
        endPos = string.length;
```

The getParm() function then returns the unescaped value of the substring starting at startPos and ending at endPos within the string string:

```
        return unescape(string.substring(startPos,endPos));
    }
```

Otherwise, an empty string is returned:

```
    return '';
}
```

A timer is started, which after 10 seconds, invokes the check-framed() function:

```
    setTimeout('checkframed()',10000);
```

We then output the complete frameset using JavaScript, dynamically assigning the name and src attributes of each frame, so as to include the key character sequence as a prefix to each frame's name, and to include either the default frame pages or the pages supplied as part of the location object's search property:

```
document.write(
    '<frameset onLoad="checkframed()" cols="150,*">' +
    '<frame name="' + key + 'menu" src="' + menu + '">' +
    '<frameset rows="150,*">' +
    '<frame name="' + key + 'title" src="' + title + '">' +
    '<frame name="' + key + 'main" src="'+ main + '">' +
    '</frameset>' +
    '</frameset>'
);
```

Note that the outer frameset element contains an onLoad event handler to call the checkframed() function when the contents of the frames have completely loaded.

Just in case the browser doesn't support JavaScript, we include a normal frameset definition inside <noscript> and </noscript> tags:

```
<noscript>
<frameset cols="150,*">
<frame name="ergi87143548_menu" src="menu.htm">
<frameset rows="150,*">
<frame name="ergi87143548_title" src="title.htm">
<frame name="ergi87143548_main" src="main.htm">
</frameset>
</frameset>
</noscript>
```

The `checkframed()` function, invoked either after the 10-second timer has expired or when all of the frame contents have loaded, checks to make sure that the current page is not contained within a frameset. It does this by comparing the current or `self` window object reference with the `top` window object reference. If they are the same, then the current window is the topmost window in the window hierarchy. If not, then the current window is held in a frameset, in which case the `loadtop()` function is invoked to load the current page into the `top` window:

```
function checkframed() {
  if (top != self) loadtop(self.location.href);
}
```

The `loadtop()` window loads the page represented by the passed `url` parameter into the `top` window:

```
function loadtop(url) {
```

If the browser supports the `document` object's `images` property, then it is assumed that it also supports the `location` object's `replace()` method. In this case the `location` object's `replace()` method is used to load the `url` page into the `top` window, at the same time as replacing the current entry in the `top` window's `history` object with the requested page:

```
if (document.images)
  top.location.replace(url);
```

A window object's `history` object contains the history of pages visited. When the user presses the Back button, the browser loads the previous entry in the `history` object. By replacing the current entry with a new entry, we effectively remove the last page visited from the history. This removes the offending frameset page that held our page from the browsers history.

If the `replace()` method is not supported, we simply change the `top` window's `location` object's `href` property to equal the value of the `url` parameter:

```
      else
         top.location.href = url;
   }
```

The `synchronize()` function, not actually used in the *frameset.htm* page, is used by pages loaded into the `main` frame to synchronize the contents of the `menu` and `title` frames. The passed `menu` and `title` parameters contain the pages to be loaded:

```
function synchronize(menu, title) {
```

If the current contents of the two frames are not the same as the passed parameters, then the new pages are loaded into the frames:

```
   if (window[key +'menu'].location.href.indexOf(menu) == -1)
      window[key +'menu'].location.href = menu;
   if (window[key +'title'].location.href.indexOf(title) == -1)
      window[key +'title'].location.href = title;
}
```

## Un-Framing and Re-Framing Source Code— main.htm

 ../chapter6/unframing/main.htm

The *main.htm* page, typical of all other pages loaded into the main frame, first defines several global variables.

The global `frame` variable contains the name of the frame:

```
var frame = 'main';
```

The global `key` variable contains the same unique `key` value as that contained in the *frameset.htm* page:

```
var key = 'ergi87143548_';
```

The global `search` variable contains the value to be passed as part of the `location` object's `search` property when it is realized that the current page is not correctly framed, and that the *frameset.htm* page should be loaded into the `top` window:

```
var search = 'menu=menu.htm&title=title.htm&main=main.htm';
```

The `redirect()` function, when and if called, actually performs the reload, passing an absolute *frameset.htm* URL to a copy of the `load-top()` function held in the *frameset.htm* page, with the value of the global `search` variable appended to the URL as a search argument following the question mark character:

```
function redirect() {
  loadtop(
    self.location.protocol + '//' + self.location.host +
    getFullPath(self.location.pathname) + 'frameset.htm?' +
    search
  );
}
```

The `onLoad` event handler in the body element invokes the `check-forframe()` when the page has completely loaded:

```
<body onLoad="checkforframe()">
```

The `checkforframe()` performs several tests before deciding whether the `redirect()` function should be called to load the *frameset.htm* page into the `top` window:

```
function checkforframe() {
```

If Netscape Navigator 4 is used to print a page that contains JavaScript code, amazingly the code is executed. This can cause a slight problem, as the redirection code attempts to load the printing page into a frame. This needs to be prevented. Testing for this requires detection of the `document` object's `images` and `layers` properties. If these two properties exist, then testing that the current or `self` window has `innerHeight` and `innerWidth` properties of zero will indicate that the page is being printed. In this case, we exit the function using the `return` statement:

```
if (document.images && document.layers)
  if (self.innerHeight == 0 && self.innerWidth == 0)
    return;
```

If the current or `self` window is equivalent to the `top` window, then the current window is not framed when it should be. Therefore, the `redirect()` function is invoked:

```
if (top == self) redirect();
```

Otherwise, if the name of `this` window does not contain the unique `key` character sequence, or it does not contain the value of the global `frame` variable, then although the page is framed, it is either not framed by one of our framesets or it is contained within the wrong frame. In this case, the `redirect()` function is invoked:

```
else if (this.name.indexOf(key) == -1 ||
         this.name.indexOf(frame) == -1) redirect();
```

Otherwise, it is framed correctly, in which case the `parent` frame's `synchronize()` function is invoked to load *menu.htm* into the `menu` frame, and *title.htm* into the `title` frame:

```
else parent.synchronize('menu.htm', 'title.htm');
}
```

With other pages that are loaded into the main frame, you'll include all of the above code, but you will possibly want to change the call to the `synchronize()` function to load other pages into the `menu` and `title` frames.

## Un-Framing and Re-Framing Source Code— title.htm

**../chapter6/unframing/title.htm**

The *title.htm* and *menu.htm* pages contain similar JavaScript code to the *main.htm* page. There are, however, one or two differences. Here we only show the changes to the *title.htm* page.

A `base` tag is included with a `target` attribute specifying the `main` frame prefixed with the unique `key` character sequence. This ensures that any hypertext links in this frame target the results into the `main` frame:

```
<base target="ergi87143548_main">
```

The `checkforframe()` exits if the current page is being printed, but then only invokes the `redirect()` function if the `self` frame is equivalent to the `top` frame:

```
function checkforframe() {
  if (document.images && document.layers)
    if (self.innerHeight == 0 && self.innerWidth == 0)
      return;

  if (top == self) redirect();
}
```

## Summary

This chapter gave you a practical grounding in many different uses for frames and pop-up windows. Use both with caution, as overuse of either is likely to offend the sensibilities of visitors to your site. They should be used for a specific and well-reasoned intention.

# Date and Time

This chapter covers the use of dates and times within JavaScript. The built-in `Date` object allows dates in the Gregorian calendar to be easily generated. The "Current Date and Time" section covers the `Date` object constructor and the `Date` object methods in detail. Despite this, there are many occasions when it is unnecessary or impractical to use the built-in `Date` object, and algorithms can be used instead. In these circumstances, it may only be necessary to use the `Date` object to create a date for the current date and time.

Some of the older versions of Netscape Navigator and Internet Explorer have certain features or bugs with regard to the `Date` object. For example, the following script attempts to create and display a `Date` object for February, 1960, but using Netscape 2, this will cause problems:

```
var date = new Date(1960,1,1);
document.write(date);
```

This causes problems because the built-in `Date` object in the first release of JavaScript stores dates internally as the number of milliseconds since January 1, 1970 00:00:00. The actual JavaScript documentation states that "Dates prior to 1970 are not allowed."

Dates after 1999 also cause problems with older browsers. The following script attempts to create and display a `Date` object for February 1, 2000, but using Microsoft Internet Explorer 3, this may produce a negative value:

```
var date = new Date(2000,1,1);
document.write(date);
```

Many of the applications within this chapter make use of reusable external JavaScript source files, containing libraries of functions, object constructors, arrays, and global variables.

This chapter also explains the `HowOld()` function used in the Family Tree application and the *calendar.js* library used in the Popup Date Selector application in Chapter 6 "Windows and Frames."

## Current Date and Time

This section discusses the Date object constructor, some of its methods, how to enhance the built-in Date object with extra prototype methods, and how to format the output of a date string.

 ../chapter7/current/test.htm

The built-in Date constructor can be invoked in several ways. The current date and time are returned when no arguments are passed to the Date object constructor:

```
var date = new Date();
document.write(date);
```

Year dot, or January 1, 1970 00:00:00, will be returned when zero is passed as an argument—that is, the number of milliseconds since year dot:

```
var date = new Date(0);
document.write(date);
```

The year, month, and day of month can be passed as input arguments. Note, however, that the value of the month argument is represented as 0–January, 1–February, 2–March, 3–April, 4–May, 5–June, 6–July, 7–August, 8–September, 9–October, 10–November and 11–December. So a Date object for December 25, 2000 is generated using

```
var date = new Date(2000,11,25);
document.write(date);
```

Additionally, the hours, minutes, seconds, and milliseconds can also be passed as input arguments. So a Date object for January 1, 2001 at 02:03:04.005 is generated using

```
var date = new Date(2001,0,1,2,3,4,5);
document.write(date);
```

As well as specific numeric parameters, a string representing a date can be passed as an input argument:

```
var date = new Date('Fri, 21 July 2000 21:57:46');
document.write(date);
```

The document object's lastModified property returns a string representing the last modified date of the document. This can therefore be passed as input to the Date object constructor:

```
var date = new Date(document.lastModified);
document.write(date);
```

There is not much point to creating a Date object unless it is possible to retrieve the various components that make up the date. Once created, the Date object's get methods can be used to retrieve the year, month, day of month, hours, minutes, and seconds:

```
var date = new Date();
document.write(
  'Year = ' + date.getFullYear() + ' ' +
  'Month = ' + date.getMonth() + ' ' +
  'Day = ' + date.getDate() + ' ' +
  'Hours = ' + date.getHours() + ' ' +
  'Minutes = ' + date.getMinutes() + ' ' +
  'Seconds = ' + date.getSeconds() + ' ' +
  'Time = ' + date.getTime() + ' ' +
  'Day = ' + date.getDay()
);
```

You can also use some of the Date object methods to directly set parts of the date it represents—for example the year, month, day of month, hours, minutes, and seconds—using the appropriate set methods. The following first creates a Date object, which initially holds the current date and time, and then proceeds to alter the Date object to January 1, 1999 at 23:59:59:

```
var date = new Date();
date.setFullYear(1999);
date.setMonth(0);
date.setDate(1);
```

```
date.setHours(23);
date.setMinutes(59);
date.setSeconds(59);
document.write(date);
```

The `getTime()` method can be used to retrieve the number of milliseconds since year dot:

```
var date = new Date();
document.write('Time = ' + date.getTime());
```

The `setTime()` method can be used to set the time based on the input argument representing the number of seconds since year dot:

```
var date = new Date();
date.setTime(0);
document.write('Time = ' + date.getTime());
```

When a date is created using the `Date` object constructor, the resultant date is based on the local time settings of the operating system that the browser is running within. For example, when the following is run on Windows 98 in GMT+0100, the date when displayed shows `Fri Jul 21 21:57:46 GMT+0100 (GMT Daylight Time) 2000`:

```
var date = new Date(2000,6,21,21,57,46);
document.write('Local date/time: ' + date);
```

Using the `Date` object's `UTC()` static method, you can generate a time in milliseconds, which when used as input to the `Date` object constructor, creates a date in the local time settings, but one that is based on the time in GMT (Greenwich mean time) time zone or UTC (universal Time coordinated). When the following is run on Windows 98 in GMT+0100, the displayed date shows `Fri Jul 21 22:57:46 GMT+0100 (GMT Daylight Time) 2000`. That is, the time in the local time zone GMT+0100 is one hour ahead of UTC:

```
var date = new Date(Date.UTC(2000,6,21,21,57,46));
document.write('UTC date/time: ' + date);
```

The `Date` object's `getTimezoneOffset()` method retrieves the number of minutes offset of the local time zone from UTC:

```
var date = new Date();
document.write('Timezone = ' + date.getTimezoneOffset());
```

The results of all the previous script snippets are shown in Figure 7-1.

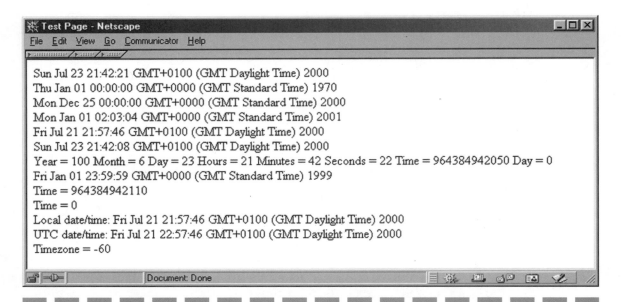

**Figure 7-1** Creating and displaying dates using the Date object constructor.

The remainder of this section shows how to manipulate the return values of the Date object methods to format dates for output to the page. Because many of these functions will be reused throughout the remainder of the chapter, they and others are included in external JavaScript source files, which can then be embedded into any and all of your HTML pages.

Figure 7-2 shows the results of displaying the value of the Date object, and then three different formats using hand-crafted functions that accept the values of the dates year, month, and day of month values.

## Current Date and Time Source Code—current.js

../chapter7/current/current.js

The getFullYear() and getMilliseconds() Date object methods were both introduced in JavaScript 1.2. However, we can add our own object methods to existing objects using the object's prototype property. First, we define the function to take the place of the missing method—in

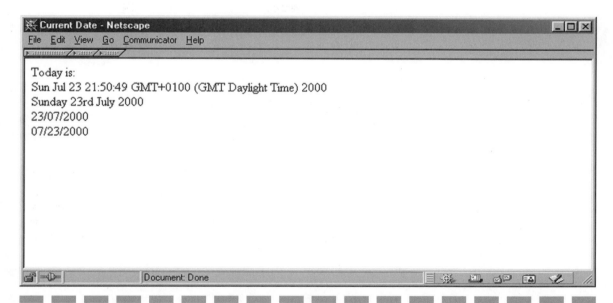

**Figure 7-2**    *Current Date and Time—Three formatted dates.*

this case, the `getFullYear()` function. This function uses the `Date` object's deprecated `getYear()` method to retrieve the year of the referenced `this` object. It then adds 1900 to the year if the year is less than 900 before returning the revised value:

```
function getFullYear() {
  var year = this.getYear();
  if (year < 1000) year += 1900;
  return year;
}
```

Then we use the `Date` object's `prototype` property to set the `getFullYear` object reference to the `getFullYear` function name, but only if the `Date` object does not already have a `getFullYear` method defined:

```
if (!Date.getFullYear)
  Date.prototype.getFullYear = getFullYear;
```

Likewise with the `getMilliseconds()` function, which subtracts the value returned from the `getTime()` method on a date created using a zero milliseconds input argument, from the value returned by the `getTime()` method on the referenced `this` object:

```
function getMilliseconds() {
  var date = new Date(
    this.getFullYear(), this.getMonth(), this.getDate(),
    this.getHours(), this.getMinutes(), this.getSeconds(), 0
  );
  return this.getTime() - date.getTime();
}
```

Again, the `Date` object's `prototype` property is used to set the `getMilliseconds` object reference to the `getMilliseconds` function name:

```
if (!Date.getMilliseconds)
  Date.prototype.getMilliseconds = getMilliseconds;
```

The actual names of the days of the week are not accessible using the `Date` object. Therefore, we create our own `daysOfWeek` array to hold the full names:

```
var daysOfWeek = new Array(
  'Sunday','Monday','Tuesday','Wednesday',
  'Thursday','Friday','Saturday'
);
```

Again, we do the same with the months of the year with the `monthsOfYear` array:

```
var monthsOfYear = new Array(
  'January','February','March','April','May','June',
  'July','August','September','October','November','December'
);
```

Although the day of the week can be retrieved from a `Date` object using the `getDay()` method, which returns a value 0–Sunday, 1–Monday, 2–Tuesday, 3–Wednesday, 4–Thursday, 5–Friday, 6–Saturday, there are times when it is inconvenient to have to first create a `Date` object and then retrieve the day of the week using the `getDay()` method. The following was taken from The Calendar FAQ at http://www.tondering.dk/claus/calendar.html:

> To calculate the day on which a particular date falls, the following algorithm may be used (the divisions are integer divisions, in which the remainders are discarded):
>
> a = (14 - month) / 12
>
> y = year - a
>
> m = month + 12*a - 2
>
> d = (day + y + y/4 - y/100 + y/400 + (31*m/12) % 7
>
> The value of d is 0 for a Sunday, 1 for a Monday, 2 for a Tuesday, etc.

This, as well as other algorithms, can easily be converted to JavaScript to create the following `dayOfWeek()` function, which returns the day of week for any day, month, and year input arguments:

```
function dayOfWeek(day,month,year) {
  var a = Math.floor((14 - month)/12);
  var y = year - a;
  var m = month + 12*a - 2;
  var d = (day + y + Math.floor(y/4) - Math.floor(y/100) +
          Math.floor(y/400) + Math.floor((31*m)/12)) % 7;
  return d;
}
```

The `nths()` function returns the date ordinal for the passed day of month integer argument—that is, the st, th, nd, or rd, in 1st, 2nd, 3rd, or 4th, all the way up to 31st:

```
function nths(day) {
  if (day == 1 || day == 21 || day == 31) return 'st';
  if (day == 2 || day == 22) return 'nd';
  if (day == 3 || day == 23) return 'rd';
  return 'th';
}
```

The `formatFullDate()` function uses the previous `dayOfWeek()` and `nth()` functions, along with the `daysOfWeek` and `monthsOfYear` arrays to return a fully formatted date string—for instance, 25th December 2000:

```
function formatFullDate(day,month,year) {
  var dow = dayOfWeek(day,month,year);
  return daysOfWeek[dow] + ' ' +
         day + nths(day) + ' ' +
         monthsOfYear[month-1] +' '+ year;
}
```

The `formatShortDate()` function uses the ubiquitous `padout()` function to return a date in a short format—for instance, 25/12/2000:

```
function formatShortDate(day,month,year) {
  return padout(day) + '/' + padout(month) + '/' + year;
}
```

The `formatShortDateUS()` function, on the other hand, returns a date in a short U.S. date format—that is, month before day of month, such as 12/25/2000:

```
function formatShortDateUS(day,month,year) {
  return padout(month) + '/' + padout(day) + '/' + year;
}
```

Once the general concept of concatenating strings and day, month, and year integers together has been grasped, then it is fairly easy to see how further date formatting functions can be created.

## Current Date and Time Source Code— index.htm

All that remains is an application to make use of the formatting functions in the *current.js* file.

 **../chapter7/current/index.htm**

First, we include all the JavaScript code contained in the external JavaScript source file *current.js*:

```
<script src="current.js" language="JavaScript"></script>
```

Before using any of the functions in the *current.js* library, we first check that the current window has a formatFullDate property—that is, a defined formatFullDate() function:

```
if (window.formatFullDate) {
```

If there is, then we proceed with the code, first retrieving the day, month, and year of the current date and time:

```
var date = new Date();
var day = date.getDate();
var month = date.getMonth() + 1;
var year = date.getFullYear();
```

These are then all used as input to the formatFullDate(), formatShortDate(), and formatShortDateUS() functions, the return values of which are then output as part of the document.write() statement:

```
document.write(
  'Today is:<br>' +
  date + '<br>' +
  formatFullDate(day,month,year) + '<br>' +
  formatShortDate(day,month,year) + '<br>' +
  formatShortDateUS(day,month,year) + '<br>'
);
}
```

# Monday's Child Is Fair of Face

This short and sweet example shows how retrieving the day of the week, using the dayOfWeek() function described in the previous Current Date and Time example, can be used to retrieve the relevant line from the following "Monday's Child" poem:

> Monday's child is fair of face,
> Tuesday's child is full of grace,
> Wednesday's child is full of woe,
> Thursday's child has far to go,
> Friday's child is loving and giving,
> Saturday's child works hard for a living,
> And the child that is born on the Sabbath day
> Is bonny and blithe and good and gay.

Figure 7-3 shows the result of running this example on Monday the 24th of July 2000.

## Monday's Child Is Fair of Face Source Code—monday.js

The *monday.js* library contains both a child array holding the pertinent extracts from the preceding poem, and a childOfWeek() function that returns the relevant entry in the child array based on the passed dayofweek parameter:

**Figure 7-3**    Monday's Child—Run on Monday the 24th of July 2000.

../chapter7/monday/monday.js

```
var child = new Array(
  'is bonny and blithe and good and gay',
  'is fair of face',
  'is full of grace',
  'is full of woe',
  'has far to go',
  'is loving and giving',
  'works hard for a living'
);
```

The `childOfWeek()` function accepts as input a `dayofweek` parameter:

```
function childOfWeek(dayofweek) {
```

The `dayofweek` parameter is used to retrieve the corresponding entries in both the `daysOfWeek` (described in the preceding Current Date and Time example) and `child` arrays, and then returns a string representing the entry in the poem:

```
  return daysOfWeek[dayofweek] + '\'s child ' +
         child[dayofweek];
}
```

# Monday's Child Is Fair of Face Source Code— index.htm

../chapter7/monday/index.htm

To use this example within our code, we have to include both the *current.js* and *monday.js* libraries in our code:

```
<script src="current.js" language="JavaScript"></script>
<script src="monday.js" language="JavaScript"></script>
```

The code body is only processed if the `window` object has `formatFullDate` and `dayOfWeek` properties—that is, both the `formatFullDate()` and `dayOfWeek()` function definitions are loaded from the external JavaScript source code libraries:

```
if (window.formatFullDate && window.dayOfWeek) {
```

Today's date is obtained using the default `Date` object constructor, and then the `day`, `month`, and `year` values are retrieved:

```
var today = new Date();
var day   = today.getDate();
var month = today.getMonth() + 1;
var year  = today.getFullYear();
```

The return value of the `childOfWeek()` function is output to the document, using the return value of the `dayOfWeek()` function as an input parameter:

```
document.write(
  'Today - ' + formatFullDate(day,month,year) + '<br>' +
  childOfWeek(dayOfWeek(day,month,year)) + '<br>'
);
}
```

# Valid Date

Validating user-entered dates can cause problems. For example, who is to tell whether when a user enters the date as `01/02/03`, they mean February 1, 2003, or January 2, 1903. Unless the user is explicitly told what format to enter the date (e.g., MM/DD/YYYY), then it can be difficult to predict what they may enter. Even then, the user may enter invalid dates—for example, the 30th February, or perhaps years outside our expected range, such as 1899 or 9999. Controlling how the user enters the date and then validating the date is explained in this section.

Figure 7-4 shows a simple interface for controlling how a user can

**Figure 7-4**
Valid Date interface.

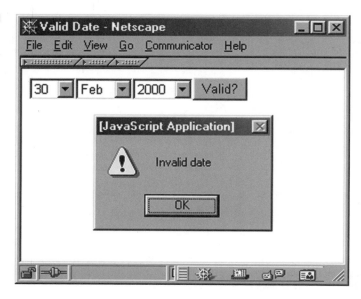

**TABLE 7-1**

Number of days in each month.

| Month | Days in Month | Month | Days in Month |
|-------|---------------|-------|---------------|
| January | 31 | July | 31 |
| February | 28—29 in a leap year | August | 31 |
| March | 31 | September | 30 |
| April | 30 | October | 31 |
| May | 31 | November | 30 |
| June | 30 | December | 31 |

enter a date. It uses three select option lists, one each for the day of month, the month, and the year. By default, it shows the current date in its initial state and allows the user to select any date 50 years on either side of the current date.

It is impossible for users to enter a date in the wrong format. However, it is still possible for them to enter an invalid date, such as 31st September. The remainder of this section shows how to construct the form interface using JavaScript and then how to ensure only a valid date combination is selected.

Before we delve into the code, let's look at a couple of known facts about dates. A year contains 12 months. Each month has a fixed number of days—except, of course, February, which has 29 days in a leap year—as shown in Table 7-1. Every year that is exactly divisible by 4 is a leap year, except for years that are exactly divisible by 100; these century years are leap years only if they are exactly divisible by 400. Therefore, 2000 is a leap year, whereas 2100 is not.

## Valid Date Source Code—validate.js

The *validate.js* library holds the arrays and functions necessary to validate dates.

../chapter7/validate/validate.js

The `daysOfMonth` array holds the number of days in each month for a non-leap year:

```
var daysOfMonth = new Array(
  31, 28, 31, 30, 31, 30, 31, 31, 30, 31, 30, 31
);
```

The `daysOfMonthLY` array holds the number of days in each month for a leap year:

```
var daysOfMonthLY = new Array(
  31, 29, 31, 30, 31, 30, 31, 31, 30, 31, 30, 31
);
```

The `isLeapYear()` function returns a Boolean `true` or `false` value indicating whether the passed year parameter is divisible by 4 and not 100, unless it is also divisible by 400:

```
function isLeapYear(year) {
```

First, we ensure that we convert any `year` string value to an integer value by subtracting zero:

```
year = year - 0;
```

If the floating-point value of `year` divided by 4 is not equal to the integer value of `year` divided by 4 (i.e., rounded down to the nearest integer value using the `Math` object's `floor()` method), then `false` is returned:

```
if ((year/4)   != Math.floor(year/4))   return false;
```

If the floating-point value of `year` divided by 100 is not equal to the integer value of `year` divided by 100, then `true` is returned:

```
if ((year/100) != Math.floor(year/100)) return true;
```

If the floating-point value of `year` divided by 400 is not equal to the integer value of `year` divided by 400, then `false` is returned:

```
if ((year/400) != Math.floor(year/400)) return false;
```

Otherwise, `true` is returned:

```
  return true;
}
```

The `isValidateDate()` function returns a Boolean `true` or `false` value indicating whether the passed day, month, and year parameters represent a valid date:

```
function isValidDate(day, month, year) {
```

First, the parameters are converted to integers by subtracting zero:

```
day = day - 0; month = month - 0; year = year - 0;
```

The function returns `false` if either the `isLeapYear()` function returns `true` *and* the value of `day` is greater than the value of the entry in the `daysOfMonthLY` array, *or* the `isLeapYear()` function returns `true` *and* the value of `day` is greater than the value of the entry in the `daysOfMonth` array:

```
if ((isLeapYear(year) && day > daysOfMonthLY[month-1]) ||
    (!isLeapYear(year) && day > daysOfMonth[month-1]))
  return false;
```

Otherwise, the function returns `true`:

```
else
  return true;
}
```

## Valid Date Source Code—index.htm

**../chapter7/validate/index.htm**

To use the arrays and functions defined in the *validate.js* library, we must include both the *validate.js* and *current.js* libraries in our application:

```
<script src="current.js" language="JavaScript"></script>
<script src="validate.js" language="JavaScript"></script>
```

The select-option list uses abbreviated month names as defined in the `mthsOfYear` array:

```
var mnthsOfYear = new Array(
  'Jan','Feb','Mar','Apr','May','Jun',
  'Jul','Aug','Sep','Oct','Nov','Dec'
);
```

An `output` variable is defined and initialized:

```
var output = '';
```

Only if the window object has both the `formatFullDate` and `isValidDate` properties is the body of the JavaScript code processed:

```
if (window.formatFullDate && window.isValidDate) {
  var today = new Date();
  var month = today.getMonth();
  var day   = today.getDate();
  var year  = today.getFullYear();
```

The HTML code necessary to display the three select option form fields is built up using the `output` variable:

```
output += '<form>';
```

A `select` option list named day is created:

```
output += '<select name="day">';
```

Thirty-one `option` elements are included; the value of each is set to the number of the day of the month (using the ubiquitous `padout()` function):

```
for (var days=1; days <= 31; days++) {
  output += '<option value="' + padout(days) + '"';
```

The `option` element that corresponds to the current `day` is selected as the default option:

```
  if (days == day) output += ' selected';
  output += '>' + days;
}
output += '</select>';
```

A `select` option list named month is created:

```
output += '<select name="month">';
```

An `option` element for each month of the year is included; the value of each is set to the value of the month:

```
for (var months=0; months<12; months++) {
  output += '<option value="' + padout(months+1) + '"';
```

The `option` element that corresponds to the current `month` is selected as the default option:

```
    if (months == month) output += ' selected';
    output += '>' + mnthsOfYear[months];
  }
  output += '</select>';
```

A `select` list named `year` is created:

```
  output += '<select name="year">';
```

An `option` element for 50 years on either side of the current `year` is included:

```
  for (var years=year-50; years<year+50; years++) {
    output += '<option value="' + years + '"';
```

The current `year` is selected as the default:

```
    if (years == year) output += ' selected';
    output += '>' + years;
  }
  output += '</select>';
```

The HTML for an input button is appended to the output variable. The `onClick` event handler invokes the `valid()` function, passing the current form reference (`this.form`) as an input argument:

```
  output += '<input type="button" value="Valid?" ' +
    'onClick="valid(this.form)">';
  output += '</form>';
}
```

The `valid()` function is invoked when the date is required to be validated. It is passed the reference to the form to be validated (i.e., `what`):

```
function valid(what) {
```

It uses the `getAnOptionValue()` function, described in the "Jump Box Tool" section of Chapter 6, to retrieve the day, month, and year values of the selected options:

```
  var day = getAnOptionValue(what.day);
  var month = getAnOptionValue(what.month);
  var year = getAnOptionValue(what.year);
```

The day, `month`, and `year` are passed as input to the `isValidDate()` function, which returns `true` if the date is valid. Otherwise, it returns `false`.

```
if (isValidDate(day, month, year))
  alert('Valid date');
else
  alert('Invalid date');
}
```

The HTML built up in the `output` variable is written out to the document:

```
document.write(output);
```

An amended version of the `valid()` function could be used to cancel the user's form submission, prompting the user to correct the date selection, thus only allowing the form to be submitted when a valid date has been selected. Examples of form cancellation are included in Chapter 8 "Forms."

## Time of Day

The previous sections showed how to format dates. This section shows how to format time. The first example explains how to update form fields to display the current time in three different formats. Once the current time has been retrieved, the second example demonstrates how it can be used to affect the display of the page. The third example shows how a digital clock can be displayed on the page using images.

## Time of Day Source Code—form.htm

The *form.htm* page contains a form with three text-input fields. The value of each are updated with the current time displayed in the formats: `00:00:00` - `23:59:59`, or a full 24-hour clock showing the time in hours, minutes, and seconds; `00:00` - `23:59`, or a full 24-hour clock but without the seconds; and `0:00` - `12:59`, or a 12-hour clock without the seconds. Figure 7-5 shows the results of *form.htm*.

 ../chapter7/timeofday/form.htm

The `updateClock()` function retrieves the current time, manipulates the values, and then updates the form's text-input fields:

**Figure 7-5**
The form.htm—
Current time in three
different formats.

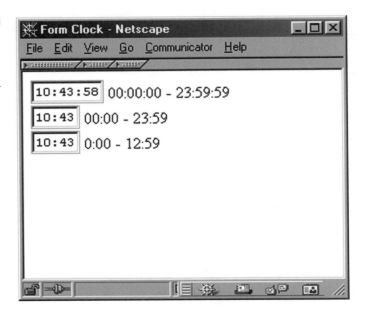

```
function updateClock() {
```

The current date and time is retrieved using a default `Date` object constructor, and is assigned to the `time` variable:

```
var time = new Date();
```

The seconds, minutes, and hours values are retrieved and assigned to the `s`, `m`, and `h` variables. The `padout()` function is used to ensure each value is padded out with a leading zero if the original value is less than 10:

```
var s = padout(time.getSeconds());
var m = padout(time.getMinutes());
var h = padout(time.getHours());
```

The `display1` variable holds the current time representing the full 24-hour clock with hours, minutes, and seconds:

```
var display1 = h + ':' + m + ':' + s;
```

The `clock` form's `time1` input field is updated with the value of `display1`, but only if the current value of the input field is not already equal to the value of `display1`. This stops any flickering when the same value is repeatedly written to the input field:

```
if (document.clock.time1.value != display1)
   document.clock.time1.value = display1;
```

The `display2` variable holds the current time representing the full 24-hour clock less the seconds.

```
var display2 = h + ':' + m ;
```

Again, the `time2` input field is updated if it does not already contain the value of `display2`:

```
if (document.clock.time2.value != display2)
   document.clock.time2.value = display2;
```

The `display3` variable holds the time representing a 12-hour clock less the seconds. To achieve this, a *tertiary* test is performed on the value of h. If it is greater than 12 (i.e., it's the afternoon), then 12 is subtracted from h. Otherwise, h is left as is.

```
var display3 = ((h > 12) ? h-12 : h) + ':' + m;
```

Again, the `time3` input field is updated if it does not already contain the value of `display3`:

```
if (document.clock.time3.value != display3)
   document.clock.time3.value = display3;
```

Finally, the `updateClock()` function starts a timer, which reinvokes the `updateClock()` function after 100 milliseconds have elapsed:

```
setTimeout('updateClock()',100);
}
```

The initial call to the `updateClock()` function is made from the body element's `onLoad` event handler. This ensures that the function is only invoked once the HTML for the form has been generated and the JavaScript code has all been defined:

```
<body onLoad="updateClock()">
```

Finally, the HTML code for the `clock` form is included within the page:

```
<form name="clock">
<input type="text" name="time1" size="8"> 00:00:00 - 23:59:59
```

```
<br>
<input type="text" name="time2" size="5"> 00:00 - 23:59
<br>
<input type="text" name="time3" size="5"> 0:00 - 12:59
</form>
```

# Time of Day Source Code—nightandday.htm

The *nightandday.htm* page detects the current time and then outputs a different title tag, loads in a different external cascading style sheet, and displays an image based on whether the time is between 6:00 a.m. and 6:00 p.m. (i.e., daytime) or 6:01 p.m. and 5:59 a.m. (i.e., nighttime). Figure 7-6 shows the effect of the page being loaded between 6:00 a.m. and 6:00 p.m., and Figure 7-7 shows the effect of the same page being loaded between 6:01 p.m. and 5:59 a.m.

**Figure 7-6**
Daytime—Between 6:00 a.m. and 6:00 p.m.

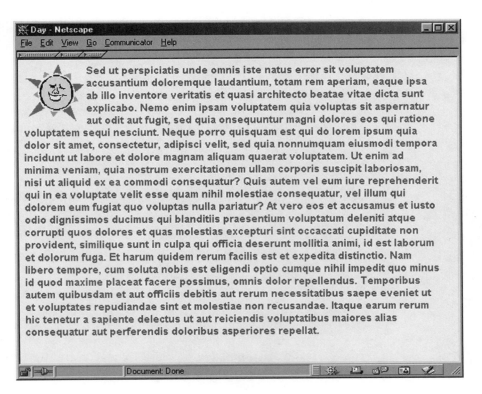

**Figure 7-7**
Nighttime—Between
6:01 p.m. and
5:59 a.m.

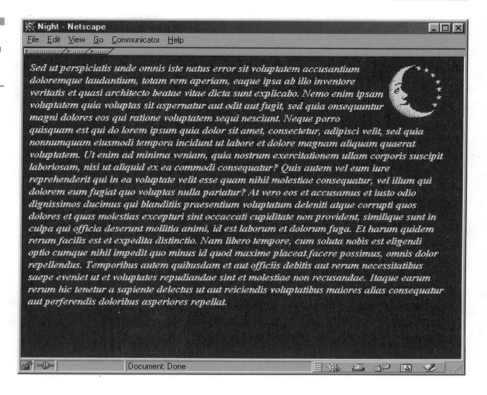

 On the CD     **../chapter7/timeofday/nightandday.htm**

First, the current date and time is retrieved using a default `Date` object constructor, assigning the result to the `date` variable:

```
var date = new Date();
```

Next, the `getHours()` method is used to retrieve the `hours` value:

```
var hours = date.getHours();
```

A Boolean `daytime` variable is defined and initialized to `true`:

```
var daytime = true;
```

If the value of `hours` is less than 6 or greater than 18 then the `daytime` Boolean variable is set to `false`:

```
if ((hours < 6) || (hours > 18))
  daytime = false;
```

If `daytime` is `true`, the code outputs a title indicating *Day*, and a link element referencing an external *day.css* cascading style sheet:

```
if (daytime) {
  document.write('<title>Day</title>');
  document.write('<link rel="stylesheet" href="day.css" >');
}
```

Otherwise, the code outputs a title indicating *Night*, and a line element referencing an external *night.css* cascading style sheet:

```
else {
  document.write('<title>Night</title>');
  document.write('<link rel="stylesheet" href="night.css" >');
}
```

Later on in the code, after the opening body tag, more JavaScript code is included to output a left aligned *sun.gif* image if `daytime` is `true`. Otherwise, it outputs a right-aligned *moon.gif* image:

```
if (daytime)
  document.write('<img src="sun.gif" align="left">');
else
  document.write('<img src="moon.gif" align="right">')
```

As you can see, the code to detect and alter the display of the page as it loads is extremely simple. It can be easily extended to detect the hour of the day or be used to load different pages using the `location` object's `href` property.

## Time of Day Source Code—timeofday.js

The Time of Day example uses two files, the *timeofday.js* library, described here, and the *timeofday.htm* page, described afterwards. Figure 7-8 shows a snapshot of the Time of Day application—over time, the clock updates itself.

**../chapter7/timeofday/timeofday.js**

**Figure 7-8**
Time of Day—Digital
image clock.

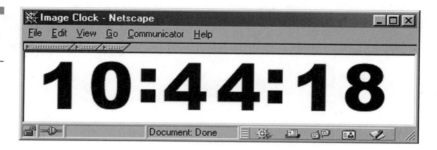

**Figure 7-8**
Time of Day—Digital
image clock.

The *timeofday.js* library contains the code necessary to preload all the images used in the digital clock and the function necessary to update the clock.

First, the code defines a `myImages` array:

```
var myImages = new Array();
```

If the document `object` has an `images` property—indicating that the document supports an array of images held in the current document—the code proceeds to load 10 images into the `myImages` array, using the `Image` object constructor, and passing the width and height of each image:

```
if (document.images) {
  myImages[0] = new Image(64,64);
  myImages[0].src = "0.gif";
  myImages[1] = new Image(64,64);
  myImages[1].src = "1.gif";
  myImages[2] = new Image(64,64);
  myImages[2].src = "2.gif";
  myImages[3] = new Image(64,64);
  myImages[3].src = "3.gif";
  myImages[4] = new Image(64,64);
  myImages[4].src = "4.gif";
  myImages[5] = new Image(64,64);
  myImages[5].src = "5.gif";
  myImages[6] = new Image(64,64);
  myImages[6].src = "6.gif";
  myImages[7] = new Image(64,64);
  myImages[7].src = "7.gif";
  myImages[8] = new Image(64,64);
  myImages[8].src = "8.gif";
  myImages[9] = new Image(64,64);
  myImages[9].src = "9.gif";
}
```

Chapter 9 "Images" will cover the use of the `Image` constructor and image-swapping techniques in more detail.

The `updateClock()` function retrieves the current date and time, extracts the separate digits of the current time, and then proceeds to swap the existing images displayed in the *timeofday.htm* page with the images reflecting the current time:

```
function updateClock() {
```

The `time` variable is assigned the current date and time:

```
var time = new Date();
```

The `s1` variable holds the number of seconds modulo 10:

```
var s1 = time.getSeconds() % 10;
```

The `s10` variable holds the number of seconds divided by 10 and rounded down to the nearest integer:

```
var s10 = Math.floor(time.getSeconds() / 10);
```

The `m1` variable holds the number of minutes modulo 10:

```
var m1 = time.getMinutes() % 10;
```

The `m10` variable holds the number of minutes divided by 10 and rounded down to the nearest integer:

```
var m10 = Math.floor(time.getMinutes() / 10);
```

The `h1` variable holds the number of hours modulo 10:

```
var h1 = time.getHours() % 10;
```

The `h10` variable holds the number of hours divided by 10 and rounded down to the nearest integer:

```
var h10 = Math.floor(time.getHours() / 10);
```

Again, if the `document` object supports the `images` property, the function then proceeds to swap the images named `s1`, `s10`, `m1`, `m10`, `h1`, and `h10`, using the new values of `s1`, `s10`, `m1`, `m10`, `h1`, and `h10`, to reference the appropriate images in the `myImages` array:

```
if (document.images) {
  document.images['s1'].src   = myImages[s1].src;
  document.images['s10'].src  = myImages[s10].src;
  document.images['m1'].src   = myImages[m1].src;
  document.images['m10'].src  = myImages[m10].src;
  document.images['h1'].src   = myImages[h1].src;
  document.images['h10'].src  = myImages[h10].src;
}
```

Finally, the `updateClock()` function uses a timer to reinvoke the `updateClock()` function after 100 milliseconds:

```
setTimeout('updateClock()',100);
}
```

## Time of Day Source Code—image.htm

 **../chapter7/timeofday/image.htm**

The *image.htm* page contains the HTML for the initial digital clock images. First, the *timeofday.js* library is loaded:

```
<script src="timeofday.js" language="JavaScript"></script>
```

The start body tag invokes the `updateClock()` function from within the `onLoad` event handler, if and only if the `window` object has an `updateClock` property. In other words, the `updateClock()` function definition contained in the *timeofday.js* library has been successfully loaded into the page:

```
<body onLoad="if (window.updateClock) updateClock()">
```

The HTML `img` elements for the named images `h10`, `h1`, `m10`, `m1`, `s10`, and `s1` are written out to the document from JavaScript—if the `document` object supports the `images` property and the `window` object contains an `updateClock` property:

```
if (document.images && window.updateClock) {
  document.write(
    '<img src="0.gif" name="h10" height="64" width="64">' +
    '<img src="0.gif" name="h1" height="64" width="64">' +
    '<img src="sep.gif" height="64" width="24">' +
    '<img src="0.gif" name="m10" height="64" width="64">' +
    '<img src="0.gif" name="m1" height="64" width="64">' +
```

```
    '<img src="sep.gif" height="64" width="24">' +
    '<img src="0.gif" name="s10" height="64" width="64">' +
    '<img src="0.gif" name="s1" height="64" width="64">'
  );
}
```

This test ensures that, where a browser either doesn't support the Images object or where JavaScript has been disabled, the default *0.gif* images are not displayed on the page. This avoids the user seeing something that the browser does not support.

# Year Calendar

The Year Calendar project displays a 12-month calendar from January to December in a 4 by 3 grid for the current year, with the current day of the current month highlighted. It uses the *calendar.js* library briefly mentioned in the Popup Date Selector project in Chapter 6. The *calendar.js* library is completely reusable. It can be used to display a single month of any year, as shown in the Popup Date Selector, all 12 months of any year, or any other combination you wish to show.

The *calendar.js* library provides three basic reusable functions:

- CalendarHead(Month,Year,Select)    This returns the HTML for displaying the heading of a calendar month, indicated by the Month and Year parameters. The Boolean Select parameter controls whether or not two drop-down select options lists are included for choosing other months and years.

- CalendarMonth(M,Y,offset)    This returns the HTML for the actual calendar month, indicated by the M and Y parameters. The offset parameter controls the first day of the week. For example, 0 indicates Sunday as the first day of the week, 1 indicates Monday, and 6 indicates Saturday.

- CalendarSelect(Month,Year,offset)    This returns the HTML for displaying a calendar month, including drop-down select-option lists for choosing other months and years. It reuses the CalendarHead() and CalendarMonth() functions.

The Popup Date Selector project in Chapter 6 uses the CalendarSelect() function, passing the month and year to be displayed, along with zero as the offset for the first day of the week. The resulting HTML includes an enclosing form with the two drop-down select-option lists. Figure 7-9 shows the multiple use of both the CalendarHead() function, with a false Select parameter, and the CalendarMonth() function, with a zero offset parameter, to show a Year Calendar. Notice how the look and feel of the Year Calendar is totally different from the Popup Date Selector. This is a result of the use of a separate external cascading style sheet—in this case, *calendar.css*—

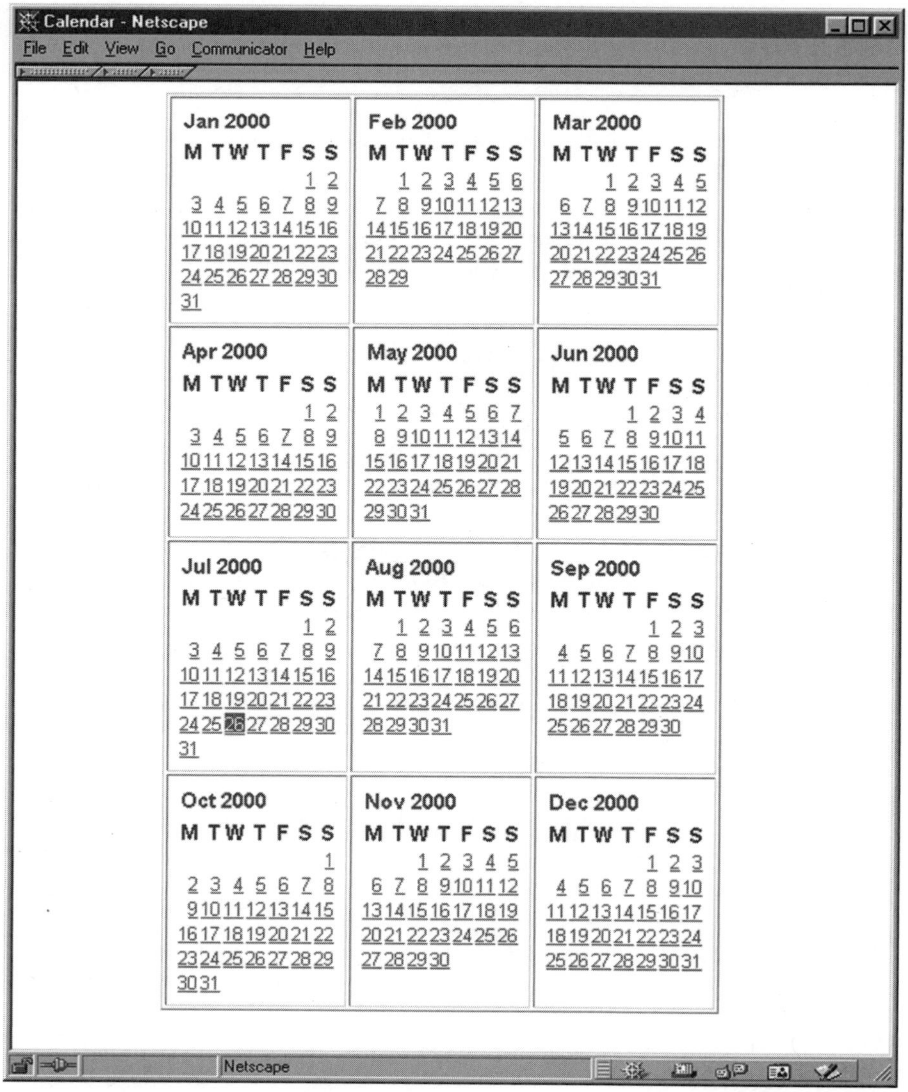

**Figure 7-9**
Year Calendar—
The 12 months
of 2000.

and the overriding of certain arrays held in the *calendar.js* library with different values held in the *index.htm* page.

## Year Calendar Source Code—calendar.js

The *calendar.js* library contains the default values of several arrays; three global variables to hold the currently selected day, month, and year; three helper functions to decouple the calendar application from any surrounding application (as seen in the Popup Date Selector); and the three functions necessary to build the HTML.

../chapter7/calendar/calendar.js

The `moy` array holds the names of the months to be displayed within the calendar application. By default, the values are the full names of the months:

```
var moy = new Array(
  'January','February','March',
  'April','May','June','July',
  'August','September','October',
  'November','December'
);
```

The `dow` array holds the names of the days to be used in the calendar application. By default, the values are abbreviations of the names of the days. Notice that the array holds extra entries. This makes it easier to use the `offset` parameter.

```
var dow = new Array('Sun','Mon','Tue','Wed','Thu','Fri','Sat',
                    'Sun','Mon','Tue','Wed','Thu','Fri');
```

The global `size` variable holds a string indicating the width and height attributes to be used for each table cell:

```
var size = 'width="50" height="30"';
```

The global `border` variable holds the border attribute to be used for each table:

```
var border = 'border="1"';
```

The three global variables `CalendarMonth`, `CalendarYear`, and `CalendarDay` are defined. They are used by the helper functions to enable the decoupling of the calendar application from any surrounding application:

```
var CalendarMonth;
var CalendarYear;
var CalendarDay;
```

The three helper functions `CalMonth()`, `CalYear()`, and `CalDay()` are invoked whenever the calendar application detects the user selecting a different month, year, or day. The three helper functions extract the value of the changed item, update the value of the corresponding global variable, and then invoke user-supplied functions. In other words, the `changeMonth()`, `changeYear()`, and `changeDay()` functions, if present, will be invoked by the calendar application. The three functions are provided independently of the calendar application.

The `CalMonth()` helper function retrieves the value of the selected `Month` option from the `Cal` form, using the `getAnOptionValue()` utility function, subtracts zero to convert the string value to a numerical value, assigns the result to the global `CalendarMonth` variable, and then invokes the `changeMonth()` function, passing the value of `CalendarMonth` as an input parameter:

```
function CalMonth() {
  CalendarMonth = getAnOptionValue(document.Cal.Month) - 0;
  changeMonth(CalendarMonth);
}
```

The `CalYear()` helper function does a similar job to the `CalMonth()` function but uses the year instead of the month:

```
function CalYear() {
  CalendarYear = getAnOptionValue(document.Cal.Year) - 0;
  changeYear(CalendarYear);
}
```

The `CalDay()` helper function accepts three parameters—day, `month`, and year—assigns the values to the `CalendarDay`, `CalendarMonth`, and `CalendarYear` global variables, and then invokes the `changeDay()` function, passing the three global variables as input parameters:

```
function CalDay(day,month,year) {
  CalendarDay = day;
  CalendarMonth = month;
  CalendarYear = year;
```

```
      changeDay(CalendarDay,CalendarMonth,CalendarYear);
}
```

The `CalendarSelect()` function is used to generate a complete header with two drop-down select-option lists for months and years, and a month calendar, using the passed `Month` and `Year` parameters to indicate the month to be displayed, and the passed `offset` parameter to indicate the first day of the week:

```
function CalendarSelect(Month,Year,offset) {
```

If the `offset` parameter is null (i.e., a value has not been passed), then the `offset` variable is defaulted to zero:

```
if (offset == null) offset = 0;
```

The HTML output generated by the `CalendarSelect()` function requires the three user-defined functions `changeMonth()`, `changeYear()`, and `changeDay()` to have been declared prior to invoking the function. If the `window` object does not contain a property for any of the three functions, then a suitable error message is sent to the user (or more usually the developer of the JavaScript application making use of the *calendar.js* library), and the function immediately exits:

```
if (window.changeMonth) { }
else {
  alert('A changeMonth() function has not been defined');
  return '';
}

if (window.changeYear) { }
else {
  alert('A changeYear() function has not been defined');
  return '';
}

if (window.changeDay) { }
else {
  alert('A changeDay() function has not been defined');
  return '';
}
```

An `output` variable is defined and initialized:

```
var output = '';
```

The `output` variable is appended with the HTML necessary to build a form named `Cal`, plus the return value of the `CalendarHead()` and `CalendarMonth()` functions:

```
output += '<form name="Cal">';
output += CalendarHead(Month,Year,true);
output += CalendarMonth(Month,Year,offset);
output += '</form>';
```

The call to the `CalendarHead()` function passes as input the value of the `Month` and `Year` parameters, along with a third parameter set to `true`.

The value of the `output` variable is returned back to whomever called the `CalendarSelect()` function:

```
return output;
}
```

The `CalendarHead()` function builds up the table to hold the month calendar, and optionally includes two drop-down select-option lists. The function accepts three parameters, `Month`, `Year`, and `Select`:

```
function CalendarHead(Month,Year,Select) {
```

An `output` variable is defined and initialized:

```
var output = '';
```

The HTML necessary to build a table around the header information is appended. The first cell of the first row contains the name of the month using the `moy` array and the value of the `Month` parameter, followed by the value of the `Year` parameter:

```
output +=
  '<table cellspacing="0" class="cal">' +
  '<tr><td align="left" width="100%" class="head">' +
  moy[Month-1] + ' ' + Year +
  '</td>';
```

If the third input parameter, `Select`, is `true`, then the HTML to build the two select-option lists is additionally appended:

```
if (Select) {
```

First, a `select` element named `Month` is appended. It has an `onChange` event handler that invokes the `CalMonth()` helper function when the user changes the current selection in the list:

```
output += '<td width="50%" align="right">' +
  '<select name="Month" onChange="CalMonth()">';
```

An `option` element for each month of the year is appended. The element that corresponds to the current value of `Month` is selected as the default option:

```
for (var month=1; month<=12; month++) {
  output += '<option value="' + month + '"';
  if (month == Month) output += ' selected';
  output += '>' + moy[month-1] + '</option>';
}
```

Next, a `select` element named `Year` is appended. It also has an `onChange` event handler, but this time it invokes the `CalYear()` function. Again, an `option` element for each year from 1900 to 2100 is appended, and the entry that corresponds to the current value of `Year` is selected as the default option:

```
output += '</select>' +
  '<select name="Year" onChange="CalYear();">';

for (var year=1900; year<=2100; year++) {
  output += '<option value="' + year + '"';
  if (year == Year) output += ' selected';
  output += '>' + year + '</option>';
}

output += '</select>';
}
```

Finally, the HTML for the table is closed, and the value of `output` is returned:

```
output += '</td></tr></table>';

return output;
}
```

The `CalendarMonth()` function builds and returns the HTML necessary to display a month calendar using the passed `M` and `Y` parameters as the month and year to be displayed, as well as the `offset` variable to indicate the first day of the week:

```
function CalendarMonth(M,Y,offset) {
```

As with the `CalendarSelect()` function, if the `offset` parameter is null (i.e., a value has not been passed), then the `offset` variable is defaulted to zero:

```
if (offset == null) offset = 0;
```

The day of the 1st of the month, `startDay`, is retrieved using the `dayOfWeek()` function:

```
var startDay = dayOfWeek(1,M,Y);
```

If this is less than the value of `offset`, then `startDay` is increased by 7.

```
if (startDay < offset) startDay += 7;
```

A local `days` variable is defined and assigned a copy of the `daysOfMonth` array reference:

```
var days = daysOfMonth;
```

If the `Y` year is a leap year, determined by the `isLeapYear()` function, then the local `days` variable is updated with a copy of the `daysOfMonthLY` array:

```
if (isLeapYear(Y)) days = daysOfMonthLY;
```

An `output` variable is defined and initialized:

```
var output = '';
```

The remainder of the function builds up the table HTML necessary to display the month calendar:

```
output +=
  '<table ' + border + ' cellpadding="0" class="cal"><tr>';
```

The first table row contains the names of each day of the week from the `dow` array:

```
for (var i=0; i<7; i++)
  output += '<td ' + size + ' class="days">' +
    dow[i + offset] + '</td>';

output += '</tr><tr>';
```

The second row starts to display the days of the month. However, the second row may contain days from the previous month, in which case they need to first be included before we can start on the current month. The value of the last month (`lastM`) is calculated by subtracting from `M`.

If this results in 0, then it is altered to 12 (i.e., the current month is January; therefore, the previous month is December):

```
var column = 0;
var lastM = M - 1;
if (lastM == 0) lastM = 12;
```

For each day from the previous month that encroaches into the first partial week of this month, a table cell is appended to the output variable:

```
for (var i=0+offset; i<startDay; i++, column++)
  output += '<td ' + size + ' class="grey">' +
    (days[lastM-1]-startDay+i+1) + '</td>';
```

Once this is complete, the code can continue to append each day of the current month to the output variable:

```
for (var i=1; i<=days[M-1]; i++, column++) {
```

A local style variable holds the class attribute to be used by all the table cells containing a day in the current month:

```
var style = ' class="links"';
```

If, however, the current cell being appended (identified by the local variables i, M, and Y), is identical to the current day (identified by global variables day, month, and year), then the style variable is replaced with another value. This has the effect of highlighting the current day within the current month within the current year:

```
if (day == i && month == M && year == Y)
  style = ' class="today"';
```

If the user supplied a changeDay() function—that is, the window object has a changeDay property—then the table cell includes a hypertext link, which invokes the CalDay() helper function, passing the value of i, M, and Y as input parameters when the hypertext link is clicked:

```
if (window.changeDay)
  output += '<td ' + size + '>' +
    '<a href="javascript:CalDay('+i+','+M+','+Y+')"' +
    style + '>' + i + '</a></td>';
```

Otherwise, the cell simply contains the value of the day of the month:

```
else
  output += '<td ' + size + style + '>' + i + '</td>';
```

After each block of seven table cells, a new table row is appended:

```
    if (column == 6) {
      output += '</tr><tr>';
      column = -1;
    }
  }
```

As at the start of the month, it is possible that days from the following month appear in the last partial week of the current month. A table cell for each one is appended:

```
    if (column > 0) {
      for (var i=1; column<7; i++, column++)
        output += '<td ' + size + ' class="grey">' + i + '</td>';
    }
```

Finally, the HTML table is closed, and the value of the output variable is returned:

```
    output += '</tr></table>';

    return output;
}
```

## Year Calendar Source Code—calendar.css

 ../chapter7/calendar/calendar.css

Note that the code uses various HTML class attributes: cal, head, grey, links, today, and days. The definition of these class styles is held in the *calendar.css* file. By amending the definitions of the class styles, it is possible to affect the presentation of the calendar independently of the JavaScript code:

```
.cal {
  background-color: #ffffff;
}

.head {
  color: #bb0000;
  font-family: Arial;
  font-weight: bold;
  text-align: left;
}
```

```
.days {
  color: #0000bb;
  font-family: Arial;
  font-weight: bold;
  text-align: right;
}

.grey {
  color: #ffffff;
  font-family: Arial;
  font-size: small;
  text-align: right;
}

.links {
  color: #ff0000;
  font-family: Arial;
  font-size: small;
  text-align: right;
}

.today {
  color: #ffffff;
  background-color: #ff0000;
  font-family: Arial;
  font-size: small;
  text-align: right;
}
```

## Year Calendar Source Code—index.htm

 ━ ━ ━ ━ ━ ━ ━ ━ ━ ━ ━ ━ ━ ━ ━ ━ ━ ━ ━

**../chapter7/calendar/index.htm**

The *index.htm* page, like the *index.htm* page in the Popup Date Selector detailed in Chapter 6, is a wrapper application that makes use of the generic code within the *calendar.js* library. Unlike the Popup Date Selector wrapper application, the Year Calendar wrapper application simply uses the *calendar.js* library to display all the months of the current year, as shown in Figure 7-9.

First we include the *calendar.css* style sheet:

```
<link rel="stylesheet" href="calendar.css" type="text/css">
```

Next, we include the *current.js* and *calendar.js* libraries:

```
<script language="JavaScript" src="current.js"></script>
<script language="JavaScript" src="calendar.js"></script>
```

We then override the values of the global variables `size` and `border` and the `dow` and `moy` arrays with our preferred values:

```
size = '';
border = 'border="0"';
dow = new Array('S','M','T','W','T','F','S',
                'S','M','T','W','T','F');
moy = new Array(
  'Jan','Feb','Mar','Apr','May','Jun',
  'Jul','Aug','Sep','Oct','Nov','Dec'
);
```

We define just the `changeDay()` function. This user-defined function, optional in this particular wrapper application, simply creates a `Date` object using values of the passed `day`, `month`, and `year` parameters and then highlights its value using an alert:

```
function changeDay(day, month, year) {
  alert(new Date(year, month, day));
}
```

An `output` variable is defined and initialized:

```
var output = '';
```

The main body of the code is processed only if both the JavaScript libraries have been loaded successfully:

```
if (window.formatFullDate && window.CalendarSelect) {
```

The `day`, `month`, and `year` global variables are defined and initialized using the current date:

```
var today = new Date();
var day   = today.getDate();
var month = today.getMonth() + 1;
var year  = today.getFullYear();
```

The code then proceeds to build up the HTML for a three wide by four high table. Each table cell contains the results of a call to the `CalendarHead()` and `CalendarMonth()` functions, and the results are appended to the `output` variable. The code loops 12 times, once for each month of the year, each time incrementing the value of the local `i` variable. The value of `i` is used as the `Month` input parameter to both the `CalendarHead()` and `CalendarMonth()` functions. Since the third parameter to the `CalendarHead()` function is absent (the `Select` parameter), the drop-down select-option lists are not included in the function's return value. The third parameter to the `CalendarMonth()` function (the `offset` parameter) is passed as the numeric value `1`. This indicates that the function should use Monday as the first day of each week.

```
output +=
  '<table class="cal" border="1"><tr><td valign="top">';
for (var i = 1; i <= 12; i++) {
  output += '<table><tr><td>' +
    CalendarHead(i,year) +
    CalendarMonth(i,year,1) +
    '</td></tr></table>';

  if (i != 12) {
    if (i % 3 == 0)
      output += '</td></tr><tr><td valign="top">';
    else
      output += '</td><td valign="top">';
  }
}

output += '</td></tr></table>';
}
```

Once all HTML has been built, the value of the output variable is written to the document:

```
document.write(output);
```

The action generated when the user clicks on one of the days in the calendar is entirely flexible. All you need to do is amend the `changeDay()` function to remove the `alert()` message and replace it with something of your own choosing, perhaps a pop-up window that displays events for that particular day.

# Date Countdown

For the last few years prior to December 31, 1999, many websites had simple countdowns to the date from 1999 to 2000. Now that January 1, 2000 has come and gone, many of these countdowns are still running but now incorrectly state the time left to January 1, 2000 as a negative amount. The code presented here shows how to use general-purpose code to count down or count up from one arbitrary date. Figure 7-10 shows the countdown and count-up timers for four different dates.

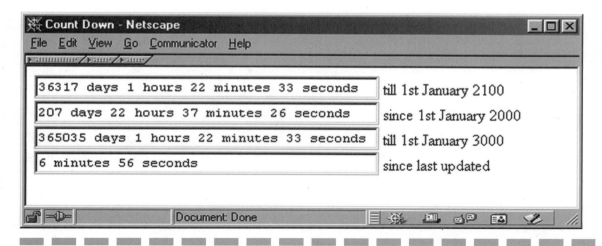

**Figure 7-10** Countdown and count-up timers in operation.

## Date Countdown Source Code—countdown.js

The *countdown.js* library includes the generic JavaScript functions used in the later *index.htm* page.

**../chapter7/countdown/countdown.js**

The formatObjectDate() function acts as a generic object method. It returns the days, hours, minutes, and seconds properties of the this object reference as a formatted string:

```
function formatObjectDate() {
  return ((this.days != 0) ? this.days + ' days ' : '') +
    ((this.hours != 0) ? this.hours + ' hours ' : '') +
    ((this.minutes != 0) ? this.minutes + ' minutes ' : '') +
    ((this.seconds != 0) ? this.seconds + ' seconds ' : '');
}
```

The countdown() function accepts the passed when Date object parameter and passes it as input along with another Date object representing the current time to the `difference()` function. The returned object reference is then reused with its `formatDate()` method to format the time remaining until the `when` date and time:

```
function countdown(when) {
  return difference(when, new Date()).formatDate();
}
```

The process is the same with the `countup()` function, except that the order of the input parameters to the `difference()` function is reversed:

```
function countup(when) {
  return difference(new Date(), when).formatDate();
}
```

The `difference()` function accepts two `Date` object parameters—`older` and `newer`—and creates a default `myObject` Object. It then calculates the difference between the `older` and `newer` dates in days, hours, minutes, and seconds and assigns the values to properties of the `myObject` Object:

```
function difference(older,newer) {
```

First, the `difference()` function uses the generic `Object` constructor to create an `Object` object with no inherent properties or methods and assigns the object reference to the `myObject` variable:

```
var myObject = new Object();
```

The time difference (`dif`) in milliseconds between the two dates is calculated by subtracting the times in milliseconds from one another, retrieved by using the `getTime()` method:

```
var dif = older.getTime() - newer.getTime();
```

The number of day's difference between the two dates is achieved by dividing the `dif` variable by 86,400,000 milliseconds (i.e., the number of milliseconds in a whole day: 1000 milliseconds by 60 seconds by 60 minutes by 24 hours). The result is then rounded down to the nearest integer and then assigned to the `myObject` object's `days` property:

```
myObject.days = Math.floor(dif/1000/60/60/24);
```

The `dif` variable is then amended to reduce the value by the number of milliseconds in the number of days difference:

```
dif = dif - myObject.days*1000*60*60*24
```

Likewise, the same type of calculations are performed to obtain the hours, minutes, and seconds difference between the two dates:

```
myObject.hours = Math.floor(dif/1000/60/60);

dif = dif - myObject.hours*1000*60*60

myObject.minutes = Math.floor(dif/1000/60);

dif = dif - myObject.minutes*1000*60

myObject.seconds = Math.floor(dif/1000);
```

The `myObject` object's `formatDate` property is assigned the reference of the `formatObjectDate()` function. This then makes the `formatDate()` a method of the `myObject` object:

```
myObject.formatDate = formatObjectDate;
```

Finally, the `myObject` object reference is returned:

```
return myObject;
}
```

## Date Countdown Source Code—index.htm

The *index.htm* page holds the HTML and specific JavaScript code necessary to show four different and unrelated date countdowns running alongside one another.

**../chapter7/countdown/index.htm**

First, the *countdown.js* library is included in the page:

```
<script src="countdown.js" language="JavaScript"></script>
```

Four separate date objects are created and assigned to four global variables—`time1` for January 1, 2100, `time2` for January 1, 2000, `time3` for January 1, 3000, and `time4` for the document's last modification date:

```
var time1 = new Date(2100, 0, 1);
var time2 = new Date(2000, 0, 1);
var time3 = new Date(3000, 0, 1);
var time4 = new Date(document.lastModified);
```

The autoUpdate() function calls the countdown() and countup() functions using the previously defined global time variables as input parameters. The return values are then used to update the value of four different input form fields:

```
function autoUpdate() {
```

The body of the autoUpdate() function is only processed in the countdown(), and countup() functions have been successfully loaded from the *countdown.js* library:

```
if (window.countdown && window.countup) {
```

The first timer uses the countdown() function to retrieve and format the time remaining until time1:

```
var dif1 = countdown(time1);
if (document.timeForm.field1.value != dif1)
  document.timeForm.field1.value = dif1;
```

The second timer uses the countup() function to retrieve and format the time since time2:

```
var dif2 = countup(time2);
if (document.timeForm.field2.value != dif2)
  document.timeForm.field2.value = dif2;
```

The third timer uses the countdown() function to retrieve and format the time remaining until time3:

```
var dif3 = countdown(time3);
if (document.timeForm.field3.value != dif3)
  document.timeForm.field3.value = dif3;
```

The fourth timer uses the countup() function to retrieve and format the time since time4:

```
var dif4 = countup(time4);
if (document.timeForm.field4.value != dif4)
  document.timeForm.field4.value = dif4;
```

In each case the relevant form field value is updated only if the value has changed. The `autoUpdate()` function then starts a timer to reinvoke the `autoUpdate()` function after 500 milliseconds:

```
    setTimeout('autoUpdate()',500)
  }
}
```

The `onLoad` event handler in the start `body` tag starts the whole process off by invoking the `autoUpdate()` function when the entire page has completely loaded:

```
<body onLoad="autoUpdate()">
```

# 32 Years 8 Months and 24 Days

This application shows how to calculate the difference between two dates in years, months, and days. The actual `HowOld()` function described and used in this application was previously used in the "Family Trees" section in Chapter 6.

Calculating the difference between two dates can be achieved using the techniques shown in the previous Date Countdown application. However, the code in the `HowOld()` function simply calculates the difference by subtracting the number of years, months, and days in one date from the other. Figure 7-11 shows the results achieved when calculating

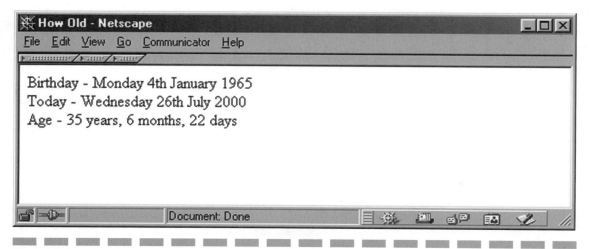

**Figure 7-11**  *The age in years, months, and days of someone born on January 4, 1965 on July 26, 2000.*

the age of someone born on the January 4, 1965, when the page is loaded into the browser on the July 26, 2000.

## 32 Years 8 Months and 24 Days Source Code—howold.js

The *howold.js* library contains the single HowOld() function. The function uses simple subtraction to determine the years, months, and days of one date from another.

 ../chapter7/howold/howold.js

The HowOld() function accepts six parameters: day, month, and year representing the older date (e.g., a birth date), and Day, Month, and Year representing the newer date (e.g., today's date).

```
function HowOld(day,month,year,Day,Month,Year) {
```

Three local variables, years, months, and days, are defined. Straight away the value of years is set to the difference between Year minus year, and the value of months and days is set to zero:

```
var years = Year - year, months = days = 0;
```

The difference between Month and months is calculated. If need be, one year is borrowed from years and added as 12 months to Month:

```
if (Month >= month) months = Month - month;
else { years—; months = Month + 12 - month; }
```

Likewise, the difference between Day and day is calculated and assigned to days, except this time there may also be a need to not only borrow one month from months and add it as 31 days to day, but alternatively to borrow one year from years and add it as 11 months to months and then 31 days to Day:

```
if (Day >= day) days = Day - day;
else {
  if (months > 0) months—;
  else { years—; months+=11; }
  days = Day + 31 - day;
}
```

If any of the calculations has resulted in years being less than zero, or years, months, and days all being equal to zero, then the input data is assumed to be incorrect, in which case, an empty string is returned.

```
if (years < 0) return '';
if ((years == 0) && (months == 0) && (days == 0)) return '';
```

Otherwise, a formatted string indicating the difference in years, months, and days is returned:

```
return years  + ' years, ' +
       months + ' months, ' +
       days   + ' days';
}
```

## 32 Years 8 Months and 24 Days Source Code—index.htm

The *index.htm* page shows how to use the *howold.js* library to calculate the age of someone born on January 4, 1965.

**../chapter7/howold/index.htm**

Both the *current.js* and *howold.js* libraries are loaded into the page:

```
<script src="current.js" language="JavaScript"></script>
<script src="howold.js" language="JavaScript"></script>
```

The code is only processed if both the libraries have successfully loaded:

```
if (window.formatFullDate && window.HowOld) {
```

The day, month, and year variables hold the date for January 4, 1965.

```
var day   = 4;
var month = 1;
var year  = 1965;
```

The formatFullDate() function is used to display the birth date:

```
document.write(
  'Birthday - ' + formatFullDate(day, month, year) + '<br>'
);
```

The `today` variable holds the current date and time created using a default `Date` object constructor:

```
var today = new Date();
```

The `Day`, `Month`, and `Year` variables hold the retrieved day, month, and year values of the `today` date:

```
var Day   = today.getDate();
var Month = today.getMonth()+1;
var Year  = today.getFullYear();
```

The `formatFullDate()` function is used to display today's date:

```
document.write(
  'Today - ' + formatFullDate(Day, Month, Year) + '<br>'
);
```

Finally, the two sets of dates are passed as input to the `HowOld()` function. The return value is then output to the document:

```
document.write(
  'Age - ' + HowOld(day,month,year,Day,Month,Year)
  )
};
```

The Family Tree application described in Chapter 6 showed how the return value of the `HowOld()` function could be used to update the value of object properties, and then be used to display the age of the people in the family tree.

# What Zodiac Sign Are You?

Many, many people are intrigued by horoscopes, their date of birth, what star sign they fall under, and the current star sign for today. This application shows how to determine which star sign a particular date falls under, including the symbol, birthstone, and quality usually associated with a star sign, and generates a date range for the particular star sign. Figure 7-12 shows the result of the application being run on July 27, 2000.

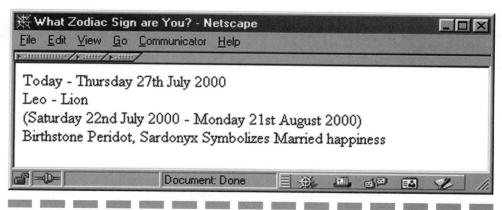

**Figure 7-12**    Zodiac Sign—For the 27th of July 2000.

## What Zodiac Sign Are You? Source Code—zodiac.js

The *zodiac.js* library contains the necessary object constructors, arrays, and functions to calculate the star sign of any date.

**../chapter7/zodiac/zodiac.js**

The Zodiac() function is actually an object constructor for Zodiac objects. It assigns the passed parameters as properties of the Zodiac object, one each for the day in the month that the zodiac star sign ends, the sign, the symbol, the birthstone, and the quality associated with the star sign:

```
function Zodiac(day, sign, symbol, birthstone, quality) {
this.day = day;
this.sign = sign;
this.symbol = symbol;
this.birthstone = birthstone;
this.quality = quality;
}
```

The setZodiac() function is used to create instances of the Zodiac object and assign the object reference to the myZodiac object array.

```
function setZodiac(day, sign, symbol, birthstone, quality) {
  myZodiac[zodiacIndex++] =
    new Zodiac(day, sign, symbol, birthstone, quality);
}
```

The zodiacIndex array index and myZodiac array are defined and initialized:

```
var zodiacIndex = 0;
var myZodiac = new Array();
```

The setZodiac() function is then invoked 12 times, once for each sign in the Zodiac:

```
setZodiac(20,'Capricorn','Goat','Garnet','Constancy');
setZodiac(19,'Aquarius','Water Bearer','Amethyst','Sincerity');
setZodiac(
  21,'Pisces','Fishes','Aquamarine, Bloodstone','Courage');
setZodiac(21,'Aries','Ram','Diamond','Innocence');
setZodiac(21,'Taurus','Bull','Emerald','Love, success');
setZodiac(
  21,'Gemini','Twins','Pearl, Alexandrite, Moonstone','Health'
);
setZodiac(22,'Cancer','Crab','Ruby','Contentment');
setZodiac(
  22,'Leo','Lion','Peridot, Sardonyx','Married happiness');
setZodiac(22,'Virgo','Virgin','Sapphire','Clear thinking');
setZodiac(23,'Libra','Balance','Opal, Tourmaline','Hope');
setZodiac(22,'Scorpio','Scorpion','Topaz','Fidelity');
setZodiac(
  21,'Sagittarius','Archer','Turquoise, Zircon','Prosperity');
```

The starSign() function is used to return a numeric value for the star sign (e.g., 0 for Capricorn, 11 for Sagittarius, and so on) that corresponds with the day and month input parameters:

```
function starSign(day,month) {
```

A local zodiac variable is assigned the value of the month parameter:

```
var zodiac = month;
```

If the passed day parameter is less then the day property of the Zodiac object that corresponds to the passed month parameter, then the zodiac variable is decreased by 1:

```
if (day < myZodiac[month-1].day) zodiac—
```

If the value of the zodiac variable is still equal to 12, then the star sign must fall into next year's zodiac calendar, in which case the value of `zodiac` is adjusted to 0 (i.e., Capricorn:):

```
if (zodiac==12) zodiac=0;
```

The value of the `zodiac` variable is returned:

```
    return zodiac;
}
```

The `starDateRange()` function returns a string of two formatted dates representing the start and end dates of the star sign that the passed `day`, `month`, and `year` dates fall within:

```
function starDateRange(day,month,year) {
```

The `beginYear`, `endYear`, and `beginMonth`, `endMonth` local variables are initialized to the values of the passed `year` and `month` parameters:

```
    var beginYear = endYear = year;
    var beginMonth = endMonth = month;
```

The `beginMonth` variable is decreased by one if the `day` of the `month` is earlier than the `day` property of the relevant `Zodiac` object; otherwise, the `endMonth` variable is increased by 1:

```
    if (day < myZodiac[month-1].day)
      beginMonth—; else endMonth++;
```

If `beginMonth` equals 0, then `beginMonth` and `beginYear` are adjusted to the last month of the previous year. Otherwise, if the `endMonth` equals 13, then `endMonth` and `endYear` are adjusted to the first month of the next year:

```
    if (beginMonth == 0) {
      beginMonth = 12; beginYear—;
    }
    else if (endMonth == 13) {
      endMonth = 1; endYear++;
    }
```

Both the `beginDay` and `endDay` variables are assigned the `day` property or `day` property minus 1 of the relevant `Zodiac` object:

```
    beginDay = myZodiac[beginMonth-1].day;
    endDay = myZodiac[endMonth-1].day - 1;
```

Finally, a string of the formatted begin and end dates is returned:

```
return formatFullDate(beginDay,beginMonth,beginYear) +
       ' - ' +
       formatFullDate(endDay,endMonth,endYear);
}
```

## What Zodiac Sign Are You? Source Code—index.htm

The *index.htm* page shows the details of the star sign for the current date.

..**/chapter7/zodiac/index.htm**

Both the *current.js* and *zodiac.js* libraries are loaded into the page:

```
<script src="current.js" language="JavaScript"></script>
<script src="zodiac.js" language="JavaScript"></script>
```

The code is processed only if the two libraries have successfully loaded:

```
if (window.formatFullDate && window.Zodiac) {
```

The day, month, and year variables are assigned the values for the current date:

```
var today = new Date();
var day   = today.getDate();
var month = today.getMonth() + 1;
var year  = today.getFullYear();
```

The starsign() function is passed the day and month input parameters, and the result is assigned to the star variable:

```
var star = starSign(day,month);
```

The relevant properties of the Zodiac object located within the myZodiac object array at position star are written out to the document, along with the return value of the starDateRange() function:

```
document.write(
  myZodiac[star].sign + ' - ' +
  myZodiac[star].symbol +
  '<br>(' + starDateRange(day,month,year) + ')<br>' +
  'Birthstone ' + myZodiac[star].birthstone +
  ' Symbolizes ' + myZodiac[star].quality
);
}
```

# The Chinese New Year

This particular application is similar to the previous What Zodiac Sign Are You? application because it displays the details of a particular date and how it relates to the Chinese calendar. The Chinese New Year falls sometime between January 10th and February 19th of the Gregorian calendar. The initial year (jia-zi) of the current 60-year cycle began on February 2, 1984. The full list of the sexagenary year names is shown in Table 7-2.

**TABLE 7-2**

The Chinese sexagenary year names from 1984 to 2043.

| Year | Year Name | Year | Year Name | Year | Year Name | Year | Year Name |
|------|-----------|------|-----------|------|-----------|------|-----------|
| '84 | jia-zi | '99 | ji-mao | '14 | jia-wu | '29 | ji-you |
| '85 | yi-chou | '00 | geng-chen | '15 | yi-wei | '30 | geng-xu |
| '86 | bing-yin | '01 | xin-si | '16 | bing-shen | '31 | xin-hai |
| '87 | ding-mao | '02 | ren-wu | '17 | ding-you | '32 | ren-zi |
| '88 | wu-chen | '03 | gui-wei | '18 | wu-xu | '33 | gui-chou |
| '89 | ji-si | '04 | jia-shen | '19 | ji-hai | '34 | jia-yin |
| '90 | geng-wu | '05 | yi-you | '20 | geng-zi | '35 | yi-mao |
| '91 | xin-wei | '06 | bing-xu | '21 | xin-chou | '36 | bing-chen |
| '92 | ren-shen | '07 | ding-hai | '22 | ren-yin | '37 | ding-si |
| '93 | gui-you | '08 | wu-zi | '23 | gui-mao | '38 | wu-wu |
| '94 | jia-xu | '09 | ji-chou | '24 | jia-chen | '39 | ji-wei |
| '95 | yi-hai | '10 | geng-yin | '25 | yi-si | '40 | geng-shen |
| '96 | bing-zi | '11 | xin-mao | '26 | bing-wu | '41 | xin-you |
| '97 | ding-chou | '12 | ren-chen | '27 | ding-wei | '42 | ren-xu |
| '98 | wu-yin | '13 | gui-si | '28 | wu-shen | '43 | gui-hai |

**Figure 7-13**
Chinese Year of the
Dragon—February 5,
2000 to January 23,
2001.

The year name is obtained using the cycle of the 12 *terrestrial branches* (zi, chou, yin, mao, and so on) and the 10 *celestial stems* (jia, yi, bing, and so on). The branches are the Chinese equivalents of the westernized animal names of the 12 years. Figure 7-13 shows the results for any date between February 5, 2000 and January 23, 2001.

## The Chinese New Year Source Code—chinese.js

The *chinese.js* library contains all the functions and arrays necessary to calculate and return the details of any date.

../chapter7/chinese/chinese.js

The Chinese() function acts as a Chinese object constructor, assigning each one of the passed parameters as a property of the this object reference:

```
function Chinese(animal,animalI,branch,branchI,stem,stemI) {
  this.animal = animal; this.animalImage = animalI;
  this.branch = branch; this.branchImage = branchI;
  this.stem = stem; this.stemImage = stemI;
}
```

The setChinese() function creates instances of the Chinese object and assign the object reference to the next entry in the myChinese object array:

```
function setChinese(animal,animalI,branch,branchI,stem,stemI) {
  myChinese[chineseIndex++] =
    new Chinese(animal,animalI,branch,branchI,stem,stemI);
}
```

The `chineseIndex` variable and `myChinese` array are defined and initialized:

```
var chineseIndex = 0;
var myChinese = new Array();
```

The `setChinese()` function is invoked 12 times, once for each Chinese branch, passing the westernized animal name, an animal image name, the branch name, a branch image name, a stem name, and a stem image name:

```
setChinese(
'Pig','pig.gif','hai','hai4.gif','gui','gui3.gif');
setChinese('Rat','rat.gif','zi','zi3.gif','jia','jia3.gif');
setChinese('Ox','ox.gif','chou','chou3.gif','yi','yi3.gif');
setChinese(
  'Tiger','tiger.gif','yin','yin2.gif','bing','bing3.gif');
setChinese(
  'Rabbit','rabbit.gif','mao','mao3.gif','ding','ding1.gif');
setChinese(
  'Dragon','dragon.gif','chen','chen2.gif','wu','wu4.gif');
setChinese('Snake','snake.gif','si','si4.gif','ji','ji3.gif');
setChinese(
  'Horse','horse.gif','wu','wu3.gif','geng','geng1.gif');
setChinese(
 'Goat','goat.gif','wei','wei4.gif','xin','xin1.gif');
setChinese(
  'Monkey','monkey.gif','shen','shen1.gif','ren','ren2.gif');
setChinese('Rooster','rooster.gif','you','you3.gif');
setChinese('Dog','dog.gif','xu','xu1.gif');
```

**NOTE**:   *Note that although there is not a one-to-one mapping between branch and stem, rather than create a separate array for the stem information, we have reused the first 10 entries in the* `myChinese` *array to hold the stem information.*

Four additional images are used for the Chinese equivalent of the English phrases *branch* and *stem*:

```
var branchImage1 = 'di4.gif';
var branchImage2 = 'zhi1.gif';

var stemImage1 = 'tian1.gif';
var stemImage2 = 'gan1.gif';
```

Rather than calculate the Chinese New Year's day for each year, something that would require a complex calculation using the phases of the moon, we have instead precalculated the Chinese New Year's day for the years 1900 through to 2051 and stored the values in the cnys array:

```
var cnys = new Array(
  1.31, 2.19, 2.08, 1.29, 2.16, 2.04, 1.25, 2.13, 2.02, 1.22,
  2.10, 1.30, 2.18, 2.06, 1.26, 2.14, 2.03, 1.23, 2.11, 2.01,
  2.20, 2.08, 1.28, 2.16, 2.05, 1.25, 2.13, 2.02, 1.23, 2.10,
  1.30, 2.17, 2.06, 1.26, 2.14, 2.04, 1.24, 2.11, 1.31, 2.19,
  2.08, 1.27, 2.15, 2.05, 1.25, 2.13, 2.02, 1.22, 2.10, 1.29,
  2.17, 2.06, 1.27, 2.14, 2.03, 1.24, 2.12, 1.31, 2.18, 2.08,
  1.28, 2.15, 2.05, 1.25, 2.13, 2.02, 1.21, 2.09, 1.30, 2.17,
  2.06, 1.27, 2.15, 2.03, 1.23, 2.11, 1.31, 2.18, 2.07, 1.28,
  2.16, 2.05, 1.25, 2.13, 2.02, 2.20, 2.09, 1.29, 2.17, 2.06,
  1.27, 2.15, 2.04, 1.23, 2.10, 1.31, 2.19, 2.07, 1.28, 2.16,
  2.05, 1.24, 2.12, 2.01, 1.22, 2.09, 1.29, 2.18, 2.07, 1.26,
  2.10, 2.03, 1.23, 2.10, 1.31, 2.19, 2.09, 1.28, 2.16, 2.05,
  1.25, 2.12, 2.01, 1.22, 2.10, 1.29, 2.17, 2.06, 1.26, 2.13,
  2.03, 1.23, 2.11, 1.31, 2.19, 2.08, 1.28, 2.15, 2.04, 1.24,
  2.12, 2.01, 1.22, 2.10, 1,30, 2.17, 2.06, 1.26, 2.14, 2.02,
  1.23, 2.11
);
```

The month and day of the month are held as a floating-point number, the integer part indicates the month, and the decimal part of the day of the month (e.g., 2.11) indicates the 11th of February.

The CNY() object constructor calculates all the information for a particular date, passed as d, m, and y, and assigns the information to properties on the this object reference:

```
function CNY(d,m,y) {
```

The start and end properties, which will hold the start and end dates of the Chinese year that the passed date falls within, are defined and initialized:

```
this.start = '';
this.end = '';
```

The start and end dates can only be calculated if the passed y year falls within the range 1900 to 2051:

```
if ((y > 1900) && (y < 2051)) {
```

The floating-point value representing the month and day of month of the New Year is retrieved from the cnys array, subtracting 1900 from the y parameter to get the correct position within the array, assigning the value to the newYear variable:

```
var newYear = cnys[y - 1900];
```

The integer and decimal portions of the `newYear` variable are extracted and assigned to the `newMonth` and `newDay` variables:

```
var newMonth = Math.floor(newYear);
var newDay = Math.round((newYear*100)-(newMonth*100));
```

To calculate the Chinese branch, you must first subtract 3 from the year before dividing by `12` to find out which animal is associated with the year: `branch = (year - 3)%12`. So, for example, for 1997, `(1997 - 3)%12` returns the integer value `2`. To retrieve the Chinese stem, it is necessary to subtract 3 from the year and then divide by `10`: `stem = (year - 3)%10`. So for 1997, `(1997 - 3)%10` returns the integer value 4. Therefore, 1997 was the Chinese year chou-ding, or the year of the Ox—that is, `myChinese[2].branch`, `myChinese[4].stem`, and `myChinese[2].animal`. However, life is not that simple. As mentioned, the start of the Chinese New Year varies from January 10th to February 19th. People always think that because I was born in 1965, that means I was born in the year of the snake. But because I was born on January 4, I was actually born in the year of the dragon.

Therefore, the code determines if the value of the `m` parameter is greater then the `newMonth` variable. If it is, then the code proceeds to calculate the `start` date property based on the passed `y` parameter and the `end` date property based on the `y` parameter plus 1 (i.e., the following year):

```
if ((m > newMonth) ||
    ((m == newMonth) && (d >= newDay))) {
// this year
this.branch = (y-3) % 12;
this.stem = (y-3) % 10;

var nextYear = cnys[y - 1900 + 1];
var nextMonth = Math.floor(nextYear);
var nextDay = Math.round((nextYear*100)-(nextMonth*100));

var lastDay = nextDay - 1;
if (lastDay == 0) {
  lastMonth = nextMonth - 1;
  lastDay = 31;
}
else lastMonth = nextMonth;

this.start = formatFullDate(newDay,newMonth,y);
this.end   = formatFullDate(lastDay,lastMonth,y+1);
}
```

Otherwise, the code proceeds to calculate the start date property based on the value of the y parameter minus 1 (i.e., the previous year) and the end date property based on the y parameter:

```
else {

  // last year
  this.branch = (y-4) % 12;
  this.stem = (y-4) % 10;

  var oldYear = cnys[y - 1900 - 1];
  var oldMonth = Math.floor(oldYear);
  var oldDay = Math.round((oldYear*100)-(oldMonth*100));

  var lastDay = newDay - 1;
  if (lastDay == 0) {
    lastMonth = newMonth - 1;
    lastDay = 31;
  }
  else lastMonth = newMonth;

  this.start = formatFullDate(oldDay,oldMonth,y-1);
  this.end   = formatFullDate(lastDay,lastMonth,y);
  }
}
```

If the y parameter falls outside or on the borders of the range 1900 to 2051, then only the general branch and stem properties for the year as a whole are calculated:

```
else {
  this.branch = (y-3) % 12;
  this.stem = (y-3) % 10;
  }
}
```

# The Chinese New Year Source Code— index.htm

The *index.htm* pages shows the Chinese year details for the current date.

**../chapter7/chinese/index.htm**

Both the *current.js* and *chinese.js* libraries are loaded into the page:

```
<script src="current.js" language="JavaScript"></script>
<script src="chinese.js" language="JavaScript"></script>
```

The code is only processed if both libraries were successfully loaded:

```
if (window.formatFullDate && window.CNY) {
```

The current date is obtained:

```
var today = new Date();
var day   = today.getDate();
var month = today.getMonth() + 1;
var year  = today.getFullYear();
```

A CNY object is created, passing the values of the day, month, and year variables as input and assigned to the cny variable:

```
var cny = new CNY(day,month,year);
```

The various properties of the cny object reference are retrieved and output to the document as either text or as src attributes of img elements:

```
document.write(
   '<img src="' + myChinese[cny.branch].animalImage +
   '" width="48" height="48">' +
   '<img src="' + stemImage1 +
   '" width="48" height="48">' +
   '<img src="' + stemImage2 +
   '" width="48" height="48">' +
   '<img src="' + myChinese[cny.stem].stemImage +
   '" width="48" height="48">' +
   '<img src="' + branchImage1 +
   '" width="48" height="48">' +
   '<img src="' + branchImage2 +
   '" width="48" height="48">' +
   '<img src="' + myChinese[cny.branch].branchImage +
   '" width="48" height="48">' +
   '<br>Chinese year of the ' + myChinese[cny.branch].animal +
   ' (' + myChinese[cny.stem].stem + '-' +
   '<br>Chinese year of the ' + myChinese[cny.branch].animal +
   '<br>(' + cny.start + ' - ' + cny.end + ')'
   );
}
```

# Born on the 4th of July

Storing the birth dates of famous people and dates of religious events or holidays that occur throughout the year is the topic of this section. Birth dates and other fixed dates are simple to hold in an array. We just need the day of month, month, and year (in the case of birth dates), or just day of month and month for repeating religious events or holidays. Religious or other events where the date changes from year to year—for example, dates that are dependent on the nth day of a month—or dates that depend on the lunar month—for example, Easter are the subject of the 3rd Saturday in November and Easter applications later in this chapter.

## Born on the 4th of July Source Code— july4th.js

The *july4th.js* library contains the object constructors and functions necessary to build the arrays for both the birth dates and the event dates. The library also contains the data necessary to construct the objects associated with each of the religious events and special holidays. The date to build the objects for the birth dates are contained in other, smaller library files—one for each month of the year.

**../chapter7/july4th/july4th.js**

The `Event()` object constructor, `setEvent()` function, `eventIndex`, and `myEvent` array, defined the code necessary to construct `Event` objects and hold them within the `myEvent` array:

```
function Event(day,month,what) {
  this.day = day;
  this.month = month;
  this.what = what;
}

function setEvent(day,month,what) {
  myEvent[eventIndex++] = new Event(day,month,what);
}

var eventIndex = 0;
var myEvent = new Array();
```

The `setEvent()` function is then used to populate the `myEvent` array with calendar events:

```
setEvent( 1, 1,'New Year\'s Day');
setEvent( 1, 1,'Mary - Mother of God');
setEvent( 6, 1,'Epiphany');
setEvent( 2, 2,'Groundhog Day');
setEvent(12, 2,'Lincoln\'s Birthday');
```

```
setEvent(14,  2,'Valentine\'s Day');
setEvent(22,  2,'Washington\'s Birthday');
setEvent(29,  2,'Leap Year\'s Day');
setEvent(17,  3,'St. Patrick\'s Day');
setEvent(19,  3,'St. Joseph');
setEvent( 1,  4,'April Fools\'s Day');
setEvent(15,  4,'Tax Day');
setEvent(14,  6,'Flag Day');
setEvent(29,  6,'St. Peter & St. Paul');
setEvent( 4,  7,'Independence Day');
setEvent(12,  7,'Battle of the Boyne (N. Ireland)');
setEvent(15,  8,'Assumption');
setEvent(12,10,'Columbus Day');
setEvent(24,10,'United Nations Day');
setEvent(31,10,'Halloween');
setEvent( 1,11,'All Saint\'s Day');
setEvent( 5,11,'Guy Fawkes Night');
setEvent(11,11,'Veteran\'s Day');
setEvent( 8,12,'Immaculate Conception');
setEvent(24,12,'Christmas Eve');
setEvent(25,12,'Christmas Day');
setEvent(26,12,'Boxing Day - St Stephen\'s Day');
setEvent(31,12,'New Year\'s Eve');
```

The showEvent() function can be used to retrieve any and all events that match the supplied day and month input parameters:

```
function showEvent(day,month) {
```

An output variable is defined and initialized:

```
var output = '';
```

The function then loops through each entry in the myEvent array:

```
for (var i=0; i < eventIndex; i++) {
```

If the day and month input parameters match the day and month properties of the current Event object, then the Event object's what property is appended to the output variable:

```
    if ((day == myEvent[i].day) && (month == myEvent[i].month))
      output += myEvent[i].what + '<br>';
  }
  return output;
}
```

The Birthday() constructor, setBirthday() function, birthday Index variable, and myBirthday array perform a similar function as the event versions:

```
function Birthday(day,month,year,who) {
  this.day = day; this.month = month; this.year = year;
  this.who = who;
}

function setBirthday(day,month,year,who) {
  myBirthday[birthdayIndex++] = new Birthday(day,month,year,who);
}

var birthdayIndex = 0;
var myBirthday = new Array();
```

The showBirthday() function can be used to retrieve the name and date of birth of any and all persons born on the same day as the passed day and month input parameters:

```
function showBirthday(day, month) {
```

An output variable is defined and initialized:

```
var output = '';
```

The function loops through all the entries in the myBirthday array:

```
for (var i=0; i < birthdayIndex; i++) {
```

Four local variables are assigned the values of the current Birthday object's day, month, year, and who properties:

```
var birthDay = myBirthday[i].day;
var birthMonth = myBirthday[i].month;
var birthYear = myBirthday[i].year;
var who = myBirthday[i].who;
```

If the day and month input parameters match the birthDay and birthMonth local variables, then the value of the Birthday objects who property and formatted date of birth is appended to the output variable:

```
if (day == birthDay && month == birthMonth) {
  output += who + ' (' +
    formatFullDate(birthDay,birthMonth,birthYear) +
    ')<br>';
  }
}

return output;
}
```

Note that at this point we have not actually created any Birthday objects. This is performed later. Figure 7-14 shows the results of running this script on December 25, 2000.

**Figure 7-14**
Christmas Day and
Sir Isaac Newton,
born on the 25th of
December.

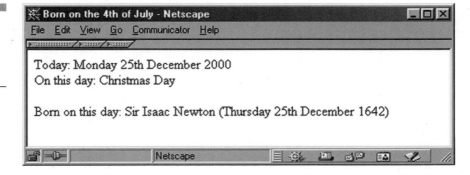

**Figure 7-14**
Christmas Day and
Sir Isaac Newton,
born on the 25th of
December.

## Born on the 4th of July Source Code—index.htm

The *index.htm* page retrieves the current date and loads an external JavaScript source file to create the `Birthday` objects for each person born in the current month. These are used along with the generically defined `Event` objects to display any special events or birthdays occurring today.

**../chapter7/july4th/index.htm**

Both the *current.js* and *july4th.js* libraries are loaded into the current page:

```
<script src="current.js" language="JavaScript"></script>
<script src="july4th.js" language="JavaScript"></script>
```

The code is only executed if both the *current.js* and *july4th.js* libraries have been loaded successfully:

```
if (window.formatFullDate && window.setBirthday) {
```

First, we retrieve the current dates day, month, and year values:

```
var today = new Date();
var day   = today.getDate();
var month = today.getMonth()+1;
var year  = today.getFullYear();
```

Next, the external JavaScript source file, which contains the calls to the `setBirthday()` function for the current month, is loaded. The filenames are `birthjan.js`, `birthfeb.js`, `birthmar.js`, `birthapr.js`, `birthmay.js`, `birthjun.js`, `birthjul.js`, `birthaug.js`, `birthsep.js`, `birthoct.js`, `birthnov.js`, and `birthdec.js`. The three-character month name (m) is retrieved as a substring of the current `month` in the `monthsOfYear` array and then converted to lowercase:

```
var m = monthsOfYear[month-1].substring(0,3).toLowerCase();
```

A script element is written out to the document to load the required *birthXXX.js* library:

```
document.write(
  '<script src="birth' + m + '.js"><\/script>'
);
}
```

To ensure that the library is loaded and processed immediately the current JavaScript code is ended with an end `script` tag:

```
//--></script>
```

Once the relevant *birthXXX.js* library has loaded and defined all the `Birthday` objects, the page then proceeds to output the details for today, again only if both the *current.js* and *july4th.js* libraries have been successfully loaded:

```
if (window.formatFullDate && window.setBirthday) {
```

First, the current date is formatted and output to the page:

```
document.write(
  'Today: ' + formatFullDate(day, month, year) + '<br>'
);
```

The `showEvent()` function is invoked with the current `day` and `month` variables. The result is assigned to the `events` variable:

```
var events = showEvent(day,month);
```

If the `events` string variable is not empty, then the contents are output to the document:

```
if (events != '')
  document.write(
    'On this day: ' +
    events + '<br>'
  );
```

Next, the `showBirthday()` function is invoked, again with the current `day` and `month` variables, and the result is assigned to the `births` variable:

```
var births = showBirthday(day,month);
```

Again, if the `births` variable is not empty, then the contents are output to the document:

```
if (births != '')
  document.write(
    'Born on this day: ' +
    births + '<br>'
  );
}
```

## Born on the 4th of July Source Code— birthjan.js

To show how the *birthXXX.js* libraries create `Birthday` objects, a snippet of the *birthjab.js* library is shown below.

 **../chapter7/july4th/birthjan.js**

The `setBirthday()` function is invoked for each person born in January:

```
setBirthday(01,01,1895,"J. Edgar Hoover");
setBirthday(02,01,1920,"Isaac Asimov");
setBirthday(03,01,1892,"J.R.R. Tolkien");
...
...
setBirthday(28,01,1912,"Jackson Pollock");
setBirthday(29,01,1880,"W.C. Fields");
setBirthday(30,01,1882,"Franklin D. Roosevelt");
```

## The 3rd Saturday in November

This application shows how to calculate the 1st, 2nd, 3rd, 4th, 5th, and last weekdays of any month. This is then used to calculate the dates of various variable calendar events or special holidays. For example, Thanksgiving Day occurs on the fourth Thursday of every November—regardless of the year.

## The 3rd Saturday in November Source Code—saturday.js

The *Saturday.js* library contains the nthDay() function that returns the day of the month that corresponds to the *n*th week day of a particular month and year. It also contains global variables can be used to enable easier usage of the function. For example, instead of using nthDay(3,3,12,2000), we can use nthDay(third,tue,dec,2000)—which can be more readily identified as requesting the 3rd Tuesday in December 2000.

../chapter7/saturday/saturday.js

The library defines all the global variables. First, the weekdays:

```
var sun=1,mon=2,tue=3,wed=4,thu=5,fri=6,sat=7;
```

Then the months:

```
var jan=1,feb=2,mar=3,apr=4,may=5,jun=6,
    jul=7,aug=8,sep=9,oct=10,nov=11,dec=12;
```

Then the first to fifth and last variables:

```
var first=1,second=2,third=3,fourth=4,fifth=5,last=-1;
```

The nthDay() function, as mentioned previously, returns the day of the month that corresponds to the requested nth weekday of the month for any particular year:

```
function nthDay(nth,weekday,month,year) {
```

If the `nth` input parameter is greater than zero—that is, we have not been requested to return the last `weekday` of the month—then the mathematical algorithm used returns the relevant day of the month:

```
if (nth > 0)
   return (nth-1)*7 + 1 +
      (7 + weekday - dayOfWeek((nth-1)*7 + 1,month,year)-1)%7;
```

If the last `weekday` of the month has been requested, then the function must first account for the `year` parameter possibly being a leap year:

```
if (isLeapYear(year))
   var days = daysOfMonthLY[month];
else
   var days = daysOfMonth[month];
```

The modified version of the mathematical algorithm then returns the relevant last day of the month:

```
return days -
   (dayOfWeek(days,month + 1,year) - weekday + 7)%7;
}
```

## The 3rd Saturday in November Source Code—index.htm

The *index.htm* page uses the `nth` function in the *saturday.js* library to calculate the dates of the following special days:

- Martin Luther King Day—The third Monday in January
- Daylight Saving time begins—The first Sunday in April
- Mother's Day—The second Sunday in May
- Armed Forces Day—The third Saturday in May
- Thanksgiving Day—The fourth Thursday in November
- Daylight savings time ends—The last Sunday in October

Figure 7-15 shows the results of this page for 2000.

../chapter7/saturday/index.htm

**Figure 7-15**
The 3rd Saturday in
November—Output
results.

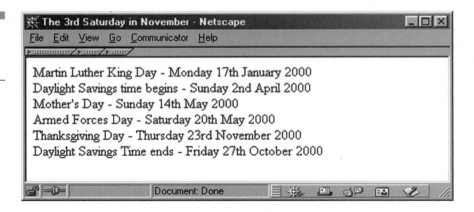

The page loads the contents of the *current.js*, *validate.js*, and *saturday.js* libraries:

```
<script src="current.js" language="JavaScript"></script>
<script src="validate.js" language="JavaScript"></script>
<script src="saturday.js" language="JavaScript"></script>
```

The code is only processed if all three libraries have been successfully loaded:

```
if (window.formatFullDate && window.nthDay
  && window.isLeapYear) {
```

The current date is retrieved:

```
var today = new Date();
var day   = today.getDate();
var month = today.getMonth() + 1;
var year  = today.getFullYear();
```

For each special holiday, the output from the nthDay() function is used as input to the formatFullDate() function. The output of this is then written out to the document:

```
document.write(
  'Martin Luther King Day - ' +
  formatFullDate(nthDay(third,mon,jan,year),jan,year) +
  '<br>'
);

document.write(
```

```
      'Daylight Savings time begins - ' +
      formatFullDate(nthDay(first,sun,apr,year),apr,year) +
      '<br>'
  );

  document.write(
    'Mother\'s Day - ' +
    formatFullDate(nthDay(second,sun,may,year),may,year) +
    '<br>'
  );

  document.write(
    'Armed Forces Day - ' +
    formatFullDate(nthDay(third,sat,may,year),may,year) +
    '<br>'
  );

  document.write(
    'Thanksgiving Day - ' +
    formatFullDate(nthDay(fourth,thu,nov,year),nov,year) +
    '<br>'
  );

  document.write(
    'Daylight Savings Time ends - ' +
    formatFullDate(nthDay(last,sun,oct,year),oct,year) +
    '<br>'
  );
}
```

# Calculating Easter

This example shows how to calculate the date of *Easter Sunday*, which according to the *Oxford English Dictionary*, is "held on a variable Sunday in March or April." This date will then be used to calculate the date of other religious occasions dependent on Easter Sunday. Figure 7-16 shows the date of Easter Sunday in 2000 along with the dates of all the other religious occasions surrounding Easter.

## Calculating Easter Source Code—easter.js

The *easter.js* library contains the arrays, object constructors, and functions necessary to calculate the date of Easter Sunday and all the other associated dates.

**Figure 7-16**
Calculating Easter—
The date of Easter
Sunday and other
religious occasions.

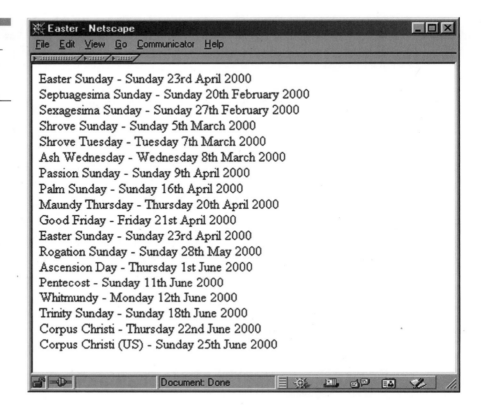

Easter Sunday - Sunday 23rd April 2000
Septuagesima Sunday - Sunday 20th February 2000
Sexagesima Sunday - Sunday 27th February 2000
Shrove Sunday - Sunday 5th March 2000
Shrove Tuesday - Tuesday 7th March 2000
Ash Wednesday - Wednesday 8th March 2000
Passion Sunday - Sunday 9th April 2000
Palm Sunday - Sunday 16th April 2000
Maundy Thursday - Thursday 20th April 2000
Good Friday - Friday 21st April 2000
Easter Sunday - Sunday 23rd April 2000
Rogation Sunday - Sunday 28th May 2000
Ascension Day - Thursday 1st June 2000
Pentecost - Sunday 11th June 2000
Whitmundy - Monday 12th June 2000
Trinity Sunday - Sunday 18th June 2000
Corpus Christi - Thursday 22nd June 2000
Corpus Christi (US) - Sunday 25th June 2000

On the CD    ../chapter7/easter/easter.js

The two arrays `julian` and `julianLY` contain the increasing number
of days for each month of the year. For example, for a normal year, there
are 59 days prior to the 1st of March (the third entry in the arrays),
whereas for a leap year, there are 60 days prior to the 1st of March:

```
var julian =
  new Array(0,31,59,90,120,151,181,212,243,273,304,334);
var julianLY =
  new Array(0,31,60,91,121,152,182,213,244,274,305,335);
```

The following algorithm is taken from *Calendars and Their History* at
http://astro.nmsu.edu/~lhuber-leaphist.html:

The following algorithm for computing the date of Easter is based on the
algorithm of Oudin (1940). It is valid for any Gregorian year, Y. All vari-

ables are integers, and the remainders of all divisions are dropped. The final date is given by M, the month, and D, the day of the month.

$$C = Y/100,$$
$$N = Y - 19*(Y/19),$$
$$K = (C - 17)/25,$$
$$I = C - C/4 - (C - K)/3 + 19*N + 15,$$
$$I = I - 30*(I/30),$$
$$I = I - (I/28)*(1 - (I/28)*(29/(I + 1))*((21 - N)/11)),$$
$$J = Y + Y/4 + I + 2 - C + C/4,$$
$$J = J - 7*(J/7),$$
$$L = I - J,$$
$$M = 3 + (L + 40)/44,$$
$$D = L + 28 - 31*(M/4).$$

This can be converted into the following `Easter()` object constructor, where the `Math` object's `floor()` method is used to convert floating-point numbers to integers:

```
function Easter(Y) {
  var C = Math.floor(Y/100);
  var N = Y - 19*Math.floor(Y/19);
  var K = Math.floor((C - 17)/25);
  var I = C - Math.floor(C/4) -
    Math.floor((C - K)/3) + 19*N + 15;
  I = I - 30*Math.floor((I/30));
  I = I - Math.floor(I/28) *
    (1 - Math.floor(I/28) * Math.floor(29/(I + 1)) *
    Math.floor((21 - N)/11));
  var J = Y + Math.floor(Y/4) + I + 2 - C + Math.floor(C/4);
  J = J - 7*Math.floor(J/7);
  var L = I - J;
  var M = 3 + Math.floor((L + 40)/44);
  var D = L + 28 - 31*Math.floor(M/4);
```

Once the D and M values have been calculated, the `Easter()` object constructor sets the day, month, and year properties of the this object reference to the value of the D, M, and Y variables, and then assigns the result of the `formatFullDate()` function call to the date property:

```
  this.day = D;
  this.month = M;
  this.year = Y;
  this.date = formatFullDate(D,M,Y)
}
```

The `daysInYear()` function returns the number of days in the year represented by the passed year parameter—366 in a leap year or 365 in a non-leap year:

```
function daysInYear(year) {
  if (isLeapYear(year)) return 366; else return 365;
}
```

The addDays() object constructor is used to calculate the various associated dates surrounding Easter Sunday. The addDays() function accepts four parameters—the date represented by the day, month, and year parameters, and the number of days to be added to the date (addition):

```
function addDays(day,month,year,addition) {
```

The current date is converted to a Julian Day format as used by NASA—that is, the number of days since the beginning of the year. The function first tests for a leap year and then updates the local number variable with the value of the day parameter, plus the value of the either the julianLY or julian arrays month minus 1 entry plus the extra addition parameter value:

```
if (isLeapYear(year))
  var number = day + julianLY[month-1] + addition;
else
  var number = day + julian[month-1] + addition;
```

The number of days in the year represented by the year parameter is obtained using the daysInYear() function and assigned to the local days variable:

```
var days = daysInYear(year);
```

If the value of number is greater than days, then the function continually increments the value of year and adjusts the value of days until the number of days in the updated year variable is less than or equal to the updated number variable:

```
while (number > days) {
  number -= days;
  days = daysInYear(++year);
}
```

If, on the other hand, the value of the addition parameter was negative, then the reverse process needs to occur in order to decrease the value of year and increase the value of number, until the value of number is greater than or equal to:

```
while (number < 1) {
  days = daysInYear(-year);
  number += days;
}
```

At this point, we have the correct `year` value, but only the Julian date with the current year (i.e., the number of days since the start of the year). The function now needs to convert this to a day of month and `month` within the year. The month variable is initialized to:

```
month = 1;
```

Depending on whether `year` represents a leap year, the function then continually increases the value of `month` until the value of `number` is no longer greater than the appropriate entry within the `julianLY` or `julian` array. The value of the `day` variable is then set to the difference between `number` and the entry within the `julianLY` or `julian` array:

```
if (isLeapYear(year)) {
  while (number > julianLY[month-1]) { month++; }
  day = number - julianLY[-month-1];
}
else {
  while (number > julian[month-1]) { month++; }
  day = number - julian[-month-1];
}
```

Once the new date has been calculated, the `day`, `month`, and `year` properties of the `this` object reference are updated, along with the `date` property, which is set to the return value of the `formatFullDate()` function:

```
  this.day = day;
  this.month = month;
  this.year = year;
  this.date = formatFullDate(day,month,year)
}
```

**NOTE**:  *The* `addDays()` *object constructor can be used to add or subtract any number of days from any date. It is not restricted just to calculating dates surrounding Easter Sunday.*

## Calculating Easter Source Code—index.htm

The *index.htm* page calculates the date of Easter Sunday for the current year using the `Easter()` object constructor, and then uses the properties of the `Easter` object along with the `addDays()` object constructor to calculate the date of the other religious occasions surrounding Easter Sunday.

**On the CD**

**../chapter7/easter/index.htm**

Both the *current.js* and *easter.js* libraries are loaded within the page:

```
<script src="current.js" language="JavaScript"></script>
<script src="easter.js" language="JavaScript"></script>
```

The remaining code is only processed if both libraries have been loaded successfully:

```
if (window.formatFullDate && window.Easter) {
```

The details of the current date are obtained:

```
var today = new Date();
var day   = today.getDate();
var month = today.getMonth() + 1;
var year  = today.getFullYear();
```

The `Easter (/)` object constructor is used to create an `Easter` object for the current year, which is then assigned to the `easter` object reference:

```
var easter = new Easter(year);
```

The value of the `easter` object's `date` property is then output to the document:

```
document.write('Easter Sunday - ' + easter.date + '<br>');
```

The `easter` object's `day` and `month` property, along with the value of the `year` variable, and the appropriate `addition` parameter value (-63) are passed to the `addDays ()` object constructor to create an `addDays` object for Septuagesima Sunday, which is then assigned to the `when` object reference:

```
var when = new addDays(easter.day,easter.month,year,-63);
```

The `when` object's `date` property is then output to the document:

```
document.write('Septuagesima Sunday - ' + when.date +'<br>');
```

This process is repeated for the remaining religious occasions:

```
var when = new addDays(easter.day,easter.month,year,-56);
document.write('Sexagesima Sunday - ' + when.date +'<br>');

var when = new addDays(easter.day,easter.month,year,-49);
document.write('Shrove Sunday - ' + when.date +'<br>');

var when = new addDays(easter.day,easter.month,year,-47);
document.write('Shrove Tuesday - ' + when.date +'<br>');

var when = new addDays(easter.day,easter.month,year,-46);
document.write('Ash Wednesday - ' + when.date +'<br>');

var when = new addDays(easter.day,easter.month,year,-14);
document.write('Passion Sunday - ' + when.date +'<br>');

var when = new addDays(easter.day,easter.month,year,-7);
document.write('Palm Sunday - ' + when.date +'<br>');

var when = new addDays(easter.day,easter.month,year,-3);
document.write('Maundy Thursday - ' + when.date +'<br>');

var when = new addDays(easter.day,easter.month,year,-2);
document.write('Good Friday - ' + when.date +'<br>');

document.write('Easter Sunday - ' + easter.date +'<br>');

var when = new addDays(easter.day,easter.month,year,35);
document.write('Rogation Sunday - ' + when.date +'<br>');

var when = new addDays(easter.day,easter.month,year,39);
document.write('Ascension Day - ' + when.date +'<br>');

var when = new addDays(easter.day,easter.month,year,49);
document.write('Pentecost - ' + when.date +'<br>');

var when = new addDays(easter.day,easter.month,year,50);
document.write('Whitmundy - ' + when.date +'<br>');

var when = new addDays(easter.day,easter.month,year,56);
document.write('Trinity Sunday - ' + when.date +'<br>');

var when = new addDays(easter.day,easter.month,year,60);
document.write('Corpus Christi - ' + when.date +'<br>');

var when = new addDays(easter.day,easter.month,year,63);
document.write('Corpus Christi (US) - ' + when.date +'<br>');
}
```

# The 24 Hour Clock

This application shows how to use the time component of a Date object—along with the value of the time zone offset, which is retrieved using the Date object's getTimezoneOffset() method—to show the time anywhere in the world.

The value returned by the getTimezoneOffset() method is the number of minutes difference between GMT or UTC time zone and the local time zone of the operating system on which the browser is running. If the local time zone is in advance of GMT (i.e., to the east of Greenwich, England, located on longitude 0° and referred to as the prime meridian), then the value returned by the getTimezoneOffset() method will be a negative number. Otherwise, for time zones that are behind GMT (i.e., to the west of the prime meridian), the values will be positive. Once the offset has been retrieved, it can be added to the local time to calculate the time at the prime meridian. It is then possible to calculate the time for any known time zone around the world.

Each international time zone spans 15° of longitude, resulting in 24 international time zones. Within each time zone, all clocks are set to the same time. Each time zone is generally referenced from GMT. For example, England is within GMT+0000, New York, United States, is within GMT-0500 (i.e., 5 hours behind, or west of, GMT), and Tokyo, Japan, is within GMT+0900 (i.e., 9 hours ahead, or east, of GMT). There are, however, variants to this to allow for boundaries and frontiers, as well as for economic and social reasons.

The time calculated in GMT does not for daylight saving time or summertime. For example, when used during the summer, the time returned for GMT+0000 is one hour behind the actual time in London. There is no accurate way to calculate the start and end of summertime for all countries around the world, since there are differences in the date for clocks that spring forward or leap back. To allow for this, the following code includes a checkbox that can be used to turn on and off the addition of an extra hour to accommodate summertime. Figures 7-17 and 7-18 show the effects of showing the current time in Arizona, both with the summertime checkbox left unchecked and then checked.

**Figure 7-17**
Time in Arizona—
non-summertime

**Figure 7-18**
Time in Arizona—
summer time

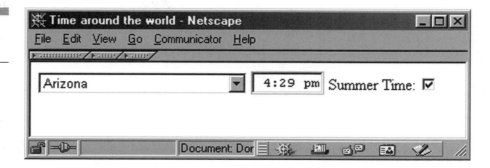

## The 24 Hour Clock Source Code—index.htm

The *index.htm* page contains all the JavaScript code and HTML necessary to allow the user to select one of many different localities. Once selected, the time shown in the form field will automatically update to reflect the time of the selected locality.

**../chapter7/clock24/index.htm**

A form named `zone` is output using HTML. It contains a select-option list named `offset`, containing an `option` element for each locality. Each `option` element contains a `value` attribute that holds, in hours, the time zone offset value from GMT:

```
<form name="zone">
<select name="offset">
<option value="4">Abu Dhabi</option>
<option value="9.5">Adelaide</option>
<option value="-9">Alaska</option>
<option value="6">Almaty</option>
<option value="1">Amsterdam</option>
<option value="-7">Arizona</option>
```

To conserve space, we only show the first and last six `option` elements.

```
<option value="1">Vienna</option>
<option value="10">Vladivostok</option>
<option value="4">Volgograd</option>
<option value="1">Warsaw</option>
<option value="12">Wellington</option>
<option value="9">Yakutsk</option>
</select>
```

The form also includes an input text field named `time`:

```
<input type="text" size="8" name="time">
```

And a checkbox field named `summer`:

```
Summer Time: <input type="checkbox" name="summer">
</form>
```

The `ampm()` function returns a formatted value of the passed `h` and `m` parameters, signifying the hour and minutes, in an `am` or `pm` format (e.g., `9:15am` or `10:45pm`):

```
function ampm(h, m) {
  var a = (h==0)?12:((h<13)?h:h-12);
  var output =
    ((a<10)?' ':'')+a+':'+padout(m)+((h<12)?' am':' pm');
  return output;
}
```

The `updateForm()` function updates the form display to show the current time of the selected locality:

```
function updateForm() {
```

First, the current local date and time is obtained:

```
var date = new Date();
```

Next, the value of the time zone offset is retrieved using the `Date` object's `getTimezoneOffset()` method:

```
var TimezoneOffset = date.getTimezoneOffset();
```

Using the ubiquitous `getAnOptionValue()` function, the value of the `zone` form's `offset` selected option element is retrieved, converted to a numeric value by subtracting zero, and then assigned to the `gmt` variable:

```
var gmt = getAnOptionValue(document.zone.offset) - 0;
```

Next, the `Date` object's `setTime()` method is used to update the date and time using the value returned by the `getTime()` method, plus the time zone offset converted from minutes to milliseconds, plus the value of the `gmt` variable converted to milliseconds, plus an extra 60 minutes (converted to milliseconds) if the `zone` form's `summer` checkbox is checked:

```
date.setTime(
  date.getTime() + TimezoneOffset*60*1000 + gmt*60*60*1000 +
  ((document.zone.summer.checked) ? 60*60*1000 : 0)
);
```

The `ampm()` function is then invoked, passing the `date` object reference's `getHours()` and `getMinutes()` method return values, assigning the result to the `time` variable:

```
var time = ampm(date.getHours(), date.getMinutes());
```

If the value of the `zone` form's `time` input text field is not already equal to the value of `time`, then the form field value is updated:

```
if (document.zone.time.value != time)
  document.zone.time.value = time;
```

The `updateForm()` function then starts a timer to reinvoke the `updateForm()` function half a second from now:

```
setTimeout("updateForm()",500);
}
```

Once the form HTML has been output to the document and all the JavaScript code has been defined, the self-updating time zone display is started by an initial call to the `updateForm()` function:

```
updateForm();
```

## Summary

As seen throughout this chapter, the examples made extensive use of libraries of functions, object constructors, arrays, and global variables. In many cases, these libraries defined in one example were repeatedly used throughout subsequent examples. By reusing libraries of established and tested code you can quickly build more complex applications from the foundations of small, discrete, but generic, code.

# Forms

Forms are a means of interaction in which the user can input text similar to what would be found on paper-based forms. The forms are subsequently processed either on the client or on the server side. JavaScript provides a powerful complement to form processing on the client side. By intercepting users interaction with the graphical user interface (GUI) that forms provide, JavaScript can be used to validate the user's input and respond to certain events, such as the mouse click on a button or the loading of another page when an option in a select list has been chosen. JavaScript can also be used to populate form fields, by updating the value properties of text fields and adding, amending, or updating entries in a select list. The scope for interaction is endless.

As forms provide a very visible use of JavaScript, examples of forms can be found in almost every chapter of this book. This chapter provides many instances of JavaScript interfacing with forms and the user's interaction. These sample applications can be reused within other larger applications to build very sophisticated GUIs. This chapter also reuses code from previous chapters, in particular the *current.js* library used in Chapter 7 "Date and Time" and the number formatting functions in Chapter 2 "Number Utilities."

JavaScript and Forms ../chapter8/general/index.htm
Sending Mail from Forms ../mailto/simple.htm and ../chapter8/mailto/multiple.htm
Dynamic Drop-Down Menus ../chapter8/dynamic/single.htm and ../chapter8/ dynamic/multiple.htm and ../chapter8/dynamic/transfer.htm and ../chapter8/ dynamic/colors.htm
Passing Data from One Form to Another ../chapter8/passing/index.htm
Dynamic Thank You Page ../chapter8/thankyou/index.htm
Form -> Cookie -> Form ../chapter8/cookie/index.htm
Form -> Email -> Form ../chapter8/mailform/index.htm
Disabling Form Fields ../chapter8/disable/index.htm
Controlling Data Entry Using Form Fields ../chapter8/entry/index.htm
Filtering Data Input ../chapter8/filter/index.htm
Date Spinner ../chapter8/spinner/index.htm and ../chapter8/spinner/index2.htm
Sales Order Form ../chapter8/sales/index.htm

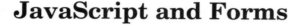

# JavaScript and Forms

Before diving into the applications used in this chapter, a brief summary of the important aspects of forms and form fields in our context is included. Forms is a broad topic, and covering all of the possible HTML attributes and their potential values would require an entire chapter on its own. We will just concentrate on the commonly used event handlers.

**chapter8/general/index.htm**

The following is a typical instance of a form, discussed throughout this section:

```
<form name="myform" action="index.htm" method="GET"
  enctype="application/x-www-form-urlencoded">

<input type="text" name="t1" value="">
<input type="password" name="t2" value="">
<input type="hidden" name="t3" value="">
<input type="file" name="t4" value="">

<input type="checkbox" name="c1" value="on"> - on
<input type="checkbox" name="c2" value="off"> - off

<input type="radio" name="r1" value="1" checked> - 1
<input type="radio" name="r1" value="10"> - 10
<input type="radio" name="r1" value="100"> - 100
<input type="radio" name="r1" value="1000"> - 1000

<select name="s1">
<option value="r">Red     <option value="o">Orange
<option value="y">Yellow <option value="g">Green
<option value="b">Blue    <option value="i">Indigo
<option value="v">Violet
</select>

<select name="s2" multiple size="3">
<option value="r">Red     <option value="o">Orange
<option value="y">Yellow <option value="g">Green
<option value="b">Blue    <option value="i">Indigo
<option value="v">Violet
</select>

<textarea name="t4" cols="60" rows="10" wrap="virtual"></textarea>

<input type="button" name="b1" value="Show Multiple"
  onClick="showMultiple(this.form)">
```

```
<input type="button" name="b1" value="Show Radio"
  onClick="showRadio(this.form)">

<input type="reset" name="b2" value="Reset">

<input type="submit" name="b3" value="Submit">

</form>
```

Each form that is included within an HTML page is entered in the document object's forms array. This array allows access to the form, either by its name (if one is given) or by the order within the page. Therefore, to access the form named myform, we can use document.forms['myform'] or the alternative document.forms.myform as the myform object is also a property of the forms object. To access the third form in a page, we may use document.forms[2], remembering that arrays start from zero. A form can also refer to itself from with event handlers in the form element using the this keyword. Therefore, an onSubmit event handler can pass a reference of the current form onto a function. For example:

```
<form onSubmit="formFunction(this)">
```

Note that we don't have to give a form a name if we never refer to the form by name. Form fields within a form can also refer to themselves using the this keyword. For example, a text field can pass its reference onto a function within the onChange event handler using

```
<input type="text" onChange="fieldFunction(this)">
```

A form field can also reference the form that it is within using the this keyword's form property. For example:

```
<input type="text" onChange="formFunction(this.form)">
```

This passes a reference to the containing form to the function, rather than a reference to the form field.

Once we have a reference to a form, or to a form field, we can access all the properties of the form or form field. For example, in the following fieldFunction(), which is passed a reference to a form field, we can update its value using the form reference's value property:

```
function fieldFunction(field) {
  field.value = 'The quick brown fox...';
}
```

Not only can we modify the properties of form fields, we can also modify properties of the form itself. For example, the form element can contain action, method, and enctype attributes that specify the target action of the form, the method to be used when submitting the form, and the encoding to be used. These three attributes can be accessed using the form object's action, method, and encoding properties. This is covered in detail later in this chapter in "Sending Mail from Forms."

The action attribute can contain one of several different values, a typical HTTP schema URL, either using an absolute or relate URL, or a mailto schema. The method attribute can contain either POST or GET. POST is used to post data to a server-side process, whereas GET is used to retrieve a document, although their use is quite often blurred. The enctype attribute specifies how the browser should encode the data:

- The standard application/x-www-form-urlencoded encoding converts any spaces to plus characters and any nonalphanumeric characters into the form %xx (where xx is the Latin-1 encoding of the character). This encoding is used with the GET method.

- The multipart/form-data encoding, used in the POST method, encapsulates each form field in separate MIME message.

- The text/plain encoding, which can be optionally used with the GET method and a mailto schema URL, places each form field's name and value separated by an equal sign on a separate line in the generated e-mail. This encoding is more suitable when the intended target is a human.

Each form field within a form appears within the form object's elements array and can be accessed either by the name of the form field or by its position within the form. A form field named t1 within the form myform can be accessed as document.myform.elements['t1'], or as document.myform.t1, as the field is a property of the form, or if it's the first field in the form, by using document.myform.elements[0].

There are two types of form fields that can select their own arrays of objects. The select object that represents a select list contains an array of all the enclosed options. The select list named s1 contains an options array that can be accessed by using document.myform['s1'].options or by using document.myform.s1.options. The number of options in the array can be accessed using its length property. The first option in the array can be accessed by using document.myform.s1.options[0], and the last by using document.myform.s1.options[document.myform.s1.options.length-1].

The text description of an option can be retrieved using the text property. For example, document.myform.s1.options[3].text retrieves the text of the fourth entry (Green). Likewise, the value of an option can be retrieved using the `value` property. For instance, `document.myform.s1.options[5].value` retrieves the value of the sixth entry (`i`).

The currently selected option in a single select list can be retrieved using the `options` array's `selectedIndex` property—for example, `document.myform.s1.options.selectedIndex`. A multiple select list is slightly harder, as there may be more than one option selected. In this case, we need to loop through all the options, testing each `option` object's `selected` property:

```
function multipleSelect(fRef) {
  var output = '';
  for (var i=0; i<fRef.s2.options.length; i++) {
    if (fRef.s2.options[i].selected)
      output += i + ' ';
  }

  alert('options selected: ' + output);
}
```

The `radio` object also contains an array of all the like-named radio buttons. Radio buttons act in groups—in effect like the radio buttons on Granny's wireless radio, where pressing one meant the previously selected button popped up. Grouping radio buttons together requires them to have identical names. It is this name that forms the name of the array of radio objects. To find the currently checked radio button within a group, we need to loop through all the radio objects in the array:

```
function showRadio(fRef) {
  for (var i=0; i<fRef.r1.length; i++) {
    if (fRef.r1[i].checked)
      alert('radio button checked: ' + i)
  }
}
```

Event handlers can be used on all the different types of form field to trap the users' interaction with the form. Table 8-1 shows the different form elements and the event handlers that they support. In our example HTML markup, the `onClick` event handlers within the two button form fields are used to invoke the `showMultiple()` and `showRadio()` functions.

# Sending Mail from Forms

This particular application shows how forms can be used to send mail to one of several different e-mail addresses, perhaps to the sales or support

**TABLE 8-1**

Form elements and their event handlers.

| HTML element | Event Handler |
|---|---|
| form | onSubmit, onReset |
| text | onFocus, onBlur, onKeyDown, onKeyUp, onChange |
| hidden | |
| password | onFocus, onBlur, onKeyDown, onKeyUp, onChange |
| textarea | onFocus, onBlur, onKeyDown, onKeyUp, onChange |
| file | onFocus, onBlur, onChange |
| radio | onFocus, onBlur, onClick |
| checkbox | onFocus, onBlur, onClick |
| button | onFocus, onBlur, onClick,  onDblClick, onMouseDown, onMouseUp |
| submit | onFocus, onBlur, onClick,  onDblClick, onMouseDown, onMouseUp |
| reset | onFocus, onBlur, onClick,  onDblClick, onMouseDown, onMouseUp |
| select | onFocus, onBlur, onChange |

**Figure 8-1**

Simple mail form.

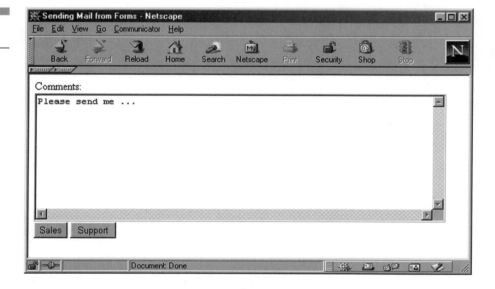

department. Rather than creating individual forms for each of the departments, the user can enter his or her correspondence on the one form and then submit the form contents to the appropriate department.

There are two examples presented here: a *simple* version that mails the form to one e-mail address, as shown in Figure 8-1, and a *multiple*

**Figure 8-2**

Multiple mail form.

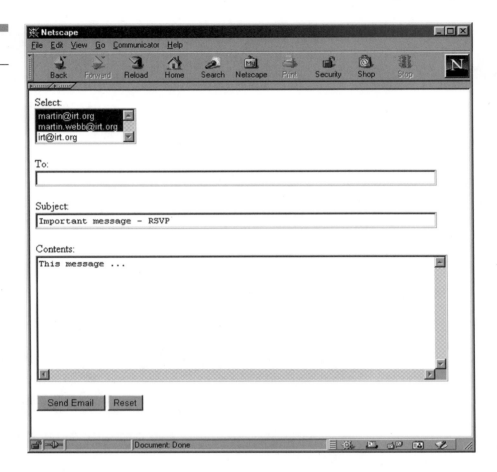

example that allows the user to select one or more addresses from a drop-down list and additionally enter another address in a text input field, as shown in Figure 8-2.

Both examples make use of the onClick event handler to update the form's action attribute. As this action attribute is read only in Microsoft Internet Explorer 3, these examples will not work on that particular browser.

## Sending Mail from Forms Source Code—
## *simple.htm*

On the CD

**chapter8/mailto/simple.htm**

The `alter()` function updates the `encoding`, `action`, and `method` properties of the passed object form reference. These three properties correspond to the `enctype`, `action`, and `method` attributes of the `form` element. The `action` property is updated with the value of the passed `where` argument:

```
function alter(object,where) {
  object.encoding = 'text/plain';
  object.action = where;
  object.method = 'POST';
}
```

The form element includes empty `action`, `method`, and `enctype` attributes, although the `method` and `enctype` attributes could have been prefilled with values of `POST` and `text/plain`:

```
<form action="" method="" enctype="">
```

The form includes two `submit input` elements, both of which include `onClick` event handlers to invoke the `alter()` function when the submit buttons are clicked. The submit button's `click` event occurs before the form's `submit` event. Therefore, the form's `action` property is amended prior to the form being submitted. This has the affect of updating the form element's `action` attribute, with the mailto scheme URL passed to the `alter()` function, immediately prior to submitting the form. The action of the form is then to request that the registered mail agent send the form details to the e-mail address within the `mailto:` URL.

```
<input type="submit" value="Sales"
  onClick="alter(this.form,'mailto:yy@yy.yy.yy')">
<input type="submit" value="Support"
  onClick="alter(this.form,'mailto:zz@zz.zz.zz')">
```

This example shows two submit buttons, but of course, the example could be extended to have many different submit buttons or, as shown in the next example, use other types of input fields.

## Sending Mail from Forms Source Code— *multiple.htm*

This *multiple* mail example uses two separate forms: one to allow the user to select the desired recipients (the control form) and the other to hold the data to be transmitted to the selected recipients (the e-mail form). When a form is submitted, each named form field along with its value is sent as part of the submitted data—for instance, a list of selected e-mail addresses—we need to either leave the form field unnamed or where we wish to access the form field by name, place the form field in a completely separate form that is never submitted. This example takes the latter approach.

 **chapter8/mailto/multiple.htm**

The control form contains a drop-down list (selectName) containing an option element for each e-mail address we may wish to send e-mails. The to text input field is used to hold the e-mail address for the current e-mail being sent. It uses an onFocus event handler to trap the user attempting to type text into this field, and immediately loses the focus (that is, the text caret) by calling the text field's (referenced as this) blur() method. There is also a separate text input field (subject) for the user to enter the subject heading for the generated e-mail:

```
<form name="controlForm">
<select multiple name="selectName">
<option value="martin@irt.org">martin@irt.org
<option value="martin.webb@irt.org">martin.webb@irt.org
<option value="irt@irt.com">irt@irt.com
</select>
<input type="text" name="to" size="72" onFocus="this.blur()">
<input type="text" name="subject" size="72">
</form>
```

The e-mail form (the actual form that is submitted) contains a textarea for the user's comments, along with submit and reset buttons. The form's action attribute is left empty, to be set from within the sendEmail() function invoked by the onSubmit event handler:

```
<form name="emailForm" action="" method="POST"
  enctype="text/plain" onSubmit="sendEmail()">
<textarea name="content" cols="72" ROWS="10"></textarea>
<input type="submit" name="mysubmit" value="Send eMail">
<input type="reset" value="Reset">
</form>
```

The code loops through all the entries within a drop-down list, looking for selected entries. To remember its position within the loop, the current global variable is defined and initialized:

```
var current = 0;
```

The `sendEmail()` function, like the `alter()` function in the single mail example, updates the action property of a form. However, unlike the `alter()` function, this function is invoked multiple times, once for each e-mail in the list. Whereas in the *simple* mail example, we generate one e-mail, here we generate one e-mail per e-mail address selected from a list. To be able to send more than one e-mail from a form, we must delay each form submission long enough to allow the previous form submission to complete successfully. The `sendemail()` function, invoked when the e-mail form is submitted, therefore sets up a timer to resubmit the e-mail form after a five-second delay. As long as the user's mail application successfully sends the previous e-mail within the five seconds, there shouldn't be a problem. Unfortunately, there is no mechanism available from within JavaScript to detect the success or failure of a form submission. Therefore if failures do occur or large delays are present on the network, then there is no way to trap and resend:

```
function sendEmail() {
```

The first time the `sendEmail()` function is invoked, the value of `current` is zero. If the current option within control form's select list is selected, then the `action` property of the e-mail form is updated, the `current` variable is incremented, and if it is less than the number of option entries in the select list, a timer is set up to programmatically "click" the control form's submit button after a five second delay. Otherwise, the `current` variable is reinitialized:

```
if (document.controlForm.selectName[current].selected) {
  document.emailForm.action =
    'mailto:' +
    document.controlForm.selectName[current].value +
    '?subject=' +
    document.controlForm.subject.value;
  document.controlForm.to.value =
    document.controlForm.selectName[current].value;
  current++;
  if (current < document.controlForm.selectName.length)
    setTimeout('document.emailForm.mysubmit.click()',5000);
  else current = 0;
}
```

If the current option isn't selected, then the `current` variable is incremented, and if less than the number of option entries in the select list, the control form's submit button is "clicked" straight away. Otherwise, the `current` variable is reinitialized:

```
    else {
      current++;
      if (current < document.controlForm.selectName.length)
        document.emailForm.mysubmit.click();
      else current = 0;
    }
}
```

Note that we use the submit button's `click` method rather than the more obvious `submit` method, as the `submit` method is not guaranteed to invoke the form's `onSubmit` event handler. We must invoke the `onSubmit` event handler, as it is this that invokes the `sendEmail()` function.

The e-mail form's `action` property is set within the `sendEmail()` function. Unlike the previous *simple* mail example where the action was set to the format `mailto:name@exampledomain.com`, this example extends the mailto schema URL to include the subject of the e-mail using the format `mailto:name@exampledomain.com?subject=text`. This should set the subject heading in the generated e-mail to the value of the control form's `subject` text input field. It is also possible to directly set the `to`, `cc`, and `bcc` headers:

```
mailto:?to=name@exampledomain.com
mailto:?cc=name@exampledomain.com
mailto:?bcc=name@exampledomain.com
mailto:?newsgroups=comp.javascript.lang
```

It is also possible to combine all of these using ampersand characters:

```
mailto:name@exampledomain.com&cc=name2@exampledomain.com&bcc=name3@
exampledomain.com&newsgroups=comp.javascript.lang&subject=Important
```

# Dynamic Drop Down Menus

Up until now we have been dealing with drop-down menus that are static once defined; however, you can also add extra options to a select list, as well as delete and amend existing options. This enables interesting user interfaces to be generated, perhaps allowing the user to add additional entries to an existing list of options or to move options from one list to another.

This section uses four examples: *single*, shown in Figure 8-3, which uses a drop-down list to add, delete, or update single entries one at a time; *multiple*, shown in Figure 8-4, which does the same but with multi-

**Figure 8-3**
Single drop-down
menu.

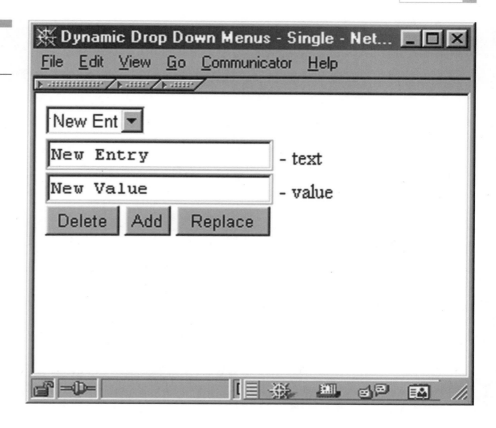

ple entries in a multiple select form field; *transfer*, shown in Figure 8-5, which allows the user to move options backward and forward between two select lists; and *color*, shown in Figure 8-6, which allows the user to select a main color from the first drop-down list and then choose a particular shade from a dynamic second drop-down list that changes the background color of the document.

## Dynamic Drop-Down Menus Source Code— *single.htm*

**chapter8/dynamic/single.htm**

The HTML markup used in this example contains a form with a select list (select1), two text input fields (text1 and value1), and three but-

**Figure 8-4**
Multiple drop-down
menu.

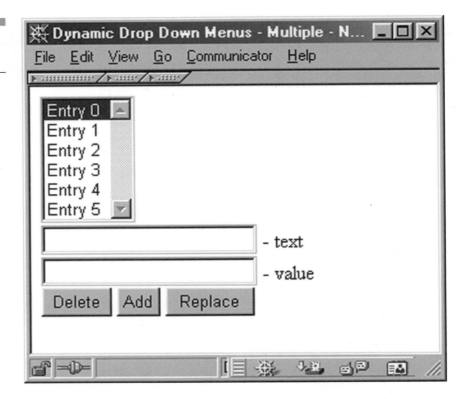

tons to delete, add, and replace an option. The select list includes an
onChange event handler that invokes the onChange() function, passing
a reference to this form, the name of the select list, and text input fields.
The onChange() function updates the contents of the two text input
fields with the value and text properties of the currently selected list
option. The three buttons contain onClick event handlers to invoke the
appropriate deleteOption(), addOption(), and replaceOption()
functions, again passing a reference to this form, and the name of the
select list, and in the case of the add and replace functions, the values of
the two text input fields. These values are used when creating new or
amending existing options.

```
<form>
<select name="select1"
  onChange="onChange(this.form, 'select1', 'text1', 'value1')">
<option value="Option 0" selected>Entry 0
<option value="Option 1">Entry 1
```

**Figure 8-5**
Transfer drop-down
menus.

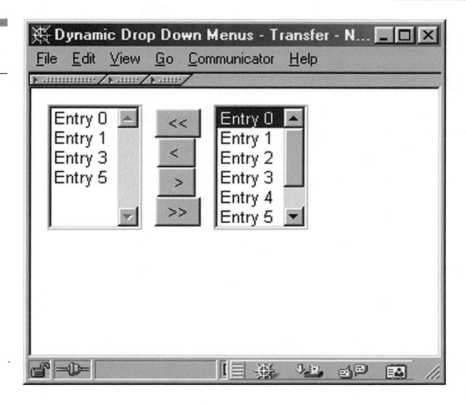

```
<option value="Option 2">Entry 2
<option value="Option 3">Entry 3
<option value="Option 4">Entry 4
<option value="Option 5">Entry 5
</select>
<input name="text1" type="text" value=""> - text
<input name="value1" type="text" value=""> - value
<input type="button" value="Delete"
  onClick="deleteOption(this.form, 'select1')">
<input type="button" value="Add"
  onClick="addOption(this.form, 'select1',
    this.form['text1'].value, this.form['value1'].value)">
<input type="button" value="Replace"
  onClick="replaceOption(this.form, 'select1',
    this.form['text1'].value, this.form['value1'].value)">
</form>
```

The onChange() function retrieves the selectedIndex property
value of the fRef form's sName select list and assigns the value to the
local i variable. The text and value properties of the selected i option

**Figure 8-6**
Color drop-down
menus.

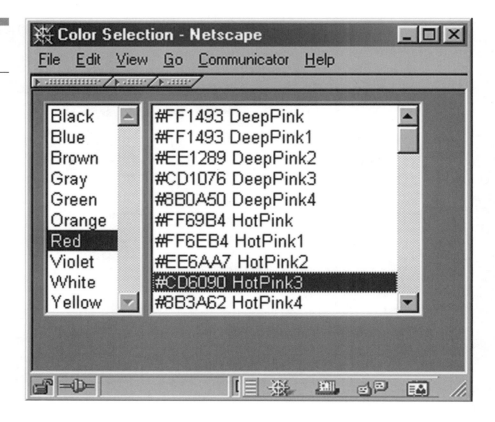

are then retrieved and used to update the value properties of the tName
and vName text input fields:

```
function onChange(fRef, sName, tName, vName) {
  var i = fRef[sName].selectedIndex;
  fRef[tName].value = fRef[sName].options[i].text;
  fRef[vName].value = fRef[sName].options[i].value;
}
```

The deleteOption() function similarly retrieves the selected option,
but it then sets the selected option object to null. In other words, the
*whole* option object is nullified—not just one of its properties. This, in
effect, causes the option to be removed from the select list:

```
function deleteOption(fRef, sName) {
  var i = fRef[sName].selectedIndex;
  fRef[sName].options[i] = null;
}
```

The addOption() function creates a new Option object using the
Option() constructor. The Option() constructor accepts four optional

arguments: the value of the `text` property, the `value` of the value property, a Boolean value specifying the `defaultSelected` property, and a Boolean value specifying the `selected` property. The current length of the passed `fRef` form's `sName` select list is obtained and used to append the newly created `Option` to the end of the current options in the list:

```
function addOption(fRef, sName, sText, sValue) {
  var def = true;
  var sel = true;
  var optionName = new Option(sText, sValue, def, sel);
  var length = fRef[sName].length;
  fRef[sName].options[length] = optionName;
}
```

The `replaceOption()` function updates the `text` and `value` properties of the currently selected option with the passed `sText` and `sValue` arguments:

```
function replaceOption(fRef,sName,sText,sValue) {
  var i = fRef[sName].selectedIndex;
  fRef[sName].options[i].text = sText;
  fRef[sName].options[i].value = sValue;
}
```

## Dynamic Drop-Down Menus Source Code— *multiple.htm*

 **chapter8/dynamic/multiple.htm**

This *multiple* example uses a similar form to the previous *single* example. The main difference is the use of the `multiple` attribute within the `select` element. This allows the user to select one or more of the options in the select list. As the user may now select more than one option, the functions we use to delete and replace options must accommodate this. We can, however, reuse the `onChange()` and `addOption()` functions used in the single example. The delete and replace buttons invoke the `deleteOptions()` and `replaceOptions()` functions, respectively:

```
<form>
<select name="select1" multiple
  onChange="onChange(this.form, 'select1', 'text1', 'value1')">
<option value="Option 0" selected>Entry 0
</select>
<input name="text1" type="text" value=""> - text
<input name="value1" type="text" value=""> - value
```

```
<input type="button" value="Delete"
  onClick="deleteOptions(this.form, 'select1')">
<input type="button" value="Add"
  onClick="addOption(this.form, 'select1',
    this.form['text1'].value, this.form['value1'].value)">
<input type="button" value="Replace"
  onClick="replaceOptions(this.form, 'select1',
    this.form['text1'].value, this.form['value1'].value)">
</form>
```

The deleteOptions() function needs to loop through each of the options in the passed fRef form's sName select list, checking each option's selected property, and if equal to true, to set the option to null. If, however, we were to loop forward from the first option to the last, then as we delete options in the list, we run the danger of hitting the end of the list as the list shrinks. Therefore, the code loops backward from the last entry to the first entry:

```
function deleteOptions(fRef, sName) {
  for (var i=0; i<fRef[sName].options.length; i++) {
    if (fRef[sName].options[i].selected) {
      fRef[sName].options[i] = null;
      length--;
      i--;
    }
  }
}
```

The replaceOptions() function loops through all the options in the passed fRef form's sName select list, updating the text and value properties of each selected option using the passed sText and sValue arguments:

```
function replaceOptions(fRef,sName,sText,sValue) {
  for (var i=0; i<fRef[sName].options.length; i++) {
    if (fRef[sName].options[i].selected) {
      fRef[sName].options[i].text = sText;
      fRef[sName].options[i].value = sValue;
    }
  }
}
```

## Dynamic Drop-Down Menus Source Code—
### *transfer.htm*

**chapter8/dynamic/transfer.htm**

This *transfer* example allows the user to move options backward and forward between two select lists, either just all the selected options or all the options in the list whether selected or not. The form contains four buttons labeled <<, <, > and >>. The << button moves all options from the `select2` list to `select1`, whereas >> moves all options from the `select1` list to `select2`. The < button moves all *selected* options from the `select2` list to `select1`, and > moves all *selected* options from the `select1` list to `select2`.

Each button's `onClick` event handler invokes the `moveOption()` function, but with different arguments: this current form, the name of select list where options are to moved from, the name of the select list where options are to be moved to, and a Boolean value indicating whether all options are to be moved regardless of their `selected` property:

```
<form>
<select name="select1" multiple>
<option value="Option 0" selected>Entry 0
</select>
<input type="button" value=" << "
  onClick="moveOption(this.form,'select2','select1',true)">
<input type="button" value=" <  "
  onClick="moveOption(this.form,'select2','select1',false)">
<input type="button" value="  > "
  onClick="moveOption(this.form,'select1','select2',false)">
<input type="button" value=" >> "
  onClick="moveOption(this.form,'select1','select2',true)">
<select name="select2" multiple>
<option value="Option 0" selected>Entry 0
<option value="Option 1">Entry 1
</select>
</form>
```

The `moveOption()` function loops though the passed `fRef` forms `sNameFrom` select list invoking the `addOption()` function, where either the current option is `selected` or the `force` argument is `true`, passing to the `addOption()` function, described in the earlier *single* example, the `fRef` argument, the name of the select list that the option is to be added to (i.e., the `sNameTo` select list), and the `text` and `value` properties of the current option in the loop. Once all options have been copied from one list to another, the `deleteOptions()` function is invoked, passing as arguments the passed `fRef`, `sNameForm`, and `force` arguments.

```
function moveOption(fRef, sNameFrom, sNameTo, force) {
  for (var i=0; i<fRef[sNameFrom].options.length; i++) {
    if (fRef[sNameFrom].options[i].selected || force) {
      addOption(
        fRef,sNameTo,
        fRef[sNameFrom].options[i].text,
        fRef[sNameFrom].options[i].value
      );
```

```
      }
    }
    deleteOptions(fRef,sNameFrom,force);
  }
```

The revised `deleteOptions()` function accepts the additional `force` argument and proceeds to delete all the *selected* options in the passed `fRef` form's `sName` select list, or all the options if the passed `force` argument is equal to `true`:

```
function deleteOptions(fRef, sName, force) {
  var length = fRef[sName].options.length;
  for (var i=0; i<fRef[sName].options.length; i++) {
    if (fRef[sName].options[i].selected || force) {
      fRef[sName].options[i] = null;
      length--;
      i--;
    }
  }
}
```

# Dynamic Drop-Down Menus Source Code— *colors.htm*

**chapter8/dynamic/colors.htm**

This next *colors* example contains two select lists. The `select1` select list holds a list of colors—Black, Blue, Brown, Gray, Green, Orange, Red, Violet, White, and Yellow—and the `select2` select list initially contains just the one entry holding nonbreaking spaces (i.e., the   HTML entity) to pad out the otherwise very narrow select list.

When the user selects one of the color options in `select1`, the select element's `onChange` event handler invokes the `updateColors()` function to populate the `select2` list with a long list of color shade names and hexadecimal color values, all of which are held in one of 10 arrays.

```
<form>
<select name="select1" size="10"
  onChange="updateColors(this.form, 'select1', 'select2')">
<option value="black">Black
<option value="blue">Blue
<option value="brown">Brown
<option value="gray">Gray
<option value="green">Green
<option value="orange">Orange
<option value="red">Red
```

```
<option value="violet">Violet
<option value="white">White
<option value="yellow">Yellow
</select>
```

When the user then subsequently selects one of the options in select2, the select element's onChange event handler invokes the showColor() function to alter the background color of the document to match the option selected:

```
<select name="select2" size="10"
  onChange="showColor(this.form, 'select2')">
<option>
          
          
          
          
</option>
</select>
</form>
```

The JavaScript code on the CD-ROM contains a complete list of colors and color hexadecimal values for each of the following arrays. To save space, we have only shown the first entries in each array.

```
var black = new Array('black', '#000000', ...);
var blue = new Array('AliceBlue', '#F0F8FF', ...);
var brown = new Array ('RosyBrown', '#BC8F8F', ...);
var gray = new Array ('DarkSlateGray', '#2F4F4F', ...);
var green = new Array ('DarkGreen', '#006400', ...);
var orange = new Array ('DarkOrange', '#FF8C00', ...);
var red = new Array ('DeepPink', '#FF1493', ...);
var violet = new Array ('DarkOrchid', '#9932CC', ...);
var white = new Array ('AntiqueWhite', '#FAEBD7', ...);
var yellow = new Array ('BlanchedAlmond', '#FFEBCD', ...);
```

The getAnOptionValue() utility function, seen in previous chapters, is used to retrieve the value property of the selected option in a select list:

```
function getAnOptionValue(what) {
  return what.options[what.options.selectedIndex].value;
}
```

The updateColors() function first deletes all the entries in the passed fRef form's sName2 select list using the deleteOptions function seen in the previous *transfer* example. It passes a true value for the force argument, therefore deleting all the options regardless of the value of their selected property. The function then uses the getAnOptionValue() function to retrieve the value of the selected option in the sName1 select list, and then uses the returned color value to create a colorObject array based on the appropriate array of colors. The eval() statement converts the color string value into the like-named array of colors. In other words, it evaluates the string expression—say, "red"—which results in the red array, defined previously, being assigned to the colorObject variable. The function then loops through every other entry in the colorObject array invoking the addOption() function to add an option to the sName2 select list, using hexadecimal color value and color name as the text property, and the hexadecimal color value as the value property of the new option. Finally, the first entry in the list is selected, and the showColor() function is invoked:

```
function updateColors(fRef, sName1, sName2) {
  deleteOptions(fRef,sName2,true);

  var color = getAnOptionValue(fRef[sName1]);
  var colorObject = eval(color);

  for (var i=0; i<colorObject.length;i+=2) {
    addOption(fRef, sName2, colorObject[i+1] + ' ' +
      colorObject[i], colorObject[i+1]);
  }
  fRef[sName2].options.selectedIndex = 0;
  showColor(fRef, sName2);
}
```

The showColor() function retrieves the value of the currently selected option from the fRef form's sName select list, and if not an empty string uses it to update the bgColor property of the document object—that is, the background color of the document:

```
function showColor(fRef, sName) {
  var sValue = getAnOptionValue(fRef[sName]);
  if (sValue != '') document.bgColor = sValue;
}
```

# Passing Data from One Form to Another

When a form is submitted, the data can be submitted in one of two different methods: POST, which posts the data to the server-side program identified in the form's action attribute for server-side processing, or

GET, which passes the data as part of the URL to the page or program identified in the form's `action` attribute.

With GET, the data is passed as encoded name/value pairs within the URL. For example, the following form when submitted requests the URL:

```
program?title=Passing+%27Data%27&name=Martin+Webb.
```

The browser has converted the spaces to plus signs and encoded the single quote characters into their two-digit hexadecimal Latin-1 encoding value. It is then up to the target program or page to decode the data passed in the URL:

```
<form action="program" method="get">
<input type="text" name="title" value="Passing 'Data'">
<input type="text" name="name" value="Martin Webb">
<input type="submit">
</form>
```

With POST the encoded name/value pairs follow the URL as separate HTTP headers. It is only possible to retrieve this data using a program on the server.

The following application shows how to submit an input form using POST with an action targeting an output HTML page containing JavaScript code. When downloaded to the browser, the data passed in the URL is extracted, as shown in Figure 8-7.

## Passing Data from One Form to Another Source Code—*index.htm*

 **chapter8/passing/index.htm**

To save space, we do not show the full HTML markup for the input page. The example on the CD-ROM includes a form field for each of the different form field types. As long as the form targets the *output.htm* page and, by default, uses a method of GET, then the hard work is performed within the *output.htm* page:

```
<form name="formname" action="output.htm">
```

**Figure 8-7**
Output page
showing the passed
data within
a duplicate form.

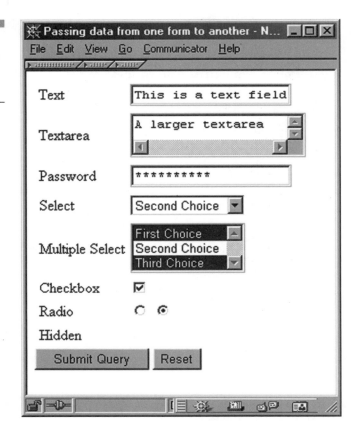

## Passing Data from One Form to Another
## Source Code—*output.htm*

chapter8/passing/output.htm

Again, to save space we do not show the HTML markup for the output form. The getNthParm() function retrieves the *nth* name/value pair from the passed string argument. For example, if the string argument contains a=1&b=2&a=3, and parm is set to a and nth is set to 1, the returned value is 3—that is, the value of the second of the two a name/value pairs.

```
function getNthParm(string,parm,nth) {
  if (!string) return";
  var count = 1;
  var startPos = 0 + string.indexOf(parm + '=');
  while (startPos > -1) {
    startPos = startPos + parm.length + 1;
    var endPos = 0 + string.indexOf('&',startPos);
    if (endPos == -1)
      endPos = string.length;
    if (count == nth)
      return unescape(string.substring(startPos,endPos));
    startPos = 0 + string.indexOf(parm + '=',endPos);
    count++;
  }
  return '';
}
```

The `location` object's `search` property is retrieved and assigned to the `passed` variable. The leading question mark is then stripped, and if the length is greater than zero—that is, data has been passed in the URL—the `reloadForm()` function is invoked, passing a reference to the `formname` form, plus the value of the `passed` variable once all plus characters have been converted back to space characters:

```
var passed = location.search;
passed = passed.substring(1);
if (passed.length > 0)
  reloadForm(document.formname, passed.replace(/\+/g,' '));
```

The `reloadForm()` function, uses the `getNthParm()` function to retrieve the required value from the appropriate name/pair held in the `passed` argument, and then assigns the returned value to the appropriate `fRef` form field. Form fields of type `text`, `textarea`, and `password` are fairly straightforward; the return value from the `getNthParm()` function is simply assigned to the appropriate form field's `value` property. Likewise, checkboxes are also straightforward; the value returned by `getNthParm()` function is assigned to the checkboxes' `checked` property. Single and multiple select lists, along with groups of radio buttons, need to be treated differently. The value returned from the `getNthParm()` function is used to find a matching entry within the options or radio arrays, and if found, the matched entries `selected` or `checked` property is set to `true`. For multiple select lists, because there may be more than one option selected, the code calls the `getNthParm()` function once for each option entry in the select list, incrementing the *nth* input parameter each time, to find the next identically named name/value in the `passed` variable.

```
function reloadForm(fRef, passed) {
  fRef.textname.value = getNthParm(passed,'textname',1);
```

```
fRef.textareaname.value = getNthParm(passed,'textareaname',1);
fRef.passwordname.value = getNthParm(passed,'passwordname',1);
fRef.checkboxname.checked = getNthParm(passed,'checkboxname',1);

var value = getNthParm(passed,'selectname',1);
if (value != '') {
  for (var i=0; i<fRef.selectname.length; i++) {
    if (fRef.selectname[i].value == value) {
      fRef.selectname[i].selected = true;
    }
  }
}

for (var i=1; i<=fRef.multipleselectname.length; i++) {
  var value = getNthParm(passed,'multipleselectname',i);
  if (value != '') {
    for (var j=0; j<fRef.multipleselectname.length; j++) {
      if (fRef.multipleselectname[j].value == value) {
        fRef.multipleselectname[j].selected = true;
      }
    }
  }
}

var value = getNthParm(passed,'radioname',1);
if (value != '') {
  for (var i=0; i<fRef.radioname.length; i++) {
    if (fRef.radioname[i].value == value) {
      fRef.radioname[i].checked = true;
    }
  }
}
}
```

This application could easily be extended to concatenate a series of forms together, placing the data passed from the previous form into hidden form fields. These fields are then passed along with the new data to the next, until eventually all the data has been collected. It can then be posted to a server-side program for processing.

# Dynamic Thank You Page

Up until now we have only used forms' submissions to another page. However, in practice many forms are submitted to a server-side program to collect and store the data. This application uses a CGI script written in Perl to generate an e-mail with the submitted data, and then it redirects the output to HTML page containing JavaScript, which displays to the user the data that has been successfully received and processed.

Unfortunately, as mentioned in Chapter 5 "Location and Links," not everyone has administrative-level access to run CGI scripts. Fret not. Many web hosting accounts include a simple CGI script that accepts a form submission that generates an e-mail and then redirects the output to a page of your choice. As long as the CGI script works with the GET method, then this application should work on your web hosting account.

If you do not have such a CGI script but have administrative level access to run CGI scripts, we also include a simple CGI script that you can use.

## Dynamic Thank You Page Source Code— *index.htm*

**chapter8/thankyou/index.htm**

This application will work with any input form. All that is needed is the location of the CGI script (e.g., /cgi-bin/userform.cgi), two text input fields to collect the user's e-mail address and name, and a hidden form field named redirect with the relative or absolute location of the output page (e.g., /thanks.htm):

```
<form method="GET"
  action="/cgi-bin/userform.cgi">
<input type="text" name="name">
<input type="text" name="email">
<input type="hidden" name="redirect" value="/thanks.htm">
...
</form>
```

Figure 8-8 shows the input form used in this example.

## Dynamic Thank You Page Source Code— *userform.cgi*

**chapter8/thankyou/userform.cgi**

This simple CGI script is all that is needed to pipe the output from any input form to a mail application, and then redirect the browser to another page. Figure 8-9 shows the e-mail generated by this CGI script.

**Figure 8-8**
Dynamic Thank You
Page input form.

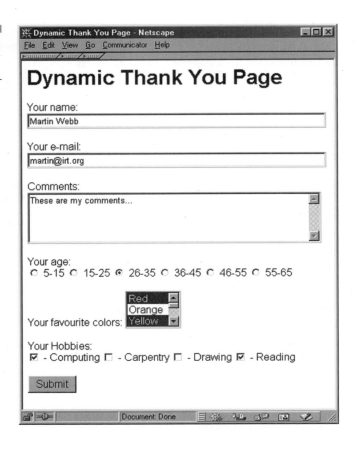

```perl
#!/usr/bin/perl

use strict;
use CGI qw(:standard);
use CGI::Carp qw(fatalsToBrowser);

my $query = new CGI;
my @names = $query->param;

my $email = param("email");
my $name = param("name");
my $redirect = param("redirect");

open (MAIL, "|/usr/lib/sendmail -t") or die "error: $!";

print MAIL "To: martin\@irt.org\n";
print MAIL "From: $email ($name)\n";
print MAIL "Subject: Dynamic Thank You Page\n";

print MAIL "Output of Dynamic Thank You Page:\n";
print MAIL "-" x 75 . "\n\n";
```

**Figure 8-9**
Dynamic Thank You
Page e-mail output.

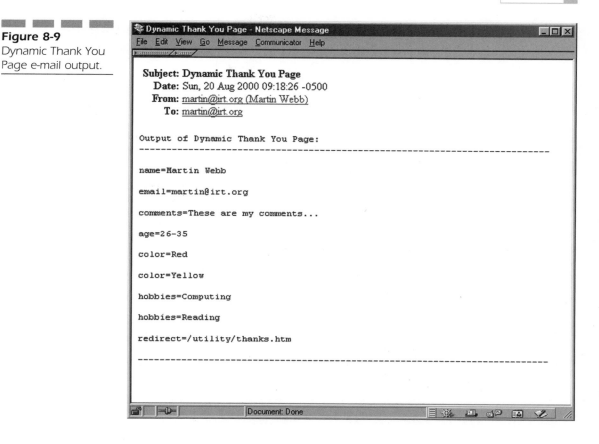

```
my $name;
my $value;

foreach $name (@names) {
  my @values = $query->param($name);
  foreach $value (@values) {
    print MAIL "$name=$value\n\n";
  }
}

print MAIL "-" x 75 . "\n\n";
close MAIL;
print "Location: $redirect\n\n";

exit;
```

For further reading I recommend *CGI Programming on the World Wide Web* by Shishir Gundavaram (ISBN 1-56592-419-3, published by O'Reilly & Associates, 2000).

## Dynamic Thank You Page Source Code— *thanks.htm*

chapter8/thankyou/thanks.htm

The *thanks.htm* page, which should be located in the root directory on the same server as the *userform.cgi* script, contains JavaScript code to extract the data passed in the URL. As the original input form is posted to the server using the GET method, then each of the named form fields contained in the input form is passed as encoded name/value pairs in the URL. We could use similar JavaScript code contained in the previous "Passing Data from One Form to Another" application, but unlike the previous application, the code here will extract any data passed in the URL. Figure 8-10 shows the output generated by this page.

**Figure 8-10**
Dynamic Thank You
Page output results.

First, six global variables are defined and initialized. If the `length` of the `location` object's `search` property is greater than zero, then its value, minus the leading question mark, is assigned to the `input` variable. All plus characters are then converted back to spaces. While the length of the input variable remains greater than zero, the code then proceeds to extract each name/value pair in the order they occur in the `input` variable, using the equal sign as an indication of the end of the name, and the ampersand character (or the lack of one) as the end of the value. The `name` and `value` values are decoded using the global `escape()` function. Then, any ampersand, greater-than, or less-than characters are converted to their respective HTML entities, before being finally written out to the document.

```javascript
var input = output = name = value = equal = ampersand = '';

if (location.search.length > 0)
  input = location.search.substring(1);

input = input.replace(/\+/g,' ');

while (input.length > 0) {
  equal = input.indexOf('=');
  name = unescape(input.substring(0,equal));
  input = input.substring(input.indexOf('=')+1);

  ampersand = input.indexOf('&');
  value = input.substring(0,ampersand);
  input = input.substring(input.indexOf('&')+1);

  if (value == '' && ampersand == -1) {
    value = input;
    input = '';
  }

  value = unescape(value);
  value = value.replace(/&/g,'&amp');
  value = value.replace(/</g,'&lt;');
  value = value.replace(/>/g,'&gt;');

  if (name != 'redirect')
    output += '<p><b>' + name + '=</b>' + value + '</p>';
}

document.write(output);
```

## Form -> Cookie -> Form

Cookies are items of data held by browser on behalf of a website. Only the domain that is registered against the cookie can retrieve the data held in the cookie. Originally, only server-side programs when returning a response to a request wrote cookies, but with the introduction of JavaScript, the ability to write cookies was extended to the page downloaded to the browser. Chapter 10 "Cookies" covers cookies in more detail.

With the ability to read and write cookies from within JavaScript, it is possible for forms to interact with cookies. The application presented here writes a cookie immediately prior to a form being submitted—capturing the state of the form. When the page is reloaded, if the cookie already exists, then the form is repopulated with the data held in the cookie. Figure 8-11 displays the form used to capture the user input and then redisplay the data from the cookie when reloaded.

## Form -> Cookie -> Form Source Code— *index.htm*

**chapter8/cookie/index.htm**

**Figure 8-11**
Input/output form for the Form -> Cookie -> Form application.

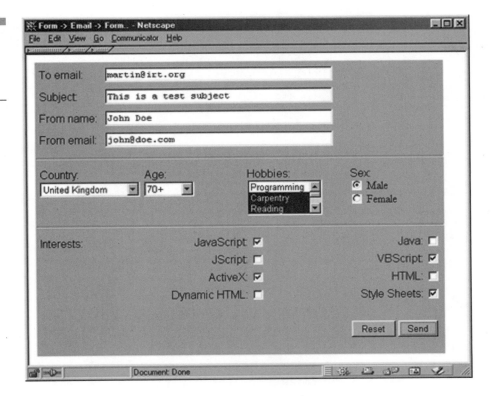

This application uses three generic cookie functions: `getCookie()`, `setCookie()`, and `deleteCookie()`, all of which are detailed in Chapter 10 "Cookies." The application also reuses the `getNthParm()` function detailed in the "Passing Data from One Form to Another" application earlier in this chapter. The cookie functions are held in an external JavaScript library, *cookie.js*. This application loads this library:

```
<script language="JavaScript" src="cookie.js"></script>
```

The first task the code attempts to perform is retrieve the value of any existing `userProfile` cookie and assign it to the global `userProfile` variable. If no cookie exists by that name, then the `getCookie()` function simply returns a `null` value:

```
var userProfile;

if (window.Cookie)
  userProfile = getCookie("userProfile");
```

Note that before attempting to use any of the cookie functions in the *cookie.js* library, a check is made to ensure that the library has loaded and defined a `Cookie` property on the `window` object.

If the `userProfile` cookie does not exist, then the code writes out a general welcome message:

```
if (!userProfile) {
  document.write(
    '<p>Welcome, According to your records you have not set' +
    ' your user profile:</p>'
  );
}
```

If the cookie does exist, then the code writes out a different message:

```
else {
  document.write(
    '<p>Welcome back, According to your records the following' +
    ' settings are held in your profile:</p>'
  );
}
```

When the page has completely loaded, the `onLoad` event handler in the `body` element invokes the `setupForm()` function, passing a reference to the `pForm` form and the value of the `userProfile` variable:

```
<body onLoad="setupForm(document.pForm, userProfile)">
```

The `setupForm()` function populates any form from any name/value pair's string passed to it. There is no need to amend this function for your own form, as the code loops through all the elements in the passed `fRef` form reference and extracts the like-named name/value pair from the passed `string` parameter, assigning the value to the form element:

```
function setupForm(fRef, string) {
```

Each form has an `elements` array, containing an entry per form element. This `elements` array allows access to the form fields by index as well as by name. The `setupForm()` function loops through all the entries in the `elements` array, first retrieving the value of the `name` property:

```
for (var e=0; e<fRef.elements.length; e++) {
  name = fRef.elements[e].name;
```

Since JavaScript 1.1, each form field contains a `type` property. This is a read-only property that specifies the type of the form element: `button`, `checkbox`, `file`, `hidden`, `password`, `radio`, `reset`, `select-one`, `select-multiple`, `submit`, `text`, and `textarea`.

The `switch` statement allows the code to switch to one or more `case` labels, depending on the value of the form element's `type` property:

```
switch (fRef.elements[e].type) {
```

Each `case` label precedes a block of code, which retrieves the appropriate value from the name/value pair's `string` variable using the `getNthParm()` function. Then depending on the element `type`, it either assigns the value to the form field's `value`, `checked`, `selected`, or `selectedIndex`.

Form elements that are simply text-based have their `value` property updated with the value returned by the `getNthParm()`, which in all cases is passed the value of the `string` variable and the value of the form element's `name` property. The `break` statement ensures that the code skips the remaining case blocks and jumps to the end of the `switch` statement:

```
case 'text':
case 'textarea':
case 'password':
case 'hidden':
  fRef.elements[e].value = getNthParm(string,name,1);
  break;
```

For checkboxes, if the value returned from the getNthParm() function is not an empty string (i.e., a value exists), then the checked property of the checkbox is set to true:

```
case 'checkbox':
  if (getNthParm(string,name,1) != '')
    fRef.elements[e].checked = true;
  break;
```

For radio buttons, if the value returned by the getNthParm() function minus zero does not result in zero, then the i object entry in the radio object array has its checked property set to true:

```
case 'radio':
  var i = getNthParm(string,name,1) - 0;
  if (value != 0) fRef[name][i].checked = true;
  break;
```

For select lists, the value returned by the getNthParm() function minus zero is used to update the selectedIndex property:

```
case 'select-one':
  fRef[name].selectedIndex = getNthParm(string,name,1) - 0;
  break;
```

For multiple select lists, the code loops through each option in the select list, invoking the getNthParm() function to retrieve the value of the *nth* entry in the name/value pairs string. If the v variable is not an empty string, then the selected property is set to true; otherwise, it is set to false:

```
case 'select-multiple':
  for (var i=0; i<fRef[name].length; i++) {
    var v = getNthParm(string,name,i+1);
    if (v != '') fRef[name][v - 0].selected = true;
  }
  break;
      }
    }
  }
```

The saveForm() function performs the reverse of the setupForm() function, it loops through all the form elements in the elements array, extracting the name and value of each form field to create a name/value pairs string, which is then used to create a userProfile cookie:

```
function saveForm(fRef) {
  var string = '';
```

```
for (var e=0; e<fRef.elements.length; e++) {
  name = fRef.elements[e].name;

  switch (fRef.elements[e].type) {

    case 'text':
    case 'textarea':
    case 'password':
    case 'hidden':
      if (string != '') string += '&';
      string += name + '=' + fRef.elements[e].value;
      break;
    case 'checkbox':
      if (fRef.elements[e].checked) {
        if (string != '') string += '&';
        string += name + '=' + fRef.elements[e].value;
      }
      break

    case 'radio':
      for (var i=0; i<fRef[name].length; i++) {
        if (fRef[name][i].checked) {
          if (string != '') string += '&';
          string += name + '=' + fRef[name][i].value;
        }
      }
      break;

    case 'select-one':
      if (string != '') string += '&';
      string += name + '=' + fRef[name].selectedIndex;
      break;

    case 'select-multiple':
      for (var i=0; i<fRef[name].length; i++) {
        if (fRef[name][i].selected) {
          if (string != '') string += '&';
          string += name + '=' + fRef[name][i].value;
        }
      }
      break;
  }
}
```

When writing cookies, we need to, among other things, set an expiration date. If no expiration date is given, then the cookie expires at the end of the current browser session. The saveForm() function defines an expires variable based on today's date plus 365 days (where 1 day equals 86,400,000 milliseconds):

```
var today = new Date();
var expires = new Date(today.getTime() + (365 * 86400000));
```

The setCookie() utility function is invoked to create a userProfile cookie with the value of the string variable with an expires expiration date:

```
      if (window.Cookie)
        setCookie("userProfile",string,expires);
    }
```

The actual HTML markup for the form is irrelevant, except for the onSubmit event handler, which invokes the saveForm() function, passing a reference to this form, as well as the reset button, which invokes the deleteCookie() utility function to delete the userProfile cookie:

```
<form name="pForm" action="index.htm"
  onSubmit="saveForm(this)">
...
<input type="reset" value="Delete Profile"
  onClick="if (window.Cookie) deleteCookie('userProfile')">
<input type="submit" value="Update Profile">
</form>
```

# Form -> Email -> Form

This particular application is very different from the preceding examples. The e-mail that is generated by this application contains, in the body of the e-mail, JavaScript code that, once cut and pasted into a file and then loaded into a browser, will show you the form as seen by the user. The form can then be amended, perhaps with further information being added to that entered by the first user, and then sent onward to yet another person.

As it is not possible for an HTML page to add an attachment to an e-mail, this application is as close as you can get to adding an attachment to a document without resorting to a server-side program.

## Form -> Email -> Form Source Code— *index.htm*

**chapter8/mailform/index.htm**

To avoid large amounts of HTML markup needing to be contained within the resultant e-mail, all of the code necessary to display the form is contained within the external JavaScript source file *mailform.js*. Therefore, the HTML markup only needs to include this and any other JavaScript code necessary to set the values of each of the form fields. In fact, the contents of the generated e-mail look very much like the contents of the *index.htm* page. The input functions used in the *index.htm* page are all defined in the *mailform.js* file. Each function accepts the name of the form field and the value to be assigned to it. The inputMultiple() functions, which select options in a multiple select list, additionally accept the index of the multiple select list to be selected:

```
<script src="mailform.js"></script>

<script language="JavaScript"><!--
inputText("to","someone@somewhere.com");
inputText("subject","This is a test subject");
inputText("name","John Doe");
inputText("email","john@doe.com");
inputSelect("country",62);
inputSelect("age",8);
inputMultiple("hobbies",false, 0);
inputMultiple("hobbies",true, 1);
inputMultiple("hobbies",true, 2);
inputMultiple("hobbies",true, 3);
inputMultiple("hobbies",false, 4);
inputMultiple("hobbies",false, 5);
inputMultiple("hobbies",false, 6);
inputMultiple("hobbies",false, 7);
inputCheckBox("i0",true);
inputCheckBox("i1",false);
inputCheckBox("i2",false);
inputCheckBox("i3",true);
inputCheckBox("i4",true);
inputCheckBox("i5",false);
inputCheckBox("i6",false);
inputCheckBox("i7",true);

inputRadio("sex",true,0);
inputRadio("sex",false,1);
//--></script>
```

# Form -> Email -> Form Source Code— *mailform.js*

**chapter8/mailform/mailform.js**

The *mailform.js* library contains JavaScript code necessary to display two forms: the data form and the email form. The data form is the form that collects all the required input from the user and can therefore contained any relevant HTML markup. To save space we have only shown the start and end form tags:

```
document.write(
  '<form name="data">' +
  '</form>'
);
```

The `email` form is the form that is actually submitted. It contains a reset and a submit button, along with a hidden form field name `<script src`. Because this is a very unusual name for a form field (it contains a less-than sign and a space character), it is necessary to access the properties of this form field using the form's `elements` array.

Remember that when a form is submitted, each *named* form field is included in the form submission, including the name of the form field. Here we are using the name of the form field itself to start part of the JavaScript code to be embedded within the resultant e-mail. The equal sign is appended to the name of the form field by the browser, followed by the value of the form field. As there is only one named form field in the e-mail form, then the generated e-mail will contain the name of the form field followed by an equal sign, followed by the value of the hidden form field:

```
document.write(
  '<form name="emailForm" method="post" enctype="text/plain">' +
  '<input type="button" value=" Reset " onClick="' +
  'document.data.reset();document.emailForm.reset()"> ' +
  '<input type="submit" value=" Send " onClick="populate()"> ' +
  '<input type="hidden" name="<script src">' +
  '</form>'
)
```

When the e-mail form is submitted, the `onClick` event handler in the submit button invokes the `populate()` function. Note that the reset button in the e-mail form resets the contents of both the visible fields in the data form and the hidden form field in the e-mail form.

The `populate()` function extracts the data from the `data` form and first updates the `action` property of the `email` form, using a `mailto:` schema with the value of the `data` form's `to` and `subject` form fields:

```
function populate() {
  document.emailForm.action =
    'mailto:' + document.data.to.value +
    '?subject=' + document.data.subject.value;
```

A local `output` variable is used to concatenate the value to be used to updated the value of the strangely named <script src hidden form field:

```
var output = '';
```

The absolute location of the *mailform.js* library is first appended to the output variable. As the resultant e-mail could eventually be loaded into any browser, the HTML markup needs to contain the full absolute location of the JavaScript source file:

```
output += '"http://www.domain.com/mailform.js"><\/SCRIPT>';
```

Next, a start script tag is appended to the output variable:

```
output += '<script language="JavaScript">';
```

The results of several function calls, one each for each of the named form fields in the data form, are then appended to the output variable:

```
output += outputText('emailAddress');
output += outputText('subjectField');
output += outputText('name');
output += outputText('email');
output += outputSelect('country');
output += outputSelect('age');
output += outputMultiple('hobbies');
output += outputCheckBox('i0');
output += outputCheckBox('i1'); .
output += outputCheckBox('i2');
output += outputCheckBox('i3');
output += outputCheckBox('i4');
output += outputCheckBox('i5');
output += outputCheckBox('i6');
output += outputCheckBox('i7');
output += outputRadio('sex');
```

Finally, a closing script tag is append to the output variable:

```
output += '<\/script>';
```

The value of the output variable is then assigned to the value property of the <script src form field:

```
document.emailForm.elements["<script src"].value = output;
}
```

The output functions used in the previous populate() function, each accept the name of a form field in the data form and retrieve either the value, selectedIndex, checked, or selected property for the type of form field they represent, and use this to return a string value that equates to the necessary JavaScript code to invoke the corresponding input function. For example, when the outputText() function is invoked with the parameter to, the string returned looks like:

```
inputText("to","martin@irt.org")
```

where martin@irt.org is the value of the to form field.

```
function outputText(name) {
  var value = document.data.elements[name].value;
  return '\ninputText("'+name+'","'+value+'");';
  }

function outputSelect(name) {
  var value = document.data.elements[name].selectedIndex;
  return '\ninputSelect("'+name+'",'+value+');';
}

function outputCheckBox(name) {
  var value = document.data.elements[name].checked;
  return '\ninputCheckBox("'+name+'",'+value+');';
}

function outputRadio(name) {
  var output = '', value;
  for (var i=0; i<document.data.elements[name].length;i++) {
    value = document.data.elements[name][i].checked;
    output += '\ninputRadio("'+name+'",'+value+','+i+');';
  }
  return output;
}

function outputMultiple(name) {
  var output = '', value;
  var length = document.data.elements[name].options.length;
  for (var i=0; i<length;i++) {
    value = document.data.elements[name].options[i].selected;
    output +=
      '\ninputMultiple("'+name+'",'+value+','+i+');';
  }
  return output;
}
```

The input functions, used in the *index.htm* page and then eventually in the email generated by this application, update the passed name argument named form field in the data form, with the passed value argument:

```
function inputText(name,value) {
  document.data.elements[name].value = value;
}

function inputSelect(name,value) {
```

```
          document.data.elements[name].selectedIndex = value;
      }

      function inputCheckBox(name,value) {
        document.data.elements[name].checked = value;
      }

      function inputRadio(name,value,index) {
        document.data.elements[name][index].checked = value;
      }

      function inputMultiple(name,value,i) {
        document.data.elements[name].options[i].selected = value;
      }
```

Figure 8-12 shows the typical contents of an e-mail generated by this application.

# Disabling Form Fields

With the introduction of the HTML 4 standard, it is now possible to disable form fields so that the user cannot interact with them. A new `disabled` attribute can be included in the `input`, `select`, or `textarea` HTML elements. This ensures that the form field is disabled by default. However, you can also set and unset the `disabled` property on each of the objects that represent the form fields using JavaScript. Both Netscape Navigator 6 and Internet Explorer 4 and above fully support the `disabled` attribute; unfortunately, earlier browser versions do not. Figures 8-13 and 8-14 show disabled form fields (colored gray) for Netscape Navigator 6 and for Internet Explorer 5.

## Disabling Form Fields Source Code— *index.htm*

**chapter8/disable/index.htm**

This sample application uses each different type of form field in the *data* form, although the JavaScript functions used in the sample application can be reused with any mix of form fields without requiring any changes:

**Figure 8-12**
Contents of a typical
generated e-mail.

```
<form name="data">
Button <input name="button" type="button" value="Button">
Checkbox <input name="checkbox" type="checkbox">
File <input name="file" type="file">
Password <input name="password" type="password">
Radio <input name="radio" type="radio">
<input name="radio" type="radio">
```

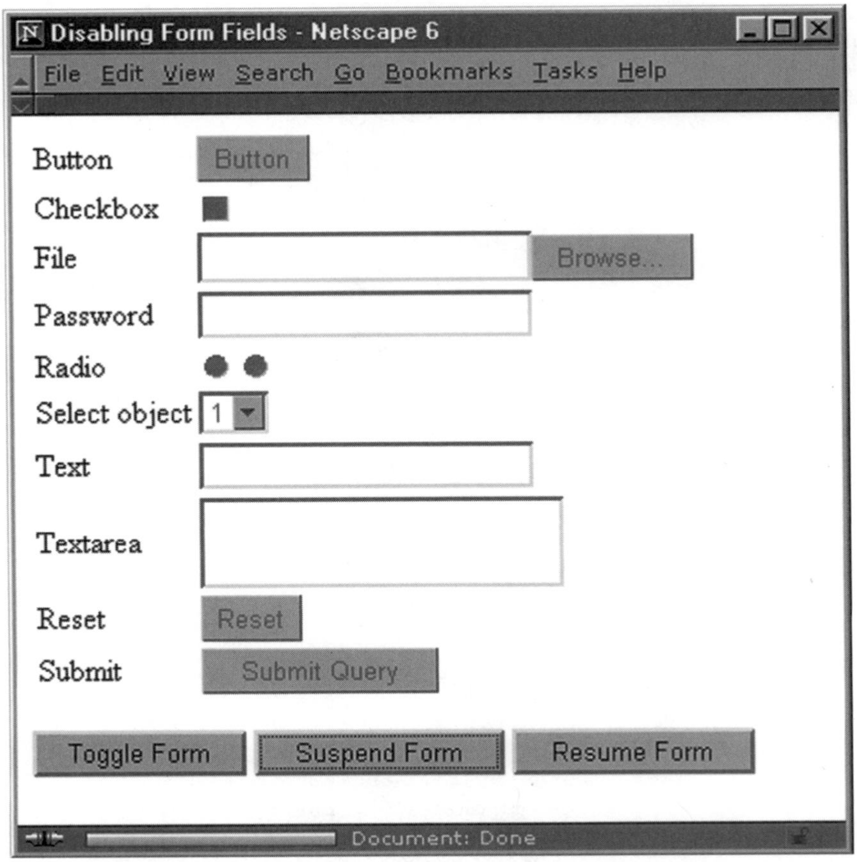

**Figure 8-13**
Disabled form fields
in Netscape
Navigator 6.

```
Select object <select name="select">
<option>1<option>2<option>3
</select>
Text <input name="text" type="text">
Textarea <textarea name="textarea"></textarea>
Reset <input name="reset" type="reset">
Submit <input name="submit" type="submit">
</form>
```

A separate form controls the disablement of the data form:

```
<form>
```

The Toggle form button invokes the toggleForm() function, passing a reference to the data form:

```
<input type="button" value="Toggle Form"
  onClick="toggleForm(document.data)">
```

The Suspend form button invokes the ableForm() function, passing a reference to the data form and a Boolean true value:

```
<input type="button" value="Suspend Form"
  onClick="ableForm(document.data,true)">
```

The Resume form button invokes the ableForm() function, passing a reference to the data form and a Boolean false value:

```
<input type="button" value="Resume Form"
  onClick="ableForm(document.data,false)">
</form>
```

The `ableForm()` function first checks that the browser supports either the `document` object's `getElementById` or `all` properties. If it does, then the code assumes that the browser supports the HTML 4 standard and in particular the disabled form field attribute. The function then proceeds to loop through all the form fields in the passed `fRef` form reference's `elements` array, setting the disabled property of each form field to the value of the passed disable argument:

```
function ableForm(fRef, disable) {
  if (document.getElementById || document.all) {
    for (var i=0; i<fRef.elements.length; i++) {
      fRef.elements[i].disabled = disable;
    }
  }
}
```

The `toggleForm()` function works in a similar fashion to the `ableForm()` function, except that it reverses the value of the form field's own disabled property:

```
function toggleForm(fRef) {
  if (document.getElementById || document.all) {
    for (var i=0; i<fRef.elements.length; i++) {
      var disable = fRef.elements[i].disabled;
      fRef.elements[i].disabled = !disable;
    }
  }
}
```

# Controlling Data Entry Using Form Fields

This application shows how difficult it can be to control data input. The code demonstrates the capturing of an 11-character string or number, a character at a time—perhaps a telephone number or a social security number. Each character is entered in its own form field. After the user enters a character into the form field, the focus instantly moves from the current form field to the next one in sequence. As far as the user is concerned, he or she can type all 11 characters without tabbing between fields, as this is automatically done for the user. Figure 8-15 shows the user halfway through entering the required data.

**Figure 8-15**
Data Entry—entering
a sequence of
numbers.

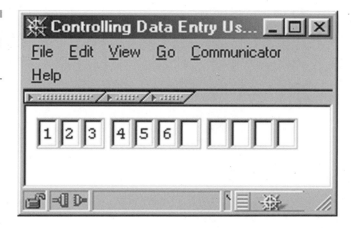

## Controlling Data Entry Using Form Fields Source Code—*index.htm*

**chapter8/entry/index.htm**

The `myForm` form contains 11 text input fields, each with `maxlength` and `size` attributes set to 1. The fields each use an `onKeyUp` event handler to invoke the `advance()` function, passing a reference to `this` current form field and the name of the next form field to move on to:

```
<form name="myForm">

<input type="text" maxlength="1" name="f1" size="1"
  onKeyUp="advance(this,'f2')"
><input type="text" maxlength="1" name="f2" size="1"
  onKeyUp="advance(this,'f3')"
><input type="text" maxlength="1" name="f3" size="1"
  onKeyUp="advance(this,'f4')">
<input type="text" maxlength="1" name="f4" size="1"
  onKeyUp="advance(this,'f5')"

><input type="text" maxlength="1" name="f5" size="1"
  onKeyUp="advance(this,'f6')"
><input type="text" maxlength="1" name="f6" size="1"
  onKeyUp="advance(this,'f7')"
><input type="text" maxlength="1" name="f7" size="1"
  onKeyUp="advance(this,'f8')">

<input type="text" maxlength="1" name="f8" size="1"
  onKeyUp="advance(this,'f9')"
```

```
><input type="text" maxlength="1" name="f9" size="1"
  onKeyUp="advance(this,'f10')"
><input type="text" maxlength="1" name="f10" size="1"
  onKeyUp="advance(this,'f11')"
><input type="text" maxlength="1" name="f11" size="1">

</form>
```

The code includes `currentField` and `nextField` global variables:

```
var currentField, nextField;
```

The `advance()` function accepts the `this` form reference as the c argument and the name of the next form field as the n argument:

```
function advance(c,n) {
```

The `currentField` and `nextField` global variables are updated with the values of the local c and n arguments:

```
currentField = c, nextField = n;
```

The `myForms` form's `f11` input field gains the current focus using its `focus()` method—that is, the text caret leaves the current form field and is moved into the `f11` form field:

```
document.myForm['f11'].focus();
```

A timer is started to invoke the `effect()` function after a millisecond delay (the minimum delay possible). The current JavaScript "thread" then ends, giving the browser the opportunity to update itself. This ensures that in Netscape Navigator, the `value` property of the current form field is correctly updated with the text just entered by the user:

```
    setTimeout('effect()',1);
}
```

The `effect()` function, when invoked after a millisecond delay, checks the `length` of the `value` property of the form field reference by the global `currentField` variable. If it is equal to 1, then the form field with the name held by the global `nextField` variable gains the text focus using its `focus()` method; otherwise, the original form field regains focus:

```
function effect() {
  if (currentField.value.length == 1)
```

```
        document.myForm[nextField].focus();
    else currentField.focus();
}
```

# Filtering Data Input

A textarea within a form can act like a very simplistic text editor. The application presented here shows how simple filters can be created that can be used to search and replace unsuitable words prior to publication, or replace common spelling or typing mistakes, and expand abbreviations and correct the capitalization of nouns.

## Filtering Data Input Source Code—*index.htm*

 **chapter8/filter/index.htm**

Three filter arrays are populated with pairs of regular expression patterns and text strings. The two regular-expression attributes g and i are used to indicate that all matches (g) are to be replaced, regardless of case (i):

```
var filter1 = new Array(
   /terrible/gi,   'nice',
   /bad/gi,        'sweet',
   /awful/gi,      'innocent',
   /nasty/gi,      'lovely'
);

var filter2 = new Array(
   /teh/gi,        'the',
   /mispelt/gi,    'misspelt',
   /isn;t/gi,      'isn\'t',
   /wot/gi,        'what',
   /dun/gi,        'done'
);

var filter3 = new Array(
   /javascript/gi, 'JavaScript',
   /(\W)re(\W)/gi, '$1Regular Expressions$2'
);
```

That last regular-expression pattern demands an explanation. The pattern matches any re text surrounded by nonword (i.e., \W) characters.

The nonword characters on either side of the re text are grouped within parentheses as subexpressions. The value of the first nine subexpressions can be referenced and used within the replacement string using $1, $2, ..., $9.

The filterText() function accepts a text string argument and a filter array reference. The function loops through the filter array a pair of regular-expression pattern and text string at a time, using the String object's replace() method to replace any regular-expression pattern matches with the replacement string, before finally returning the value of the amended text string:

```
function filterText(text, filter) {
  for (var i = 0 ; i < filter.length ; i +=2) {
    text = text.replace(filter[i], filter[i+1]);
  }
  return text;
}
```

The sample application contains a textarea form field, prefilled with spelling errors and typing mistakes, along with nonsuitable words, abbreviations, and words requiring capitalization:

```
<form>

<textarea name="input" cols="70" rows="10" wrap="virtual">
This text area is prefilled with a selection of bad, awful,
nasty, terrible words in amongst some innoculous words. By
pressing teh filter button teh bads words are replaced with
good words. Not only can this be used to replace bad words
but also words that are commonly mispelt or mistyped,
abbreviated or in the wrong case. There isn;t a limit to
wot can be dun. Even words that are in upper case (e.g. BAD,
AWFUL, NASTY, or Bad, Awful, nASTY) will be replaced. This
is all done using javascript and re
</textarea>
```

The three button input fields use onClick event handlers to invoke the filterText() function, passing the value property of the input textarea and one of the three filter arrays. The string value returned by the filterText() function is used to update the input textarea's property value:

```
<input type="button" value="Bad -&gt; Nice"
  onClick="this.form.input.value=
    filterText(this.form.input.value,filter1)">

<input type="button" value="Spellings & typos"
  onClick="this.form.input.value=
    filterText(this.form.input.value,filter2)">
```

```
<input type="button" value="Caps. & Abbs."
  onClick="this.form.input.value=
    filterText(this.form.input.value,filter3)">

</form>
```

Of course, it would be perhaps more suitable to invoke the filterText() function from the form element's onSubmit event handler immediately prior to form submission.

# Date Spinner

Although it may look like we are restricted to creating graphical user interfaces (GUIs) using the 11 different types of form fields, we can with the use of images create our own "buttons." The two sample applications in this section show how to make form controls using an image and an image map, as shown in Figure 8-16, and using traditional image links, as shown in Figure 8-17, that control the date displayed in a text form field.

**Figure 8-16**
Date Spinner with an image map.

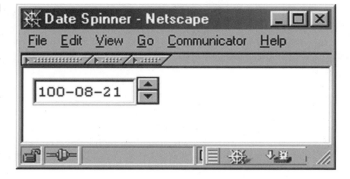

**Figure 8-17**
Date Spinner with image links.

Creating images that look like traditional form fields with their gray background color allows us to create diverse and interesting interfaces. In Chapter 11 "Dynamic HTML," we show how to make slider controls.

## Date Spinner Source Code—*index.htm*

**chapter8/spinner/index.htm**

Both sample applications reuse the *current.js* library described in Chapter 7 "Date and Time":

```
<script src="current.js" language="JavaScript"></script>
```

The date form contains a text input field named spinner, an image link with an onMouseOver event handler to reset the window object's status property, and an image with a usemap attribute set to #spinner-map:

```
<form name="date">
<input name="spinner" type="text" size="10" value="9999-99-99"
><a href="JavaScript:" onMouseOver="self.status='';return true"
><img src="date.gif"  border="0" width="19" height="24"
  align="top" usemap="#spinner-map" alt="Click"></a>
</form>
```

The usemap attribute indicates that the image is a special "mouse-selectable" image with one or more hypertext links defined in a client-side map element, and in this case, it is located in the current document (as specified by the pound character).

The following map element defines the "mouse-selectable" areas within the spinner-map map. Two rectangular area elements are defined, the first area from coordinates 0,0 to 18,10, and the second from 0,12 to 18,23. Each area element includes an href attribute that contains a javascript schema URL to invoke either the nextDay() or prevDay() functions and to also reset the window object's status property:

```
<map name="spinner-map">
<area shape="rect" coords="0,0,18,10"
  href="javascript:nextDay()"
  onMouseOver="self.status='';return true">
<area shape="rect" coords="0,12,18,23"
  href="javascript:prevDay()"
  onMouseOver="self.status='';return true">
</map>
```

The current time in milliseconds is retrieved and assigned to the global `milliseconds` variable:

```
var date = new Date();
var milliseconds = date.getTime();
```

The `formatDate()` function uses the value of the global `millisec-onds` variable to create a new `Date` object. The year, month, and day of the new date are retrieved and formatted before being used to update the `value` property of the `spinner` text input field:

```
function formatDate() {
  date = new Date(milliseconds);
  var year = date.getYear();
  var month = date.getMonth() + 1;
  var day = date.getDate();
  document.date.spinner.value =
    year + '-' + padout(month) + '-' + padout(day);
}
```

The `prevDay()` function decreases the value of the global `millisec-onds` variable by 86,400,000 milliseconds (i.e., one day) and then invokes the `formatDate()` function to update the spinner form field with the new `milliseconds` value:

```
function prevDay() {
  milliseconds -= 86400000;
  formatDate();
}
```

The `nextDay()` does a similar job but increases the value of the global `milliseconds` variable by 86,400,000 milliseconds:

```
function nextDay() {
  milliseconds += 86400000;
  formatDate();
}
```

To initialize the value of the `spinner` form field, the `body` element's `onLoad` event handler invokes the `formatDate()` function when the page has completely loaded:

```
<body onLoad="formatDate()">
```

When the user clicks one of the two areas within the "mouse-selec-table" image, the `prevDay()` or `nextDay()` functions are invoked to alter the contents of the `spinner` form field by one day on either side of its current value.

## Date Spinner Source Code—*index2.htm*

 chapter8/spinner/index2.htm

The only difference in the second sample application is that instead of using an image map, two separate image links are both used with onClick event handlers, one that invokes the prevDay() function and the other that invokes the nextDay() function:

```
<form name="date">
<a href="#" onMouseOver="self.status='';return true"
  onClick="prevDay();return false"
><img src="prev.gif" border="0" width="17" height="23"
  align="top" alt="Click"></a
><input name="spinner" type="text" size="10"
  value="9999-99-99"
><a href="#" onMouseOver="self.status='';return true"
  onClick="nextDay();return false"
><img src="next.gif" border="0" width="17" height="23"
  align="top" alt="Click"
></a>
</form>
```

# Sales Order Form

The need to accept product orders over the Internet continues to grow every day, B2C (business-to-consumer) as well as B2B (business-to-business) transactions are well into the billions of dollars per year, with B2B expected to far overtake B2C in the coming months. Being able to offer client-side calculations of product totals, subtotals, tax, and grand totals before dispatching the order to the server allows the user to see an immediate cause and effect when entering his or her order.

The application presented here, shown in Figure 8-18, demonstrates how different quantities of several different products can be chosen, with the totals all automatically updated—almost like a spreadsheet package.

## Sales Order Form Source Code—*index.htm*

 chapter8/sales/index.htm

The products array contains pairs of product descriptions and prices. To adapt this application for your purposes, all you need to do is amend, delete, or add entries to the products array:

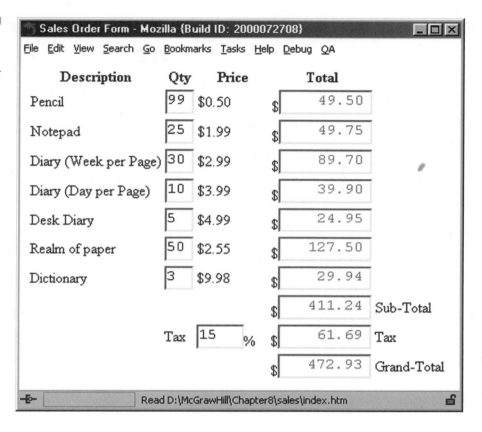

**Figure 8-18**
Sales Order Form—
an order in progress.

```
var products = new Array(
  'Pencil', 0.50,
  'Notepad', 1.99,
  'Diary (Week per Page)', 2.99,
  'Diary (Day per Page)', 3.99,
  'Desk Diary', 4.99,
  'Realm of paper', 2.55,
  'Dictionary', 9.98
);
```

A global output variable is defined and initialized:

```
var output = '';
```

The code then loops through the pairs of descriptions and prices in the `products` array, increasing the `i` loop integer by 2 each time. The `j` loop integer is used to count the number of pairs within the `products` array; therefore, it is incremented by 1 each time through the loop:

```
for (var i=0, j=0; i<products.length; i+=2, j++) {
```

For each product in the `products` array, the HTML markup for a table row is appended to the `output` variable:

```
output +=
```

The row contains the product description:

```
'<tr><td>' + products[i] + '</td><td>' +
```

A text input field is named with a `quantity` prefix plus the value of the `j` integer, containing an `onChange` event handler that invokes the `calc()` function and passes a reference to `this` current form:

```
'<input type="text" name="quantity' + j + '" ' +
'size="2" maxlength="2" onChange="calc(this.form)">' +
```

The product price is formatted using the `cents()` function:

```
'</td><td>$' + cents(products[i+1]) +
```

A hidden text field is named with a `price` prefix plus the value of the `j` integer, with its `value` attribute set to the product price:

```
'<input type="hidden" name="price' + j + '" value="' +
products[i+1] + '">' +
'</td><td>' +
```

A disabled text input field is named with the `total` prefix plus the value of the `j` integer:

```
'$<input type="text" name="total' + j +
'" size="9" disabled>' +
'</td></tr>';
}
```

The HTML markup is written out to the document:

```
document.write(output);
```

Several text input fields are included. Among them are three disabled fields named: `subTotal`, `taxTotal`, and `grandTotal`, as well as a text field named `tax` containing an `onChange` event handler that invokes the `calc()` function, again passing a reference to `this` current form:

```
<input type="text" name="subTotal" size="9" disabled>
<input type="text" name="tax" value="7" size="4" maxlength="4"
  onChange="calc(this.form)">
<input type="text" name="taxTotal" size="9" disabled>
<input type="text" name="grandTotal" size="9" disabled>
</form>
```

The `calc()` function, invoked when any of the input form fields' `onChange` event handlers detect a change in the quantity of products being ordered or a change in the rate of tax, loops once per product in the application, first calculating the product `total` price using the `cents()` function to format the result and updating the relevant *total* form field. It adds the `total` to the running `subTotal`, before updating the `value` property of the `subTotal` form field. The tax rate is then retrieved from the `value` property of the `tax` input field, and then it is used to calculate the `taxTotal` amount. Finally, the `grandTotal` is calculated and used to update the `value` property of the `grandTotal` form field:

```
function calc(what) {
  var subTotal = 0;
  for (var i=0;i<products.length/2;i++) {
    var quantity = what.elements['quantity' + i].value - 0;
    var price = what.elements['price' + i].value - 0;
    var total = quantity * price;
    total = cents(total);
    what['total' + i].value = padwith(total,9,' ');
    subTotal += total - 0;
  }
  subTotal = cents(subTotal);
  what.subTotal.value = padwith(subTotal,9,' ');
  var taxrate = what.tax.value - 0
  var taxTotal = cents((subTotal - 0) / 100 * taxrate);
  what.taxTotal.value = padwith(taxTotal,9,' ');
  var grandTotal = cents((subTotal - 0) + (taxTotal - 0));
  what.grandTotal.value = padwith(grandTotal,9,' ');
}
```

Note that whenever a value is retrieved from a form field, it is first converted from a string to an integer by subtracting zero. Whenever a form field is updated, the value is first formatted using the `cents()` function and then is padded with leading spaces using the `padwith()` function:

```
function padwith(num, size, chr) {
  num = '' + num;
  while (num.length < size) num = chr + num;
  return num;
}
```

The `cents()` function used in this application is described in detail in Chapter 2 "Number Utilities."

# Summary

Forms can provide a useful framework when developing applications, allowing the user to enter and select data. Forms can interact with cookies and data passed from previous pages. They can also be used simply to capture data to be processed by a server-side process or simply sent as an e-mail. In addition, with the use of JavaScript, forms can become applications in the true sense of the word—for instance, for comparing the calculator examples in Chapter 2 with the desktop calculator provided in Windows, and the previous "Sales Order Form" with simple spreadsheet applications.

With the use of Dynamic HTML (DHTML) techniques, form interfaces can become even more sophisticated, with form fields appearing and disappearing at will. In addition, with the use of images, new *widgets* can be created to extend the existing form field types. See Chapter 11 "Dynamic HTML" for examples.

# Images

This chapter presents many different uses of images and JavaScript—from simple image highlighting code to complex fading images. Slides shows, not unlike automated Microsoft PowerPoint presentations, can also be achieved using JavaScript. Although JavaScript has very limited capabilities when it comes to creating graphics, we show how, with the aid of 1x1-pixel-sized images, both horizontal and vertical bar charts can be created. Examples are included to show a simple but effective counter, along with a progress display of images being downloaded to the browser's cache. The chapter ends with two different image toolbars, one of which only requires a single line of HTML to all the pages that need to display the toolbar.

**Highlighting Images ../chapter9/highlight/index.htm**
**Fast Image Rollovers ../chapter9/fast/index.htm**
**Fading Images In and Out ../chapter9/fade/index.htm**
**Image Maps ../chapter9/imagemap/index.htm**
**Slide Show ../chapter9/slide/index.htm**
**Bar Charts ../chapter9/barchart/index.htm**
**Image Percentage Download ../chapter9/download/index.htm**
**Image Popup ../chapter9/popup/index.htm**
**Image Counter ../chapter9/counter/index.htm**
**Random Banner Adverts ../chapter9/banner/index.htm**
**Image Toolbar ../chapter9/toolbar1/section-a.htm and ../chapter9/toolbar2/section-a.htm**

# Highlighting Images

Highlighting images or "image swapping" is probably one of the most infamous uses of JavaScript. With the introduction of the Image object in Netscape Navigator 3, overnight developers were able to make their pages active, swapping one image with another when the mouse pointer ventured over what would have otherwise been a static image link. Unfortunately, the version of Internet Explorer around at that time (Internet Explorer 3) did not support the Image object. Therefore, developers included code to detect the browser being used. If the browser was Netscape Navigator 3, image swapping was allowed. If not, the code was skipped.

Of course, when Netscape Navigator 4 came along, image-swapping code using this approach suddenly ground to a halt. Likewise, when Internet Explorer 4 was released with support for the Image object, image swapping still did not occur. This happened just because of the check for a particular version of a particular browser, when all along a test for the Image object would have sufficed.

The code presented here is a general-purpose image-highlighting code that can be used to change the src attribute of an image using the onMouseOver and onMouseOut event handlers in an anchor element, for any browser that supports the Image object. Figure 9-1 shows the effects of the mouse pointer moving over one of the many image links contained in the HTML markup.

**Figure 9-1**
Highlighting Images—swapping the src property of one image in an image link.

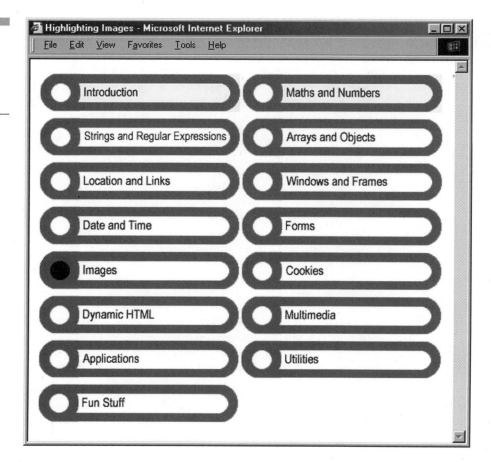

# Highlighting Images Source Code—*index.htm*

 **chapter9/highlight/index.htm**

The first thing the JavaScript code in the *index.htm* page does is attempt to preload *circle-off.gif* and *circle-on.gif* images. A test is made to see if the browser supports the `document` object's `images` array. The `images` array contains an `Image` object reference to all the images in the current document. If this array exists, we assume that the browser supports the `Image` object. This may be a faulty assumption, as other JavaScript code in the document might have created a `document` property named `images` (a variable, method, object, or array). Care must be taken not to create a `document` property named `images`, where you later test for `Image` object support. Another test would perhaps be to test for the `window` object's `Image` object constructor, but as the test for the `document` objects images `array` is more common, this is used in preference.

If the `document` object contains an `images` property, the code creates two `Image` objects, specifying the `width` and `height` of the images as parameters to the `Image` constructor and assigning the object references to the global variables `circleOff` and `circleOn`. After each `Image` object has been created, the `Image` object's `src` property is updated with the relative URL of an image file. This then causes the browser to download the images from the server to the browser's cache, where they are immediately available for use.

```
if (document.images) {
  var circleOff = new Image(50,50)
  circleOff.src = 'circle-off.gif';
  var circleOn = new Image(50,50)
  circleOn.src = 'circle-on.gif';
}
```

If we did not preload images, then there might be a perceptible delay when first swapping the `src` property of an image to an image not already in the browser's cache, while waiting for the image to be downloaded from the server. Once downloaded to the browser's cache, there is no delay.

To simplify the code, we only show the first four image links. Each of the four following links include `onMouseOver` and `onMouseOut` event handlers within the anchor tag. The `onMouseOver` event handlers invoke the `swapOn()` function, passing an integer indicating part of the `img` element's name attribute—likewise with the `onMouseOut` event handlers that invoke the swapOff() function. Note that each image link contains two images—one named and one unnamed. The named image will be swapped when the mouse moves over either of the two images in the image link.

The first image link includes an image named c0; the value passed to both the swapOn() and swapOff() functions is 0:

```
<a href="1.htm" onMouseOver="swapOn(0)" onMouseOut="swapOff(0)"
><img src="circle-off.gif" name="c0"
><img src="chapter1.gif"></a>
```

The second image link includes an image named c1; the value passed to both the swapOn() and swapOff() functions is 1:

```
<a href="2.htm" onMouseOver="swapOn(1)" onMouseOut="swapOff(1)"
><img src="circle-off.gif" name="c1"
><img src="chapter2.gif"></a>
```

The third image link includes an image named c2; the value passed to both the swapOn() and swapOff() functions is 2:

```
<a href="3.htm" onMouseOver="swapOn(2)" onMouseOut="swapOff(2)"
><img src="circle-off.gif" name="c2"
><img src="chapter3.gif"></a>
```

The last image link includes an image named c3; the value passed to both the swapOn() and swapOff() functions is 3:

```
<a href="4.htm" onMouseOver="swapOn(3)" onMouseOut="swapOff(3)"
><img src="circle-off.gif" name="c3"
><img src="chapter4.gif"></a>
```

The swapOn() function, invoked by one of the four onMouseOver event handlers, accepts the passed integer as the name parameter. Another check is made to ensure that the document object's images array is supported. If it is, then the src property of one of the Image objects contained in the document object's images array is changed to the src property of the circleOn object Image reference:

```
function swapOn(name) {
  if (document.images) {
    document.images['c' + name].src = circleOn.src;
  }
}
```

The actual Image object changed depends on the concatenated string value of the character c plus the integer value of the name parameter. In other words, if 0 is passed to the swapOn() function, then the src property of the c0 image is altered.

**NOTE**.  *It is possible to use the index position of images within the images array, but this suffers from problems in early versions on Netscape Navigator and has the potential to cause problems when documents are changed and the relative positions of images within the document are changed.*

The swapOff() function is almost identical to the swapOn() function, except that it changes the src property of the "highlighted" image to the src property of the circleOff object Image reference instead:

```
function swapOff(name) {
  if (document.images) {
    document.images['c' + name].src = circleOff.src;
  }
}
```

**NOTE**.  *It is not necessary to swap one of the images within the image link. Any named image can be swapped anywhere in the page.*

# Fast Image Rollovers

In the previous "Highlighting Images" example, we restricted the image swapping to just two images: *circle-on.gif* and *circle-off.gif*. The preloading of these two small images (approximately 1 Kb in size) does not impose any effect upon the loading of the rest of the page. However, if lots of larger images are preloaded in anticipation of being required for image swapping, then the time taken to download these images may vary drastically, sometimes resulting in the "highlighted" versions of the images being available before the "unhighlighted" versions. This results in very patchy image swapping where the "highlighted" image is shown by the onMouseOver event, but then is not replaced by an as-yet-unavailable "unhighlighted" image by the onMouseOut event.

The code presented here uses techniques to only download the "highlighted" versions of the images once the page has completely loaded (i.e., after the document has been rendered and the "unhighlighted" images downloaded and displayed) and then only perform the image swapping

**Figure 9-2**

Fast Image
Rollovers—swapping
the `src` property
of two images in
an image link.

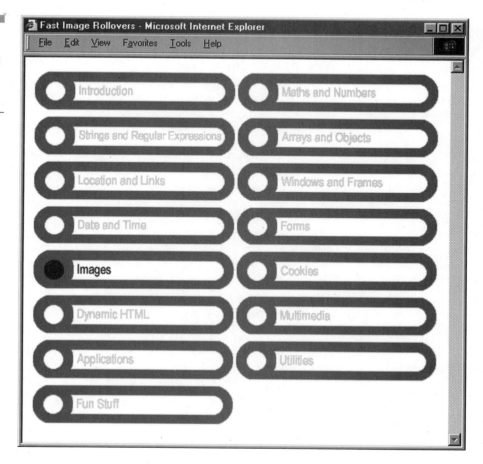

on the images if the preloading of the "highlighted" versions has started. The code now swaps both of the images in each of the image links on mouse over, as shown in Figure 9-2.

## Fast Image Rollovers Source Code—*index.htm*

**chapter9/fast/index.htm**

The global `loaded` variable is defined and initialized with a `false` Boolean value. This variable is set to `true` once the page has completely loaded; it is used to control the image swapping:

```
var loaded = false;
```

An `imageOff` array is defined. It is used to hold `Image` object references of all the "unhighlighted" images. This is not unlike the `document` object's `images` array, except that it bears no resemblance to the images contained in the document, just the images we intend on preloading:

```
var imageOff = new Array();
```

If the `document` object's images array is supported, the code continues to preload the original *circle-off.gif* and *circle-on.gif* images:

```
if (document.images) {
  var circleOff = new Image(50,50)
  circleOff.src = 'circle-off.gif';
  var circleOn = new Image(50,50)
  circleOn.src = 'circle-on.gif';
```

Next, the code loads 15 images, first creating a new `Image` object using the `Image` object constructor and assigning the object reference to the current position within the `imageOff` array, and then it continues to preload one of 15 images named *chapter0off.gif* through to *chapter14off.gif*:

```
  for (var i=0; i<15; i++) {
    imageOff[i] = new Image(200,50);
    imageOff[i].src = 'chapter' + (i+1) + 'off.gif';
  }
}
```

An `imageOn` array is then defined to hold the `Image` object references of all the "highlighted" images:

```
var imageOn = new Array();
```

These images are not preloaded immediately; the code to preload them is contained within the `imageLoad()` function, which also sets the global `loaded` variable to `true`, signifying it is now acceptable to allow image swapping to occur:

```
function imageLoad() {
  if (document.images) {
    for (var i=0; i<15; i++) {
      imageOn[i] = new Image(200,50);
      imageOn[i].src = 'chapter' + (i+1) + '.gif';
    }
  }
  loaded = true;
}
```

The revised `swapOn()` function swaps the original images (with the name prefix of `c`) as before, but now additionally swaps the larger images (with the name prefix of `ch`), but only if the `loaded` variable is set to `true`:

```
function swapOn(name) {
  if (document.images) {
    document.images['c' + name].src = circleOn.src;
    if (loaded)
      document.images['ch' + name].src = imageOn[name].src;
  }
}
```

Likewise with the revised `swapOff()` function:

```
function swapOff(name) {
  if (document.images) {
    document.images['c' + name].src = circleOff.src;
    if (loaded)
      document.images['ch' + name].src = imageOff[name].src;
  }
}
```

The `imageLoad()` function, which starts the preloading of all the "highlighted" images, is triggered by the `onLoad` event handler in the `body` element. The `onLoad` event usually fires once all the HTML markup and inline images, and other associated inline files have completely downloaded. This ensures that the default static state of the document is completely visible before attempting to download the "extra" images needed for image swapping:

```
<body onLoad="imageLoad()">
```

As before, we only show the first four image links contained in the full example. They have all been revised to include a `name` attribute in the second of the two images in all of the image links, named `ch0` through to `ch3`, or `c14` in the full example on the CD-ROM:

```
<a href="1.htm" onMouseOver="swapOn(0)" onMouseOut="swapOff(0)"
><img src="circle-off.gif" name="c0"
><img src="chapter1off.gif" name="ch0"></a>

<a href="2.htm" onMouseOver="swapOn(1)" onMouseOut="swapOff(1)"
><img src="circle-off.gif" name="c1"
><img src="chapter2off.gif" name="ch1"></a>

<a href="3.htm" onMouseOver="swapOn(2)" onMouseOut="swapOff(2)"
><img src="circle-off.gif" name="c2"
><img src="chapter3off.gif" name="ch2"></a>

<a href="4.htm" onMouseOver="swapOn(3)" onMouseOut="swapOff(3)"
><img src="circle-off.gif" name="c3"
><img src="chapter4off.gif" name="ch3"></a>
```

# Fading Images In and Out

Image-swapping techniques can be used to do more than simply swap one or two images between two different states. They can also be used to swap between many different states, perhaps replacing the image over time with a slightly different version of the previous one. The images used in this next example show a color fade between each image. However, the example could just as easily be used with images that morph between two slightly different images.

The trick is using a timer that invokes the image "highlighting" swapping code after a set delay ad nauseam until the sequence is completed, but to then cancel this if the mouse moves off the image and replace it with another timer that invokes the image "unhighlighting" swapping code—again after a set delay ad nauseam, until the sequence returns to its original state.

There is a second subsequent trick, and that is remembering that while one image may be fading up through the sequence of images, one or more other images may be fading back down through the sequence, as shown in Figure 9-3. This therefore requires sophisticated management of multiple timers and multiple states.

## Fading Images In and Out Source Code— *index.htm*

**chapter9/fade/index.htm**

To make it easy to manage the multiple timers and multiple states, we define a `Rollover` object constructor, which is used to create a `Rollover` object for an image link to fade up and down through a sequence of images, each initially defined with default properties: i representing the current image sequence, inFade, and outFade Booleans, that when set to `true` indicates that the image is fading up through or back down the image sequences, and inTimeout and outTimeout, which are used to hold the timer's reference for controlling the fading up through and back down the image sequences:

```
function Rollover() {
    this.i = 0;
    this.inFade = false;
```

**Figure 9-3**
Multiple fading images each in one of many states.

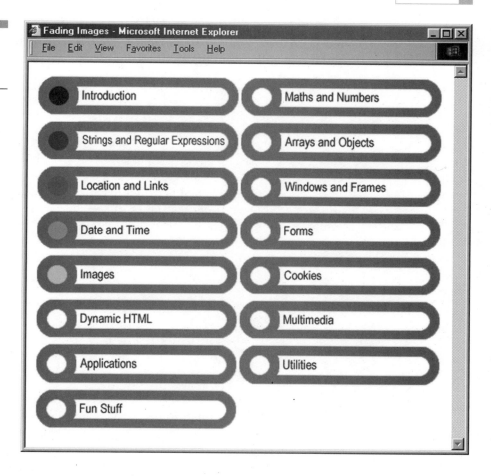

```
    this.outFade = false;
    this.inTimeout = null;
    this.outTimeout = null;
}
```

If the document object's images array is supported, then an image array is defined to hold six preloaded images, named *circle-0.gif* through to *circle-1.gif*:

```
if (document.images) {
  var image = new Array();
  for (var i=0; i<6; i++) {
    image[i] = new Image(50,50);
    image[i].src = 'circle-' + i + '.gif';
  }
```

A `rollovers` array is then defined to hold 15 `Rollover` object references created using the `Rollover()` object constructor, one for each of the image links used in the full example:

```
var rollovers = new Array();
for (var i=0; i<15; i++) rollovers[i] = new Rollover();
}
```

Whenever the `swapOn()` function is invoked from any one of the image link's `onMouseOver` event handlers with the integer `name` parameter suffix for the named image to be swapped, the `window` objects `clearTimeout()` method is called to cancel any previous timers started in the `fadeOut()` function, using the `outTimeout` property of the relevant `Rollover` object in the `rollovers` arrays. This immediately halts any existing fade out sequence. The `inFade` property is set to `true` and the `outFade` property is set to `false` before the `fadeIn()` function is invoked, passing as input the `name` parameter:

```
function swapOn(name) {
  if (document.images) {
    clearTimeout(rollovers[name].outTimeout);
    rollovers[name].inFade = true;
    rollovers[name].outFade = false;
    fadeIn(name);
  }
}
```

The `swapOff()` function performs a similar role, except that it cancels any timer started in the `fadeIn()` function, sets the `outFade` property to `true`, and sets the `inFade` property to `false` before invoking the `fadeOut()` function:

```
function swapOff(name) {
  if (document.images) {
    clearTimeout(rollovers[name].inTimeout);
    rollovers[name].outFade = true;
    rollovers[name].inFade = false;
    fadeOut(name);
  }
}
```

The `fadeIn()` function performs the fade up image swapping, swapping the `src` of the required image to the next image in the sequence, based on the value of the `Rollover` object's `i` property, which is incremented each time the `fadeIn()` function is called, as long as the `inFade` property is still set to `true` and the value of the `i` property is less than 5. A timer is then created using the `window` object's `setTimeout()` function to reinvoke the `fadeIn()` function after 50 milliseconds, passing as input the current value of the n parameter and assigning the generated timer reference to the `Rollover` object's `inTimeout` property. The repeated use of the `fadeIn()` function causes the image to fade up from the first in the sequence to the last in the sequence, unless the mouse pointer is moved off the image link, in which case the `onMouseOut` event handler invokes the `swapOff()` function, which clears the timer referenced by the `inTimeout` property:

```
function fadeIn(n) {
  if (rollovers[n].inFade && rollovers[n].i<5) {
    document.images['c' + n].src = image[++rollovers[n].i].src;
    rollovers[n].inTimeout = setTimeout('fadeIn("'+n+'")',50);
  }
}
```

The `fadeOut()` function performs the fade *back* image swapping, swapping the `src` of the required image to the *previous* image in the sequence, based on the value of the `Rollover` object's i property, which is *decreased* each time the `fadeOut()` function is called, as long as the `outFade` property is still set to `true` and the value of the i property is *greater* than zero. A timer is then created using the window object's `setTimeout()` function to reinvoke the `fadeOut()` function after 150 milliseconds, passing as input the current value of the n parameter and assigning the generated timer reference to the `Rollover` object's `outTimeout` property. The repeated use of the `fadeOut()` function causes the image to fade *back down* from the *last* in the sequence to the *first* in the sequence. If the mouse pointer is moved *back over* the image link, however, the `onMouseOver` event handler invokes the `swapOver()` function yet again, which clears the timer referenced by the `outTimeout` property:

```
function fadeOut(n) {
  if (rollovers[n].outFade && rollovers[n].i>0) {
    document.images['c' + n].src = image[-rollovers[n].i].src;
    rollovers[n].outTimeout = setTimeout('fadeOut("'+n+'")',150);
  }
}
```

The actual image links simply require the appropriate integer suffix value of the named image to be passed as input to the `swapOn()` and `swapOff()` functions as in previous examples. Only the first four image links contained in the full example are shown:

```
<a href="1.htm" onMouseOver="swapOn(0)" onMouseOut="swapOff(0)"
><img src="circle-0.gif" name="c0"
><img src="chapter1.gif"></a>

<a href="2.htm" onMouseOver="swapOn(1)"
```

```
onMouseOut="swapOff(1)"
><img src="circle-0.gif" name="c1"
><img src="chapter2.gif"></a>

<a href="3.htm" onMouseOver="swapOn(2)" onMouseOut="swapOff(2)"
><img src="circle-0.gif" name="c2"
><img src="chapter3.gif"></a>

<a href="4.htm" onMouseOver="swapOn(3)" onMouseOut="swapOff(3)"
><img src="circle-0.gif" name="c3"
><img src="chapter4.gif"></a>
```

# Image Maps

The usemap attribute in an img element indicates that the image is a "clickable image" of one or more hyperlinks, referred to as an *image map*.

There are occasions where we only need to swap an image when the mouse moves over a small region within an image. Using the onMouseOver and onMouseOut event handlers within an anchor element of an image link does not enable us to perform this lower-level granularity; it swaps the images when the mouse pointer moves anywhere over the images contained in the image link. A solution is to use images maps. We define a mapping of one or more "hot spots"—that is, regions of the map where we require interaction to occur. Image maps can include onMouseOver and onMouseOut event handlers, so that when the mouse pointer moves over one of the hot spots, the event handlers can be used to swap the source of the image.

In this example, we have the illusion of one very large image, shown in Figure 9-4, which is actually made up of many smaller images, and we only perform the image swapping when the mouse pointer moves over the areas of the images, which have a white background. As the shapes of these areas range from very simple (circular) to very complex (a rectangle with concave and convex ends), we define several different areas.

As in previous examples, the example is made up from two basic images. The first basic image is the spot image (*circle-off.gif*).

The white background of the *circle-off.gif* forms two different regions: the simple circular shape in the middle of the image and the more complicated area on the right-hand edge of the image. The HTML map markup necessary to define these areas is included in the following:

```
<map name="map-name">
<area shape="circle" coords="25,25,12">
<area shape="poly" coords="47,13,49,13,49,18">
<area shape="poly" coords="49,31,47,37,49,37">
</map>
```

**Figure 9-4**
Image maps,
swapping images
using hot spots.

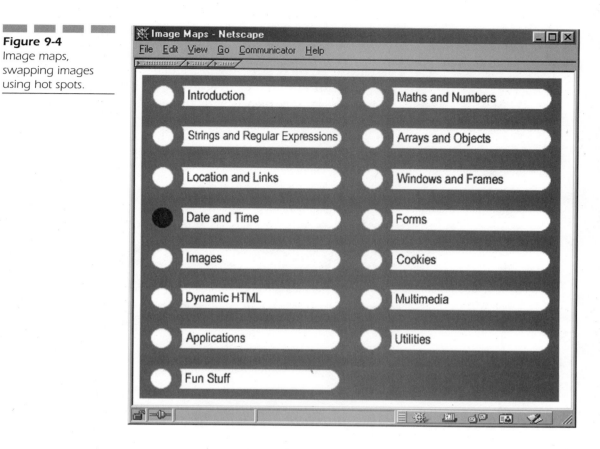

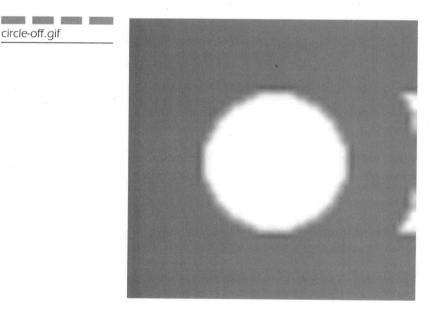

We've actually used three `area` elements to define three `shape` areas: a `circle` shape with a center x:y coordinate of 25:25 and radius of 12 pixels, and two `poly` shapes, each with three sets of x:y coordinates to mark the boundary of the polygon.

The second of the two basic images (of which there are many different versions) can be illustrated using the *chapter1.gif*.

chapter1.gif

The *chapter1.gif* contains one region of white background, although we use two `area` elements within the HTML `map` markup:

```
<map name="map-name">
<area shape="rect" coords="0,13,178,37">
<area shape="circle" coords="175,25,12">
</map>
```

The fact that the areas overlap is unimportant.

The area elements can contain an `href` attribute that dictates the target page to be loaded when that region of the map is clicked, along with `onMouseOver` and `onMouseOut` event handlers.

## Image Maps Source Code—*index.htm*

On the CD **chapter9/imagemap/index.htm**

The JavaScript code necessary to perform the actual image swapping is identical to that used in the previous "Highlighting Images" example. We first preload the "highlighted" and "unhighlighted" versions of the image to be swapped:

```
if (document.images) {
  var circleOff = new Image(50,50)
  circleOff.src = 'circle-off.gif';
  var circleOn = new Image(50,50)
  circleOn.src = 'circle-on.gif';
}
```

The `swapOn()` function simply updates the `src` property of the required image with the "highlighted" image `src` property:

```
function swapOn(name) {
  if (document.images) {
    document.images['c' + name].src = circleOn.src;
  }
}
```

The `swapOff()` function simply updates the `src` property of the required image with the "unhighlighted" image `src` property:

```
function swapOff(name) {
  if (document.images) {
    document.images['c' + name].src = circleOff.src;
  }
}
```

Whereas in previous examples we have used image links where the anchor elements use the `onMouseOut` and `onMouseOver` event handlers to invoke the `swapOn()` and `swapOf()` functions, here we omit the anchor element and instead include a `usemap` attribute in each `img` element, referencing a relative map definition:

```
<img src="circle-off.gif" name="c0" usemap="#circle1"
><img src="chapter1.gif" usemap="#bar1">

<img src="circle-off.gif" name="c1" usemap="#circle2"
><img src="chapter2.gif" usemap="#bar2">

<img src="circle-off.gif" name="c2" usemap="#circle3"
><img src="chapter3.gif" usemap="#bar3">

<img src="circle-off.gif" name="c3" usemap="#circle4"
><img src="chapter4.gif" usemap="#bar4">
```

Each of the images references a unique map definition. This is required, as the `onMouseOver` and `onMouseOut` event handlers need different parameters for the `swapOn()` and `swapOff()` functions.

The `circle1` and `bar1` maps pass an integer value of 0 to the `swapOn()` and `swapOff()` functions, and contain `href` attributes that specify `1.htm` as the target page to load when the user clicks the hot spots:

```
<map name="circle1">
<area shape="circle" coords="25,25,12"          href="1.htm"
onMouseOver="swapOn(0)" onMouseOut="swapOff(0)">
<area shape="poly" coords="47,13,49,13,49,18" href="1.htm"
onMouseOver="swapOn(0)" onMouseOut="swapOff(0)">
<area shape="poly" coords="49,31,47,37,49,37" href="1.htm"
onMouseOver="swapOn(0)" onMouseOut="swapOff(0)">
</map>
```

```
<map name="bar1">
<area shape="rect" coords="0,13,178,37"          href="1.htm"
onMouseOver="swapOn(0)" onMouseOut="swapOff(0)">
<area shape="circle" coords="175,25,12"          href="1.htm"
onMouseOver="swapOn(0)" onMouseOut="swapOff(0)">
</map>
```

The `circle2` and `bar2` maps pass an integer value of 1 to the `swapOn()` and `swapOff()` functions, and contain `href` attributes that specify `2.htm` as the target page to load when the user clicks the hot spots:

```
<map name="circle2">
<area shape="circle" coords="25,25,12"           href="2.htm"
onMouseOver="swapOn(1)" onMouseOut="swapOff(1)">
<area shape="poly" coords="47,13,49,13,49,18" href="2.htm"
onMouseOver="swapOn(1)" onMouseOut="swapOff(1)">
<area shape="poly" coords="49,31,47,37,49,37" href="2.htm"
onMouseOver="swapOn(1)" onMouseOut="swapOff(1)">
</map>
```

```
<map name="bar2">
<area shape="rect" coords="0,13,178,37"          href="2.htm"
onMouseOver="swapOn(1)" onMouseOut="swapOff(1)">
<area shape="circle" coords="175,25,12"          href="2.htm"
onMouseOver="swapOn(1)" onMouseOut="swapOff(1)">
</map>
```

The `circle3` and `bar3` maps pass an integer value of 2 to the `swapOn()` and `swapOff()` functions, and contain `href` attributes that specify `3.htm` as the target page to load when the user clicks the hot spots:

```
<map name="circle3">
<area shape="circle" coords="25,25,12"           href="3.htm"
onMouseOver="swapOn(2)" onMouseOut="swapOff(2)">
<area shape="poly" coords="47,13,49,13,49,18" href="3.htm"
onMouseOver="swapOn(2)" onMouseOut="swapOff(2)">
<area shape="poly" coords="49,31,47,37,49,37" href="3.htm"
onMouseOver="swapOn(2)" onMouseOut="swapOff(2)">
</map>
```

```
<map name="bar3">
<area shape="rect" coords="0,13,178,37"          href="3.htm"
onMouseOver="swapOn(2)" onMouseOut="swapOff(2)">
<area shape="circle" coords="175,25,12"          href="3.htm"
onMouseOver="swapOn(2)" onMouseOut="swapOff(2)">
</map>
```

The `circle4` and `bar4` maps pass an integer value of 3 to the `swapOn()` and `swapOff()` functions, and contain `href` attributes that specify `4.htm` as the target page to load when the user clicks the hot spots:

```
<map name="circle4">
<area shape="circle" coords="25,25,12"              href="4.htm"
onMouseOver="swapOn(3)" onMouseOut="swapOff(3)">
<area shape="poly" coords="47,13,49,13,49,18" href="4.htm"
onMouseOver="swapOn(3)" onMouseOut="swapOff(3)">
<area shape="poly" coords="49,31,47,37,49,37" href="4.htm"
onMouseOver="swapOn(3)" onMouseOut="swapOff(3)">
</map>

<map name="bar4">
<area shape="rect" coords="0,13,178,37"              href="4.htm"
onMouseOver="swapOn(3)" onMouseOut="swapOff(3)">
<area shape="circle" coords="175,25,12"              href="4.htm"
onMouseOver="swapOn(3)" onMouseOut="swapOff(3)">
</map>
```

The integer value passed to the swapOn() and swapOff() functions dictates which named image has its src property amended. Obviously, the HTML markup required to support the 15 different sets of images in the full example is extremely repetitive, but imagine the possibilities where a table of images, perhaps a map of a state, each with a different image map with hidden hot spots, reveals information about the location currently under the mouse pointer.

# Slide Show

Slide presentations can very effectively convey through images a large amount of information. The code presented here shows how to traverse through a series of images at the readers' pace, or, for those that require it, automatically using a "hands-off" approach.

The code controls the slide show all from within the one page. Therefore, there is no delay while waiting for the next page to be downloaded, and thus the process does not require the page to be rendered between each slide. The code uses image-swapping techniques to replace the current slide with another, and to update the visual representation of the current position within the slide sequence. Image preloading techniques are also used to ensure that the slides are loaded one at a time in the order they appear in the slide show.

As an added bonus, the code also examines the URL used to load the page, so that external references can be made to a specific slide in the sequence. For example, the third slide can be shown using a relative URL of index.htm?3. This also allows the code to reload the page specifying a value in the search portion of the URL, providing an alternative solution for those older browsers that do not support the Image object (i.e., Internet Explorer 3 and Netscape Navigator 2 and below).

Figure 9-5 shows the third slide in a sequence of five, with the third button image highlighted. If the user clicks any one of the five button images, then the relevant slide is displayed. If the user clicks the sixth button (the auto-play button), then the code automatically displays the next slide in the sequence up until the end of the slide show, when it then restarts at the beginning. Figure 9-6 shows the slide show in its automated state, with the auto-play button highlighted.

**Figure 9-5**

Slide Show—the third slide in the sequence.

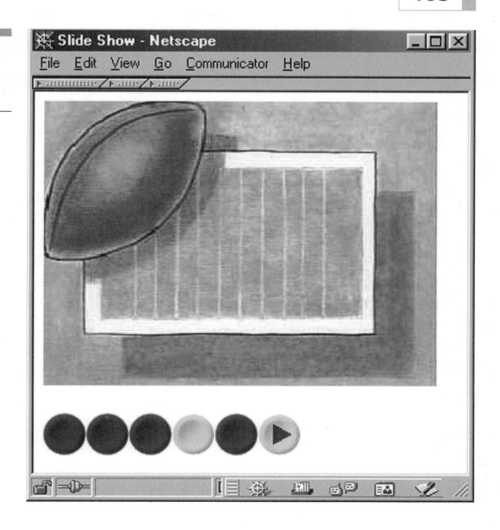

Figure 9-6
Slide Show—
the fourth slide in
an automated
sequence.

## Slide Show Source Code—*index.htm*

**chapter9/slide/index.htm**

To hold the details of the images, an `image` array is created and then subsequently populated with the object references returned from the `myImage()` function, each of which are passed the relative location of the image URL, plus the previous entry in `image` array:

```
var image = new Array();

image[0] = myImage('image1.jpg',null);
image[1] = myImage('image2.jpg',image[0]);
image[2] = myImage('image3.jpg',image[1]);
image[3] = myImage('image4.jpg',image[2]);
image[4] = myImage('image5.jpg',image[3]);
```

The first call to the myImage() function is passed a null value as the second parameter as there is not a previous entry in the array to pass to the function.

The myImage() function accepts the passed url and last parameters, and then proceeds to create a new Image object (if supported) and sets various properties of the Image object just created, before finally returning the Image object reference or null (if not supported). The img object's url property is set to the url parameter, onLoad event handler is defined and set to invoke the imageLoaded() function, and the next property initially set to null.

If the passed last parameter is not null (and, remember, the first one always is), then the last object entry in the image array has its next property updated with the current img object reference. This in effect links each object in the image array with the next in the array using the object's next properties—rather like a linked-list common in the C programming language:

```
function myImage(url,last) {
  if (document.images) {
    var img = new Image();
    img.url = url;
    img.onload = imageLoaded;
    img.next = null;
    if (last) last.next = img;
    return img;
  }
  return null;
}
```

Both the url and next properties are user-added properties of the Image object. In other words, they would not exist unless the myImage() function adds them to the object.

The first Image object in the image array then has its src property updated with the value of its url property. This causes the image to start downloading from the server:

```
if (document.images)
  image[0].src = image[0].url;
```

When the image has loaded the `onLoad` event handler (defined in the `myImage()` function) executes the `imageLoaded()` function. This function uses the passed `this` object reference to start downloading the next image, by updating the `src` property of the `next` object reference with the value of its `url` property:

```
function imageLoaded(e) {
    if (this.next != null) this.next.src = this.next.url;
}
```

The way this is coded ensures that the successful downloading of one image triggers the next, until the last image to be downloaded has a `null` value as its `next` property.

The value of any passed search parameter is retrieved from the location object's `search` property and assigned to the `number` variable:

```
var search = location.search.substring(1);
var number = 0;
if (search != '') number = search - 1;
```

As arrays start from zero, the value of `number` is set to 1 less than any value passed. If a value is not passed, then `number` defaults to zero.

An `img` element is then output to the document, using the `url` property of the `number` object in the `image` array as its `src` attribute, and is given the name `slide`:

```
document.write(
    '<img src="' + image[number].url + '" name="slide">'
);
```

An output variable is defined and initialized:

```
var output = '';
```

For each object within the `image` array the HTML markup for an image link is added to the `output` variable, each one containing an `href` attribute that would reload the current page with a search parameter equal to the value of the `i` variable, an `onClick` event handler that invokes the `load()` function passing the value of the `i` variable, and an `onFocus` event handler that invokes the link's `blur()` method (avoiding the unsightly dashed outlines present in Internet Explorer when an image link is clicked):

```
for (var i=0; i<image.length; i++) {
  (i == number) ? img = 'on.gif': img = 'off.gif';
  output +=
    '<a href="index.htm?' +i+ '" ' +
    'onClick="return load(' +i+ ')" onFocus="this.blur()">' +
    '<img src="' +img+ '" name="d' +i+ '"></a>';
}
```

Additional coding is included in the preceding code to use either the
*on.gif* image, if the value of the i variable equals the value of the number variable, or the *off.gif* image. This ensures that if the page is loaded
with a value passed in the URL, the initial state of the relevant button
image is highlighted.

Only if the document object's images array is supported is the HTML
markup necessary for the auto-play button added to the output variable, with an onClick event handler in the anchor element that invokes
the show() function to start the auto-play feature, and an img element
named play:

```
if (document.images)
  output +=
    '<a href="#" onClick="return show()" onFocus="this.blur()">' +
    '<img src="play-off.gif" name="play"></a>';

document.write(output);
```

The load() function, invoked when one of the button images is clicked,
accepts the passed name parameter, and then assigns the value to the
global number variable, making it available for other code in the page. The
src property of the slide image is then updated with the src property of
the name object within the image array. Each of the button images are then
reset to their "unhighlighted" state by swapping them all to the *off.gif*
image, before the current slides button image is set to its "highlighted"
state by swapping it to the *on.gif* image. If the document object's images
array is supported, then the function returns false to the event handler
and thus cancels the normal action of the link; otherwise, the function
returns true, and the page identified in the link's href attribute is loaded:

```
function load(name) {
  if (document.images) {
    number = name;
    document.images['slide'].src = image[name].src;
    for (var i=0; i<image.length; i++)
      document.images['d' + i].src = 'off.gif';
    document.images['d' + name].src = 'on.gif';
    return false;
  }
```

```
    return true;
}
```

The auto-play feature requires two global variables: `playing` to indicate the status and `timeout` to hold a timer reference:

```
var playing = false;
var timeout = null;
```

The `show()` function, invoked when the auto-play button is clicked,
first toggles the value of the `playing` variable and then sets the `src`
property of the `play` image to one of two states, depending on the new
value of the `playing` variable. If set to `true`, then the image is swapped
to the *play-on.gif* image and the `nextSlide()` function invoked. Else, if
`false`, the image is swapped to the *play-off.gif* image and the window
object's `clearTimeout()` method is used to cancel any `timeout` timer
set in the `nextSlide()` function:

```
function show() {
  playing = !playing;
  if (document.images) {
    if (playing) {
      document.images['play'].src = 'play-on.gif';
      nextSlide();
    }
    else {
      document.images['play'].src = 'play-off.gif';
      clearTimeout(timeout);
    }
  }
  return false;
}
```

The `nextSlide()` function increments the value of the global `number`
variable, and if it is now equal to the total number of slides the function
resets the value to zero before passing the value onto the `load()` function. The `load()` function loads the required slide and adjusts the state
of the button images. The `nextSlide()` function then starts a delayed
timer using the `window` object's `setTimeout()` function to reinvoke
itself after 1000 milliseconds, assigning the returned reference to the
global `timeout` variable:

```
function nextSlide() {
  number++;
  if (number == image.length) number = 0;
  load(number);
  timeout = setTimeout('nextSlide()',1000);
}
```

# Bar Charts

JavaScript has very little support for manipulating graphics at the pixel level. Since Netscape Navigator 2, Netscape supports XBM, a scripted monochrome graphics format, but this is too complex a format and too limited for the occasional business chart. Java applets would be far more suitable for a cross-browser-compatible graphing application, but you would need to find, buy, or write an applet—perhaps a bit of an overkill for a bar chart of the current server load.

To create a bar chart in JavaScript, we need something that can be stretched horizontally and vertically. The `colspan` and `bgcolor` attributes of the table cell element will do nicely for horizontal bars, and a single-pixel GIF image can be used for either horizontal or the vertical bars.

The decision to use either table cell element attributes or GIF images for sizing can depend on how many rows or columns you expect to render. We have a few choices when it comes to formatting the chart. Since Internet Explorer will collapse an empty table cell element unless the `height` attribute is specified, we can specify one in the table row element. Netscape Navigator normally ignores this, so here we would need a sized 1x1-pixel transparent GIF image if we wanted to specify cell height other than the default height of a nonbreaking space entity (` `). However, if you attempt to render a lot of rows, some browsers, notably Netscape Navigator 3, can slow to a crawl if each cell contains a GIF image.

When first starting to write JavaScript to output HTML markup, we first create the HTML and then split it up, replacing the variable parts with placeholders:

```
<table width="200" bgcolor="#FFFFCC">
<tr>
<td bgcolor="red" colspan="12">
123
</td>
</tr>
</table>
```

In JavaScript we could generate a similar HTML markup using something like:

```
output +=
  '<table width=' + w + ' bgcolor="' + tbbg + '">' +
  '<tr>' +
  '<td bgcolor="'  + tdbg + '" colspan="'  + tdcs + '">' +
  data +
  '</td>' +
  '</tr>' +
  '</table>';
```

where the value of the variables w, tbbg, tdbg, and tdcs would be supplied at runtime. We have to decide how many of the attributes we want to script and how much functionality to give the script. In this example, we have chosen to parameterize most of the attributes, so as to make the JavaScript code as reusable as possible.

## Bar Charts Source Code—*barchart.js*

**chapter9/slide/barchart.js**

All of the reusable JavaScript code is located in the external *barchart.js* library. The setParms object constructor uses the tertiary operator (test ? true_value : false_value) to assign default values. In other words, if any one of the passed parameters is null, then the relevant property value is set with a hard-coded literal value, else we use the value of the supplied parameter:

```
function setParms(spacing, width, cellWidth, cellType, bgColor){
   this.spacing   = (spacing)   ? spacing   : 1;
   this.width     = (width)     ? width     : 100;
   this.cellWidth = (cellWidth) ? cellWidth : 5;
   this.cellType  = (cellType)  ? cellType  : 'i';
   this.bgColor   = (bgColor)   ? bgColor   : '#FFFFFF';
   this.defaultColor = "#000000";
}
```

The cellWidthType property defaults to 'i', representing *image*. The only other possible setting is 'w', representing *width*.

The getCellWidth() helper function creates the row of table *spacing* cells, using the passed width parameter to control a loop, which creates table cells with either a width attribute if type equals w, or with an enclosed w.gif image if type equals i. Otherwise, a table cell is created that contains the characters ----+----+:

```
function getCellWidth(width,cellWidth,type) {
  var text = '';

  for (var i=1;i<=width;i++) {
    if (type=='w')
      text += '<td width="' + cellWidth + '">';
    else if (type == 'i')
      text += '<td>' +
        '<img src="w.gif" width="' + cellWidth + '" height="1">'
    else {
      text += '<td>';
```

```
      if (i%10==0)
        text += i.toString().substring(0,1);
      else if (i%5==0)
        text += '+';
      else
        text += '-';
    }
    text += '</td>';
  }

  return text
}
```

The horizontal chart `hChart()` function accepts an array of values (`vals`), an indication of how wide the table should be (`maxVal`), and an array of colors (`barColor`):

```
function hChart(vals,maxVal, barColor) {
```

First, we call the `getCellWidth()` function to retrieve the HTML markup necessary for a row of table *spacer* cells and assign the returned result to the `cellWidthText` variable, using as input arguments the `maxVal` parameter and the `cellWidth` and `cellType` properties of the global `parms` object reference:

```
var cellWidthText =
  getCellWidth(maxVal, parms.cellWidth, parms.cellType);
```

If the length of the two arrays `barColor` and `vals` do not match, then the `barColor` array is padded out with the color value of the global `parms` object's `defaultColor` property:

```
if (barColor.length != vals.length)
  for (var i=0;i<vals.length;i++)
    barColor[i] = parms.defaultColor;
```

The function then proceeds to build the HTML markup necessary to display the graph:

```
var text = '';
```

The first row of the table holds the *spacing* `cellWidthText` HTML. This creates a table with enough table cells for the maximum value held in the `vals` array:

```
text +=
  '<table border="0" cellspacing="' + parms.spacing + '"' +
  ' cellpadding="0" width="' + parms.width + '"' +
  ' bgcolor="' + parms.bgColor + '">' +
  '<tr>' + cellWidthText + '</tr>';
```

Then the code loops over the length of the `vals`, adding a new table row element for each entry in the `vals` array, where each row contains just two table cell elements. The first table cell element contains a `colspan` attribute set to the value of the current entry in the `vals` array, and a `bgcolor` attribute set to the current entry in the `barColor` array. This causes the table cell to stretch over one or more of the table cells in the `spacer` row. The second table cell is then stretched over the remaining table cells using a `colspan` attribute set to the value of `maxVal` minus the current entry in the `vals` array, and a `bgcolor` attribute set to the `bgColor` property of the global `parms` object reference:

```
for (var i=0, n=vals.length;i<n;i++) {
  text +=
    '<tr><td bgcolor="' + barColor[i] + '"' +
    ' colspan="' + vals[i] + '"> </td>' +
    '<td bgcolor="' + parms.bgColor + '"' +
    ' colspan="' + (maxVal-vals[i]) + '">' + vals[i] +
    '</td></tr>';
}

text += '</table>';

return text;
}
```

The vertical chart `vChart()` function works in much the same way. It accepts an array of values (`vals`), a maximum value (`maxVal`), a number of pixels (`units`), and top and bottom legend Boolean values (`topLegends` and `bottomLegends`):

```
function vChart(vals,maxVal,units,topLegends,bottomLegends) {
```

If the `units` parameter is not specified, we default to 1 pixel

```
units = (units) ? units : 1;

var text = '';
```

The start of the table HTML markup is created, using the various properties of the global `parms` variable to set the attributes:

```
text +=
  '<table border="0" cellspacing="' + parms.spacing + '"' +
  ' cellpadding="0" width="' + parms.width + '"' +
  ' bgcolor="' + parms.bgColor + '">';
```

If a `topLegends` Boolean parameter is set to `true`, then a table row element is created, with each table cell element containing the individual values in the `vals` array:

```
if (topLegends) {
  text +=
    '<tr valign="bottom" bgcolor="' + parms.bgColor + '"' +
    ' align="center">' +
    '<td><img src="w.gif" width="1" height="1"></td>';

  for (var i=0;i<vals.length;i++) {
    text += '<td class="t">' + vals[i] + '</td>';
  }
  text += '</tr>';
}
```

The code then proceeds to create the table row element that contains the table cell elements representing the visual components of the various values in the `vals` array. Note the use of the `valign` attribute. With a value set to `bottom`, then the contents of each table cell element will be bottom aligned:

```
text +=
  '<tr valign="bottom" bgcolor="' + parms.bgColor + '"' +
  ' align="center">';
```

First, a table *spacing* cell element is created with a `height` attribute set to the value of the `maxVal` parameter multiplied by the value of `units` parameter. This ensures that all the following table cells in this row inherit this height:

```
text +=
  '<td><img src="w.gif" width="1"' +
  ' height="' + (maxVal*units) + '"></td>';
```

A table cell element is then created for each value in the `vals` array. Each one containing an `r.gif` image with a `width` attribute set to the global `parms` object's `width` property, and more importantly, a `height` attribute set to the value of the current `vals` array value multiplied by the value of `units`:

```
for (var i=0;i<vals.length;i++) {
  text +=
    '<td><img src="r.gif" width="' + parms.width + '"' +
    'height="' + (vals[i]*units) + '"></td>'
}

text += '</tr>';
```

If a `bottomLegends` Boolean parameter is set to `true`, then a table row element is created, with each table cell element containing the column number:

```
    if (bottomLegends) {
      text += '<tr><td><img src="w.gif" width="1" height="1"></td>'

      for (var i=0;i<vals.length;i++) {
        text += '<td>' + (i+1) + '</td>'
      }

      text += '</tr>';
    }

    text += '</table>'

    return text;
}
```

## Bar Charts Source Code—*index.htm*

**chapter9/slide/index.htm**

The code required to request the generation of bar charts is fairly simple. The first thing is to ensure that the *barchart.js* library is loaded:

```
<script language="JavaScript" src="barchart.js"></script>
```

Next, a `setParms` object is created using the `setParms` object constructor, the result of which is assigned to the `parms` global variable, but only if the *barchart.js* library has been successfully loaded to define the object constructor:

```
if (window.setParms)
  var parms = new setParms();
```

The `setParms` object constructor accepts five optional parameter values (cell spacing, width cell width, cell width type, and background color). If any parameter is not supplied or set to null, then the `setParms` object constructor uses in-built default values to set the missing values. Therefore, to set the parameters to use cell spacing of 5 pixels and a red background color, the following could be used:

```
if (window.setParms)
  var parms = new setParms(5, null, null, null, 'red');
```

First, to generate a horizontal chart using default parameters, shown in Figure 9-7, the following JavaScript code creates a `chartValues`

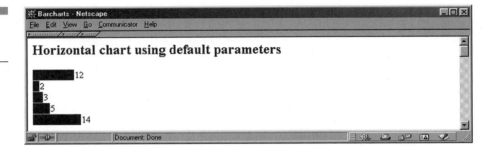

**Figure 9-7**
Default horizontal
chart.

array, which is passed to the `hChart()` function along with a `maxValue` of 20 and an empty `barColor` array, the return value of which is written out to the document:

```
<script language="JavaScript"><!--
if (window.setParms)
  var parms = new setParms();

var chartValues = new Array(12,2,3,5,14);

if (window.hChart)
  document.write(hChart(chartValues,20,new Array()));
//--></script>
```

We can generate another horizontal chart with changed parameters and different colors, shown in Figure 9-8, quite simply be providing parameters to the `setParms` object constructor and creating a `barColor` array holding the color for each row:

```
<script language="JavaScript"><!--
if (window.setParms)
  var parms = new setParms(2,200,null,'w','beige');

var barColor = new Array(
  'Red','ForestGreen','Blue','SandyBrown','DeepPink','lightgrey'
```

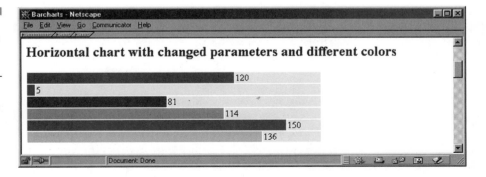

**Figure 9-8**
Horizontal chart with
overridden
parameters.

```
);

var chartValues = new Array(120,5,81,114,150,136);
if (window.hChart)
document.write(hChart(chartValues,170,barColor));
//--></script>
```

A vertical chart with default settings shown in Figure 9-9, can be created using the vChart() function, passing the chartValues array, a maxVal of 200, a units multiplier of 1, and Boolean true or false values for the topLegends and bottomLegends parameters:

```
<script language="JavaScript"><!--
if (window.setParms)
  var parms = new setParms();

var chartValues = new Array(120,5,81,114,150,136,119);

if (window.hChart)
  document.write(vChart(chartValues,200,1,false,true));
//--></script>
```

A vertical chart, shown in Figure 9-10, can also use user-supplied parameters in the setParms object constructor:

```
<script language="JavaScript"><!--
if (window.setParms)
  var parms = new setParms(2,30,null,null,'lightgrey');

var chartValues = new Array(120,5,81,114,150,136,119);

if (window.vChart)
  document.write(vChart(chartValues,200,2,true,true));
//--></script>
```

**Figure 9-9**
Default vertical chart.

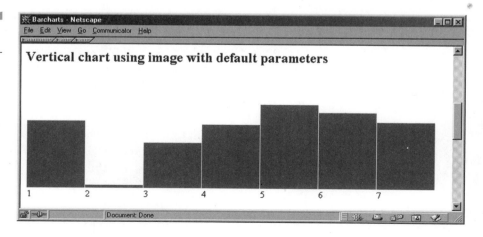

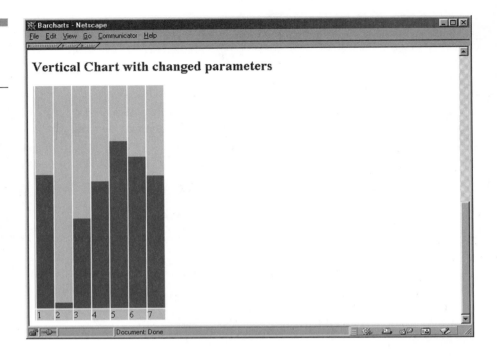

**Figure 9-10**
Vertical chart with overridden parameters.

# Image Percentage Download

Nothing can be worse than a user giving up while waiting for a page to download and deciding to go somewhere else. While images are being downloaded to the browser, some visual indication of how long the user will need to wait until the page is ready may prevent the user from giving up.

The code presented here downloads 36 images. While they are downloading, a pop-up window, shown in Figure 9-11, indicates the percentage of images downloaded. Once all the images are downloaded, a simple image-swapping application immediately starts running (see Figure 9-12).

While the images are downloading, the image-swapping application is inactive. This is so that any missing images do not detract from the visual effect. The side effect of this is that the user may feel that the page is broken. The pop-up window indicates otherwise.

**Figure 9-11**
Pop-up window
showing the
percentage of
images downloaded.

**Figure 9-12**
Image-swapping
application running
after all images
downloaded.

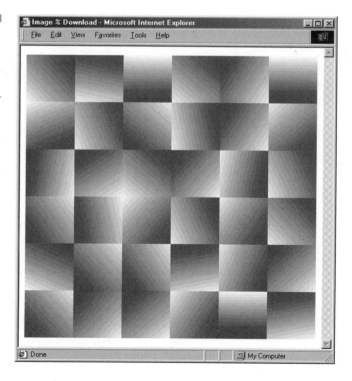

## Image Percentage Download Source Code—
## *index.htm*

**chapter9/download/index.htm**

Several global variables are defined and initialized: `count` is used to hold the number of images downloaded, `percent` is used to hold the percentage value of images downloaded, and the `imagesLoaded` and `bodyLoaded` Boolean variables are used to indicate when all the images have been loaded and the initial static page has been loaded:

```
var count = 0;
var percent = 0;
var imagesLoaded = bodyLoaded = false;
```

A global `popup` object is created. We create an object instead of a variable, as we want to assign the `popup` object a `closed` property set to `true`. The `popup` object will later be reused as a variable to hold a window object reference. To be able to detect whether the window is still open, we would normally test the value of its `closed` property. However, prior to the window being opened for the first time, there will not be a window object reference with a `closed` property. Therefore, we fake one:

```
var popup = new Object();
popup.closed = true;
```

We define an `image` array to hold 36 images:

```
var image = new Array(36);
```

If the `document` object's `images` array is supported, then for the `length` of the `image` array, a new `Image` object is created using the `Image` object constructor and is assigned to the current `image` array entry. The properties of the object are then populated: the `onload` event handler property is set to invoke the function named `imageLoad`, the `src` property is updated to the relative image file name from `0.gif` to `35.gif`, and the `no` property (a user-defined property) is set to a random integer from 0 to 35 using the `rndInteger()` function described in the "Random Quote of the Day" application in Chapter 2:

```
if (document.images) {
   for (var i=0; i<image.length; i++) {
```

```
    image[i] = new Image();
    image[i].onload = imageLoad;
    image[i].src = i +'.gif';
    image[i].no = rndInteger(image.length);
  }
}
```

The `imageLoad()` function is invoked whenever one of the `onload` event handler properties of the `Image` objects held in the `image` array is triggered. The function increments the global `count` variable. Then it uses this to work out the percentage number of images successfully downloaded, stores the result in the global `percent` variable, and proceeds to open a new window, referenced as `popup`, to display the value of percent. If the new value of `count` is equal to the `length` of the `image` array, then all the images will have successfully downloaded. In this case, as long as the `bodyLoaded` global variable has been set to `true` by the `onLoad` event handler in the body element, then the `start()` function is invoked to start the image-swapping application; otherwise, the global `imagesLoaded` Boolean is set to `true`:

```
function imageLoad() {
  percent = Math.floor(100 * (count+1) / image.length);
  popup =
    window.open('about:blank','wName','width=100,height=100');
  popup.document.open();
  popup.document.write(percent + '%');
  popup.document.close();

  count++;
  if (count == image.length) {
    if (bodyLoaded) start();
    else imagesLoaded = true;
  }
}
```

The `start()` function, invoked from either the `imageLoad()` function or from the `onLoad` event handler in the body element, closes any open window using the `popup` window reference and then invokes the `play()` function:

```
function start() {
  if (!popup.closed) popup.close();
  play();
}
```

The `play()` function, invoked by the `start()` function, alters the src property of each of the named images `image0` through to `image35`, to the next image in the sequence—using the `no` property of the relevant `Image` object held in the `image` array to decide which is the next image to show. The `window` object's `setTimeout()` method is then used to reinvoke the `play()` function after the minimum delay possible (1 millisecond—although in reality the delay is much longer than this):

```
function play() {
  for (var i=0; i<image.length; i++) {
    var no = image[i].no;
    no = (++no) % image.length;
    image[i].no = no;
    document.images['image' + i].src = image[no].src;
  }
  setTimeout('play()',1);
}
```

The `onLoad` event handler in the body element invokes the `start()` function if the `imagesLoaded` Boolean is set to `true`. In other words, if all the images have already loaded, start the image-swapping application. Otherwise, the `bodyLoaded` Boolean is set to `true`, which delays the start of the image-swapping application until the previous described `imageLoad()` function detects that all the images are subsequently loaded:

```
<body onLoad="if (imagesLoaded) start(); else bodyLoaded = true">
```

The body of the document is created using JavaScript. It contains a table of six rows each containing six columns, where each table cell element contains one image named from `image0` to `image35`:

```
var output = '';

var i=0;

for (var x=0; x<6; x++) {
  output += '<tr><td>';
  for (var y=0; y<6; y++)
    output +=
      '<img src="blank.gif" name="image' + (i++) + '">';
}

document.write(output);
```

## Image Pop-Up

How to open up remote windows that are sized exactly to fit the image displayed inside is often requested. The code presented here shows two different techniques for opening a remote window to the exact size of one of more different-sized images. The first technique uses the width and height properties of an `Image` object to open a remote window to the required size. The second technique opens a remote window and then from within the remote window resizes the window to fit the image.

Figure 9-13 shows the main window with two select lists that can be used to load one of several images in a remote window using one of the two different techniques, with a remote window sized to hold the contained image.

## Image Pop-Up Source Code—*index.htm*

 **chapter9/popup/index.htm**

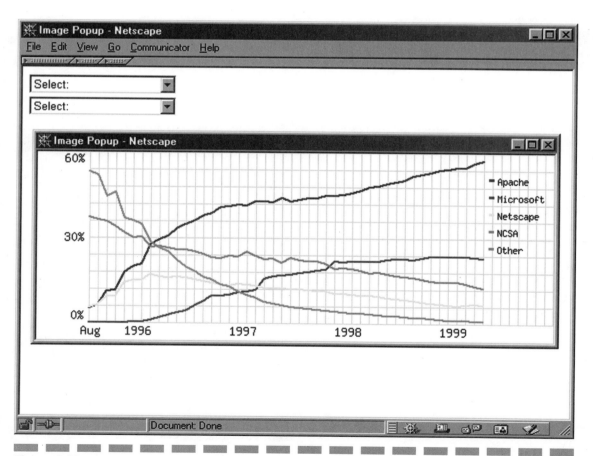

**Figure 9-13**    Image Popup—remote window sized to image dimensions.

As in the previous "Image Percentage Download" example, the code defines a popup object with a closed property set to true to fake a closed remote window reference:

```
var popup = new Object();
popup.closed = true;
```

In our example, four images are preloaded using the Image object constructor. Then the images are held in the image array:

```
var image = new Array();

if (document.images) {
   image[0] = new Image(378,475);
   image[0].src = 'book.gif';

   image[1] = new Image(595,231);
   image[1].src = 'irt.png';

   image[2] = new Image(400,400);
   image[2].src = 'lake.jpg';

   image[3] = new Image(591,221);
   image[3].src = 'survey.gif';
}
```

The form contains two select option lists, both with onChange() event handlers that detect when the user selects one of the options. Then the form invokes either the loadUsingImage() or the loadUsingName() functions, in each case passing a this object reference—that is, an object reference to the appropriate select object:

```
<form>
<select onChange="loadUsingImage(this)">
<option value="">Select:
<option value="0">Instant ASP book cover
<option value="1">irt.org Logo
<option value="2">Picture of a Lake
<option value="3">Server survey
</select>
```

The previous option select list uses incrementing integers as the value attribute of the option elements, whereas the second uses the relative URL of the images:

```
<select onChange="loadUsingName(this)">
<option value="">Select:
<option value="book.gif">Instant ASP book cover
<option value="irt.png">irt.org Logo
<option value="lake.jpg">Picture of a Lake
<option value="survey.gif">Server survey
</select>
</form>
```

The `openPopup()` function first closes any opened `popup` window reference and then proceeds to open a new `popup` window using the passed `file` parameter as the file to be loaded, and the `width` and `height` parameters as the width and height of the new window:

```
function openPopup(file,width,height) {
  if (!popup.closed) popup.close();
  popup = window.open(file, 'wName',
    'width=' + width + ',height=' + height + ',resizable');
}
```

A global `display` variable is defined and initialized for use with the `loadUsingImage()` function. It is used to hold data shared between the main window and the remote window:

```
var display = null;
```

The `loadUsingImage()` function accepts the passed `what` parameter as a reference to the changed select object and uses it to retrieve the `value` property of the selected option (as identified by the value of the `select` object's `selectedIndex` property), which is assigned to the local i variable. If the `document` object's `images` array is supported and the value of the i variable is not an empty string, then a new `Image` object is constructed and assigned to the global `display` variable. The `Image` object constructor is passed the `width` and `height` properties of the relevant `Image` object in the `image` array. The `display` object's onload event handler property is then set to invoke the `openPopup()` function (passing the three parameters `'popup.htm'`, and the `width` and `height` properties of the global `display Image` object), and its `src` property set to the `src` property of the `Image` object stored in the `image` array. This ensures that the `openPopup()` function call is delayed until the image is actually loaded:

```
function loadUsingImage(what) {
  var i = what.options[what.selectedIndex].value;

  if (document.images && i != '') {
    what.selectedIndex = 0;
    display = new Image(image[i].width,image[i].height);
    display.src = image[i].src;
    display.onload =
      openPopup('popup.htm',display.width,display.height);
```

Internet Related Technologies         http://www.irt.org/
                                      http://developer.irt.org/

```
  }
}
```

A global `filename` variable is defined and initialized for use with the `loadUsingName()` function. It is also used to hold data shared between the main window and the remote window:

```
var filename = null
```

The loadUsingName() function also accepts the passed what parameter as a reference to the changed select object. It retrieves the relative URL held in the selected option object's value property and assigns the value to the global filename variable. If the document object's images array is supported and the value of filename is not an empty string, the function then first unsets the selected entry and invokes the openPopup() function, passing the three parameters: 'resize.htm' (the file to be opened in the remote window), and the width and height properties, both nominally set to 100 pixels:

```
function loadUsingName(what) {
  filename = what.options[what.selectedIndex].value;

  if (document.images && filename != '') {
    what.selectedIndex = 0;
    openPopup('resize.htm',100,100);
  }
}
```

## Image Pop-Up Source Code—*popup.htm*

The first technique, used in the loadUsingImage() function in *index.htm*, loads the *popup.htm* page into a remote window with the same width and height of the image to be displayed.

chapter9/popup/popup.htm

To ensure that there are no white margins surrounding the image, the body elements' margin attributes are all set to 0:

```
<body topmargin="0" leftmargin="0"
  marginwidth="0" marginheight="0">
```

JavaScript code is then used to write out to the document the HTML markup necessary to display the image, using the src property of the display object held in the remote window's opener window as the src attribute value:

```
document.write('<img src="' + opener.display.src + '">');
```

Finally, for neatness, if the window object's screen object is supported, the remote window is repositioned to the center of the screen:

```
if (window.screen)
  self.moveTo(
    (screen.availWidth - opener.display.width)/2,
    (screen.availHeight - opener.display.height)/2
  );
```

## Image Pop-Up Source Code—*resize.htm*

The second technique, used in the loadUsingName() function in *index.htm*, loads the *resize.htm* page into an initial 100 × 100-pixel remote window.

**chapter9/popup/resize.htm**

The value of the filename property of the remote window's opener property is assigned to the global img variable:

```
var img = opener.filename;
```

Again, to ensure that there are no white margins surrounding the image, the body elements' margin attributes are all set to 0. In addition, an onLoad event handler invokes the resizeMe() function, but only if the document object's images array is supported:

```
<body topmargin="0" leftmargin="0"
  marginwidth="0" marginheight="0"
  onLoad="if (document.images) resizeMe();">
```

The HTML markup necessary to display the img image is then output to the document:

```
document.write('<img name="img1" src="' + img + '">');
```

The resizeMe() function retrieves the width and height properties of the image named img1 and assigns them to the local width and height variables. If Internet Explorer is being used, the values of the width and height variables are adjusted (this is required, as Internet Explorer includes the size of the window chrome when resizing), and then the remote window (self) is resized using the resizeTo() method. Again for neatness, the window is centered:

```
function resizeMe() {
  var width = document.images['img1'].width;
  var height = document.images['img1'].height;

  if (document.all) {
    width += 10; height += 25;
  }

  self.resizeTo(width, height);

  if (window.screen)
    self.moveTo(
      (screen.availWidth - width)/2,
      (screen.availHeight - height)/2
    );
}
```

# Image Counter

The idea for an image counter came some years ago when I wanted to make a splash page featuring a fake boot-up screen for a fictitious PC dealer. I wanted a memory counter counting up to 256 MB of RAM (cutting-edge in 1998), and I soon realized it would mean either a very large animated GIF image or a JavaScript manipulating multiple smaller images. The following illustrates the image counter counting up to 256 MB of RAM:

The following script can be used in any situation where you want numbers of your own design changing dynamically—for example, clocks, monetary amounts, or game counters.

Only 20, 971, 520 bytes counted

Now 199, 229, 440
bytes counted

All 268, 435, 456
bytes counted ok

## Image Counter Source Code—*index.htm*

On the CD

**chapter9/counter/index.htm**

Several global variables are defined and initialized: nine (maxImages) images to hold a maximum theoretical display of 999,999,999, a count starting at 0, an upper limit of 256 MB (bytes), a speed of 5 milliseconds, and an increment of 1 MB.

```
var maxImages = 9;
var count = 0;
var bytes = 256 * 1024 * 1024;
var speed = 5;
var increment = 1024 * 1024;
```

A `pics` array is used to hold 10 images to represent the digits 0 through 9:

```
var pics = new Array(9);
```

The code preloads all 10 images, but only if the `document` object's `images` array is supported:

```
if (document.images) {
   for (i=0; i<=9; i++) {
     pics[i] = new Image();
     pics[i].src = '' + i + '.gif';
   }
```

The additional `ok` and `blank` images are preloaded so they will appear immediately when needed:

```
   pics['ok'] = new Image();
   pics['ok'].src = 'ok.gif';
   pics['blank'] = new Image();
   pics['blank'].src = 'blank.gif';
}
```

The counting is started once the page has fully loaded—that means the preloading of all the images has also taken place and all images should be available in the browsers' cache. The `onLoad` event handler in the `body` element triggers the `countUp()` function:

```
<body onLoad="if (document.images) countUp()">
```

We reuse the value of the global `maxImages` variable to write the required number of images out to the document, named from `count0` to `countN` (where `N` is 1 less than the value of `maxImages`):

```
for (i=0;i<maxImages;i++)
   document.write(
     '<img src="0.gif" name="count' + i + '">'
   );
```

A *blank.gif* image is also included in the HTML markup, named `ok`. This is where the *ok.gif* image will appear once the count has finished:

```
<img src="blank.gif" name="ok">
```

The `countUp` function, invoked from the body element's `onLoad` event handler, uses image-swapping techniques to update the `src` properties of all the images in the counter:

```
function countUp() {
```

The value of global `count` variable is increased by the value of the global `increment` variable. Then two local variables are defined: `theDigitPos` represents the position of each character in a string and `theDigitValue` represents the value of said character:

```
count += increment;
var theDigitPos;
var theDigitValue;
```

The value of the `count` variable is then converted into a string and held in the local `Counter` variable, which is then prefixed with enough leading zeros to extend its length to a maximum of `maxImages` characters:

```
var Counter = '' + count;
for (var j=0; Counter.length < maxImages; j++)
  Counter = '0' + Counter;
```

The function then loops over the length of the string of nine digits, extracting the value of the character (`theDigitalValue`) at each position (`theDigitPos`) using the `String` object's `charAt()` method:

```
for (j=0; j<Counter.length; j++) {
  theDigitPos   = Counter.length - j - 1;
  theDigitValue = Counter.charAt(theDigitPos);
```

This is then used to change the `src` property of the appropriately named image:

```
document.images['count' + theDigitPos].src =
  pics[theDigitValue].src;
}
```

Once the global `bytes` variable limit is reached, the `src` property of the image named `ok` is changed to the *ok.gif* image, and the function is ended using a `return` statement:

```
if (count >= bytes) {
  document.images['ok'].src = 'ok.gif';
  return;
}
```

If the limit has not been reached, then the `setTimeout()` method is used to reinvoke the `countUp()` function after a number (`speed`) of milliseconds

```
setTimeout('countUp()',speed);
}
```

# Random Banner Adverts

We have included many examples within this chapter that show how easy it is to alter the src property of a named image. The code presented here shows how to also change the href property of the surrounding anchor element so that not only the visible image changes, but also the target page that would be loaded if the user clicks the image link. An ideal use of this application would be a rotating or random banner advert—where both the image and target page change once every few seconds.

We can identify the image using its name property, but the only way to identify the anchor element that surrounds the banner image, in as many browsers as possible, is to test the href property of all the links in the document object's links array, searching for a known value. The links array is covered in detail in Chapter 5 "Location and Links."

Figure 9-14 shows three banner adverts. The middle one of three changes both its image and target page every few seconds.

**Figure 9-14**
Random Banner Adverts—three adverts, one of which is constantly changing.

# Random Banner Adverts Source Code— *index.htm*

 **chapter9/banner/index.htm**

To hold the details of all the banner images, a `Banner` object constructor is defined. It accepts `href`, `src`, and `text` parameters, which are used to populate the values of like-named properties:

```
function Banner(href, src, text) {
  this.href = href;
  this.src = src;
  this.text = text;
}
```

The `setBanner()` function is used to create a `Banner` object, assigning the object reference to the next entry in the `myBanner` array:

```
function setBanner(href, src, text) {
  myBanner[bannerItems++] = new Banner(href, src, text);
}
```

A `myBanner` array is then defined and populated with several `Banner` objects created using the `setBanner()` function. Each call to the `setBanner()` function includes the URL of the page to be loaded, the URL of the image to be displayed, and a text value to be displayed in the window's status bar:

```
var bannerItems = 0;
var myBanner = new Array();

setBanner('1.htm','banner1.gif','Events');
setBanner('2.htm','banner2.gif','Location');
setBanner('3.htm','banner3.gif','Source');
setBanner('4.htm','banner4.gif','Windows');
setBanner('5.htm','banner5.gif','Mail');
setBanner('6.htm','banner6.gif','Date and Time');
setBanner('7.htm','banner7.gif','Forms');
setBanner('8.htm','banner8.gif','Images');
setBanner('9.htm','banner9.gif','Password');
setBanner('10.htm','banner10.gif','Cookies');
```

Two global variables (`random` and `lastrandom`) are defined and initialized to `-1`:

```
var random = lastrandom = -1;
```

Two further global variables are defined: bannerLink, which is the location of the banner advert anchor element in the links array and bannerStatus, which is used to hold the current text value to be displayed in the window's status bar:

```
var bannerLink = -1;
var bannerStatus = 'Advert';
```

The startBanners() function, described later, is invoked once the page has completely loaded:

```
<body onLoad="startBanners()">
```

Three image links are included in this example code. Only one of the image links acts as a random banner advert; the first and last image links are static banner adverts. The second image link includes an href attribute value of javascript:bannerWait(). If the user clicks this image link before the application has finished initializing, then a "Please wait" message is output by the bannerWait() function:

```
<a href="dummy.htm" name="banner"
   onMouseOver="window.status='';return true"
   onMouseOut="window.status='';return true"
><img src="banner1.gif"></a>

<a href="javascript:bannerWait()" name="banner"
   onMouseOver="window.status=bannerStatus;return true"
   onMouseOut="window.status='';return true"
><img src="banner1.gif" name="banner"></a>

<a href="dummy.htm" name="banner"
   onMouseOver="window.status=bannerStatus;return true"
   onMouseOut="window.status='';return true"
><img src="banner1.gif"></a>
```

The startBanners() function, invoked from the body element's onLoad event handler, loops through each of the entries in the document object's links array, testing the href property of each with the string value javascript:bannerWait(), the value of the href attribute in the random banner image link. Once found, the value of the global bannerLink variable is set to its position (i) within the links array. If the document object's images array is supported and the value of bannerLink is not -1, then the bannerReplace() function is invoked:

```
function startBanners() {
  for (var i=0; i<document.links.length; i++) {
    if (document.links[i].href == 'javascript:bannerWait()') {
      bannerLink = i;
```

```
      break;
    }
  }

  if (document.images && bannerLink != -1)
    bannerReplace();
}
```

The `bannerReplace()` function, invoked from the `startBanners()` function, first generates a random integer using the `rndInteger()` function described in the "Random Quote of the Day" application in Chapter 2. The function repeatedly creates a random number, while the value returned is equal to the value of the global `lastrandom` variable:

```
function bannerReplace() {
  while (random == lastrandom)
    random = rndInteger(bannerItems);
```

Both the `src` property of the image named `banner`, and the `href` property of the `bannerLink` link are replaced with the `src` and `href` properties of the random `Banner` object in the `myBanner` array. The value of the global `bannerStatus` variable is updated with the `Banner` object's `text` property:

```
document.images['banner'].src    = myBanner[random].src;
document.links[bannerLink].href = myBanner[random].href;
bannerStatus = myBanner[random].text;
```

The `setTimeout()` method is used to continually reinvoke the `bannerReplace()` function at 1-second intervals:

```
setTimeout('bannerReplace()',1000);
```

The `lastrandom` variable is then updated with the value of the `random` variable. This ensures that the same banner advert is not shown two times in a row:

```
  lastrandom = random;
}
```

The `bannerWait()` function, invoked if the random banner image link is clicked before the page has completely loaded, simply requests that the user should "please wait." This could be replaced with additional functionality:

```
function bannerWait() {
  alert('Please wait');
}
```

# Image Toolbar

Most of the image swapping performed within this chapter has swapped an image from its "unhighlighted" state to its "highlighted" state, apart from the "Fading Images In and Out" example, where images morphed between several different states. The two examples presented here show how a third status can be used to indicate the last toolbar image selected.

Figure 9-15 shows the first type of image toolbar with *Section B* loaded and the image for *Section C* in its "highlighted" state, and Figure 9-16 shows an alternative JavaScript library-based image toolbar, with *Section C* loaded and the image for *Section D* in its "highlighted" state.

## Image Toolbar #1 Source Code—*section-a.htm*

 **chapter9/toolbar1/index.htm**

The first of the two image toolbars contains a copy of the following JavaScript code in each and every page that displays the toolbar. The `swapOn()` and `swapOff()` functions swap the images from `onMouseOver`

**Figure 9-15**
Image Toolbar #1—
Section B is displayed
and Section C is
"highlighted."

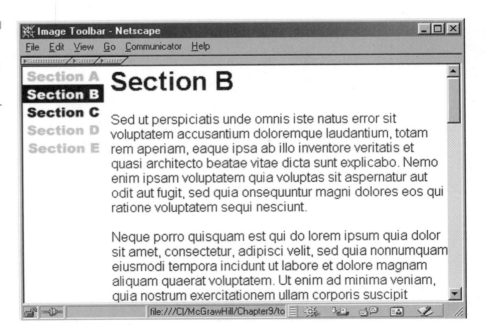

Figure 9-16
Image Toolbar #2—
Section C is displayed
and Section D is
"highlighted."

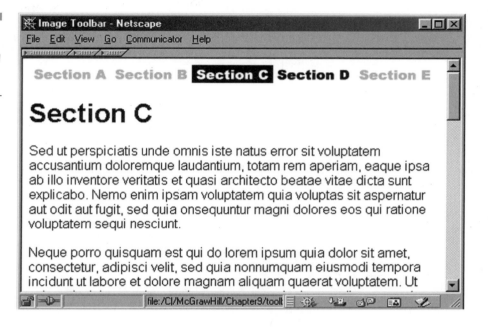

**Figure 9-16**
Image Toolbar #2—
Section C is displayed
and Section D is
"highlighted."

and `onMouseOut` event handlers from, say, the *a-off.gif* image to the *a-over.gif* image and back again:

```
function swapOn(name) {
  if (document.images) {
    document.images[name].src = name + '-over.gif';
  }
}

function swapOff(name) {
  if (document.images) {
    document.images[name].src = name + '-off.gif';
  }
}
```

For *Section A*, we simply display the *a-on.gif* toolbar image without a surrounding anchor element:

```
<img src="a-on.gif" name="a">
```

The remaining toolbar images are enclosed in anchor elements containing `onMouseOver` and `onMouseOut` event handlers that invoke the `swapOn()` and `swapOff()` functions passing the name of the image to swap:

```
<a href="section-b.htm"
onMouseOver="swapOn('b')" onMouseOut="swapOff('b')"
><img src="b-off.gif" name="b"></a>

<a href="section-c.htm"
onMouseOver="swapOn('c')" onMouseOut="swapOff('c')"
><img src="c-off.gif" name="c"></a>

<a href="section-d.htm"
onMouseOver="swapOn('d')" onMouseOut="swapOff('d')"
><img src="d-off.gif" name="d"></a>

<a href="section-e.htm"
onMouseOver="swapOn('e')" onMouseOut="swapOff('e')"
><img src="e-off.gif" name="e"></a>
```

## Image Toolbar #1 Source Code—*section-b.htm*

 **chapter9/toolbar1/section-b.htm**

The next section, *Section B*, is almost identical to *Section A*, except that the toolbar image for *Section A* is now surrounded by an appropriate anchor element, whereas the toolbar image for *Section B* is not:

```
<a href="section-a.htm"
onMouseOver="swapOn('a')" onMouseOut="swapOff('a')"
><img src="a-on.gif" name="a"></a>

<img src="b-off.gif" name="b">

<a href="section-c.htm"
onMouseOver="swapOn('c')" onMouseOut="swapOff('c')"

><img src="c-off.gif" name="c"></a>
<a href="section-d.htm"
onMouseOver="swapOn('d')" onMouseOut="swapOff('d')"

><img src="d-off.gif" name="d"></a>
<a href="section-e.htm"
onMouseOver="swapOn('e')" onMouseOut="swapOff('e')"
><img src="e-off.gif" name="e"></a>
```

## Image Toolbar #2 Source Code—*section-a.htm*

 **chapter9/toolbar2/section-a.htm**

The second of the two image toolbars uses an external JavaScript source file to hold all the necessary JavaScript code to both control the toolbar and display it in the first place. Therefore, all that is needed in each page that is required to display the toolbar is the following reference to the *toolbar.js* library:

```
<script language="JavaScript" src="toolbar.js"></script>
```

## Image Toolbar #2 Source Code—*toolbar.js*

 **chapter9/toolbar2/toolbar.js**

The *toolbar.js* library contains two slightly revised copies of the `swapOn()` and `swapOff()` functions. Rather than holding the names of the images to swap to within the function, the names are held in an array of `Image` objects (`imageOver` and `ImageOff`):

```
function swapOn(name) {
  if (document.images) {
    document.images[name].src = imageOver[name].src;
  }
}

function swapOff(name) {
  if (document.images) {
    document.images[name].src = imageOff[name].src;
  }
}
```

The library also includes an additional `swapClick()` function, invoked from `onClick` event handlers, used to temporarily swap the toolbar image from its initial "highlighted" state to its third status, using the `imageOn` array of `Images`:

```
function swapClick(name) {
  if (document.images) {
    document.images['s' + name].src = imageOn[name].src;
  }
}
```

Three arrays of `Image` objects are created to preload all the images required for the image toolbar (`imageOff`, `imageOver`, and `imageOn`). The `Image` objects held in the `imageOff` array have an additional user-supplied property (`href`) set to the relative URL of the target page to be loaded by clicking the toolbar image:

```
if (document.images) {
var imageOff = new Array();
```

```
imageOff[0] = new Image(97,22);
imageOff[0].src = 'a-off.gif';
imageOff[0].href = 'section-a.htm';
imageOff[1] = new Image(97,22);
imageOff[1].src = 'b-off.gif';
imageOff[1].href = 'section-b.htm';
imageOff[2] = new Image(97,22);
imageOff[2].src = 'c-off.gif';
imageOff[2].href = 'section-c.htm';
imageOff[3] = new Image(97,22);
imageOff[3].src = 'd-off.gif';
imageOff[3].href = 'section-d.htm';
imageOff[4] = new Image(97,22);
imageOff[4].src = 'e-off.gif';
imageOff[4].href = 'section-e.htm';

var imageOver = new Array();
imageOver[0] = new Image(97,22);
imageOver[0].src = 'a-over.gif';
imageOver[1] = new Image(97,22);
imageOver[1].src = 'b-over.gif';
imageOver[2] = new Image(97,22);
imageOver[2].src = 'c-over.gif';
imageOver[3] = new Image(97,22);
imageOver[3].src = 'd-over.gif';
imageOver[4] = new Image(97,22);
imageOver[4].src = 'e-over.gif';

var imageOn = new Array();
imageOn[0] = new Image(97,22);
imageOn[0].src = 'a-on.gif';
imageOn[1] = new Image(97,22);
imageOn[1].src = 'b-on.gif';
imageOn[2] = new Image(97,22);
imageOn[2].src = 'c-on.gif';
imageOn[3] = new Image(97,22);
imageOn[3].src = 'd-on.gif';
imageOn[4] = new Image(97,22);
imageOn[4].src = 'e-on.gif';
```

An `output` variable is defined and initialized:

```
var output = '';
```

The `window` object's `location` object's `href` property is assigned to the `href` variable:

```
var href = location.href;
```

For each of the toolbar images, the appropriate HTML markup is generated. If the value of the `href` property of the current `Image` object held in the `imageOff` array appears anywhere within the value of the `href` variable, then the current page is loaded for that toolbar image, in which case just the HTML markup for the image element is included. Otherwise, the HTML markup includes the anchor element with the three event handlers `onMouseOver`, `onMouseOut`, and `onClick`, along with the `image` element:

```
for (var i=0; i<5; i++) {

  if (href.indexOf(imageOff[i].href) > -1) output +=
    '<img src="' + imageOn[i].src + '" name="' + i + '"'
  else output +=
    '<a href="' + imageOff[i].href + '" ' +
    'onMouseOver="swapOn(' + i +')"' +
    'onMouseOut="swapOff(' + i + ')" ' +
    'onClick="swapClick(' + i +')">' +
    '<img src="' + imageOff[i].src + '" name="' + i + '"</a>'
}

document.write(output);
}
```

## Summary

Images, or as some people describe them, "eye candy," can be used to great effect. Combined with JavaScript graphics can make a huge difference. Apart from the examples seen in this chapter, possible applications abound: banner advertising in e-commerce, image-map-based navigation systems, and so on. As long as tests are carried out to check that the browser being used supports the `Image` object, then you should be able to write image manipulation techniques that can disregard what browser or version of browser is being used. Images combined with Dynamic HTML techniques can produced stunning results. Dynamic HTML is covered in Chapter 11.

# Cookies

As the use of the Web becomes ubiquitous and permeates daily activities, from online shopping to banking, the personalization of user information has increasingly become important. The mechanism of cookies allows a developer to facilitate such an environment on a website.

*Cookie* is the term given by Netscape to persistent data stored by the browser on the user's machine. The original intended use of cookies was as a storage mechanism for data to be supplied by the server with its response to a HTTP request. This would allow, among other things, for session data to be held by the browser and then to be supplied by the browser back to the server with further requests, thus getting around the stateless nature (where the server cannot distinguish one request from another) of the HTTP protocol.

Netscape's Persistent Client State HTTP Cookies Specification is available online at http://www.netscape.com/newsref/std/cookie_spec.html. The important points within the specification are the *minimum* browser specifications:

- Support for 300 total cookies
- 4 kilobytes per cookie, where the name and value combine to form the 4-kilobyte limit.
- 20 cookies per server or domain

When a cookie is stored, there are six items associated with the cookie: name and value with the four attributes—expires, domain, path, and secure. The name and value are used as a traditional name=value pair. The remaining optional attributes follow the name=value pair, separated from one other using semicolons.

The expires attribute determines how long the cookie is held before being expired. If no expires attribute is specified, then the cookie expires at the end of the current browser session.

The domain attribute controls which domains or hosts can retrieve the cookie from the browser. The match is made using the tail of the domain or host, so that a domain attribute of example.com would match example.com, www.example.com, and thirdlevel.example.com.

The path attribute specifies the subset of URLs in a domain for which the cookie is valid. For example, if the domain attribute is set to example.com and the path attribute is set to /directory1/, then only URLs matching example.com/directory1/ would be allowed access to the cookie.

The `secure` attribute, when present, indicates that the cookie should only ever be transmitted back to the domain when a secure HTTP-over-SSL (Secure Sockets Layer) connection is used. For example, a cookie named `myCookie` with a value of `Hello World`, which expires on September 17, 2000, belonging to the `example.com` domain and only accessible from within the `/directory1/` directory of that domain, and that must only ever be sent back to the domain on a secure connection, would be represented with the following string value:

```
Set-Cookie: myCookie=Hello%20World; expires=Sunday, 17-Sep-00
23:12:40 GMT; domain=example.com; path=/directory1/; secure
```

Note that nonalphanumeric characters in the cookie's name or value are usually encoded in their corresponding Latin-1 encoding. This is especially true of cookies generated using JavaScript.

Any JavaScript-enabled browser can also use JavaScript to store, retrieve, and delete cookies through the `document` object's `cookie` property, as already seen in the "Form -> Cookie -> Form" application in Chapter 8. This chapter shows how to use a cookie to record the last time the visitor visited your page and how to use it the next time the visitor returns to highlight new material since his or her last visit.

Because of the possible sensitive nature of data being held in a cookie, it is extremely important that leaks do not occur. Browser vendors try their utmost to prevent leakage, but there have been occasions in the past where bugs in browsers have opened up security holes allowing access to cookies. As the browser vendors can never 100 percent guarantee that future bugs will not reveal further security holes, either through existing unfound bugs or as a result of code changes in new versions of browsers, a small minority of security-conscious users use the browser's ability to disable or warn about cookies. By doing this, they can either totally reject cookies or accept cookies on a case-by-case basis. The "Intelligent Cookies" application in this chapter covers techniques to avoid pestering the user with multiple cookie warnings.

This chapter also shows how to use cookies to track visitors around a site and how to personalize the "Year Calendar" application described in Chapter 7 "Date and Time" to store diary activities.

# General-Purpose JavaScript Cookie Routines

The cookies available to any particular page are available using the `document` object's `cookie` property. For example, the cookies associated with a document can be highlighted using

```
alert(document.cookie);
```

The `cookie` property provides a string value of `name=value` pairs separated with semicolons of all the cookies that are valid for the current document. This means that cookies associated with one domain are not made available to a page from another. The `cookie` property acts as a filter to the actual cookies held by the browser.

The simple application presented here shows how to store, retrieve, and delete cookies from JavaScript using general-purpose JavaScript functions held in an external JavaScript library. These functions are then used throughout the remainder of this chapter within the more advanced applications.

## General-Purpose JavaScript Cookie Routines Source Code—*index.htm*

chapter10/index.htm

To make use of the general-purpose JavaScript cookie routines, the *cookie.js* library must first be loaded in to the current page:

```
<script language="JavaScript" src="cookie.js"></script>
```

The library creates a `Cookie` object, which we can then use to check if the library has successfully loaded before proceeding:

```
if (window.Cookie) {
```

Before storing a persistent cookie—that is, a cookie that outlasts the current browser session—we first need to create an expiry date. The following two lines create a `Date` object for the current date and time. They then create a `Date` object named `expires` set to a year from now, using the `Cookie` object's `year` property:

```
var today = new Date()
var expires = new Date(today.getTime() + Cookie.year);
```

The `setCookie()` function contained in the *cookie.js* library can then be used to store a cookie—in this case, a cookie named `myCookie` with a value of `Hello World`, and a cookie named `myOtherCookie` with a value of `123456789.00`, both set to expire a year from now:

```
setCookie('myCookie', 'Hello World', expires);

setCookie('myOtherCookie', '1234567890.00', expires);
```

To see if the cookies were actually stored successfully, we can examine the `document` object's `cookie` property:

```
document.write(document.cookie + '<br>');
```

To retrieve the value of a cookie, we can use the `getCookie()` function in the *cookie.js* library. All that is needed is the name of the cookie to retrieve:

```
var myCookie = getCookie('myCookie');

document.write(myCookie + '<br>');
```

Likewise, to delete a cookie, we can use the `deleteCookie()` function:

```
deleteCookie('myCookie');
```

The cookie will now no longer be present in the `document` object's `cookie` property:

```
document.write(document.cookie + '<br>');
}
```

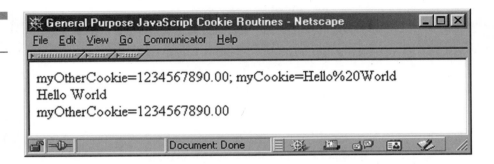

myOtherCookie=1234567890.00; myCookie=Hello%20World
Hello World
myOtherCookie=1234567890.00

## General-Purpose JavaScript Cookie Routines Source Code—*cookie.js*

 **chapter10/cookie.js**

The *cookie.js* library first creates a new `Object` named `Cookie`, and then sets four properties equal to the number of milliseconds in a `day`, `week`, `month`, and `year`:

```
var Cookie     = new Object();
Cookie.day     = 86400000;
Cookie.week    = Cookie.day * 7;
Cookie.month   = Cookie.day * 31;
Cookie.year    = Cookie.day * 365;
```

First, the `setCookie()` function accepts the six parameters that form a cookie. The `name` and `value` are mandatory parameters, whereas the `expires`, `path`, `domain`, and `secure` parameters are optional. The `value` parameter is first converted, so that any nonalphanumeric characters are converted to their corresponding Latin-1 value, using the `escape()` method. Then the tertiary operator is used to prefix the four optional parameter with their appropriate identifier, if a non `null` value has been passed. Otherwise, they are simply set to empty string values. The formatted cookie string is then assigned to the `document` object's `cookies` property:

```
function setCookie(name, value, expires, path, domain, secure) {
  value = escape(value);
  expires = (expires) ? ';expires=' + expires.toGMTString() :'';
  path    = (path)    ? ';path='    + path                 :'';
  domain  = (domain)  ? ';domain='  + domain               :'';
  secure  = (secure)  ? ';secure'                          :'';
```

```
document.cookie =
   name + '=' + value + expires + path + domain + secure;
}
```

The getCookie() function attempts to extract the value of the matching cookie name within the document object's cookie property. As the cookie property may hold none, one, or more than one name=value pairs, then string manipulation techniques are required to extract the relevant portion of the string, before then replacing any Latin-1 encoded characters with the original characters using the unescape() function. If the named cookie cannot be found, then a null value is returned. Otherwise, the value of the cookie is returned. Note that it is not possible to extract data from cookies stored by nonmatching domains or paths, and then only the name of the held cookies and their value attributes may be extracted:

```
function getCookie(name) {
   var cookies = document.cookie;
   var start = cookies.indexOf(name + '=');
   if (start == -1) return null;
   var len = start + name.length + 1;
   var end = cookies.indexOf(';',len);
   if (end == -1) end = cookies.length;
   return unescape(cookies.substring(len,end));
}
```

The deleteCookie() function simply sets the expires attribute of the cookie to year dot—that is, 1 second past January 1, 1970. This causes the cookie to be expired immediately. As the cookie may have been stored with different values for the path and domain attributes, then the function also optionally accepts these as input parameters. A check is made using the getCookie() function to ensure that we are not attempting to delete a nonexistent cookie, before finally assigning the formatted cookie string to the document object's cookie property:

```
function deleteCookie(name, path, domain) {
   var expires = ';expires=Thu, 01-Jan-70 00:00:01 GMT';
   (path)   ? ';path='   + path      : '';
   (domain) ? ';domain=' + domain    : '';

   if (getCookie(name))
      document.cookie = name + '=' + expires + path + domain;
}
```

Note that as well as not being able to retrieve the data, we can also not update or delete a cookie stored by another domain. This is a wise security mechanism to prevent data leaking from one domain to another. If, however, you have two domains with a different third-level tier—say, aaa.example.com and bbb.example.com—then you can share cookies between these two domains by setting the domain attribute of cookies to be shared to example.com.

Note also that when hosting a website on an Internet service provider's domain, unless the path attribute is correctly set, cookies may be accidentally shared across multiple websites. For example, if multiple websites are hosted on a domain such as www.example.com and your web-site is hosted at www.example.com/~mysite/, it is possible to restrict access to your cookies by specifying a path attribute value of /~mysite/, thus ensuring that your cookies are not accessible from another site at, say, www.example.com/~anothersite/.

# Cookies and Auto New

The current date and time can be held quite easily within a cookie using the number of milliseconds since year dot (midnight on January 1, 1970). Every time a user visits the home page of your website, you can store the current time in a cookie and use any previous value held in the cookie to highlight any new material added to the site since the user's last visit.

The application presented here highlights content as new if the content was added since the user's previous visit, as show in Figure 10-1.

## Cookies and Auto New Source Code— *index.htm*

**chapter10/autonew/index.htm**

Both the *cookie.js*, described earlier in this chapter, and the *calendar.js* libraries, described in the "Current Date and Time" application in Chapter 7, are loaded into the current page:

```
<script language="JavaScript" src="cookie.js"></script>
<script language="JavaScript" src="current.js"></script>
```

The formatValue() function, used to preformat the value stored in a cookie, accepts the three passed parameters today, last, and visit and returns a text string of the three values concatenated together with separating comma characters:

**Figure 10-1**    Cookies and Auto New—highlighting new content.

```
function formatValue(today,last,visit) {
   return today + ',' + last + ',' + visit;
}
```

The `getLastHere()` function attempts to retrieve the value of any existing `autoNew` cookie, using the `getCookie()` function.

```
function getLastHere(delay) {
```

The function first retrieves the current date (`now`) and time since year dot (`today`) and uses this to create a new date object (`expires`) based on the current time plus the value of the passed input parameter (`delay`):

```
var now = new Date();
var today = now.getTime();
var expires = new Date(today + delay);
```

The value of the `autoNew` cookie is retrieved:

```
var autoNew = getCookie('autoNew');
```

If the cookie does not already exist, then a new one is created using the `setCookie()` function with a `value` created using the `formatValue()` function, passing the values of `today`, `last` (set to `today` minus the `delay`), and `visit` (initialized to 1). The function then terminates by returning a new `Date` object representing the `last` date:

```
if (!autoNew) {
  var last = today - delay;
  var value = formatValue(today, last, visit=1);
  setCookie('autoNew', value, expires);
  return new Date(last);
}
```

If the cookie exists, then the three components `last`, `previous`, and `visit` are extracted using the comma characters as separators. If the value of `today` is not equal to `last`, then the cookie is updated with the new values of `today`, `last`, and `visit`. This check avoids the danger of updating the cookie twice within any one day—that is, all visits during the same day are counted as one visit. The function then terminates by returning a new `Date` object representing the date of the user's previous visit:

```
else {
  var comma1 = autoNew.indexOf(',');
  var comma2 = autoNew.lastIndexOf(',');

  var last = autoNew.substring(0,comma1) - 0;
  var previous = autoNew.substring(comma1 + 1,comma2) -` 0;
  visit = autoNew.substring(comma2 + 1,autoNew.length) - 0;

  if (today != last) {
    var value = formatValue(today, last, ++visit);
    setCookie('autoNew', value, expires);
  }
  return new Date(previous);
  }
}
```

The `isNew()` function compares two passed `date` objects, using the value returned by the `Date` object's `getTime()` method to return a `true` Boolean value if `date1` is greater than or equal to `date2`. Otherwise, the function returns a `false` Boolean value:

```
function isNew(date1, date2) {
  if (date1.getTime() >= date2.getTime())
    return true;
  return false;
}
```

The `formatDate()` function uses the `formatFullDate()` function held in the *calendar.js* library, described in detail in the "Current Date and Time" application to generate HTML markup to highlight the passed date parameter, but only if the *calendar.js* library has successfully loaded and defined the `formatFullDate()` function:

```
function formatDate(date) {
  if (window.formatFullDate)
    return '<b>' +
      formatFullDate(
        date.getDate(),
        date.getMonth()+1,
        date.getFullYear()) +
      '</b>';
  return '';
}
```

A global `visit` variable is defined and initialized to 0. This variable is used to hold the number of times the user has visited this page. A global `autoNewDate` variable is defined and initialized to `null`:

```
var visit = 0;
var autoNewDate = null;
```

If the `window` object's `Cookie` property has been successfully created by the loading of the *cookie.js* library, then the `getLastHere()` function is invoked, passing as input the number of milliseconds in 14 days. The function returns a `Date` object representing the date of the user's last visit, which is then assigned to the `autoNewDate` variable:

```
if (window.Cookie)
  autoNewDate = getLastHere(14 * Cookie.day);
```

To highlight content, a date that the content was added to the document must first be defined. The `itemDate` variable is used to hold a `Date` object reference representing the arbitrary date of December 25, 2001:

```
var itemDate = new Date(2001,12-1,25);
```

The `isNew()` function is used to indicate whether the date held in the `itemDate` variable is greater than or equal to date the held in the `autoNewDate` variable. If the function returns a `true` Boolean variable, then a *new.gif* image is written out to the document:

```
if (isNew(itemDate, autoNewDate)) {
  document.write('<img src="new.gif">');
}
```

The output of the `formatDate()` function, passed the value of the `itemDate` variable, is also written out to the document:

```
document.write(formatDate(itemDate));
```

# Intelligent Cookies

Cookies, when used sensibly, have a place within websites—for example, to store user preferences. However, cookies that are served from third-party websites, typically from banner advertising agencies, can be used to track users browsing habits over a wide network of websites that share a common ad agency. For this reason, users may be reluctant to accept carte blanche access to websites to write cookies. These users may either deny cookies outright, or they may wish to be warned prior to cookies being added to their browser. In either case, the user is in control.

Many websites can, however, drown the user in cookies, with each one having the potential to prompt the user with a warning that a cookie is about to be written. An example is shown in Figure 10-2. The user may at any point deny one of more of these cookies. Unfortunately, a badly designed website will not notice this and may continue to request cookies that the user doesn't want. This may cause the user to soon lose patience with the website and never revisit it.

This application shows how to utilize multiple cookies in your website without forcing cookies on those visitors that don't want them. A check is performed after every cookie is written to make sure that the cookie actually exists. If it does, then we proceed to set further cookies. If it doesn't, we prompt the user, indicating that cookies are essential and

**Figure 10-2**
Netscape Navigator warning the user that the server wants to store a cookie.

**Figure 10-3**
Intelligent Cookies—
prompting the user
after denial of
a cookie.

requesting that we are allowed to attempt to write the cookie again, as shown in Figure 10-3. If the user agrees, the cookie is written again. If the user disagrees, we do not bother the user again.

To be able to satisfy the user's like or dislike of cookies over many pages or many visits to the website, we need to store at least one cookie, a master cookie. When the user accepts cookies, the master cookie's value is set to `yesCookies`. If the user doesn't accept cookies, the code attempts to set just the one master cookie with a value of `noCookies`. The user is informed that this one cookie is required so as to prevent disturbing the user with cookie warnings in the future.

## Intelligent Cookies Source Code—*index.htm*

**chapter10/intelligent/index.htm**

The *cookie.js* library is included, along with an *intelligent.js* library that extends the cookie functionality:

```
<script language="JavaScript" src="cookie.js"></script>
<script language="JavaScript" src="intelligent.js"></script>
```

If both the libraries have loaded correctly, then the `window` object will have both a `Cookie` and `setMCookie` property. In this case, it is safe to invoke the `setMCookie()` function to attempt to store the master cookie and then attempt to store many sample cookies using the setICookie() function, passing the name and value of the cookie to be stored. Both of these functions are held in the *intelligent.js* library:

```
if (window.Cookie && window.setMCookie) {
  setMCookie();

  setICookie('cookie_name1','cookie value 1');
  setICookie('cookie_name2','cookie value 2');
  setICookie('cookie_name3','cookie value 3');
  setICookie('cookie_name4','cookie value 4');
  setICookie('cookie_name5','cookie value 5');
  setICookie('cookie_name6','cookie value 6');
  setICookie('cookie_name7','cookie value 7');
}
```

## Intelligent Cookies Source Code— *intelligent.js*

**chapter10/intelligent/intelligent.js**

The *intelligent.js* library extends the functionality held in the *cookie.js* library. For this reason, the *intelligent.js* library must follow the *cookie.js* library when loaded from within an HTML page.

The existing Cookie object is extended by defining a new MExpires date property set to 23:59:59 on December 31, 2099, an excepts property set to a false Boolean value, and a question string property:

```
Cookie.MExpires = new Date(2099,11,31,23,59,59);

Cookie.excepts = false;

Cookie.question =
  'We have detected that you do not allow cookies.\n' +
  'However, for this application to work correctly\n' +
  'cookies must be stored.\n\n' +
  'Please click \'OK\' to try again or \'Cancel\' to\n' +
  'set one preference cookie so that no further cookies\n' +
  'will be written by this site.';
```

The setMCookie() function is used to create the master cookie. It first attempts to retrieve the value of any existing master cookie (MCookie). If one does not exist, it then attempts to create a new master cookie with a value of yesCookie, using the value of the Cookie object's MExpires property as the expires input parameter. The value of the just-created cookie is then retrieved using the getCookie() function and assigning the result to the local MCookie variable. If the MCookie exists and its value is equal to yesCookies, then the Cookie object's excepts property is set to a true Boolean value, overriding its default false value:

```
function setMCookie() {
  if (!getCookie('MCookie'))
    setCookie('MCookie', 'yesCookies', Cookie.MExpires);

  var MCookie = getCookie('MCookie')

  if (MCookie && MCookie == 'yesCookies')
    Cookie.excepts = true;
}
```

To intelligently create cookies, instead of directly using the setCookie() function provided in the *cookie.js* library, we must instead use the setICookie() function. The setICookie() function accepts the same name, value, expires, path, domain, and secure parameters as the setCookie() function and actually uses these as input to the setCookie() function.

```
function setICookie(name, value, expires, path, domain, secure) {
```

The value of the master cookie is first retrieved and assigned to the MCookie local variable. If the Cookie object's excepts property is set to true, the MCookie object exists, and its value is equal to yesCookies, then the function proceeds to store the requested intelligent cookie:

```
var MCookie = getCookie('MCookie')

if (Cookie.excepts && MCookie && MCookie == 'yesCookies') {
```

The getCookie() function is used to attempt to retrieve the value of the cookie we are being requested to write.

```
var ICookie = getCookie(name);
```

If it does not exist, or its existing value is not equal to the new value, then the function proceeds to store the cookie using the setCookie() function. This prevents storing the cookie when it already exists with the required value—avoiding one possible warning that the user may reject:

```
if ((!ICookie) || (ICookie != value)) {
  setCookie(name, value, expires, path, domain, secure);
```

The value of this cookie is then immediately retrieved using the getCookie() function:

```
ICookie = getCookie(name);
```

If it does not exist or its value is not the same as expected, then a confirmation window is opened using the window object's confirm() method and passing the value of the Cookie object's question property. This creates a pop-up window with the question property text displayed above an OK and Cancel button. If the user clicks the OK button, the confirm() method returns a true value. If the user clicks the Cancel button, the method returns a false value:

```
if ((!ICookie) || (ICookie != value)) {
  var tryAgain = confirm(Cookie.question);
```

In addition, if the user clicks the OK button, the code attempts to store the cookie again using the setCookie() function and then retrieve its value again using the getCookie() function. If the cookie still does not exist or its value is still not as expected, then the code gives up at this point and sets the Cookie object's excepts property to false, thus preventing any further cookies from being stored by the code:

```
if (tryAgain) {
  setCookie(name, value, expires, path, domain, secure);
  var temp = getCookie(name);
  if (!temp || temp != value)
    Cookie.excepts = false;
}
```

If the user clicks the Cancel button, then the code attempts to store the master cookie, but this time with a value of noCookies, and sets the Cookie object's excepts property to false, again preventing any further cookies from being stored:

```
else {
    setCookie('MCookie', 'noCookies', Cookie.MExpires);
    Cookie.excepts = false;
    }
  }
 }
}
```

If the user prevents the master cookie from being stored, then the code will still avoid storing any further cookies, but only while the current page is loaded. If the page is reloaded, or the user moves on to further pages in the website or revisits the website at a later time, then as the master cookie is missing the next page to make use of the intelligent cookie, the code will again attempt to store the master cookie.

# Cookie Tracker

Being able to track the pages that one user has visited can provide opportunities for recommending additional pages that the user may have missed on his or her journey. Storing information within a cookie allows the data to be made available to all pages on a website, no matter what route the user takes (thus avoiding the need to pass the data across through the location's search property) and at a later date. Using one cookie to store the details of one visited page quickly becomes nonsensical, as browsers will soon drop older cookies to make room for new cookies. We therefore need to use compression techniques to store information about many visited pages in one cookie.

When storing many individual items of data in a single cookie, we must use a technique that enables the data to be easily extracted. One approach is to use fixed-length items of data—for instance, where every item of data is 4 bytes long. We could then use string-splicing techniques to extract the data. Care must be taken to ensure that when searching for data we match at word boundaries. For example, if using data fixed at 4 bytes long, then searching for 1234 within the string 212344451234 may mismatch on the 1234 substring at 2*1234*4451234, whereas it should have matched 212344445*1234*.

Another approach would be to use a separator character (say, a comma or a semicolon), which would then allow searches to be made using the separator character as a terminating character. Care must also be taken to ensure that false matches do not arise. For instance, searching for the phrase 3;within the string 33;93;3; may match 3*3;*93;3; substring, whereas we may have actually required the match 33;93;*3;*.

To ensure we avoid the problems inherent in both of these two approaches, we use a mixture of the two: fixed-length data items terminated with a separator character. To store as many items of data within the one cookie, the length of the data items must be as short as possible, but at the same time offer a large enough range of values. A four-digit integer would allow 10,000 different values (0000 through to 9999), but it would first require leading zeros to pad the numbers out to four characters and would only, with the addition of the separator character, allow a maximum of 819 data items in a 4-kilobyte cookie (4096 divided by 5). Using a two-character data item made up of alphanumeric characters (i.e., 0 through to 9, A through Z, and a through z), would allow 2116 different values (46 multiplied by 46) and allow a maximum of 1365 data items in a cookie (4096 divided by 3).

To ensure that the data being stored in a cookie does not grow in length because of the escape() method converting nonalphanumeric characters to their Latin-1 encoding value, we must be careful to choose a separator character that the escape() method does not convert. One such possible character is the plus character (+).

The application presented here tracks visitors around nine different pages, highlighting which pages they have yet to visit and which pages they have already visited, as shown in Figure 10-4. Each page is given a unique two-character code, which is prefixed to the value of a cookieTracker cookie to indicate which pages the user has visited and in which order. For example:

```
4h+4h+df+aB+Za+B4+AC+63+F0+00+00+F0+00+
```

**Figure 10-4**
Cookie Tracker—
which of nine pages
has the user visited.

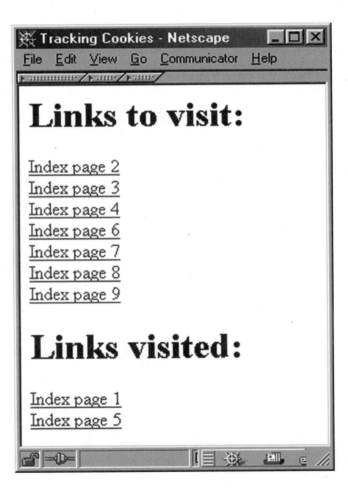

## Cookie Tracker Source Code—*index1.htm*

**chapter10/tracker/index1.htm**

Each page that is required to update the `cookieTracker` cookie must include both the *cookie.js* and *tracker.js* libraries:

```
<script language="JavaScript" src="cookie.js"></script>
<script language="JavaScript" src="tracker.js"></script>
```

To add a two-character code to the `cookieTracker` cookie, the page simply invokes the `addCookieCode()` function, passing the value of the two-character code, after first checking that both the two external libraries have successfully loaded:

```
if (window.Cookie && window.addCookieCode)
   addCookieCode('00');
```

Any page that wishes to show which pages have been visited can simply include the sample *tracking.js* library:

```
<script language="JavaScript" src="tracking.js"></script>
```

## Cookie Tracker Source Code—*index2.htm*

**chapter10/tracker/index2.htm**

The code is almost identical in each and every page that needs to update the `cookieTracker` cookie. The only change needed to the code shown in *index1.htm* is the replacement of the original two-character code with a different value:

```
if (window.Cookie && window.addCookieCode)
   addCookieCode('63');
```

## Cookie Tracker Source Code—*tracker.js*

**chapter10/tracker/tracker.js**

The *tracker.js* library extends the objects defined in the *cookie.js* library, so it must therefore be loaded after the *cookie.js* library. If the Cookie object exists, then the getCookie() function retrieves any existing cookieTracker value and assigns the value to the Cookie object's tracker property. If the cookie does not already exist, then the tracker property is set to an empty string:

```
if (window.Cookie) {
  Cookie.tracker = getCookie('cookieTracker');
if (!Cookie.tracker)
  Cookie.tracker = '';
}
```

An expires variable is defined and initialized to a date one year from today:

```
var today = new Date();
var expires = new Date(today.getTime() + Cookie.year);
```

The addCookieCode() function, invoked whenever a page requires to be added to the cookieTracker cookie, accepts the passed code parameter and prefixes it to the existing value of the Cookie object's tracker property, along with a separating plus character. If the length of the tracker property value is greater than 4096 bytes minus the length of the cookieTracker name, then the last three characters are chopped from the end of the tracker property. The cookie is then stored using the setCookie() function, passing as input to the path parameter the string '/'. This indicates that the cookie is available for update by any page anywhere from the root directory on down and is finally retrieved using the getCookie() function:

```
function addCookieCode(code) {
  Cookie.tracker = code + '+' + Cookie.tracker;

  if (Cookie.tracker.length > (4096 - 13))
    Cookie.tracker =
      Cookie.tracker.subString(0,Cookie.tracker.length - 3);

  setCookie('cookieTracker', Cookie.tracker, expires, '/');
    Cookie.tracker = getCookie('cookieTracker');
}
```

## Cookie Tracker Source Code—*tracking.js*

**chapter10/tracker/tracking.js**

The code contained in the *tracking.js* library is a very simple example of what can be achieved by examining the entries in the `cookieTracker` cookie and then building two lists, one of visited links and one of unvisited links. The code creates an array of user-defined `Link` objects, each with three properties: `href`, `text`, and `code`. The `code` property of each `Link` object is then checked against the value of the `Cookie` object's `tracker` property:

```
function Link(href, text, code) {
  this.link = '<a href="' + href + '">' + text + '</a><br>';
  this.code = code + '+';
}

function setLink(href, text, code) {
  myLink[item++] = new Link(href, text, code);
}

var item = 0;
var myLink = new Array();

setLink('index1.htm','Index page 1','00');
setLink('index2.htm','Index page 2','63');
setLink('index3.htm','Index page 3','AC');
setLink('index4.htm','Index page 4','B4');
setLink('index5.htm','Index page 5','F0');
setLink('index6.htm','Index page 6','Za');
setLink('index7.htm','Index page 7','aB');
setLink('index8.htm','Index page 8','df');
setLink('index9.htm','Index page 9','4h');

var newLinks = oldLinks = '';

for (var i=0; i<myLink.length; i++) {
  if (window.Cookie &&
    Cookie.tracker.indexOf(myLink[i].code) > -1)
    oldLinks += myLink[i].link;
  else
    newLinks += myLink[i].link;
}

if (newLinks != '')
  document.write('<h1>Links to visit:</h1>' + newLinks);
if (oldLinks != '')
  document.write('<h1>Links visited:</h1>' + oldLinks);
```

# Personal Calendar

This application combines the calendar application described in the "Pop-up Date Selector" application in Chapter 6 and the "Year Calendar" application in Chapter 7 with cookies to create a personalized calendar to store

**Figure 10-5**
Personal Calendar—
typical entries for
December 2000.

activities against any day in the calendar. Figure 10-5 shows typical entries stored against several days in December 2000. The figure shows eight entries underneath the calendar display, with each day in the calendar that contains an entry highlighted with larger font sizes.

The user is able to click on any day in the visible month to open a new window to add, update, or delete an entry against that day, as shown in Figure 10-6.

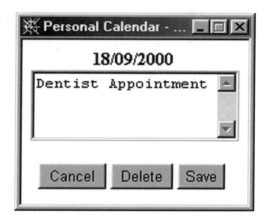

**Figure 10-6**
*Personal Calendar—*
*an entry for*
*September 18, 2000.*

The Personal Calendar uses storing techniques similar to the previous "Cookie Tracker" application to store all entries for the current month in one cookie. This allows a maximum possible 20 months' worth of entries. Whereas in the previous application the plus character was used as a terminating separator character, because it is quite likely that the user could enter a plus character as part of an entry, we must use a character sequence that the user is unlikely to enter. Since the application needs to identify which day of the month the entry is stored against, the day of the month has to also be included as part of the separator. Therefore, this application uses the character sequence @@ followed by the day of the month as separator followed by an equal sign—for instance, @@17=. Each cookie stored is given the name built from the year and month. Therefore, for September 2000, the cookie stored will be named 200009. When the maximum number of cookies that the browser can hold for any one domain is surpassed, then the browser automatically deletes the oldest cookie first.

## Personal Calendar Source Code—*index.htm*

**chapter10/calendar/index.htm**

Unlike the "Pop-Up Date Selector" application in Chapter 7, this application resides in the main window. It does, however, reload the contents of this window when the user selects another month or year from the calendar, or when the user adds, updates, or deletes an entry in the calendar. The page passes year and month values from one page to the next using the `location` object's `search` properties, but if required, the application can be adapted to reside in a pop-up window, as in the "Pop-Up Date Selector" application, for use offline in Internet Explorer—which does not support passing data in the URL while offline.

The *index.htm* page uses the *calendar.css* style sheet to define the styles to be used in the calendar:

```
<link rel="stylesheet" href="calendar.css" type="text/css">
```

The *calendar.js* library, described in the "Year Calendar" application in Chapter 7, and the *cookie.js* library are both loaded:

```
<script language="JavaScript" src="calendar.js"></script>
<script language="JavaScript" src="cookie.js"></script>
```

An `entries` array is defined to hold the entries for a maximum 31 days:

```
var entries = new Array(31);
```

The `getPersonal()` function, passed the value of the appropriate year and month, is used to extract any entries stored in the cookie for this year and month. The function uses the `getCookie()` function to retrieve the value of the cookie with the name of the year and month parameters (e.g., `200009` for September 2000) and assigns the value returned to the `monthValue` local variable. The code then attempts to retrieve a maximum 31 entries from the `monthValue` variable, using the `@@` character sequence along with day of the month and an equal sign. If the entry is not found, then the `dayValue` variable is set to an empty string. Otherwise, it is set to the value following the separator sequence up to the next separator sequence or until the end of the `monthValue` variable value. The value of the `dayValue` variable is then assigned to the appropriate entry in the `entries` array.

```
function getPersonal(year,month) {
  var monthValue;

  if (window.Cookie)
    monthValue = getCookie(year + pad(month,2));

  if (monthValue == null) monthValue = '';
    var dayValue;

  for (var i=1; i<=31; i++) {
```

```
      var start = monthValue.indexOf('@@' + i + '=');
      var len = start + ('@@' + i + '=').length;
      if (start == -1) dayValue = '';
      else {
        var end = monthValue.indexOf('@@',len);
        if (end == -1) end = monthValue.length;
        dayValue = monthValue.substring(len, end)
      }
      entries[i] = dayValue;
    }
  }
```

As described in Chapter 7, the "Year Calendar" application requires three functions to be defined to support the user changing the year or month, or clicking on one of the hypertext links representing the days. The following changeMonth() and changeYear() functions intercept the user changing the month or year, and reload the *index.htm* page, passing the value of the new year and month as data held in the URL:

```
function changeMonth() {
  location.href =
    'index.htm?year=' + year + '&month=' + CalendarMonth;
}

function changeYear() {
  location.href =
    'index.htm?year=' + CalendarYear + '&month=' + month;
}
```

The changeDay() function, invoked when the user clicks on one of the hypertext links, first checks if the window object has a Cookie property, and if so, it proceeds to open a new window to load the *cookie.htm* page. The function also updates the value of the global day variable with the value of the "Year Calendar" application's CalendarDay variable:

```
function changeDay() {
  if (window.Cookie) {
    day = CalendarDay;

    var popupCookie =
      window.open('cookie.htm','cookie','width=200,height=150');

    if (popupCookie.opener == null)
      popupCookie.opener = self;
  }
}
```

This application defines three global variables for use in the above three change functions: day, month, and year. Initially, they are all set to today's date. However, if data has been passed in the URL, then the year and month values are retrieved from the location object's search property using the `getNthParm()` function described in Chapter 8, "Passing Data from One Form to Another":

```
var today = new Date();
var day   = today.getDate();
var month = today.getMonth() + 1;
var year  = y2k(today.getYear());

var search = location.search;

if (search.length > 1) {
  year = getNthParm(search, 'year', 1);
  month = getNthParm(search, 'month', 1);
}
```

The `getPersonal()` function is invoked to populate the `entries` array with the calendar entries for the passed `year` and `month`:

```
getPersonal(year,month);
```

The "Year Calendar" application's `CalendarSelect()` function is invoked to generate the HTML markup for the passed `month` and `year`:

```
if (window.CalendarSelect)
  document.write(CalendarSelect(month,year,0));
```

All the entries in the `entries` array are then formatted for output, using the ubiquitous `pad()` function to pad the value of the `day` and `month` variables with leading zeros characters:

```
var output = '';

for (var i=1; i <= 31; i++) {
  var dayValue = entries[i];

  if (dayValue != '')
    output += pad(i,2) + '/' + pad(month,2) + '/' + year +
      ' - ' + dayValue + '<br>';

}
document.write('<p>' + output + '</p>');
```

## Personal Calendar Source Code— *calendar.js*

**chapter10/calendar/calendar.js**

One small change needs to be made to the *calendar.js* library described in the "Year Calendar" application in Chapter 7. The code that highlights the current day in the calendar is commented out:

```
//    if (day == i && month == M+1 && year == Y)
//      style = ' class="today"';
```

It is then replaced with code that highlights any day in the month that contains a nonempty string in the `entries` array, with a style `class` attribute of `cookie`:

```
if (entries[i] != '')
  style = ' class="cookie"';
```

## Personal Calendar Source Code—*calendar.css*

**chapter10/calendar/calendar.css**

Likewise, the *calendar.css* style sheet contains a new `cookie` class to highlight entries in the calendar with a large font:

```
.cookie {
  color: #0000FF;
  font-family: Arial;
  font-size: large;
  text-align: center;
}
```

## Personal Calendar Source Code—*cookie.htm*

**chapter10/calendar/cookie.htm**

The *cookie.htm* page is loaded into a small pop-up window whenever the user clicks one of the hypertext links in the calendar. This allows the user to enter, update, or delete an entry using a text form field.

To save reloading the *cookie.js* library into the pop-up window, and to save creating another `entries` array and then having to populate it with all the entries in the relevant cookie, the code in the *cookie.htm* page reuses the objects, methods, functions, and variables held in the `opener` window, as long as the `opener` property contains a non-null object reference:

```
if (opener) {
  var Cookie = opener.Cookie;
  var setCookie = opener.setCookie;

  var entries = opener.entries;

  var pad = opener.pad;

  var year  = opener.year;
  var month = opener.month;
  var day   = opener.day;
}
```

The `setPersonal()` function performs the reverse of the `getPersonal()` function in the *index.htm* page. It first updates the day entry in the `entries` array with the passed `value` parameter, and then concatenates all the entries in the `entries` array together using the `@@` character sequence, the day of the month, and an equal sign, before using the `setCookie()` function to create or update the existing cookie for the `year` and `month`:

```
function setPersonal(year,month,value) {
  entries[day] = value;

  var monthValue = '';
  for (var i=1; i<=31; i++) {
    if (entries[i] != '')
      monthValue += '@@' + i + '=' + entries[i];
  }

  if (window.Cookie) {
    var today = new Date()
    var expires = new Date(today.getTime() + Cookie.year);

    setCookie(year + '' + pad(month,2), monthValue, expires);
  }
}
```

The `showEntry()` function updates the value of the `form1` form's data form field with the value of the day entry in the `entries` array, as long as the current window has a non-null `opener` property, and the opener window's `entries` array exists:

```
function showEntry(day) {
  if (opener && entries)
    document.form1.data.value = entries[day];
}
```

The `saveEntry()` function invokes the `setPersonal()` function to update the current day entry in the `entries` array based on the value of the `form1` form's data form field. It then reloads the page in the opener window, before finally closing the current (`self`) window. Note that the `setPersonal()` function is only invoked and the `opener` window reloaded if both the `opener` and `entries` object references are not null and if the existing entry in the `entries` array is not already equal to the value of the form field:

```
function saveEntry(year,month) {
  if (opener && entries &&
    entries[day] != document.form1.data.value) {
    setPersonal(year,month,document.form1.data.value);
    opener.location.href = opener.location.href;
  }
  self.close();
}
```

The `deleteEntry()` function performs a similar role to the `saveEntry()` function, except that rather than using the value of a form field, it instead uses an empty string value:

```
function deleteEntry(year,month) {
  if (opener && entries[day] != '') {
    setPersonal(year,month,'');
    opener.location.href = opener.location.href;
  }
  self.close();
}
```

The `showEntry()` function is invoked from the `body` element's `onLoad` event handler to load the value of the current `day` entry in the `entries` array into the visible form field. The `onBlur` event handler ensures that the pop-up window remains on top of all other browser windows:

```
<body onLoad="showEntry(day)" onBlur="this.focus()">
```

The `form1` form contains a textarea named data, and three buttons that either close the current (`self`) window or invoke the `deleteEntry()` or `saveEntry()` functions:

```
<form name="form1">
<textarea name="data" cols="20" rows="3" wrap="virtual"></textarea>
<br>
<input type="button" value="Cancel" onClick="self.close()">
<input type="button" value="Delete"
  onClick="deleteEntry(year,month,day)">
<input type="button" value="Save"
  onClick="saveEntry(year,month,day)">
</form>
```

# Summary

Cookies are an ideal mechanism for storing and sharing persistent data across multiple pages and multiple visits. Capturing user preferences and storing them in a cookie, and then using the data to provide a customized view of your website may entice the user to come back again and again.

The use of cookies opens up new vistas in convenience for users in a variety of situations. For a frequently visiting user, it allows quick access to restricted areas of a website without repeated need for logging in, thereby saving time. For an Internet shopper, it provides the comfort of browsing (and selecting items) in an online portal without losing track. For an avid reader, it helps maintain the list of electronic books chosen from an online library to a personal account, once he or she has logged out. For a user with a visual disability, it makes the environment accessible (by maintaining font and color preferences). It should therefore come as no surprise that many of the successful portals today widely implement cookies.

Despite their power and widespread use, there are a certain drawbacks to cookies (apart from the possibility that the user may reject your attempt to store them in the first place), including limitations over the number of cookies that any one domain can store (20) and the maximum size of a cookie (4 kilobytes). Cookies are therefore not suitable for storing large amounts of crucial data, as they may subsequently be deleted to make way for other cookies.

Cookies are used in the "Dynamic Style Sheets" application in Chapter 11, "Dynamic HTML", and in the shopping cart applications in Chapter 12 "Applications".

# Dynamic
# HTML

The combination of HTML, JavaScript, cascading style sheets, and the Document Object Model is collectively known as Dynamic HTML, or DHTML. Up until this chapter, we have concentrated on the usage of JavaScript with forms, images, cookies, and so on. In this chapter, we turn our attention to the model that enables access to more than just these objects, to the very objects that make up the page. Particularly with the latest browsers (Internet Explorer 5 and Netscape Navigator 6), it is possible with the use of the World Wide Web Consortium's (W3C) Document Object Model (DOM) specification to access any components of HTML markup, element, and attribute via the Document Object Model. Various helper methods exist to provide easy access to the elements or nodes in the model. The model acts very much like a tree, with each node having other attached nodes, until eventually you reach the end of the branch, where, perhaps, a text node is found.

The W3C DOM effort is to provide a standard, nonproprietary way to access objects (nodes) of a document and is independent of any software implementation (such as by browsers or otherwise) or a programming language. Bindings for W3C DOM exist for ECMAScript (the standardization of JavaScript), among other languages.

This chapter only skims the surface of the facilities available in the W3C DOM specification and focuses on producing applications that work on as many browsers as possible. Unfortunately, there are fundamental differences between browsers in use today. Therefore, instead of requiring applications to be written that work with just one browser—or worse, requiring three times the coding to work with the three major models in existence—we first introduce a Document Object Model interface. The resultant *dom.js* library will hopefully hide the unnecessary complication from the application layer and will instead allow the easy creation of applications by understanding one simple interface.

This chapter presents a collapsible hierarchical Web page that can be used to show smaller portions of a much larger page. It shows how to change a page's style sheet on the fly and how to place a dynamic tool tip relative to a hypertext link.

In addition, the chapter demonstrates how to split a form into several parts, but display each part on the same page without requesting the next from the server and still allow the user to go back and amend any of the previous forms without losing data already entered.

The chapter also covers a toolbar menu with drop-down menus and how to generate an automatic table of contents built from the header elements already present in the document. Techniques are shown to slide content from the top and side of the page and how to show and control a dynamic menu system, before rounding off with a banner advert more interesting than most in use today.

All the applications covered in this chapter work on Netscape Navigator 4 and 6, as well as Internet Explorer 4 and 5, except for the "Dynamic Style Sheets" and "Automated Table of Contents" applications, which, although they fail gracefully, do not work on Netscape Navigator 4 or Internet Explorer 4 because of the limited DOM support on those particular browsers.

**Collapsible Content** ../chapter11/content/index.htm
**Dynamic Style Sheets** ../chapter11/stylesheet/index.htm
**Floating Tool Tips** ../chapter11/tooltips/index.htm
**Multi-Dialog Forms** ../chapter11/Dialog/index.htm
**Toolbar Menus** ../chapter11/toolbar/index.htm
**Automated Table of Contents** ../chapter11/toc/index.htm
**Tab Slider** ../chapter11/slide/index.htm
**Menu System** ../chapter11/menu/index.htm
**Dynamic Adverts** ../chapter11/advert/index.htm

# Document Object Model Interface

Three different Document Object Models are currently supported by browsers in use today: the simple "layer" approach in Netscape Navigator 4, the more advanced "all" object in Internet Explorer 4, and the standardized W3C DOM supported in both Netscape Navigator 6 and Internet Explorer 5.

To provide support for older browsers, it is necessary to provide three solutions, as all three models have differences from one other. Only Netscape Navigator 4 supports "layers" of content generated by absolutely positioned layer and ilayer elements, and only Internet Explorer 4 and 5 have an all object that provides access to nearly all elements based on their position within the all object or via their id attribute.

For example, to access an element in Netscape Navigator 4, we must first make the element absolutely positioned using a style attribute:

```
<div id="myDiv" style="position: absolute;">....</div>
```

To access the div element identified as myDiv, we must use one of three different mechanisms depending on the browser being used. For Netscape Navigator 4:

```
document.layers['myDiv']
```

For Internet Explorer 4 or 5:

```
document.all['myDiv']
```

For Internet Explorer 5 and Netscape Navigator 6:

```
document.getElementById('myDiv')
```

When writing code that could be run on any browser, we need to detect the support for particular objects before attempting to use any one of the preceding mechanisms:

```
if (document.layers) {
  // Internet Explorer 4 and 5
}
else if (document.all) {
  // Netscape Navigator 4 only
}
else if (document.getElementById) {
  // W3C DOM - Internet Explorer 5 and Netscape Navigator 6
}
```

Rather than coding three separate solutions in each application that you write, it is more practical to write a generic interface to the three models—once and once only—and then to use this interface instead of the three models directly.

This section introduces the *dom.js* library, used throughout the remainder of this chapter, which provides objects and functions to hide the differences between each model. Learn how to make use of the interface, and you do not need to worry about the details within.

# Document Object Model Interface Source Code—*dom.js*

**chapter11/dom.js**

The *dom.js* library defines a global DOMObjects object array. This is used to first detect that the *dom.js* library has been loaded successfully by the browser, and to then hold objects of interest to a DHTML application:

```
var DOMObjects = new Object();
```

The `DOMInitialize()` function is invoked by a DHTML application to populate the `DOMObjects` array with elements that match the passed `type` parameter. For example, an application may wish to access all the `div` elements, in which case the function is invoked as `DOMInitialize('div')`. In this case, if the W3C DOM is supported, then the `getElementsByTagName()` method is used to populate the `DOMObjects` object array with references to all the `div` elements in the document. However, if just the Internet Explorer `all` object is supported, then the `all` object's `tags` method is used to retrieve the `div` elements instead. Finally, if just the Netscape Navigator "layers" model is supported, then the `DOMObjects` object is assigned the reference to the `layers` object. Thus, in Netscape Navigator 4, the `type` parameter is ignored and only those absolutely positioned objects that appear in the `layers` object are available for use. If none of the object models are supported, then `DOMObjects` is set to `null`:

```
function DOMInitialize(type) {
  if (document.getElementById)
    DOMObjects = document.getElementsByTagName(type);
  else if (document.all) DOMObjects = document.all.tags(type);
  else if (document.layers) DOMObjects = document.layers;
  else DOMObjects = null;
}
```

After an application has invoked the `DOMInitialize()` function, a further check must be made on the `DOMObjects` object to ensure that it is not `null` before attempting to make use of any of the functions in the *dom.js* library. To save space, only a few of the more common functions available in the *dom.js* library are described. The remaining functions are just variations on a theme and can be examined by reading the source of the *dom.js* library.

The `DOMElementHide()` function can be used to hide an element. It accepts an object reference (`o`), and then tests the browsers support for the three object models. If the `getElementById()` method or the `all` object is supported, then the `o` object's `style` properties, `visibility` and `display`, are set to `hidden` and `none`, effectively causing the element to disappear. Otherwise, if the `layers` object is supported, then the `visibility` property of the `o` object is set to `hidden`:

```
function DOMElementHide(o) {
  if (document.getElementById || document.all) {
    o.style.visibility = 'hidden';
    o.style.display = 'none';
```

```
    }
    else if (document.layers)     o.visibility = 'hidden';
  }
```

The `DOMElementShow()` function performs the reverse of the `DOMElementHide()` function:

```
function DOMElementShow(o) {
  if (document.getElementById || document.all) {
    o.style.visibility = 'visible';
    o.style.display = 'block';
  }
  else if (document.layers)     o.visibility = 'visible';
}
```

The `DOMElementSetTop()` function sets the `o` object's `top` property to the value of the passed `val` variable. This causes the object (whether visible or not) to be repositioned at the new position, whereas the `DOMElementGetTop()` retrieves the value of the `top` property:

```
function DOMElementSetTop(o,val) {
  if (document.getElementById) o.style.top = val;
  else if (document.all)       o.style.top = val;
  else if (document.layers)    o.top = val;
}

function DOMElementGetTop(o) {
  if (document.getElementById) return o.style.top;
  else if (document.all)       return o.style.top;
  else if (document.layers)    return o.top;
}
```

The `DOMElementSetInnerHTML()` function uses the value of the passed `html` parameter to update the contents of the `o` object with new HTML markup—extremely useful for replacing existing content on the screen with new content:

```
function DOMElementSetInnerHTML(o,html) {
  if (document.getElementById)     o.innerHTML = html;
  else if (document.all)           o.innerHTML = html;
  else if (document.layers) {
    o.document.open();
    o.document.write(html);
    o.document.close();
  }
}
```

All bar one of the applications make use of the extended version of the *dom.js* library available on the CD-ROM. Writing and debugging one instance of the library allows the confidence that more complicated applications that make use of the library are not only simpler but are less likely to break on different browser than the one developed on. They are also much easier to maintain, as only the library needs to be amended when differences between two or more object models are discovered.

# Collapsible Content

This application demonstrates three separate uses for showing and hiding content on the page. As long as the page content is placed within HTML `div` tags with a class attribute set to 1, then the content will be used in a collapsible structure. The `id` attribute of the `div` tag indicates the levels that the content can be displayed in, the position within the structure, and the section it belongs in.

In this application the value of the `div` tag's `id` attribute is made up of three discrete parts. For example, a `div` tag of `<div id="L321-0/0+" class="1">` indicates the various levels that the contents of the `div` tag are displayed—in this case, any of the three levels 3, 2, and 1. It also indicates its position within the structure—in this case, item zero (i.e., the first position). Finally, it indicates the section that the content belongs in—again in this case, section 0. The characters L, -, /, and + are used as separators to allow the JavaScript code to intelligently extract the information from the `id` attribute.

The `div` tag `<div id="L32-6/1+" class="1">` indicates that it is visible in levels 3 and 2, is the item 6, and is in section 1. The div tag `<div id="L3-10/5+" class="1">` indicates that it is visible only in level 3, is the item 10, and is in section 5.

Figure 11-1 shows the application in action. The hypertext links at the top of the page allow the user to show the content based on its level, item number, or section number. Figure 11-1 currently shows the content that matches level 1 only—that is, those `div` tags with an `id` attribute starting with the sequence L321. All other `div` tags are hidden from view, and those remaining are shifted together to run one after another down the page.

## Collapsible Content Source Code—*index.htm*

**chapter11/content/index.htm**

**Figure 11-1**
Collapsible Content—
displaying just level 1
content.

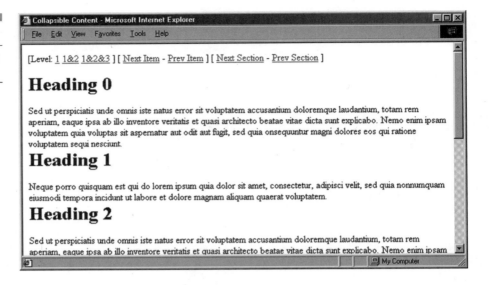

The *dom.js* library is loaded into the *index.htm* page. This ensures that all the functions described in the previous section are available to the JavaScript code in the rest of the page:

```
<script language="JavaScript" src="dom.js"></script>
```

Three global variables are initialized: the offset of the first visible content from the top of the page, and the initial values for I and S, the item and section values:

```
var offset = 50, I = S = -1;
```

The reveal() function accepts level and type parameters, which it uses to hide or reveal visible items represented by the entries in the global DOMObjects array:

```
function reveal(level, type) {
```

A check is first made to ensure that the window object's DOMObjects property is defined and is not equivalent to null:

```
    if (window.DOMObjects) {
```

The code then loops through each of the entries, passing each one in turn to the DOMElementHide() function to initially hide all the items:

```
for (var i=0; i<DOMObjects.length; i++)
    DOMElementHide(DOMObjects[i]);
```

The global `offset` variable is reinitialized to 50:

```
offset = 50;
```

Again, the code loops through all the DOMObjects entries, trying to find a match against the entry's id attribute and the passed `level` parameter. If the type passed is `l` (i.e., match on the level), the level value is found immediately after the `L` character, or if the type is `i` (i.e., match on the item number), and the level value is found between the `-` and `/` characters, or if the type is `s` (i.e., match on the section number), and the level value is found between the `/` and `+` characters, then the `DOMElementSetTop()` and `DOMElementShow()` functions are used to reposition the item at the `offset` position and to reveal the items content, before finally increasing the value of `offset` by the value returned by the `DOMElementsGetHeight()` function:

```
for (var i=0; i<DOMObjects.length; i++) {
    var id = DOMObjects[i].id;
    if ((type == 'l' && id.indexOf('L'+level)>=0) ||
        (type == 'i' && id.indexOf('-'+level+'/')>=0) ||
        (type == 's' && id.indexOf('/'+level+'+')>=0)) {
        DOMElementSetTop(DOMObjects[i], offset);
        DOMElementShow(DOMObjects[i]);
        offset += DOMElementGetHeight(DOMObjects[i]);
    }
  }
}
    return false;
}
```

The `start()` function, invoked by the `body` tag's `onLoad` event handler, invokes the `DOMInitialize()` function, passing a string containing the HTML markup tag to be loaded into the DOMObjects array:

```
function start() {
  if (window.DOMObjects)
    DOMInitialize('div');
}
```

The inline `l` class style is used to immediately hide all DHTML markup that has a `class` attribute set to `l`:

```
<style><!--
.l { position: absolute; visibility: hidden; display: block; }
//--></style>
```

In Netscape Navigator 4, although DHTML techniques are supported, the browser does not rerender the page to take account of changes. It is necessary to ensure that the initial page length is long enough to display all the content when visible. Therefore, an `img` tag is output to the document with a very narrow width, but with a very long height, high enough to cater for the maximum length of the viewable but initially collapsed content:

```
if (document.layers)
  document.write(
    '<img src="blank.gif" width="1" height="3500" align="left">'
);
```

The hypertext links contain `onClick` event handlers to pass the necessary `level` and `type` parameters to the `reveal()` function:

```
[Level: <a href="" onClick="return reveal(321,'l')">1</a>
<a href="" onClick="return reveal(32,'l')">1&2</a>
<a href="" onClick="return reveal(3,'l')">1&2&3</a> ]

[<a href="" onClick="return reveal(++I,'i')">Next Item</a> -
<a href="" onClick="return reveal(--I,'i')">Prev Item</a> ]

[<a href="" onClick="return reveal(++S,'s')">Next Section</a> -
<a href="" onClick="return reveal(--S,'s')">Prev Section</a> ]
```

Note that the item and section links use the prefix increment and decrement operators to adjust the values of the `I` and `S` global variables prior to being passed to the functions.

All that remains is to split the page into several levels, items, and sections:

```
<div id="L321-0/0+" class="l">
<h1>Heading 0</h1>
...
</div>

<div id="L321-1/1+" class="l">
<h1>Heading 1</h1>
...
</div>

<div id="L32-2/1+" class="l">
<h2>Heading 1.1</h2>
...
</div>

<div id="L32-3/1+" class="l">
<h2>Heading 1.2</h2>
...
</div>

<div id="L3-4/1+" class="l">
```

```
<h3>Heading 1.2.1</h3>
...
</div>

<div id="L3-5/1+" class="l">
<h3>Heading 1.2.2</h3>
...
</div>

...
```

## Dynamic Style Sheets

With the advent of Internet Explorer 4 and Netscape Navigator 6, it has been possible to access the style sheets loaded within a document using the `document` object's `stylesheets` array, and then disable or enable one or more of the loaded style sheets using the `disabled` property.

Any external style sheet loaded using a `link` tag with a `rel` attribute set to `style` and any inline styles defined within individual `style` tags are referenced via the entries in the `document` object's `stylesheet` array. This application combines this with a cookie so that the user may elect which one of any loaded style sheets to use as default for the remainder of the site. Figure 11-2 shows the initial effects of the user selecting an option

**Figure 11-2**
Dynamic Style Sheets—style sheet one.

from the select list form element. Figure 11-3 shows the effects of the user selecting a different option, saving the chosen style, and then moving on to a different page. Each time the use selects a style sheet, all style sheets are disabled except the one chosen. When the user clicks the Save button, a cookie is written to remember the current selection.

## Dynamic Style Sheets Source Code— *index.htm*

**chapter11/stylesheet/index.htm**

The *index.htm* page first loads three separate external style sheets and then defines inline styles using a style element. Note that each style sheet uses the title attribute to identify each separate style sheet using the syntax styleX, where X is an increasing integer value starting at 1:

```
<link rel="stylesheet" href="style1.css" title="style1">
<link rel="stylesheet" href="style2.css" title="style2">
<link rel="stylesheet" href="style3.css" title="style3">
```

```
<style title="style4"><!--
...
//--></style>
```

The *cookie.js* library, described in detail in Chapter 10, "Cookies," is loaded along with a new *stylesheet.js* library, explained later in this section:

```
<script language="JavaScript" src="cookie.js"></script>
<script language="JavaScript" src="stylesheet.js"></script>
```

The `update()` function, invoked from the `select` list's `onChange` event handler, accesses the value of the selected option, assigns the value to the global `mySheet` variable, and then invokes the `enableStyle()` function, passing the value of the `mySheet` variable to the function. Both the `mySheet` global variable and `enableStyle()` function are defined in the *stylesheet.js* library:

```
function update(o) {
  if (window.enableStyle)
    enableStyle(mySheet = o.options[o.selectedIndex].value);
}
```

The `save()` function, invoked from the Save button's `onClick` event hander, uses the `setCookie()` function to store a cookie named `stylesheet` with the value of the `mySheet` global variable:

```
function save() {
  if (window.Cookie && mySheet)
    setCookie('stylesheet', mySheet, expires, '/');
}
```

The remainder of the JavaScript code in the *index.htm* page creates the necessary HTML markup to output the form containing the `select` list and Save button, using the value of the `mySheet` global variable to highlight the currently saved style sheet preference. The `title` property of the `stylesheet` object is used as the value of the `option` element's `value` attribute:

```
var output = '';
if (document.styleSheets) {
  output +=
    '<form>' +
      '<select name="style" onChange="update(this)">' +
      '<option value="" selected>Choose a stylesheet:';

  for (var i=0; i<document.styleSheets.length; i++) {
```

```
      var title = document.styleSheets[i].title;
      var selected = (title == mySheet) ? ' selected' : '';
      output +=
        '<option value="' + title + '"' + selected + '>' + title;
    }

  output +=
    '</select>' +
    ' <input type="button" value="Save" onClick="save()">' +
    '</form>';
}
document.write(output);
```

## Dynamic Style Sheets Source Code— *stylesheet.js*

The *stylesheet.js* library contains all the code to retrieve any existing style sheet preference, and then disable and enable one of the style sheets in the *stylesheets* array. First, the `mySheet` global variable is defined:

```
var mySheet;
```

If the *cookie.js* library has loaded, then an expires date is defined (one year from now) and the value of any existing `stylesheet` cookie is retrieved:

```
if (window.Cookie) {
  var today = new Date();
  var expires = new Date(today.getTime() + Cookie.year);
  mySheet = getCookie('stylesheet');
}
```

The `enableStyle()` function accepts the `title` parameter passed from the `update()` function in the *index.htm* page, and then it proceeds to set the `stylesheet` object's `disabled` property to `true` if the passed `title` parameter does not equal the `stylesheet` object's `title` property. Otherwise, the `disabled` property is set to `false`, as both titles match:

```
function enableStyle(title) {
  if (document.styleSheets) {
    for (var i=0; i<document.styleSheets.length; i++) {
      document.styleSheets[i].disabled =
        (document.styleSheets[i].title != title);
    }
  }
}
```

The `enableStyle()` function is then used to enable just the style sheet that corresponds to the non-null value of the `mySheet` global variable. This then immediately disables all style sheets except the preferred one:

```
if (mySheet) enableStyle(mySheet);
```

Note that the value of the `mySheet` global variable and thus the value stored in the `stylesheet` cookie matches the value of one of the style sheet's `title` attributes.

### Dynamic Style Sheets Source Code—*next.htm*

To ensure that the user's style sheet preference is observed throughout the remainder of the website, the style sheets all need to be included and identified using the title attribute, and then followed by the inclusion of first the *cookie.js* and then the *stylesheet.js* library:

```
<link rel="stylesheet" href="style1.css" title="style1">
<link rel="stylesheet" href="style2.css" title="style2">
<link rel="stylesheet" href="style3.css" title="style3">

<style title="style4"><!--
...
//--></style>

<script language="JavaScript" src="cookie.js"></script>
<script language="JavaScript" src="stylesheet.js"></script>
```

## Floating Tool Tips

Floating tool tips appear in almost all applications, even in browsers and especially in Internet Explorer with the title attribute of a link element. Yet the tool tip available within Internet Explorer is limited, as it does not allow the use of HTML markup within the attribute element.

The application presented here shows how to use a positioned element to contain any HTML markup that is revealed whenever the mouse pointer moves across a "sensitive" hypertext link. The code adjusts the position of the tool tip to take account of the position of the link relative to the sides of the browser window.

Figure 11-4 shows a typical tool tip in action after the mouse pointer has moved across the "accusantium" hypertext link.

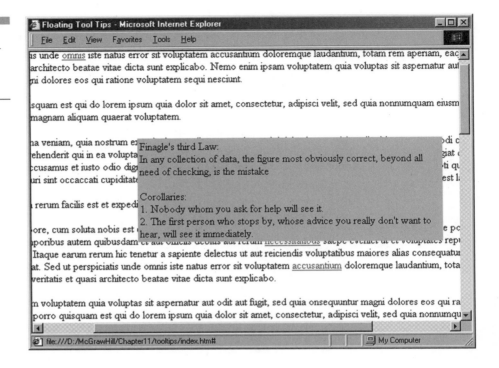

## Floating Tool Tips Source Code—*index.htm*

**chapter11/tooltip/index.htm**

The *index.htm* page makes use of the *dom.js* library:

```
<script language="JavaScript" src="dom.js"></script>
```

The `show()` function, invoked by the `onMouseOver` event handler, is used to first make the tool tip visible and then position the tool tip relative to the location of the mouse pointer. The `show()` function accepts an `id` and `e` parameter, representing the `id` attribute of the tool tip and the `window` object's `event` object, which contains all the properties of the mouse-over event that triggered the `onMouseOver` event handler:

```
function show(id,e) {
  if (window.DOMObjects) {
```

First, the tool tip is made visible using the `DOMElementShow()` function:

```
DOMElementShow(DOMObjects[id]);
```

Next, the x and y coordinates of the mouse-over event are retrieved using the `DOMEventGetOffsetX()` and `DOMEventGetOffsetY()` functions and increased by adding a 50-pixel offset to each, so that by default, the tool tip will appear below and slightly to the right of the mouse-over location:

```
var x = DOMEventGetOffsetX(e) + 50;
var y = DOMEventGetOffsetY(e) + 50;
```

The width and offset from the top of the page of the tool tip and the inner width of the browser window are then retrieved using various functions in the *dom.js* library:

```
var width = DOMElementGetWidth(DOMObjects[id]);
var innerWidth = DOMWindowGetInnerWidth();
var xOffset = DOMWindowGetXOffset();
```

The height and offset from the left-hand side of the page and the inner height browser window are also retrieved:

```
var height = DOMElementGetHeight(DOMObjects[id]);
var innerHeight = DOMWindowGetInnerHeight();
var yOffset = DOMWindowGetYOffset();
```

The values of the x and y coordinates are then adjusted if there is not enough room to the left and beneath the current position to contain the tool tip, so that the tool tip may appear above or to the right of the hypertext link:

```
if (x > innerWidth + xOffset - width)
  x = innerWidth + xOffset - width - 25;

if (y > innerHeight + yOffset - height)
  y = y - height - 75;
```

Finally, the `DOMElementSetLeft()` and `DOMElementSetTop()` functions are used to reposition the tool tip to the new x and y coordinates:

```
DOMElementSetLeft(DOMObjects[id], x);
DOMElementSetTop(DOMObjects[id], y);
  }
}
```

The `hide()` function, invoked by `onMouseOut` event handlers, is used to loop through all the objects in the `DOMObjects` array and uses the `DOMElementHide()` function to hide each positioned element:

```
function hide() {
  if (DOMObjects && DOMObjects.length>0)
    for (var i=0; i<DOMObjects.length; i++)
      DOMElementHide(DOMObjects[i]);
}
```

The `start()` function, invoked from the `body` element's `onLoad` event handler, invokes the `DOMInitialize()` function to populate the `DOMObjects` array:

```
function start() {
  if (window.DOMObjects)
    DOMInitialize('div');
}
```

To initially hide all the tool tips, the `l` class style is defined and then used in each `div` element's `class` attribute:

```
.l { position: absolute; visibility: hidden; display: block; }
```

Each tool tip is contained within its own `div` element. The `class` attribute matches the `l` class style defined previously. The `style` attribute specifies the approximate width and height of the tool tip, which allows the `show()` function to adjust the position of the tool tip depending on the size of its contents. The tool tips can contain HTML markup. In the following four examples, table HTML markup has been included:

```
<div id="myLayer1" class="l" style="width:350; height:75">
<table bgcolor="#c0c0c0" width="350"><tr><td>
...
</td></tr></table></div>

<div id="myLayer2" class="l" style="width:300; height:200">
<table bgcolor="#c0c0c0" width="300"><tr><td>
...
</td></tr></table></div>

<div id="myLayer3" class="l" style="width:350; height:75">
<table bgcolor="#c0c0c0" width="350"><tr><td>
...
</td></tr></table></div>

<div id="myLayer4" class="l" style="width:350; height:75">
```

```
<table bgcolor="#c0c0c0" width="350"><tr><td>
...
</td></tr></table></div>
```

Finally, to make use of the tool tips, `onMouseOver` and `onMouseOut` event handlers are used to invoke the `show()` and `hide()` functions, respectively, and in the case of the `show()` function call, the value of the required tool tips `id` attribute is passed along with the `window` object's event object:

```
<a href="..." onMouseOver="show('myLayer1',event)"
onMouseOut="hide()">...</a>
<a href="..." onMouseOver="show('myLayer2',event)"
onMouseOut="hide()">...</a>
<a href="..." onMouseOver="show('myLayer3',event)"
onMouseOut="hide()">...</a>
<a href="..." onMouseOver="show('myLayer4',event)"
onMouseOut="hide()">...</a>
```

# Multi-Dialog Forms

Good web design dictates small pages, small enough to fit the most important information in the first visible part of the page. Collecting information from users (e.g., name and address, preferences, and so on) may require a large expanse of page space. Asking users to complete a long, data-intensive form may discourage them from even starting to complete the form. Breaking the form up into smaller, more digestible chunks is preferred.

The downside to this is that between each "chunk," a round-trip to the server is required each time, to both send the results of the current form and retrieve the page for the next form. Delays in the network can cause this to take longer than desired. It is also difficult, if not impossible, for the user to backtrack several pages to fix an error or omission in the data and then page forward without having to reenter all the data in the intervening pages.

The "Multi-Dialog Forms" application presented here overcomes both these problems, by first ensuring that the HTML markup is delivered in one page and then using Dynamic HTML techniques to present the form in manageable chunks to the user, using a tabbed dialog user interface, similar to that used in most modern applications, which allows to the user to move through the dialogs in any order he or she chooses. Figure 11-5 shows the user currently entering data into a Skills dialog tab.

**Figure 11-5**
Multi-Dialog Forms—
showing the Skills tab
dialog.

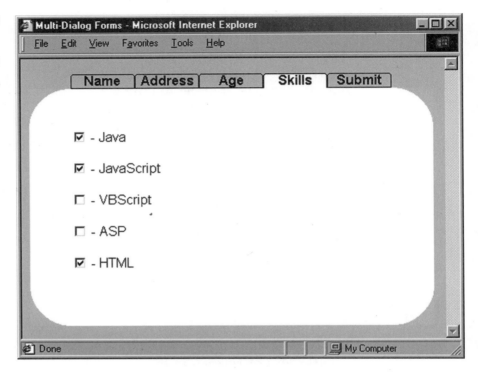

## Multi-Dialog Forms Source Code—*index.htm*

**chapter11/dialog/index.htm**

First, the *dom.js* library is loaded:

```
<script language="JavaScript" src="dom.js"></script>
```

The global `tab` variable holds the value of the currently visible dialog:

```
var tab = 1;
```

The `copyForm()` function copies the data from any form (referenced as `fRef1`) to any other form (referenced as `fRef2`). It is similar, but not identical, to the `setupForm()` function in the "Form -> Cookie -> Form" application in Chapter 8, which populated a form from name/value pairs contained in a string. The difference here is that the second form (`fRef2`) must contain an identically named field for each field in the first form (fRef1):

```
function copyForm(fRef1, fRef2) {
  for (var e=0; e<fRef1.elements.length; e++) {
    var name = fRef1.elements[e].name;

    switch (fRef1.elements[e].type) {
      case 'text':
      case 'textarea':
      case 'password':
      case 'hidden':
        fRef2[name].value = fRef1.elements[e].value;
        break;

      case 'checkbox':
        if (fRef1.elements[e].checked)
          fRef2[name].value = fRef1.elements[e].name;
        break;

      case 'radio':
        for (var i=0; i<fRef1[name].length; i++)
          if (fRef1[name][i].checked)
            fRef2[name].value = fRef1[name][i].value;
        break;

      case 'select-one':
        fRef2[name].value =
          fRef1[name].options[fRef1[name].selectedIndex].text;
        break;

      case 'select-multiple':
        var output = '';
        for (var i=0; i<fRef1[name].length; i++)
          if (fRef1[name][i].selected)
            fRef2[name].value = fRef1[name][i].text + ',';
        fRef2[name].value = output;
        break;
    }
  }
}
```

The input form is actually made up from separate forms contained within div elements, each with an id attribute and a class attribute set to 1. Each form contains a unique name attribute value:

```
<div id="div1" class="1"><form name="form1">
...
</form></div>

<div id="div2" class="1"><form name="form2">
...
</form></div>

<div id="div3" class="1"><form name="form3">
...
</form></div>
```

```
<div id="div4" class="l"><form name="form4">
...
</form></div>
```

Note that none of the preceding forms have a submit button—these forms and their contents are not submitted back to the server. Instead, the `copyForm()` function in the preceding code is used to copy the contents of each one of the preceding forms into a hidden form, named `hiddenForm`. It is this form that is submitted to the server. Again, it does not have a submit button:

```
<form name="hiddenForm" method="get">
...
</form>
```

The actual dialog tabs are made from image text links. The first four represent the four visible form dialogs. The `onClick` event handlers invoke the `change()` function, passing the value of a global `tab` variable and the number of the dialog to show (one through five). The last dialog tab is the Submit tab, which invokes the `submit()` function:

```
<a href="" onClick="return change(tab,1)"><img src="tab1-on.gif">
<a href="" onClick="return change(tab,2)"><img src="tab2-off.gif">
<a href="" onClick="return change(tab,3)"><img src="tab3-off.gif">
<a href="" onClick="return change(tab,4)"><img src="tab4-off.gif">
<a href="" onClick="return submit(tab,5)"><img src="tab5-off.gif">
```

The `change()` function accepts the current/old value of the `tab` variable as `o` and the next/new value for the `tab` variable as `n`. It then invokes the `update()` function to copy the contents of the current/old visible form to the hidden form, the `show()` function to reveal the next/new form dialog for the tab just clicked, and the `swapOff()` and `swapOn()` functions to perform simple image swapping on the tab images, before eventually updating the value of the global `tab` variable with the value of the `n` parameter:

```
function change(o,n) {
  update(o);
  show(n);
  swapOff(o);
  swapOn(n);
  tab = n;

  return false;
}
```

The `submit()` function performs a similar role, except that rather than show a different dialog, it invokes the hidden form's `submit()` method, causing the form and its contents to be submitted back to the server:

```
function submit(o,n) {
  update(o);
  swapOff(o);
  swapOn(n);
  tab = n;

  document.hiddenForm.submit();

  return false;
}
```

The `update()` function, invoked from the `change()` function, is simply a wrapper for the `copyFrom()` function. In Netscape Navigator 4, the `div` elements that hold the dialog forms generate their own document object. Therefore, the object reference is slightly different from that in Netscape Navigator 6 and Internet Explorer. A test is made on the `document` object's `layers` object, which is only supported in Netscape Navigator 4. If present, the input to the `copyForm()` function uses a reference to the `div` element's `document` for the first parameter:

```
function update(o) {
  if (document.layers)
    copyForm(document['div' + o].document['form' + o],
             document.hiddenForm);
  else
    copyForm(document['form' + o],document.hiddenForm);
}
```

The `show()` function uses the `DOMElementHide()` function in the *dom.js* library to first hide all the `div` elements and then the `DOMElementShow()` function to reveal the next/new dialog:

```
function show(n) {
  if (window.DOMObjects) {
    for (var i=0; i<DOMObjects.length; i++)
      DOMElementHide(DOMObjects[i]);

    DOMElementShow(DOMObjects['div' + n]);
  }
}
```

The `start()` function, invoked from the `body` element's `onLoad` event handler, initializes the application by invoking the `DOMInitialize()` function and then invokes the `show()` function to reveal the first of the four dialogs:

```
function start() {
  if (window.DOMObjects)
    DOMInitialize('div');

  if (window.DOMObjects)
    show(1);
}
```

# Toolbar Menus

This application shows how to generate menus that drop down from a toolbar when the mouse pointer moves over the toolbar. Several techniques are employed in this application to ensure that the menus always align with the toolbar and that the menus remain open even if the mouse wanders of the menu then back on within a predetermined delay interval. The code allows for the absolute positioning of the toolbar, thus allowing space to be reserved above the toolbar for items like banner adverts or company logos. Figure 11-6 shows one active menu from the example application.

**Figure 11-6**
Toolbar Menus— showing the menu for the Software toolbar item.

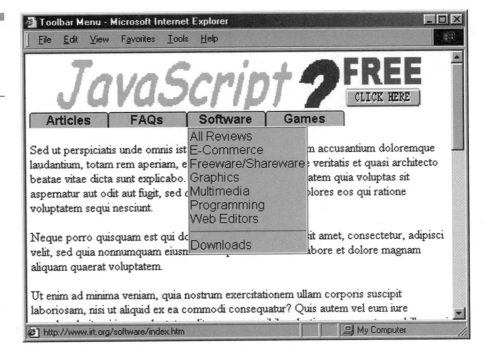

## Toolbar Menus Source Code—*index.htm*

 **chapter11/toolbar/index.htm**

The code contained in the *dom.js* library is loaded into the *index.htm* page:

```
<script language="JavaScript" src="dom.js"></script>
```

First, we'll look at the toolbar. It consists of image links contained within a span element, identified as `toolbar`. The `toolbar` has a `class` attribute set to v and a `style` attribute specifying the top and left positions of the toolbar. The links include `onMouseOver` and `onMouseOut` event handlers to invoke the `openMenu()` and `closeMenu()` functions. The `openMenu()` function is passed the name of the menu to open, along with its x and y offsets from the toolbar:

```
<span id="toolbar" class="v" style="top: 77; left: 5;">
<a href="..." onMouseOver="openMenu('menu1',0,20)"
onMouseOut="closeMenu()"><img src="menu1.gif" width="100"></a>
<a href="..." onMouseOver="openMenu('menu2',100,20)"
onMouseOut="closeMenu()"><img src="menu2.gif" width="100"></a>
<a href="..." onMouseOver="openMenu('menu3',200,20)"
onMouseOut="closeMenu()"><img src="menu3.gif" width="100"></a>
<a href="..." onMouseOver="openMenu('menu4',300,20)"
onMouseOut="closeMenu()"><img src="menu4.gif" width="100"></a>
</span>
```

The menus are all contained within span elements that contain layer elements that contain a table element. This complicated structure is needed to ensure that the application works properly on all the major browsers. The layer and table elements both contain `onMouseOver` and `onMouseOut` event handlers that invoke the `keepOpen()` and `closeMenu()` functions. Both are required, as Netscape Navigator 4 does not support event handlers in a table element and Internet Explorer does not support the layer element. Each span element has a class attribute set to l and an id attribute to identify the menu. The menu items are made from simple hypertext links:

```
<span id="menu1" class="l">
<layer onMouseOver="keepOpen()" onMouseOut="closeMenu()">
<table onMouseOut="closeMenu()" onMouseOver="keepOpen()"><tr><td>
<a href="...">...</a><br>
...
```

```
</td></tr></table></layer></span>

<span id="menu2" class="l">
<layer onMouseOver="keepOpen()" onMouseOut="closeMenu()">
<table onMouseOut="closeMenu()" onMouseOver="keepOpen()"><tr><td>
<a href="...">...</a><br>
...
</td></tr></table></layer></span>

<span id="menu3" class="l">
<layer onMouseOver="keepOpen()" onMouseOut="closeMenu()">
<table onMouseOut="closeMenu()" onMouseOver="keepOpen()"><tr><td>
<a href="...">...</a><br>
...
</td></tr></table></layer></span>

<span id="menu4" class="l">
<layer onMouseOver="keepOpen()" onMouseOut="closeMenu()">
<table onMouseOut="closeMenu()" onMouseOver="keepOpen()"><tr><td>
<a href="...">...</a><br>
...
</td></tr></table></layer></span>
```

Two inline style classes are used in this application. The l class immediately hides all the menus, whereas the v class is used to mark the toolbar as being absolutely positioned—essential for Netscape Navigator 4:

```
.l { position: absolute; visibility: hidden; display: block; }
.v { position: absolute; visibility: visible; display: block; }
```

The start() function, invoked from the body element's onLoad event handler, first initializes the application using the DOMInitialize() function held in the *dom.js* library and then retrieves the left and top position of the toolbar and assigns the values to the global xOffset and yOffset variables:

```
var xOffset = yOffset = 0;

function start() {
  if (window.DOMObjects)
    DOMInitialize('span');

  if (window.DOMObjects) {
    xOffset = DOMElementGetOffsetLeft(DOMObjects['toolbar']);
    yOffset = DOMElementGetOffsetTop(DOMObjects['toolbar']);
  }
}
```

The openMenu() function, invoked from one of the onMouseOver event handlers in the toolbar image links, accepts the name of the menu, along with the x and y offset from the toolbar. It first loops through all the items in the DOMObjects array and uses the DOMElementHide()

function to hide the item unless the id property matches either the toolbar or the menu being opened. The keepOpen() function is then invoked before positioning the menu using the DOMElementSetLeft() and DOMElementSetTop() functions, passing the value of the x and y parameters plus the value of the xOffset and yOffset global variables, and then revealing the menu using the DOMElementShow() function:

```
function openMenu(menu, x, y) {
  if (window.DOMObjects) {
    for (var i=0; i<DOMObjects.length; i++)
      if (DOMObjects[i].id != 'toolbar' &&
          DOMObjects[i].id != menu)
        DOMElementHide(DOMObjects[i]);

    keepOpen();

    DOMElementSetLeft(DOMObjects[menu],xOffset + x);
    DOMElementSetTop(DOMObjects[menu],yOffset + y);
    DOMElementShow(DOMObjects[menu]);
  }
}
```

Two further global variables are defined: timer, which is used to hold a reference to a timer created using the setTimeout() function, and closing, a Boolean indicating whether the menu is in the process of being closed:

```
var timer, closing = true;
```

The keepOpen() function is used to set the global closing variable to false and to cancel any running timer:

```
function keepOpen() {
  closing = false;
  clearTimeout(timer);
}
```

The closeMenu() function is used to set the global closing variable to true and to start a timer to invoke the closeMenuAll() function after a 500-millisecond delay:

```
function closeMenu() {
  closing = true;
  timer = setTimeout('closeMenuAll()',500);
}
```

The closeMenuAll() function closes all the menus, as long as the global closing variable is still set to true. Note that a check is made on the `id` property of each item in the `DOMObjects` array to ensure that the function does not inadvertently hide the `toolbar`:

```
function closeMenuAll() {
  if (window.DOMObjects && closing) {
    for (var i=0; i<DOMObjects.length; i++) {
      if (DOMObjects[i].id != 'toolbar')
        DOMElementHide(DOMObjects[i]);
    }
  }
}
```

# Automated Table of Contents

Have you ever written a long page with many levels of headings, and then had to manually build a table of contents at the start of the document? Well, this application demonstrates how to automate this process. It works similar to the way Microsoft Word inserts a table of contents in a Word document.

This application uses techniques introduced as part of the W3C DOM specification, supported by both Microsoft Internet Explorer 5 and Netscape Navigator 6. As such, this application does not work on earlier versions of these browsers.

The code walks through the nodes in the DOM representing the current page, extracts information about any heading element found, along with any nested anchor elements, and builds up the necessary HTML markup to create a nested list of text links to each of the headings in the document. Figure 11-7 shows a dynamically generated table of contents at the top of the document.

## Automated Table of Contents Source Code— *index.htm*

**chapter11/toc/index.htm**

Again, we include the *dom.js* library:

```
<script language="JavaScript" src="dom.js"></script>
```

**Figure 11-7**
Automated Table
of Contents—
dynamically
generated from
H1–H6 HTML
markup tags.

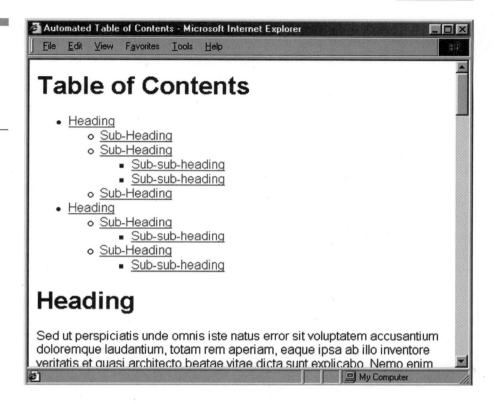

Three global variables are defined: anchor is used to hold the details of any nested anchor name, level holds the depth of current heading, and headings holds a list of heading elements that are suitable for the table of contents. Note the leading two spaces are required, as the position of the heading element is divided by 2 to get the depth of the heading:

```
var anchor, level = 0, headings = '  H1H2H3H4H5H6';
```

The retrieveToc() function, invoked from the start() function, is passed a node within the DOM "tree," where the function is to start searching for heading elements. The function recurses (i.e., repeatedly invokes itself) down through all the lower level branches of this "tree" (represented by nodes of nodeType 1 in the current node's childNodes array), looking for heading elements listed in the global headings property. When found, the function builds HTML markup output for the table of contents, made up of either text or hypertext links in nested unordered lists:

```
function retrieveToc(node) {
  var output = '';
```

The function loops through all the entries in the current node's `childNodes` array, passing each node to another instance of the `retrieveToc()` function, the output of which is appended to the local `output` variable:

```
for (var i=0; i<node.childNodes.length; i++)
  output += retrieveToc(node.childNodes[i]);
```

If the current node's `nodeType` property is equal to 1—that is, it is an element node as opposed to, say, a text node which has a value of 3, then the `nodeName` property of the node is examined to see if it is a suitable heading element:

```
if (node.nodeType == 1) {
```

The position of the `nodeName` value in the `headings` global string variable is divided by 2 and assigned to the `sublevel` variable. If the `nodeName` does not appear within the string, then the `sublevel` value will be set to 0:

```
var sublevel = headings.indexOf(node.nodeName) / 2;
```

If the value of `sublevel` is greater than zero, than a suitable heading element has been found. In this case, the `output` variable is appended with the necessary unordered list and list item HTML markup, and then the `retreiveText()` function invoked, passing the current node as input:

```
if (sublevel > 0) {
  if (sublevel > level)
    output += '<ul>\n';
  else
    output += '</li>\n';

  if (sublevel < level)
    output += '</ul>\n';
  level = sublevel;
  output += '<li>';
  anchor = null;
  var text = retrieveText(node);
```

The `retrieveText()` function, described later, extracts the text from the heading element, and extracts the name of any enclosed anchor element and assigns it to the global `anchor` variable. If the anchor vari-

able is not `null`, then the `output` variable is appended with a suitable
hypertext link to the heading. Otherwise, just the text of the heading is
appended:

```
if (anchor != null)
  output += '<a href="#' + anchor + '">' + text + '</a>';
else
  output += text;
  }
}
```

As the `retrieveToc()` function invokes itself for each element node it
encounters, the `output` returned by one instance of the `retrieveToc()`
function is appended to the `output` of the invoking function:

```
return output;
}
```

The `retrieveText()` function, passed the `node` representing the
found heading element, effectively retrieves all the text within the found
heading, no matter what HTML markup is contained within the heading.
At the same time, it identifies any anchor elements. The function iterates
through each of the nodes in the `node` node's `childNodes` array, looking
for anchor elements (`nodeType` of 1 and `nodeName` of A). When found, the
function invokes the `retireveAnchor()` function, passing the current
node as input, and looks for text nodes (`nodeType` of 3), appending the
value of the `nodeValue` property to the local `output` variable:

```
function retrieveText(node) {
  var output = '';

  for (var i=0; i<node.childNodes.length; i++)
    output += retrieveText(node.childNodes[i]);

  if (node.nodeType == 1 && node.nodeName == 'A')
    retrieveAnchor(node);

  if (node.nodeType == 3)
    output += node.nodeValue;

  return output;
}
```

The `retrieveAnchor()` function, passed the `node` representing the
found anchor element, loops through each of the entries in the `attrib-
utes` array, looking for a `nodeName` property equal to `name` (i.e., the
`name` attribute of the anchor) and then assigns the value of the
`nodeValue` to the global `anchor` variable:

```
function retrieveAnchor(node) {
  for (var i=0; i<node.attributes.length; i++) {
    if (node.attributes[i].nodeName == 'name') {
      anchor = node.attributes[i].nodeValue;
    }
  }
}
```

The start() function, invoked from the body element's onLoad event handler, tests for support of the document object's getElementById property. If supported, then the output from the retrieveToc() function, which is passed the document object's body node, is added to the necessary number of closing list items and unordered list tags, as many as the current depth level, before being used to update the contents of the toc element using the DOMElementSetInnerHTML() function:

```
function start() {
  if (document.getElementById) {
    var output = retrieveToc(document.body);

    for (var i=level; i>0; i--)
      output += '</li>\n</ul>\n';
    if (output != '')
      output = '<h1>Table of Contents</h1>' + output;

    var toc = document.getElementById('toc');
    DOMElementSetInnerHTML(toc, output);
  }
}
```

The div element, identified with the id attribute of toc, is used as an initial place holder. It is subsequently updated with the HTML markup generated by the application:

```
<div id="toc"></div>
```

The remainder of the page contains the normal page content, sprinkled with heading elements containing optional anchor elements:

```
<h1><a name="1">Heading</a></h1>
...
<h2><a name="1.1">Sub-Heading</a></h2>
...
<h2><a name="1.2">Sub-Heading</a></h2>
...
<h3><a name="1.2.1">Sub-sub-heading</a></h3>
...
<h3><a name="1.2.2">Sub-sub-heading</a></h3>
...
<h2><a name="1.3">Sub-Heading</a></h2>
...
```

```
<h1><a name="2">Heading</a></h1>
...
<h2><a name="2.2">Sub-Heading</a></h2>
...
<h3><a name="2.2.1">Sub-sub-heading</a></h3>
...
<h2><a name="2.3">Sub-Heading</a></h2>
...
<h3><a name="2.3.1">Sub-sub-heading</a></h3>
...
```

# Tab Slider

Imagine being able to build additional user interfaces that supplement the existing browser toolbars. This is exactly what this application does. Figure 11-8 shows three items of content attached to the side and top of the browser window. Only two of the three are actually open, but clicking

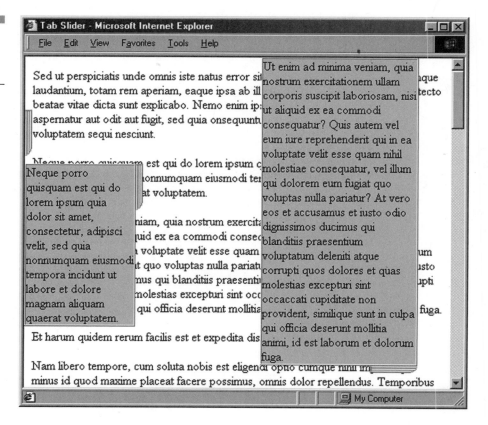

**Figure 11-8**
Tab Slider—showing extended horizontal and vertical sliders.

the tab on either of the three causes the content to gracefully slide out from or back into the edges of the page.

The example application presented here uses simple text as the content of the sliders, but it could easily have been more interesting content, such as a feedback form or a navigational toolbar.

## Tab Slider Source Code—*index.htm*

**chapter11/slide/index.htm**

The code within the *dom.js* library is loaded into the *index.htm* page:

```
<script language="JavaScript" src="dom.js"></script>
```

The three tab sliders used in this example are contained with separate div elements, each with an id, class, and style attribute. The id attribute enables easy identification of the div element, the class attribute of 1 causes the content to be initially invisible, and the style attribute positions the content using a positive top or left value, along with a corresponding negative left or top value. Those div elements with a positive top style value will be attached to the side of the document, and those with a positive left style value will be attached to the top of the document. Each div element contains a image text link of either a *bar-x.gif* or a *bar-y.gif* image, each with an onClick event handler that invokes the slide() function, passing an integer representing the div element's position within the DOMObjects array, as well as an indication of the direction that the slider should be moved (either in the x or y axis):

```
<div id="tab01" class="l" style="top: 70; left: -1;">
<table width="200" border="0" cellspacing="0" cellpadding="0">
<tr><td>
. . .
</td><td valign="top">
<a href="" onClick="return slide(0,'x')"><img src="bar-x.gif"></a>
</td></tr></table>
</div>

<div id="tab1" class="l" style="top: 140; left: -1;">
<table width="150" border="0" cellspacing="0" cellpadding="0">
<tr><td>
. . .
</td><td valign="top">
<a href="" onClick="return slide(1,'x')"><img src="bar-x.gif"></a>
</td></tr></table>
</div>
```

```
<div id="tab2" class="l" style="top: -1; left: 300;">
<table width="200" border="0" cellspacing="0" cellpadding="0">
<tr><td>
...
</td></tr>
<tr><td align="right">
<a href="" onClick="return slide(2,'y')"><img src="bar-y.gif"></a>
</td></tr></table>
</div>
```

The `start()` function, invoked from the `body` element's `onLoad` event
handler, initializes the application by first calling the `DOMInitialize()`
function in the *dom.js* library. Then the function loops through each of the
items in the `DOMObjects` array, retrieving the x an y offset values of the
item using the `DOMElementGetOffsetLeft()` and `DOMElementGet`
`OffsetTop()` functions, and the width and height using the `DOMElement`
`GetWidth()` and `DOMElementGetHeight()` functions. If the x or y offset
is less than zero, then they are amended to 9 minus the `width` or `height`
values, respectively, and the new values are used to update the properties
using the `DOMElementSetLeft()` and `DOMElementSetTop()` functions.
This ensures that no matter how wide or how long the content is, it always
sits 9 pixels proud of either the side or top of the document. Finally, the
`DOMElementShow()` function is invoked to reveal the content in its new
position, before creating a `Slider` object with the values of the `width` and
`height` values minus the 9 pixels for the tab image:

```
function start() {
  if (window.DOMObjects)
    DOMInitialize('div');

  if (window.DOMObjects) {
    for (var i=0; i<DOMObjects.length; i++) {
      var xOffset = DOMElementGetOffsetLeft(DOMObjects[i]);
      var yOffset = DOMElementGetOffsetTop(DOMObjects[i]);

      var width = DOMElementGetWidth(DOMObjects[i]);
      var height = DOMElementGetHeight(DOMObjects[i]);
      if (xOffset < 0) xOffset = 9 - width;
      if (yOffset < 0) yOffset = 9 - height;

      DOMElementSetLeft(DOMObjects[i], xOffset);
      DOMElementSetTop(DOMObjects[i], yOffset);
      DOMElementShow(DOMObjects[i]);

      sliders[i] = new Slider(width-9,height-9);
    }
  }
}
```

The `Slider()` object constructor creates a `Slider` object based on the
passed `width` and `height` parameters. This `Slider` object contains
additional properties to hold the state of each slider content:

```
function Slider(width,height) {
  this.inSlide = false;
  this.outSlide = false;
  this.timeout = null;
  this.width = width;
  this.height = height;
}
```

A global `sliders` array is defined to hold the `Slider` objects:

```
var sliders = new Array();
```

The `slide()` function, invoked when the tab image is clicked, controls the movement of the slider. The current values for the x and y offsets are first retrieved, and the `inSlide` and `outSlide` properties of the `Slider` object are set to `false`. If the passed `dir` parameter is set to the character string x, then the `slideX()` function is invoked and passed the n integer parameter. Otherwise, the `slideY()` function is invoked. If either of the x or y offsets are less than zero, then it is assumed that the user has clicked a partially hidden slider tab and requires the slider to slide inwards. Therefore, the `inSlide` property is set to `true`. Otherwise, the `outSlide` property is set to `true`:

```
function slide(n,dir) {
  if (window.DOMObjects) {
    var xOffset = DOMElementGetOffsetLeft(DOMObjects[n]);
    var yOffset = DOMElementGetOffsetTop(DOMObjects[n]);

    sliders[n].inSlide = false;
    sliders[n].outSlide = false;

    if (dir == 'x') {
      if (xOffset < 0)
        sliders[n].inSlide = true;
      else
        sliders[n].outSlide = true;
      slideX(n);

    }
    else {
      if(yOffset < 0)
        sliders[n].inSlide = true;
      else
        sliders[n].outSlide = true;
      slideY(n)
    }
  }

  return false;
}
```

The slideX() function, invoked from the slide() function, accepts the passed n integer parameter and uses it to retrieve the x offset of the relevant item in the DOMObject array, using the DOMElementGet OffsetLeft() function. The remainder of the function then manipulates the value of the xOffset variable to move the content in small steps either inward or outward, depending on the values of the inSlide and outSlide properties. The function also starts a timer to invoke the slideX() function after a short delay, repeatedly until the slider has reached its fully extended or hidden state. This causes the content to slide smoothly across the page in front of the user. Finally, the DOMElementSetLeft() function is used to reposition the content based on the new value of the xOffset variable:

```
function slideX(n) {
  var xOffset = DOMElementGetOffsetLeft(DOMObjects[n]);

  if (sliders[n].inSlide && xOffset < 0) {
    xOffset += sliders[n].width/10;
    if (xOffset > 0) xOffset = 0;
    sliders[n].timeout = setTimeout('slideX("'+n+'")',5);
  }
  else if (sliders[n].outSlide && xOffset > -sliders[n].width) {
    xOffset -= sliders[n].width/10;
    if (xOffset < -sliders[n].width)
      xOffset = -sliders[n].width;
    sliders[n].timeout = setTimeout('slideX("'+n+'")',5);
  }

  DOMElementSetLeft(DOMObjects[n], xOffset);
}
```

The slideY() function performs a similar role to the slideX() function, except that it works in the *y* axis:

```
function slideY(n) {
  var yOffset = DOMElementGetOffsetTop(DOMObjects[n]);

  if (sliders[n].inSlide && yOffset < 0) {
    yOffset += sliders[n].height/10;
    if (yOffset > 0) yOffset = 0;
    sliders[n].timeout = setTimeout('slideY("'+n+'")',5);
  }
  else if (sliders[n].outSlide && yOffset > -sliders[n].height) {
    yOffset -= sliders[n].height/10;
    if (yOffset < -sliders[n].height)
      yOffset = -sliders[n].height;
    sliders[n].timeout = setTimeout('slideY("'+n+'")',5);
  }

  DOMElementSetTop(DOMObjects[n], yOffset);
}
```

**Figure 11-9**
Menu System—
a dynamic menu
with both the Home
menu and Document
submenu opened.

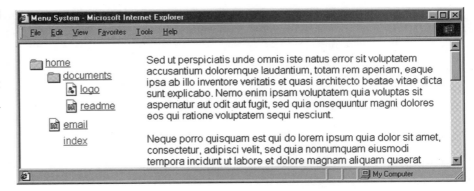

# Menu System

The "Menu System" application presented here is not unlike the "Dynamic Table of Contents" shown earlier in this chapter. The major difference is that the contents of the menu are built up from JavaScript objects as opposed to parsing the contents of the document, and the menu is interactive—that is, the menu system can be used to open and close leaves of the menu. Figure 11-9 shows a typical menu that can be generated by this application. The initially closed "document" submenu has been subsequently opened by the user.

## Menu System Source Code—*menu.js*

The "Menu System" application uses an external *menu.js* library to hold all the application-specific code. It contains object constructors for Menu and File objects, an add() method to add File and Menu objects to other Menu objects, a show() function to recurse down through all the menus, submenus, and menu entries in a menu system to build up the HTML markup necessary to display the current state of the system, and an openMenu() function to toggle the open status of a particular menu before requesting that the entire menu system be rebuilt and redisplayed.

**chapter11/menu/menu.js**

The `File` object constructor accepts three parameters: `href`, the `href` attribute of the generated image and text link; the `name` to appear in the hypertext link; and the `type` of menu entry. There are several types available, each with its own image supplied as part of the "Menu System" application: `binary`, `image`, `index`, `movie`, `sound`, `telnet`, `text`, and `unknown`. The `File` constructor creates a maximum of two object properties—an imageLink property if a non-null `type` has been passed and a `textLink` property:

```
function File(href,name,type) {
  if (type != null) {
    var image = '<img src="' + type + '.gif">';
    this.imageLink = '<a href="' + href + '">' + image + '</a>';
  }
  else
    this.imageLink = ' ';

  this.textLink = '<a href="' + href + '">' + name + '</a>';
}
```

The `add()` function, used as a method of the `Menu` object, is used to add an object reference to a `Menu` object's `Contents` array:

```
function add(obj) {
  this.Contents[this.index++] = obj;
}
```

The `Menu` object constructor accepts three parameters: `ref`, which is a text string identical to the textual representation of the objects reference that is used so that the object can reference itself, the `name` to appear in the hypertext link, and the `open` status, either `true` or `false`. The constructor creates the two `textLink` and `imageLink` properties, as with the `File` constructor, but it also defines several other properties: `ref` and `open`, which are assigned the like-named parameter values, an `add` method assigned the reference of the `add()` function, an `index` property of zero, and an empty `Object` object, used to allow submenu and menu entries to be added to `Menu` objects using the `add()` method. Note that the `href` attribute of the text and images links is a JavaScript call to the `openMenu()` function, passing a string `ref` value:

```
function Menu(ref,name,open) {
  var href = 'javascript:openMenu(' + ref + ')';
  var image = '<img src="menu.gif">';

  this.textLink = '<a href="' + href + '">' + name + '</a>';
  this.imageLink = '<a href="' + href + '">' + image + '</a>';

  this.ref   = ref;
```

```
      this.open = open;
      this.add = add;
      this.index = 0;
      this.Contents = new Object();
}
```

The show() function, invoked whenever the HTML markup for the menu system needs to be rebuilt, recurses down through all the open menus, creating nested tables for each menu and subsequent submenu, along with table rows for each menu item. It uses the imageLink and textLink properties of the passed obj object as the content of the table cells. If a submenu is found with an open property set to true, then the show() method is invoked on each entry within its Contents array in turn and its return value is appended to the output variable:

```
function show(obj) {
  var output =
    '<table><tr><td valign="top" width="20">' + obj.imageLink +
    '</td><td class="menulink">' + obj.textLink;
  if (obj.open)
  for (var i=0; i<obj.index; i++)
    output += show(obj.Contents[i]);

  return output + '</td></tr></table>';
}
```

The openMenu() function, invoked by the hypertext links for menus and submenus, toggles the value of the passed obj object's open property, before invoking the updateMenu() function defined in the *index.htm* page in the next section. This causes the menu system to be rebuilt and redisplayed on the page with the new open property value of the clicked menu:

```
function openMenu(obj) {
  obj.open = !obj.open;
  updateMenu();
}
```

## Menu System Source Code—*index.htm*

**chapter11/menu/index.htm**

To use the "Menu System" application within a page, both the *dom.js* and *menu.js* libraries must be loaded:

```
<script language="JavaScript" src="dom.js"></script>
<script language="JavaScript" src="menu.js"></script>
```

A menulink class is used to define the style of the links that appear in the menu:

```
.menulink { font-family: Arial; }
```

The updateMenu(), invoked from the start() function described a little later in this section, and from the menu system's openMenu() function, invokes the show() function, passing as input the rootMenu reference. It then uses the returned value of this function as input to the DOMElementSetInnerHTML() to update the contents of the menu object:

```
function updateMenu() {
  DOMElementSetInnerHTML(DOMObjects['menu'], show(rootMenu));
}
```

If the *menu.js* library has loaded successfully—that is, the window object has a Menu property—then the Menu() and File() object constructors contained in the *menu.js* library are used to build menus (rootMenu and docMenu), and then menu entries. The docMenu is subsequently made a submenu of the rootMenu by using its add() method. The menu entries are assigned to the required Menu objects by also using the add() method:

```
if (window.Menu) {
  rootMenu = new Menu('rootMenu','home',true);

  docMenu = new Menu('docMenu','documents',false);

  docMenu.add(new File('logo.gif','logo','image'));

  docMenu.add(new File('readme.txt','readme','text'));

  rootMenu.add(docMenu);
  rootMenu.add(new File('mailto:xxx@yyy.zzz','email','text'));
  rootMenu.add(new File('index.htm','index'));
}
```

***NOTE***.  *To use a different menu on a different page, simply adjust the preceding JavaScript code to generate the required menus and menu items.*

The start() function, invoked from the body element's onLoad event handler, initializes the application by invoking the DOMInitialize()

function, and then by invoking the `updateMenu()` function, but only if the two external libraries have successfully loaded:

```
function start() {
  if (window.DOMObjects)
    DOMInitialize('div');

  if (window.Menu && window.DOMObjects)
    updateMenu();
}
```

The `div` element that holds the output of the menu system is identified with the `id` attribute of `menu` and is held in one cell of a table that is wide enough to hold the deepest submenu:

```
<table><tr><td valign="top" width="180">
<div id="menu" align="left"></div>
</td><td valign="top">
...
</td></tr></table>
```

# Dynamic Adverts

Banner advertising generally uses animated GIF images in an attempt to get a message across to the visitor. The application presented here makes use of Dynamic HTML to provide a more interactive experience for the user. When the mouse moves over what appears to be a typical banner advert, shown in Figure 11-10, another area is immediately revealed beneath the banner advert in a seamless connection, as shown in Figure 11-11.

**Figure 11-10**
Dynamic Adverts—
the banner advert in
its initial state.

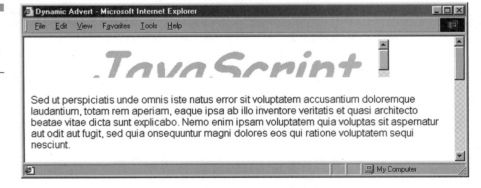

**Figure 11-11**
Dynamic Adverts—
opened up by the
mouse moving
across the banner
advert.

## Dynamic Adverts Source Code—*index.htm*

**chapter11/advert/index.htm**

First, the *dom.js* library is loaded into the *index.htm* page:

```
<script language="JavaScript" src="dom.js"></script>
```

The initial banner advert is contained within a span element, with an id attribute set to advert, a class attribute set to v, and a style attribute with initial top and left values. The image link includes onMouseOver and onMouseOut event handlers to invoke the openAdvert() and closeAdvert() functions:

```
<span id="advert" class="v" style="top: 5; left: 100;">
<table><tr><td>
<a href="..." onMouseOver="openAdvert()" onMouseOut="closeAdvert()">
<img src="advert1.gif"></a>
</td></tr></table></span>
```

The dynamic portion of the banner advert is also contained in a span element, but with an id attribute set to dynamic and a class attribute set to 1. The span element contains a layer element that contains a table element, both of which include onMouseOver and onMouseOut event handlers to invoke the keepOpen() and closeAdvert() functions. The layer element is required for Netscape Navigator 4, which does not support event handlers in the table element; the table element is required for Internet Explorer and Netscape Navigator 6, which do not support the layer element:

```
<span id="dynamic" class="l" style="top: 65; left: 100;">
<layer onMouseOver="keepOpen()" onMouseOut="closeAdvert()">
<table onMouseOver="keepOpen()" onMouseOut="closeAdvert()">
<tr><td>
...
</td></tr></table></layer></span>
```

Two global variables are defined: `timer`, which holds a reference to a timer set within the `closeAdvert()` function to close the dynamic advert after 500 milliseconds, and the Boolean `closing` variable used to indicate that the dynamic advert is closing:

```
var timer, closing = true;
```

The `start()` function, invoked from the `body` element's `onLoad` event handler, initializes the application by invoking the `DOMinitialize()` function and then proceeds to reposition both the advert and dynamic span elements so that they are centered across the viewable portion of the page. The code makes use of the `DOMWindowGetInnerWidth()` function in the *dom.js* library to retrieve the inner width of the window and the `DOMElementGetWidth()` function to retrieve the width of the advert. The `DOMElementSetLeft()` function is then used to reposition both of the span elements:

```
function start() {
  if (window.DOMObjects)
    DOMInitialize('span');

  if (window.DOMObjects) {
    var innerWidth = DOMWindowGetInnerWidth();
    var width = DOMElementGetWidth(DOMObjects['advert']);
    var x = (innerWidth - width) / 2;

    DOMElementSetLeft(DOMObjects['advert'], x);
    DOMElementSetLeft(DOMObjects['dynamic'], x);
  }
}
```

The `closeAdvert()` function, invoked by the `onMouseOut` event handlers, sets the global `closing` Boolean variable to `true` and then creates and assigns a timer to the global `timer` variable to invoke the `closeDynamic()` function after a 500-millisecond delay:

```
function closeAdvert() {
  closing = true;
  timer = setTimeout('closeDynamic()',500);
}
```

The keepOpen() function, invoked by the onMouseOver event handlers in the dynamic advert, sets the global closing variable to false and cancels the timer:

```
function keepOpen() {
  closing = false;
  clearTimeout(timer);
}
```

The closeDynamic() function, invoked after a 500-millisecond delay, uses the DOMElementHide() function to hide the dynamic advert, as long as the global closing variable is still set to true:

```
function closeDynamic() {
  if (window.DOMObjects && closing) {
    DOMElementHide(DOMObjects['dynamic']);
  }
}
```

The openAdvert() function, invoked from the static advert's onMouseOver event handler, invokes the keepOpen() function to cancel any existing timer that may be running and then uses the DOMElementShow() function to reveal the dynamic advert:

```
function openAdvert() {
  if (window.DOMObjects) {
    keepOpen();
    DOMElementShow(DOMObjects['dynamic']);
  }
}
```

## Summary

Although DHTML applications can be somewhat complicated and sophisticated at first, once a DOM interface library has been written and mastered, the creation of applications is simply a matter of joining the various DOM functions together to build the functionality required.

DOM implementation (and therefore the expected behavior on the client side) can vary across browsers. By using the features that are common to the browsers, such idiosyncrasies can be somewhat avoided.

This chapter has only skimmed the surface of the capabilities of the W3C DOM. For more information, refer to the online W3C DOM documentation for more information at http://www.w3.org/DOM/.

# Applications

This chapter shows how larger applications can be created based on the many libraries of reusable JavaScript code that we have built in previous chapters. The fully fledged applications within this chapter show how to store persistent data on the client browser to represent an online shopping basket, drag and drop items around the page onto a shopping cart, turn a Web page into a component so as to allow the user to reconfigure the web page based on their own preferences, and build a database of related product parts that allow a customer to select and configure one of several base products.

The final application presented in this chapter takes a break from the norm. It uses JavaScript within an XML document, something that is now possible with Internet Explorer 5 and Netscape Navigator 6, to show how JavaScript can be used to work with a document object model that isn't composed of the HTML elements that we typically deal with.

This chapter also uses the `for/in` statement, for example: `for (var propertyName in objectName)`. This type of `for` loop does not loop through the length of the object, but instead it loops through all the properties of the object.

**Shopping Basket ../chapter12/basket/index.htm**
**Drag 'n Drop Shopping Cart ../chapter12/dragdrop/index.htm**
**myPage.com ../chapter12/mypage/index.htm**
**Online Computer Builder ../chapter12/builder/index.htm**
**Book Catalog—XML the DOM and style sheets ../chapter12/catalog/catalog.xml**

# Shopping Basket

Shopping on the Internet, one facet of B2C (business to customer) has rapidly expanded over the last few years. Amazon.com is a prime example, in which people can order books, CDs, software, and so on and have them delivered to their doorstep. While the customer is selecting purchases on the online website, their choices are placed in a virtual shopping basket or cart, reminiscent of the shopping cart used in supermarkets.

We have previously seen in Chapter 10 "Cookies" how cookies can store information on the client computer. This application uses cookies to store persistent data on the client browser. If the user comes back within the 14-day expiry period used in the application, then the data will still be held in the shopping basket.

Figure 12-1 shows the "checkout" page used in this application. The first page allows the user to add and remove items from the shopping basket, and the "checkout" page allows the user to confirm the items and optionally add or remove further products before submitting his or her order.

**Figure 12-1**
Shopping Basket—
The "checkout" page.

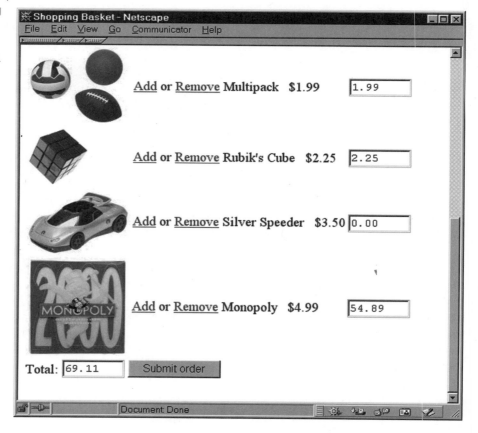

# Shopping Basket—*shopping.js*

 — — — — — — — — — — — — — — — — — —

**chapter12/shopping/shopping.js**

The *shopping.js* library uses the *cookie.js* library to hold all the items in the shopping basket in a cookie. Cookies are covered in detail in Chapter 10. A global `expiryDate` variable is initialized to 14 days from the current date:

```
var today = new Date();
var expiryDate = new Date(today.getTime() + (2 * Cookie.week));
```

A `totamt` local variable is declared. This is used to hold the total price of all the products currently held in the shopping basket:

```
var totamt;
```

A global Boolean `basket` variable is declared and initialized to `false`. This is used to indicate whether the *shopping.js* library is being used to capture or display the shopping basket contents:

```
var basket = false;
```

To hold the individual items for sale, we create a `product` object constructor. The `product()` function accepts six parameters, each of which become a property of the new `product` object: an identification number (`pid`), a product name, a URL of an image (`img`), the width and height of the image (`w` and `h`), and a product `price`. The constructor initializes an additional `quantity` property and declares two methods— `add()` and `remove()`, which are later defined by the `add()` and `remove()` functions:

```
function product(pid,name,img,w,h,price) {
    this.pid        = pid;
    this.name       = name;
    this.img        = img;
    this.w          = w;
    this.h          = h;
    this.price      = price;
    this.quantity   = 0;
    this.add        = add;
    this.remove     = remove;
}
```

Then we create a `catalog` array to hold all the `product` objects created by the `product` constructor:

```
catalog = new Array(
new product (0,'Furby',        'furby.gif',      132, 150,25.99),
new product (1,'Helicopter',   'helicopter.gif',150, 141, 3.99),
...
)
```

The `product` object's `add()` method increments the `product` object's `quantity` property and invokes the `saveBasket()` function. The `remove()` method, decrements the `quantity` property and invokes the `saveBasket()` function:

```
function add() {
  this.quantity++;
  if (window.Cookie) saveBasket();
}

function remove() {
  this.quantity--;
  if (this.quantity < 0) this.quantity = 0;
  if (window.Cookie) saveBasket();
}
```

The `getPage()` function builds and returns HTML markup to display the shopping basket and all the `product` objects in the `catalog` array. The function first initializes the value of the global `totamt` variable, and then updates the local `output` variable with the start of the HTML markup by first adding a `form` element, named `basket`, to invoke a server-side CGI *billing.cgi* process.

As this book is about JavaScript, the actual implementation of *billing.cgi* is outside the scope of this book; therefore, the `onSubmit` event handler captures and cancels the form submission by returning `false`:

```
function getPage(basket) {
  totamt = 0;

  var output =
    '<form name="basket" action="billing.cgi"' +
    ' onSubmit="alert(\'We should send the form to billing\');'+
    'return false">';
```

The function then loops through all the `product` objects in the `catalog` array, building up the HTML markup necessary to display both image and text links to be able to add or remove products, one at a time, to and from the shopping cart. The `onClick` event handler of each link invokes either the `add()` or `remove()` method on the appropriate `product` in the `catalog` array, and then invokes the `setAmt()` function to update the `totamt` global variable. The `onMouseOver` and `onMouseOut` event handlers invoke the `show()` function to update the window's `status` text.

```javascript
for (var i = 0; i < catalog.length; i++) {
  var link1 =
    '<a href="javascript:;"' +
    ' onClick="catalog['+i+'].add();setAmt('+i+');' +
    'return false"' +
    ' onMouseOver="return ' +
    'show(\'Add \'+catalog['+i+'].name)"' +
    ' onMouseOut="return show(\'\')">';

  var link2 =
    '<a href="javascript:;"' +
    ' onClick="catalog['+i+'].remove();setAmt('+i+');' +
    'return false"' +
    ' onMouseOver="return ' +
    'show(\'Remove \'+catalog['+i+'].name)"' +
    ' onMouseOut="return show(\'\')">';

  output +=
    link1 + '<img src="' + catalog[i].img +
    '" name="img' + i +
    '" width="'  + catalog[i].w +
    '" height="' + catalog[i].h +
    '" border=0"></a>' +
    link1 +'Add</a> or ' +
    link2 + 'Remove</a> ' + catalog[i].name +
    '$' + cents(catalog[i].price);
```

The function then calculates the amount for each item and adds it to the `totamt` variable:

```javascript
var amt = catalog[i].quantity * catalog[i].price;
totamt += amt;
```

Only if an item appears in the shopping basket is it then subsequently shown on the checkout page:

```javascript
if (!basket || (basket && catalog[i].quantity > 0)) {
```

If the page that requests the script is the actual "checkout" `basket`, then the function also includes a subtotals form field for each `product` in the `catalog` array to display the value of the local `amt` variable after being passed to the `cents()` function. The name of the form field includes a `pid` string prefix followed by the object's `pid` property value:

```
      if (basket) {
       output +=
          '<input type="text" size="8"' +
          ' name="pid' + catalog[i].pid + '"' +
          ' value="' + cents(amt) + '">';
       }
     }
   }
```

The function includes a `totamt` form field to display the value of the global `totamt` variable after being passed to the `cents()` function:

```
  output +=
    'Total: <input type="text" size="8"' +
    ' name="totamt" value="' + cents(totamt) + '">';
```

If the `basket` variable is set to `true`, then a Submit form button is included. This would normally cause the form data to be sent to the server-side *basket.cgi* process:

```
  if (basket)
    output += '<input type="submit" value="Submit order">';

  output += '</form>'
  return output;
}
```

The `setAmt()` function, invoked by the `onClick` event handlers in the image and text links generated by the `getPage()` function, first confirms that the `basket` form contains a text form field for the `product` object, identified by the passed `idx` parameter, and if not, it exits using the `return` statement. The function then updates the `value` property of the relevant form field in the `basket` form with the value of the `price` property of the identified `product`, multiplied by the value of the `quantity` property. The function then invokes the `setTotAmt()` function:

```
function setAmt(idx) {
  if (!document.basket['pid'+idx]) return
  document.basket['pid'+idx].value=
    cents(catalog[idx].quantity * catalog[idx].price);
  setTotAmt()
}
```

The `setToAmt()` function, invoked from several places in the code, first confirms that the `basket` form contains a `totamt` text form field, then reinitializes the global `totamt` variable, and loops through each of the `product` objects in the `catalog` array, updating the `totamt` variable with the sum of the `price` properties multiplied by the `quantity`

properties, before finally updating the value of the relevant form field
with the output of the cents() function:

```
function setTotAmt() {
  if (!document.basket.totamt) return
  totamt = 0;
  for (var i = 0; i < catalog.length; i++) {
     totamt += catalog[i].quantity * catalog[i].price;
  }
  document.basket.totamt.value=cents(totamt);
}
```

The show() function, invoked by the onMouseOver event handlers,
updates the window object's status property:

```
function show(msg) {
   status=msg;
   return true;
}
```

The cents() and round() functions, not shown here but included on
the CD-ROM, are used in conjunction with one another to format and
return the passed input value to two decimal places suitable for displaying monetary amounts.

The saveBasket() function, invoked whenever an item is added or
removed from the shopping basket, first tests that cookies are enabled
using the isCookieEnabled() function. If the return result is false,
then the functions immediately exits. If cookies are enabled, then the
function proceeds to build a local saved string variable of *name=value*
pairs separated by the bar character (|), where the *name* represents the
pid property of the product object, and the *value* the quantity property, for each product in the catalog array that has a nonzero quantity property. The setCookie() function is then used to store the cat
cookie, and the setToAmt() function is invoked to update the totamt
variable:

```
function saveBasket() {
  if (!isCookieEnabled()) return;

  totamt = 0;
  var saved = '';
  for (var i = 0; i < catalog.length; i++)
    if (catalog[i].quantity > 0)
      saved += '|' + catalog[i].pid+'='+catalog[i].quantity;
  if (saved.length > 0)
    setCookie('cat',saved.substring(1),expiryDate);

  setTotAmt();
}
```

The getBasket() function is used to retrieve the details of items in the cookie. The String object's split() method is used to first split the string at each bar character (|) into the various *name=value* pairs and to hold the results in a catArray array. Then, while looping through all the entries in this entry, the split() method is used again to split the *name=value* pairs at the equal character (=) and to hold the results in a catItem array. The quantity property of the product object within the catalog array identified by the *name* is updated with the *value* of the *name=value* pair:

```
function getBasket() {
  var saved = getCookie('cat');
  if (!saved) return;

  var catArray = saved.split('|');
  for (var i = 0; i < catArray.length; i++) {
    var catItem = catArray[i].split('=');
    catalog[catItem[0]].quantity = catItem[1];
  }
}
```

## Shopping Basket—*cookie.js*

**chapter12/shopping/cookie.js**

The *cookie.js* library includes an additional function not yet seen. The isCookieEnabled() function is used to test that the browser and user allow cookies to be stored before attempting to store any further cookies. The isCookieEnabled() function makes use of the navigator object's cookieEnabled property supported in Internet Explorer. If the document object supports the all property (in other words, the browser being used is Internet Explorer), then the value of the cookieEnabled property is returned. For browsers that don't support the cookieEnabled property, a test cookie is stored and retrieved, and its value is compared with the current time. A new navigator object property (cookieEnabled) is then generated with the results of this test, along with another property (tested), which is set to true to indicate that this test does not need to be performed again:

```
function isCookieEnabled() {
  if (document.all || navigator.tested)
    return navigator.cookieEnabled;
  setCookie('testcookie',today.getTime());
  navigator.tested = true;
  navigator.cookieEnabled =
```

```
    (getCookie('testcookie') == today.getTime());
  return navigator.cookieEnabled;
}
```

## Shopping Basket—*index.htm*

**chapter12/shopping/index.htm**

The *index.htm* page allows the customer to add or remove items to the shopping basket. Once completed, the customer can proceed to the *basket.htm* page to confirm the purchases and add or remove items from the basket.

The *cookie.js* and *shopping.js* libraries are loaded into the *index.htm* page:

```
<script language="JavaScript" src="cookie.js"></script>
<script language="JavaScript" src="shopping.js"></script>
```

Then any existing cookie data is retrieved using the getBasket() function, and the body of the page is produced by writing the return value of the getPage() function to the document:

```
if (window.getBasket && window.Cookie) {
  getBasket();
  document.write(getPage());
}
```

A "checkout" image link is used to allow the customer to proceed to the "checkout" *basket.htm* page:

```
<a href="basket.htm"><img src="cart.gif">Check out</a>
```

## Shopping Basket—*basket.htm*

**chapter12/shopping/basket.htm**

The *basket.htm* page retrieves the details of the items added to the shopping cart in the *index.htm* page and displays the results so that the customer can confirm the order, or add or remove further items.

Again, the *cookie.js* and *shopping.js* libraries are loaded:

```
<script language="JavaScript" src="cookie.js"></script>
<script language="JavaScript" src="shopping.js"></script>
```

The items added to the shopping basket are retrieved using the getBasket() function, and the total price is initialized (totamt). The basket variable is set to true to indicate to the getPage() function that it is being used within the *basket.htm* page, and that the subtotal details of the items in the shopping basket and a Submit form button should be included in the output:

```
if (window.getBasket && window.Cookie) {
  getBasket();
  var totamt = 0;
  var basket = true;
  document.write(getPage());
}
```

 **NOTE:** *For information on how to process form data using CGI, I recommend* CGI Programming with Perl *by Scott Guelich, Shishir Gundavaram and Gunther Biranieks* (ISBN 1-56592-419-3, published by O'Reilly & Associates, 2000).

# Drag 'n Drop Shopping Cart

The application presented here takes this idea of a shopping cart a stage further by allowing the customer to click the mouse pointer on an image of the product and then drag and drop it into a visual shopping cart. The shopping cart then expands to show a smaller version of the product image. Once the product is in the cart, the customer can remove the product by again dragging and dropping the image outside of the cart. A form select list is also included in this application to allow the customer an alternative means of removing items from the cart. This application does not use cookies to hold persistent data; instead, the data is passed from one page to another using data held in the form submission.

Figure 12-2 shows a typical session in progress, with the customer having already dropped products into the shopping cart.

# Drag 'n Drop—*index.htm*

**chapter12/dragdrop/index.htm**

The *dom.js* library, discussed in Chapter 11, is reused with this application:

```
<script language="JavaScript" src="dom.js"></script>
```

Several global variables are defined and initialized: `code` and `anti` are used to hold the product code of the item currently being dragged into or out of the shopping cart. The `fRef` variable is used to hold a simple reference to the form used in this application. The `id` variable is hard-coded to `cart`, the identity of the shopping cart. The `dndPrefix` and `dndAnti` variables hold the string prefixes attached to the items that can be dragged into or back out of the shopping cart:

```
var code = anti = null;
var fRef;
var id = 'cart';
var dndPrefix = 'DND-';
var dndAnti = 'dnd-';
```

Two arrays are defined: `catalog` is a list of all the products that are displayed on the page, and `products` is a list of all the products currently in the shopping cart:

```
var catalog = new Array();
var products = new Array();
```

The `catalog` array holds instances of the `product` objects, each built using the following `product()` constructor. A property is defined for each of the passed parameters, plus two additional `miniWidth` and `miniHeight` properties, which are set to a third of the passed `width` and `height` parameters:

```
function product(code, name, src, width, height) {
   this.code = code;
   this.name = name;
   this.src = src;
   this.width = width;
   this.height = height;
   this.miniWidth = Math.floor(width/3);
   this.miniHeight = Math.floor(height/3);
}
```

The addProduct() function is used to assign the product object created by the product() constructor to the catalog array, using the value of the code parameter. In other words, instead of a simple array of indexed objects, we create an array of named objects, accessible via their name in the array. In Perl and other languages, this is described as a *hash table:*

```
function addProduct(code, name, src, width, height) {
  catalog[code] = new product(code, name, src, width, height);
}
```

Six products are then created using the addProduct() function:

```
addProduct('fby', 'Furby',       'furby.gif',      132, 150);
addProduct('hlc', 'Helicopter',  'helicopter.gif', 150, 141);
...
```

In Netscape Navigator 4 we need to capture *all* the mouse down or mouse up events and to invoke a corresponding down() or up() function. The code to do this is wrapped up within a test for the document object's layers property, only supported in Netscape Navigator 4. For other browsers we can simply use event handlers in the body element:

```
if (document.layers) {
  window.captureEvents(Event.MOUSEDOWN | Event.MOUSEUP);
  window.onmousedown=down, window.onmouseup=up;
}
```

The down() function, invoked whenever the user clicks the mouse button, is used to capture the name (if available) of the object that the mouse pointer was clicked on. The DOMEventGetName() function in the *dom.js* library does this. If the returned name contains the dndPrefix string at position zero, then the object is suitable for dragging and therefore the global code variable is set to the value of name minus the leading dndPrefix string. Otherwise, if the name contains the dndAnti prefix, then the object is suitable for dragging out of the shopping cart, and therefore, the global anti variable is set instead. In either case, the function returns a false value to cancel the effect of the mouse down event:

```
function down(e) {
  if (window.DOMObjects) {
    var name = DOMEventGetName(e);

    if (name && name.indexOf(dndPrefix) == 0) {
      code = name.substring(dndPrefix.length);
      return false;
    }

    if (name && name.indexOf(dndAnti) == 0) {
```

```
            anti = name.substring(dndAnti.length);
            return false;
        }
    }
}
```

The up() function, invoked when the user subsequently releases the mouse button, attempts to identify the x and y coordinates of the mouse pointer in relation to the shopping cart. If the global code variable has been set and the mouse pointer is within the boundaries of the shopping cart, then the product is added to the cart. However, if the global anti variable is set and the mouse pointer is outside the boundaries of the shopping cart, then the product is removed from the cart; otherwise, the drag-and-drop process is ignored. Several functions in the *dom.js* library are used to find the position of the mouse pointer using the e event passed into the function, and the top left and bottom right x and y coordinates of the shopping cart (id) object.

When adding a product to the cart, the addOption() function is invoked, passing a reference to the form, name of the select list (cart), name property of the cataloged product, and the product code. The refresh() function is then invoked to update the contents of the shopping cart.

When removing a product from the cart, the select() function is invoked, passing the product anti code. In addition, the deleteOptions() function is invoked, passing a from reference, select list name, and a false value, and then the refresh() function is invoked.

The final job of the up() function is to reset both the code and anti global variables to null:

```
function up(e) {
  if (window.DOMObjects) {
    var x = DOMEventGetClientX(e);
    var y = DOMEventGetClientY(e);

    var x1 = DOMElementGetOffsetLeft(DOMObjects≡);
    var y1 = DOMElementGetOffsetTop(DOMObjects≡);

    var x2 = x1 + DOMElementGetWidth(DOMObjects≡);
    var y2 = y1 + DOMElementGetHeight(DOMObjects≡);

    if (x>=x1 && x<=x2 && y>=y1 && y<=y2) {
      if (code && !products[code]) {
        addOption(fRef, 'cart', catalog[code].name, code);
        refresh();
      }
    }
    else if (anti) {
      select(anti);
```

```
      deleteOptions(fRef, 'cart', false);
      refresh();
    }
    code = anti = null;
  }
}
```

The addOption(), deleteOptions(), and deleteOption() functions
from the Dynamic Drop-Down Menus application in Chapter 8 are
included within this application. Their purpose is to add and remove
selected options to and from a form select list. However, the functions have
been adapted to additionally populate the products array in the
addOption() function, and to set the relevant entry in the products
array to null in the deleteOptions() and deleteOption() functions:

```
function addOption(fRef, sName, sText, sValue) {
  var def = false;
  var sel = false;
  var optionName = new Option(sText, sValue, def, sel);
  var length = fRef[sName].length;
  fRef[sName].options[length] = optionName;
  fRef[sName].options[length].selected = false;
  products[sValue] = sValue;
}

function deleteOptions(fRef, sName, force) {
  var length = fRef[sName].options.length;
  for (var i=0; i<fRef[sName].options.length; i++) {
    if (fRef[sName].options[i].selected || force) {
      if (products[fRef[sName].options[i].value])
        products[fRef[sName].options[i].value] = null;
      fRef[sName].options[i] = null;
      length--;
      i--;
    }
  }
}

function deleteOption(fRef, sName) {
  var i = fRef[sName].selectedIndex;
  if (products[fRef[sName].options[i].value])
    products[fRef[sName].options[i].value] = null;
  fRef[sName].options[i] = null;
}
```

The highlight() function ensures that all bar the first option in
the cart select list are selected, by setting the selected property to
true:

```
function highlight() {
  for (var i=1; i<fRef.cart.length; i++)
    fRef.cart[i].selected = true;
}
```

The `select()` function ensures that only the option in the `cart` select list that matches the passed `sValue` is selected, by setting the `selected` property to the Boolean result of the comparison of the `code` property of the cataloged product represented by the current `select` option with the value of the `sValue` parameter:

```
function select(sValue) {
  for (var i=1; i<fRef.cart.length; i++)
    fRef.cart[i].selected =
      (catalog[fRef.cart[i].value].code == sValue);
}
```

The `remove()` function first sets the `selected` property of the first option in the `cart` select list to `false`, before invoking the `deleteOptions()` function to remove the products represented by the remaining selected `select` options from the shopping cart. It then invokes the `refresh()` function to update the visible display of the shopping cart:

```
function remove() {
  fRef['cart'].options[0].selected = false;
  deleteOptions(fRef, 'cart', false);
  refresh();
}
```

The `wipe()` function is used to remove all products from the shopping cart. It invokes the `highlight()` function to select all bar the first option in the select list, and then invokes the `remove()` function, which removes all the selected products:

```
function wipe() {
  highlight();
  remove();
}
```

The `refresh()` function, invoked whenever a product has been added or removed from the shopping cart, loops through all the entries in the `products` array, building up the HTML markup and using the `DOMElementSetInnerHTML()` function in the *dom.js* library to update the `id` shopping cart:

```
function refresh() {
  var output = '';

  for (var i in products)
    if (products[i] != null)
      output += '<img src="' + catalog[products[i]].src +
        '" name="' + dndAnti + catalog[products[i]].code +
        '" width="' + catalog[products[i]].miniWidth +
        '" height="' + catalog[products[i]].miniHeight + '">';
```

```
if (output != '') output =
  '</td><td><table><tr><td>' + output + '</td></tr></table>';

var html = '<table><tr><td><img src="cart.gif">' +
  output + '</td></tr></table>';

DOMElementSetInnerHTML(DOMObjects≡,html)
}
```

The `start()` function, invoked from the `onLoad` event handler in the `body` element, initializes the `DOMObjects` object with all the `span` elements in the document, and sets the global `fRef` variable to the `shopping` form, either via the `content` layer in the case of Netscape Navigator or directly for all other browsers. The `wipe()` function is invoked to initialize the `shopping` form and the `id` shopping cart:

```
function start() {
  if (window.DOMObjects)
    DOMInitialize('span');

  if (document.layers)
    fRef = document.content.document.shopping;
  else
    fRef = document.shopping;

  wipe();
}
```

A style class (a) is defined and used throughout the HTML markup to indicate an absolutely positioned element. This is really just needed for Netscape Navigator 4, which requires an element to be absolutely positioned to be included within the `document` object's `layers` object array:

```
.a { position: absolute; }
```

The `body` element is simply bulging with event handlers. The most unusual one is the `onDragOver`, supported in Microsoft Internet Explorer, which is used to set the `window` object's `event` object's `returnValue` to `false`, enabling the ability to drop (or release the mouse button) over a target object. The `onLoad` event handler invokes the `start()` function to initialize the application, and the various `onMouseOver`, `onMouseUp`, and `onDrop` event handlers invoke the relevant `down()` or `up()` functions, passing the `window` object's `event` object reference:

```
<body onLoad="start()" onMouseDown="down(event)"
  onMouseUp="up(event)" onDrop="up(event)"
  onDragOver="window.event.returnValue = false">
```

The shopping cart is located within an absolutely positioned (class="a") span element identified as cart:

```
<span class="a" id="cart">
<table><tr><td>
<img src="cart.gif">
</td></tr></table>
</span>
```

As the shopping cart is absolutely positioned, it does not reserve any space in the document. Therefore, the following content must be positioned (again, absolutely) to take account of this. The remainder of the document content is held within an absolutely positioned (class="a) div element, with a style attribute specifying the absolute top and left style values:

```
<div id="content" class="a" style="top: 250px; left: 8px;">
```

The shopping form is used to both submit the shopping cart contents to the next page (*next.htm* is not implemented by this application, although you could use techniques similar to that discussed in the Dynamic Thank You Page in Chapter 8) and to display the products in the shopping cart in a dynamic select options list. The onSubmit event handler, invoked when the user clicks on the Submit button, ensures that all bar the first descriptive option in the cart select list are selected and thus forwarded on to the action target. The Remove button invokes the remove() function, which removes any selected options from the shopping cart. The Reset button, on the other hand, invokes the wipe() function to remove all the products from the shopping cart:

```
<form name="shopping" action="next.htm" onSubmit="highlight()">
<select name="cart" multiple size="7">
<option value="">Shopping Cart Contents:</option>
</select>
<input type="button" value="Remove" onClick="remove()">
<input type="button" value="Reset" onClick="wipe()">
<input type="submit" value="Submit">
</form>
```

Rather than hard-coding all the products that can be dragged into the shopping cart, the various properties of the product objects held within the catalog array are used to generate the necessary HTML markup. The contents of the catalog array are looped through using the unusual for/in statement. The for/in statement loops through all the properties of the catalog object. As each property corresponds to a named object within the catalog array, then the returned property values correspond to the names of each of the objects in the array in turn, which are allocated to the `i` variable. Each `product` object in the `catalog` array is used to build HTML markup for an image with a `src` attribute set to the `src` property of the `product` and a `name` attribute set to the value of the global `dndPrefix` string variable plus the `i` variable string value:

```
var output = '';

for (var i in catalog)
  output += '<img src="' + catalog[i].src +
            '" name="' + dndPrefix + i +
            '" width="' + catalog[i].width +
            '" height="' + catalog[i].height + '">';

document.write(output);
```

Finally, the closing `div` element:

```
</div>
```

# myPage.com

Once a visitor arrives at your website, keeping the visitor there is critical. "Stickiness," a term used to indicate a website in which users stick around, can be achieved in several ways. This application, which is a demonstration of website personalization, shows how to make a *myPage.com* web page configurable by the visitors to their own preferences—similar to the many *my.acme.com* websites in existence (e.g., my.yahoo.com).

Once a visitor has spent time configuring a page to his or her own preference, then it is more likely that the visitor will return again and again. Figure 12-3 shows a customized page in which the visitor has decided to collapse the content for headings one, three, seven, and eight and has closed the content for heading four. Each time the user interacts with the content headings, the cookie that stores the user's preferences is automatically updated so that when the visitor returns, the content is redisplayed as he or she left it.

This application makes use of inline frames, generated using the `iframe` element. As such, this particular application does not work in Netscape Navigator 4, because inline frames support was introduced in Internet Explorer 4 and 5 as a browser-specific feature. It has since been

**Figure 12-3**
myPage.com—
collapsed and closed
content.

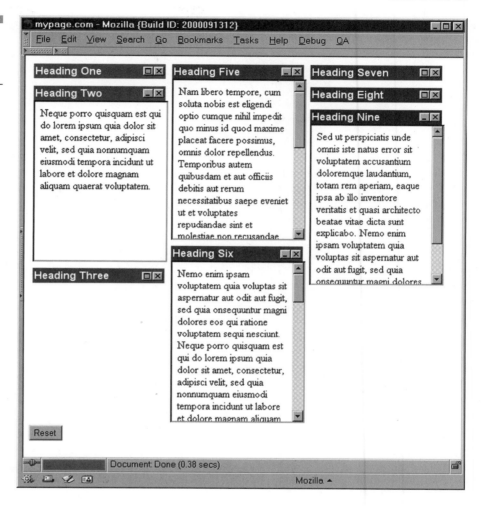

adopted by the W3C in the HTML 4 recommendation, so is therefore supported in Netscape Navigator 6.

## myPage.com—*index.htm*

**chapter12/dragdrop/index.htm**

The myPage.com application makes use of code in both the *dom.js* and *cookie.js* libraries described in Chapter 11 and 10, respectively:

```
<script language="JavaScript" src="dom.js"></script>
<script language="JavaScript" src="cookie.js"></script>
```

Two global variables are defined and initialized: myPage, a Boolean variable to state the readiness of application and initially set to false, and an item array:

```
var myPage = false;
var item = new Array();
```

Several functions are defined to control the effect of the user clicking the mouse on one of the three icons in the top right-hand corner of each heading bar. Each function is passed a single parameter, accepted into the i variable.

The toggle() function, invoked whenever the user clicks the collapse or expand icons, is used to toggle the state of the content from and to its expanded and collapsed states. If the application has been readied (i.e., myPage is set to true), then the src property of the image named with the passed i variable plus the suffix -a is retrieved. If it contains the string *shrink.gif*, then as the *shrink* image is currently displayed, it is assumed that the content is currently expanded, in which case the shrink() function is invoked to collapse the content. Otherwise, the expand() function is invoked, passing in either case the value of the i variable as input. The toggle() function then returns false to cancel the default action of the mouse click:

```
function toggle(i) {
  if (myPage) {
    var src = document.images[i+'-a'].src;

    if (src.indexOf('shrink.gif') > -1)
      shrink(i);
    else
      expand(i);
  }

  return false;
}
```

The kill() function, invoked whenever the visitor clicks on the close icon, again tests the readiness of the application. If ready, it changes the src property of the clicked image (named with the value of the passed i parameter plus the -b suffix) to *close.gif*, sets the relevant entry in the item array to closed, invokes the setPrefs() function, invokes the hide() function, passing the value of the i parameter as input, and then finally returns false to again cancel the default action of the mouse click:

```
function kill(i) {
  if (myPage) {
    document.images[i+'-b'].src = 'close.gif';
    item[i] = 'closed';
    setPrefs();
    hide(i);
  }

  return false;
}
```

The expand() and shrink() functions set the src of the clicked image to *shrink.gif* and *open.gif*, respectively. They also set the relevant item array entry to open or small, before invoking the setPrefs() function, and then either invoking the show() or hide() functions, passing the value of the i parameter concatenated with the -f suffix:

```
function expand(i) {
  document.images[i+'-a'].src = 'shrink.gif';
  item[i] = 'open';
  setPrefs();
  show(i+'-f');
}

function shrink(i) {
  document.images[i+'-a'].src = 'open.gif';
  item[i] = 'small';
  setPrefs();
  hide(i+'-f');
}
```

The start() function, invoked from the body element's onLoad event handler, checks that the browser first supports images, has loaded the *cookie.js* library, and that the page contains at least one embedded frame. It does this by testing the length property of the document object's frames object. If either of these conditions is false, then the application is not readied, and therefore, the functionality is, by default, not enabled. If all three conditions are true, then the application is readied by setting the global myPage Boolean variable to true, and then the getPrefs() function is invoked:

```
function start() {
  if (document.images && window.Cookie &&
    window.frames.length > 0) {
    myPage = true;
    getPrefs();
  }
}
```

The hide() and show() functions use the DOMElementHide() and DOMElementShow() functions in the *dom.js* library to either hide or show the content represented by the passed i parameter. If the document object's getElementById() method is supported, then the element with the matching id property is passed as input to the two *dom.js* functions; otherwise, if the browser being used is Internet Explorer 4 (i.e., only supports the document object's all object), then the all object entry that corresponds to the passed i parameter is passed as input:

```
function hide(i) {
  if (document.getElementById)
    DOMElementHide(document.getElementById(i));
  else if (document.all)
    DOMElementHide(document.all(i));
}

function show(i) {
  if (document.getElementById)
    DOMElementShow(document.getElementById(i));
  else if (document.all)
    DOMElementShow(document.all(i));
}
```

A slightly revised version of the getNthParm() function, discussed in the Passing Data from One Form to Another application in Chapter 8, is used by this application. Instead of using an ampersand (&) separator, a semicolon (;) separator is used:

```
function getNthParm(string,parm,nth) {
  if (!string) return";
  var count = 1;
  var startPos = 0 + string.indexOf(parm + '=');
  while (startPos > -1) {
    startPos = startPos + parm.length + 1;
    var endPos = 0 + string.indexOf(';',startPos);
    if (endPos == -1)
      endPos = string.length;
    if (count == nth)
      return unescape(string.substring(startPos,endPos));
    startPos = 0 + string.indexOf(parm + '=',endPos);
    count++;
  }
  return '';
}
```

The getPrefs() function, invoked from the start() function, retrieves the value of any mypage.com cookie stored by the browser assigning its value to the local myCookie variable, and then proceeds to extract the status of each content heading from the cookie to populate the item array. The function loops through the contents of the document object's images array, testing the src property of each image to see if it contains the string *dot-a.gif*.

When found, the name property of the image minus the last two characters is assigned to the local `name` variable and the local `pref` variable is then initialized to open. If the local `myCookie` variable is not null, then `getNthParm()` function is used to retrieve the first value of any matching *name/value* pair from the unescaped value of the `myCookie` variable and assign it to the `pref` variable. Then depending on the value of `pref` variable, one of the three functions, `expand()`, `shrink()`, or `kill()` is invoked, passing the value of the `name` variable as input.

```
function getPrefs() {
  var myCookie = getCookie('mypage.com');

  for (var i=0; i<document.images.length; i++) {
    var src = document.images[i].src;

    if (src.indexOf('dot-a.gif') > -1) {
      var name = document.images[i].name;
      name = name.substring(0,name.length-2);
      var pref = 'open';

      if (myCookie)
        pref = getNthParm(unescape(myCookie),name,1);

      if (pref == 'open')        expand(name);
      else if (pref == 'small')  shrink(name);
      else if (pref == 'closed') kill(name);
    }
```

If, however, the `src` property of the image contains the string *dot-a.gif*, then the `src` property of the image is changed to *close.gif*:

```
    else if (src.indexOf('dot-b.gif') > -1)
      document.images[i].src = 'close.gif';
  }
}
```

The `setPrefs()` function, invoked when any of the heading icon images are clicked, updates the `mypage.com` cookie with the current values held in the `item` array:

```
function setPrefs() {
  var myCookie = '';

  for (var i in item)
    myCookie += i + '=' +item[i] + ';';

  var today = new Date()
  var expires = new Date(today.getTime() + Cookie.year);
  setCookie('mypage.com',escape(myCookie), expires);
}
```

The `resetPrefs()` function, invoked when the Reset Form button is clicked, deletes the `mypage.com` cookie and resets all the closed content by invoking the show() function on any entries in the item array that are set to closed. It then invokes the getPrefs() function, which—as the mypage.com cookie has just been deleted—proceeds to display all the content in the default expanded state:

```
function resetPrefs() {
  if (myPage) {
    deleteCookie('mypage.com');

    for (var i in item) {
      document.images[i+'-a'].src = 'dot-a.gif';
      if (item[i] == 'closed')
        show(i);
    }

    getPrefs();
  }
}
```

An inline style sheet is used to initially set all iframe elements display style to none so that they are invisible:

```
iframe { display: none; }
```

The body elements onLoad event handler invokes the start() function:

```
<body onLoad="start()">
```

Each customizable item used within this application is held within a table element, each with an id attribute set to an increasing integer starting from 1 with an x prefix. In an effort to conserve space, only the first three tables are shown here, and the table row and cell tags omitted. The first table (x1) contains two image links named x1-a and x1-b and one iframe element named x1-f. The image links contain the images *dot-a.gif* and *dot-b.gif*. The actual contents of the iframe element are loaded from a separate external *x1.htm* file (although this file can be called anything and may even be an absolute URL to the same or different server):

```
<table id="x1">
<href="#" onClick="return toggle('x1')">
<img src="dot-a.gif" name="x1-a"></a>
<a href="#" onClick="return kill('x1')">
<img src="dot-b.gif" name="x1-b"></a>
<iframe src="x1.htm" id="x1-f"></iframe>
</table>
```

The second table (x2) contains two image links named x2-a and x2-b and one iframe element named x2-f, which loads the external *x2.htm* file:

```
<table id="x2">
<a href="#" onClick="return toggle('x2')">
<img src="dot-a.gif" name="x2-a"></a>
<a href="#" onClick="return kill('x2')">
<img src="dot-b.gif" name="x2-b"></a>
<iframe src="x2.htm" id="x2-f"></iframe>
</table>
```

The third table (x3) contains two image links named x3-a and x3-b and one iframe element named x3-f, which loads the external *x3.htm* file:

```
<table id="x3">
<a href="#" onClick="return toggle('x3')">
<img src="dot-a.gif" name="x3-a"></a>
<a href="#" onClick="return kill('x3')">
<img src="dot-b.gif" name="x3-b"></a>
<iframe src="x3.htm" id="x3-f"></iframe>
```

 **NOTE:**  *It is possible to place HTML markup between the opening and closing* iframe *tags, which would be displayed by those older browsers (e.g., Netscape Navigator 4) that do not support inline frames, providing a fallback static page.*

To enable the visitor to reset their preferences, a simple form button with an onClick event handler that invokes the resetPrefs() function is included:

```
<form>
<input type="button" value="Reset" onClick="resetPrefs()">
</form>
```

There is one feature with the beta version of Netscape Navigator 6 used to develop this particular application, which may or may not be present in the production version. When iframe elements have all been collapsed by setting their display style to none, as defined in the inline style sheet, then the inline frame no longer is available via the document object's frames object. This means that the value returned by document.frames.length when used in the start() function will be zero. This means that the start() function will incorrectly identify the browser as not supporting inline frames. To avoid this, we include an additional iframe element that overrides the inline style sheet with a style attribute setting the display style to block. To ensure that this otherwise redundant inline frame does not affect the visual page, the width, height, and frameborder attributes are all set to zero:

```
<iframe style="display:block" src="blank.htm"
  width="0" height="0" frameborder="0"></iframe>
```

## Online Computer Builder/Selector

Many online stores include the ability to build a product based on selectable subcomponents. For example, the Dell PC manufacturer allows potential buyers to select one of many basic PC systems and then choose among the options that each base system has. While the user makes changes, the current price is reloaded into a separate frame.

The application presented here takes this concept and adapts it. Rather than using frames, the price is dynamically output to an area of the current page. To avoid duplication across many similar pages, the database of products and configurable options is held in a single JavaScript external file (*database.js*). The database is further supplemented by individual JavaScript files (*windows.js*, *redhat.js*, *cobalt.js*, and *solaris.js*), one for each of the base products.

This application allows the user to select and configure a virtual web server. Figure 12-4 shows the initial page that allows the user to select one of the four basic servers.

**Figure 12-4**
Builder—select
a configuration.

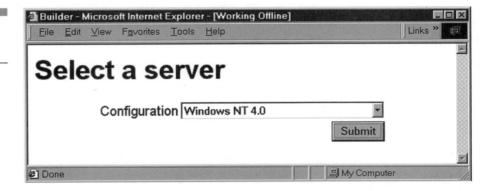

# Online Computer Builder/Selector—*builder.js*

**chapter12/builder/builder.js**

The *builder.js* library contains object constructors for user-defined
Form, Option, and Select objects, which correspond to the form,
select, and option elements. The object constructors define add()
methods to allow Select objects to be attached to Option objects, and
Option objects to Form objects, along with getHTML1() and getHTML2()
methods to retrieve the HTML markup necessary to build the form elements that are required to build a visual representation of the objects. Also
defined are getString1() and getString2() methods to retrieve the
HTML markup to display the objects as simple text within table elements.

The Form() object constructor populates name and action properties
from the passed name and action parameters, declares an add() method
defined by the addSelect() function, and defines an Object array
called Contents to later hold Option objects. Then it declares the four
methods getHTML1(), getHTML2(), getString1(), and getString2()
defined by the two functions formHTML1() and formHTML2():

```
function Form(name, action) {
  this.name = name;
  this.action = action;

  this.add = addSelect;
  this.index = 0;
  this.Contents = new Object();

  this.getHTML1 = formHTML1;
  this.getHTML2 = formHTML2;

  this.getString1 = formHTML1;
  this.getString2 = formHTML2;
}
```

The addSelect() function implements the Form object's add()
method. It adds the passed code Select object to the current (this)
Form object's Contents array, and then sets the Select object's value
property to the passed value parameter:

```
function addSelect(code, value) {
  this.Contents[this.index++] = selects[code];
  selects[code].value = value;
}
```

The `formHTML1()` function implements the `Form` object's `getHTML1()` and `getString1()` methods. It returns the HTML markup necessary for an opening form tag with the `name` and `action` attributes set to the `Form` object's `name` and `action` properties, as well as for an opening table tag:

```
function formHTML1() {
  return '<form name="' + this.name +
    '" action="' + this.action + '"><table>\n';
}
```

Likewise, the `formHTML2()` function implements the `Form` object's `getHTML2()` and `getString2()` methods. It returns the HTML markup necessary for a submit form button within its own table row, the closing table and form tags:

```
function formHTML2() {
  return '<tr><td colspan="2" align="right">' +
    '<input type="submit" value="Submit">' +
    '</td></tr>\n</table></form>\n';
}
```

The `createSelect()` function is used to create new `Select` objects and assign the object reference to the `selects` object array:

```
function createSelect(code, text) {
  selects[code] = new Select(code, text);
}
```

The `Select()` object constructor is similar to the `Form()` object constructor, it populates the `code` and `text` properties, initializes a `value` property to zero, declares an `add()` method defined by the `addOption()` function, defines an `Object` array called `Contents` to later hold `Option` objects, and then declares the four methods `getHTML1()`, `getHTML2()`, `getString1()`, and `getString2()` defined by the four functions `selectHTML1()`, `selectHTML2()`, `selectString1()`, and `selectString2()`:

```
function Select(code, text) {
  this.code = code;
  this.text = text;

  this.value = 0;

  this.add = addOption;
  this.index = 0;
  this.Contents = new Object();

  this.getHTML1 = selectHTML1;
```

```
      this.getHTML2 = selectHTML2;

    this.getString1 = selectString1;
    this.getString2 = selectString2;
}
```

The addOption() function implements the Select object's add() method. It adds the passed code Option object to the current (this) Select object's Contents array, and then sets the Option object's selectCode property to the Select object's code property and the selected property to true if the value of the passed selected parameter is also true. Finally, the function returns the value of the Option object's value property:

```
function addOption(code, selected) {
  this.Contents[this.index++] = options[code];
  options[code].selectCode = this.code;
  if (selected) options[code].selected = true;
  return options[code].value;
}
```

The selectHTML1() function implements the Select object's getHTML1() method. It returns the HTML markup necessary to generate a table row of two columns containing the text property of the Select object and an opening select tag with a name attribute set to the code property and an onChange event handler to invoke the total() function, passing a reference to the form (this.form):

```
function selectHTML1() {
  return '<tr><td>' + this.text + '</td><td>' +
    '<select name="' + this.code +
    '" onChange="total(this.form)">\n';
}
```

The selectHTML2() function implements the Select object's getHTML2() method. It returns the HTML markup for the closing select, table cell, and row tags:

```
function selectHTML2() {
  return '</select></td></tr>\n';
}
```

The selectString1() function implements the Select object's getString1() method. It returns the Select object's text property wrapped in table tags:

```
function selectString1() {
  return '<tr><td>' + this.text + '</td><td>';
}
```

The `selectString2()` function implements the `Select` object's `getString2()` method. It returns the closing table cell and row tags:

```
function selectString2() {
  return '</td></tr>\n';
}
```

The `createOption()` function is used to create new `Option` objects and assign the object reference to the `options` object array:

```
function createOption(code, text, value) {
  options[code] = new Option(code, text, value);
}
```

Again like the `Form()` and `Select()` object constructors, the `Option()` constructor populates several properties, one for each of the passed parameters, and two additional properties `selectCode` and `selected` initialized to an empty string and `false`. The constructor declares the usual four `get` methods:

```
function Option(code, text, value) {
  this.code = code;
  this.text = text;
  this.value = value;
  this.selectCode = '';
  this.selected = false;

  this.getHTML1 = optionHTML1;
  this.getHTML2 = optionHTML2;

  this.getString1 = optionString1;
  this.getString2 = optionString2;
}
```

The `optionHTML1()` function implements the `Option` object's `getHTML1()` method. It returns the HTML markup for an opening option tag. The value attribute is set to the `Option` object's `code` property, and if the `selected` property is set to `true`, a `selected` attribute is added. The `Option` object's `text` property is appended so as to appear as the option tags visible textual component, and if the `value` property is not an empty string, the `value` property is also appended as a price within brackets:

```
function optionHTML1() {
  var output = '<option value="' + this.code + '"';
  if (this.selected) output += ' selected';
  output += '>' + this.text;
  if (this.value != '') output += ' (Add $' + this.value + ')';
  return output;
}
```

The `optionHTML2()` function implements the `Option` object's `getHTML2()` method. It simply returns a closing option tag:

```
function optionHTML2() {
  return '</option>\n';
}
```

The `optionString1()` function implements the `Option` object's `getString1()` method. It returns the HTML markup necessary for a hidden form field, instead of the opening option tag returned in the `optionHTML1()` function, and the visible textual component:

```
function optionString1() {
  var output = '<input type="hidden" name="' + this.selectCode +
    '" value="' + this.code + '">' + this.text;
  if (this.value != '') output += ' (Add $' + this.value + ')';
  return output;
}
```

The `optionString2()` function implements the `Option` object's `getString2()` method, which simply returns an empty string:

```
function optionString2() {
  return '';
}
```

The `showHTML()` function iterates through all the nested objects contained in the passed `obj` object's `Contents` array. When given a `Form` object reference, the function will iterate down through all the attached `Select` objects, and then all their attached `Option` objects, using the `getHTML1()` and `getHTML2()` object methods to retrieve the HTML markup necessary to generate a visual representation of the form data held in the various objects:

```
function showHTML(obj) {
  var output = obj.getHTML1();

  for (var i=0; i<obj.index; i++)
    output += showHTML(obj.Contents[i]);

  return output + obj.getHTML2();
}
```

The `showString()` function performs a similar function to the `showHTML()` function, except that instead of using the `getHTML1()` and `getHTML2()` object methods, it uses the `getString1()` and `getString2()` object methods, thus returning the HTML markup for a non-form-based visual representation of the object data:

```
function showString(obj) {
  var output = obj.getString1();

  for (var i=0; i<obj.index; i++)
    output += showString(obj.Contents[i]);

  return output + obj.getString2();
}
```

The total() function is invoked by the onChange event handlers in the various generated select elements. This traps the user making configuration changes, which have an impact on the price of the base product. The total() function is passed a form object reference:

```
function total(form) {
```

The two local variables monthly and setup are defined and initialized to zero; they hold the monthly and initial setup prices:

```
var monthly = 0;
var setup = 0;
```

The function then loops through all the elements in the form object. In this application, we are only interested in single select elements (single-one) or hidden elements. For select elements the selected option is first identified. For both select and hidden elements, the value property is assigned to the local code variable and the name property of the select element is assigned to the local selectCode variable:

```
for (var i = 0; i<form.elements.length; i++) {
    var code = '';
    var selectCode = '';
    if (form.elements[i].type == 'select-one') {
      var selected = form.elements[i].selectedIndex;
      code = form.elements[i].options[selected].value;
      selectCode = form.elements[i].name;
    }
    else if (form.elements[i].type == 'hidden') {
      code = form.elements[i].value;
      selectCode = form.elements[i].name;
    }
```

If both the code and selectCode variables are nonempty strings, then either the setup or monthly local variables are incremented by the numeric value of the code Option object's value property. The setup price is updated if the `selectCode` (i.e., the name of the `select` element) matches the string `setup`. Otherwise, the `monthly` price is updated:

```
if (code != '' && selectCode != '') {
  if (selectCode == 'setup')
    setup += options[code].value - 0;
  else
    monthly += options[code].value - 0;
}
}
```

Once all the form elements have been examined, the local `total` variable is updated with the sum of the `monthly` and `setup` values:

```
var total = monthly + setup;
```

If the `formatMoney()` function held in the *money.js* library has been successfully loaded, then the function is used to format the `monthly`, setup, and `total` numeric values into fully formatted money strings (e.g., from `9999.99` to `$9,999.00`):

```
if (window.formatMoney) {
    monthly = formatMoney(monthly);
    setup = formatMoney(setup);
    total = formatMoney(total);
}
```

The function then updates either a dynamic area of the page using the `DOMElementSetInnerHTML()` and `DOMElementShow()` functions held in the *dom.js* library if the `DOMObjects` object is not null, or updates the value properties of the `outputForm` form's `monthly`, setup, and `total` input form fields:

```
if (window.DOMObjects) {
  var html = '<p>Setup: ' + setup +
    ' Monthly: ' + monthly + ' Total: ' + total + '</p>';
  DOMElementSetInnerHTML(DOMObjects['dynamicArea'],html)
  DOMElementShow(DOMObjects['dynamicArea']);
}
else if (document.outputForm) {
  document.outputForm.monthly.value = monthly;
  document.outputForm.setup.value = setup;
  document.outputForm.total.value = total;
}
}
```

## Online Computer Builder/Selector— *database.js*

  chapter12/builder/database.js

The *database.js* library builds objects for each of the select lists available across the various base products, and objects for each of the options that appear in the select lists. It first ensures that the Select() object constructor in the *builder.js* library is available before proceeding:

```
if (window.Select) {
```

A global selects array is defined:

```
var selects = new Array();
```

All the Select objects are then created using the createSelect() function, which uses the Select() object constructor to first create a Select object and then add it to the selects object array. Each Select object is given a code and text property:

```
createSelect('choice', 'Configuration');
createSelect('setup', 'Setup');
createSelect('os',     'Operating System');
createSelect('procs', 'Processor');
createSelect('mem',    'Memory');
createSelect('hd1',    'Hard Drive');
createSelect('hd2',    '2nd Hard Drive');
createSelect('hd3',    '3rd Hard Drive');
createSelect('hd4',    '4th Hard Drive');
createSelect('data',   'Data Transfer');
```

A global options array is defined:

```
var options = new Array();
```

All the Option objects are then created using the createOption() function, which uses the Option() object constructor to first create an Option object and then add it to the options object array. Each Option object is given a code, text, and value property:

```
createOption('setupNT',   'Setup', '250.00');
createOption('setupRH',   'Setup', '250.00');
...
```

```
        createOption('osNT4.0', 'Windows NT 4.0', '');
        createOption('osRH7.0', 'Red Hat 7.0',    '');
        ...

        createOption('p600',    '600 Mhz',  '70.00');
        createOption('p700',    '700 Mhz', '100.00');
        ...

        createOption('m64',     '64Mb RAM',  '10.00');
        createOption('m128',    '128Mb RAM', '20.00');
        ...

        createOption('--', '--', '');
        createOption('h10eide', '10 Gb EIDE',  '40.00');
        createOption('h20eide', '20 Gb EIDE',  '80.00');
        ...

        createOption('b10',    '10Gb/Month',       '');
        createOption('b25',    '25Gb/Month', '25.00');
        ...
    }
```

# Online Computer Builder/Selector—
# *index.htm*

**chapter12/builder/index.htm**

The *index.htm* page presents a form select list containing all the base products. Once chosen, the user is then directed to the *choice.htm* page to configure the base product. The *builder.js* and *database.js* libraries are included in the *confirm.htm* page:

```
<script language="JavaScript" src="builder.js"></script>
<script language="JavaScript" src="database.js"></script>
```

If the Select() object constructor in the *builder.js* library has loaded successfully, then the page can be built. A user-defined Form object is created using the Form() constructor in the *builder.js* library, passing the name of the form (form) and the required action attribute value (choice.htm), and the object is assigned to the global form variable. Then the Select object's add() method is used to add Option objects to the choice Select object, before it itself is added to the form object using the Form object's add() method:

```
if (window.Select) {
  var form = new Form('form', 'choice.htm');
```

```
selects['choice'].add('osNT4.0');
selects['choice'].add('osRH7.0');
selects['choice'].add('osRAQ4');
selects['choice'].add('osSOL7');
form.add('choice', 0);
}
```

The HTML markup generated by passing the `form` object reference to the `showHTML()` function is then written to the document. This effectively generates the HTML markup for a `form` element containing a `select` element named `choice` with four `option` elements:

```
if (window.form) document.write(showHTML(form));
```

# Online Computer Builder/Selector— *windows.js*

**chapter12/builder/windows.js**

The *windows.js* library is one of four similar but different libraries that are used to build the four base products. They include one function that can be called by the application to create a `Form` object, which is then used to add different combinations of the available `Select` objects, which are then subsequently used to add different combinations of the `Option` objects.

As with the JavaScript code in the *index.htm* page, if the `Select()` object constructor in the *builder.js* library has loaded successfully, then the page can be built. A user-defined `Form` object is created using the `Form()` constructor in the *builder.js* library, passing the name of the form (`form`) and the required action attribute value (`confirm.htm`), and the object is assigned to the global `form` variable:

```
function buildWindows () {
  if (window.Select) {
    var value;

    var form = new Form('form', 'confirm.htm');
```

Then the `Select` object's `add()` method is used to add the `setupNT` `Option` object to the `setup` `Select` object, before it itself is added to the `form` object using the `Form` object's `add()` method. The `Select` object's `add()` method is passed a second parameter set to `true`. This indicates to the method that this option should be selected by default. The return value from the method is then used as the second parameter to the Form object's add() method:

```
value = selects['setup'].add('setupNT',true);
form.add('setup', value);
```

Likewise with the osNT4.0 Option object; however, it is added to the os Select object:

```
value = selects['os'].add('osNT4.0',true);
form.add('os', value);
```

A more interesting example is where more than one Option object is added to a Select object. Only the first Option object added to the Select object passes a second parameter set to true, as there can only be one option selected in a select-one type select list. In this example the Option objects are added to the procs Select object, and again only the first add() method has its return value captured and passed to the Form object's add() method:

```
value = selects['procs'].add('p600',true);
selects['procs'].add('p700');
...
form.add('procs', value);
```

The next example is similar to the previous, the only difference being that the Option objects are added to the mem Select object:

```
value = selects['mem'].add('m64',true);
selects['mem'].add('m128');
...
form.add('mem', value);
```

Several different Select objects can reuse the same Option objects. The following examples reuse the various hard disk Option objects when added to the four separate hd1, hd2, hd3, and hd4 Select objects:

```
value = selects['hd1'].add('h10eide',true);
selects['hd1'].add('h20eide');
...
form.add('hd1', value);

value = selects['hd2'].add('--',true);
selects['hd2'].add('h20eide');
...
form.add('hd2', value);
value = selects['hd3'].add('--',true);
```

```
selects['hd3'].add('h20eide');
...
form.add('hd3', value);
value = selects['hd4'].add('--',true);
selects['hd4'].add('h20eide');
...
form.add('hd4', value);
```

Finally, the last Select object (data) for this base product has its own Option objects added:

```
value = selects['data'].add('b10',true);
selects['data'].add('b25');
...
form.add('data', value);
}
```

The form object reference is then returned:

```
return form;
}
```

The three additional external JavaScript libraries *redhat.js*, *cobalt.js*, and *solaris.js* perform a similar role. The options and selections attached to the Form object are, however, different in each case, and the names of the functions are different to reflect the base product that they are generating: buildRedHat(), buildCobalt(), and buildSolaris().

## Online Computer Builder/Selector— *choice.htm*

**chapter12/builder/choice.htm**

The user selects a base product shown in the *index.htm* page and submits the form to the *choice.htm* page. This page extracts the chosen base product from the URL and then invokes one of the builder functions in the four libraries (*windows.js*, *redhat.js*, *cobalt.js*, and *solaris.js*) to build the object hierarchy to represent the selections and objects that the user can configure. Once built, the showHTML() function is used to build the HTML markup for the visual representation of the Form, Select, and Option objects, as shown in Figure 12-5. While the user is configuring the base product, as shown in Figure 12-6, the setup, monthly, and total price are constantly updated and redisplayed.

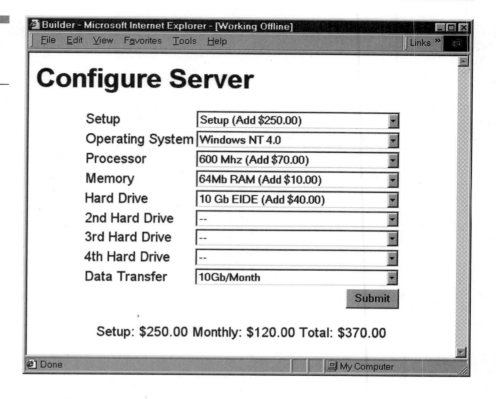

**Figure 12-5**
Builder—
default settings for
configuration.

An inline style sheet is used to define a l class as a hidden, collapsed, and absolutely positioned style:

```
.l { position: absolute; visibility: hidden; display: block; }
```

The *builder.js*, *database.js*, *dom.js*, and *money.js* libraries are all included in the *confirm.htm* page:

```
<script language="JavaScript" src="builder.js"></script>
<script language="JavaScript" src="database.js"></script>
<script language="JavaScript" src="dom.js"></script>
<script language="JavaScript" src="money.js"></script>
```

along with the additional *windows.js*, *redhat.js*, *cobalt.js*, and *solaris.js* libraries, each of which represents a different configurable base product:

```
<script language="JavaScript" src="windows.js"></script>
<script language="JavaScript" src="redhat.js"></script>
<script language="JavaScript" src="cobalt.js"></script>
<script language="JavaScript" src="solaris.js"></script>
```

**Figure 12-6**
Builder—overridden
settings.

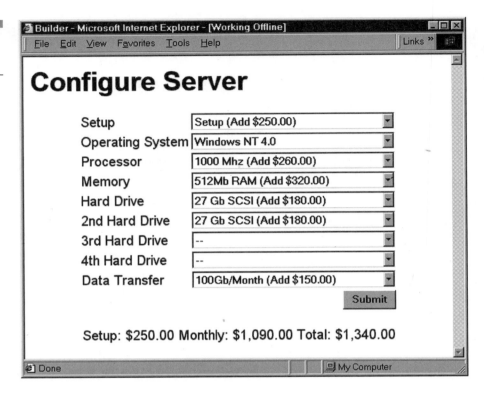

The `location` object's `search` property is stripped of the leading question mark character and assigned to the global `passed` variable:

```
var passed = location.search.substring(1);
```

As long as the `Select()` object constructor held in the *builder.js* library has successfully loaded, then the page can be built. Depending on the value of the `passed` variable and whether the required `build` function has been successfully loaded, the relevant `build` function is invoked and the return results assigned to the global `form` variable. If no match is found, then the `buildWindows()` function is used by default:

```
if (window.Select) {
  if (passed == "choice=osNT4.0" && window.buildWindows)
    var form = buildWindows();
  else if (passed == "choice=osRH7.0" && window.buildRedHat)
    var form = buildRedHat();
  else if (passed == "choice=osRAQ4" && window.buildCobalt)
```

```
      var form = buildCobalt();
   else if (passed == "choice=osSOL7" && window.buildSolaris)
      var form = buildSolaris();
   else if (window.buildWindows)
      var form = buildWindows();
}
```

The `start()` function, invoked from the `body` element's `onLoad` event handler, initializes the application, and if the global `form` object variable is defined and initialized and the `total()` function is loaded from the *builder.js* library, then the `total()` function is invoked, passing a reference to the *form.name* form as input. This updates the dynamic content with the setup, monthly, and total values:

```
function start() {
   if (window.DOMObjects)
      DOMInitialize('div');

   if (window.form && window.total)
      total(document.forms[form.name]);
}
```

The `body` element's `onLoad` event handler invokes the `start()` method:

```
<body onLoad="start()">
```

If the global `form` object variable is defined and initialized, then the `showHTML()` function is invoked, passing the `form` object reference as input and the returned result written out to the document:

```
if (window.form) document.write(showHTML(form));
```

A `div` element named `dynamicArea` is included, with a fallback `outputForm` form, to enable the monthly, setup, and total values to be displayed. If the browser is advanced enough to support it, then the contents of the `dynamicArea` are overwritten from within the `total()` function with HTML markup to replace the fallback `outputForm` form with simple text output:

```
<div id="dynamicArea" class="l">
<form name="outputForm">
<input type="text" name="monthly" size="10">
<input type="text" name="setup" size="10">
<input type="text" name="total" size="10">
</form>
</div>
```

## Online Computer Builder/Selector—
## *confirm.htm*

**chapter12/builder/confirm.htm**

Once the user has configured the base product, displayed by the *choice.htm* page, to their required specifications, the user submits the form to the *confirm.htm* page. This page extracts the passed data from the URL and then builds a simpler version of the Form, Select, and Option objects, only using the data passed between the two pages and not the full data from any one base product. It then uses the showString() function, held in the *builder.js* library, to show a non-forms-based view of the selected options, as shown in Figure 12-7. If the user is happy with details shown on the confirmation screen, then the user can submit the results to a server-side process (not included here) for processing.

**Figure 12-7**
Builder—
confirm settings.

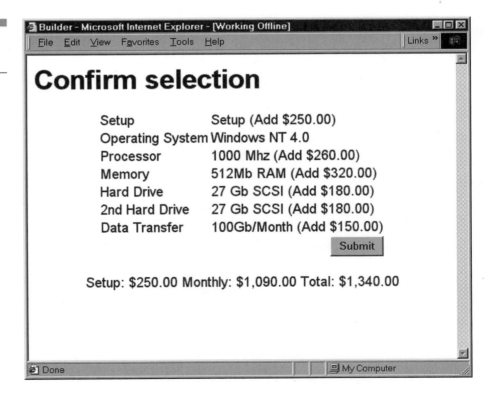

The *builder.js*, *database.js*, *dom.js*, and *money.js* libraries are all included in the *confirm.htm* page:

```
<script language="JavaScript" src="builder.js"></script>
<script language="JavaScript" src="database.js"></script>
<script language="JavaScript" src="dom.js"></script>
<script language="JavaScript" src="money.js"></script>
```

A user-defined `Form` object is created using the `Form()` constructor in the *builder.js* library, passing the name of the form (`form`), and the required action attribute value (`nextpage.htm`—although this has not been implemented in this application) and assigned to the global `form` variable:

```
var form = new Form('form', 'nextpage.htm');
```

The following code is an almost exact copy of the code used in the Dynamic Thank You Page application in Chapter 8. The only difference is that instead of outputting the passed *name/value* pairs to the document, the `value` is added to the corresponding `name` `selects` object array using the `add()` method and the `price` retrieved. Then along with the `name` object, the `value` is added to the form using the `Form` object's `add()` method:

```
var input = output = name = value = equal = ampersand = '';
if (location.search.length > 0)
  input = location.search.substring(1);

input = input.replace(/\+/g,' ');

while (input.length > 0) {
  equal = input.indexOf('=');
  name = unescape(input.substring(0,equal));
  input = input.substring(input.indexOf('=')+1);

  ampersand = input.indexOf('&');
  value = input.substring(0,ampersand);
  input = input.substring(input.indexOf('&')+1);

  if (value == '' && ampersand == -1) {
    value = input;
    input = '';
  }

  value = unescape(value);
  value = value.replace(/&/g,'&amp');
  value = value.replace(/</g,'&lt;');
  value = value.replace(/>/g,'&gt;');

  if (value != '--') {
    var price = selects[name].add(value);
    form.add(name, price);
  }
}
```

The start() function, invoked from the body element's onLoad event handler, initializes the application, and as long as both the form object and the total() function have been defined and loaded, the start() function invokes the total() function, passing as input a reference to the form named with the value of form object's name property:

```
function start() {
  if (window.DOMObjects)
    DOMInitialize('div');

  if (window.form && window.total)
    total(document.forms[form.name]);
}
```

The body element's onLoad event handler invokes the start() function:

```
<body onLoad="start()">
```

If the form object exists, and therefore all the external JavaScript libraries have successfully loaded, then the output from the showString() function, passing the form object reference as input, is written to the document:

```
if (window.form) document.write(showString(form));
```

As in the *choice.htm* page, a div element named dynamicArea is included, with a fallback outputForm form, to enable the monthly, setup, and total values to be displayed:

```
<div id="dynamicArea" class="l">
<form name="outputForm">
...
</form>
</div>
```

## Online Computer Builder/Selector—*money.js*

**chapter12/builder/money.js**

The *money.js* library contains copies of the three functions commas(), round(), and cents() described in Chapter 2, along with the following formatMoney() function, which uses the aforementioned functions to format the passed amount parameter into a recognizable money format (e.g., from `9999.99` to `$9,999.00`):

```
function formatMoney(amount) {
  return '$' + commas(Math.floor(amount)) +
         cents(amount - Math.floor(amount)).substring(1);
}
```

# Book Catalog—XML the DOM and Style Sheets

JavaScript is not restricted to working with just HTML. It can also, with the introduction of XML support in Internet Explorer 5 and Netscape Navigator 6, work with XML files. The W3C document object model (DOM) supported by these two browsers enables JavaScript to access any node within the document.

The Book Catalog application presented here shows how to work with XML data structures by using JavaScript to walk through the nodes that make up the page to extract data from the file, used to allow the user to search through the catalog. JavaScript code is also used to hide and reveal portions of the XML structure, hiding the books in the catalog that do not match the search criteria.

Four cascading style sheets are included within the application to vary the visual presentation of the XML data. The first style sheet loaded (*catalog1.css*) initially hides all the books, as shown in Figure 12-8. When a search is performed, the second style sheet (*catalog2.css*) is used to reveal all the books that have not been hidden, as shown in Figure 12-9. The final two style sheets (*catalog3.css* and *catalog4.css*) allow the user to view the search results in different formats.

**Figure 12-8**
Book Catalog—initial display with stylesheet1.

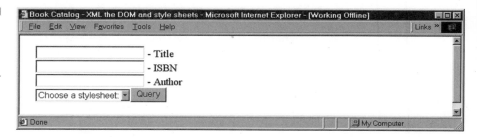

# Book Catalog—*catalog.xml*

**chapter12/catalog/catalog.xml**

As this application is working with XML, the file extension must be *.xml* and the document should include an XML declaration that specifies the version of XML being used:

```
<?xml version="1.0" encoding="UTF-8"?>
```

We will be working with a specific XML vocabulary, XHTML 1.0, which is a reformulation of HTML 4 in XML, a stepping stone, you might say, between the loose definition and usage of HTML and the more data-oriented usage of XML.

The four external cascading style sheets are included using the `xml-stylesheet` processing instruction:

```
<?xml-stylesheet type="text/css" href="catalog1.css"?>
<?xml-stylesheet type="text/css" href="catalog2.css"?>
<?xml-stylesheet type="text/css" href="catalog3.css"?>
<?xml-stylesheet type="text/css" href="catalog4.css"?>
```

An XML document must be *well formed*. This means that, whereas in HTML (because of its SGML legacy) tags can be omitted (such as in the case of the `</p>` tag), in XML both start and end tags must be included (in short, tag minimization is not allowed in XML). It should also be mentioned that attribute minimization is not allowed either—that is, attributes must be quoted. All start and end tags must be nested correctly within their enclosing element—that is, the XML markup `<a><b></a></b>` is invalid, whereas `<a><b></b></a>` is valid.

This application uses an `html` root element that specifies that all elements with `html:` prefixes are part of the W3C XHTML namespace; this allows HTML to be embedded within XML. If a namespace is not defined, then the browser would not know that the HTML elements are to be rendered as per the XHTML document template definition—for instance, that a `p` element is a paragraph, and that a `script` element contains or references a scripting language:

```
<html xmlns:html="http://www.w3.org/1999/xhtml">
```

All HTML elements within the remainder of the *catalog.xml* file, except the final closing `html` element, are then prefixed with `html`. For example, the following element is identified as an HTML `title` element, as specified by the `html` namespace:

```
<html:title>Book Catalog - XML the DOM and style sheets</html:title>
```

An HTML `body` open element is included:

```
<html:body>
```

An empty HTML `div` element identified as `picker` is included within the XML document. The contents of the `div` element are subsequently updated by the JavaScript code to include HTML markup to display a search form:

```
<html:div id="picker"></html:div>
```

An HTML `script` element is included to load the external *catalog.js* library:

```
<html:script src="catalog.js"></html:script>
```

Each book definition is included within an HTML `div` element that then contains a nested structure of XML elements that mark up the details of the book into an undetermined but recognizable format. The `image` element contains a nested HTML `img` element, which easily allows images to be rendered within an XML document. Note that the `img` element, which is an empty element—that is, it does not contain any other elements—ends with a space character followed by `/>`. In XML `<img />` is an abbreviation of `<img></img>`; however, unlike the latter, the former is compatible on older browsers:

```
<html:div>
  <book>
    <isbn>0072127309</isbn>
    <title>Instant ASP Scripts</title>
    <image>
      <html:img src="0072127309.jpg" width="110" height="140" />
    </image>
    <synopsis>
    Active Server Pages (ASP) technology represents...
    </synopsis>
    <authors>
      <author>Buczek, Greg</author>
    </authors>
    <pages>928pp</pages>
    <price>$49.99</price>
    <publisher>Osborne McGraw-Hill</publisher>
  </book>
</html:div>
```

In the code on the accompanying CD-ROM, there are four books defined in total. To conserve space, we only show two. The second example includes three `author` elements within the `authors` element and omits the `synopsis` and `image` elements:

```
<html:div>
  <book>
    <isbn>007212994x</isbn>
    <title>Instant JavaScripts</title>
    <authors>
      <author>Webb, Martin</author>
      <author>Plungjan, Michel</author>
      <author>Drakard, Keith</author>
    </authors>
    <pages>700pp</pages>
    <price>$49.99</price>
    <publisher>Osborne McGraw-Hill</publisher>
  </book>
</html:div>
```

Finally, the closing `body` and `html` element are included:

```
    </html:body>

  </html>
```

# Book Catalog—*catalog.js*

 **chapter12/catalog/catalog.js**

The *catalog.js* library contains all the JavaScript code necessary to interact with the XML catalog. The *catalog.xml* file loads it once the four external style sheets have been declared. The code uses an adapted enableStyle() function, discussed in the Dynamic Style Sheets application in Chapter 11. Rather than accept a title string that represents the style sheet to be enabled, it accepts an integer j value specifying which of the style sheets in the document object's styleSheets array should be enabled:

```
function enableStyle(j) {
  if (j != 0 && document.styleSheets) {
    for (var i=0; i<document.styleSheets.length; i++) {
      if (i == j-1)
        document.styleSheets[i].disabled = false;
      else
        document.styleSheets[i].disabled = true;
    }
  }
}
```

The first style sheet is then enabled by invoking the enableStyle() function, which also disables the remaining style sheets:

```
enableStyle(1);
```

Each node within a DOM has a nodeType property indicating the type of node (e.g., an element code or a text node). This can be compared against the Node object's defined constants. However, certain versions of Internet Explorer do not include the window object's Node object; therefore, the code tests for this and creates a Node object using the Object constructor and then defines the entire list of constants:

```
if (!window.Node) {
  var Node = new Object();
  Node.ELEMENT_NODE = 1;
  Node.ATTRIBUTE_NODE = 2;
  ...
}
```

The `query()` function, invoked when the user submits a query, extracts the ISBN, title, and author values from the like-identified elements using the `getElementById()` method and assigns the values to the local `iisbn`, `ititle`, and `iauthor` variables:

```
function query() {
  var iisbn = document.getElementById('isbn').value;
  var ititle = document.getElementById('title').value;
  var iauthor = document.getElementById('author').value;
```

An object array of all the `book` elements/tags is obtained using the `getElementsByTagName()` method and assigned to the local `books` variable:

```
var books = document.getElementsByTagName('book');
```

Each object reference within the books array is then examined in turn using the `item()` method to retrieve each `book` object reference:

```
for (var i=0; i<books.length; i++) {
  var book = books.item(i);
  var title = isbn = author = '';
```

As long as the `id` attribute returned by the `getAttribute()` method is not equal to `picker`, a cautious but necessary check, the code walks through all the child nodes of the `book` object reference, thereby extracting the title, ISBN, and author details. Where a node is found to be another element node (`nodeType` equals `Node.ELEMENT_NODE`), then the code continues to walk through that node's child nodes. The code is specific to the book structure used within the *catalog.xml* file:

```
if (book.getAttribute('id') != 'picker') {
  var attributes = book.childNodes;

  for (var j=0; j<attributes.length; j++) {
    var attribute = attributes[j];

    if (attribute.nodeType == Node.ELEMENT_NODE) {

      if (attribute.tagName == 'title')
        title = attribute.firstChild.data;
      else if (attribute.tagName == 'isbn')
        isbn = attribute.firstChild.data;
      else if (attribute.tagName == 'authors') {
        authors = attribute.childNodes;

        for (var k=0; k<authors.length; k++) {
          var attribute = authors[k];
```

```
                if (attribute.nodeType == Node.ELEMENT_NODE) {
                  if (attribute.tagName == 'author') {
                    author += attribute.firstChild.data + '\n';
                  }
                }
              }
            }
          }
        }
      }
```

Once all the nodes have been examined for one particular book element, then the retrieved ISBN, title, and author details are compared against the query data. If there are any matches, then book element's parent node (parentNode; i.e., the enclosing div element) has its style object's display property set to block. Otherwise, it is set to none, thus collapsing the content from view:

```
      if (
          (iisbn != '' && isbn.indexOf(iisbn) > -1) ||
          (ititle != '' && title.indexOf(ititle) > -1) ||
          (iauthor != '' && author.indexOf(iauthor) > -1)
          )
        book.parentNode.style.display = 'block';
      else
        book.parentNode.style.display = 'none';
    }
  }
```

Whether or not there are any matches, the second style sheet is enabled to give a listing of all the books found, as shown previously in Figure 12-9:

```
  enableStyle(2);
}
```

While the page is still loading, the HTML markup necessary to display the query form is added to the output variable:

```
var output =
  '<form name="search">' +
  '<input type="text" id="title" value="" /> - Title' +
  '<input type="text" id="isbn" /> - ISBN' +
  '<input type="text" id="author" /> - Author';
```

If the styleSheets object is supported, then the HTML markup necessary to allow the user to select one of the four style sheets is appended to the output variable. A select element is added with an onChange event handler that invokes the enableStyle() function, passing the value of the selected index. The code then loops through the entries in the `styleSheets` object array, adding an `option` element for each entry, with a `value` attribute set to the style sheet's indexed position within the array and the visible text portion set to the style sheet's filename minus the domain and directory path:

```
if (document.styleSheets) {
  output +=
    '<select onchange="enableStyle(this.selectedIndex)">' +
    '<option value="">Choose a stylesheet:</option>';

  for (var i=0; i<document.styleSheets.length; i++) {
    var href = document.styleSheets[i].href;
    var text = href.substring(href.lastIndexOf('/')+1);
    output +=
      '<option value="' + i + '">' + text + '</option>';
  }
  output +=
    '</select>';
}
```

The `output` variable is then appended with the HTML markup for a button form field with an `onclick` event handler (note the lowercase `onclick`, as opposed to the usual `onClick`) that invokes the `query()` function:

```
output +=
  '<input type="button" value="Query" onclick="query()" />' +
  '</form>';
```

Finally, the `innerHTML` property of the `div` element identified as `picker` is updated with the value of the `output` variable. This has the effect of replacing the existing nodes within the `div` element with the new HTML markup:

```
document.getElementById('picker').innerHTML = output;
```

## Book Catalog—*catalog1.css*

**chapter12/catalog/catalog1.css**

The cascading style sheet *catalog1.css*, the default, initially hides all the `book` elements and their contents, as the display attribute for `book` elements is set to `none`:

```
root { display: block; }
book { display: none; }
root { margin: 1em; }
```

## Book Catalog—*catalog2.css*

 **chapter12/catalog/catalog2.css**

The *catalog2.css* style sheet, when enabled, reveals the contents of the book. The style sheet also defines the styles for all the remaining elements used in the XML file:

```
root, book, title, synopsis { display: block; }
author, image { display: inline; }
isbn, pages, price, publisher { display: none; }
root { margin: 1em; }
book { text-align: justify; width: 300px; margin: 10px; }
image { float: right; margin: 10px; }
title { font-size: x-large; color: #009900; }
synopsis { color: #999900; }
author { color: #009999; }
```

The two further style sheets, *catalog3.css* and *catalog4.css*, perform a similar role, except that the styles of the remaining elements are different to display the XML markup in different ways, as shown in Figures 12-10 and 12-11.

## Summary

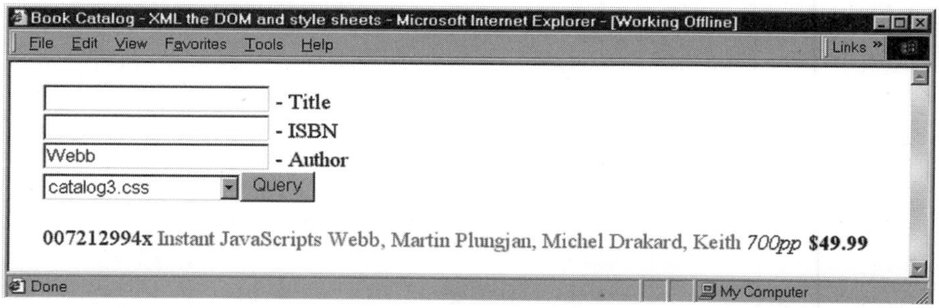

**Figure 12-10**
Book Catalog—
search results with
stylesheet3 applied.

| | |
|---|---|
| | - Title |
| | - ISBN |
| Webb | - Author |
| catalog3.css ▼ | Query |

007212994x Instant JavaScripts Webb, Martin Plungjan, Michel Drakard, Keith *700pp* **$49.99**

**Figure 12-11**
Book Catalog—
search results with
stylesheet4 applied.

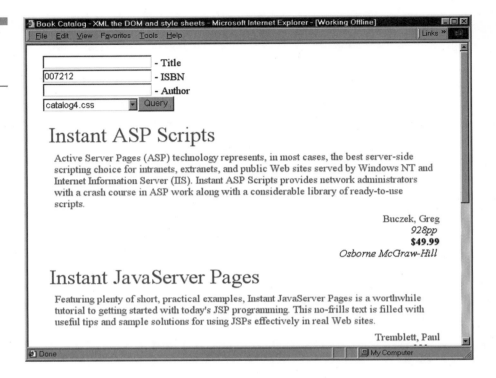

This chapter demonstrated how to build complex applications based on smaller reusable libraries of JavaScript code. The amount of code necessary to build complex applications can quite often be very short. You should be able to build even more complicated applications by adapting or reusing the ideas and techniques used in this chapter.

# Utilities

Up until this point we have been looking at various aspects of JavaScript, from mathematics and string manipulation to the more advanced uses of dynamic HTML. The previous chapter showed how to easily use the techniques learned throughout the book to build complex applications. The applications in this chapter represent a mixture of different uses of JavaScript, from a simple color picker to detecting plug-ins and ActiveX support, which extend the basic features of the browser.

**Color Picker** ../chapter13/color/index.htm
**Onscreen Keyboard** ../chapter13/keyboard/index.htm
**Automated Scrolling** ../chapter13/autoscroll/index.htm
**HomePage Script** ../chapter13/homepage/index.htm
**Detecting Plug-ins and ActiveX Components** ../chapter13/plugin/index.htm

# Color Picker

Lately it has become increasingly important to let the user customize the experience of visiting a website. This is especially important if you run a portal website. Following is a script designed to capture the user's preference in foreground and background color. When users click a link on the preference page, a pop-up window allows users to select the foreground and background colors, experimenting with their choice of colors, before finally updating the colors on the main page.

We stick to the 216 browser-safe colors in the so-called *Netscape Color Cube*. If you use only these colors, your page will not be dithered on screens with low color depth. These 216 colors represent the color values 0, 51, 102, 153, and 204, and for each primary color (i.e., red, green, and blue). The hexadecimal values corresponding to the decimal values are 0×00, 0×33, 0×66, 0×99, 0×CC, and 0×FF. Thus, in HTML color attributes, black would be #000000, pure green would be #00FF00, while white would be #FFFFFF. Figure 13-1 shows the Color Picker in action, with the user having selected #0033CC as the foreground color and #FFCC33 as the background color.

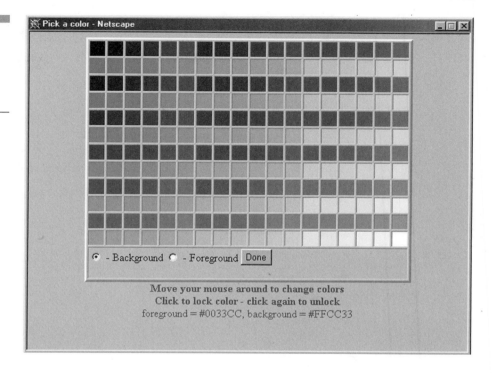

## Color Picker—*index.htm*

chapter13/color/index.htm

First the dom.js library is loaded, discussed in Chapter 11 "Dynamic HTML":

```
<script language="JavaScript" src="dom.js"></script>
```

An absolutely positioned class style (1) is defined:

```
.1 { position: absolute; display: block; }
```

The global text variable holds sample text that is later used to display the user's preferred foreground and background colors:

```
var text =
  'Sed ut perspiciatis unde omnis iste natus error sit' +
  ...
  'consequatur aut perferendis doloribus asperiores repellat.';
```

The setColor() function, when invoked, is passed the values of the foreground (fg) and background (bg) colors. As long as the *dom.js* library has loaded, the function proceeds to build the html variable to contain a table to display the value of the text variable in the selected colors, before using the DOMElementSetInnerHTML() function to update the contents of the HTML element identified as dynamicArea:

```
function setColor(fg,bg) {
  if (window.DOMObjects) {

    var html =
      '<table style="background-color:' + bg + ';">' +
      '<tr><td><font color="' + fg + '">' +
      text + '</font></td></tr></table>';
    DOMElementSetInnerHTML(DOMObjects['dynamicArea'],html)
  }
}
```

The getCol() function opens a new pop-up to display the *picker.htm* page, and returns false to cancel the default action of the event handler used to invoke this function:

```
function getCol() {
  window.open('picker.htm','colmap','width=640,height=480');
  return false;
}
```

The start() function, invoked when the page is loaded, initializes the *dom.js* library:

```
function start() {
  if (window.DOMObjects) DOMInitialize('div');
}
```

To invoke the Color Picker, a simple text link is included in the page, which when clicked invokes the getCol() function from the onClick event handler:

```
<a href="#" onClick="return getCol()">Select a color</a>
```

An absolutely positioned element (dynamicArea) is included to display the results of the user's preferences:

```
<div id="dynamicArea" class="l" style="width: 100%;"></div>
```

## Color Picker—*picker.htm*

On the CD

**chapter13/color/picker.htm**

The *picker.htm* page, loaded by the *index.htm* page into a pop-up window whenever the user clicks the Select a Color text link, first loads the *dom.js* library:

```
<script language="JavaScript" src="dom.js"></script>
```

An absolutely positioned class style (l) is defined:

```
.l { position: absolute; display: block; }
```

A `locked` global variable, used to indicate whether the current foreground or background color is locked, is initialized to `false`, and the initial values of the colors `fg` and `bg` are set:

```
var locked = false;
var bg = '#ffffff', fg = '#000000';
```

The global `text` variable is set to a simple message string:

```
var text =
  'Move your mouse around to change colors<br>' +
  'Click to lock color - click again to unlock';
```

The `updateColor()` function, invoked whenever the user moves the mouse over one of the visible colors on the page, first checks that the user has not `locked` the current foreground or background color, and if not, proceeds to display the passed `rgb` color as either the background (`bg`) color, if the first entry in the `what` radio group is checked, or the foreground (`fg`) color, using techniques similar to those used in the `setColor()` function held in the *index.htm* page:

```
function updateColor(rgb) {
  if (!locked) {

    if (document.what.color[0].checked)
      bg = rgb; else fg = rgb;

    document.bgColor = bg;

    if (window.DOMObjects) {
```

```
    var html =
      '<p align="center"><font color="' + fg + '">' +
      '<strong>' + passed + '</strong><br>' +
      'foreground = ' + fg + ', background = ' + bg +
      '</font></p>';

    DOMElementSetInnerHTML(DOMObjects['dynamicArea'],html)
  }
 }
 return true;
}
```

The `toggleLock()` function, invoked whenever the user clicks one of the visible colors on the page, toggles the value of the `locked` global variable and returns a `false` value to cancel the default action of the event handler used to invoke this function:

```
function toggleLock(col) {
  locked =! locked;
  return false;
}
```

The `start()` function, invoked when the page has loaded, sets the current pop-up window as the focused window—that is, it brings it to the top of the stack of windows—and then initializes the *dom.js* library:

```
function start() {
  window.focus();

  if (window.DOMObjects) DOMInitialize('div');
}
```

The code then loops in increments of 51 (33 hex) over the three colors: red (`r`), green (`g`), and blue (`b`), converting the decimal value to a hexadecimal value and building the `output` HTML necessary to hold table cells for each of the 216 colors. Each color contains an image link with `onMouseOver` and `onClick` event handlers to invoke the `updateColor()` and `toggle()` functions, respectively. In each case, the code passes the value of the current color (`col`) as input to the functions:

```
var count = 0;
var output = '';

for (var r = 0 ; r <= 255; r += 51) {
  for (var g = 0; g <= 255; g += 51) {
    for (var b = 0; b <= 255; b += 51) {
      if (count == 18) {
        document.write(output + '</tr>\n<tr>');
        count = 0;
```

```
        output = '';
    }

    var col = '#' +
      ((r==0) ? '00' : r.toString(16).toUpperCase()) +
      ((g==0) ? '00' : g.toString(16).toUpperCase()) +
      ((b==0) ? '00' : b.toString(16).toUpperCase());

    output +=
      '<td bgcolor="' + col + '">' +
      '<a href="#" onClick="return toggleLock(\''+col+'\')"' +
      ' onMouseOver="return updateColor(\''+col+'\')">' +
      '<img src="w.gif" height="20" width="20"></a></td>';

    count++;
    }
  }
}
```

The value of the `output` variable is then written out to the document:

```
document.write(output);
```

Two radio form buttons, held in the same radio group (`color`), are used to control whether the foreground or background color is changed:

```
<input type="radio" name="color" onClick="locked=false" checked>
- Background
<input type="radio" name="color" onClick="locked=false">
- Foreground
```

The `Done` button, when clicked, invokes the `setColor()` function in the `opener` window, as long as both the `opener` window exists and it still contains the `setColor()` function. Then the button closes the current pop-up window:

```
<input type="button"
  onClick="if (opener && opener.setColor) opener.setColor(fg,bg);
  self.close()" value="Done">
```

The absolutely positioned element (`dynamicArea`) is included to display the interim results of the user's preferences:

```
<div id="dynamicArea" class="l" style="width: 100%;">
<p align="center"><strong>
Move your mouse around to change colors<br>
Click to lock color - click again to unlock
</strong></p>
</div>
```

# Onscreen Keyboard

Not all computers have keyboards. Internet kiosks—that is web browsers that are located in public locations—may instead have touch-screen capabilities. The application presented here demonstrates how to allow the user to enter text data without using a keyboard. Figure 13-2 shows a keyboard made out of form fields. When the user interacts with the keyboard, either by a touch-sensitive screen or with a tracking or pointing device, the keyboard application inserts the relative character into the text input field.

Figure 13-3 shows the effect that selecting the Caps Lock key (represented by the /\ form button) has on the application. The application allows the user to toggle between the lowercase and uppercase views of

**Figure 13-2**

Onscreen Keyboard—lowercase view with Caps Lock off.

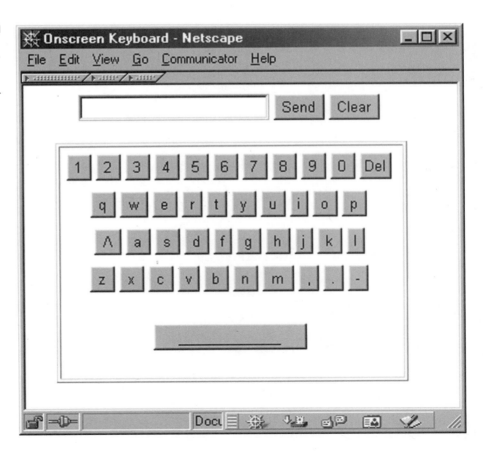

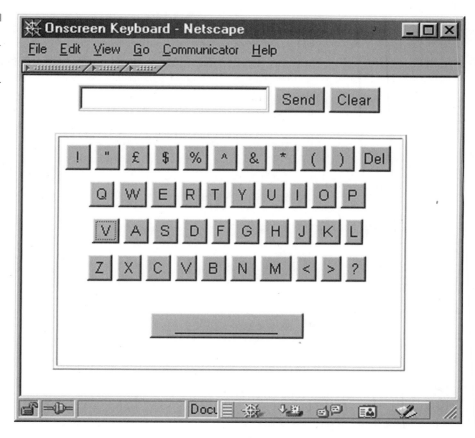

**Figure 13-3**
Onscreen Keyboard—
uppercase view with
Caps Lock on.

the keyboard. Obviously, this application can be extended to provide any character keys that you require.

## Onscreen Keyboard—*index.htm*

**chapter13/keyboard/index.htm**

The *index.htm* page contains two separate forms. The first (search) is used to hold the data entered by the user. It could be amended to submit the data to a search engine; however, at the moment, it simply alerts the value of the data to the user, before canceling the form submission by returning false:

```
<form name="search" onSubmit="alert(this.data.value);return false">
<input name="data" size="20">
<input type="submit" value="Send">
<input type="reset" value="Clear">
</form>
```

The second form (keyboard) contains all the keyboard form button fields. The entire interaction behind the Onscreen Keyboard has been implemented using onClick event handlers inside every form button field. When clicked, each form button field passes a two-character string to the add() function. The first character is to be used when the Caps Lock is off, and the second is to be used when the Caps Lock is on. For example, the a or A button uses:

```
<input type="button" name="a" value="a" onClick="add('aA')">
```

There are a couple of exceptions to this. The Caps Lock form field button simply invokes the toggle() function, passing a reference to the current (this) form:

```
<input type="button" name="caps" value="/\"
  onClick="toggle(this.form)">
```

The other exception is the Delete form field button, which invokes the del() function:

```
<input type="button" value="Del" onClick="del()">
```

The code starts by storing a double quote character within the dbquote global variable, initializing the global capsLock variable to false and holding all the lowercase letters of the alphabet in the global letters variable:

```
var dbquote = '"';
var capsLock = false;
var letters = 'abcdefghijklmnopqrstuvwxyz';
```

The add() function, invoked whenever any of the form field buttons (except the Caps Lock and Delete buttons) are clicked, adds the first character of the passed letter parameter to the search form's data field's value property if the capsLock global variable is set to false. Otherwise, it adds the second character:

```
function add(letter) {
  if (!capsLock)
    document.search.data.value += letter.substring(0,1);
```

```
   else
      document.search.data.value += letter.substring(1,2);
}
```

The `del()` function, invoked whenever the Delete form button field is clicked, retrieves the `value` property of the `search` form's `data` field. If the `length` property is greater than zero, the function removes the last character before updating the `value` property with the new value:

```
function del() {
  var input = document.search.data.value;
  if (input.length > 0)
    document.search.data.value =
      input.substring(0, input.length-1);
}
```

The `toggle()` function, invoked when the Caps Lock form button field is clicked, accepts the passed form reference (`fRef`) and then changes the `value` property of each of the form button fields from one value to another, depending on the current value of the `capsLock` global variable. The function first toggles the value of the `capsLock` global variable and, if the resultant value is equal to `true`, proceeds to update the keyboard to display the uppercase version. Otherwise, the function updates the keyboard to display the lowercase version. Rather than update the alphabetic form field buttons individually, instead, a loop through all the characters in the global `letter` variable is performed, to set the button form field value to either the uppercase value using the `String` object's `toUpperCase()` function or simply the value as is:

```
function toggle(fRef) {
  capsLock = !capsLock;

  if (capsLock) {
    fRef.caps.value = ' \\/ ';

    fRef.n1.value = ' ! ';
    fRef.n2.value = ' " ';
    fRef.n3.value = ' f ';
    fRef.n4.value = ' $ ';
    fRef.n5.value = ' % ';
    fRef.n6.value = ' ^ ';
    fRef.n7.value = ' & ';
    fRef.n8.value = ' * ';
    fRef.n9.value = ' ( ';
    fRef.n0.value = ' ) ';

    fRef.comma.value = ' < ';
    fRef.dot.value = ' > ';
    fRef.dash.value = ' ? ';

    for (var i = 0; i < letters.length; i++) {
      var letter = letters.substring(i,i+1)
```

```
        fRef[letter].value =
            ' ' + letter.toUpperCase() + ' ';
      }
    }
    else {
      fRef.caps.value = ' /\\ ';

      fRef.n1.value = ' 1 ';
      fRef.n2.value = ' 2 ';
      fRef.n3.value = ' 3 ';
      fRef.n4.value = ' 4 ';
      fRef.n5.value = ' 5 ';
      fRef.n6.value = ' 6 ';
      fRef.n7.value = ' 7 ';
      fRef.n8.value = ' 8 ';
      fRef.n9.value = ' 9 ';
      fRef.n0.value = ' 0 ';

      fRef.comma.value = ' , ';
      fRef.dot.value = ' . ';
      fRef.dash.value = ' - ';

      for (var i = 0; i < letters.length; i++) {
        var letter = letters.substring(i,i+1)
        fRef[letter].value =
            ' ' + letter + ' ';
      }
    }
  }
```

# Automated Scrolling

This application provides an attractive companion to the previous Onscreen Keyboard. Rather than requiring the user to interact with the browser to scroll down the page, this application scrolls automatically through the entire length of the document. When it reaches the end, it starts to scroll back through the document to the top. As it stands, this application repeats this process ad infinitum. The application can easily be adapted to scroll just once, or to vary the speed of the scrolling, or even to scroll on the horizontal rather than the vertical axis.

## Automated Scrolling—*index.htm*

chapter13/autoscroll/index.htm

To enable all browsers to correctly identify the length of the document, the visible contents of the page must be included with an absolutely positioned `div` element. The *dom.js* library, which includes functions to retrieve the length of elements, is included within the *index.htm* page:

```
<script language="JavaScript" src="dom.js"></script>
```

An absolutely positioned class (1) is defined:

```
.1 { position: absolute; display: block; }
```

Four global variables are used in this application—`yLength` to hold the length of the document, `yPosition` to hold the current position in the y-axis, `scrollAmount` to hold the amount to scroll each time, and `scrollInterval` to hold the delay between each scroll:

```
var yLength;
var yPosition = 0;
var scrollAmount = 15;
var scrollInterval = 100;
```

The `myScroll()` function controls the entire scrolling process. The `yPosition` global variable is incremented by the value of `scrollAmount`. The `window` object's `scroll()` method is used to reposition the document at the new coordinates (identified by zero and `yPosition`). If the ends of the document have been reached, then the value of `scrollAmount` is multiplied by `-1` to change the direction of the scroll. Finally, the `setTimeout()` method is used to invoke the `myScroll()` function after the delay specified by the `scrollInterval` global variable:

```
function myScroll() {
  yPosition += scrollAmount;
  window.scroll(0,yPosition);
  if (yPosition > yLength || yPosition == 0)
    scrollAmount *= -1;
  setTimeout('myScroll()',scrollInterval);
}
```

The `start()` function, invoked when the page has loaded, first initializes the *dom.js* library and then calculates the length of the visible document by subtracting the value returned by the `DOMWindowGetInnerHeight()` function from the value returned by the `DOMElementGetHeight()` function, both of which are held in the *dom.js* library. The whole automated scrolling process is then started by invoking the `myScroll()` function:

```
function start() {
  if (window.DOMObjects) DOMInitialize('div');

  if (window.DOMObjects) {
    yLength = DOMElementGetHeight(DOMObjects['bodyArea']) -
      DOMWindowGetInnerHeight();
    myScroll();
  }
}
```

The preceding call to the `DOMElementGetHeight()` function uses as input the `bodyArea` entry in the `DOMObjects` array. This maps to the following absolutely positioned `div` element, which is used to hold all of the document's visible content:

```
<div id="bodyArea" class="l" style="width: 100%;">
...
</div>
```

# Home Page Script

If you have a portal website, then you might want to allow your visitors to make your page the default home page they see when they open their browser. Don't panic though, as this application will not force a home page on you; the browser still confirms (independently of this application) whether or not you as the user of the browser wish to allow the default home page preference to be updated.

Internet Explorer has over time added several behaviors, one of them being `url(#default#homepage)`, supported in Internet Explorer 5, which makes the behavior of object clicked set the default home page to the requested URL. Netscape Navigator 4 allows the preferences held in the *prefs.js* file to be updated, as long as the JavaScript code requests and is granted extra privileges from the user. Requesting privileges in Netscape Navigator was covered in detail in Chapter 5 "Location and Links" in the Site Link Crawler application. Here the required privilege is the `UniversalPreferencesWrite` privilege, which as its name implies, allows universal write access to the browser's preferences.

Figure 13-4 shows the browser dialog window shown when using the `url(#default#homepage)` behavior. This allows the user the opportunity to deny the request.

Figure 13-5 shows the browser dialog window shown when requesting the `UniversalPreferencesWrite` privilege in Netscape Navigator 6.

Unfortunately, the details of the request are not as clear as the

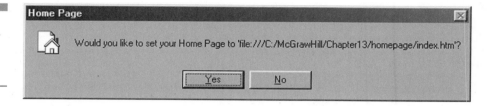

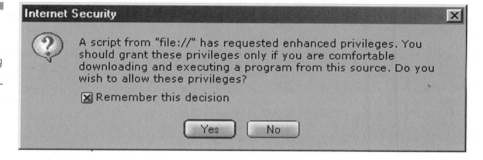

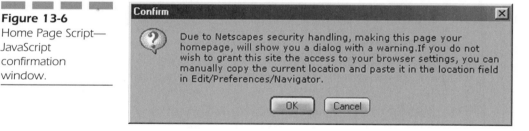

Internet Explorer version. Therefore, the Home Page Script application confirms with the user prior to requesting the extra privilege, informing the user why he or she is being consulted. Figure 13-6 shows the JavaScript-generated prompt window.

If the user cancels the initial confirmation window, then the application does not attempt to request the extra privilege.

# Home Page Script—*index.htm*

**chapter13/homepage/index.htm**

The reusable code for setting a default home page is located in the external *homepage.js* library, which is then loaded by the *index.htm* page:

```
<script language="JavaScript" src="homepage.js"></script>
```

The *index.htm* page includes a hypertext link to invoke the code to set the default home page. Rather than display this link irrespective of the browser being used, we instead test for support of the desired functionality, and then only display the link in browsers that are capable of setting the default home page. First, the location object's href property of the URL in the top frame is retrieved and assigned to the global page variable. This ensures that we do not use the URL of a frame, but rather the URL of the outer frame set:

```
var page = top.location.href;
```

If the *homepage.js* library has successfully loaded, the code tests the browser to see if it supports either the document object's layers property (Netscape Navigator 4) or the document object's getElementById property (Internet Explorer 5 and Netscape Navigator 6). Only then do we write out a hypertext link to the document, which when clicked invokes the setHomepage() function, held in the *homepage.js* library, passing a reference to the current link object (this) and the value of the global page variable:

```
if (window.setHomepage) {
    if (document.layers || document.getElementById) {
      document.write(
        '<p>' +
        '<a href="#" onClick="return setHomepage(this, page)">' +
        'Make this page your Home Page</a>' +
        '</p>'
      );
    }
}
```

The setHomepage() function returns a false value, which cancels the default action of the above onClick event handler.

## Home Page Script—*homepage.js*

On the CD    **chapter13/homepage/homepage.js**

Because the two browsers, Netscape Navigator and Internet Explorer, set the default home page using entirely different mechanisms, the setHomePage() function simply detects which browser is being used and alternates the code between either the setHomepageExplorer() or setHomePageNetscape() functions, passing onward the input parameters what and url:

```
function setHomepage(what, url) {
  if (navigator.appName == 'Microsoft Internet Explorer'
      && document.getElementById)
    setHomepageExplorer(what, url);
  else if (document.layers || document.getElementById)
    setHomepageNetscape(what, url);
  return false;
}
```

The setHomepageNetscape() function first warns the user using the window object's confirm() method, the return value of which is either true if the user clicks OK or false if the user clicks Cancel. The request to enable the UniversalPreferencesWrite privilege is only carried out if the confirm() method returns true. The navigator object's preference() method is then used to update the value of the browser.startup.homepage preference with the value of the passed url parameter, before finally disabling the privilege:

```
function setHomepageNetscape(what, url) {
  var warn =
    'Due to Netscapes security handling, making this page ' +
    'your homepage, will show you a dialog with a warning.' +
    'If you do not wish to grant this site the access to ' +
    'your browser settings, you can manually copy the ' +
    'current location and paste it in the location field in ' +
    'Edit|Preferences|Navigator.';

  if (confirm(warn)) {
    netscape.security.PrivilegeManager.enablePrivilege(
      "UniversalPreferencesWrite"
    );

    navigator.preference('browser.startup.homepage', url);

    netscape.security.PrivilegeManager.disablePrivilege(
      "UniversalPreferencesWrite"
    );
  }
}
```

The setHomepageExplorer() function first sets the passed what object reference's style object's behavior property to the url(#default#homepage) behavior, before invoking the what object's setHomePage() behavior method, passing as input the passed url parameter:

```
function setHomepageExplorer(what, url) {
  what.style.behavior = 'url(#default#homepage)';
  what.setHomePage(url);
}
```

**NOTE:** *Behaviors provide a means to extend Internet Explorer's current object model. A number of behaviors have been implemented as part of Internet Explorer 5 (referred to as* default behaviors*) and are detailed at* http://msdn.microsoft.com/workshop/author/behaviors/reference/reference.asp.

# Detecting Plug-ins and ActiveX Components

A browser natively knows a limited number of file types, such as HTML, TEXT, GIF, and JPEG. If it encounters a file type it does not support, it looks to see if the browser has any additionally installed plug-ins or helper applications that are registered against the unsupported file type. The difference between a *plug-in* and a helper application is that a plug-in will be given an area of the browser window where it can render its output and a *helper application* will normally open outside the browser window. A plug-in extends a browser's capabilities, whereas a helper application does not. A helper application is a program that resides on the client's computer and is capable of processing the corresponding file format in some manner (for example, rendering it).

A plug-in is a Netscape Navigator-specific feature, which although technically supported by Internet Explorer, is not as useful to JavaScript developers, since Internet Explorer does not provide the ability to detect what plug-ins are installed. Instead, in Internet Explorer you must detect if a given ActiveX is installed. ActiveX is Microsoft's alternative to Netscape's plug-ins, and in most cases, it works the same.

The application presented here detects if the browser supports Macromedia's very popular Shockwave Flash player. It combines this with a test for the version of Flash supported and then loads the appropriate Flash file to play. Figure 13-7 shows a simple Shockwave Flash movie, whereas Figure 13-8 shows the effect where the browser does not support Flash.

Before we describe the Shockwave Flash detector, we'll first describe how to work with the `plugins` object.

**Figure 13-7**
Detecting plug-ins and ActiveX components— a sample Flash movie.

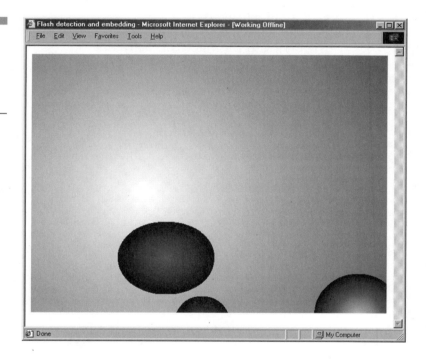

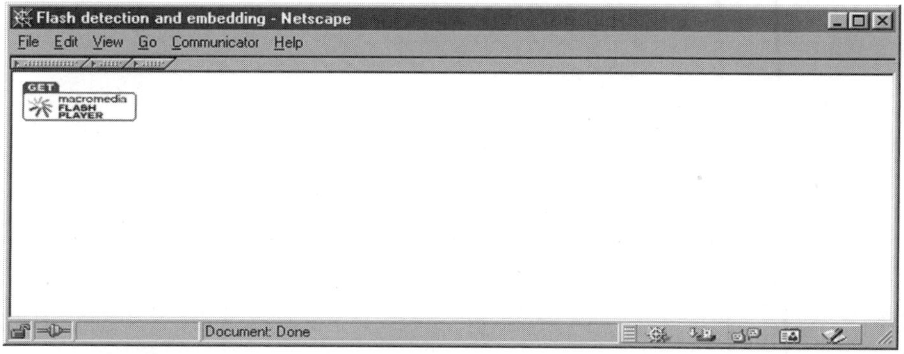

**Figure 13-8**
Detecting plug-ins and ActiveX components—Flash not supported.

## Examining the plugins Array

Both Internet Explorer and Netscape Navigator have a navigator object with a plugins property. In Netscape Navigator, this property is an array of all the installed Plugin objects. Unfortunately, in Internet Explorer it is only included for compatibility reasons and is not populated. Table 13-1 shows all the properties of the Plugin object. For Netscape Navigator you can loop through the plugins array, looking for the information you need.

A loop to show all the Plugin objects supported in Netscape Navigator, with the values of their name, filename, and description properties, along with a list of the MimeType objects that they each support, would look like this:

**chapter13/plugins/plugin1.htm**

```
for (var i = 0; i < navigator.plugins.length; i++) {
    var output = '';

    output += '<strong>Name of Plugin:</strong> ';
    output += navigator.plugins[i].name;
```

**TABLE 13-1**

All the properties of the Plugin object.

| Plug-in Properties | Description |
| --- | --- |
| description | The vendor-provided description of the plug-in. For example, "Netscape Navigator Plug-in for Acrobat." |
| filename | The complete filename of the plugin. On a Windows platforms, this would typically be<br><br>c:\program files\netscape\communicator\program\plugins\npxxxxxx.dll<br><br>where xxxxxx for an Adobe Acrobat plugin is pdf32. |
| length | Number of mime types supported |
| name | Vendor given name for the plug-in, e.g., "Adobe Acrobat" for PDF. |
| mimetype | The mime type of the file, the plug-in handles. This is an object array and can be accessed using navigator.plugins [x] [y], where y ranges from 0 to navigator.plugins.length. |

```
output += '<br><strong>File name:</strong> ';
output += navigator.plugins[i].filename;

output += '<br><strong>Description:</strong> ';
output += navigator.plugins[i].description;

for (var j = 0; j < navigator.plugins[i].length; j++) {
    output += '<br>' + navigator.plugins[i][j].type;
}

output += '<hr>';
document.write(output);
}
```

To detect whether a specific plug-in is supported then the following code can be used:

**chapter13/plugins/plugin2.htm**

```
function retrievePlugin(Plugin) {
    for (var i = 0; i < navigator.plugins.length; i++) {
        if (navigator.plugins[i].name == Plugin) {
            return true;
        }
    }
    return false;
}

var Plugin = 'Shockwave Flash';

if (retrievePlugin(Plugin))
    document.write(
      'Plugin <strong>' + Plugin + '</strong> is supported.'
    );
else
    document.write(
      'Plugin <strong>' + Plugin + '</strong> is not supported.'
    )
```

Alternatively, you can use the `navigator` object's `mimetypes` property, which is an array of all the `MimeType` objects, which if you know the mime type (for example, the plug-in for the mime type `text/pdf`) can be used to find the plug-in that supports it by testing the existence of `navigator.mimeTypes['text/pdf']` and its `enabledPlugin` property, which is a reference to one of the `Plugin` objects in the `plugins` array if there is an enabled plug-in, or `null` if there is not. Table 13-2 shows all the properties of the `MimeType` object.

A loop to show all the `MimeType` objects supported in Netscape Navigator, with the values of their `type`, `suffixes`, and `description`

**TABLE 13-2**

All the properties of the `MimeType` object.

| MimeType Properties | Description |
|---|---|
| description | The vendor-provided description of the plug-in. For example, "FutureSplash Player." |
| enabledPlugin | The `Plugin` object if available. |
| suffixes | The file extensions supported. |
| type | Mime type. |

properties, along with any supporting `enabledPlugin` object, would look like the following:

**chapter13/plugins/plugin3.htm**

```
for (var i = 0; i < navigator.mimeTypes.length; i++) {
    var output = '';
    output += "<strong>Type of mime type:</strong> ";
    output += navigator.mimeTypes[i].type;

    output += "<br><strong>Suffixes:</strong> ";
    output += navigator.mimeTypes[i].suffixes;

    output += "<br><strong>Description:</strong> ";
    output += navigator.mimeTypes[i].description;

    if (navigator.mimeTypes[i].enabledPlugin)
        output += navigator.mimeTypes[i].enabledPlugin.name;
    else output += ' N/A';

    output += "<hr>";
    document.write(output);
}
```

If you only know the file type extension or you suspect that the name of the plug-in may change, you can loop through all of the elements in the `mimeTypes` array, checking the file type extension against the list of comma-separated `suffixes` held in the `suffixes` property to find out what plug-in supports which file type extension.

The following code shows how a file type extension (e.g., `swf`) can be used to retrieve the name of the `Plugin` object that supports it:

**chapter13/plugins/plugin4.htm**

```
function retrieveMimeType (suffix) {
    for (var i = 0; i < navigator.mimeTypes.length; i++) {
        var suffixes = navigator.mimeTypes[i].suffixes;
        if (suffixes.indexOf(suffix) != -1 &&
            navigator.mimeTypes[i].enabledPlugin)
                return navigator.mimeTypes[i].enabledPlugin.name;
    }
    return '';
}

var suffix = 'swf';

var plugin = retrieveMimeType (suffix);

if (plugin != '')
    document.write(
      'The file type extension <strong>' + suffix +
      '</strong> is supported by the <strong>' +
      plugin + '</strong> plugin.<br>'
    );
else
    document.write(
      'The file type extension <strong>' + suffix +
      '</strong> is not supported.<br>'
    )
```

## Detecting ActiveX Components

With Internet Explorer you first need to create an ActiveX object for the file type you wish to support and then test if the creation was successful. In Internet Explorer 4 we have the additional problem of the lack of comprehensive error handling. The feature we lack is a localized `on error resume next` construct. Since a failed attempt to create an ActiveX object will result in an error message, we need to have any errors ignored at the time of testing. We only have one choice in Internet Explorer 4: VBScript. So to create the object, we use the following VBScript:

 **chapter13/plugins/plugin4.htm**

```
<script language="VBScript"><!--
Dim object
object = "rmocx.RealPlayer G2 Control"
on error resume next
RealPlayerG2 = (NOT IsNull(CreateObject(object)))
//--></script>
```

The syntax here is very JavaScript-like. The `IsNull()` is a built-in function to test the result of the object creation, using the built-in

`CreateObject()` function that attempts to create an ActiveX object and using the identity used by the ActiveX vendor to register their product in the Windows Registry.

From within JavaScript we can test the results of the above object creation by using

```
<script language="JavaScript"><!--
if (window.RealPlayerG2)
  document.write('RealPlayer found');
else
  document.write('RealPlayer NOT found');
//--></script>
```

## Detecting Plug-ins and ActiveX Components —*index.htm*

**chapter13/plugins/index.htm**

The code initializes a Flash version variable (`ver`) and then detects whether the page has been loaded into a Macintosh. Unfortunately, ActiveX objects are not supported by Internet Explorer on the Mac:

```
var ver = -1;
var mac =
  (navigator.appVersion.toLowerCase().indexOf('mac') != -1);
```

For Netscape Navigator we use plug-in detection:

```
if (navigator.appName == 'Netscape') {
  if (navigator.plugins["Shockwave Flash 2.0"]) ver = 2;
  else if (navigator.plugins["Shockwave Flash"]) {
    var desc = navigator.plugins["Shockwave Flash"].description;
    var verPos = desc.lastIndexOf('.');
    ver = parseInt(desc.substring(verPos - 1, verPos));
  }
}
```

For Internet Explorer we use VBScript to detect what object support is present:

```
<script language="VBScript"><!--
Dim shockwave
shockwave = "ShockwaveFlash.ShockwaveFlash."
```

```
on error resume next

if (NOT IsNull(CreateObject(shockwave & "2"))) Then ver=2
if (NOT IsNull(CreateObject(shockwave & "3"))) Then ver=3
if (NOT IsNull(CreateObject(shockwave & "4"))) Then ver=4
if (NOT IsNull(CreateObject(shockwave & "5"))) Then ver=5
//--></script>
```

Now we can use the knowledge gained up to this point to load the appropriate Flash file. For Internet Explorer the code outputs an `object` element for an ActiveX object, but only if the page is not loaded on a Macintosh. The `object` element's `classid` attribute value has been gleaned from the Macromedia site support pages. For Netscape Navigator an `embed` element is output:

```
if (ver > -1) {
    if (navigator.appName == 'Microsoft Internet Explorer') {
        if (!mac)
          document.write(
            '<object classid="clsid:' +
            'D27CDB6E-AE6D-11cf-96B8-444553540000">' +
            '<param name="movie" value="flash' +ver+ '.swf">' +
            '<param name="play" value="true">' +
            '<param name="loop" value="true">' +
            '</object>'
          );
    }
    else if (navigator.appName == 'Netscape') {
        document.write(
          '<embed src="flash' + ver + '.swf">'
        );
    }
}
```

In each case a Flash file with the version number in the filename is used. For example, for browsers that support Flash 4, the movie *flash4.swf* is loaded.

If Flash is not supported, the code outputs HTML markup to request that the user download a copy of Flash from the Macromedia website:

```
else {
    document.write(
      '<a href="http://www.macromedia.com/go/getflashplayer/">' +
      '<img src="get_flashplayer.gif" width="88" height="31"'+
      ' alt="Download Flash"></a>'
    );
}
```

A special `noscript` element rounds off the script, just in case the browser does not support JavaScript or where the user has disabled JavaScript support:

```
<noscript>
<img src="sample.gif" width="640" height="480"
  alt="A screenshot from the Flash movie">
</noscript>
```

## Summary

This chapter has shown that there is more to JavaScript than simply working with the basic document object model. JavaScript can, especially in the case of the Onscreen Keyboard and Automated Scrolling applications, change the way people view or interact with the browser. The Color Picker shows how JavaScript can be used to generate tools for developers. It is highly likely that this type of application does not ever become visible to the users of a website, but the tool can quite easily be used to decide what two colors work well together.

# Fun Stuff

If you've made it this far, then you have learned some useful JavaScript techniques and principles. Creating games is a good way to put them into practice and develop new methods of solving coding problems, which we'll do in this chapter.

This chapter describes a few of the games possible with JavaScript and shows how code written once is reused in later games. It also demonstrates how ordinary image swapping can lead to the appearance of motion in games like Tetris and Columns.

Icon Match ../chapter14/match/index.htm
Icon Match 2 players ../chapter14/match/index2.htm
Tetris ../chapter14/tetris/index.htm
Columns ../chapter14/columns/index.htm
Mouse Trail ../chapter14/trail/index.htm
Personality Quiz ../chapter14/personality/index.htm

## Icon Match

Based on an old card pastime, this game consists of matching various pairs of icons together. The icons are randomly arranged, facedown, on a grid. The player then tries to find all the matching pairs in the fewest number of moves by selecting two icons per turn. A JavaScript version of this game is fairly straightforward because the game does not involve moving any pieces around the screen—click on a grid square to reveal one icon, then click on another square to show a second icon. If the second icon matches the first, then remove them both; if not, hide the two icons again. Repeat until all the icons have been removed from the grid. Figure 14-1 shows an Icon Match game in progress.

A two-player version of this game is also included on the CD, along with a sample set of icons. If you want to create your own custom icons, try basing them around a theme, and if you want to make the game harder, use similar-shaped icons and have multiple sets in different colors. Figure 14-2 shows the two-player version of Icon Match.

## Icon Match—*index.htm*

chapter14/match/index.htm

**Figure 14-1**
Icon Match—
a single-player game
in progress.

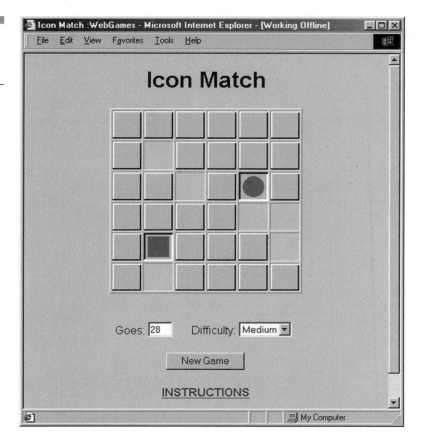

We'll start by looking at the main variables used throughout the game. Initially, we zero the game state (whether it is running or not) and the counter of matched icons, and set the currently selected tile to indicate nothing. Then we define the length of time that the tiles stay revealed and state that we have a number of sets of icons (typically, just color variations of the same tiles) and the number of icons in a set.

To give the player some flexibility, we allow the difficulty level (diff) to be passed in the URL, as discussed in Chapter 8 in the Passing Data from One Form to Another application. If the difficulty was not passed, then we set it to the middle setting by default. We then use the difficulty level to determine the number of tiles in play and the dimensions of the board. One thing to watch is that howmany * 2 must equal width * height.

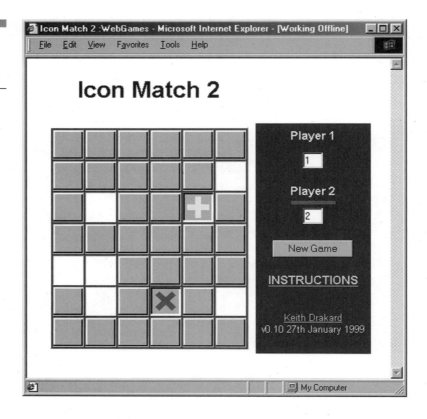

**Figure 14-2**
Icon Match—
a two-player version
in progress.

```
var running = 0;
var count;
var tiles = 6;
var sets = 4;
var howmany;
var width;
var height;

var passed = window.location.search.substring(1);
var diff = getParm(passed,'d') - 0;
if (diff == 0) diff =2;

if (diff == 1) {
  howmany = tiles * (sets - 2);
  width = 6;
  var height = 4;
}
else if (diff == 2) {
  howmany = tiles * (sets - 1);
  width = 6;
  var height = 6;
}
else {
```

```
   howmany = tiles * sets;
   width = 6;
   var height = 8;
}

var board = new Array(width * height);
var sel = -1;
var delay = 750;
```

The preload() function preloads the images and sets up the board, ready for a new game. One image is used to represent a hidden icon (tile[0]), one to represent a removed icon (blank), and the rest from loading image icon files in the format s_t.gif, where s is the set number and t the tile number:

```
function preload() {
  if (document.images) {
    tile = new makeArray(tiles * sets + 1);
    tile[0].src= 'images/tileup.gif';

    for (var s = 1; s <= sets; s++) {
      for (var t = 1; t <= tiles; t++) {
        tile[((s-1)*tiles)+t].src = 'images/'+s+'_'+t+'.gif';
      }
    }

    blank = new Image();
    blank.src = 'images/blank.gif';

  }
}
```

The newgame() function is called every time we start a new game. Normally, we can just reset all the variables and put the board back to the starting position. However, we need to detect if the player has changed the tmp_d difficulty level, as this means we have to create a different-sized board. The simplest way to do that is to simply reload the page with the new difficulty level passed in the URL. On the other hand, if reloading the page is not needed, then we can just blank out the internal representation of the board and the images that the player actually sees. We then only have to hide all the icons and their corresponding pair on the grid.

The method used to hide these icons is slightly over the top—there's no real need to randomly pick an icon to randomly be hidden on the board. While keeping track of exactly which ones we've already placed, we loop over the available icons (selecting at random) and hide two copies in unoccupied board spaces. Note that we don't simply mark the board square as being occupied; instead, we remember exactly which icon occupies it. This comes in handy when comparing two squares, as it eliminates the need to look up extra variables. After we've placed our icons on the board, we finish setting up the new game by resetting three game variables and making the first reference to the user interface by ensuring that the number of turns that the player sees he or she has taken is set to zero:

```
function newgame() {
  var index = document.user.diff.selectedIndex;
  var tmp_d = document.user.diff.options[index].value;
  if (tmp_d != diff) {
    window.location.href = 'index.htm?d=' + tmp_d;

  }
  else {
    for (var i = 0; i < (width*height); i++) {
      board[i] = 0;
      document.images['' + i].src = tile[0].src;
    }

    var temp = new Array(tiles * sets + 1);
    for (var i = 0; i < tiles * sets + 1; i++)
      temp[i] = 0;
    var what = (rand(sets) * tiles) + rand(tiles) + 1;
    var where = rand(width * height);

    for (var i = 0; i < howmany; i++) {
      while (temp[what])
        what= (rand(sets) * tiles) + rand(tiles) + 1;
      temp[what] = 1;
      while (board[where])
        where = rand(width * height);
      board[where] = what;
      while (board[where])
        where = rand(width*height);
      board[where] = what;
    }

    document.user.goes.value = 0;
    sel = -1;
    count = 0;
    running = 1;
  }
}
```

After setting all the variables and creating the board, we are ready for the main function of the game. First off, because of the way JavaScript and HTML work, we can't be sure which phase of the game the `select()` function has been invoked within, so we check that we are currently playing a game and exit the function if we're not.

Once that's been established, we look to see if we are selecting the second icon in the turn or just the first. If it is the first icon of the turn, then we don't need to do anything but check we aren't trying to select a blank square, show the icon to the player, and remember that we now have something selected.

What happens when the second icon has been chosen is the key part of the `select()` function. It's important to try to cover all the different things that the player can do at any one point—in this case, we look to see if he or she has attempted to pick a previously revealed icon. If the player is actually selecting a hidden tile, we check it to see if it matches the previous icon. If it does, then we increment the number found and see if that's all the icons found. In either eventuality, we show the second icon to the player, then reset the currently selected tile and note that we've taken another go.

We also set a timer to invoke the `clear()` function, which either hides the selected pair from the player or removes them from the board. Because there is a delay before this function is activated (in order to give the player time to see the second icon), we again have to be vigilant, this time in case the player selects another icon during the delay. To get around this, we set the `running` state of the game to 0 before we set the timer to call the `clear()` function, and we'll put it back to 1 after the `clear()` function completes:

```
function select(pos) {
  if (!running) return;

  if (sel>= 0) {

    if (document.images['' + pos].src == tile[0].src) {

      document.images['' + pos].src = tile[board[pos]].src;

      if (board[pos] == board[sel]) {
        running = 0;
        document.user.goes.value++;
        count++;
        setTimeout('clear(' + sel + ',' + pos + ',1)', delay);
        if (count == howmany) {
          setTimeout('alert("Well done!\\n")', delay+10);
        }
      }
      else {
        running = 0;
        document.user.goes.value++;
        setTimeout('clear(' + sel + ',' + pos + ',0)', delay);
      }
      sel = -1;
    }

  }

  else if (document.images[pos].src != blank.src) {

    document.images['' + pos].src = tile[board[pos]].src;
    sel = pos;
  }
}
```

The clear() function, called to remove or hide a pair of icons, sets the two board positions to be blank or back to the "hidden tile" image. Finally, it resets the game running state back to 1:

```
function clear(posA, posB, flag) {
  var clear = (flag) ? blank.src : tile[0].src
  document.images['' + posA].src = clear;
  document.images['' + posB].src = clear;
  running = 1;
}
```

There are also some miscellaneous functions that are used throughout the game. One is the same random number generator described in Chapter 2 "Maths and Numbers":

```
function rand(n) {
  return Math.floor(Math.random() * n);
}
```

In addition are two other general-purpose functions that we can reuse to easily create all the icon images and pull out any parameters passed in the URL, such as the difficulty level:

```
function makeArray(n) {
  this.length = n;
  for (i = 0; i < n; i++)
    this[i] = new Image();
  return this;
}

function getParm(string,parm) {
  var startPos = string.indexOf(parm + '=');
  if (startPos > -1) {
    startPos = startPos + 2;
    var endPos = string.indexOf("&",startPos);
    if (endPos == -1) endPos = string.length;
    return unescape(string.substring(startPos,endPos));
  }
  return '';
}
```

The visual front end of the game is now the only element left, and it is simply a matter of wrapping the game board in a table and a form for the user interface. Rather than calling document.write() every few lines, it is easier (and quicker) to store up all the desired output in one variable and then just write that out at the end.

The board is created by looping through the values of the height and width variables set at the start of the game and placing a "hidden tile" image on each grid square. Each image is named and has a link placed around it to call the `select()` function with its position on the board, as determined by the useful expression `(y*width)+x`:

```
var output = '';

for (y = 0; y < height; y++) {
  for (x = 0; x < width; x++) {
    pos = (y * width) + x;
    if (x == 0) output += '<tr>';
    output += '<td><a href="javascript:select('+pos+')">';
    output += '<img src="tileup.gif"';
    output += ' name="'+pos+'"</a></td>';
    if (x == width - 1) output += '</tr>';
  }
}

document.write(output);
```

Additional form fields, used to hold and display the state of the game and to allow the player to start a new game, are additionally added to the output variable before being written out to the document, although not shown here this code is present in the version on the CD.

The game is initiated by invoking the `preload()` function to preload the images and then the `newgame()` function to initialize the game, ready for the player interaction:

```
preload();
newgame();
```

## Icon Match—*index.htm2*

 **chapter14/match2/index.htm**

As previously mentioned, there is a two-player version of the Icon Match game on the CD that provides additional functionality over and above the single-player version.

# Tetris

A desktop classic, Tetris (originally by Alexey Pajitnov) showed how a simple idea could have good game play and be enormously addictive to boot. A quick recap of the game: Tetris involves guiding a stream of

**Figure 14-3**
Tetris—a game in progress.

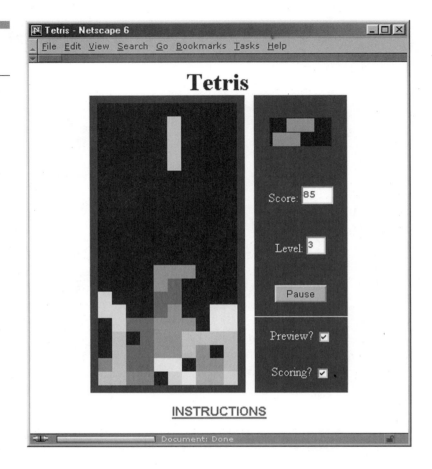

falling shapes in order to make as many complete lines as possible. As lines are completed, they are removed, and any pieces above them drop down to fill their place. The shapes fall quicker as the score increases until the shapes come too fast and they reach the top of the playing area. Figure 14-3 shows a Tetris game in progress.

## Tetris—*index.htm*

**chapter14/tetris/index.htm**

We'll start again with the global variables used throughout the game. First, we set two game-state variables to indicate that the game hasn't been started yet and that the game isn't paused. We then defined both the `width` and `height` of the playing area, and also the dimensions of the tiles. Next, we create space for information about our falling blocks—the color of the current piece and the color and shape of the next piece. The shape of the current piece needs to be represented in more detail than just one number; we need to know its location in the playing area. We also set up the "heap" of pieces—that is, what the shape drops onto when it reaches the bottom of the board.

After assigning ordinary ASCII key values to the various directions and rotations that the player can perform on a falling piece, we reserve a variable to hold the interval between a piece falling from one line of the board to the next (and in order to pause the game, we need something to identify the timer we use for this as well). Finally, we set the level (or, in game terms, the rate at which the blocks fall) and an array to hold the scores needed to reach the next level:

```
var running = 0;
var paused = 0;
var width = 10;
var height = 21;
var tilex = tiley = 18;
var c_color;
var nextp; var nextc;
var heap = new Array(width * height);
var DOWN = 50;
var LEFT = 52;
var RIGHT = 54;
var ROTATE_C = 56;
var ROTATE_A = 53;
var interval;
var id;
var level = 1;
var lev = new Array(0,20,45,90,200,400,800,1600,3200,6400,9800);
```

We have left out the definition of the `preload()` function, since it is almost exactly the same as all the other image preloading functions used throughout the book. In this case, we read in a transparent 1-pixel GIF and seven colored, single-pixel GIFs into an array called `color[]`.

To get some semblance of the original game, it was necessary to use the `onKeyPress` events of JavaScript 1.2. Unfortunately, at the time of writing, Netscape Navigator and Internet Explorer use different ways of capturing key-press information, so we need to cater for both. For Internet Explorer and Netscape Navigator 6, the `keyPress()` function is called from an `onKeyPress` handler in the `body` element, passing both the `window` object's `event` object reference and the event handler's `event` object reference (required for Netscape Navigator 6):

```
<body onKeyPress="keyPress(window.event, event)">
```

For Netscape Navigator prior to version 6, we require the following lines to capture the KEYPRESS event and then to set the window object's onKeyPress event handler to invoke the keyPress() function:

```
if (navigator.appName == 'Netscape' && !document.getElementById) {
  window.captureEvents(Event.KEYPRESS);
  window.onKeyPress = keyPress;
}
```

The KeyPress() function passes the value of the pressed key to the play() function. For Internet Explorer, the window object's event object's keyCode property contains the value of the key pressed. In Netscape Navigator prior to version 6, the passed e event object reference's which property contains the value, whereas for Netscape Navigator 6, the value is held in the passed event object's which property:

```
function keyPress(e, event) {
  if (running) {
    if (window.event && window.event.keyCode)
      play(window.event.keyCode);
    else if (e && e.which)
      play(e.which);
    else if (event && event.which)
      play(event.which);
  }
}
```

The play() function determines what result, if any, the passed key parameter has on the current piece by calling one of the movement or rotation functions:

```
function play(key) {
  if (key == LEFT) move(-1);
  if (key == RIGHT) move(1);
  if (key == DOWN) move_down();
  if (key == ROTATE_C) rotate(1);
  if (key == ROTATE_A) rotate(-1);
}
```

Unlike more static games like Icon Match, whenever a new game is started, we need to constantly keep moving pieces. In JavaScript, we can do this by having one function call itself after execution, using a timer so the game is not inhumanly quick for the player.

The step() function acts as the main game loop. If a piece is in play, then it is moved down one line and the step() function is called again. Otherwise, we try to make a new piece and do this all over. However, if we detect that there is no more room at the top of the board to create a new piece, then the newpiece() function will fail and the game is over, so the heap of pieces is turned to a single color, the preview screen is blanked, and along with the current block variables, the running state of the game is reset:

```
function step() {
  if (block[0] != -1) {
    move_down();
    id = setTimeout('step()', interval);
  }
  else {
    if (newpiece(nextp)) {
      nextp = rand(7);
      nextc = rand(7);
      preview();
      id = setTimeout('step()', interval);
    }
    else {
      c_color = rand(7);
      for (c = 0; c < width * height; c++)
        if (heap[c])
          document.images['' + c].src = color[c_color].src;
      for (i = 0; i < 8; i++)
        document.images['preview' + i].src = color[0].src;
      document.user.b.value = ' New Game ';
      running = 0;
      block = null;
    }
  }
}
```

The newpiece() function is normally called from the step() function with the value of the next piece to be created. Once the piece has been created and the block[] array set with the shape of the piece, we move the piece from a default position by a random amount. If this brings it into conflict with the existing heap of pieces, then the game is over and we return zero. Otherwise, we display the piece on the board and exit the function successfully:

```
function newpiece(flag) {
  var w = (flag) ? flag : rand(7);
  var m = rand(width - 3);

  switch (w) {
    case 1 :
      block[0]  =   8;
      block[1]  =  18;
      block[2]  =  28;
      block[3]  =  38;
      break;
    case 2 :
      block[0]  =   7;
      block[1]  =   8;
      block[2]  =   9;
      block[3]  =  17;
```

```
        break;
      case 3 :
        block[0]  =   7;
        block[1]  =   8;
        block[2]  =   9;
        block[3]  =  19;
        break;
      case 4 :
        block[0]  =   8;
        block[1]  =  17;
        block[2]  =  18;
        block[3]  =  28;
        break;
      case 5 :
        block[0]  =   7;
        block[1]  =  17;
        block[2]  =  18;
        block[3]  =  28;
        break;
      case 6 :
        block[0]  =   8;
        block[1]  =  17;
        block[2]  =  18;
        block[3]  =  27;
        break;
      case 7 :
        block[0]  =   7;
        block[1]  =   8;
        block[2]  =  17;
        block[3]  =  18;
    }

    for (i = 0; i < 4; i++) {
      block[i] -= m;
      if (heap[block[i]]) return(0);
    }

    if (flag) {
      c_color = nextc;
      for (i = 0; i < 4; i++)
        document.images['' + block[i]].src = color[c_color].src;
    }
    return(w);
}
```

The next group of functions are the functions called from the play()
function to control the motion of the falling block. The move() function
is called when the left or right keys are pressed. As for all the motion
functions, we first check to see if a block is in play, or if it is that brief
period between pieces. Assuming a piece is still falling, we simulate the
desired direction on each of the four component squares that make up a
Tetris block. If any of the squares would then intersect an edge of the
board or the heap of previous pieces, we break out of our test and no
action is taken. Otherwise, we know we can carry out the motion safely
and redisplay the piece:

```
function move(dir) {
  if (block[0] == -1) return(0);

  for (i = 0; i < 4; i++) {
    edge = (dir==1) ? ((block[i] % width) == width-1)
      : ((block[i] % width) == 0)
    if (edge || heap[block[i] + dir]) return(0);
  }

  display(dir);
  return(1);
}
```

The `move_down()` function is broadly similar to the previous function, in that we check if we've reached the edge of the board (in this case the bottom of the playing area) or if we've come to rest on the `heap`. However, instead of not carrying out the motion, we merge the piece into the rest of the `heap`.

One key point is the parameter that is passed to the `display()` function. The way in which the pieces are represented on the board has a direct effect on how easy it is to manipulate those pieces. Rather than describe the board and the pieces as a set of x and y values, we simply number each square consecutively, starting from 0 in the top left corner and ending with the product of the width and height in the bottom right corner. From this representation, we can call the `move()` function with a direction of -1. If it is safe to move, then the `display()` function is called with the same parameter, 1 is subtracted from all the squares of the piece, and the piece is moved one square to the left.

Alternatively, we can call it with the width of the board (as a positive value) and, in effect, move the piece down one line:

```
function move_down() {
  if (block[0] == -1) return(0);

  for (var i = 0; i < 4; i++) {
    if ((block[i] >= (height - 1) * width) ||
        (heap[block[i] + width])) {
      if (document.user.scoring.checked)
        document.user.score.value =
          document.user.score.value * 1 + level;
      merge();
      return(0);
    }
  }

  display(width);
  return(1);
}
```

Rotating the pieces is a bit more complicated than just altering each of the coordinates of the piece by the same value. To rotate a piece, we need to work out a pivot point from the positions of the squares that make it up. We can then apply a simple transformation to each of the squares and make the piece rotate.

The pivot point is calculated by converting the four single values that describe the piece's position into four x and y coordinate pairs and then averaging the values. The difference between the pivot and each of the four squares is then either added to or subtracted depending on which direction we are rotating. Finally, we check, as before, whether this movement has brought the piece into the edge of the board or onto the heap. If the movement is okay to continue, then we redisplay the piece at the new position:

```
function rotate(dir) {
  if (block[0] == -1) return(0);

  var x = new Array(3);
  var y = new Array(3);
  var xt = 0;
  var xp;
  var xn;
  var yt = 0;
  var yp;
  var yn;
  var pos;
  var newpos = new Array(3);

  for (i = 0; i < 4; i++) {
    x[i]= (block[i] % width);
    xt += x[i];
    y[i]= Math.floor(block[i] / width);
    yt += y[i];
  }
  xp = Math.floor((xt / 4) + 0.5);
  yp = Math.floor((yt / 4) + 0.5);

  for (i = 0; i < 4; i++) {
    xn = (dir == 1) ? (xp - (y[i] - yp)) : (xp + (y[i] - yp))
    yn = (dir == 1) ? (yp + (x[i] - xp)) : (yp - (x[i] - xp))
    pos = (yn * width) + xn;
    if ((xn<0 || xn>=width) || (yn<0 || yn>=height) ||
      heap[pos]) return(0);
    newpos[i] = pos;
  }

  for (i = 0; i < 4; i++)
    document.images['' + block[i]].src = color[0].src;
  for (i = 0; i < 4; i++) {
    block[i] = newpos[i];
    document.images['' + newpos[i]].src = color[c_color].src;
  }

  return(1);
}
```

The display() function is only used by the horizontal and vertical move functions, since rotate() needs its own, near-identical display method because the positional modifier is not the same for each of the four squares of the piece. However, the principal is the same in each case— blank all of the old positions, move the block to the new one, and redisplay:

```
function display(modifier) {
  for (i = 0; i < 4; i++)
    document.images['' + block[i]].src = color[0].src;

  for (i = 0; i < 4; i++) {
    block[i] += modifier;
    document.images['' + block[i]].src = color[c_color].src;
  }
}
```

After a piece has come to rest, it is merged into the rest of the heap. Merging a piece into the heap is straightforward—mark the position of the piece on the heap, reset the current block, and test to see if any complete lines have been formed by the addition of this new piece. If a line has been made, then we need to remove it. First, we can provide the player with some feedback by making all of a row change color (matching the piece that completed it). Then we score the row and delete it, giving just enough time for the player to register the color change before the game continues:

```
function merge() {
  var count;
  var x = 0;

  for (i = 0; i < 4; i++) {
    heap[block[i]] = 1;
    block[i] = -1;
  }

  for (y = 0; y < height; y++) {
    count = 0;
    while (heap[(y * width) + x]) { count++; x++; }

    if (count >= width) {
      for (x = (y * width); x < (y * width) + width; x++)
        document.images['' + x].src = color[c_color].src;
      score(height - y);
      setTimeout('del(' + y + ')', 50);
    }
    x = 0;
  }
}
```

The del() function accepts the y position of the row to be deleted, removes that row from the heap and from the screen, and then looks to see if there are any blocks above each x position of the removed line that need to be moved down:

```
function del(y) {
  var ymod;
```

```
for (x = (y * width); x < (y * width) + width; x++) {
  document.images['' + x].src = color[0].src;
  heap[x] = 0;
}

for (c = (y * width) - 1; c >= 0; c--) {
  if (heap[c]) {
    while (!heap[c + width]) {
      document.images['' + (c+width)].src =
        document.images['' + c].src;
      document.images['' + c].src = color[0].src;
      heap[c + width] = 1;
      heap[c] = 0;
    }
  }
}
}
```

The score() function is invoked with the height of the row that has just been completed. Depending on whether or not the player has the scoring option selected, the function either just counts the number of rows removed or uses a combination of the height of the row, the current level, and whether the "preview piece" option is enabled to determine a score:

```
function score(modifier) {
  var cs = (document.user.score.value) * 1;

  if (document.user.scoring.checked) {
    var score = (Math.floor(modifier / 5) + 1) * level;
    if (document.user.preview.checked)
      score = Math.floor(score / 2 + 0.5);

    cs += score;
    if (cs > lev[level] && level < 12)
      level++;
  }
  else {
    cs += 1;
    if (cs > ((lev[level] / 10) * 3) && level < 12)
      level++;
  }

  document.user.score.value = cs;
  document.user.level.value = level;

  interval = 300 - (20 * level);
}
```

Tetris includes an option to see what the next piece to drop will be—the preview facility mentioned above. Since the player can turn this preview facility on and off during the game, we always need to clear the preview screen, then check to see if we need to redraw it. If we do, then some of the squares in the preview need to be set to reflect the shape of the next piece.

We can do this more easily by taking advantage of the way in which they appear in the `newpiece()` function and of what the shapes actually are:

```
function preview() {
  var c = color[nextc].src;
  for (i = 0; i < 8; i++)
    document.images['preview' + i].src = color[0].src;

  if (!document.user.preview.checked) return(0);

  if (nextp != 5) document.images['preview0'].src = c;
  document.images['preview1'].src = c;
  if (nextp < 6) document.images['preview2'].src = c;
  if (nextp == 1) document.images['preview3'].src = c;
  if (nextp == 2 || nextp == 5 || nextp == 7)
    document.images['preview4'].src = c;
  if (nextp > 3) document.images['preview5'].src = c;
  if (nextp % 3 == 0) document.images['preview6'].src = c;

  return(1);
}
```

The `newgame()` function doubles up as the function that pauses (and recontinues) the game. All of this is invoked from a form button, which changes its lettering depending on the running state of the game. If the function is to pause the game, then we just need to clear the main loop timer. If we need to continue the game, then we restart this timer (with double the normal interval to give the player a chance to move from pausing the game to playing it again):

```
function newgame() {
  if (! document.images) return(0);

  if (! running) {
    if (! paused) {
      document.user.score.value = 0;
      document.user.level.value = 1;
      block = new Array(3);
      for (i = 0; i < 4; i++) block[i] = -1;
      for (c = 0; c < width * height; c++) {
        document.images['' + c].src = color[0].src;
        heap[c] = 0;
      }
      nextc = rand(7);
      newpiece(rand(7));
      nextp = rand(7);
      nextc = rand(7);
      preview(nextp);
      level = 1;
      interval = 300;
    }
    running = 1;
    paused = 0;
    document.user.b.value = ' Pause ';
    id = setTimeout('step()', interval * 2);
  }
```

```
  else {
    running = 0;
    paused = 1;
    document.user.b.value = ' Continue ';
    clearTimeout(id);
  }
}
```

Like most JavaScript games, the easiest way to create the playing area is to loop over the x and y dimensions of the board within a table:

```
for (y = 0; y < height; y++) {
  for (x = 0; x < width; x++) {
    if (x == 0)
      output += '<tr>';
    output += '<td><img src="blank.gif" name="'+((y*width)+x);
    output += '" width="'+tilex+'" height="'+tiley+'"></td>';
    if (x == width - 1)
      output += '</tr>\n';
  }
}
```

The preview screen area is created in much the same fashion:

```
output += '<tr>'
for (i = 0; i < 8; i++) {
  output += '<td><img src="blank.gif" name="preview'+i+'" ';
  output += 'width="'+tilex+'" height="'+tiley+'"></td>';
  if (i == 3)
    output += '</tr>\n<tr>';
}
output += '</tr>\n';
```

The final part of the game is the HTML form that provides feedback on the score and current level of the game and allows the user to pause or start the game and to choose whether or not new pieces are previewed first and if scoring is enabled:

```
output += 'Score: <input type="text" size="4" name="score"';
output += ' value="0" onFocus="blur()">\n';
output += 'Level: <input type="text" size="2" NAME="level"';
output += ' value="1" onFocus="blur()">\n';
output += '<input type="button" name="b" value=" New Game "';
output += ' onClick="newgame()" onFocus="blur()">\n';
output += 'Preview? <input type="checkbox" size="2"';
output += ' name="preview" checked onFocus="blur()">\n';
output += 'Scoring? <input type="checkbox" size="2"';
output += ' name="scoring" checked onFocus="blur()">\n';
```

These form elements need to have an onFocus event handler to blur the current focus. Otherwise, Netscape Navigator will not detect the key presses if any of them are selected with the mouse, which would be a slight problem when the user started playing.

# Columns

There are many variants of Tetris, which can now be made without having to code everything from scratch again. This version differs in that each piece is a line of three blocks, and each block may be a different color. Removing blocks is done by forming lines, of three or more and in any direction, of the same color. Finally, if there is an empty space underneath a block, then the block will fall down, leading to cascades as new lines are formed and removed. Figure 14-4 shows a Columns game in progress.

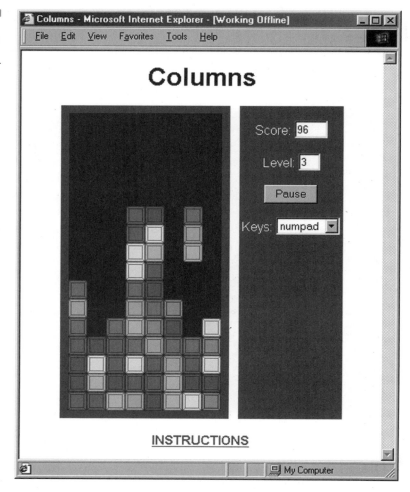

**Figure 14-4**
Columns—a game in progress.

Setup takes place as normal—the game state is set, the board and tile sizes are defined, and space is set up for the heap. The remove array is used during the line-detection function to flag which blocks are due to be removed from play. An enhancement over the original Tetris framework is the addition of extra key settings, so the player isn't forced to use the number-pad keys. The variable keychoice reflects which setting the player is using—changing this will alter the key/variable mapping:

```
var running = 0;
var paused = 0;
var width = 8;
var height = 16;
var tilex = tiley = 24;
var heap = new Array(width * height);
var remove = new Array(width * height);
var timeout_id;
var keychoice = 1;
var DOWN = 50;
var LEFT = 52;
var RIGHT = 54;
var ROTATE_C = 56;
var ROTATE_A = 53;
var interval;
var level = 0;
var lev = new Array(0,10,70,140,210,270,340,410);
```

This is where we can start reusing chunks of the Tetris code. Here we simply need to remove the redundant preview code from the step() function, and our main loop is written. The newpiece() function called from the loop is similar in principal to the equivalent Tetris function, but now there is just one shape to move to a random starting position at the top of the board. The rand() function, used to pick the starting modifier and the three colors, has now been in all three of the games in this chapter:

```
function newpiece() {
  var m = rand(width);
  block[0] = 8;
  block[1] = 8 + width;
  block[2] = 8 + (2 * width);
  for (var i = 0; i < 3; i++) {
    block[i] -= m;
    if (heap[block[i]]) return(0);
  }

  cblock[0] = rand(7);
  cblock[1] = rand(7);
  cblock[2] = rand(7);
  for (var i = 0; i < 3; i++)
    document.images['' + block[i]].src = color[cblock[i]].src;

  return(1);
}
```

Like the main loop, we can reuse most of the previous movement functions with little changes. The method of detecting and responding to key presses does not change—although instead of rotating the piece, we will now be cycling the three colors up or down:

```
function rotate(dir) {
  if (block[0] == -1) return(0);

  if (dir == 1) {
    var temp = cblock[0];
    cblock[0] = cblock[1];
    cblock[1] = cblock[2];
    cblock[2] = temp;
  } else {
    var temp = cblock[2];
    cblock[2] = cblock[1];
    cblock[1] = cblock[0];
    cblock[0] = temp;
  }

  display(0);
  return(1);
}
```

The `move()` function remains unchanged, and the only alteration to the `move_down()` function is to remove the scoring check and to loop over only three blocks instead of four. Likewise, only this change needs to be made to the `display()` function.

## Heap Control

The main internal difference between Columns and Tetris lies in what happens when a piece finishes moving. In Tetris, detecting completed lines was only a matter of scanning horizontally for the absence of any block. Here, though, we must check in eight directions and keep track of the color of each block in the heap. After the piece lands, the positions in the heap are flagged with the color of each block and then the game is paused briefly, so that the player can register that the blocks have been deleted before the next piece drops, before the board is checked for completed lines:

```
function merge() {
  for (var i = 0; i < 3; i++) {
    heap[block[i]] = cblock[i];
    block[i] = -1;
    cblock[i] = -1;
  }
  paused = 1;
  setTimeout('mycheck()', 100);
}
```

The actual line-checking function is called from within the `mycheck()` parent function. If any lines of three or more of the same color are found, they are scored and deleted, and then the function calls itself again to check for newly formed lines. Otherwise, control is passed back to the player and the game resumes:

```
function mycheck() {
  var howmany = check();
  if (howmany > 0) {
    score(howmany);
    del();
    setTimeout('mycheck()', 100);
  }
  else
    paused = 0;
}
```

It would be possible to just check around the piece and then around any blocks dropping into the vacated spaces. However, with modern computing power, the easiest way to check is to simply scan the whole board.

The `check()` function looks in four directions—respectively, horizontally, top left to bottom right, vertically, and top right to bottom left—which cover all the possible lines. The loops work by taking these x and y coordinates and converting them to the positioning number used in the internal board representation. The four `diff` settings control the direction of the scan—a multiple of this number will be added to the original position to give the position of the next square in the line. Because of the shape of the board and the way in which the `chk()` function works, the diagonals require two separate scans—one for lines coming from the top of the board and one for lines coming from the side:

```
function check() {
  var pos;
  var diff;
  var count = 0;

  diff = 1;
  for (var y = 0; y < height; y++) {
    for (var x = 2; x < width; x++) {
      pos = (y * width) + x;
      count += chk(pos, diff);
    }
  }

  diff = 1 + width;
  for (var i = 1; i < width - 2; i++) {
    for (var j = 2; j < Math.min(width, width - i); j++) {
      pos = i + (j * diff);
      count += chk(pos, diff);
    }
  }
```

```
      }
      for (var i = 0; i <= (height-1) * width; i += width) {
        for (var j=2; j < Math.min(width, height-(i/width)); j++) {
          pos = i + (j * diff);
          count += chk(pos, diff);
        }
      }

      diff = width;
      for (var x = 0; x < width; x++) {
        for (var y = 2; y < height; y++) {
          pos = (y * width) + x;
          count += chk(pos, diff);
        }
      }

      diff = width - 1;
      for (var i = 2; i < width; i++) {
        for (var j = 2; j < Math.min(width, width - i); j++) {
          pos = i + (j * diff);
          count += chk(pos, diff);
        }
      }

      for (var i = width - 1; i < height * width; i += width) {
        for (var j=2; j < Math.min(width, height-(i/width)); j++) {
          pos = i + (j * diff);
          count += chk(pos, diff);
        }
      }

      return (count);
    }
```

Finally, the chk() function is the one that actually compares the squares to each other. It takes a position on the board and a directional modifier and uses these two numbers to work from two squares back to the passed position. Matching squares are marked for removal and counted, assuming that we haven't already just matched them:

```
function chk(p, d) {
  var c = 0;
  if (heap[p]==heap[p-d] && heap[p-d]==heap[p-(2*d)] &&
    heap[p]!=0) {
    if (remove[p] != 1)
      remove[p] = 1;
    c++;
    if (remove[p - d] != 1)
      remove[p - d] = 1;
    c++;
    if (remove[p - (2 * d)]!= 1)
      remove[p - (2*d)] = 1;
    c++;
  }
  return (c);
}
```

After the board has been checked and the count returned to the parent function, any matched lines are set for deletion. Again, the game is paused for the sake of playability, and then the squares are removed from the board. At the end of the current round of deletion, the gravity() function is called to ensure no square remains hovering above an empty space:

```
function del() {
  pause(200);
  for (var i = 0; i < width * height; i++) {
    if (remove[i] == 1) {
      document.images['' + i].src = color[0].src;
      remove[i] = 0;
      heap[i] = 0;
    }
  }
  gravity();
}
```

The gravity() function scans each column on the board from bottom to top, looking for a blank square. If it finds one, it remembers the height of it and then goes looking for nonblank squares above it. Finding one filled in leads to the squares being swapped over and the height of the blank space moved upward by one:

```
function gravity() {
  var mark, pos, oldpos;
  for (var x = 0; x < width; x++) {
    mark = -1;
    for (var y = height - 1; y >= 0; y--) {
      pos = (y * width) + x;
      if (mark == -1 && heap[pos] == 0)
        mark = y;
      else if (mark > -1 && heap[pos] > 0) {
        oldpos = (mark * width) + x;
        document.images['' + oldpos].src =
          document.images['' + pos].src;
        heap[oldpos] = heap[pos];
        mark--;
        document.images['' + pos].src = color[0].src;
        heap[pos] = 0;
      }
    }
  }
}
```

Like Tetris, there are a few miscellaneous functions not already covered. The score() and newgame() functions are broadly similar to the previous ones, the only differences being that a simplified scoring system is used and that upon starting a new game, the player's choice of keys is detected.

The pause() function is only called from within the del() function and is only included as a separate function because it too has been reused, but not from Tetris. It takes one argument—a delay in milliseconds—and waits in a loop until the delay is over:

```
function pause(ms) {
  var when = new Date();
  var then = when.getTime() + ms;
  var now;
  do {
    when = new Date();
    now = when.getTime();
  } while (now < then);
}
```

Another piece of code is reused from Tetris, the form HTML, only with the addition of a select box to choose the key combination:

```
output+= 'Keys: <select name="keychoice"><option value="1"';
output+= (keychoice == 1) ? ' SELECTED>' : '>'
output+= 'numpad';
output+= '<option value="2"';
output+= (keychoice == 2) ? ' SELECTED>' : '>'
output+= 'a-x-d-s-w';
output+= '<option value="3"';
output+= (keychoice == 3) ? ' SELECTED>' : '>'
output+= 'j-m-l-k-i</select>\n';
```

# Mouse Trail

This application tracks the mouse pointer around the browser window, placing twinkling-star images all around its current location. The images then gradually move in toward the stationary pointer, until they finally all cluster around the pointer before disappearing. As soon as the user moves the mouse pointer, the star images instantly begin tracking again. This particular application serves no real useful purpose, but it does show how to track and position content around the mouse pointer. Whether or not this application is suitable for your website depends upon the intended audience, a kids website might be ideal, whereas a news site might not. Figure 14-5 shows the star images tracking the mouse pointer.

## Mouse Trail—*index.htm*

chapter14/trail/index.htm

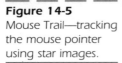

**Figure 14-5**
Mouse Trail—tracking
the mouse pointer
using star images.

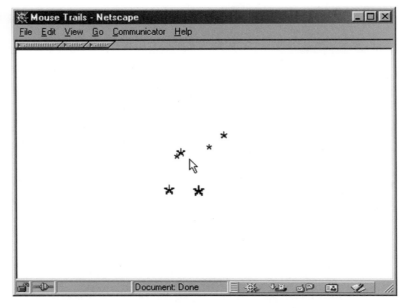

The ubiquitous *dom.js* library is included in the *index.htm* page:

```
<script language="JavaScript" src="dom.js"></script>
```

An absolutely positioned and initially hidden class (1) is defined:

```
.l { position: absolute; visibility: hidden; display: block; }
```

The global variables masterscale and scale dictate the maximum distance from the mouse pointer, timer to hold the reference to a running timer, and x and y the current latest coordinates of the mouse pointer:

```
var masterscale = scale = 50;
var timer;
var x, y;
```

Netscape Navigator 4 (which supports the layers object) uses the document object's captureEvents() method to register which events on the document object are to be captured—in this particular application, the mouse-move event—although note that the event must appear as an uppercase property of the Event object:

```
if (document.layers) document.captureEvents(Event.MOUSEMOVE);
```

The `document` object's `onmousemove` property is assigned the `trackMouse` object reference. In other words, the `trackMouse()` function is invoked whenever the `document` object's `onMouseMove` event handler is triggered:

```
document.onmousemove = trackMouse;
```

The `trackMouse()` function—passed an `event` object in Netscape Navigator, which is accepted as the `e` parameter—retrieves the coordinates of the mouse pointer, using the `DOMEventGetX()` and `DOMEventGetY()` functions held in the *dom.js* library. The function then assigns the values to the global `x` and `y` variables. If the value of the global `timer` variable is not set to `false` (i.e., a timer is currently running), then the current timer is cleared using the `setTimeout()` method, and the value of the global `scale` variable is reset to the `masterscale` value. Finally, the function invokes the `mouseTrail()` function, passing the value of the `x` and `y` global variables:

```
function trackMouse(e) {
  if (window.DOMObjects) {
    x = DOMEventGetX(e);
    y = DOMEventGetY(e);

    if (timer) {
      clearTimeout(timer);
      scale = masterscale;
    }

    mouseTrail(x, y);
  }
}
```

The `mouseTrail()` function, invoked from the `trackMouse()` function, loops through all the element entries in the `DOMObjects` array, generating random `rndX` and `rndY` numbers for each entry between the range `-scale` to `+scale`. These values are then used to set the position of the elements identified as `star0` through `star5` (this example Mouse Trail application uses six different elements) around the `x` and `y` coordinates of the mouse pointer, using the `DOMElementSetLeft()` and `DOMElementSetTop()` functions in the *dom.js* library. If the global `timer` variable is not equal to `false`, the `DOMElementShow()` function is used to reveal the hidden element. Finally, a `timer` is started using the `setTimeout()` method, to invoke the `clusterTrail()` function after a `100`-millisecond delay:

```
function mouseTrail(x, y) {
  for (var i = 0; i < DOMObjects.length; i++) {
    var rndX = Math.floor(Math.random() * 2 * scale) - scale;
    var rndY = Math.floor(Math.random() * 2 * scale) - scale;

    DOMElementSetLeft(DOMObjects['star' + i], x + rndX);
    DOMElementSetTop(DOMObjects['star' + i], y + rndY);

    if (!timer)
      DOMElementShow(DOMObjects['star' + i]);
  }

  timer = setTimeout('clusterTrail()',100);
}
```

The clusterTrail() function, invoked after a 100-millisecond delay, divides the scale value by 2 and invokes the mouseTrail() function, passing the global x and y values, as long as the value of scale is greater than or equal to 1. Therefore, the mouseTrail() and clusterTrail() functions continually trigger one another until the value of scale is less than 1. This has the effect of gradually centering the elements on the mouse pointer coordinates. When eventually that position is reached, the global scale variable is reset to the value of the masterscale value, the timer is set to null, and each element in the DOMObjects array is hidden using the DOMElementHide() function:

```
function clusterTrail() {
  if (scale >= 1) {
    scale = scale / 2;
    mouseTrail(x, y);
  }
  else {
    scale = masterscale;
    timer = null;

    for (var i = 0; i < DOMObjects.length; i++) {
      DOMElementHide(DOMObjects['star' + i]);
    }
  }
}
```

The start() function, invoked when the page has completely loaded, initializes the *dom.js* library:

```
function start() {
  if (window.DOMObjects) DOMInitialize('div');
}
```

The div elements identified as star0 through star5, all of which use a class attribute value of 1, are initially hidden when the page is loaded. Once the mouse pointer starts to move, the copies of the *star.gif* image contained in each div element follow and cluster around the mouse pointer:

```
<div id="star0" class="l"><img src="star.gif"></div>
<div id="star1" class="l"><img src="star.gif"></div>
<div id="star2" class="l"><img src="star.gif"></div>
<div id="star3" class="l"><img src="star.gif"></div>
<div id="star4" class="l"><img src="star.gif"></div>
<div id="star5" class="l"><img src="star.gif"></div>
```

**NOTE:** *You may use as many or as few images as you wish with the Mouse Trail application, and you may also use different images for each* div *element, as long as the* div *elements are identified with a* star *prefix and with a sequential number starting from zero.*

# Personality Quiz

This application is not unlike the Multiple Choice Test application in Chapter 4. However, whereas the Multiple Choice Test tallied up the total number of correct answers, this application gives each potential answer a score. Then the individual scores are tallied up at the end and are used to give a simplistic personality rating. The other main difference is that this application uses the *dom.js* library to work on as many browsers as possible, whereas the Multiple Choice Test application was specifically written to work with just Netscape Navigator 4 and Internet Explorer. By comparing the two applications, you can appreciate the simplicity of using a library of browser-compatible functions instead of individually coding solutions that work on individual browsers. Figure 14-6 displays the output of just one of the questions within the quiz.

This chapter is supposed to be fun; therefore, we suggest that you don't take the results of the personality quiz too seriously.

## Personality Quiz—*index.htm*

**chapter14/personality/index.htm**

The quiz makes use of the *dom.js* library to display the questions one at a time on the page, along with the *personality.js* library, which contains the majority of the JavaScript code to drive the quiz:

```
<script language="JavaScript" src="dom.js"></script>
<script language="JavaScript" src="personality.js"></script>
```

**Figure 14-6**
Personality Quiz—
one question within
the quiz.

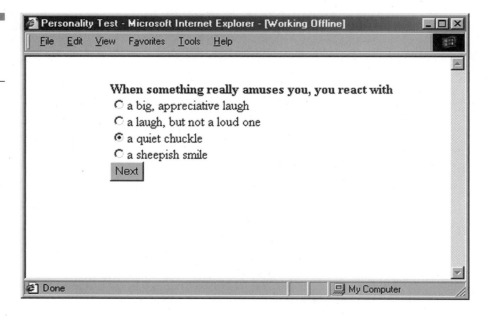

**Figure 14-6**
Personality Quiz—
one question within
the quiz.

An absolutely positioned class (1) is defined:

```
.l { position: absolute; display: block; }
```

The `start()` function, invoked when the page has completely loaded, first initializes the *dom.js* library and then invokes the `show()` function to display the first question in the quiz:

```
function start() {
  if (window.DOMObjects) DOMInitialize('div');

  if (window.DOMObjects && window.tallyScore && window.show)
    show();
}
```

The *questions.js* library, which holds all the questions, is loaded:

```
<script language="JavaScript" src="questions.js"></script>
```

A `div` element identified as `myDiv` is used as a placeholder for the questions:

```
<div id="myDiv" class="l" style="left:100; top:30;"></div>
```

## Personality Quiz—*personality.js*

 **chapter14/personality/personality.js**

The *personality.js* library contains all the JavaScript code necessary to drive the quiz. The code is similar but not identical to that used in the Multiple Choice Test application. As a result, only the major differences are highlighted.

The `Choice()` object constructor does not contain a `correct` property, but it does include an extra array to hold the scores for each answer. Except for the first, the alternate parameters passed to the function are used to populate the `scores` and `answers` arrays:

```
function Choice(question) {
  this.question = question;
  this.answer = -1;
  this.scores = new Array();
  this.answers = new Array();

  for (var i=0; i < (Choice.arguments.length - 1)/2; i++) {
    this.scores[i] = Choice.arguments[i*2 + 1];
    this.answers[i] = Choice.arguments[i*2 + 2];
  }
}

var item = 0;
var myChoice = new Array();
var q = 0;
```

The `show()` function, used to generate the HTML markup for each question and set of answers and also to display the results of the quiz, has many small changes to account for the need to keep track of the score for each question, the main one being the use of the `onClick` event handler within the `input` element to update the `answers` array with the score of the selected answer. The biggest change is the use of the `DOMElementSetInnerHTML()` function, held in the *dom.js* library, to first display the questions one at a time, and finally the personality trait at the end of the quiz. This replaces the `update()` function used in the Multiple Choice Test application, which was originally written to support just Netscape Navigator 4 and Internet Explorer:

```
function show() {
  var output = '';
  var score = 0;

  if (q < myChoice.length) {
    output +=
      '<form><b>' + myChoice[q].question + '<\/b><br>';
```

```
      for (var i=0; i<myChoice[q].answers.length; i++) {
        output +=
          '<input type="radio" name="answer"' +
          'onClick="myChoice[' + q + '].answer=' +
          myChoice[q].scores[i] + '">' +
          myChoice[q].answers[i] + '<br>';
      }

      output +=
        '<input type="button" value="Next" ' +
        'onClick="if (myChoice[' + q + '].answer!=-1) show()">';
      output += '<\/form>';
      q++;
    }
    else {
      for (var i=0; i<myChoice.length; i++)
        score += myChoice[i].answer
      output = tallyScore(score);
    }

    DOMElementSetInnerHTML(DOMObjects['myDiv'], output)
}
```

## Personality Quiz—*questions.js*

**chapter14/personality/questions.js**

The *questions.js* library contains a complete set of questions and personality traits for one quiz. Each question is built using the Choice() constructor held in the *personality.js* library. Each constructor is passed the question, followed by pairs of scores and answers. The returned Choice object reference is then added to the myChoice object array:

```
myChoice[item++] = new Choice(
  'How often do you play Tetris?',
  2, 'every day',
  4, 'every week',
  6, 'never'
);

myChoice[item++] = new Choice(
  'You usually walk',
  6, 'fairly fast, with long steps',
  4, 'fairly fast, with short, quick steps',
  7, 'less fast head up, looking the world in the face',
  2, 'less fast, head down',
  1, 'very slowly'
);

...
```

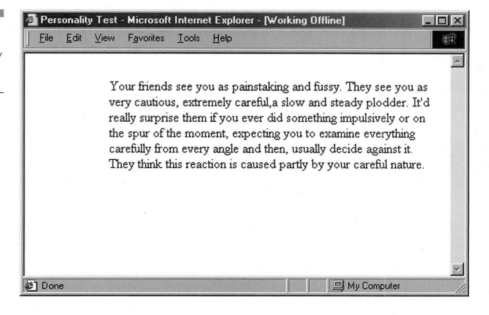

**Figure 14-7**
Personality Quiz—
a possible personality
based on the user's
input.

The `tallyScore()` function, invoked at the end of the quiz, simply tests the value of the passed score parameter and returns the appropriate personality trait, as shown in Figure 14-7:

```
function tallyScore(score) {
   if (score < 21) output = 'People think you are...';
   else if (score < 31) output = 'Your friends see you as...';
   else if (score < 41) output = 'Others see you as...';
   else if (score < 51) output = 'Others see you as...';
   else if (score < 61) output = 'Others see you as...';
   else output = 'Others see you as...';

   return output;
}
```

# Summary

This chapter has shown that we can have some fun with JavaScript and that JavaScript can be used to enhance a visitor's website experience. Although entertainment, games, or special effects might not be visitors' reasons for visiting your website in the first place; however, they may delight and capture their attention and keep them awhile. Nothing, however, can replace the interesting information that the visitor was looking for, and thus JavaScript effects should be used where appropriate. Hopefully, the games in this chapter will inspire you to write your own. If you do, then let us know about them.

Game programming, though primarily for entertainment, is usually complex. It can also serve as a useful test bed to measure the capabilities of a language. Stand-alone game programs require a lot of resources, including programming expertise, and are often strongly dependent on the client platform. As you have seen in this chapter, with the use of HTML support for interface elements and JavaScript capabilities for scripting, you can readily write game scripts that take advantage of the browser's user interface to run.

# INDEX

Index

**701**

## X

## Y

## Z

## SOFTWARE AND INFORMATION LICENSE

The software and information on this diskette (collectively referred to as the "Product") are the property of The McGraw-Hill Companies, Inc. ("McGraw-Hill") and are protected by both United States copyright law and international copyright treaty provision. You must treat this Product just like a book, except that you may copy it into a computer to be used and you may make archival copies of the Products for the sole purpose of backing up our software and protecting your investment from loss.

By saying "just like a book," McGraw-Hill means, for example, that the Product may be used by any number of people and may be freely moved from one computer location to another, so long as there is no possibility of the Product (or any part of the Product) being used at one location or on one computer while it is being used at another. Just as a book cannot be read by two different people in two different places at the same time, neither can the Product be used by two different people in two different places at the same time (unless, of course, McGraw-Hill's rights are being violated).

McGraw-Hill reserves the right to alter or modify the contents of the Product at any time.

This agreement is effective until terminated. The Agreement will terminate automatically without notice if you fail to comply with any provisions of this Agreement. In the event of termination by reason of your breach, you will destroy or erase all copies of the Product installed on any computer system or made for backup purposes and shall expunge the Product from your data storage facilities.

## LIMITED WARRANTY

McGraw-Hill warrants the physical diskette(s) enclosed herein to be free of defects in materials and workmanship for a period of sixty days from the purchase date. If McGraw-Hill receives written notification within the warranty period of defects in materials or workmanship, and such notification is determined by McGraw-Hill to be correct, McGraw-Hill will replace the defective diskette(s). Send request to:

Customer Service
McGraw-Hill
Gahanna Industrial Park
860 Taylor Station Road
Blacklick, OH 43004-9615

The entire and exclusive liability and remedy for breach of this Limited Warranty shall be limited to replacement of defective diskette(s) and shall not include or extend to any claim for or right to cover any other damages, including but not limited to, loss of profit, data, or use of the software, or special, incidental, or consequential damages or other similar claims, even if McGraw-Hill has been specifically advised as to the possibility of such damages. In no event will McGraw-Hill's liability for any damages to you or any other person ever exceed the lower of suggested list price or actual price paid for the license to use the Product, regardless of any form of the claim.

THE McGRAW-HILL COMPANIES, INC. SPECIFICALLY DISCLAIMS ALL OTHER WARRANTIES, EXPRESSED OR IMPLIED, INCLUDING BUT NOT LIMITED TO, ANY IMPLIED WARRANTY OF MERCHANTABILITY OR FITNESS FOR A PARTICULAR PURPOSE. Specifically, McGraw-Hill makes no representation or warranty that the Product is fit for any particular purpose and any implied warranty of merchantability is limited to the sixty day duration of the Limited Warranty covering the physical diskette(s) only (and not the software or information) and is otherwise expressly and specifically disclaimed.

This Limited Warranty gives you specific legal rights; you may have others which may vary from state to state. Some states do not allow the exclusion of incidental or consequential damages, or the limitation on how long an implied warranty lasts, so some of the above may not apply to you.

This Agreement constitutes the entire agreement between the parties relating to use of the Product. The terms of any purchase order shall have no effect on the terms of this Agreement. Failure of McGraw-Hill to insist at any time on strict compliance with this Agreement shall not constitute a waiver of any rights under this Agreement. This Agreement shall be construed and governed in accordance with the laws of New York. If any provision of this Agreement is held to be contrary to law, that provision will be enforced to the maximum extent permissible and the remaining provisions will remain in force and effect.